To Live Among the Stars

This wide-ranging history of Catholic and Protestant origins in Oceania works forces and people into a single narrative of church growth to 1900, with special attention to the role of Islanders. The book is designed for the general reader and for students and teachers, in the belief that this fascinating story needs to be more widely known.

John Garrett, whose previous book, *Roger Williams*, New York, 1970, has become standard, has taught church history in Sydney and at Suva's Pacific Theological College, Fiji. He is a minister of the Uniting Church in Australia, lives in Fiji and has worked for the World Council of Churches, Geneva.

To Live Among the Stars

Christian Origins in Oceania

John Garrett

World Council of Churches
in association with the Institute of Pacific Studies
University of the South Pacific
Geneva and Suva

WCC PUBLICATIONS
P.O. BOX 66
150 ROUTE DE FERNEY
1211 GENEVA 20, SWITZERLAND

INSTITUTE OF PACIFIC STUDIES
P.O. BOX 1168
SUVA, FIJI

REPRESENTATIVES IN THE US:
FRIENDSHIP PRESS
ROOM 772
475 RIVERSIDE DRIVE
NEW YORK, N.Y. 10015

BV
3640
.G3

COPYRIGHT © 1982 JOHN GARRETT
ISBN 2-8254-0692-9
COVER DESIGN: KIM GRAVELLE
PRINTED IN FIJI
OCEANIA PRINTERS LTD, SUVA

FOR ROBERTA

FOR ROBERTA

Contents

Pictures		viii
Maps		viii
Foreword		xi
1	A Curious New God	1
	The Marianas, Tahiti and to Leeward	
2	Christians in Hawaii	32
	Protestants, Catholics	
3	Points of Progress	60
	Sydney, New Zealand, Tonga, The Cook Islands	
4	Ave Maria or Hallelujah?	88
	Mangareva, Wallis/Futuna, Fiji	
5	Securing Polynesia	116
	The Cooks, Samoa, Niue	
6	Micronesia: Missions Meet	139
	Carolines, Marshalls, Kiribati, Tuvalu	
7	Melanesian Footholds I	161
	Vanuatu	
8	Melanesian Footholds II	179
	Solomon Islands, New Caledonia	
9	The Lure of New Guinea	206
	The LMS in Papua, Wesleyans in New Britain	
10	Partitioning Papua	230
	Wesleyans, Roman Catholics, Anglicans	
11	Each Church Distinct I	253
	The Societies, Hawaii, Cooks, Tonga, Samoa	
12	Each Church Distinct II	279
	Fiji, Kiribati, Vanuatu, New Caledonia, Solomons	
13	Toward Regional Identity	302
	The Twentieth Century	
	Acknowledgments	312
	Glossary	314
	Abbreviations	317
	Sources	319
	Notes	340
	Index	383

Pictures

	facing page
Tahiti: source of missionary endeavour	1
Original mission house, Honolulu	40
Villa Maria, Marists' Australian base	101
Clydesdale seminary building, New South Wales	132
The printery, Lahainaluna, Maui	143
Samuel McFarlane's house, Lifou	199
Ruatoka—Cook Island missionary to Papua	208
from Joseph King, *W.G. Lawes*	
W.G. Lawes, LMS pioneer missionary	218
from Joseph King, *W.G. Lawes*	
Peter Rautamara, first Papuan Anglican priest	251
from Tomkins & Hughes, *Road from Gona*	
Henri Vernier at Pastoral School, Tahiti	258
Roman Catholic cathedral, Papeete	260
Wailuku church, Maui	264
Joeli Bulu, Tongan missionary to Fiji	282
Paton Memorial Church, Vila, Vanuatu	293
Joel and Céline Hoioré, PTC graduates	306
Vanuatu leaders Walter Lini, Sethy Rengenvanu	308

PICTURES: JOHN GARRETT

Maps

	page
Tahiti	14
Society Islands	23
Moorea	25
Hawaiian Islands	45
New Zealand/Bay of Islands	63
Tonga and Its Neighbours	72
Tongatapu	76
Gambier Islands	90
Futuna	98
The Lau Group	104
Fiji	108
Viti Levu Rewa Coast	115
Rarotonga	117

Lower Cook Group	118
Northern Cooks (Atolls)	119
Samoa	123
Savai'i	125
Tutuila	127
Upolu	130
Micronesian Islands	140
Ponape	144
Marshall Islands	147
Kiribati and Tuvalu	149
Vanuatu	163
Erromanga	165
Aneityum	171
Solomon Islands	180
New Caledonia	191
Lifou	196
Ouvea	202
Mare	203
Papua	214
Bismarck Archipelago	224
Papua Islands Region	232
Marquesas Islands	267
Vanua Levu and Taveuni (Fiji)	282

REALIZATION OF MAPS: GARY WINTER

Foreword

TO LIVE AMONG THE STARS is an account of Christian origins in the Pacific Islands to 1900 and slightly beyond. A full and detailed history would call for several volumes. Some constant themes emerge.

In almost every island group, mission and church growth are intertwined with the voluntary migrations of several thousand Pacific Islanders under the guidance of small groups of white missionaries. Diffusion of Christianity has been largely by the contacts of Islanders with Islanders in everyday life. From the time of the first baptisms the churches struggled to be free, to embody their Oceanic environments and customs. Names of Islander pioneers in this book resemble ensigns at mastheads. They indicate the presence of long passenger lists in the ships. Historians have already begun to make members of this company more widely known.

Political and social history and ethnography have been brought to bear on the analysis. Theological interpretation is vital. Pacific societies can be understood only by close attention to a wide diversity of Christian thought and worship.

An ecumenical element has been latent in the meetings of divided Christians in the Pacific. The ecumenical movement has come from both differences and agreements. In the Pacific the adoption of Christianity eventually spelt peace when Islanders came to know each other. The conclusion of *To Live Among the Stars* depicts a gradual flowering of the process into deeper understanding and unity in the present century.

Geography is a normal prerequisite for history. Pacific Christian history is partly an essay in oceanography. The environment of the small but vivacious communities of the islands is the nourishing, at times threatening, sea. Pacific Islander Christians have a special way of comprehending the world. Most human beings look outward on solid earth. Islanders live on small pieces of earth surrounded by the wealth — and menace — of the sea. Travel and arrival, life and death, the Good News and the prospect of "life among the stars" have distinctive meanings for Church and people. Christ is the Pacific Prince, chief of chiefs come from afar. The paradox of an ocean of suffering, barely dispelled by the beliefs and rites of older religious systems, seems illuminated suddenly by the cross. The symbol of the Last Things also holds out hope in the end for island ancestors who appeared to await a covenant of grace.

Certain clear limits have had to be set for this book. The Latter Day Saints, the Seventh-day Adventists and Pentecostal and Faith missions are only marginally included. The churches mainly described now belong to the

FOREWORD

Pacific Conference of Churches. Many Pacific island cults and religious reactions demand full treatment by others. The Lutheran missions in New Guinea and parts of Micronesia have stories of their own. In this book the general movement of mission from Tahiti to Papua has pride of place. After 1900 Lutherans gradually entered the mainstream of the Islander community so formed.

Previous accounts of Christianity in Oceania have been dominated by the assumption that church growth came mainly from Europe and North America. In reality, early in the development, Latin America, Australia and New Zealand were important sub-bases for missionary initiative and cooperation with the islands. Their role should be plain when account is taken of the narrative and indication of sources in *To Live Among the Stars*.

The writer, in describing Roman Catholic, Protestant and Anglican traditions, has tried to do so with a kind of critical affection for them all. The aim is not to praise or blame, but to understand and describe. Dwellers in the islands and others have filled out and corrected the survey. The result is published in the hope that many members of this wide family may soon reconstruct the detail of a fascinating and little known story with a sure hand.

*I will lotu that I may
live among the stars.*

JOELI BULU

To Live Among the Stars

1

A Curious New God

The Marianas
Tahiti and to Leeward

WHEN THE SPANISH EXPEDITION of Ferdinand Magellan crossed the ocean from the southern tip of South America to the Mariana Islands eastward of the Philippines in 1521, its members brought the banners, crosses and incense of the mass for the first time into the Pacific.

Mendaña and Quiros, Magellan's successors, were commissioned to share their faith and worship with the peoples they met. The procession of Spanish ships on the route between the South American possessions of the Conquistadors and the Philippine Islands was a sign of the expansion of Catholic pre-Reformation Europe. By a papal bull of 1493 Alexander VI granted the right to the kings of Portugal and Spain to propagate the Catholic religion in the new territories they were opening up. He drew a line dividing East from West through Brazil and gave Portugal this right of royal patronage to the east of it, Spain to the west. The fact that the world was round led to later unseemly dispute about where the two met and diverged. Alexander intended to propagate Christianity among all peoples.

In the Pacific the landings — and shipwrecks — of Spaniards acquainted scattered groups of island-dwellers with the processions, plainsong and ritual actions of the white men. It has been argued that their impact, and the permanent traces of their religious observance, have been pervasive in the

Tahiti: source of missionary endeavour.

TO LIVE AMONG THE STARS

Tuamotus, Raiatea, Hawaii, New Zealand and Easter Island. Genetics and the study of blood-groupings have been called into the argument. Animal populations, boat-building, scripts, artifacts and cultural traces of Christian doctrine and worship may indicate some early process of rapid intermarriage and the acculturation of marooned Spaniards, though the extent and value of the evidence are debated.

The first organized Catholic mission came from the opposite direction. In 1668 the Spanish queen mother and regent, Mariana, sent a Jesuit mission from the Philippines to Guam in the Ladrones Islands, which were renamed in Mariana's honour. The missionaries accompanied a military garrison intended to protect Spanish trade and assist the mission where necessary to prevent Spanish depredations on the local people. Father Diego Luis de Sanvitores had been moved to pity on previous visits by the cruelties of Spanish transients. His entreaties for a mission were heard at court, but the soldiers who arrived with him foreboded a mixture of cross and sword.

Sanvitores made his first contacts with Quipuha, the *chamorri* (chief), of Agana. The first Catholic approach to the society thus came at the apex of a social pyramid with the *chamorri* at the top, served by a middle group below them and serfs at the base. Extension of baptism to classes below the *chamorri* threatened the whole structure; resentment broke out among the chiefs after a first remarkable year of Catholic successes. Thirteen thousand people were baptized within the year. The supernatural efficacy of the rite was assumed; the natural reaction of the populace was not. When Guamanians were told that Christianity would call for abandoning the traditional sexual freedom of their "bachelor houses" and the cults of their ancestors, resistance to the mission stiffened on Guam and Tinian, where Sanvitores' group — four priests, a lay brother and a group of Filipino cathechists — were at work. Quipuha, the mission's patron, died early in 1669. In January 1670 resentment hardened into resistance. Father Luis de Medina and a catechist, Hipolito de la Cruz, were killed on Saipan. By July Spanish soldiers had taken punitive action. When open revolt flared at Agana, many Chamorros were killed; no Spanish lives were lost. Hatred of the garrison and its Mexican and Filipino foot-soldiers began to cancel the impact of the Christian message of peace.

Sanvitores, true while he lived to his desire to curb excessive force, continued his labours. When he secretly baptized a child of the leading *chamorri*, Matapang of Guam, against the will of the father, who by then had become a lapsed convert, an angry crowd, incited by Matapang, killed Father Sanvitores and a young Filipino catechist, Pedro Cesar, who was with him. The death of the mission's founder removed his restraining hand and precipitated the long Chamorro wars, carried on by a succession of severe and fanatical commanders. In the insurrection begun by Matapang, fighting

A CURIOUS NEW GOD

swept both northern and southern islands until the completion of Spanish conquest by 1694. It has been estimated that about 5,000 of a pre-war population of 100,000 survived the violence and accompanying epidemics. The remnant, intermarried with Spanish settlers and mercenaries, became a nucleus of subsequent Catholic Guam. Traces only of pre-christian culture survived. Sanvitores' evangelical intentions underwent ironic change.

In the next 100 years Spanish ships were largely supplanted in the Pacific by incoming explorers and scientific expeditions sent out by the Dutch, the British and the French. Curiosity made common cause with prospects for commerce as the successive expeditions of Roggeveen, Byron, Wallis and Bougainville arrived in search of the Great South Land. Their efforts culminated in the three great voyages of James Cook. None of them took particular interest in converting the peoples they met. Spain contemplated British exploration in Tahiti with some alarm as an incursion on islands too close to their South American empire for comfort. Their attempt to create a settlement in Tahiti followed close to Cook's first voyage, when he observed the transit of the planet Venus across the sun in 1768. The Spaniards came twice to Tahiti — in 1772 and 1774; their aim was partly to convert the Tahitians to their faith.

The vessel *Aguila* made a reconnaissance of the island under orders from Spain in 1772. As a result the Governor of Peru arranged for two Spanish Franciscans, accompanied by a lay interpreter, Maximo Rodriguez, and two Tahitians brought back to Peru on the *Aguila's* first expedition, to undertake a serious mission to Tahiti.

The attempt failed. A landing was made near Tautira, on the northern coastline of Tahiti's smaller peninsula. The chiefs of the area were hospitable to the missionaries; but immediately, the two Franciscan priests drew back, as celibates, from the traditional Tahitian offer of women. Their Tahitian companions soon re-entered their own society after what had been for them a straitened stay in Peru. Only Rodriguez, the interpreter, who had enough Tahitian to fraternize, felt free to roam round the coast and avail himself of offers of food, company and conversation. His diary survived, to be translated into English and French in the present century.

This Spanish mission, terminated after twelve months by the removal of the friars by the *Aguila*, revealed some of the perplexities facing Catholic enterprise in the Pacific in the ensuing 200 years. A celibate, stationary and relatively enclosed life, punctuated by prayer and the liturgy and practised by persons under religious vows, was not easily comprehended in societies where journeying, group activities, sexuality, family life and communications with the spirit world had been parts of an indivisible communal whole. Nevertheless, Rodriguez had been popular. A promise to renew the mission, made by the commander of the *Aguila*, was coincidentally fulfilled at Tautira, when French Catholic priests landed there in 1836 on their way to Papeete.

TO LIVE AMONG THE STARS

BRITISH UNDER Wallis, Cook and Bligh visited Tahiti and excited interest in its conversion to Christianity. The officers were usually members of the Church of England. They and the occasional chaplains carried by their ships for the most part observed the religion of the Book of Common Prayer and could be seen reading the services on board. After 1750, when the Evangelical Revival in Britain had affected the southern seaport towns and London, more ships' captains and other ranks had been touched by the effects of the revival's great preachers, George Whitefield and John Wesley. Religious services on board were more likely by then to be visibly pious, less formal and Erastian. Captain William Bligh of the *Bounty* became an associate of the Calvinistic Evangelicals, who formed and supported Methodist chapels under the aegis of Selina, Countess of Huntingdon. The Rev. Dr Thomas Haweis, chaplain to the Countess, derived information about Tahiti from Bligh. On the basis of Haweis' roseate account of the people and environment, his fellow-founders and Directors of the London Missionary Society were persuaded to send the ship *Duff* with the Society's first missionaries to the South Seas (page 13).

They were not without predecessors. Some common sailors were wrecked or left behind. Others deserted ship. Escaped convicts from the British penal colonies in Australia sometimes reached Pacific islands. The castaways brought new skills to local societies. Some astutely observed the religious sanctions of the cultures they adopted. It is difficult to distinguish between sincerity and charlatanry in the reports we have of such religions as the Sio Vili cult of Samoa. Dominant sailor personalities fused the Bible reading and hymn-singing of their former environments with the cultic expectations of their hosts to form an amalgam. To some extent all subsequent Pacific Island Christian practice has combined aspects of local custom and culture with the European forms of Christian observance imported by missionaries. In this sense Christianity has been both "sailor cult" and local church from its early days in the Pacific.

THE POLYNESIAN SOCIETIES first reached by Christians were a novel mission-field. Visitors had to come over long distances by sea to reach any island group. Whether the newcomers were from other Pacific islands, or from a continent, they needed to overcome fatigue and replenish their supplies. Visits were rare; therefore local people treated any ship's company as a break in the normal round and a source of curious people and objects. Custom almost everywhere dictated the need for warm welcomes, exchanges of gifts, and an invitation to remain.

Since magic and religion governed so much of local life a particularly cordial welcome awaited the white man's religion. High chiefs variously styled *ali'i, ari'i, ariki, 'eiki,* in the Polynesian groups of the eastern Pacific, frequently traced their ultimate descent from sky gods and heroes. They were treated as divine personalities. Commoners bowed or squatted before them and never touched their persons in a familiar way or raised themselves higher than the chief's head. The chief's *mana*, or power, was thought to be due to the presence of divinity.

Similar mythology in Europe surrounded the persons of British royalty and the Bourbon kings of France. Divine right carried with it "the divinity that hedges a king." The peoples of the Society Islands, Hawaii, the Cook Islands, Tonga, and later Fiji, responded intuitively to the connections on board naval vessels between royally conferred rank and official religion. Receptiveness to the new religion sprang from readiness to believe that the God of the newcomers, like the ships, must be more powerful than their own.

Local "prophets," charismatic men or women whose function in the local religions was to consult the gods and predict the future, are reported in many islands as having foreseen the arrival of the ships and of new religious leaders who would fulfil the old Pacific religions. In Tahiti, Hawaii, the Cook Islands and Samoa memories of these ecstatic forecasts were probably filled out in detail after the arrival of Christianity, but the prophetic activities point toward a fever of expectation, set going by report and rumour of the presence of seemingly supernatural ships and people. When nails, iron tools, clothing, glass objects and firearms began to be exhibited they were naturally coveted. For this reason the early prophets in island societies have been correctly described as precursors of the later charismatic figures who precipitated so-called cargo cults. Polynesians at the close of the eighteenth century and the beginning of the nineteenth were not, however, necessarily trying to get the material possessions of the white invaders by cynically adopting their religion. For the most part they genuinely desired to test the God who seemed to be the source and controlling power behind a floating society of marvels. When missionaries eventually arrived, island peoples quickly distinguished between Christ's reported humility, fair dealing and peace, and the unashamed rapacity of crews of many trading vessels, or missionary meanness in paying for land, goods and services. The gospel of peace and reconciliation was understood. On the other hand many societies were at first perplexed by the refusal of white missionaries to accept the sexual favours of their women. In general, the first recipients of Christianity were intrigued by missionary ways of worship and glad that missionaries were willing to stay longer than other kinds of white men and learn local languages. From the beginning, the context of mission activity was set by local chiefly leaders, who extended the first invitation to stay and influenced the majority of their people to reject or adopt the Christian Gospel and worship.

When carvings and ceremonial objects associated with the old gods were destroyed at the instigation of missionaries the chiefs did it themselves. Local leaders became convinced that the *mana* of the old deities was no longer worth taking seriously. Their ritual gesture and the attitude of the missionaries have robbed the world of many finely crafted religious artifacts; but in the early stages of many missions in the Pacific efforts were sometimes made to save representative specimens from the hands of local people who had become disenchanted about the power of their old gods and wanted to exorcise them. Mission influence on the practice of other related local crafts was not normally as negative as the introduction by traders of industrial methods of production or the diversion of labour into the organized export of items such as bêche-de-mer, sandalwood or pearls.

White sailors, particularly any who stayed on to assist local chiefs, became advisers, interpreters, and in many cases participants, in local wars. In Hawaii, John Young, an Englishman captured by the high chief Kamehameha from an American ship, assumed an important advisory role and became a contributor through his marriage to the blood of Hawaiian royalty. In Tahiti, Peter Hagerstein, a Swedish subject from Helsinki, attached himself to the high chief Tu (Pomare I). When Polynesians saw how effective cannon and muskets could be in war they wanted both. Soon they observed that communications at a distance and storage of information could be achieved by the miraculous signs committed to paper by print or writing — a revolutionary discovery in oral cultures.

At first many chiefs coveted European weapons, to achieve ascendancy in situations where no one chief had yet become paramount in an island group. They assumed that missionaries would provide more firearms; they were disappointed when their requests were turned down on the ground that missions were friends of peace. In time it became clear to the chiefs, in spite of this, that alliance with missionaries brought benefits in local power struggles: naval vessels came to protect the missionaries and therefore tended to be on the side of the missionaries' local protectors; the missionaries themselves, by abstaining from spurring on contestants in the local wars, helped to provide longer breathing spaces between battles. The regulatory function of the Christian religion became a benefit when forces had to be re-grouped in preparation for major engagements. The careers of Pomare II, who threw in his lot with the London Missionary Society in Tahiti, and Taufa'ahau (George Tupou I) of Tonga, who joined forces with the Wesleyan mission at a later period, showed the relationship between personal conversion and the furtherance of ambition; both men showed genuine regard for the mission and its message and a clear recognition of the advantages to be gained. In Tahiti, Tonga and Futuna missionaries were also king-makers; the future kings were patrons of missionaries; the missions depended on them for ultimate success. Where local high chiefs strove for permanent ascendancy, the missionaries saw themselves as Samuels to rising Polynesian Davids and Solomons (pages 27 and 74). Religion in the Pacific was already changing when organized

A CURIOUS NEW GOD

missions arrived. Foretastes of a greater source of *mana* and *tapu*, and of more coherent accounts of the world, created a climate of readiness.

THE CONDITION OF TAHITI as envisaged by the Directors of the Missionary Society was superficially correct, but misleading in depth and details. They knew that on the main island of Tahiti the chief Tu (or Otoo as they called him) had built a house for Bligh, which was offered to the missionaries for their use when they landed. What they did not know was that the position of Tu in Tahitian society was not kingly supremacy as had been thought by British navigators. Under his name of Pomare, Tu, whose current authority largely derived from the Leeward Island of Raiatea to the west, was really still engaged in tense and intermittent struggle with other rival chiefs (*ari'i*), who did not accept his title as paramount.

On arrival the mission party found that Tu's power was shared increasingly by his son, the younger Tu, who by then dominated the western areas of the island of Tahiti. Neither Tu was personally a great warrior, but the younger, the later Pomare II, was intelligent and able to see that he could win in the wars if he had the benefit of cannon, muskets, better ships for sea fighting and transport, and the aid of Europeans as soldiers and advisers. He had already enlisted two Scandinavian deserters, Andrew Cornelius Lind and Peter Hagerstein. The first came from the ship *Matilda*, the second from the *Daedalus*. Both had been tattooed, spoke Tahitian and some English, and helped members of the party from the *Duff* in their early contacts.

Only gradually did the missionaries come to see the importance of the links between the cult of the fertility god Oro of Raiatea and the fortunes of Tu on Tahiti. Oro, a spirit celebrated in partly phallic dance-drama believed to ensure the fruitfulness of crops, was served by travelling groups of dedicated players, the society of the Arioi. Their sexual favours were freely available among the chiefs, but they contracted no permanent marriages and their children were killed at birth. Their religious observances had largely overlaid the older sacrificial practices of the priests of Ta'aroa and Tane, the gods of ocean and sky. Oro, who was worshipped through a fetish of highly prized red feathers, was also a fierce war god. His wandering companies of dancing and singing players travelled with representatives of the high chiefs of Raiatea from their headquarters at the great *marae* of Opoa on Raiatea, a sacred seaside stone temple-space, open to the sky. They frequented similar *marae* on the island of Tahiti and were the attendants of the Raiateans in the celebration of marriage alliances and conduct of wars during the eighteenth century on Tahiti. Cook and Bligh had been told the Pomare line was supreme among the Tahitian chiefs, accepting a claim as a fact. The mission soon came to see that the claim had yet to be made good by final conquest.

British misconceptions about the power of the Pomare line on Tahiti proved to be one of the mission's gravest problems for the first eighteen years of its work. The missionaries found in time that as protégés of Pomare II they first had to work for his conversion, then share the sharp reversal of his fortunes in war, as exiles with him on the island of Moorea and in the Leeward group. They had to resist Pomare's urgent attempt to get them to obtain firearms for his wars; at the same time they could not help being desperately anxious for his ultimate political success. They were appalled by his chiefly sexual conduct with both men and women, by his addiction to alcohol, and by his early indifference to their moral objections to infanticide and human sacrifice. But they knew they had to stay with him; if they could convert him they would probably witness a landslide in favour of their preaching on Tahiti, Moorea and Raiatea, the home island of the Pomares' titles and power, mediated in large measure through the female lines.

THE MISSIONARY SOCIETY

MISSIONARY ACTIVITY was a product of great religious changes in Europe and America. The Evangelical Revival in Britain, coinciding chronologically with a parallel advance of rationalism and the scientific spirit, stressed the conversion of the individual, through recognition of the gravity of sin, heartfelt repentance, and trust in the self-sacrifice of Christ to restore the believer to union with God. As a result the heart was warmed; the whole life, especially the will, felt directed again, by the grace of God and the help of the Holy Spirit, toward love and service of God and fellow-man. This redirection, sensitive to the parting command of Christ *(Matthew 28.19)*, included sharing the message of going "into all the world to preach the Gospel to every living creature."

The practical recovery of this Great Commission flowed from the revival of individual religion in the formal and often deist atmosphere of the churches in the British Isles. People of all classes, men and women, followed the example of the Northamptonshire cobbler William Carey, whose concern led to the formation of the Baptist Missionary Society, the first non-conformist body of its kind in Britain. Carey had himself been roused by reading of the missions undertaken from Germany and Denmark in the earlier part of the eighteenth century as a result of the slightly earlier Pietist movement in Lutheran circles in those countries. He in turn partly inspired the founders of the Missionary Society, later known as the London Missionary Society.

Carey was a Particular Baptist. His church, unlike the General Baptists, who were Arminians, was Calvinist. The Calvinists believed that Christ died for the salvation of the predestinate; Calvinist missionaries therefore preached the Gospel to all nations for the locating and awakening of the Elect. They

A CURIOUS NEW GOD

believed in double predestination — that Christ died in intention for all men, but that some would inevitably be hardened and lost by rejecting the Gospel, others equally inevitably saved. Arminians, among them the Wesleyan Methodists, believed that Christ died for the salvation of all men: "whosoever will may come and taste of the water of the fountain of life freely" *(Revelation 22.17)*. Double predestination in its rigid form was anathema to Wesleyans; but although Calvinists and Arminians found themselves in marginal conflict over the doctrine of predestination, they were united by other common convictions, especially the desire to obey the Great Commission.

George Whitefield and John Wesley, the two dominant preachers of the Revival in England, were both priests of the established Church of England. Whitefield's followers became Calvinistic Methodists when it was clear that they were not welcome within the Establishment as a whole and would need their own church buildings and connexional organization. Wesley too, was forced into what he fervently hoped would be temporary secession; he ultimately founded the Methodist Conference in the British Isles. Wesleyan Methodism developed in Britain with such speed that its energies were largely concentrated there in home mission until the close of the Napoleonic Wars in 1815.

The Calvinist wing of the revival spread most dramatically in North America, following the spectacular preaching campaigns of Whitefield among Congregationalists and Presbyterians. In Britain its efforts were made largely in upper class and prosperous merchant circles, though its influence also spread among the rural artisans and small townsmen grouped around ,its richer converts. These "godly mechanicks" provided a first source of manpower for foreign missionary enterprise.

Calvinistic Methodists, clustered about Lady Huntingdon's Connexion — the converts of Whitefield, and those of several preachers who preceded him in Wales — became the nucleus for a missionary society drawing its support from within several Calvinistic British evangelical churches. Lady Huntingdon's preachers and the Wesleyan Methodists believed themselves to be raised up for the Establishment's eventual good. They joined forces for foreign mission with fellow-Calvinists — Scottish Presbyterians and Congregational Independents.

Calvinist Anglicans supported their aims. Together in 1795 they formed the Missionary Society, to be known from 1818 as the London Missionary Society. They met in an atmosphere of excitement created by the publication of Cook's and Bligh's voyages to Tahiti. Not surprisingly, they chose Tahiti, in the inviting Society Islands claimed for Britain by Cook in 1769, as their first field. The Society's foundation in London was celebrated in a speech made on the occasion by the Rev. David Bogue of Gosport, one of the founders, as "the funeral of bigotry." In case it should raise its head after the interment, the society in May 1796 gave out as its Fundamental Principle:

> our design is not to send Presbyterianism, Independency, Episcopacy, or any other form of Church Order and Government, about which there may be differences of opinion among serious persons, but the Glorious Gospel of the Blessed God to the Heathen: and that it should be left (as it ought to be left) to the minds of the persons whom God may call into the fellowship of his Son from among them to assume for themselves such form of church government, as to them shall appear most agreeable to the Word of God.

A formula of this kind united the parties to the missionary adventure and transcended their theological differences concerning church, ministry, sacraments and the propriety of an established national religion. Beyond these considerations, the founding fathers were influenced by other important theological currents leading them into missionary activity. In England, as across the Atlantic in New England, the writings of the American philosopher-theologian Jonathan Edwards, who was both a Calvinist in theology and a disciple of the influential English philosopher John Locke, had helped to shape a generation of new thinkers. Most of them, like Edwards himself, had been touched by the evangelical awakening. The description of Christian duty as "disinterested benevolence" played its part in shaping a school of moderate Calvinists — people who combined gripping awareness of a divine call with scientific curiosity and a passion for the eternal welfare of the human race.

The founders of the London Missionary Society and the American Board of Commissioners for Foreign Missions also shared a belief that the world must be evangelized promptly; not that they expected universal conversion, but their reading of the New Testament persuaded them that their duty included the sharing of the message of salvation with all nations as a necessary prelude to the final coming of Christ and the end of "the present age." What they felt was not exactly millennial fever, though their normal seriousness and sobriety were definitely tinged with heightened excitement; they lived and made their missionary decisions at a time when calm faith in the triumph of reason had been set trembling in Europe by the successive earthquakes of the American and French Revolutions, to be followed by the wars of Napoleon.

The shadow of the conflict between the European nations hung over the entire period of the arrival and establishment of the Protestant Church in Tahiti; its European accompaniment of dismay became magnified in the Society Islands as grim despair when, after 1800, ships, men, supplies and letters failed to arrive for almost six years. The Directors of the Missionary Society during that time appear to have become so preoccupied with the problems of straitened trade and finance in Europe, and so intimidated by

A CURIOUS NEW GOD

Napoleon's blockade of shipping, as to have fallen out of touch with the ominous situation of their representatives in the Pacific. From the standpoint of the earliest missionaries in the new field the wars on Tahiti and its neighbour islands, and on Tonga, with hardened resistance to their message everywhere, could equally have been imagined as signs of the imminent end of the age, the approaching Millennium.

WHAT KIND OF PERSONS planned and were sent out to do the work?

The Directors, drawn from London and other parts of Britain, were mostly merchants and ministers of religion. Their more noble patrons included titled persons and the gentry, to whom the ministers were deferential spiritual advisers. Intellectually, they took an interest in nature and geography, but related it to biblical revelation. They urgently sought to share with "the heathen" the transformation wrought in their own lives by their conversions.

Dr Thomas Haweis, their dominating early leader and planner, was sure that it was unnecessary to send highly educated men to do the work of winning the people of Tahiti for Christ. His conversations with Captain Bligh led him to conclude that the natives of the islands, as distinct from their "kings" and "nobles," were fundamentally tractable persons who would quickly yield to the superior powers of his own religion, which he considered both reasonable and soul-stirring. He equally believed that the best kind of men to reach simple though benighted savages, lost in superstition, would be members of the British lower classes who worked with their hands and could rapidly prepare the ground for the religious conversion of their pupils by teaching them useful arts and trades.

The prime ideologist of the first missionary group thus saw civilization, the benefits of technology and the machine, as partial salve for savagery, as many who shared his notions of uplift and productivity have done since. However, Haweis, and probably most of his associates, blended their simplistic view of how to mould a theoretically lower culture, with the thought that Tahitian women would quickly be converted and make good wives for British "godly mechanicks." He and Bligh seem not to have foreseen that still unconverted Tahitian women would threaten the piety and chastity of unmarried men.

Contrary to later pictures of the London Missionary Society given by ardent nineteenth century Congregationalists who came to be its chief supporters, the early period of its formation was thoroughly pre-democratic; its patrons were respectable enough to appeal to the upper classes; its servants in the field were under the absolute and unquestionable authority of the

TO LIVE AMONG THE STARS

Directors, to go and do exactly as they were told, not otherwise. This pattern of unquestioned headquarters authority marked the whole life-span of the LMS, though it was often assailed, and sometimes defied, by resourceful and quirky Congregationalists who served the Society.

At the beginning, the handsome volume presented to those who sent out the ship *Duff* with the first party in 1796 concluded with an alphabetical list of the 1400 subscribers' names, in which the designation "Esquire," and "Sir," the prefix of knighthood, jostled the names of army officers in England and India, the Earl of Macclesfield, and the scientist Joseph Banks, the President of the Royal Society. The book, a considerable account of the state of Tahitian society and of the voyage, still valuable for students of the pre-christian Pacific, was dedicated by the Directors to King George III. The description of Tahiti was contributed from the journal of James Morrison of the *Bounty*.

The list of missionaries tells the other side of the story. Four ordained ministers headed the group; the Revs. James Fleet Cover (a former school teacher), John Eyre (once a blockmaker), John Jefferson (former actor and teacher), and Thomas Lewis, who "attended the hospitals and dispensaries, and understands printing." The others, with an average age of 26, make up a curious assortment of tradesmen and craftsmen. Henry Bicknell, house carpenter, sawyer, wheelwright; Daniel Bowell, shopkeeper; Benjamin Broomhall, buckle and harness maker; John Buchanan, tailor; James Cooper, shoemaker; John Cock, carpenter; William Crook, gentleman's servant, "and since tinworker"; Samuel Clode, whitesmith and gardener; John A. Gillham, surgeon; Peter Hodges, smith and brazier; William Henry, carpenter and joiner; John Harris, cooper; Samuel Harper, cotton manufacturer; Rowland Hassall, Indian weaver; Seth Kelso, weaver; Edward Main, tailor, "late of the royal artillery" says the record; Isaac Nobbs, hatter; Henry Nott, bricklayer; Francis Oakes, shoemaker; James Puckey, carpenter; William Puckey, carpenter; William Smith, linen draper; William Shelley, cabinet maker; George Vason, bricklayer; James Wilkinson, carpenter and joiner.

Cover, Eyre, Hassall, Henry and Hodges were accompanied by their wives, who were separately listed, with three children, twelve-year-old James Cover, two-year-old Thomas Hassall, and Samuel Otoo Hassall, sixteen weeks, named in honour of Otoo (Tu) chief of Pare, whom Bligh believed to be the king of Tahiti; he was in fact one of several warring high chiefs whose territory happened to include the favourite mooring place of British ships at Matavai Bay. The naming of the child suggests that it was a purpose of the expedition to show appropriate honour to the line of the Pomares in Tahiti, as to the House of Hanover in England.

There was logic in the choice of personnel for the first contingent. The strategy, by its own lights, was sound enough; what could be more appropriate than to send pious and evangelical subjects of one monarch to convert, marry and elevate the loyal subjects of another? The categories of rank and duty appeared, to readers of Captain Cook and interlocutors of Bligh, to be appropriate to descriptions of Tahiti; a happy realm, apparently recently unified, inclined to trade, debased by superstition, but ready to respond quickly to Christianity. The disparity between the earlier voyagers' reports of a Happy Isle and the realities of the subtly structured and war-racked societies of Polynesia registered in the first discouraging missionary reports. It was time for a change in thinking and planning in London.

Already in the period of formation of the Missionary Society a difference of view had emerged between Haweis, a chaplain to nobility and an Anglican, and the Rev. David Bogue, minister of the Independent Church at Gosport, near Portsmouth. Haweis advocated the recruiting of godly unlearned artisans; Bogue wanted a seminary to train persons for the work. Haweis prevailed in the beginning, because of his status and prestige, but Bogue lived to make his point as the trainer of a new kind of missionary after the Napoleonic Wars were over and Haweis' vision had given place to near disaster. Bogue, a Scot, stood in a line of Presbyterian conviction, which was now making common cause with the English Evangelical Academies of the eighteenth century to provide thorough ministerial training for English non-conformists, barred from the universities of Oxford and Cambridge. He wished to see them well grounded in arts, sciences, theology, languages, with study of foreign peoples included in the equipment of missionaries. In this he agreed with the remarkable Baptist ex-cobbler, William Carey, who taught himself this ambitious curriculum in preparation for his lifetime of achievement in India.

The tension between Haweis and Bogue represents more than an undercurrent of discord between dissenters and the Church of England; it heralds the attempt of brighter Britishers "of the lesser sort" to improve their status and powers by sound training, to climb to a place in the sun, to assert the prerogatives of the self-made democrat to property, recognition and a share in the running of the churches and the country. The conflict also reflected the dissenters' resentment of the suggestion that Holy Orders conferred following university degrees were superior to the qualifications of their own godly ministry.

PROTESTANTS IN TAHITI

WHEN THE SHIP *Duff* came in view of the green foreshore and spectacular mountains to the southwest of the island of Tahiti on what was reckoned to be Sunday 5 March 1797 those on board had been at sea since 6 August 1796.

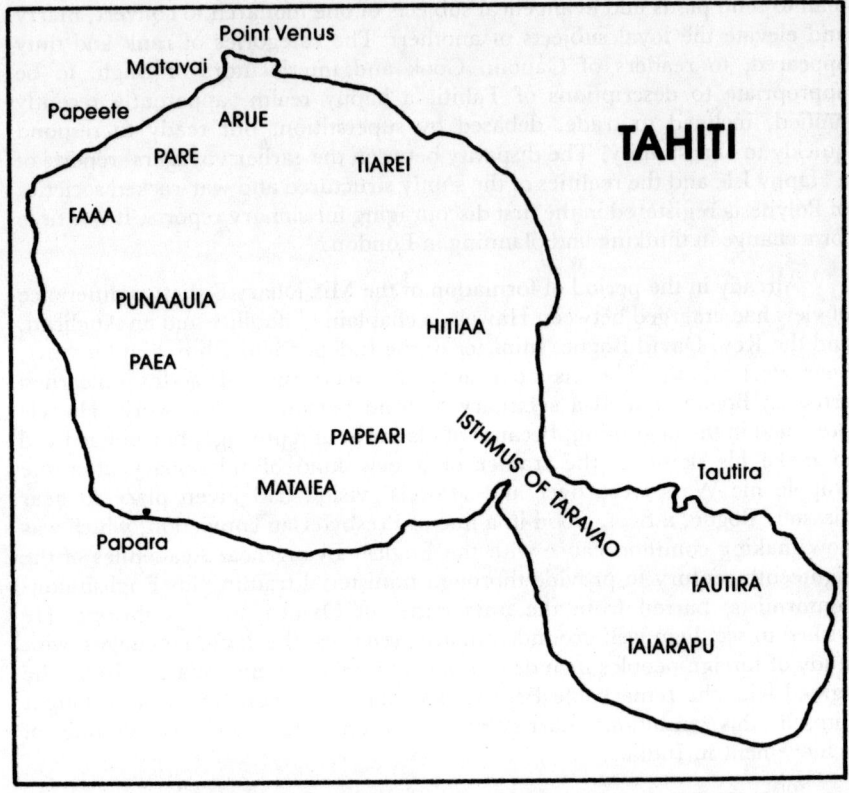

In a scene of great oddity a troupe of Arioi, led by Oro's high priest, clambered aboard. Captain Wilson put his cannon on deck; the Arioi, unarmed and in good humour, helped cheerfully to put them in position. The missionary party was disappointed because the women were not as handsome as British sailors had reported. The Tahitians who came on board to trade left early; they were astonished to hear that the religion of the new arrivals put a taboo on Sabbath barter. Forty Arioi stayed on board, to become the first South Pacific ship-board congregation at an Evangelicals' Sunday morning service. Earlier in the proceedings the Arioi had created an unfavourable impression by their "tricks"; then, forming a ring around the hymn-singing, praying missionary contingent, they stayed on:

> During sermon and prayer the natives were quiet and thoughtful; but when the singing struck up, they seemed charmed and filled with amazement; sometimes they would talk and laugh, but a nod of the head brought them to order.

A CURIOUS NEW GOD

Cover's sermon on the text "God is love," in English, was reported to be of "a peculiar solemnity and excellence." Though not understood by the Arioi, its hearers would certainly have grasped that this was the English "day of the Eatooa" (*atua,* God) which had been observed by previous ships' companies. The gaudy drama of one liturgy met the sober thanksgiving of another in the beginning of a momentous encounter involving religion.

Thirty of the Arioi stayed on board overnight as the *Duff* sailed to Matavai Bay, off Point Venus, Bligh's landfall. They had been joined soon after the Sunday service by Lind and Hagerstein. Within a few days they had met both the older and younger Tu and their wives and attendants. On 16 March, after settling in Bligh's house at Matavai, they met the chiefs, with their important consorts, in a formal ceremony of cession of the land on the point of Matavai. As in many parts of the Pacific, what was done meant that the land was made available for use so long as the friendship and mutual helpfulness of giver and recipient continued. The successors of the British, on their side, in time came to regard such transactions as permanent allotments, legal transfers of ownership. The two divergent conceptions account for many subsequent misunderstandings of what happened to the ownership of land as a result of missionary settlement in the Pacific.

As originally planned, the first venture of the Missionary Society was intended to extend to a number of widely separated stations in the South Seas. Tahiti was conceived of as headquarters for a more ambitious mission. The *Duff* landed Bowell, Buchanan, Cooper, Harper, Kelso, Nobbs, Shelley, Vason, Wilkinson and Gaulton on the southern island of Tongatapu in the Friendly Islands (Tonga). Harris and Crook were taken to the Marquesas Islands, where Harris found the food and the surroundings insupportable and came back with the ship; he had been offered the wife of a chief as his bedmate for the night, refused to sleep with her, and was investigated as to his sex by a party of women while asleep alone. He was then robbed of his belongings. Crook was not deterred by all this; he stayed on, as he had intended, to be taken off the island of Tahuata to an adjacent island a year later, then picked up by an American ship. The Marquesas, referred to by a later American missionary there as "the suburbs of hell," proved a tough missionary proposition. The persistent Crook returned to New South Wales. Later, after visiting Britain, he served between 1815 and 1830 on Moorea and Tahiti.

Damaging experiences awaited the contingent left by the *Duff* on Tongatapu. The party dispersed among the Tongan chiefs in unavailing efforts to teach and to conduct worship. They were regarded with suspicion. Beachcombers, escaped convicts from New South Wales, made the way difficult for them. Harper, Bowell and Gaulton were tragically killed in a civil war, as it swept through the village where they lived. Their deaths were vividly described in George Vason's memoirs. Vason defected. He was adopted into a chief's family, married, took part in war, and assumed the way of life of highborn Tongans. The remaining missionaries left Tonga for Sydney, where Shelley vigorously advocated resumption of the Tongan mission (page 70). Vason elected in 1801 to leave Tonga on the ship *Royal Admiral,* which had brought the second mission group to Tahiti. He repented, married, became a Baptist, wrote his arresting reminiscences, became Governor of Nottingham Town Gaol and died at 66 in 1837 after suffering from erysepalis, "nervous irritability" and finally madness.

On Tahiti early events were equally discouraging. The signs were many. Itia, wife of the elder Pomare, destroyed at birth a child conceived in a union with an Arioi; she did not take kindly to missionary remonstrances against this normal custom. Little Otoo Hassall's first birthday on 13 May 1797 was a muted celebration; the missionaries learned that it was taboo to use the name Tu of any but the king himself. Disgust followed the discovery that Tahitian "royalty" retained the services of a group of *mahu,* effeminate companions whose favours were coveted by the male chiefs. "So depraved are these poor heathens," records the narrative of the *Duff's* voyage, "that even their women do not despise those fellows, but form friendships with them." Some of the ship's company rowed ashore and had to be retrieved. The elder Pomare, after hearing a sermon from Cover on *John 3.16,* professed interest, but indicated that he would wait for the arrival of the Christians' God in person.

Troubles multiplied when the *Duff* left. The hopes of the Pomare family for ammunition, guns and trade goods remained unrealized. When the high priest of Oro, Mannemanne, who had been a leader of the Ariois' boarding party on the first day, expressed his disappointment, he spoke for the *ari'i* in general as their herald and one of their leaders: "You give me," he said, "much paraow (talk) and much prayers... but very few axes, knives, scissors, or cloth."

The family of Pomare needed ships, tools, cloth, muskets, moral support in war, the protection of the power they knew lay behind the visits of Cook and Bligh, printing and literacy, alcohol and goods for barter. Their pickings from the *Duff* proved lean. When, in March 1798 a North American ship, the *Nautilus,* arrived, they turned eagerly to its crew. The missionaries protested especially about the willingness of the people on the *Nautilus* to provide firearms and accept the favours of the women. In displeasure the younger Tu turned against the missionaries, stripped the clothes off four of their number, and threatened the mission house. After conferring on the frightening outlook, eleven of the group, married men and single waverers, decided to leave for Sydney on the *Nautilus,* with Shelley from Tonga. Three of them, Cover, Hassall and Henry, became a vanguard for a group of LMS refugees from Tahiti destined to play an important part in the life of the infant convict colony around Port Jackson and cooperate there effectively with the Rev. Samuel

A CURIOUS NEW GOD

Marsden, Sydney's perpetually busy and opinionated evangelical Anglican chaplain. There they promoted the welfare of their own mission and the beginnings of Wesleyan Methodist missions in the South Seas.

In the same year the capture of the *Duff*, on her second voyage, by a French privateer, gave warning of the coming long break in communication between the Directors of the Society in London and missionaries in the Pacific. Of fifty reinforcements captured in the Atlantic on the *Duff* and returned to England, only four, James Hayward, William Waters, Charles Wilson and John Youl, persevered. They arrived in Tahiti on 10 July 1801 on the East Indiaman *Royal Admiral* with John Davies, two Scots — James Elder and William Scott — and Samuel Tessier. Elder and Scott, recruited by the Edinburgh Missionary Society, were made available to the LMS.

Between the departure of the *Nautilus* and the arrival of the *Royal Admiral* on 10 July 1801 the few who had elected not to go to Sydney suffered more setbacks. Eyre, Bicknell, Harris, Jefferson, Nott, Lewis and Broomhall knew by then that the Tahitian language was harder to learn than they had been told before leaving England. The hope of the Missionary Society's Directors that its bachelor agents would fairly rapidly convert and marry persons of higher station in Tahitian society was not realized. Surrounded by sexual freedom, they debated whether members of their party should be allowed to marry unregenerate Tahitians. The small white church decided against. Lewis, to the distress of his colleagues, left them, to contract a customary marriage with a local woman; he was murdered in unclear circumstances among the Tahitians on 27 November 1799. Broomhall said he had come to doubt "the reality of divine influences on the human mind" and the immortality of the soul. He was excommunicated as having "embraced Deistical Principles." Eyre, Bicknell, Harris, Nott and Jefferson formed a lonely but stubborn remnant of the *Duff's* ambitious enterprise on Tahiti.

Harris left on a passing ship for Port Jackson; Broomhall was taken off on the *Royal Admiral*. Eyre, Bicknell, Nott and Jefferson (their acknowledged leader and senior until his death in 1807) weathered a six-year gap in direct communication from the Directors in London at one of the most dispiriting periods of the Napoleonic Wars in Europe. Until the fighting in Europe ended in 1815 the missionaries in Tahiti lived through war, or the threat of it, themselves. From the death of Pomare I in 1803 onward their fortunes were necessarily tied to Pomare II. They strove to make him literate and instruct him, travelled between the settlements on Tahiti and improved their command of the language. There was no avoiding that they were his guests; they depended on his friendship in a country that belonged to him and to his fellow *ari'i*. The elite leadership among Pomare's rivals and enemies were aware of them — settlers different from the beachcombers, custodians of the secret of writing, strange devotees of a god with requirements and taboos differing from their own. Yet the Tahitians were not simply using and manipulating their beleaguered sojourners. Since their own religion was powerful among them, through its ceremonies, priests and enactments, they were sensitive to the religious devotion of this odd little cluster of British missionaries, whose shoes wore out and whose clothes became tattered, during the long wait for word and supplies from London.

Davies, a Welsh schoolteacher who served the Tahitians from his arrival in 1801 until his death in 1855 at the age of 84, noted all this in the manuscript history he compiled. Of the older Pomare he observed that he was "decidedly a *religious* character, if such is to be found among heathen idolators. He was no hypocrite in his religion, but truly sincere, he feared and served his god constantly, and in all that he did, and took in hand, he had respect to the gods, never forgot them."

By 1807, when Pomare II had been under instruction and had learned to write, he addressed the LMS Directors in London promising to banish Oro to Raiatea and "cast off all evil customs." He declared he could "fully acquiesce" in the desire of the Society to instruct Tahiti and called his country "this land that knoweth not the true God." In the same letter he asked for firearms, property, cloth and writing equipment. He was evidently manipulating the situation as far as possible, for material advantage, but rightly sensed that for his fellow chiefs and people the heart of the exchange would be a religious decision.

As seen by Tahitian chiefs, and dimly by the people, the period between the first LMS landing and the arrival of the *Royal Admiral* group involved acceptance of the mission itself and resistance to its message. From 1801 onward Nott and Jefferson improved their command of Tahitian and were therefore ready to cultivate and instruct Pomare II after the death of his father in 1803.

In spite of their preoccupations with other developing mission-fields and the distractions and shortages caused by the wars in Europe, the Directors of the Missionary Society were not totally forgetful of their people in Tahiti, though Davies complained that they were. The view from London looked different; news told of a debacle on Tahiti, in the Marquesas and in Tonga. The time had come for fresh consideration and alternative strategy.

When they received word from their exiles in New South Wales, the Directors conducted an enquiry into the reasons for the early collapse in Tahiti. Missionaries who returned to England were intensively cross-questioned about the decision to quit the mission for the time being and take refuge in Sydney. Hospitality was readily given in Sydney to their errant servants. Samuel Marsden, the Church of England clergyman who received the group from Tahiti, was known to some of the London Directors as a fellow evangelical; indeed he was both a Calvinistic Methodist and a loyal Anglican. They knew he was industrious, financially astute and fully in sympathy with the Missionary Society. They appointed him to look after their affairs in the South Seas.

The relationship so formed with a fellow evangelical became crucial for the development of missionary activity from an Australian base throughout the nineteenth century and into the twentieth. Marsden's activity in aiding the Tahitian mission guaranteed shipping and advice for lonely British Christian missionaries. His personal influence during the closing phases of the Napoleonic Wars, and beyond into the 1820s, became a new focus of advice and aid for them. Some of the Tahiti missionaries such as Shelley and Hassall were deeply involved, as he was himself, in commercial affairs. Their marriages in the colony of New South Wales confirmed the link. Hassall's son Thomas, an Anglican clergyman, married one of Marsden's daughters. The group retained a lively interest in the provisioning and prosperity of the mission; soon they were busy planning and acting with Marsden to introduce Anglican and Wesleyan missions into New Zealand and Tonga. Samuel Marsden's seven voyages to New Zealand to introduce the mission of the evangelical Anglican Church Missionary Society did not deter him from being friendly toward the Wesleyans when they in turn decided to begin a mission in the North Island of New Zealand at no great distance from the Anglicans who were already there (pages 66-7).

In a curious intermixture of religion and trade, Marsden co-operated with the Sydney merchant and ship-owner Robert Campbell to supply the missionaries in Tahiti with necessities and trade goods. They sent pork and coconut oil to Sydney on vessels owned by Campbell; later they used the brig *Active*, which had been acquired by Marsden himself. At a still later stage they weathered accusations of distilling rum from Tahitian sugar they had planted and supplying it to Sydney, where the *mores* of the rough colony made it a prized item of barter.

On Tahiti there were local reasons why missionary residence continued to be precarious. After the death of Pomare on 3 September 1803 the members of the mission group were painfully aware that among the *ari'i* "many would be aspiring for superiority." Arms came in to make the problems worse "by almost every vessel." In a long and slow struggle to acquire the language, Henry Nott, the Birmingham bricklayer, from this point forward emerged as the most persistent member of the party, despite his relatively poor command of writing and learned pursuits. Nott was the teacher of the others. His familiarity with Tahitian was a result of oral practice; he became involved in some dispute with the more lettered John Davies, a teacher, over questions of orthography. But his personal friendship with Pomare II exposed him to a generally acceptable form of the language; he supervised Pomare's own progress in reading and writing. By July of 1805 the Tahitian leader had also advanced sufficiently in English to write a letter of his own to the Directors in London. "The writing is the King's, the diction is not, but he has an idea of the meaning of each sentence," Eyre told the recipients of the letter.

Pomare was, in 1806, still absorbing the skills of the mission and trying to use his patronage of its presence to strengthen his threatened hold on the Tahitian mainland. Davies was frank about what had occurred up to that point; in 1806 he lamented that there was no "sincere desire of instruction manifested by any as to the truths of the Gospel, but on the contrary much aversion." In the following two years two hard blows made things worse; on 25 September 1807 Jefferson died, and in 1808 Pomare was forced by the pressure of his chiefly opponents on Tahiti to retreat to the adjacent island of Moorea and re-group his forces by recourse to family alliances on the Leeward islands of Huahine and Raiatea.

Jefferson had acted as leader, and most frequently as secretary, for the missionaries, during the initial period in Tahiti. His letters and reports show his sane realism about the plight of the "grand design," the civilizing and conversion of the islands. His gradual recognition of the size of the remaining task transmitted itself to his colleagues. They belonged to a gathered company and viewed the church as a minority of the called, living in hope that they would be counted with the elect. Jefferson and those who worked with him regretfully became architects of a Tahitian Christian establishment; they saw that conversion of high chiefs would lead to the emergence, not of small companies of called and gathered individuals, but a large church of the multitude, endorsed by traditional leaders. The eventual conversion of Pomare II and the subsequent rush to join the church have been grandly dramatized as the story of a "second Constantine."

Pomare himself was forced to ponder his political and religious options when a "dangerous rebellion" on Tahiti was followed by his exodus with all the missionaries to Huahine. On 24 November 1809 Hayward and Nott informed the Directors in London that the other missionaries had gone to Sydney on the *Hibernia*. Nott then accompanied Pomare to the island of Moorea. In their desperate straits a symbiotic relationship of mutual interdependence was established between the two men. In theological terms, the night of adversity and dismay brought home to Pomare, with Nott's aid, a sense of his own insufficiency and the inefficacy of the power of his own religion. He began to speak of giving up Oro and accepting the Christian God. At the same time he planned the gathering of a fresh fleet and armed forces to enable him to return to Tahiti.

A CURIOUS NEW GOD

The mental and physical state of Nott at this turning point are harder to describe. He was no great writer; no journal has survived. Later evidence indicates that he probably entered into a custom marriage with a woman of chiefly status; but his resolution was not dimmed. In October 1810 he wrote to his revered early mentor Dr Haweis to counter any thought that the end had come. "The idea of the work being entirely given up is a great grief to us," he protested, and enclosed a letter in Tahitian, with his own translation, from Pomare, describing the spiritual and military aspirations of his royal companion.

Relief eventually arrived through the good offices of Marsden in Sydney. In 1810 four "pious young women" had been sent from England as wives for the missionaries. They came out to Australia in the care of the returning Bicknell, who had been to England and been married there. Three of the women eventually married Davies, Hayward and Nott. The thought of intermarrying with high-born Tahitian converts had been abandoned, but the problem of celibacy had been overcome.

In 1811 Bicknell, aided by Marsden, returned to Moorea with the group of missionaries from Sydney; Eyre stayed in New South Wales. The reconstituted group — Davies, Henry, Scott, Wilson, Bicknell, Nott and Hayward — were gaining proficiency in Tahitian and a better understanding of the complex marriage relationships and alliances between the chiefs, male and female, of Moorea, and the Leeward Islands of Huahine, Raiatea and Borabora. Pomare was away on Tahiti, patching his alliances and preparing his military return. In 1812 Nott had gone to Port Jackson to marry one of the four young women sent from England. He was back on Moorea in the month of October, when the turning point in the emergence of a Tahitian church occurred. Pomare wrote from Tahiti to the missionaries on Moorea in Tahitian, expressing his repentance for his past, his desire to be forgiven, and his attachment to the God of the Christians. On 21 October 1812 the missionaries wrote to the Directors, giving news of Pomare's conversion and his request for baptism.

The king had earlier made this request to Nott, but all the missionaries had reservations about complying. Pomare's sincerity in his change of allegiance from Oro to Christ and his grasp of the essence of his decision come through clearly in his letters; but he was a person of high social position, accustomed to long-sanctioned forms of dalliance with both sexes and fond of the alcohol he was freely offered by ships' officers. Because conversion implied a life lived in moral conformity with the Gospel, the missionaries exercised long "prudence and circumspection" in Pomare's case before he was baptized in 1819.

Society Islanders became quickly aware of the change in Pomare's religion. Already, before his conversion took place, his altered attitude toward Christ and his neglect of the cult of Oro appear to have struck a chord in two young men, Tuahine and Oito, who had been domestic servants of the missionaries at Matavai before Pomare was forced to leave Tahiti. These two, and some around them, had been influenced by the instruction they received in Davies' school at that time. By 1813 they were holding secret prayer meetings with others in the bush, in Huatana Valley, Tahiti, in the district of Pare. They were induced by the missionaries to come to Moorea and enter the school Davies had by then set up. Worship on Sundays was commenced in Tahitian as well as English. Moorea, and particularly the district of Papetoai on the leeward side of the island, where the missionaries lived, became a rallying point at this period for people coming over from Tahiti, together with the allies of Pomare from Huahine and Raiatea.

One of the more striking chiefs who came regularly for worship and instruction became the first Christian convert of high rank. Paofai a Manua, called Upaparu by Davies, was a leading Arioi, and therefore a chief under the old religion. In 1813 he had distinguished himself by personally protecting and saving the former LMS missionary Shelley, when the crew of a Sydney-based ship on which Shelley was trading was slaughtered in the Tuamotu Islands. Paofai, as a high chief of the Tahiti district of Tiarei, had conceived a deep regard for the earliest missionary party. His attachment to the growing group of people under instruction at Papetoai drew hostility from Fenuapeho, the high chief of Tahaa in the Leewards, who stood by his old religion. In view of the threats against him, Paofai went in 1815 to Tahiti to join Pomare. The influence of this intelligent chief established a pattern for a truly local church in the Society Islands. From this period forward the decisions of highly placed leaders like Paofai, and those of larger companies of the "praying people" typified by Tuahine and Oito, began to produce churches on the islands. Chiefs and commoners accepted the outward forms of missionary government and worship. But the external appearance of the church was not a reliable clue to its internal character. One of its functions was to protect part of the culture and language of the Society Islands against the inroads of white trade and conquest. The new religion became, by degrees, a repository for elements of Tahitian language and custom, as the older religions had been within pre-christian society.

Davies wrote in early 1814 from Moorea about the religious change in the people, countering the regret of Directors of the LMS that there had not been more advance in the "civilizing" of the Tahitians by artisan missionaries. Davies detected the centrality of the religious decision:

> These Islanders are Religious people, and their Religion (or if you please Superstition) influences all their affairs, their building, planting, fishing, eating, drinking, in short, everything they do ... and no material alteration *can* possibly take place without interfering with their Religious System ... As Christianity prevails a different state of things will gradually take place.

A CURIOUS NEW GOD

The gradual change was accelerated by growing literacy as Nott travelled to cultivate groups of inquirers and "praying people" on Raiatea, Huahine and other Leeward Islands. By early 1815 the number of these *bure atua*, or people who pray to God, was estimated to be between 500 and 600 in the Society Islands. They became the nucleus of the future church. The visits by Nott prefigure things to come; within four years the focus of intensive work, and of the expansion of the mission, shifted, under new influences, to Huahine, Raiatea and Borabora in the Leewards; but not before Pomare had added military conquest on Tahiti to the change in his religion.

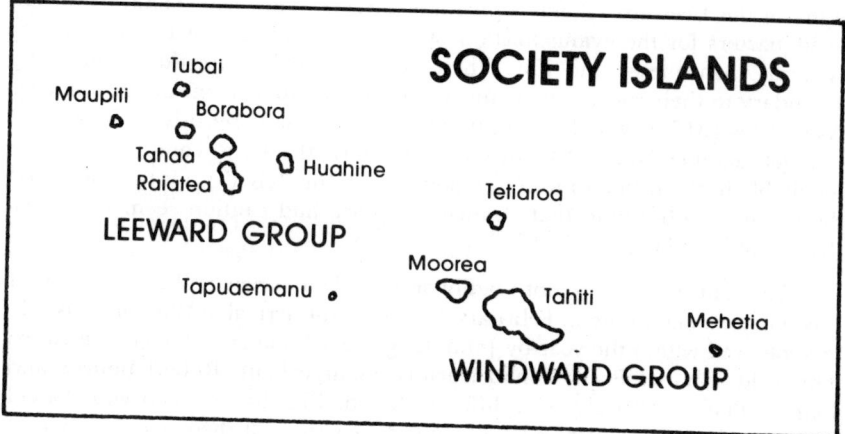

On 12 November 1815, on Tahiti, in the district of Atehuru, Pomare and his pro-christian followers, by this time collectively known as the *bure atua*, were attacked while at Sabbath worship by their opponents who still followed the old Tahitian religious system. With the aid of cannon and the use of opportunist tactics not normally sanctioned under the old conventions of war in the island, Pomare's forces won a quick battle. They had been attacked while worshipping on the assumption that they would not retaliate on a holy day, which morally may have balanced their shooting down of a chiefly spokesman before the signal to commence fighting in earnest had begun. Afterwards Pomare, in accordance with long-standing missionary counsel, did not take the usual vindictive measures against his defeated enemies. The triumph was seen on Tahiti as the victory of a superior divine *mana* and was followed by a general movement in the Leeward Islands and on Moorea in favour of abandoning old worship and some customs and adopting Christianity.

In early 1816 rolls of converts were discontinued by the mission, "the profession of Christianity having become national." Large numbers of intending church members were, however, enrolled as baptismal candidates, with the same status as Pomare, who was still on trial. He surrendered his family idols; they were sent to London. Davies, Bicknell, Nott and Hayward went to Tahiti to consolidate the position. A brief war in the Leewards against the residue of chiefly resisters led to the victory of the Christian group. A law code was drawn up by Nott to meet the need of the new order on Tahiti. From this time forward the older group of missionaries became identified with Pomare's newly inaugurated, and increasingly diluted Christian imperium. Davies and Nott translated the Bible and superintended Pompare's progress in Christianity. They did not forget their original instructions to proceed beyond their Tahitian base. They had already made preliminary preaching tours of the Leeward Islands with some success. They saw Tahiti as logical headquarters for the evangelization of the "out-stations" of the Tuamotus, Australs, Marquesas and Fiji. Their labour in these directions had to be secondary to their role as chaplains to a virtual establishment under Pomare. As early as 1817 they had, at this point, become acutely sensitive; for genuine evangelicals there was a "lie in the soul"; formalism and compromise were inevitable in the fusion of the "religious" with the "civil"; but they accepted the situation, observing that "much prudence and caution seem necessary that no offence be given."

The sentiments were not readily acceptable to a new and eager group of missionaries, beginning in February 1817 with the arrival of William Ellis. He was followed within the year by John Muggridge Orsmond, Lancelot Edward Threlkeld, Charles Barff, David Darling, George Platt, Robert Bourne and John Williams. All were of a different breed. Ellis had studied with David Bogue at Gosport. Orsmond had undertaken the full theological course of studies there and was not reticent about his superior intellectual and linguistic qualifications. The others showed the influence of Bogue, and of post-Napoleonic movements of thought in Britain. Unlike Jefferson and Nott, they were not naturally subservient to Directors brought up on high church Tory assumptions. They had greater influence with merchants of the middling sort. They felt pride in the educational traditions of Nonconformist Dissenters. Their claim to be "gentlemen" was branded as dangerous Jacobinism in England after the French Revolution and the wars. Ecclesiastically, they stood for the participation of lay deacons with the ministers in the running of each local church. Six of the group of eight were Congregational Independents; Williams, Bourne and Threlkeld — originally Calvinistic Methodists — were drawn into this way of thinking about the church as they advanced in their missionary careers.

These young and vigorous men already represented a party, styled Presbyterian for convenience, that reflected the ideas of David Bogue. Directors who adhered to the style and social connections of Dr Thomas Haweis were no longer as influential as they had been at the beginning. The

A CURIOUS NEW GOD

Calvinistic Methodists, who had made no formal renunciation of bishops, resented what they considered the high-flown educational policies of Bogue, who was interested in India and Africa rather than Haweis' treasured South Sea mission. Bogue became involved in angry brushes with Haweis over these issues. "We refuse episcopal government," wrote Bogue to George Burder of the LMS in London, "and have adopted another independent authority and set him at the head of it."

A new flavour — brusque initiative, suspicion of old guards, upward social striving — injected itself into the LMS in the Pacific with the arrival of this group. They criticized the tepid Erastianism of Pomare's establishment. Ellis, a printer, brought a press. He set it up at Afareaitu, on the windward side of Moorea; Pomare greeted it with wonder as he was invited to draw the first sheets from the marvellous machine.

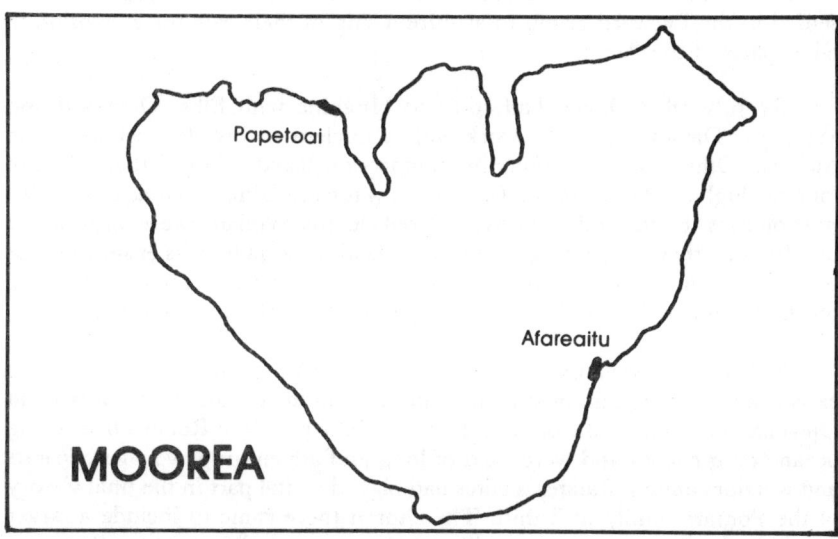

The siting of the press was a compromise. The older missionaries wanted it on Tahiti; younger men, who felt the pull of new possibilities in the Leeward Islands, wanted it there. When more printers and printing machinery arrived, the issue was resolved by placing presses where they were needed to keep pace with schooling and literacy. But the tensions between the older and younger missionaries were a symptom of things to come. Orsmond arrived on Moorea in April 1817. His superior manner, his pride in his scholastic attainments, and his premature and acid judgments on the work of his predecessors caused a stir. Personally prickly, Orsmond's analytical powers were great; his papers eventually presented a necessary, even though over-stated, critique of all that went before him. Threlkeld, who came in November, brought a stormy and officious style to the confrontation with his elders. He had been an actor, craved attention, and liked to dominate. Meetings between the two groups, as Darling, Platt, Bourne and Williams joined in the debate, pointed to the inevitable decision: the younger men, with the aid of Davies, went to the Leeward Islands to follow up important contacts established with Leeward chiefs and warriors on Moorea during the wars. They became the guides of the important local churches of Huahine, Raiatea and Borabora, and played their part in founding others on Tahaa and Maupiti.

Until 1817 inter-island transport had to be found on passing ships or on the brig *Active*, a Sydney-based vessel used by Marsden on the mission's behalf. In December 1817 the LMS launched its own ship, the *Haweis*. Pomare and the missionaries had been long in building it, for use within the Society Islands to transport workers. Its very existence stimulated those who settled in the Leeward group to acquire a ship of their own for expansion to other parts of the Pacific.

By July 1818 Davies had come to Huahine with Ellis, Orsmond and Williams. Davies began the work with a nucleus of his old "scholars" on Moorea. Other learners among his contacts on Raiatea joined them. Before long the high chief of Raiatea, Tamatoa I, was complaining that he too needed missionaries. By the end of the year Threlkeld and Williams were on Raiatea; on Huahine they chafed to get free. Threlkeld, especially, was eager to strike out on his own. They entered into a close relationship with Tamatoa, building on the foundations laid among his people by the earlier missionaries.

Raiatea was well placed to become a central point of influence and expansion for Protestant missionary enterprise in the Pacific. Its great *marae* at Opoa had been the shrine of the cult of Oro. The people of Raiatea had strong ocean-going canoes and were fond of long and adventurous voyages. Priests and warriors among Raiatea's elites had played a vital part in the final victory of the Pomare family in Tahiti. The church there came to include a larger number of converts who were willing to become travellers and missionaries, under the dynamic and restless influence of Threlkeld and Williams.

With Tamatoa's support and blessing, the people began to form auxiliary societies to recruit island teachers. The names of some became honoured in the Leeward Islands, Tahiti, and eventually all parts of the Pacific. They transformed the story of mission in the Pacific into a protracted effort by many Pacific Islanders under the official leadership of fewer white missionaries. Most of the work was done by and for the peoples of the Pacific. As pioneers, advisers and informants, their prior knowledge of island and marine environments was of decisive value to the white men they accepted and admired as their "fathers" in the new religion.

A CURIOUS NEW GOD

The auxiliary societies were financed by contributions of coconut oil, arrowroot, hogs and cotton. The local rulers were assiduous in promoting them. They were good for both religion and trade and took a burden off the London Missionary Society's London budgets. The month of May, a traditional time of the year for missionary meetings at Exeter Hall in London, was adopted with enthusiasm by the local churches in the Pacific; in the Society Islands and elsewhere it remains a continuing festival. The consequent use of small ships for trade was sharply questioned by the London Directors; however, the presentations of gifts in kind, with Bible drama and song, developed into treasured community festivities and initiatives; auxiliary societies and the recruitment of local teachers took the place of harvest and battle celebrations under the old order.

Expansion on Huahine, Raiatea and Borabora was inevitably offset by a contrasting static trend. Both the Leeward Islands Mission and the older work on Tahiti and Moorea became partly preoccupied with problems of conduct and of civil government. Recently converted high chiefs, Pomare and Tamatoa, had to be rendered the things due unto Caesar and discharge their offices in a Christian way. Law codes were needed.

Though not strictly king-makers (the chiefs themselves in battle had settled that issue) the missionaries felt obliged to be law-givers. Nott and Pomare promulgated a first code of law for Tahiti in 1819; Tamatoa's code for Raiatea followed in 1820, the Huahine code, drafted by Ellis and Barff, in 1822. The codes received the assent of the chiefs, who enforced them as judges. Lapses and offences were frequent in the recently converted society at all levels. As island teachers, recruited with enthusiasm by pastors and deacons, left to serve abroad, problems of civic order and morality became increasingly vexing among lukewarm people who stayed at home. All the disappointments were not among the rank and file; Pomare II, the chief convert, went into serious decline.

Pomare was baptized by the pouring of water at the hands of Bicknell, and in the presence of Platt, Darling, Crook, Wilson and Henry on 16 May 1819. The delayed action was performed with more hope than pride. Nott stayed beside the king in the labour of translating the Bible into Tahitian. On a small island in Papeete's harbour Nott worked the text into acceptable high Tahitian, seated beside his royal neophyte. When Crook saw Pomare in 1821, the signs of the end were already visible. He was despotic, swollen with elephantiasis, addicted to the spirits he obtained with ease from ships, and dallying, even during the translation of the Bible, with his favourite effeminate male companion, his *mahu*. To the younger group he seemed a dissolute and disgraceful fraud. He died on 7 December 1821, not long after the arrival from London of the Rev. Daniel Tyerman and George Bennet, Esquire — a two-man Deputation sent by the Directors of the LMS to visit their fields throughout the world.

TO LIVE AMONG THE STARS

On 15 October the members of the Deputation were received by Pomare himself and thus able to form a fairly favourable impression of his retinue, house and person. They noted his love of alcohol, said he showed "vain remorse and impotent resolution to shun the snare in future," found him "courteous and affable, though grave," and talked with him about European royalty.

The delegation's visit extended the rift between the Windward and Leeward missions. Attention focussed on the recent spectacular landslides into Christianity on the islands occupied by younger missionaries. Tyerman and Bennet reported favourably on the work of Ellis on Huahine, Threlkeld and Williams on Raiatea, and Orsmond on Borabora. They took Ellis with them, accompanied by a group of Christian Leeward Islanders, to visit the American missionaries who had arrived in Hawaii in 1820 and were struggling with problems of situation and language. William Ellis was an indefatigable collector of material on Polynesia. He had obtained a good command of Tahitian, which he found to be closely allied to Hawaiian. The king, chiefs and missionaries invited his group to stay and help them. In December 1822, after his return to report at Huahine, Ellis and his wife returned to Hawaii to work, travel, advise and translate. He was fully accepted by the American group, until he left for England in September 1824 (pages 39-43) on account of his wife's ill-health.

Orsmond, who had been the missionary on Borabora for three years from the end of 1820, moved back to Moorea to take charge of the newly established South Sea Academy at Afareaitu. Children born to the missionaries in the islands were becoming a problem to the mission. They grew up speaking Tahitian; tropical informality and infantile sexuality threatened British Christian standards. The academy was established to cater for the children's needs; at the same time it was intended to be a place of regal education for the young son of Pomare II, who, following Tahitian custom, had been provisionally anointed and crowned Pomare III at the age of four at Papaoa, Tahiti, on 21 April 1824. The anointing was done by Henry, and the crowning by Nott. In presenting the Bible, the missionaries used the words of the Coronation Service in the Book of Common Prayer of the Church of England. The two members of the Deputation from London were present, with most of the older missionaries. The ceremony took place in the presence of the great Tahitian chiefs Utami and Tati and an estimated 800 people. Great hopes were held for the young Pomare III, but he was not strong. He died on 11 January 1827, to be succeeded by a young and pleasure-loving queen, Pomare IV. The dream of a spiritually and morally regulated Christian kingdom, edified by Nott and Henry, tutored by Orsmond, dissolved with the young king's death. Pastoral direction of the young and flighty new queen was a more difficult assignment, assumed as the years

A CURIOUS NEW GOD

passed by George Pritchard, the missionary at Papeete and Paofai, districts where the queen resided. It fell to Pritchard to cope with the arrival of French Catholic missionaries from France, leading up to intervention by the French and British governments and the simmering of their rivalry in Tahiti into a succession of crises (pages 254-6).

From 1821 onward Raiatea, under Threlkeld, became the dynamic force in the Leeward Islands mission. Its neighbouring island of Tahaa, within the same reef, was tended from 1822 by Robert Bourne. Threlkeld struck out his own line. He altered the observation of Sunday in the Leeward Islands by one day when he discovered from ships' captains that Captain James Wilson of the *Duff* had failed to adjust the date on the voyage out. This trivial detail set up a barrier between the Leeward and Tahitian missions, which remained until the French readjusted the date to conform with ships' practice. The older missionaries insisted that their Sabbath was set to coincide exactly with Jerusalem.

Threlkeld was openly derogatory about Pomare II's backsliding. He and Williams successfully cultivated the Raiatean king, Tamatoa I, a genial and authoritative old warrior whose conversion provided a benevolent umbrella for their Congregational churches on Raiatea. Their brisk democratized arrangements stressed the function of lay deacons and auxiliary societies supported by trade. Tamatoa endorsed their efforts to get a ship; the people of Raiatea thought of it as theirs, though it was technically registered in the name of Threlkeld's colleague, John Williams.

Threlkeld and Williams indignantly protested to the Directors of the LMS in London when they decreed that trading in the name of the Society should stop and Pomare's previously built vessel, the *Haweis*, should not be used for gain. The Raiatea missionaries attempted to grow and export tobacco, but were frustrated by the imposition of customs duty in New South Wales. They felt that a little commercial skill would provide Tamatoa and his people with shipping and funds adequate to take eager converts to establish churches in the Austral and Cook Island groups, each capable of being reached within a few days sail.

John Williams was unwell during 1820. His wife's health troubled him; he himself suffered from filariasis; in 1821 he went to Sydney for medical treatment. Threlkeld, physically robust and colourful, had until then been the more aggressive leader. When William Ellis was in Hawaii with the London Deputation he suggested to the American missionaries that Williams would find the climate of the Sandwich Islands better for his health; the Americans even wrote to invite him. By then, however, he and his wife were in Sydney, negotiating with Marsden the fulfilment of the dream that possessed his teeming brain; Williams wanted a ship of his own.

TO LIVE AMONG THE STARS

In 1822 he returned to Raiatea from Sydney. While there he had bought a ship, the old schooner *Endeavour*. Tamatoa and the people of Raiatea greeted it with delight, but Threlkeld and Williams thought it a poor step toward the great goal they had conceived — Williams regarded it as a temporary expedient. He wanted a real ship, of proper tonnage. The members of the two-man LMS Deputation did not agree with Raiatea's tendency to construct its own little empire. Tyerman and Bennet brought instructions to practise economies, to depend for support on the local people, and to step up local contributions in kind to defray expenses. They brought with them a cotton artisan, Elijah Armitage, to manufacture cloth locally from cotton presumed to have been grown by his predecessor, John Giles, a planter who arrived in 1817. Pomare II frowned on both projects. Lancastrian enterprise and leisurely Polynesian subsistence gardening were incompatible. Threlkeld and Williams were scornful of the tottering project. The Deputation appealed for co-operation and unity between the missionaries in the Leeward and Windward Islands before they left in 1824; they were not impressed by Williams' longing to have a ship sent from London; hence he went to Sydney and obtained his own.

In July and August 1823 Williams and Bourne set out with six teachers and their wives on a westward cruise to the Hervey Islands (now the southern Cooks). For Williams, the voyage was psychologically important. His letters and journals began to show the tonic effect of the ocean breeze; colourful contacts with new islands restored his physical and mental health. John Williams' social origins in London as an apprentice ironworker give some clue to his knack of getting rapidly into touch with men and women of unfamiliar cultures. His favourite texts for sermons were drawn from the Gospel and First Epistle of John. They dealt with the love of Christ. Williams came out of his shell; he used the wiles and conversational techniques of the Cockney in exotic societies where he blossomed as a trail-blazing chief. He loved it; he could transcend his past. If he was driven, it was in the cause of Christ; when he became depressed he could get out of it by forming and carrying through even larger designs. Suddenly he became the most active LMS missionary in the South Seas; the Directors in London were embarrassed by his impatience, but flattered by his almost invariable success. He created — and became — a legend.

The story of Williams' first voyage, in the *Endeavour*, "the vessel belonging to the United Chiefs in the Leeward Islands," in 1823, belongs to the development of churches in the Cook Islands (page 82). Tamatoa was on board, and active with Williams in commending his faith to brother chiefs in the Cooks who spoke a closely related language. Already two Raiateans, Papeiha and Vahapata, had been left on the island of Aitutaki by Williams on his voyage to Sydney in 1821. The way was opening for him, as a chief among

A CURIOUS NEW GOD

chiefs and the honoured friend of Pacific Islander Christian teachers, to pursue his energetic path as planter of new churches, westward and northward across Polynesia, to the outskirts of the Melanesian island chains.

As he did so, his progress and reputation caused some chagrin among older missionaries. Davies and Nott found themselves relatively immobile on Tahiti. From the beginning of their careers they had earnestly tried to cultivate the Marquesas (266), the Austral Islands (page 270), Tonga (page 71) and Fiji (page 102) in accordance with their mandate; they found themselves frustrated — their Tahitian church running to seed, the queen too young and self-indulgent to govern effectively. Younger men — especially Williams — whose paths they had prepared, brashly thrust out towards islands they themselves had no ship to reach.

In 1824 Threlkeld left Raiatea with Tyerman and Bennet, never to return. His wife had died; he went to Sydney. There he was drawn into a mission among the Australian Aboriginal population and eventually left the LMS. Ellis, after his service in Hawaii, returned to England; he wrote his celebrated *Polynesian Researches* and in 1832 became Foreign Secretary of the LMS. Orsmond's removal from Borabora to Moorea made him a member, and waspish critic, of the group centered on Tahiti, where he settled in 1831. "'I said I shall die in my nest,' was the language of each of us, both Williams and myself at Raiatea, when we chose the place of our sepulchre," wrote Threlkeld many years later. Both were tempestuous birds — and finished elsewhere.

On Raiatea, when together, they had remonstrated at the "caprice of irresponsible directors"; they demanded greater independence of action and a good ship. After his return from visiting the Cook Islands in mid-1823, Williams wrote to the London Directors to express his strong dissatisfaction:

> for my part I cannot content myself within the narrow limits of a single reef, and if means are not afforded, a continent to me would be infinitely preferable, for there if you cannot ride you can walk, but in these isolated islands a ship must carry you.

The Directors were not pleased with his brand of abrupt ambition. The ways he circumvented them to gain the adulation and support of "the religious public at home" made them ambivalent about him until he died. Williams was a phenomenon; he had to be gingerly handled, but his vision in the end became a foundation of policy for missions in the Pacific.

2

Christians in Hawaii

Protestants
Catholics

BEFORE THE FIRST MISSIONARY from New England stood on Hawaiian soil the islands were already a unified kingdom under Kamehameha I. An enterprising chief, intelligent, a formidable warrior, shrewd in trade as in battle, Kamehameha the conqueror had made good use of the guns, skills and men he acquired as a result of the visits of the explorers Cook and Vancouver and the many ships that followed in their wake. Two of his retainers, Isaac Davis and John Young, Englishmen from the American fur-trading ships *Fair American* and *Eleanora,* had been waylaid and pressed into service for Kamehameha's consolidation of his gains. They were familiar with the equipment of the many ships that watered and took in supplies during the northern winter, as part of their lucrative trade with China in the pelts of sea otters, and later in sandalwood. These men married high female chiefs and were absorbed into the Hawaiian scene. Young became a forbear of later Hawaiian royalty. Their service to Kamehameha was a parallel, on a grander scale, to the way Andrew Lind and Peter Hagerstein had reinforced the rise of Pomare I on Tahiti at the same period.

In Hawaii, the scale of everything seemed more grandiose. More ships, sailors and trade goods poured into the islands. Kamehameha himself was an imposing personality. In the Sandwich Islands (as they were then called) the celebrations of war and fertility deities marked the travels and festivals of the semi-divine high chiefs and their priestly *kahuna.* Their gorgeous feather

CHRISTIANS IN HAWAII

cloaks, *kahili,* or stave banners, and elaborate headgear were symbols of intricate religious observances centered on great occasions at the *heiau,* sacred enclosures comparable with the Tahitian *marae,* and held together by the conception of *kapu,* or taboo. The *kapu* system around the chiefs prescribed a supernatural sanctioned web of custom, radiating holiness, and enforced by fear of the spirits' revenge. Sexual relations, as in other Polynesian lands, were normally extended to a far wider range of partners than in Christian Europe. A form of *hula* — an ecstatic dance frequently celebrating fruitfulness and procreation — surrounded the cult of Lono, a deity whose role in the society and external trappings recall the Oro worship of the Society Islands.

When the first American Protestant missionaries reached the shores of the largest island, Hawaii, on 30 March 1820, they entered a society in a condition of sudden and spectacular transition. They learned that Kamehameha, the old king, was dead and had been succeeded by his son, Liholiho; the *kapu* system had been suspended by Kamehameha's successors — men were eating with women "in all the islands." The *heiaus* had been dismantled and the images of the gods destroyed or secreted. "If these are facts," said the missionaries' journal for that day, "they are interesting facts. They seem to show that Christ is overturning in order to take possession, and that these isles are waiting for his law while the old and decaying pillars of idolatry are falling to the ground."

Whether viewed as providence or good fortune, the timing seemed right. The American Board of Commissioners for Foreign Missions entered the Sandwich Islands with advantages when compared with the first LMS expedition to Tahiti. They found a reasonably stable group of high chiefs, the successors of Kamehameha. The rapid changes within the old religion provided a receptive breathing space; people were in a state of questioning and expectancy in all that concerned the power of the God of white sailors and traders. Economically the ABCFM's mission could count in 1820 on steady further supplies of materials and workers from America. Their enterprise had been carefully thought out and briefed in the light of what their directing body had gleaned from across the Atlantic. They also gained by careful evaluation of the cautionary story of the LMS in the South Pacific up to that point.

Who sent them? Who were they?

The American Board of Commissioners for Foreign Missions, like the London society, grew in a climate of revival and rigorous Calvinist theological thought. After 1790, classical New England Puritanism went through a rebirth in the colleges and local churches of Massachusetts and Connecticut. In reaction against the deism, "free thinking" — and Unitarianism — that had swept some of their strongholds, Congregationalists and Presbyterians joined forces in re-asserting the teaching of Jonathan Edwards, the massive

TO LIVE AMONG THE STARS

American systematician who fused the rationality of John Locke and Calvin with the "surprising work of God," the re-kindling of frigid Christians and their conversion to disinterested works of benevolence. Their standard theologians were Jedidiah Morse and Samuel Hopkins. Young ministers in the colleges at Yale, Williams, Amherst, Dartmouth and Middlebury absorbed this heady newer thought along with a solid grounding in classical and general studies. They provided about two-thirds of the ordained missionaries in Hawaii in the first twenty years of the mission.

Another, but related, side of their preparation was absorbed from their farm backgrounds. Most of them came from communities away from the sea where as boys they had handled planes, saws and ploughs. They could keep accounts as regularly as they said their prayers. By the time their professors were through with them they were often chiselled, fitted and polished — pious and practical Yankees. All they needed was the wealth and know-how of maritime Boston and Salem to get them to their goals. Sponsors with savvy in these ports, open to the world, were not in short supply.

In the Park Street Church, facing Boston Common, and on Beacon Hill nearby, ministers and merchants forged the headquarters of an efficient missionary organization, the American Board. They were a ripe product of the revival that followed George Whitefield's intensely theatrical and effective preaching tours in North America. In the language of Puritanism, these ministers and businessmen were "practical and affectionate."

Enterprise on behalf of Christ, with whom they held daily communion in prayer, was not to them a form of getting to heaven by good works. As Calvinists they believed that only the grace they had received, when by conversion they entered the Kingdom in hope, was sufficient for their needs. Their works flowed as disinterested benevolence from the grace to which they were debtors. The debt, though a free gift without interest, had to be honoured by unquestioning obedience to the Great Commission — "preach the Gospel to every living creature."

More than that; the American and French Revolutions and the Napoleonic Wars had stirred up among some of their theologians the premonition that Napoleon, and later the resurgent papacy, might herald the end of the world. Before the return of Christ and his millennial reign they anticipated, from their study of scripture, that the Gospel would necessarily have to be proclaimed to the ends of the earth. The same general conviction had seized the minds of some of the founders of the London Missionary Society. When remarkable success crowned the early efforts of the American Board in Hawaii, the editor of the Board's *Missionary Herald* wondered whether Christ's thousand-year reign might begin in the Pacific.

CHRISTIANS IN HAWAII

When war broke out in 1812 between Britain and the United States, bad feeling between the two countries failed to disrupt the transatlantic solidarity of the evangelical "religious public," forged by fresh revivals at the turn of the century. Whatever happened to politics and trade, missionary obligation remained. Americans on the eastern seaboard eagerly read reports of early LMS efforts in several fields, including the Pacific. When the ABCFM was in process of formation in Boston its agents informed the LMS fully of its plans to send a mission to the Sandwich Islands.

Attention had been focussed on Hawaii by the presence in America of a small group of young men who had come to the United States on American ships. One of them became part of the legend of the founding of the ABCFM; Henry Opukahaia (called Obookiah in America) is the New England version of the Noble Savage. A group of fervent young college students, fired with the desire to become foreign missionaries, met Opukahaia at Yale. Their discovery led to the gathering together of five young Hawaiians, two students from India, a Canadian Indian, and two white Americans, in a Foreign Mission School at Cornwall, Connecticut. One of them, George Kaumualii, was the son of the high chief of the island of Kauai. Their most hopeful neophyte, Opukahaia, died of typhus in 1818, to the intense disappointment of the ABCFM. They had hoped he would be foremost in converting his own people. Three other Hawaiians who had studied and been trained in piety at Cornwall — Kaumualii, William Tenui and Thomas Hopu, went as assistants in the first company of missionaries on the brig *Thaddeus,* leaving Boston on 23 October 1819.

Their instructions from the Board told them "to aim at nothing short of covering those islands with fruitful fields and pleasant dwellings, and schools and churches; of raising up the whole people to an elevated state of Christian civilization," but they were "above all to convert them from their idolatries and superstitions and vices, to the living and redeeming God." As in the case of the LMS before them, they had simultaneously to civilize and convert; they were the first American missionaries to enter the country, and as such were advised to submit to the ruling chiefs and stay away from any attempt to interfere in politics. In the kingdom they entered, they were to fear God and to act as though they were "settled and contented as citizens," subject to the chiefs. They did fairly well, but there were problems.

In the earliest period of the mission they found themselves willingly received and patronized by a group of influential high chiefs. One of these was the important spokesman and agent of Kamehameha I, Kalanimoku, jocularly referred to by ships' crews as Billy Pitt, because he was indeed prime minister. Here was a highly placed Hawaiian, more than normally ready to welcome Christians. He had been baptized in the previous year by the Catholic chaplain, the Abbé de Quélen, on the French ship *Uranie,* with the commander, Louis de Freyçinet, as his godfather. He lay open to future instruction, now to be imparted by Protestants, who recognized his baptism as valid when in 1826 they eventually received him as a full communicant member of their church.

Kalanimoku's situation, following the suspension of *kapu*, was not unique. The crews of many passing ships and Hawaiian voyagers abroad had filled the islands with rumours and curiosity about the God of Cook and Vancouver. It seems highly likely that from the sixteenth century Spanish and post-Spanish influences contributed to the visions and ecstatic predictions of local Hawaiian prophets, who foretold, under the old religion, the coming of strangers from the sea who were to be taken seriously. Since Catholic influences were distasteful to the missionaries of the American Board, they tended to suppress such evidence.

Kalanimoku and Kaahumanu, the widowed queen of Kamehameha I, were therefore extending more than traditional Polynesian politeness and "desire to please" when they welcomed the American mission. They were in search of viable spiritual alternatives to the *kapu* sanctions they had suspended when they decreed the discontinuance of their old religious rites.

Surprised, delighted, yet baffled by the strangeness of the language and culture, the Americans were for an initial period unable to cope with the size of their opportunity. They had to rely on English, and for interpretation on the services of their Hawaiian-born assistants, two of whom let them down. Kaumualii, who had served in the American navy before being converted, absented himself from prayers on the *Thaddeus* and made friends with "one or two deists" on board. He returned to his father's island of Kauai, took refuge in alcohol and the easy company of locally settled white men, and finally died after trying to stage an abortive revolt against the new king, Kamehameha II, Liholiho.

The young king, from the beginning, was less willing than Kaahumanu and Kalanimoku to draw near to the American missionaries. He had abrogated *kapu* under pressure from his titled seniors. The Americans' approach to him developed gradually, by way of the powerful Kaahumanu, whose authority as *Kuhina nui,* vested in the female line, made her virtual regent. She cemented her powerful position by taking two other high chiefs from the potentially dangerous and proud island of Kauai as husbands. The missionaries sensed her importance and tried to cultivate her.

After their early investigation of the situation on the big island of Hawaii, they opted to settle for the time being at Honolulu on Oahu, a port town where ships put in for revictualling and revelry. They became acquainted with the adaptive ways of resident Honolulu foreigners, among whom they found the diminutive and acquisitive French adviser to Kamehameha II, Jean

CHRISTIANS IN HAWAII

Rives, and the Spaniard Francisco de Paula Marin, half Catholic, half adoptive Hawaiian. Marin, with several wives, was one among many who had accepted, as pleasant and familiar, island practices that seemed, to Yankee Calvinists, immoral and against the law of God.

The first company built their houses and stores as they struggled to learn the language, preach and find their way. They constructed a neat half-frame timber house as the first of the "pleasant dwellings" their commission had prescribed. A first church and school-house soon followed. Their wives, bearing children, cooking together in the cramped kitchen, sewing, receiving guests, became prototypes of an American migration destined to offset the violent and roistering ways of the traders and whalers. They soon met head-on conflict, at Honolulu and the busy port of Lahaina on Maui, with men of many nations off the whaling ships. The early days of whaling and the mission in Hawaii coincide. This first company of New Englanders was squeezed between two unfamiliar groups of residents — the chiefs, and the assorted community on the beach.

Most of the party of fourteen Americans and three Hawaiians were still in their twenties. All the American men were from rural backgrounds in New England or New York State. The two ordained ministers who led the company had been well trained; Hiram Bingham, a Vermonter, at Middlebury College and Andover Seminary, Asa Thurston at Yale and Andover. In their translation work, like many of their successors in later companies, they could work from Greek and Hebrew. Thomas Holman, a medical doctor, and his wife "did not adjust well in spirit to their fellow workers," and left for home on 20 July 1820. They were, in fact, uppish. Daniel Chamberlain, an older farmer from Massachusetts, who came with his wife and five children, also had problems settling, and left in 1823. Samuel Ruggles was a teacher and catechist from Brookfield, Connecticut; Elisha Loomis a printer and teacher who set up the first press at Honolulu. Samuel Whitney, from Branford, Connecticut had been educated at Yale and was licensed to preach; he was ordained in the islands and stayed on, with his wife, both dying in their new country, as did Asa Thurston and his wife Lucy. Thurston proved the long-stayer of the first company, making only one brief visit to California in 1863; he died in Honolulu in 1868, she in 1876.

Hiram Bingham, the missionary in charge, achieved most fame and attracted most obloquy in the islands and abroad. Set rigidly in religious and moral conclusions he considered to be revealed and unquestionable, Bingham alienated other settlers whose principles and behaviour allowed more latitude on matters such as sex and the Sabbath. His solid education and his tireless efforts to protect the people of Hawaii against white exploiters and their own excesses, nevertheless earned him the great affection he has retained within the Hawaiian church he helped to found. Bingham's make-up was short on humour, particularly the kind that can deprecate its possessor's own foibles, but he was a tireless observer and writer, a formidable organizer, a builder and an educated man. Bingham could turn his head to designing and putting up chapels and schools. After twenty years of struggle and toil he was forced in 1840 by his wife's indifferent health to return to Boston. He listed his statistics and affirmed that "the age of darkness, of wars, of infanticide, and of human sacrifices had passed away, and the age of schools, of wholesome laws, of Bibles, of spiritual sacrifices, and revivals, had come." He never returned. Scribe and colossus of the first period of the mission, he had affronted many critics; some were his enemies, others his colleagues in Hawaii and at Boston. He was firmly and fairly, but politely, denied opportunity to go back.

The first company became legendary for the Mission. They brought both Christianity and the Protestant virtues of ingenuity and hard work to the Sandwich Islands. Altogether twelve companies of American Board missionaries came, the last in 1848. Later "individual arrivals" followed, as Americans were called upon between 1848 and 1900 to serve the autonomous Hawaiian Church. "Without them the American flag would not now be flying over Hawaii," says the record of the missionaries. The children — some sent back to be educated in America, others kept to pass through schools established for them on Oahu — became important in the later staffing of Hawaiian-based missions to Micronesia and in the commercial and political evolution of Hawaiian society. Samuel Northrop Castle and Amos Starr Cooke, both members of the eighth company, arriving in 1837, became partners in Castle and Cooke, one of Hawaii's largest mercantile and financial corporations.

Among the wives were many with considerable educational attainments. Mrs Charlotte Close Knapp Dole, who came out with the eighth company, as the wife of Horton Knapp, a teacher, in 1837, was "a scholar in Hebrew, Greek, and Latin" and understood "all kitchen branches of information into the bargain." When widowed, she married the Rev. Daniel Dole, a widower and a member of the ninth company of 1840. Her combination of skills was fairly typical. Quilting, weaving, reading, praying, teaching, the women of the mission imparted special and enduring talents to generations of their converts.

The second and third companies, like the first, included "helpers" trained beforehand in America. Three Hawaiians — William Kamooula, Richard Kalaioulu and Kupelii — and one Tahitian, Stephen Popohe, came with the second in 1823. Henry Tahiti ("a Tahitian"), George Tyler Kielaa, Samuel J. Mills Paloo and John E. Phelps Kalaauluna (Hawaiians) followed in the third company in 1828. Their given names speak for themselves. The flow of islanders educated at Cornwall stopped under the influence of Ellis of the LMS, who recommended the training of island teachers in and for the islands.

CHRISTIANS IN HAWAII

So the list continues. Sober and quizzical faces of men and women whose names have been absorbed into the colourful social history of the islands look out from the portraits of members of all twelve companies in the Missionary Album compiled as a memorial of their positive achievements. Their drawings of the scattered stations they occupied reveal the forward march of printing, building and prayer among the Hawaiians. For most of their converts, and for the church they founded, they became and remain fathers and mothers in Israel. Their spiritual children honour them even when they no longer feel obliged to do exactly as they said.

In the first two years of their work the members of the first company found progress slow. As early as May 1820 they wrote to George Burder, the secretary of the LMS in London, after initiating correspondence with the "missionary brethren in the Society Islands." Bingham, who kept the journal, said: "With some anticipation we cherish the desire that this may be the commencement of a long happy and important correspondence between the two establishments."

On 15 April 1822 their wishes came true. William Ellis and his wife arrived in Honolulu from Huahine, accompanied by a group of nine converts from the Society Islands. Ellis came with the English LMS Deputation, Tyerman and Bennet (page 27), who had been offered a passage on the ship *Mermaid* when it touched at Huahine. The *Mermaid* was en route to Hawaii as convoy for the small schooner *Prince Regent*, a present from the British king to the Hawaiian king.

Two of the recently elected deacons of Ellis' church on Huahine, with their wives, were intended as leaders of the party accompanying the Deputation. Auna, their outstanding head, had been a person of consequence in Tahiti before his conversion and baptism. His father, a high chief of Raiatea, designated him as a priest. He had been a leading member of the Arioi Society and an outstanding warrior in Pomare II's campaigns on Tahiti in 1812 and 1815. He fought at the battle of Feipi in the latter year, when Pomare overcame his enemies, as he could vividly recall after he became a Christian.

Auna was one of the first people of rank in Tahiti to accept Christianity. He began to teach other inquirers at Taiarapu as early as 1814, when he was already spending time in the school established by John Davies at Papetoai on Moorea. In 1818 he went with Ellis and Davies to Huahine, and was baptized there in 1819.

His fellow-deacon, Matatore, was the other missionary assistant. He and his wife, with five other unnamed persons from the Huahine church, were intended to be sent to evangelize the Marquesas. They were not dropped there by the *Mermaid* because of adverse weather, but accompanied Ellis and the Deputation to Honolulu.

TO LIVE AMONG THE STARS

There was joy in the American mission house when they came. The British visitors were squeezed uncomfortably into the available space, while the Tahitian Christians lived nearby in grass houses. Ellis brought news of encouraging first contacts with high chiefs on the island of Hawaii where they made their first landfalls.

They had been warmly welcomed by Kuakini, the Governor of Hawaii, who responded at once to the presence among them of Tahitians. Kuakini told them excitedly that there were already Tahitians ashore on Hawaii. Ellis and his nine companions could easily be understood when they spoke Tahitian. Kuakini took Auna, "towards whom he manifested much attachment," to fraternize with Hawaiians, while the ship sailed slowly round from Kailua to Kealakekua. There Auna rejoined the ship, with word that he had talked ashore with a man named Toteta from Moorea and that Kuakini was eager to become Christian.

Even more heartening was a meeting at Honolulu, witnessed by Thurston, Chamberlain and Loomis, as the party from the *Mermaid* landed. The ship was first boarded by Kalanimoku. "On our way," Ellis afterwards reported, "we met a canoe, in which the wife of Auna recognized a brother, who had left the Society Islands in the *Bounty*, when the mutineers took possession of the ship."

This man was Moe, or Jack, who had been in the Hawaiian islands for "many years, as steward to the Queen's Brother, the Governor of the Island of Maui" (Keeaumoku). Auna's wife's brother thus opened the way instantly for the whole Tahitian group to mingle with Hawaiian high chiefs, the *ali'i*, with credentials he established for Auna, himself a Christian and a chief among chiefs.

By being introduced to Kalanimoku (Billy Pitt, the Prime Minister), Auna and his wife formed an intimate acquaintance with Kaahumanu, the highly influential Queen Mother and widow of Kamehameha the Great. She "produced for them a lodging at her house. Finding them interesting and agreeable, on acquaintance of three weeks becoming attached to them, she and Taumare, have given them a pressing invitation to remain here," Bingham noted on 9 May. Taumare was the Tahitian spelling for the name of the high chief of Kauai, Kaumualii, father of George Kaumualii, the backsliding protégé of the Mission. The elder Kaumualii had been taken in marriage by Kaahumanu — a politically astute move in her widowed state. "Nor is Auna less desirous to stay but wishes that his beloved pastor, Mr E. may remain also," Bingham went on. "The invitation, seconded by the other principal chiefs is extended to Mr E. and his family."

Original mission house, Honolulu.

TO LIVE AMONG THE STARS

The form of this invitation is a clue to the processes lying behind it. Moe, the long-lost brother of Auna's wife, after his *Bounty* adventure, most probably came from Tahiti in 1792 on the English schooner *Jenny,* the only vessel known to have travelled the route at that period. The mutineers from Bligh's *Bounty* read Christian prayers together every Sunday. Among the Tahitians who were with them "several were desirous to have the observance of Christmas explained to them." According to a member of the mutineer group, "some of them wished to learn our prayers which they all allowed to be better than their own; those who were constantly about us knew when our Sunday came, and were always prepared accordingly." The element of taboo in the observance of the Sabbath appealed to many Pacific Islanders, for whom holy and forbidden seasons were already customary in their own religions.

Moe's presence in Hawaii, at a time when interest in Christianity had been generated by events like Kalanimoku's baptism, heightened the feeling of religious expectancy. The powerful *kapu* system had been suspended by the Hawaiian chiefs; people were seeking beliefs and practices to fill what they sensed as an uneasy twilight of the gods. "Generally speaking," Ellis observed, "they have cast away their idols, but not entirely, they may truly be said to be without any religion at all and are literally waiting for a better one than that which they have just abandoned."

Auna and his wife spoke a language easily grasped by Hawaiian chiefs. All observers remark on his imposing physique; one also described his wife as "one of the most polished females I ever saw." Auna frequently led prayers in the houses of the chiefs, took prayer meetings, and participated in long conversations about his own conversion and the churches in Tahiti. Five of the Tahitians brought as servants mingled with Hawaiians, evidently at a different level, in the household of Kaahumanu, where they were invited to lodge. Auna kept a journal of part of his time in Hawaii. The king, Kamehameha II (Liholiho) and his wife were reserved at first about Auna and his group, but soon became curious and attended Tahitian family worship.

Thus the chiefs' invitation to stay in Hawaii was a direct result of the work of Auna and his fellow-Tahitians, but was extended to include Ellis. He and Tyerman and Bennet were unwilling to accept until they had consulted the Americans, who warmly endorsed the proposal, which was made only three weeks after the arrival of the LMS representatives in Honolulu. It was decided not to proceed to the Marquesas. "The voyage seemed to be marked out by the finger of God," Ellis reported to London, "and we appeared only to follow the cloudy pillar of His Providence."

How cloudy the providential coincidences appeared to be derived from more than the fortunate presence of Moe among the Hawaiian chiefs' retainers. On board the *Mermaid* Captain Kent had shown amorous attention to the wife of Matatore, Auna's fellow-deacon from Huahine. By the time the vessel reached Honolulu a seduction occurred. On 8 May Kent took the wife on board with him and refused to allow her husband to board the *Mermaid* with Ellis to get her back. On 9 May the *Mermaid* sailed for Fanning Island with Matatore's wife still on board. At that stage the members of the LMS party indignantly said they did not intend to continue their voyage on the *Mermaid*, but would wait for another ship. Eventually Kent returned, on 29 July. Matatore's wife, who was evidently a consenting partner, died at sea on her way home, after Ellis and the Deputation agreed to return with Kent to Huahine; there Ellis prepared for his return to Hawaii to take up his new station (at a salary in line with the Americans' higher scale) in February 1823.

Ellis, Tyerman and Bennet filled the providential space of the *Mermaid's* absence with a tour around Oahu. More influential in the rooting of Christianity in the Hawaiian Islands were other tours undertaken on the islands of Maui and Hawaii by Auna and his Tahitians between 11 May and 2 July. They were accompanied by Kuakini and Kaahumanu. The people collected round them as they taught reading and writing. Kaahumanu, who made fast progress in literacy on the journey, was impressed by the Tahitians' accounts of the burning of their religious effigies; she knew the hiding places on Hawaii of many of the idols used in the time of Kamehameha and had them brought out of concealment and burned in the presence of her Tahitian guests and teachers.

By 10 August George Bennet told William Hankey, the LMS treasurer in London, "the King has declared his regard for the Word of God! He himself, his queens, great numbers of chiefs, are daily receiving instruction by all hands." Ellis hoped that Liholiho, whose Hawaiian was naturally elegant, might become a second Pomare as an adviser on scripture translation; the king's fondness for spirits and other pleasurable diversions turned him eventually, however, into a Pomare of a less wished for kind.

When the *Mermaid* sailed finally back to Tahiti Auna and some of his companions were left behind to serve in Hawaii, until he also felt compelled to leave in March 1824 on account of his wife's homesickness. In cooperation with the Hawaiians Thomas Hopu and John Honolii, Auna had been influential in commending Christianity to the native Hawaiian decision-makers at a time when they needed persuading in terms they understood. The church in the Sandwich Islands owes its Tahitian visitors a large and not always fully acknowledged debt.

By the time of Ellis' return in 1823 Bingham and his co-workers believed the break-through had come in the mission's work. *Pule* (prayer) and *palapala* (literacy) were advancing among the chiefs. Both needed to be regulated, institutionalized. At Waimea on Kauai Whitney and Ruggles began the work.

TO LIVE AMONG THE STARS

Bingham, Loomis, Chamberlain and Thurston were at Honolulu. In 1823 the Rev. Charles Stewart of the second company established a station at the booming whalers' port of Lahaina on Maui, where Miss Betsey Stockton, a black American and a freed slave, worked with them as servant and teacher in a school she had established. The Stewarts were forced by Mrs Stewart's bad health to leave the islands in October 1825, taking Betsey Stockton with them. Thurston and Holman began at Kailua on Hawaii in 1820. Thurston was joined in 1824 by members of the second company, who commenced work at Hilo and Kaawaloa. Chiefs and people together flocked into the simple chapels and schoolhouses for instruction. Over half the population was estimated to be literate within the first decade.

Eli Chamberlain, the watchful and often witty accountant and administrator who came to Honolulu with the second company in 1823, deftly noted the deadening effect of the landslide of so many into the church by late 1825; he described Hiram Bingham's attempts after a large religious meeting to call for decision at a deeper level:

> *I believe* that all who were spoken to on the subject declared themselves to be of those who desired to pursue the *narrow way* — probably had *ten times* as many more been present they would all have answered the question in the same way.

Inevitably the whole period to 1830 involved busy, almost feverish activity for the American Board missionaries and their pupils: translating, teaching, catechizing, instituting discipline, framing civil codes for the chiefs and explaining them to the people. Hymns were translated and composed by Ellis, Bingham and Thurston. Modes of worship in the vernacular were devised and made familiar.

At the ports of Honolulu and Lahaina the missionaries became involved in sharp confrontations with captains of whaling ships when women in large numbers were taken on board for sex — and crews ashore took advantage of traditional Hawaiian sexual hospitality. To the mission, sex meant monogamous life-long marriage; to many sailors and Hawaiians it was a form of boisterous play. Under the circumstances venereal disease became epidemic in Hawaiian ports. In 1825 at Lahaina William Richards opposed Captain William Buckle of the English whaler *Daniel* over the issue; Richards' house was surrounded by twenty white sailors armed with knives. There were threats to burn house and inmates. Eventually the chiefs and local people prevailed on the sailors to go back to the ship. At Honolulu in February of the following year members of the crew of the American warship *Dolphin* under Lieutenant John Percival were so enraged at the taboo placed on women visiting ships that they staged a violent riot in the town, menaced Kaahumanu, Kalanimoku, and others of the high chiefs, and physically attacked Bingham,

CHRISTIANS IN HAWAII

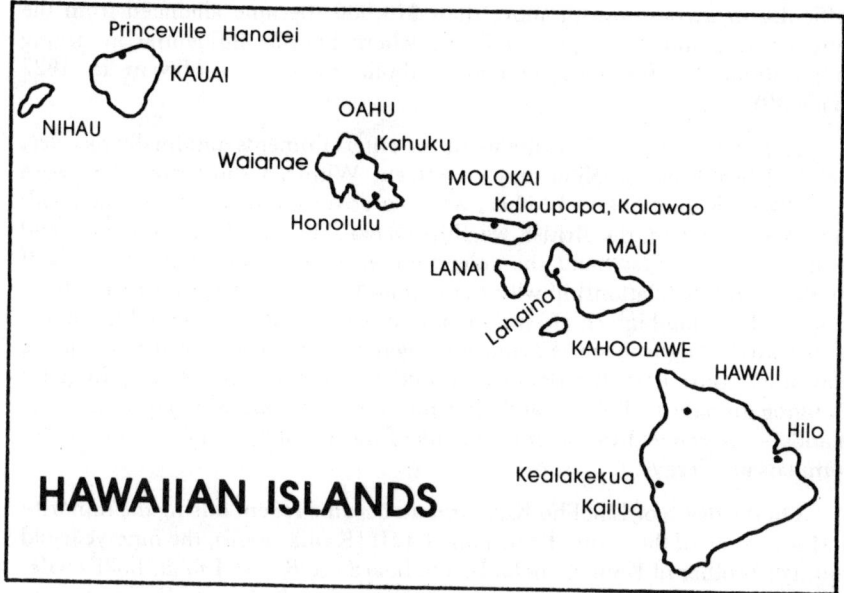

who protected himself against a blow from a club by waving his umbrella. Furious Hawaiians came to his assistance and laid out his assailants. Percival was obliged to recognize that Kaahumanu and the chiefs meant business and had in principle accepted Bingham's advice about women in ships. Some local reparations were made by Percival, but the affair was referred to the ABCFM in Boston and Percival was brought before an inquiry into the whole episode on his return to America.

Kamehameha II (Liholiho) had taken ship in 1823 with his favourite queen, Kamamalu, to visit the king of England. His love of dissipation and display drew him away from the influence of Kaahumanu and the American missionaries. The British, he knew, unlike the Americans, had a king; their religion, as he had sensed it among the generation that had known Cook and Vancouver, went better with regal style and the sort of amusements dear to some of the British residents on the beach. He would go and see King George.

Ellis, back now in Honolulu, offered to accompany the royal party as interpreter and guide, but after some vacillation the master of the ship *Aigle* on which they sailed made excuses for not taking Ellis. Instead he made common cause with the Honolulu French resident Jean Rives, who accompanied Liholiho as secretary and with the captain administered the provision of $25,000 in specie set aside for the tour. On arrival in London Rives had difficulty in accounting for more than $13,000, became alienated from the king's suite, and decamped to Paris, where he was influential in urging preparations for the first Roman Catholic mission to Hawaii in 1827 (page 49).

In London the weather, the food, the entertainments and finally measles, weighed heavy on Liholiho and his queen. Within a short time they were dead. Boki, Kalanimoku's brother, who was governor of Oahu, returned with the royal coffins on the British warship *Blonde*. He and the royal couple had seen and felt at first hand the splendour and ceremony of the Church of England and its relationship with the monarchy and nobility. He recognized, as later Hawaiian high chiefs and monarchs came to know, that old-fashioned high church Anglicanism was more congenial to the traditional *mores* of the Hawaiian court than the democracy and moral rigorism of New England Congregationalism. Boki — and after him the future kings and queens of the islands — responded to the enticements of more stately worship and a more complaisant clergy.

On the death of Liholiho Kaahumanu became regent during the minority and education of the young Kamehameha III (Kauikeaouli), the nine-year-old younger brother of Kamehameha II. On board the *Blonde*, Liliha, Boki's wife, and Kekuanoa, one of the chiefs who accompanied the king to England, were baptized by the ship's Anglican chaplain. For the young king this was not to be; the chiefs agreed in 1825 "that Kauikeaouli should receive a Christian education, and be separated as much as possible from those of his subjects whose influence would lead him to the vices which had stained the character of his brother." Sheltered schooling produced its own recoil; Kamehameha, though he treated the mission with respect and supported the legal enactments made under its influence, never became a full communicant member. The restrictive apron strings tied around him were attached by Kaahumanu, whose conversion from haughty wrath to authoritarian piety had been overwhelmingly complete.

Until her death in 1832 Kaahumanu acted as the great mother in church and state. Her authority as regent, and her close link with Kamehameha the Great, reinforced the prescriptions of the missionaries. As Congregationalists and New Englanders they insisted on a separation between ecclesiastical and civil power, but the Puritan doctrine that rulers could be nursing fathers and mothers to the Church and that Caesar was to be obeyed as "ordained by God for good" to civil subjects, suited both chiefs and missionaries. The new church, bursting with freshly literate and largely nominal adherents, laboured under an anomaly: neither the imported work ethic nor Christian morals took firm hold. When the first phase of the teaching process drew to its close after 1830 the character of Christian education changed. Most of the pupils in the quickly erected "grass hut" schools had necessarily been adults. The time then came for baptized children of the baptized, who had passed through the elementary schools, to have high schools.

The first and best known of these was established at Lahainaluna on the breezy mountain-side above Lahaina, Maui, in 1831. The school evolved into the Mission Seminary where elite generations were taught to be community leaders, writers, thinkers. Many were recruited for mission among their compatriots; some went as foreign Hawaiian missionary assistants and pastors to Micronesia and the Marquesas. During the 1830s and 1840s missionaries were slow and reluctant to license native Hawaiians as preachers. Nine were licensed before 1849; in that year James Kekela, who became a distinguished missionary in the Marquesas, was fully ordained to the pastorate (page 268).

By the mission's standards, delay in devolving the work on local people was not mere dragging of feet. Sexual behaviour evidently changed little. The missionary Lorrin Andrews reported in 1835 at Lahainaluna that "most teachers have lain with many or all of their scholars." A later comment on the situation identifies one of the paradoxes of putting adolescent Polynesian girls in neatly patterned long garments that veiled what was once familiar: "the clothes the girls put on became a source of allurement to men who all their lives had taken nudity for granted."

Other high schools, one for each main island, followed from 1836 onward. In 1839 in Honolulu a special school was begun for young chiefs; later it became the Royal School. At Punahou near Honolulu the mission established the first of the influential cluster of schools on the site; their own children were growing up and becoming attached to Hawaii, as many of them were themselves. The original school at Punahou was to provide good education for children of the mission without the need to send them on long journeys round Cape Horn to the ivy-clad and chilly colleges dear to their parents.

Before 1837 conditions in the Hawaiian churches had created an atmosphere preparatory to revival — lukewarm second-generation conformity, barely concealed acceptance of pre-christian morals, cultural exasperation caused by the suppression of local lore, missionary paternalism, a sense of bewildered displacement following in the wake of serious decline in population. Rufus Anderson, the far-sighted secretary of the American Board, had already in June 1836 rebuked the Sandwich Islands Mission for producing the strict conditions of communicant membership imposed by American Church Meetings. Although many had been baptized, only 1300 had been admitted to full communion by 1837. "*Our* standard by which to judge for piety, cannot be the one of the Sandwich Islands, nor any heathen country," Anderson wrote, "nor can our standard for conviction of sin, nor for genuine revivals."

TO LIVE AMONG THE STARS

In 1837 the revival came, partly under the spur of fervent preaching by rugged new missionaries whose own flagging faith had been fired before they came to Hawaii in the searing frontier evangelism of America's northeastern "burned over district" centered in upper New York State. New and sometimes bizarre forms of fervour took the place, in the lives of the people, of ecstasy once generated by public mass festivals and the performance of the hula. The hectic and at times hysterical enthusiasm of the Great Revival years, 1837-1840, left a permanent impression in the life of the church and established its character as belonging integrally to the Hawaiian people. The way was being paved for self-government and self-support in the church (pages 58-59).

Before the full force of the revival struck on the island of Hawaii a new and alternative Christian Church had been planted in Hawaii against many obstacles and with great pain. Roman Catholicism arrived in 1827.

ROMAN CATHOLIC ENTRY

FATHER ALEXIS BACHELOT, Father Abraham Armand and Father Patrick Short, the priests who led the small group of French and French-Irish Catholic missionaries to Honolulu, were members of the Congregation of the Sacred Hearts of Jesus and Mary. They arrived late in a field where heretics they tended to group pejoratively under the description "Methodists" had already pre-empted, or rather, summarily occupied, some of the most populous and influential centres of population. As conscious inheritors of a French Catholic revival they intended to reclaim for Christ, the Virgin and the Pope those they believed to have been subverted to heresy in the Pacific during the oppression of Catholics in the period of the French Revolution and the early years of Napoleon. Their community had been founded to continue the work of those suppressed by the Revolution. Its founders, the Rev. Pierre Marie Joseph Coudrin and the Countess Henriette de la Chevalerie, from the region of Poitou, were fervently devoted to the Sacred Hearts and the Perpetual Adoration of the Most Blessed Sacrament of the Altar.

Coudrin's desire for the revival of Catholicism in France and in northern Europe was intensely missionary — indeed a conscious re-assertion of the piety and virtue of the rural and small-town Catholicism of the *ancien régime* — closely attentive to the festivals of the Assumption, the Immaculate Conception, Corpus Christi (*fête-Dieu*) and the saints. On his deathbed and during his lifetime Coudrin, many of whose recruits came from the maritime western provinces around the mouth of the Loire, fixed his eyes on the oceans and the apostolate of the seas. Was not Mary the patron of sailors, the Star of the Sea and Queen of Heaven? Would she not reclaim her own? Direct attachment to the claims of the restored papacy was taken for granted by

CHRISTIANS IN HAWAII

Coudrin, the "good father." He also shared the ideas then current in the Roman Curia about transferring the spearhead of foreign missions from the older maritime Catholic powers, Portugal and Spain, to the France of the restored monarchy, the new favourite child of the Church. Pope Pius VII approved the new congregation in 1817; in 1825 Leo XII endorsed a plan to send French missionaries to Oceania for the first time.

An aspect of the project had been conceived in the fertile brain of Jean Rives, once bosom associate of Kamehameha I, a French Catholic with political and commercial plans for the future of Hawaii, and companion of the young king and queen, Liholiho and Kamamalu, on their ill-starred visit to London in 1824 (page 46). When the displeasure of the royal party fell on Rives he went to France to confer with ship-owners and investors. By the pleasure of Kamehameha he had been granted extensive lands in the Sandwich Islands. He regarded them as ready for cultivation. With many other foreign residents of Honolulu he cast a jaundiced glare on the straitened morality and narrow biblicism of the American missionaries. He induced a group of French bankers to buy a ship, the *Héros,* and outfit her at Le Havre, with trade goods and equipment. At Bordeaux the French Foreign Affairs Ministry prepared another ship, the *Comète,* to carry missionaries without charge, priests and lay brothers. In Rome, at the College of Propaganda, Coudrin gained papal approval. With the three priests and a choir-brother, he sent two lay brothers and a group of technicians. Rives went ahead of them from Le Havre on the *Héros* in company with a lawyer, Philippe A. de Morineau, who was supposed to oversee the financial and legal details of settling.

On the coast of California, en route, the expedition changed its character. It appears that Rives heard of the death of Liholiho and the ascendancy of Kaahumanu and Kalanimoku, the regent and prime minister who were already attached to the Sandwich Islands Mission and not friends of Rives. His design was probably to exploit the adherents of the High Chief Boki, Governor of Oahu, who had been baptized a Catholic on Freycinet's French ship *l'Uranie* in 1819 shortly after his brother Kalanimoku (page 35). Boki had been in London with Rives and was still restless and seeking. Rives could sense from a distance that his lands and his intended investment were in jeopardy. He disembarked in California on the pretext of trading engagements there, spent a large part of the capital entrusted to him for the Hawaiian adventure, and failed to rejoin the *Héros* at Monterey as had been intended. He never returned to Hawaii. Because of his defection the bottom fell out of the whole plan of settlement. Bachelot and Short, landing on 7 July 1827, found themselves from the beginning in embarrassing straits. Boki received them guardedly as Governor of Oahu, but told them, as they set up house on a ceded piece of land, that permission to stay was provisional and depended on the chiefs — which meant in effect Kaahumanu and Kalanimoku. The two priests had waited first on the American Consul, John Coffin Jones, a Unitarian known to be more sympathetic to traders on the beach than to the American Board missionaries, whom he disliked heartily. He and the British Consul, Richard Charlton, who detested Bingham even more, were friends of commerce and therefore pro-Catholic in the new partly commercial venture. Bachelot, leader of the group, with papal authority as Prefect Apostolic for the Sandwich Islands, found himself uncomfortably teetering on his beachhead, stripped of his budget, in trouble with the captain of his ship who needed his payment out of Rives' alienated funds, dependent on the quixotic local authority of Boki, waiting anxiously on the pleasure of powerful Protestant chiefs who had Bingham as their active grey eminence. Bachelot attended on the nominal Catholic Don Francisco de Paula Marin, and found him, with his two wives and his fondness for precautionary Hawaiian sorcery, an unwilling and weak sponsor.

Until 1840, when religious liberty was granted to Roman Catholics, these were the unpromising conditions within which the tiny new church struggled to be born and survive.

From the beginning there were other built-in disadvantages. The expedition had been fitted out and transported by the French government, laying the missionaries under suspicion of being simply the spiritual arm of broader French plans for the occupancy of Hawaii; the British and Americans offered protection and trade, but the French? The chiefs found the intrusion of a new power bewildering; the members of the American Mission advised them in print and by word of mouth that they thought French naval power and — more sinister — the Pope of Rome, had designs on their small kingdom. The mission compound of the Catholics was referred to as the *hale Palani,* the French House. It became difficult for Bachelot and his colleagues to explain the distinction between their commissions for the French king and the King of Kings. They had little English on arrival; even Short, despite his Anglo-Irish name. Kaahumanu, given her advice by Bingham, determined in her own right to order the priests to depart. Her authority to do so, under the Law of Nations, was not seriously questioned. The Catholics made their request for residence, but were asked not to stay. They did, however, pointing out that it was at the behest of Christ for the eternal good of their little flock; whatever the chiefs' instructions, they considered they must remain at the posts to which their Church assigned them. Their first mass on Hawaiian soil was celebrated on Bastille day, 14 July. When, years later in 1837, the power of French guns had forced the chiefs to accept the mission they established, that event too was celebrated on shore by another mass on the same significant date. Not until the 1880s would the Roman Catholic Church in Hawaii shed its pervasive French character and become "anglicized," though around the priests an authentically Hawaiian minority church was growing slowly.

CHRISTIANS IN HAWAII

There were two good reasons for putting down roots in Hawaiian soil: Boki, alienated, dissatisfied, was seeking a spiritual home, attended mass sporadically, and drew with him into the Catholic circle a group of simple followers from his own lands at Wainanae on Oahu. With others who clung to memories of the days before the great queen-widow Kaahumanu broke *kapu* in 1819, they developed a small but tight nucleus of disaffected people, persecuted mainly because the chiefs thought they were seditious.

The second reason for their attachment to Catholicism, readily visible to the American Protestants who considered any graven image as an idol, was that their very souls, steeped in Hawaiian ceremonial and pageantry, were hungry for a religion that communicated direct with an oral culture. They responded to ritual movement, imposing vestments, medals, crucifixes and statues, the cults of the Virgin and the saints. When they were persecuted it was usually for violating the chiefs' Protestant-inspired law against bowing down before graven images of any kind, old or new.

Alarms shook the small and still tentative American Sandwich Islands Mission. Their conceptions of Roman Catholicism were shaped by long unfamiliarity and horror sterotypes. They and their supporters knew nothing of the inwardness and suffering of the French Catholics at the time of the Revolution. Being in the dark about the origins and aims of any religious societies younger than the Jesuits, they called the Sacred Hearts missionaries Jesuits in disguise (as did the LMS in Tahiti) — a misnomer no less inaccurate than the Catholic "Methodist" applied to themselves. In the years that followed members of the Protestant mission published various booklets outlining in both English and Hawaiian what was then current about the misdeeds of "popery."

At the same time the American Congregationalists were embarrassed. They were reminded from headquarters that they were supposed to believe in religious liberty and the separation of church and state. Their resultant tactic was subtle; they came out in favour of public toleration, but determined to oppose the Catholics by wordy pulpit warfare. If Roman Catholicism was proscribed by the chiefs, they said, it would be on account of well-based civil laws against idolatry. Later they supported the other pretext given — that the government of Hawaii did not want its kingdom divided. Behind the scenes Bingham supported the chiefs in their decision not to let the Catholics stay; though he hid behind them and pleaded that the policy was theirs, he privately encouraged them to take a firm stand.

Between 1827 and 1831 Bachelot and Short, supported in particular by Brother Melchior Bondu, succeeded in beginning oral instruction and baptizing a few children and adults. Boki's permission to reside and work was revoked in April 1829 under pressure from Kaahumanu. Boki's own situation thereafter became increasingly untenable; he was disturbed and restless. The visit of the United States worship *Vincennes,* demanding that the Hawaiian chiefs should liquidate a debt of $50,000 owing on undischarged sandalwood contracts, set him off on a fatal voyage from which he never returned. He hastily equipped a ship and set out for Erromanga in the New Hebrides where he said he hoped to establish his fame by cutting precious sandalwood and returning to restore Hawaii's fortune and his own name. His ship was lost with all on board somewhere between Rotuma and Erromanga; the second ship of the expedition returned in August 1830, with its surviving crew ravaged by privation and disease. Boki, the hoped-for prop of the Catholic mission among the chiefs, was no more; his wife Liliha, who had remained, rallied Boki's partisans and unsuccessfully tried to foment revolt against Kaahumanu. The suspicion of collusion between the mission and Boki's partisans was consolidated by these events, but already during Boki's absence Kaahumanu had taken steps to control Liliha, who had been left as governor on Maui by Boki on his departure. Kaahumanu installed another high female chief, Kinau, a widow of Kamehameha II, as a co-governor of Maui. Violent measures were used to prevent would-be worshippers in the Catholic chapel from attending. Some were brought to answer before the chiefs; three of them, Luika Kaunaka, Kimeone Paele and Akoneriko, stood firm in public and suffered for their belief. Another old man, Valeriano, had been an opponent of the unification of Hawaii under the house of Kamehameha.

Throughout 1831 the Hawaiian chiefs tried to expel the two Catholic priests, though they were ready to allow the lay brothers and another member of the party to stay. Officially they had the right to deport over-stayers; they were concerned too, about the link between the mission and Boki's people, because they thought it threatened sedition and return to idolatry. Bachelot's expressed willingness to comply was happily thwarted by his providential lack of funds sufficient to pay the master of any ship that would take him. For most of the year the priests secretly continued their work. They were under three months notice to leave, but their property was not confiscated then as had been laid down. Among their catechumens was a high female chief, Kalola, of Boki's party. In July Kaahumanu arrested twelve Hawaiians who kept their contact with the mission; they set them to work labouring on the project called the Waikiki wall, between mountains and sea. Finally the chiefs obtained and prepared a small brig, the *Waverley,* and on 24 December 1831, deported the two priests to California, where they were received and employed by the Franciscan missions. They kept in touch with their converts, some of whom contrived to visit them, and prepared for their return.

In France the founder of the Sacred Hearts Fathers soon saw that the first piecemeal approach to Hawaii had been a debacle, calling for better coordinated strategy. At his instigation the College of Propaganda at Rome in

CHRISTIANS IN HAWAII

1833 appointed a single bishop for the whole of Eastern Oceania, Etienne Rouchouze, and cut the area of his Vicariate up into two sections, north and south of the equator. Bachelot was confirmed as Prefect Apostolic of the Sandwich Islands. To the south, in Valparaiso, Chrysostome Liausu was made Prefect. The whole Vicariate was assigned to the Fathers of the Sacred Hearts. In retrospect the intention became clear: the hitherto unoccupied island group of Mangareva was treated as a base for a Catholic approach to Tahiti and an attempt to plant a more durable church in Hawaii. Several who spoke English were designated as new missionaries, notably an Irish choir-brother, Columban Murphy, who was a British subject. He and Father Arsenius Walsh, two vigorous francophile Catholics, were used by Rouchouze at intervals during the 1830s to make sallies for reconnaissance into Honolulu.

They found, in 1835 and 1836, an altered internal scene. Kaahumanu, the Protestants' royal protector-figure, died in 1832. Her successor as regent, Kinau, found Kamehameha III fractious in his resistance to the chiefs, and to Bingham, who had educated him. In 1833 the king broke out wildly, as a heavy drinker and patron of prostitutes; he defied missionary authority by showing favour to Boki's followers. Columban Murphy made a rapid visit to Honolulu in 1835; he was still not a priest, simply a tall and jovial Irish carpenter in lay clothing. On his way back to report to the members of his congregation at Valparaiso he tried to pick up Bachelot and Short in California, but found they were absent from Monterey where he called. He left a message encouraging them to re-enter, and telling them Brother Melchior and the Catholics were holding on. In September 1836 Arsenius Walsh arrived, only to meet the old objections to residence for priests; he was told by Kinau, and by a now mildly penitent king, that he must go, but was saved from deportation by a passing French ship's captain after promising the chiefs that he would officiate only for resident white Catholics in their own homes. In October and November of the same year Lord Edward Russell, in command of the British warship *Actaeon,* clarified the rights of British subjects by negotiating an agreement giving them the right to reside "with the consent of the king."

Thus the cases of Walsh and Murphy appeared to be covered; the test case for a French priest followed on 17 April 1837 with the re-entry of Bachelot and Short from California. They had orders to go on to Ponape in Micronesia if they were repelled, as repelled they were. Both priests were recognized on landing and confined to their vessel, the *Clémentine,* as prisoners in the harbour. There were spectacular protests from the British Consul, Charlton, and from the French owner of the *Clémentine,* who said she had been seized and chartered unlawfully by the chiefs. In July the commanders of two ships, one British and the other French, were in port and tried to sort out the situation. Captain Edward Belcher of the *Sulphur* and Captain Abel Du Petit-Thouars of the *Vénus* acted jointly, but with regret, to tell both Short and Bachelot that they had no power at that moment to over-ride international law; if Hawaii's king and high chiefs insisted that Short, a British subject, should leave, he must do so as soon as possible, and must not preach in the meantime. The conferences at which the matter was sorted out were small but grim, with elements of comedy. Some of the French sailors subjected Bingham to "boorish" jostling and disdain, when he came as interpreter.

Before Bachelot left, but after the departure of Short, two more priests were sent urgently by Rouchouze. One, Louis Maigret, came for the first time to the place where he would become bishop in 1848; the other, Columban Murphy, concealed the fact that he had been secretly ordained priest by Rouchouze in the Gambier Islands before setting out. He already knew the Honolulu scene from his previous visit, was regarded in Honolulu as not being a priest, and would be able to officiate surreptitiously for the faithful, and act as confessor for the stranded Walsh.

Challenged to swear they were not priests, the two men declined and were obliged to buy a re-fitted schooner which had once, ironically, been the property of the Sandwich Islands Mission. Under her new name, *Notre Dame de Paix,* she left with Maigret and Bachelot for Ponape on 23 November. Murphy remained quietly at Honolulu, to serve the mission and belatedly study up his theology with Walsh. Bachelot, who was suffering acutely from rheumatism, a final thorn in his already heavy crown of disappointments and troubles, died at sea and was buried on a small island just off Ponape, by Maigret.

Short, Bachelot and the Sacred Hearts Congregation had previously addressed strong protests to the French government over their exclusion from Honolulu. Before long the retributive climax erupted. In 1838, the year of the great Protestant revivals on Hawaii, with a ban placed on Catholic teaching and Kinau's position apparently endorsed — persecution of the Catholics relaxed. When Kinau died however, in April 1839, her insecure successor as female protector of the realm, Kekauluohi, arrested sixty-seven Catholics from Boki's lands at Waianae, fifty kilometres from Honolulu, on suspicion of collusion with Boki's widow. Catholics were chained and maltreated so severely during the following two months that some of the Protestant missionaries had to intercede for them.

By July, word was abroad that the French ship *l'Artémise* was at Tahiti to demand compensation and execute summary justice on behalf of wrongly treated French subjects. On 9 July 1839 Commandant Cyril Pierre Théodore La Place stood off Honolulu and issued an ultimatum calling for surety of $20,000 that Catholics and French subjects would be given complete liberty. He cited the Queen of Tahiti's "praiseworthy example" in having given him (under pressure) such a guarantee in April (page 254) and threatened immediate bombardment in the event of default. He offered shelter on board to all white men except American Protestant clergy, who thereupon sought and received assurance of asylum in the American consulate. All on shore, foreign residents and Hawaiians, called for calm and raised the money. Liberty of religion was guaranteed. A military mass celebrated the new order on shore on Bastille Day, 14 July, and a commercial convention was concluded under the shadow of the guns, providing that juries to try French subjects should be selected after agreement with the French Consul and French wines and spirits should be given benefit of free import at no more than five per cent duty.

As a pathetic sequel Boki's widow, the once beautiful Liliha, came forward as an enquirer to the mission; before she could progress to baptism she died, on 25 August 1839. At her funeral simple catechisms in Hawaiian were given to the remnants of Boki's supporters from other islands to sow seed for a long and slow effort now still lying ahead of the infant Catholic mission.

REVIVAL AND AFTER

AFTER THE GUARANTEE of religious liberty had been exacted in 1839 by French fire-power the dream of a homogeneous Protestant religious system upheld by the protection of the chiefs disappeared. But a more profound change burst at the same period over the Protestant Church itself. Until the great revival broke out on the island of Hawaii in February 1837, pre-baptismal discipline and the excommunication of moral offenders had been modelled on the stern traditions of New England. The revival brought change. Three remarkable missionaries of a new stamp were largely responsible for the first stage of the outbursts of mass sorrow and ecstasy that swept the big island in 1837 and moved outward to a lesser extent to affect Oahu and Maui. Titus Coan and David Lyman were stationed at Hilo; Lorenzo Lyons was at Waimea.

All three belonged to a new era — westward expansion of the American frontier. Coan, a tall and commanding man, physically tough, had spent a year in the cold wastes of Patagonia at the tip of South America before coming to Hawaii in 1834 with the seventh company of missionaries. He had been a first lieutenant of militia and was converted in an atmosphere of protracted small town revivals by Charles Grandison Finney, the archetypal American evangelist of the nineteenth century. On Hawaii he found himself in another rugged frontier landscape that appealed to his taste for ceaseless activity and his roving inclination. As a preacher he combined the attributes of actor and warrior; Hawaiian culture still vibrated to both. He found himself among simple people as he tramped on foot, climbed the mountains and forded the streams of his enormous district. His voice and gestures moved people more powerfully than the systematic teaching and sober self-examination of Bingham or Thurston. For them the *pule* and the *palapala,* prayer and literacy, had advanced together; they called for moral evidence of regeneration before they would baptize. Before 1837 the total communicant membership of their church did not exceed 2,000.

Coan, from the time of his arrival at Hilo in 1835, concentrated on *pule* rather than *palapala.* The Hawaiians who congregated in great numbers at his station nevertheless came under the teaching influence of his colleague Lyman, who established the Hilo Boys' Boarding School in 1836 for vocational training and, like Coan, made Hilo his home until his death in the 1880s. Lyman's wife, Sarah, was the practical musician. Her original instrumental band used flutes and other instruments fashioned out of vines; her singers were forerunners of the later famed choir of Hilo's Haili Church.

Lorenzo Lyons in the Waimea district, further north and inland on the same windward coast, was acknowledged among the Hawaiians he served to be a second "father of the mission" on their island. Lyons was perky and amusing, smaller than Coan, but physically strong. He too died in the 1880s, after fifty-four years at Waimea. He wrote more hymns in Hawaiian than any other writer; the language, and its lyric Polynesian resources, became his own.

Weeping, physical movement, shouts of joy and a travail of groans made their appearance during a two-week day and night gathering for preaching, prayer and praise at Hilo in February of 1837. Coan recognized the signs of Finney's campaigns — ecstasy and release let loose among people who had lost their pagan childhood certainties and felt the outpouring of the Holy Spirit as a new birth in a strange land. Hawaii sought the Mercy Seat. Old people, the diseased, the isolated, the children, broke out into weeping and shouts of joy. This was no patient submission to Bible reading and learning letters. In the mass manifestations of 1837 and 1838 spontaneous ritual movement surrounded the orchestrated repetition of the preachers' voices; music and social warmth suffused the converts with a rewarding glow. At last a sanctified substitute appeared to compensate for losing the hula and other group celebrations of the old culture.

In the revivals, living voices evoked new social joy. People felt at home, saved from themselves and the limbo of a fragmented culture, where the old taboos had waned and little took their place. From this time forward the Hawaiian church became less an awkward mirror of old New England, closer to the relaxed and questing spirit of a people in numerical decline. Feelings familiar from the past were revived by Good News of resurrection to eternal life. The church became more tolerant of sinners, but more hopeful that in spite of all they would be saved. A church run by Americans and chiefs was inwardly transformed into a church of the people, though the outer protective shell provided by missionaries and chiefs remained. The mirage of a

CHRISTIANS IN HAWAII

disciplined Israel yielded to reality: a genuinely Hawaiian version of the Promised Land, flowing with milk and honey for famished souls. Since the Great Revival the church of the Hawaiian people has born these marks. Coan had travelled to the coast and mountains to meet and challenge his future converts before he called them in to Hilo for his epic seasons of preaching and penitence. When they repented he did not put them on probation; he baptized them, and trusted God to do the rest. The subsequent leakages and moral lapses during the time of cooling-off led to many criticisms from old-time New England bystanders; but the church became a refuge, open to all who sensed that the one qualification for belonging permanently was an acknowledgement of need. The lean sobriety of the early mission gave place to a happy forgiveness and fellowship. Hawaiians made the church their own.

Since it now belonged to the multitude, Rufus Anderson, the forward-looking Boston secretary of the ABCFM, saw reason to move the church as fast as possible toward self-government and self-support. He said so repeatedly for twenty years, until he had his way.

More than other observers he sensed an anti-foreign sentiment, voiced strongly by some of the most able Hawaiian Christians, for whom David Malo, a graduate of Lahainaluna, and later an ordained minister and superintendent of schools, was the most active and articulate. Anderson asked, in 1846, for Hawaiians to take positions in the church and the government. "The most effectual rebuke to ambitious foreigners in the civil government will be the adoption of measures at all your stations for creating native pastors for all the native churches," he told the mission.

Anderson nevertheless urged the missionaries to respond to the emphasis of Kamehameha III, who took a grip on himself after 1840 and tried, with guidance from the ex-missionaries William Richards and Gerrit P. Judd, to strengthen his kingdom from within. In Rufus Anderson's view the increasing white population of traders and foreign exploiters needed to be leavened by the permanent presence of committed Christian Anglo-Saxons. By 1851 twenty-two missionaries became naturalized Hawaiian citizens. The ABCFM transferred land to them for their local support. The changes led to the founding of the Hawaiian Evangelical Association in 1854 as a home mission for the islands, to assume the former functions of the Sandwich Islands Mission of the ABCFM.

After the French intervention of 1839 the royal house of Hawaii leaned toward Britain. Anderson took a stand against all foreign interference and attempts to dominate, including American. He acted at a later period as a watchdog for the ABCFM against Robert Crichton Wyllie, the Scots-born adviser of Kamehameha IV, to introduce Anglicanism and reinforce the British connexion (pages 263-4).

TO LIVE AMONG THE STARS

For other reasons, of necessity rather than principle, Anderson did his best to speed up the localization of the Hawaiian church on account of rising prices in the islands and declining financial support in America. Congregationalism in New England was changing in the 1850s; some of its former bastions of missionary enthusiasm trembled at assaults of Unitarianism and liberalizing theology. The claims of the mid-west also competed with the less vivid need of remote Hawaii, as religion followed the expansion of the American frontier.

By 1856 Anderson was vigorously following up the new order begun in Hawaii in 1852, when the church became independent. The ABCFM had urged quick progress toward financial self-support, but pledged to make up any leeway for the time being. Anderson urged that all fully representative church meetings should be conducted in the vernacular. When the missionary Daniel Dole declined to "turn his labors and influence into a *vernacular church for the native population*" he was edged out of his ABCFM appointment at Punahou school; significantly, his son Sanford Ballard Dole became the president of the later Hawaiian Republic and first governor of the American Territory of Hawaii.

Anderson visited Hawaii in 1863 to superintend the arrangements for the final and total transfer of effective power to the Hawaiian Church and the end of superimposed missionary infusions. When he returned to Boston he pointedly contrasted the rising standard of living of the children of ABCFM missionaries to Hawaii, even those who served the church, with the simple life and low incomes of home missionaries "going West" from the New England seminaries. Vision was joined with considerations of strict economy in the process that gave early independence to the Protestant church in Hawaii.

Children of the pioneer missionaries who continued to live and work in the islands fell into two streams within the country's life. Richards, Judd and Richard Armstrong left the mission by agreement in order to serve the Kingdom in politics and education. They established a tradition of public service. Others like them, of whom Castle and Cooke were the precursors, "came to do good and did well." Much of the church land given to mission families when they took citizenship was used by their descendants to grow sugar. Those who went into trade and commerce remained in close touch with the clergy through the Mission Children's Society; they called each other "the cousins"; their marriages and business ventures prepared the way for Hawaiian annexation and statehood.

The second stream of influence flowed into expansion of Hawaiian Christianity through missions in the Marquesas Islands and Micronesia. Binghams and Gulicks, Alexanders and Clarks and Parkers, by their varied forms of identification with other Pacific islands ensured that after the foundation of the Hawaiian Missionary Society in 1851 there would be a

CHRISTIANS IN HAWAII

planning and guiding American Board role among the Hawaiian teachers who laid the foundations of the work in some other parts of the Pacific at village level (pages 140ff).

When, in 1863, Rufus Anderson paid his official visit to oversee arrangements for the full autonomy of Hawaii's church, America was in the grip of inflation and the war between the states. Contributions fell off catastrophically at Boston; independence and self-support in Hawaii had become urgent necessities. Anderson, instead of a musty report, wrote a topical book about the Sandwich Islands — a mixture of historical review, panegyric and extended pamphlet. The pamphleteering imposed itself on him because the "Christian nation" he described had become multiform in its church life. Not only had Roman Catholics arrived; Mormons were moving in and Anglicans from England were knocking on an opening royal Hawaiian door.

3
Points of Progress

Sydney, New Zealand
Tonga, The Cook Islands

VOYAGERS PASSING through Sydney's Port Jackson heads on their way to the Bay of Islands in the north of New Zealand considered themselves to be bound, at least until 1830, for a wild and dangerous part of Polynesia. Ships' companies in quest of hardwood timber and flax, or whalers looking for fresh water, meat and vegetables — they brought back similar tales. The Maori were fighters; battle was their delight. Their chiefs, of all ranks, were proud and independent. When their honour was stained they exacted revenge. Their carved wooden meeting houses and green jade artifacts were as elegant and strange as their curvilinear tatooing. Their canoes were fast. Their spirit world and mythology permeated their daily occupations and their relationships with forest, mountain and coastline. The language they spoke was close to that of the Cook Islands; their leaders believed they came, within the Christian era, from a mythic homeland called Hawaiki beyond the sunrise.

After the coming of Cook the Maoris were fascinated by the arrival of the white man's ships; they looked for the rough crews who sought their women for sex and gave them blankets and rum against the cold climate — and muskets to make their tribal wars more lethal. Some Europeans were killed and eaten. The Maori was used to human flesh; he thought the spirit of a vanquished enemy yielded up his *mana*, or power; there were no large land animals in New Zealand; man was a source of alternative protein. Some sailors stayed on the beaches at the Bay of Islands; Maoris began to take journeys around the coast and across the sea to meet the newcomer in other ports and view his world. They saw that his possessions could be good for conquest when brought back to New Zealand and put to use among the tribes. Sometimes they sensed with foreboding that a time might come when white men, whom they called Pakeha, would dispossess them of their lands and ancient chiefly prerogatives — for the high-born Maori was an aristocrat and no fool.

One man at least, under these conditions, wanted to correct this state of affairs by taking Christianity among the New Zealanders — Samuel Marsden. Maori visitors off ships were to be seen in the early years of the nineteenth century around his parsonage in Parramatta, then a growing new town twenty kilometres west of Sydney. Marsden, who was already the Australian agent of the London Missionary Society (page 19), and therefore concerned for the whole of Polynesia, was determined to act on his concern. His reactions to the Australian Aboriginal culture, particularly in the light of his attempts to domesticate Aborigines in his own ways, were negative. Finding them secretive and impervious, he called them unintelligent. By contrast the Maoris seemed to him to have style; they were assured and gregarious; he warmed to them.

As a sequel Marsden made the mission to the Maori one of the guiding passions of his life. He made seven journeys across the stormy Tasman sea on their behalf between 1814 and 1837. He acquired the brig *Active* to make the first of these journeys, but used it also in the service of the LMS, since to him the Polynesian mission-field was to be seen as a whole from its new and vital Port Jackson base. When he began in New Zealand he was pained by the slow and erratic progress of the Tahiti missionaries; nevertheless, as an Anglican who did not disdain to be known as both a Calvinist and a Methodist, he clung to what he had absorbed of the missionary strategy of his senior English counterpart, Dr Thomas Haweis. Both believed that the civilizing mission, through the use of devout mechanics, should be related to evangelism; Haweis thought the artisans should evangelize, Marsden that they should *precede* the evangelists. In Marsden's case the belief was based on the need to offset cynical exploitation of the New Zealander; philanthropy would be based on religion, but without explicit early indoctrination.

In 1808, on his one visit to England, Marsden laid his plans. He knew the Pacific was too vast a region to be assaulted by the LMS alone. Cautionary events in Tonga proved the point. Many of his contacts in England were with the founders of the Church Missionary Society, an Anglican evangelical organization formed in London in 1799 to work with the Establishment for the promotion of missions to Africa and the East. He recruited his technicians — William Hall, a carpenter from Carlisle, and John King, a shoemaker born in Oxfordshire. They turned out to be effective workers, as he desired, in wood

TO LIVE AMONG THE STARS

and iron, but more interested in earning a good living than converting Maoris; the tug-of-war between the claims of trade and evangelism came to distress Samuel Marsden; trade often won. On his return journey to Sydney, Marsden made a providential friendship with a Maori chief, Ruatara, who was being repatriated after a series of distressing events on ships during a foray abroad. He loved Marsden and treated him as a chief, as did many Maoris. Ruatara taught the minister some Maori; Marsden, reciprocating, in a letter to the CMS called Ruatara "my new leader and friend."

Between 1809 and 1814 Marsden fought to remove a barrier the Sydney colonists had thrown in the way of sending ships to New Zealand. In 1809 the whaling ship *Boyd* had been waylaid and sunk in the Bay of Islands as an act of revenge for the flogging of a Maori chief; all on board were massacred and eaten. Sydney reacted to the wreck of the *Boyd* at Whangaroa with mingled horror, fulmination and caution. Marsden at that time found himself surrounded by a small group of stranded Maoris who wanted to go home. Hall and King were working for their living in relatively civilized New South Wales. They showed no itch to depart for a life of poverty, danger and self-sacrifice. Eventually Marsden bought the *Active*. He sent her to New Zealand early in 1813 with a fearless and experienced Roman Catholic, Peter Dillon, as captain. Marsden's agent on board for this first reconnaissance (he was forbidden to go himself by Governor Lachlan Macquarie of New South Wales) was Thomas Kendall, a third CMS lay missionary who had recently arrived in Sydney. Ruatara had found a passage home to Rangihoua ahead of the *Active*, but Kendall, and Hall, who also sailed, bore him a letter from Marsden.

Kendall, a man in his thirties with a wife and five children, came from Lincolnshire. He had been soundly converted in London, was a teacher with a knowledge of farming, and had been commended to the CMS as apt at languages. In temperament he showed himself subject to sudden anger, alternating between exalted effort and black depressions. His powers of observation and unmistakable ability were thwarted by a lack of advanced education; his close relationship with Ruatara's uncle, the high chief Hongi Hika, was to be crucial for his subsequent development when he settled in the Bay of Islands. Through Hongi, a man of mercurial charm and bloody impulse, Kendall was able to fraternize with the Maoris more closely than any other missionary. His subsequent undoing was a product of his personal strengths and weaknesses.

Kendall returned and reported to Marsden that the outlook for a mission seemed favourable. The *Active*, this time with Marsden on board, sailed at the end of 1814. Hongi and Ruatara were both members of the party; Kendall had brought them back with him to Australia. The missionaries were accompanied by members of their families and by servants.

POINTS OF PROGRESS

On Christmas Day, a Sunday, in 1814, after a tumultuous welcome at Rangihoua from Ruatara's people, Marsden preached the first Protestant sermon on New Zealand soil. He was deeply moved, having spent one of his previous nights on shore at Whangaroa among the very Maoris who had slaughtered and eaten the crew of the *Boyd*. Further elation followed the auspicious settling-in process of the mission before he left New Zealand on 26 February 1815. At the same time he foresaw that Ruatara, who was severely ill, would die, as he did on 3 March.

Ruatara's contact with Marsden had partly anglicized him; he laid plans for farming and a proper settlement. After Ruatara's untimely death Hongi, whose heart was set on the exhilaration of war, became the dominant protector of the mission, intimate with Kendall. Hall, Kendall and King struggled to learn the language. They had to live — the two artisans did so by their hands. For supplies, they also had to trade. They found that necessities could be acquired only in exchange for muskets — the fatal currency most in demand. Planting, building and choice of sites occupied their thoughts between their daily prayers. Rangihoua had been chosen because it was close to ships, had been under the protection of Ruatara and was centrally placed to reach the largest number of Maoris. But the ships brought worldly distractions to Maori and mission alike.

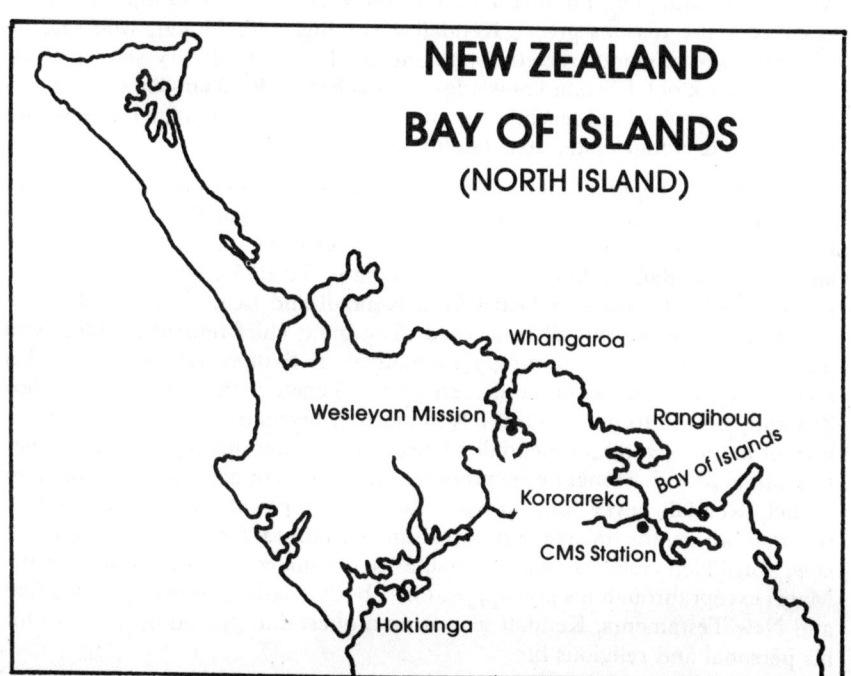

TO LIVE AMONG THE STARS

The trio bickered. Kendall worked hard on the language; he taught people to read and write. In doing so he gradually became fascinated by many aspects of Maori culture. His exploration of the world of the Maori endangered his missionary dedication. By 1816, involved in frequent short journeys away from home, Kendall found that when he was absent his wife had been unfaithful to him with Richard Stockwell, a convict who had come with them as a household servant. The grief of the event coincided with his discovery of Maori ideas about sexuality as generative and regenerative principle. In 1818 Marsden, disturbed by reports about Kendall, paid his second visit to the mission, bringing what he hoped might be the remedy for its ills in the person of a new superintendent, the Rev. John Butler.

Butler, the first ordained clergyman in New Zealand, proved, however, to be no solution. He was named as Superintendent, exciting resentment and quarrels among his more experienced colleagues. When Marsden on his next visit sought to compose matters between them, Kendall summarily announced his intention of visiting England, in company with Hongi. Having compiled a Maori vocabulary, Kendall wanted to take it to Professor Samuel Lee, an expert Cambridge linguist, in order to pave the way for an orthography, dictionary and grammar. While abroad, Kendall also wanted to seek holy orders. He was ambitious to be a cleric of consequence in New Zealand, as was Butler. Marsden, not enamoured of these projects, found himself unable to counter the reasons given; Kendall was going with Hongi, who said he wished to see England, secretly planning to add to his military arsenal along with his stock of Christian knowledge. It was harder for Marsden to say no to a chief than a school-teacher. A masterful Maori dominated the scene; Kendall and Hongi made their fateful voyage.

Marsden's reports to the CMS in London were full of practical warnings about the state of the mission; in spite of these, Hongi and Kendall together in England proved irresistible. Lee was impressed by the materials on the language; Kendall's influential clerical mentor, Basil Woodd of Paddington, was enthralled by what he heard from Kendall and Lee; Hongi worked the charm of his person on all concerned. The great chief returned, laden with many gifts, which he cunningly exchanged in Sydney for arms. Kendall received holy orders as deacon, then priest. Together they returned to New Zealand, bound to one another; Kendall had become accessory to Hongi's love of battles, Hongi to Kendall's Christian task and his quest for the inner soul of the Maori. Hongi never properly understood or accepted the Christian gospel; Kendall never fully grasped the inwardness of Maori pre-christian spiritual power, the linkage of procreation and natural fertility in a complex of *tapu*, forbidden holiness. Being unable to rationalize the mythology of the Maori except through his presuppositions about creation, drawn from the Old and New Testaments, Kendall set out on a quest that proved devastating for his personal and religious life.

POINTS OF PROGRESS

The wooden sacred houses of the Maori people, with their explicitly genital carvings, were a background to his transgression of the sexual code expected of a missionary. He was not the only Christian minister to live with a Maori woman, but his actions take on special poignancy in view of his wife's earlier behaviour, his loneliness and his serious attempt to come to grips with the interior thought-world and religious life of the people among whom he lived and worked. He succumbed to the hazards of research he intended to lead him to deeper sympathetic identification. Kendall's prolonged affair in 1821 and 1822 with Tungaroa, the seventeen-year-old daughter of a chief who was also a *tahunga*, or a priest, led to his censure and dismissal by the CMS in 1823.

Marsden personally conveyed the CMS verdict to Kendall and dismissed him. In great agitation of mind Kendall at first declined to go, then agreed. He and Marsden, leaving together, were shipwrecked on the *Brampton* before it cleared the coast. In this breathing space, Kendall stayed on, while Marsden, exasperated by Butler's angry disposition and reports of his having been drunk, removed Butler instead to Sydney. The CMS mission, after almost nine years, had been manipulated by dominant Maoris and compromised by trading in arms. Its most able representative, drawn into the thought-world of the Maori, spent the brief remainder of his days in New Zealand, in Valparaiso, Chile, and farming in New South Wales. He endured paroxysms of regret, heavy drinking and tortured repentance. Hongi, his sponsor, died unconverted; a bullet wound in his chest, received in battle, gave out a melancholy whistle when he breathed. Kendall drowned when his small boat foundered in a squall at Uladulla, New South Wales, in 1832. The one member of the earliest CMS group to last the distance was the most laconic — John King, who worked on. He died in the Bay of Islands in 1854.

Not until two ordained brothers, Henry Williams and William Williams, brought to the mission a combination of discipline and vision did the work expand southward among the Maoris. After 1840, when English colonial settlers came in droves to the North Island, Christianity and the Church became predominantly the preserve of the white man. Churches founded among the Maoris were, and continue to be, havens of the earlier culture and language of New Zealand, but they are minority churches. Leaders among the missionaries, such as Octavius Hadfield of the CMS and the Williams brothers, on one side of their careers were champions and guardians of chiefs who had accepted the pacifying and merciful content of the Christian message and liturgy. But the CMS as a whole failed to escape alignment with the settlers' hunger for land and juridical supremacy. The Treaty of Waitangi, signed in February 1840 by a majority of chiefs, ceded sovereignty to Queen Victoria in the presence of representatives of three missions, the Anglicans of the CMS, the Wesleyans and the Roman Catholics. "Do not sign the paper," said one chief. "If you do you will be reduced to the condition of slaves and be compelled to break stones on the roads. Your land will be taken from you and your dignity as chiefs will be destroyed."

WESLEYANS: NEW ZEALAND

WESLEYAN METHODISM was introduced in the Bay of Islands, and later at Hokianga on the west coast, under the aegis of Marsden and as a supplement to the work of the CMS. Its instigator was the Rev. Samuel Leigh, who inspected the field in 1818 and in 1820 persuaded the Wesleyan Methodist Missionary Society in London to begin work of its own in New Zealand and the Friendly Islands. Leigh was designated General Superintendent of Missions for both areas, which thus became closely related to each other and to Sydney.

For sixteen months from 1821 Leigh resided with the CMS missionaries at the Bay, trying and failing to learn Maori and directing detailed reports on Kendall's misconduct to Marsden. Finally, he settled on Whangaroa as the site for the Wesleyan station, Wesleydale, gazing, as he travelled there by boat, into the cavernous submerged hulk of the *Boyd*. The chief who received and sponsored them was Te Aara, or George, the very man whose flogging had been avenged in 1809 by the *Boyd* massacre. The auspices were ominous.

Leigh, who on the bulk of the evidence was self-pitying, impractical and vacillating, broke down under the strain of bad weather, Maori curiosity and pilfering, and his own forebodings. He was in the midst of a people who did not understand him and whom he did not understand. After other colleagues, James Stack and William White, had joined him and erected houses and fences he was still "unequal to the conflict"; he "began to despair of life." Nathaniel Turner and John Hobbs reinforced Wesleydale later in 1823. When Marsden came to Whangaroa in August he diagnosed the situation and took Leigh off, never to return.

The story of the mission continued to be discouraging until marauding and resentful Maoris raided and burned the mission houses at Whangaroa in 1827. The attackers were most probably remnants of the Ngatiuru tribe the Wesleyans came to convert. The missionaries had become preoccupied with their farming and their stores. They enclosed themselves in a touchy community beset by petty internal strife, having grown suspect to the Maoris immediately around them when they flogged the son of the chief George, who had been caught stealing. By the time of the flogging George had died, but George's people remembered he had himself once suffered flogging by white men. As the *Boyd* tragedy had shown, chiefs were not to be flogged; the indignity provoked eventual *utu*, revenge.

POINTS OF PROGRESS

Following the catastrophe at Whangaroa, the Wesleyan Mission was resited on the west coast, at Mangungu on the Hokianga River. Hobbs became the "second founder" on the invitation of Patuone, a chief who had been involved in the wars between Hongi and the Whangaroa tribes when Wesleydale was destroyed. He alone of the earlier company persisted in the work to the end — a physically strong and eloquent missionary, accustomed to working with his hands, but also a healer and a musician. White, like Kendall, succumbed to twin temptations — sexual adventure and money-making. He was dismissed from the mission, but ended his days in New Zealand in an aura of respectability as a prosperous and fitfully repentant citizen of Auckland. In time new workers of the calibre and staying power of James Wallis, James Buller and Thomas Buddle pushed the frontiers of the mission southward and became involved in uneasy comity disputes with the CMS. An agreement had allotted the east coast to the Anglicans and the west to the Methodists, but in Waikato the boundaries became hard to fix. Methodist Maoris and Anglican Maoris became separate spiritual subdivisions of a people. Both subdivisions were subject, after 1838, to partial attrition by Roman Catholics under their bishop, Jean Baptiste François Pompallier.

MARISTS ENTER NEW ZEALAND

THE BISHOP arrived late, but his commission was clear; he had to win the peoples of the Pacific for the Catholic Church and to restore the years the locusts of heresy had eaten. There were serious disadvantages to be overcome: Pompallier's designation as Prefect Apostolic of Western Oceania and titular bishop of Maronea gave him a vast area to supervise. His priests were professed members of the Society of Mary (page 97), but he himself never took Marist vows and believed that though he was responsible to Father Jean Claude Colin, he was answerable ultimately only to the pope. This conflict of obligations plagued him. He came to New Zealand with only rudimentary English. His dédication and spiritual depth were never in question, but his business acumen came under constant fire from his critics, and his knowledge of ships and the sea was poor.

The last point is significant. Ships and navigation were never far from the boyhood world of many of the Fathers of the Sacred Hearts in Eastern Oceania. By contrast, the origins of the Society of Mary lay mainly, with the affections of its recruits, in the inland city of Lyon, and the rural parishes of the Rhône Valley and its sub-alpine tributaries. The tang of the sea was not in the nostrils of these priests, who had for the most part known softer landscapes of sheaves and vines. Pompallier himself was a son of a bourgeois family of Lyon silk merchants; in New Zealand he took it as normal that he should be carried in a litter on the backs of willing Maoris as he journeyed through forest, fern and stream.

TO LIVE AMONG THE STARS

Pompallier came out by a tortuous route and fixed on New Zealand as his base. He toyed with several options en route. After rounding Cape Horn and reaching Valparaiso in a French naval vessel, he had to charter a ship at considerable expense. He called on the Sacred Hearts Mission at Mangareva to confer briefly — and celebrate liturgically — with Bishop Rouchouze, his fellow Vicar Apostolic for the Eastern Pacific. Going on to Papeete he chartered yet another small ship, with thoughts of trying Ponape in Micronesia as a first station. Then, touching at Vava'u in the north of Tonga he was persuaded to go with two beachcombers, the French-speaking Charles Simonet and the English-speaking Thomas Boog, to try Wallis and Futuna, where he left several Marists — Father Pierre Bataillon and Brother Joseph Luzy on Wallis, Father Pierre Chanel and Brother Marie Nizier on Futuna. He promised reinforcement and, if possible, his personal return within six months, then went on to Sydney, where the bishop, John Bede Polding, gave him letters of introduction to an Irish Catholic timber merchant named Thomas Poynton, at Hokianga, thus helping him make up his mind to go to New Zealand. By the time he arrived to celebrate the first mass in Poynton's house at Totiara on 13 January 1838, Pompallier was deep in debt, reduced to a staff of two, and exposed to Protestant alarms and distortions.

Notwithstanding the auguries, Pompallier's efforts took hold. In May 1838 and again in September, prestigious French navigators came to the Bay of Islands. They received him on board with salvoes and masses, and gave notice that he was, in the eyes of France, a protected person of high standing. The Maoris, aligned in tribes as Christians by the Anglican and Wesleyan missions, looked on him with a mixture of suspicion and curiosity. He was invited by John Roberton, a resident of Kororareka, overlooking the Bay of Islands, to move there, on land Roberton provided, in September 1839. Publications purporting to show the real nature of Roman Catholicism as antichrist flowed from the Protestant presses — fuel for the bishop's debates in his frequent journeyings among the tribes. His chants, ceremonies, sacred objects and personal insignia aroused interest among barely literate Maoris, who responded to his chiefly style and oral methods of instruction. On solemn occasions such as the signing of the Treaty of Waitangi he used his robes of office and patrician manner to good effect. Pikopo became his name and the name of his followers among the Maori people. This phonetic equivalent of *episcopos* well fitted the impression he created at the centre of the small but loyal flock he succeeded in gathering — for the most part through proselytism among those who had already been reached by the Protestants who preceded him. After a tour to the north along these lines in 1840 he wrote to Colin, the head of the Marists:

> The result of this long trip has been to make about forty tribes turn to the Catholic faith. But I must first explain to you what is understood

POINTS OF PROGRESS

here by turning to the Catholic faith. It is to recognize that our Church is the ancient society, the Mother Church, founded by the Saviour. Ordinarily it is also understood that it is the only true Church.

By commending his faith in this way and slowly building a minority Roman Catholic Maori church, Pompallier became greatly attached to "his well loved Maoris." From New Zealand, which became his home and the base of his effort, he sent out Marist assistants for the relief and reinforcement of Wallis and Futuna (page 97). In 1841, confronted with the tragic news that his Pro-Vicar Pierre Chanel had been murdered on Futuna, he visited his priests in the Wallis-Futuna group and from there hoped to deploy Marists in eastern Fiji and northern Tonga. By 1844 the responsibility for closer cultivation of the tropical Polynesian islands had been transferred to Pierre Bataillon, who was consecrated bishop there in 1843 (page 99).

By 1840 the Maoris had made Christianity their own. An estimated majority of a total population of 110,000 had become practising adherents of one of the three missions. Sunday had been accepted as the *tapu* Sabbath. Inter-tribal wars had become less frequent and savage. Literacy was widespread. Tattooing had been proscribed by the missions and was less often seen. Sexual morality conformed more closely to average white Christian standards. Maoris themselves, many drawn from the enslaved class of former war prisoners, served the missions as evangelists to their own people further south. The changes indicated acceptance, partial adoption, explanation of the Christian message in distinctive Maori categories. God was seen as the supremely powerful *Atua,* or spirit power, overcoming the many former Maori *atua.*

Even though the Maoris, in terms of crude control of their own situation in their own land, now exchanged a position of relative dominance for one of submission to the invader, their old perceptions of the supernatural shaped their understanding of Christ, the devil, angels, resurrection and the after-life. Most analyses of what occurred in the conversion of the Maoris stress the partial and distorted comprehension of Christian faith by those who adopted it, as though this is surprising. A parallel analysis of the religious belief and practice of the white settlers of New Zealand at the same period would probably have revealed, in most cases, a similar amalgam of distorted ideas. Among the Maoris, as in all Christian societies, there were those who grasped the heart of the matter, response to the self-denying love of the crucifixion by similar self-denying love; acceptance of the resurrection.

More serious losses followed the imposition of English dress, manners and nuclear family customs on traditional ways of life. When a people finds its distinctiveness being threatened by imitation of the external forms and way of life of the mission-house, reactions set in. The first Maori cult in New Zealand was instigated by a prophet who was active in the Rangihoua area, then in Hokianga, from 1833 onward. Under the name Te Atua Wera (the burning god) he gathered his followers in a religion called Papahurihia, which for a time attracted several influential chiefs. The cult incorporated many elements of Christianity, but used Maori art forms; a lizard figure, venerated in Maori lore, was retained by the cult. Missionaries were shut out of the heaven. Memories of Papahurihia beliefs, worship and leadership carried over, during the Maori wars, into the more active cultist struggle of the *Pai Marire* or *Hauhau* movement. Recent study of *Pai Marire* corrects our picture of it as a primarily horrifying and barbarous form of terrorism. As sincere and in many ways pathetic struggles for selfhood in the face of cultural supremacism, cult movements in various parts of the Pacific gave a glimpse of what forms might have been taken by genuinely local churches if missionaries had been less prone to confuse the matter of their message with its imported Anglo-Saxon or French cultural wrappings.

TONGA: WESLEYAN KINGDOM

FOR THE WESLEYAN AND ROMAN CATHOLIC missions New Zealand acted in part as base and in part as staging point in the approach to other parts of Polynesia. Because Samuel Marsden was agent for both the London and Wesleyan Societies his projects for trade and evangelization involved his circle of religious friends in Sydney. William Shelley, one of the London missionaries forced hastily to take refuge from Tonga at Port Jackson (page 18), collaborated closely with Marsden, advocating re-entry into Tonga until his death in 1817. Shelley's widow, Elizabeth, kept up his concern. A Wesleyan, Walter Lawry, fresh out from England, married a daughter of Rowland Hassall, former LMS missionary to Tahiti. Hassall's son Thomas married one of Marsden's daughters. Lawry prospered commercially in New South Wales; his first appointment to Tonga in 1822 as a Wesleyan missionary reflected Marsden's interests in mission and trade — and the urging of Elizabeth Shelley. Under the protection of a chief called Fatu, at Mu'a on Tongatapu, Lawry and his wife lived in an agricultural settlement, assisted by two artisans, but had slender success in learning Tongan. They converted nobody. The Lawrys stayed for little more than a year and withdrew to Sydney, leaving two artisans behind.

On his way to Tonga Lawry had called on Samuel Leigh, who was then in the midst of his New Zealand setbacks and trying to make up his mind how and where to settle. There was little brotherly affection between the two men; Lawry had wealth, presence and dispatch; Leigh resented him. Their personal incompatibility bedevilled the beginnings of Methodist missions in the Pacific.

POINTS OF PROGRESS

A more significant prelude to the appearance of a Tongan Wesleyan church was played out by Tahitians sent from Borabora in 1822 by J.M. Orsmond (pages 26, 28) and from Papara in early 1826 by John Davies (pages 18, 102). Orsmond's teachers, Borabora, Taute and Zorobabela, settled on the northern island of Vava'u, where the powerful chief Finau detained and "domesticated" them. Zorobabela and Taute apostatized, but Borabora extricated himself and migrated to Tongatapu. In 1826 he was unexpectedly joined there by two other Tahitians, Hape and Tafeta, who had been sent by Davies as missionaries for Lakeba in Fiji. Two chiefs, one Fijian and the other Tongan, had met Davies while voyaging in Tahiti. They requested him to send teachers to Lakeba. When their ship called at Tongatapu the teachers were appropriated by the chief of Nuku'alofa, Aleamotu'a, who became the first high-born sponsor of Christianity in Tonga and assisted the Tahitians to set up a school and conduct worship. Borabora, after joining them, died at Nuku'alofa. Tafeta returned to Tahiti in 1827, but Hape stayed on until 1828.

This group of Tahitian teachers, with their checkered record, formed a significant bridgehead at Nuku'alofa for the entry of the Wesleyans, whose discouragements bordered on despair until they found in Aleamotu'a (Tupou) at Nuku'alofa the chiefly sponsor they needed. By the time the English Wesleyans attached themselves to him he had already committed himself to Christianity, perceiving that it had roots in Tahiti, a country more akin to his own. Hape, who was a hunchback, appears to have been a resourceful and optimistic Christian emissary. He later for many years served the church at Rapa, a small island near the Australs evangelized by the LMS.

In 1826 the Wesleyans tried again. They were directed by Charles Tindall, one of Lawry's artisan helpers, who had stayed on, to seek the interest and protection of another chief, Ata, at the western tip of Tongatapu. The two pioneers in this district of Hihifo were John Thomas, a blacksmith from Hagley in Worcestershire, and John Hutchinson, whose health soon failed and forced him to leave. Thomas stayed in Tonga until 1859 and is celebrated as the missionary builder of Tongan Methodism. He lacked advanced education and suffered from feelings of acute inferiority. "What a raw, weak, uncultivated wretch I was when I left old England," he once confessed. All his life he defended obstinately the religious views he drank in from the wellsprings of John and Charles Wesley. Calvinist dissent was to Thomas a cold and lifeless business; he was appreciated by LMS missionaries such as John Williams, but did not heartily reciprocate. His politics were also of a different stamp; he was a Wesleyan high church Tory, loyal to the memory of George III and out of sympathy with democratic ideas in the air following the French and American revolutions. These cherished positions he defended in the Tongan setting throughout a career of single-minded preaching and instruction. Thomas observed, wrote about, edified and tried to control all that occurred within the juvenile church toward which he acted as proud *accoucheur* and nurse. Once his early period of frustration on Tongatapu had ended he went northward to Ha'apai, the central island cluster of Tonga, there to find his personality and aims entwined with the rise to power and religious conversion of the Tongan giant of the nineteenth century — Taufa'ahau, later to be king of all Tonga as George Tupou I.

Ata's intention at Hihifo followed a familiar pattern. He felt himself to be in competition with other Tongan chiefs in the race to acquire prestige-conferring and trade-attracting missionaries. He took Thomas, but not the gospel. In 1827, in response to a cry of near-dismay, the Sydney Methodists reinforced the mission by sending Nathaniel Turner and William Cross, with John Weiss — who did not stay. They took up residence, more strategically, with Aleamotu'a (Tupou) at Nuku'alofa, a chief who had already declared for Tahitian Christianity. With Aleamotu'a's aid they built on foundations laid by their Tahitian predecessors. Turner had passed through trauma in the New

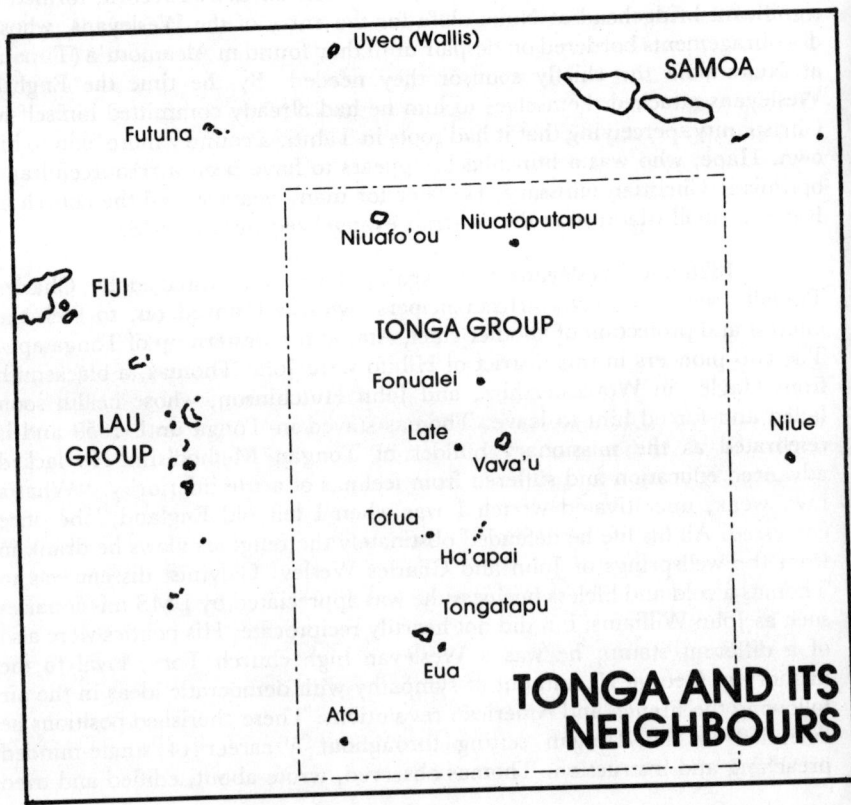

Zealand mission when the Whangaroa mission house and station had been sacked; the basic Maori language he learned in the Bay of Islands gave him a start with Tongan. At Nuku'alofa he and Cross could run their own mission; Turner felt released from the jealousy and mutual backbiting he and Leigh and Lawry had carried on between them in New Zealand. By 4 January 1829 seven young men had been baptized at Nuku'alofa, among them Pita Vi, a person of chiefly rank close to Tupou.

Not long after the baptisms, Taufa'ahau, Ha'apai's tall and imperious high chief, visited Tongatapu. The groups of the Tongan island chain, from north to south, were in regular touch through the comings and goings of large sailing canoes manned by some of the most skilful and fearless seamen of the South Seas. Taufa'ahau cast envious eyes on Turner and Cross and tried to entice Thomas away from Ata without success. Thomas had been sent to Hihifo, and felt he must stay until re-stationed from headquarters. Eventually Taufa'ahau accepted, as his teacher for the time being, Pita Vi, who was of acceptable social class. In the period between Taufa'ahau's invitation and the removal of Thomas and his wife to Lifuka on Ha'apai, Vi lived with Taufa'ahau, whose daring in publicly reviling his old gods and putting their *mana* to public tests was probably a result of the influence of foreign ships in Tongan waters and of resident beachcombers. He was also aware of the witness of the Tahitian *lotu Tahiti* — the new religion of the islands. Vi was with him when he entered the shrine of an inspired priestess of his own shark god and struck her twice in the face; subsequently he tried to spear a shark from his canoe while sailing, believing the shark to be the offended god. The shark escaped, but Pita Vi and a companion were pushed overboard to get the spear and bring it to shore. When they did so unharmed Taufa'ahau's determination to turn Christian was strengthened. His countryman Pita Vi, who afterwards became the first Tongan to be ordained to the ministry, prepared the ground for the arrival of Thomas by commending in Tongan terms the power of the new God. Most of the old *marae* on Ha'apai, sacred to the old deities, were converted into places of Christian worship while Vi was with the king. A chapel seating three hundred people was built at Lifuka on a spot still called *Pulela'a,* sanctuary.

Thomas, despondent at the limited success he had with Ata, waited at Nuku'alofa for word from Sydney sanctioning the proposal that he should go north to Ha'apai. His one baptized convert had been Lolohea, a chief related as nephew to Tupou and stepson to Ata. The baptism drew him into the orbit of Tupou, who had been active, since he first determined to become a Christian, in urging Taufa'ahau and Finau Ulukalala of Vava'u to embrace Christianity and receive missionaries. When Thomas went to Ha'apai Tonga was already stirring, as a result of chiefly initiatives, in the direction of accepting Christianity.

TO LIVE AMONG THE STARS

As a result Tupou was instructed, and baptized with the name Josiah on 18 January 1830. His conversion, and reception with his family into the church, weighted the balance in favour of the *lotu* on Tongatapu, Ha'apai and Vava'u. Three supreme titles were acknowledged in Tonga: the Tu'i Kanokupolu had come to seem supreme in government; the Tu'i Tonga was predominantly sacral; the powers of the Tu'i Ha'atakalaua, originally warlike and secular, had waned before Tu'i Kanokupolu's stronger claims by the time of the arrival of Christianity. Tupou, as holder of the crucial Tu'i Kanokupolu title at the time of his conversion, gained a certain prestige over the whole group. His own people in large numbers followed him into the church. Because his title had the force of holy investiture his decision carried weight with both Taufa'ahau and Finau. "When I turn, they all turn," Taufa'ahau is reported to have said. The mass movements into the church that followed the conversions and baptisms of these three high chiefs were associated with the intense regard for their persons. A divine authority and force surrounded each of the three Tongan rulers who embraced Christian belief and the church within a short span of time. Far from being dissipated by their new religion, the aura became all-embracing in a Christian form, as Taufa'ahau gradually established his reign over the whole of Tonga. His ally was John Thomas, for whom the British throne was surrounded with a similar halo of anointed right.

The stages of growth within the church were clearly defined by the successive baptisms of the local rulers in the three island groups; Tupou's in 1830 carried the biblical name of Josiah, a king who had broken down the idols in Israel and restored the people's allegiance to God; Taufa'ahau's, at the hands of Thomas in August 1831, conferred — at his own request, according to the missionary — the name George (Sioasi), "or (as we wrote it) Joaji — out of respect to our good old king (George III), whose memory is cherished in these islands." Finally, Finau received baptism as Zephaniah before he died in 1833, handing his power over in death to Taufa'ahau, who thus became ruler of the two northern groups.

Missionary reinforcements arrived to cope with the influx of people who came forward for instruction and baptism in the wake of the chiefs. Peter Turner, James Watkin and William Woon (who brought a printing press) arrived in 1831; Woon left in a huff in 1834 for New Zealand after he and his wife fell out with their colleagues. Watkin and Turner went north; in Vava'u in 1834 Peter Turner was joined briefly by David Cargill, a Scot educated at Aberdeen University. Both men had been through the classical Methodist experience of the "strangely warmed heart"; Cargill moved out of Presbyterianism into Wesleyanism under the impulse of the "Spirit of holiness." At Utui, near Neiafu on Vava'u on 23 July 1834, after months of prayer meetings under the ministry of Turner and Cargill, a revival broke out. In emotionally charged scenes involving physical transports, singing and ecstatic joy and sorrow, it proceeded to sweep the villages of Vava'u with the "gifts" of personal testimony to Christ and longings for "perfect love," the "glorious" inward manifestation of Wesleyan religion. A barely Christian society made up of "friendly islanders" on whose fondness for mass scenes of song and dance many voyagers had remarked, transferred its former fervent participation in occasions celebrating its ancient gods and ancestral heroes to the public rejoicings and recurrent revivals of the gospel of the people called Methodists, to whose ways most of Tonga has adhered with full allegiance since. A church that had already found chiefly sponsors received its soul back again — part Wesleyan, part Tongan; no strange mixture, but a seemingly predestinate love affair between modes of life united in underlying harmony.

In a short time the revival swept southward to both Ha'apai and Tongatapu. Taufa'ahau, who had already responded to the patient teaching style of Thomas, became moved in his depths by what occurred. A Tongan, Joeli Bulu, said he saw him writhe physically under the Spirit's power. It was as though in the process he received a new heart and became for life a man who knew his Saviour, who testified to Christ's transforming life. His renunciation of women other than Charlotte, whom he chose to be his sole queen, was firm and permanent. He became a humble and dedicated local preacher — a witness to his people. The commoners, who had been of minimal worth before, were glad that as a forgiven and restored sinner he drew closer to them; at the same time, as a ruler he lost none of his peremptory power over his people. Much still lay ahead of him in consolidating his position by conquest; in his own eyes and in the eyes of Thomas he became the King Saul of the Pacific, with Tongan-born Methodist ministers as his priests and, as his Prophet Samuel, John Thomas, a one-time village blacksmith cast by God in the role of king-maker. In the relationship between the two men Thomas did not circumvent the Tongan process of assigning high titles and consolidating chiefly powers; he merely saw what occurred in Tonga as an expression of the working of God's providence; he set God's seal on events by the actions of baptism and enthronement. Other missionaries — Peter Turner, Charles Tucker (who arrived in 1835) and James Watkin — also surrounded Taufa'ahau with Christian blessing and counsel. Thomas, if only as a result of his priority in the field and his long service, was closest.

From the year 1833 Taufa'ahau was *tu'i* (supreme ruler) of the two northern groups. He was younger than Tupou, who bore the vital dignity of Tu'i Kanokupolu, and bound to him by family relationship (Tupou was his uncle) and the obligations of support. His hopes and plans over the following ten-year period led him toward succession to the Tu'i Kanokupolu title and overlordship of Tonga. Taufa'ahau's father had held the title. During this in-between period the aspirant fell into conflict with southern chiefs who continued in the old religion and offered prolonged resistance in war. The core of this non-christian resistance on Tongatapu was provided by a group, the Ha'a Havea chiefs, who feared take-over of all Tonga and the bestowal of the status of *hau,* or winner of supreme power, on Taufa'ahau. By offering resistance to Tupou and his Christians they kept the Tu'i Kanokupolu paramountcy in question. Taufa'ahau's mother was a daughter of the head of the Ha'a Havea; in this sense they *too* were claimants.

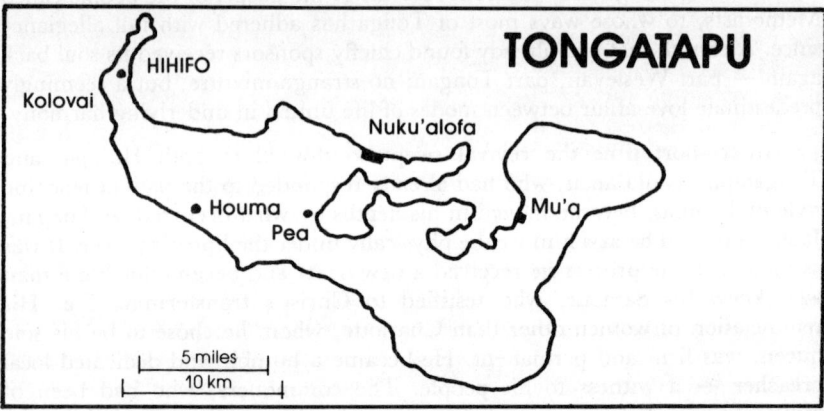

In 1837 Taufa'ahau came to Tongatapu with strong forces, to rally to the support of Tupou. His campaigns were conducted with relentless savagery; when the battles that subdued two strongholds of his opposition were over, he consolidated his gains by a surprising display of Christian clemency. The school books, sermons and journals of the missionaries — Thomas in particular — show that in the years between 1834 and 1837 the emphasis shifted in teaching Taufa'ahau and his people. Whereas, before the excitement and alarms of preparation for war against the "heathen," New Testament counsels of peace-making and gentleness prevailed, in wartime the early Old Testament theme of God's activity as the Lord of Hosts became uppermost. The books of Joshua, I Samuel, Kings, Chronicles and the imprecatory Psalms were used to accentuate God's help for Israel in the conquest of the Promised Land. Psalms of victory and physical vengeance appeared in lessons and sermons.

After the two great battles of 1837, Taufa'ahau, fired by this teaching and preaching, did not hesitate, on impulse, to slaughter and mutilate non-combatants in the stormed forts. Peter Dillon, an Irish sea-captain (page 62) and a Roman Catholic, arrived in Tongatapu not long after the battles. He wrote to Thomas, accusing him of provoking the massacres and making George Taufa'ahau his pawn. Dillon afterwards published these charges in London. David Cargill entered the pamphlet war with a refutation. The leaders of the Wesleyan Missionary Society were embarrassed and instituted an enquiry in Sydney; they had already remonstrated with Thomas about his intemperate exultation over the victory of the Christian troops.

In fact, the main charge of Dillon, that the Christian soldiers, including Taufa'ahau, had engaged in indiscriminate vengeance under orders, was true. A further charge — that Thomas had directly urged the atrocities on the spot — carried the evidence too far. The missionaries had prepared the ground for Taufa'ahau to make up his own mind to kill non-combatants. Their Old Testament teaching helped his recruiting processes and provided him with scriptural justification for what he did in the heat of battle. Thomas himself went no further than taking satisfaction in the outcome. "King George is conqueror," he wrote to his parents, "but he gives all the praise to the Lord ... I am sure that you will rejoice that God is so good to us." Thomas' king was not patronized as his creation, but saluted as his liege-lord; "a choice young man and a godly, and there was not among the people of Israel a goodlier than he, from his shoulders and upwards he was higher than any of his people," Thomas wrote enthusiastically soon after the king's conversion. In peace and war the English missionary was bound as subject and prophet to the victorious Tongan monarch.

War on Tongatapu did not cease after the trauma of 1837. The settlement and fort of Pea continued to be a stronghold of the Ha'a Havea cause. In 1840 Taufa'ahau again tried to subdue all resistance, but Pea, fortified strongly by a ring of spike-strewn ditches, could not be induced to give up. When Captain William Croker, the commander of a visiting British warship, the *Favourite*, was called in by apprehensive Wesleyan missionaries to mediate, he became exasperated and was shot in an attempt to attack the defenders of Pea. In the uneasy situation they faced after the episode the Ha'a Havea chiefs feared reprisals. When in 1842 Father Joseph Chevron of the Society of Mary came to Tongatapu under instruction from Bishop Pompallier, accompanied by an assistant, Brother Attale, they were responding to an invitation sent to them at Lakeba in Fiji, through relatives of the chief of Pea, Moeaki. After a courtesy call on Aleamotu'a as Tu'i Kanokupolu, the Roman Catholic missionaries settled at Pea, thus introducing a fresh element of Catholic-Protestant rivalry into the civil wars. Chiefs of the Ha'a Havea line at Mu'a and Houma used the Catholic mission to strengthen their resistance to Taufa'ahau, well aware that French gunboats might provide protection for the Catholic cause. The mission saw in Pea a stronghold for their spiritual struggle to reclaim Tonga from heretical error.

Moeaki's wife, Fietoa, showed sympathy toward Catholicism. Following her baptism Moeaki's followed in mid-1844, but any hopes the Catholics entertained of offsetting Taufa'ahau's power in the south were disappointed by the death of Aleamotu'a in 1845. His status as Tu'i Kanokupolu passed to

Taufa'ahau, who was enthroned on 4 December by Thomas, with the title of George Tupou I. All Tonga, by consent of the high chiefs, had a Wesleyan local preacher as king.

As though to underline the point, a second religious revival broke out in 1846. The ascendancy of the Wesleyan cause was undergirded by the introduction everywhere of the king's law code of 1839, which contained many provisions drawn from Methodist law books. These already governed the conduct of converts and were taught in Wesleyan schools. The Methodist missionaries, under the king's direction, drew up the code. They revised it in 1850.

Chevron's small and under-provided mission became restricted to the centres of Ha'a Havea resistance. Father Jérôme Grange joined Chevron in late 1842. The Marists reinforced them in 1844 by sending Father Pierre Calinon and Brother Jean, and again in 1850 by the arrival of Fathers Charles Nivelleau and Alfred Pieplu, supported by Brother Paschase. Their period of settlement in Tonga coincided, unfortunately for them, with growing tension between Bishop Pompallier and Father Colin, the Marists' superior. In 1842 Colin persuaded the College of Propaganda in Rome to subdivide the unwieldy jurisdiction of Pompallier into five smaller units. One of these, Central Oceania, embraced Wallis, Futuna, Fiji, Samoa, Tonga and neighbouring islands, and was entrusted to Pierre Bataillon, who was made a bishop for the purpose. A papal decree of 16 September 1842 confirmed the arrangement. Wallis became a new sub-base, the Catholic "Jerusalem" of the area, to be provisioned for its apostolic warfare through Sydney, where Colin established a centre in 1845 to supply and develop all the Marist missions in the Pacific.

Colin's overall plan, characteristic of the man, assumed a grand scale. In 1843 and 1844, with the help of French ship-owners and merchants, he launched a project called the Oceanian Company. He aimed to transport and supply his beleaguered priests in the Pacific with the company's ships and to make a large contribution to the financing of Catholic missions generally through the profits of trade. Poor management and the revolution of 1848 in France led to the collapse of these hopes (page 101).

Joseph Chevron of Tonga, inwardly gentle and saintly, came from the deeply Catholic town of Nantua in the cool mountain landscape on a main road between the Rhône Valley and Geneva. He was one of many Marists translated by their obedience from the changing seasons of France to overhead sun and a strange people. Kava replaced their delicate wines; taro and yams were substituted for French bread. Tongan chiefs, even those who protected the Catholic missions, could not always be relied upon in times of war and scarcity to relieve the Marists' poverty with local supplies. The missionaries were alternately annoyed and snubbed by the Wesleyans; reinforcement from

Wallis gave them moral courage, but added to their material want. At times they indulged themselves by coveting the martyr's crown, already won by Chanel on Futuna in 1841 (page 98). Amid their distresses, the Marists were inclined to dream of a brief heroic end and an instant Paradise.

During this same period of stressful Marist beginnings Taufa'ahau was preoccupied with buttressing his rule in the north. As lord over many canoes he turned his ambitions to the trade routes of his ancestors. The title Kanokupolu derived in Tongan memory from the island of Upolu in Samoa. One of Taufa'ahau's wives before his baptism was Samoan, "a fine young woman" and literate; Thomas had baptized her Salata (Charlotte); she had returned in 1832, laden with gifts, to her father, Matetau, the high chief of the strategic small Samoan island of Manono. (She is not to be confused with Taufa'ahau's eventual sole queen, who had the same name.) The large canoe that carried Salata to Samoa was estimated by John Williams, who saw it, to have a hundred and thirty Christians on board. "It is hoped," wrote Williams, "they will not imitate the example of their heathen countrymen who visit that group." By means of co-operation with Peter Turner, who went himself to Samoa in 1835, Taufa'ahau furthered his new religion there among his "kinsmen."

In 1839 Turner was obliged to withdraw, on orders from the Wesleyan Society's headquarters in London; John Williams insisted that Cross and Nathaniel Turner had promised him Samoa would be an LMS field, in return for LMS acknowledgement of Fiji as Wesleyan. Taufa'ahau was not content with the decision. He retained Benjamin Latuselu, the first ordained representative of Tongan Methodism abroad, to be his envoy in Samoa. Latuselu, a chief and "politician," maintained (and diluted) the Tongan *lotu* in preparation for the eventual re-opening of Samoa to English Wesleyan missionaries in 1857 (pages 128-9). After his enthronement in 1845 the king's motives as Methodist and as Tu'i Kanokupolu were intertwined; the advancement of the king's faith and power in Samoa and the Tongan-dominated islands of Niuatoputapu and Niuafo'ou suited John Thomas' desire to send the Methodist remnant in Samoa more white missionaries.

In Fiji, migration from Vava'u to Lakeba had intermingled Tongans with the population of Fiji's eastern Lau group of islands; the policy of Taufa'ahau was less direct but more effective. The ordained missionaries William Cross and David Cargill were sent to Lakeba in 1835, the year of the opening of the Samoan Wesleyan mission. In 1841 or 1842 one thousand Tongans were reported at Lakeba to obtain prized Fijian hardwood bowls. In 1842 Taufa'ahau himself visited Lakeba, on his way back from a journey to place Tongan Christian teachers in Samoa. In 1853 he visited Ratu Seru Cakobau of Bau, Fiji's paramount chief, to urge him to become Christian. Two years later Taufa'ahau's Tongan warriors clinched the issue in Fiji at the

TO LIVE AMONG THE STARS

battle of Kaba (page 114) when Bau, with Tongan help, defeated its enemies. The advance of Tongan Wesleyan Christianity and warlike manoeuvres proceeded simultaneously in Fiji. After the Battle of Kaba Taufa'ahau sealed his policy by despatching his cousin, Henele Ma'afu, the son of Aleamotu'a, as general of a large force of Tongan troops. They fought in the Lau Group, and on the islands of the Lomaiviti Group, Taveuni and Vanua Levu. Ma'afu's power, at its peak, extended to Kadavu, and to the Yasawas in the west. King George dramatized the placement of his handsome and adventurous cousin as a contribution from one Christian realm to another. In practice Ma'afu's power threatened Cakobau's. The English missionaries and Tongan Christian teachers in Fiji were embarrassed by the violence and off-duty licentiousness of Ma'afu's nominally Christian force (page 108). For twenty-eight years he dominated eastern Fiji, and was honoured with the title Tu'i Lau.

Following the close of the "wars of religion" on Tongatapu in 1852 King George made a treaty with France, ensuring French subjects, including the Marists, of protection and the right to reside. The period when Thomas was tutor and counsellor to the king drew to its close. Thomas visited England, told his story, and received word that the British Wesleyans, in a period of financial depression, intended pulling out of Oceania and handing over to the Methodists of the Australasian Conferences. On the recommendation of their representative Robert Young, who had toured the field and taken the Tongan king on an eye-opening and flattering tour to Sydney in 1853, they did so in 1855. When Thomas returned from England he found the Tongan king the master of his own ship of state, no longer inclined to bow easily to the advice of his veteran mentor. Thomas departed from Tonga in 1859, leaving the way open for an incoming missionary, the Rev. Shirley Waldemar Baker, to become the new confidant and Prime Minister of the king, steadying the development of government for a time, only later to throw the Wesleyan church into convulsions of schism and internal strife (pages 272-6).

Foundations had been laid for a church which, from its earliest growth under Tahitian influence, asserted its deeply Tongan character — a royal and chiefly church, with seats in the sanctuary alongside its ministers for those who bore titles of royalty, nobility or high local rank. Within its tuneful and affirmative liturgies and ceremonies an ancient Tongan pride in feasting, song and the presentation of gifts prevailed. The spirit of the Friendly Islands vibrated in harmony with the lovefeasts of Methodism — confessions of contrite need and aspirations after perfect holiness. Wars ceased in Tonga, but the love of conflict accompanied the *lotu Tonga* through its Christian soldiers (of both kinds) in Fiji — and many teachers sent later into Melanesia. The Tongan Bible, absorbed through literacy, was re-translated back into Bible drama and song. Around the festivals of the church, men and women continued their absorption in all the dances of their people, save those that celebrated the old gods or were sexually explicit. Sunday became sacred for ever in Tonga, a recurrent *tapu* day of legally enforced rest; inwardly, the worship, dressing up, eating and drinking of the Tongan Sabbath more than compensated the wide-extended family of the Wesleyan Church for what seemed to outsiders to be a strict and dull lacuna in the week. The pagan excesses of the old *'inasi*, the fertility festival of first fruits and sexual abandon, found their surrogate in mass gatherings of the newly literate for the school examination festivals, when missionaries had to watch edgily for unholy passions poking through. In time, as annual presentations of gifts in kind and cash for the mission of the church (the *Misinale* festivals) became a great event for the people, dancing, mimicry and public buffoonery in church buildings on the occasion became, and remained, celebratory expressions of popular fulfilment, manifestations of equality before God under the dispensation of grace.

Tonga had been Christianized from other bases, London, Sydney and the Bay of Islands; within Tonga, under its king, Christianity became Tongan; as the *lotu Tonga* it has left abiding marks on the Christianity of Fiji, the Western Solomons, New Britain, Papua and the New Guinea Highlands (pages 102, 300, 220, 230, 303).

THE LMS EXPANDS WESTWARD

SYDNEY, the Bay of Islands and the Tongan chain were touched at various times during the travels of LMS missionaries from Tahiti and the Leeward Islands. These three emerging bases of Anglican and Wesleyan expansion — Australia, New Zealand and Tonga — were gradually dwarfed in scale by local missionary expansion from the Society Islands and the Cooks. John Davies, William Ellis and J.M. Orsmond trained promising leaders in their churches to participate in missions to Hawaii, the Marquesas, Fiji and the Austral Islands. Davies listed out-stations of the Tahitian Mission as Anaa in the Tuamotus, Tubuai and Raivavae in the Australs, Rapa, the Marquesas and Fiji; he described in detail the sending of Tahitian teachers to these places and to others within the Society and Cook Island groups. Evidently he felt proud, writing between 1827 and 1831, that the foundations for evangelization of the Pacific by Pacific Islanders had been laid before John Williams, Lancelot Threlkeld and Orsmond began to make their noise in the world.

The noise they made was louder. The younger missionaries on Raiatea took advantage of a long tradition of intrepid voyaging by the descendants of a shadowy ancestor named Hiro, steersman of large sea-going outrigger canoes and conqueror of new worlds beyond the horizon. Love of distant battles was in the blood of the deacons, landowners and high chiefs of the Leewards. Did their passion for navigation and roving inspire John Williams, or was their vision partly inspired by his? The two wide-ranging longings coalesced when the *Endeavour* was acquired by the chiefs. Williams, as the evangelical white chief Wiriamu, a latter day Hiro, looked at western horizons from under her sails, with the trade winds blowing at his back.

In 1823 Robert Bourne and John Williams sailed, in July and August, to the island of Aitutaki, where they visited the Raiatean teachers Papeiha and Vahapata who had been left by Williams in 1821 (page 30). Both men had been deacons of the Raiatea church. The *Endeavour* picked up Papeiha from Aitutaki, where Williams and Bourne observed that the *maraes* had been destroyed and the Sabbath was observed under the forceful ministry of Papeiha. Going on to Atiu, the missionaries made good use of their "old Chief Tamatoa," who accompanied them on the voyage and told of the destruction of the *maraes* and the building of a great Christian chapel on Raiatea. The recital, and Tamatoa's chiefly presence, impressed Rongomatane, the chief of Atiu, who was acknowledged on Mitiaro. Taua and Haavi, two teachers from Bourne's station of Tahaa, adjacent to Raiatea, were "settled on the islands of Mitiaro and Mauto (Mauke) in the most satisfactory and comfortable manner."

Less satisfactory and comfortable was the shape of the *Endeavour's* reception at Rarotonga. Papeiha, with his prior knowledge of life on Aitutaki, was first ashore. When the Raiatean teachers and missionaries followed him the women were molested by "a gang of fellows lost to all sense of decency," who plucked at their long garments and threatened, during a sleepless night on shore, to go further. Makea, the high chief, was also very forward. According to Maretu, a Rarotongan Christian chronicler, who was then a young man, a local Rarotongan prophet had four months earlier predicted the arrival of a ship bearing women and Bibles and promised "when that shipload of women arrived he would share them out to all the people and they shall ravish them." The Raiatean teachers were not eager to stay. Papeiha, however, was liked by Makea, who promised him protection. "He manifested a true Missionary Spirit, sent all his clothes, property, and even his bedstead to Raiatea, to be returned when the vessel visits them again, and went on shore with nothing but what he stood upright in and a few Spelling Books under his arm."

In spite of these slender beginnings, Papeiha showed an eye for the main chance. He married on Rarotonga, into a chiefly line; his evangelistic activities were enmeshed with destruction of the old deities and with landholding. He belonged to the class of teachers Williams liked to think of as rugged levellers of the site. Later European missionaries were startled by the behaviour of Papeiha; Charles Pitman and Aaron Buzacott, who came after him on Rarotonga, complained about his lordly attitudes over the people.

They were still more critical of a second Raiatean teacher, Tiberio, who joined Papeiha four months later. Tiberio owned a gun, which he used to coerce people into giving him land. The English missionaries later gave back what he gained by these methods. Williams, who was not noticeably appalled by the deeds of his pupils, perhaps sensed that to Makea the means used were not as heinous as they seemed in English law.

Williams and Bourne were elated by their voyage. They "entered the Harbour of Raiatea decorated with trophies of Victory obtained by King Jesus; a large Idol was hung at each yard Arm — one at the bowsprit and another at the boom end." On this first exhilarating journey to new islands Williams relied on the inherited skills of Raiatean and Atiu sailors. He named Faaori of Raiatea as "our native sailor" and told how Rarotonga had been found for him without compass, by aligning landmarks with the stars. A different kind of course had been set for Williams' future by the impression Tamatoa made on his fellow-chiefs; by observing them in their relationships Williams learned to be a chiefly missionary with his own style of authority; it was "entirely of a moral character," but powerful in Polynesia to build his image and to persuade.

Bourne followed up with another voyage to inspect progress in 1825; then, on 6 May 1827 Williams returned to Rarotonga for a longer stay, bringing with him Charles Pitman and his wife as the first resident Europeans. Pitman, who settled at Ngatangiia, was a scholar with a model grounding at Gosport (page 24) in grammar and the scriptures. He translated eleven books of the New Testament and eighteen of the Old, using the Greek and Hebrew text. His admired Rarotongan versions owed much to his local pupil, Ta'unga, who became an outstanding missionary in Samoa and Melanesia (pages 190-5). Though his gifts as pastor and teacher were many, Pitman was also a hypochondriac; his letters and journals reveal a "one station" missionary of a complaining turn of mind, who remained where he was, with two furloughs, until 1854, and died in Sydney at the age of eighty-eight.

Aaron Buzacott, who joined Pitman in February 1828, was the right complement to his talents. He seemed a godsend to John Williams, who was struggling to build his own vessel at Rarotonga and helping Pitman to translate the Bible. Buzacott, like Williams, was an ingenious handyman. He had been trained to work metal; at Rarotonga, he presented himself with apron and tools on the work-site where the home-built *Messenger of Peace* was emerging out of scraps. Buzacott carried old iron he had acquired on Tahiti. "This is the man we want," Williams told Makea, who was standing by. Williams fashioned his makeshift schooner out of local materials with "a perfect genius for mechanical contrivance, and a mirthful triumph over obstacles such as paralyze ordinary minds." He sometimes exasperated Pitman by drawing off Rarotongan workers from learning to be literate

Christians, but Pitman and the practical Buzacott formed an effective team. As Buzacott taught the Rarotongans to build durable "civilized" houses of coral lime, Williams planned with him for the future. He sowed in Buzacott's mind the idea of founding a theological seminary at Takamoa for training Rarotongan teachers who would sail with Williams as missionaries to Samoa and Melanesia. People were brought in from the villages to the settlements at Ngatangiia (under Pitman) and Avarua (under Buzacott) to learn reading, writing and Christian faith. Williams' labours to acquire ships, with the steady translation work of Rarotonga's missionary triumvirate, combined to shape a plan of wider evangelization, to be copied later by the LMS in Samoa, and later again by the Wesleyans in Fiji (pages 126 and 221).

Development of the Rarotongan base coincided for Williams with lamentable decline at his Raiatea headquarters, which he visited fitfully with a sinking heart. The standards imposed when he and Threlkeld had been in charge had slipped in an atmosphere of moral rot and strife between chiefs. His wife's health was a constant trouble; she was often pregnant and a bad sailor. Williams was fathering a family during his years of wandering. It has been argued that his missionary career, toward the end, was a flight from Raiatea and from the tedium of home and fatherhood. On board ships he certainly came to life. He loved to sail, to command, to write, plan, evangelize and dream.

In 1830, in his improvised ship, he set out in the cooler mid-year weather accompanied by his colleague Charles Barff of Huahine, for the Cooks, Niue, Tonga and Samoa. They took with them for Samoa two teachers from Huahine (Moia and Boti), three from Raiatea (Taataori, Umia and Arue), one from Borabora (Taihere), and two from Aitutaki (Rake and Tuava). Of these all but two were married. "So great are the advantages on the side of a native Teacher at the commencement of a Mission over a European," Williams wrote, "one colour, almost one language, and a oneness of habit gives them these superior advantages." Passing through the Tongan islands Williams and Barff visited the Wesleyan missionaries Nathaniel Turner and Cross on Tongatapu and talked — evidently in general terms — about dividing their future labours between Fiji for the Wesleyans and Samoa for the LMS. Williams, in London in 1834, depicted the arrangement as a binding compact; he thus succeeded in having the infant Wesleyan mission in Samoa withdrawn. Wesleyan missionaries in Tonga denied any firm undertaking had been given to establish comity (pages 122 and 123).

In Tonga the expedition was joined by a Samoan chief named Fauea, a relative of the powerful Savai'i chief Malietoa. Fauea had been impressed by the Wesleyan *lotu Tonga* as seen among the people of Taufa'ahau and Siosaia Tupou (pages 70-81). He recognized the value of strengthening Malietoa's hand in the strife of districts and titles then raging in Samoa. Though he did not adopt Christianity for himself, he was instrumental, as Williams showed, in "giving the Samoans in general and his own family in particular a favourable account of the lotu, or Praying system, obtained for our native teachers a very favourable reception and turned the opinion of the Samoans much in favour of the lotu, especially as they were informed by Fauea that the chief of the Haapaes and many of his people were lotu ..."

The success of his contacts with Malietoa at Sapapali'i on Savai'i, encouraged Williams. The teachers he left there were promised protection and opportunity to instruct and evangelize. For Malietoa their very presence was a means of increasing his prestige; he was jealous at the thought that Matetau, the chief of the strategic islet of Manono in the narrow strait between Savai'i and Upolu, also sought and was sent teachers (page 122). On his second visit to Samoa in October 1832 Williams brought with him Makea, high chief of Rarotonga, who, wrote Williams, "excited much attention" at Sapapali'i, "dressed in European clothing with a fine red surtout presented by Mr. Buzacott just before our departure." Malietoa "viewed him with an eagle's eye, made many enquiries about him and then called him a handsome man and said he was not to be equalled by any Chief in the Samoas."

On his way to Savai'i on this second visit, Williams made first contacts for the mission on the eastern Samoan islands of Manua and Tutuila, where he found a beachcomber named Gray had been active in teaching rudimentary Christianity, including worship and Sabbath observance. He noted that teachers he had left on Savai'i two years before had already increased the desire for Christianity on Tutuila; he found the Sabbath strictly observed at Leone by fifty Christians using a mixture of Tahitian and Samoan, and dressed in white. Moving on to Upolu, he heard reports of "a clever, artful designing individual" named Sio Vili, who had come by a devious route from Tahiti and observed the (earlier LMS) "sixth day" Tahitian sabbath (page 29). The cult of Sio Vili, with its promises of ships, muskets and beads, revealed that Samoan expectation of Christianity was already an attempt to "appropriate from below" the white man's coveted complex of technology, trade goods and religion. Williams recognized the mixed motives.

Another passenger with Williams, Teava of Rarotonga, a pupil of Buzacott, was left to reside with Matetau on Manono. Teava was a forerunner of a line of capable inner-directed Cook Island missionaries to many parts of the Pacific. They travelled with unwearied cheerfulness in open canoes along unfamiliar shores, working with ease in new languages, building houses to be occupied later by incoming British missionaries, and leading village after village into Christianity by conversation round cooking fires and kava bowls. Teava's faith was unfeigned; he never lost or compromised it; he knew how to transmit it to fellow-Polynesians. In the time between his arrival on Manono and the coming of a group of LMS missionaries from England in 1836 he was a leader in the process of alerting the Samoan islands to the significance of the "Tahitian *lotu.*"

This voyage of 1832 brought Williams to the peak of his achievement in the South Seas. He wrote a long journal in a neat hand. By 1834 he was in England, to tell the story directly up and down the country, with the aid of large coloured pictures depicting the scenes he described. The LMS no longer shrank from allowing him the spotlight. He put the manuscript of his best selling book, *A Narrative of Missionary Enterprises in the South Seas,* in the press. By cultivating nobility and royalty as patrons he promoted the entire cause of Protestant missions in Britain. Williams achieved the standing of a Nonconformist social lion. He raised £4,000 to buy and outfit the missionary ship *Camden;* he designed her to carry enough equipment and trade goods to establish his son in business in the islands. The wavering young missionary who in 1821 had virtually limped to Sydney, in a state of indecision, for medical treatment, had developed into a celebrity.

He basked in it; his euphoria verged at times on the fulsome; but he had a right to be celebrated. In the field he had become a remarkable all-round missionary. He was a pioneer, a translator, a ship-builder, a navigator and a fraternizing evangelist with a taste for many customs of the exotic societies he revelled in describing. The detailed observations of Samoan life at the end of his 1832 journal show a clear eye and ability to record faithfully. The journal is mostly free of pious asides; it seldom attributes normal human events to special divine providence. Williams was also a bold missionary strategist; what he said of polygamous marriages in his journal prefigures late twentieth-century thinking about some of the peoples of Africa:

> a man had two wives with whom he has lived for many years and has a family by each, feels an attachment to both, and of course is at a loss which to put away ... prudence and consideration must be exercised in the management of this affair. I have thought that in some instances perhaps it might be well to allow them to retain their two wives and yet admit them into Christian communion.

Nor was Williams lacking in humour. When, on his way through Tonga, he volunteered to chew kava root in the presence of the chiefs Taufa'ahau and Makea to prepare for mixing it as a drink in the bowl, he reported:

> before it had been in my mouth half a minute I was glad to put it out again for it is extremely bitter and produces a great discharge of saliva — the Tonga people had a laugh at me and said the papalangi (Europeans) were clever at most things but not at chewing kava.

When he returned in the *Camden* in 1839 for his final voyage, through Samoa to the New Hebrides — and to death, there were signs that Williams, the builder of bases and instigator of voyages, was already weary. The handwriting of his journal was no longer full, neat and clear. The last sentence, like its author's life, broke off — sadly — in the middle (pages 164-7).

4

Ave Maria or Hallelujah?

Mangareva, Wallis/Futuna
Fiji

ROMAN CATHOLICISM came late to Eastern Polynesia, but with a sense of divine right. The French fathers of the Society of the Sacred Hearts of Jesus and Mary (Picpus Fathers) were Ultramontane, *anti-modernes*, classically trained. They unashamedly inherited the Baroque tradition, viewing the restoration of a Catholic monarchy in France as a call to their country to be once more the handmaid of the Catholic Reformation. Their religion was inseparable from their patriotism; their ideal for a mission was the assembling of non-christian populations into "reductions" — villages gathered together around a nucleus of priests who followed a religious rule. Baptism of converts was followed up by catechizing, the instilling by slow and patient rote of the fundamentals of Catholic dogma and behaviour. The forest reductions of the Jesuits in Paraguay established their general model for the small islands of the Pacific. Treasured rites, the Seven Sacraments and the feasts of Christ, Mary and the saints, visibly effected the transformation. Regular confession ensured intimate communication between missionaries and converts. Mangareva, the largest of the Gambier islands, for forty years became a singular outpost of Catholic Christendom, under Father Louis Laval (Le Père Honoré Laval), its miniature Pope Hildebrand.

In 1837, on his deathbed, Father Pierre Marie-Joseph Coudrin, the founder of Laval's Congregation, prayerfully uttered the words "Valparaiso, Gambier." Three of his young men had by then landed on Akamuru, one of

AVE MARIA OR HALLELUJAH?

the four inhabited high islands of the Gambiers, on 7 August 1834: Father François d'Assise Caret from Brittany, Laval, and as assistant and catechist, Brother Columban Murphy, an Irishman later to appear as scourge of Protestants in Hawaii (pages 53-55). Caret was thirty-one, Laval twenty-five. Soon after they landed among the virtually unclothed people Laval met his first Protestant, George Hunn Nobbs, who had come, a little ahead of the Catholics, from Pitcairn Island. Nobbs was sent as a scout of the LMS, with ideas of commencing a mission. He did not stay long; in October he left to resume his previous work among descendants of the *Bounty* mutineers on Pitcairn; eventually he accompanied them to Norfolk Island in the far western Pacific. Caret was the first superior of the Catholic mission to the Gambiers. Physically small, an emotionally tender antithesis for Laval, he died in 1844 with a reputation for gentle saintliness.

Protestants in the Pacific sought to acquaint their converts with heavenly salvation; Catholics stressed the earthly sanctification of the islands through the sacraments. On the Gambiers they began by finding and baptizing children whose parents offered no resistance. By the middle of August the missionaries were searching for children who were in danger of dying. They baptized a child of seven or eight days on 15 August, giving her the name Mary. "What could be more appropriate?" wrote Laval. The child, the first fruits of the mission, lived for two more days. A mass had been celebrated on the morning of the baptism, the first to be offered in the Gambiers. Mary's burial followed "with all the ceremonies of the Church," on 18 August. The missionaries placed a cross at the head of the grave, sure that "graces were about to flow abundantly for these peoples." No labour was spared to facilitate the flow.

On the island of Aukena, beside the grave of their "angel," Caret and Laval chanted the canonical hours each day according to rule. They sought permission from the chiefs to live on the larger island of Mangareva, but its high chief, Maputeoa, their future convert, denied the request. Caret, probably correctly sensing fear of local spirits as the dissuasive, attributed the rebuff to a devil, the spirit-god of one of the temples of the local people. On their way back to Aukena after the refusal the two priests took the precaution of making the sign of the cross many times unobserved inside this shrine. Laval even hid an image of Our Lady of Peace on the spot where "erotic compositions" were customarily sung by the *hakakarioi*, Mangarevan fertility dancers of a type similar to the Tahitian *arioi*.

Only temporarily deterred, the three men persisted with their preliminaries, countering signs of the old religion with alternative signs of the new. These small gestures, reinforced by singing the *Ave Maris Stella* in Latin and the *Holy City* in French, foreshadowed the regime to follow. Before long the small islands would be generously peppered with stone churches, a convent, schools, stone-built roads, wayside shrines and royal buildings designed to elevate the family of Maputeoa to Christian kingship. Ironically, the first interpreters the Catholic missionaries used, apart from Nobbs, were two LMS island teachers sent from the young church on the island of Rapa in the Australs to work in the Gambiers. Their services were soon dispensed with by the priests, whose ability with languages enabled them to use the vernacular for themselves and begin to write it for the first time. The rapidity of their success, after overcoming the hazards of rejection, rats, hunger and homelessness, is a tribute to tenacity.

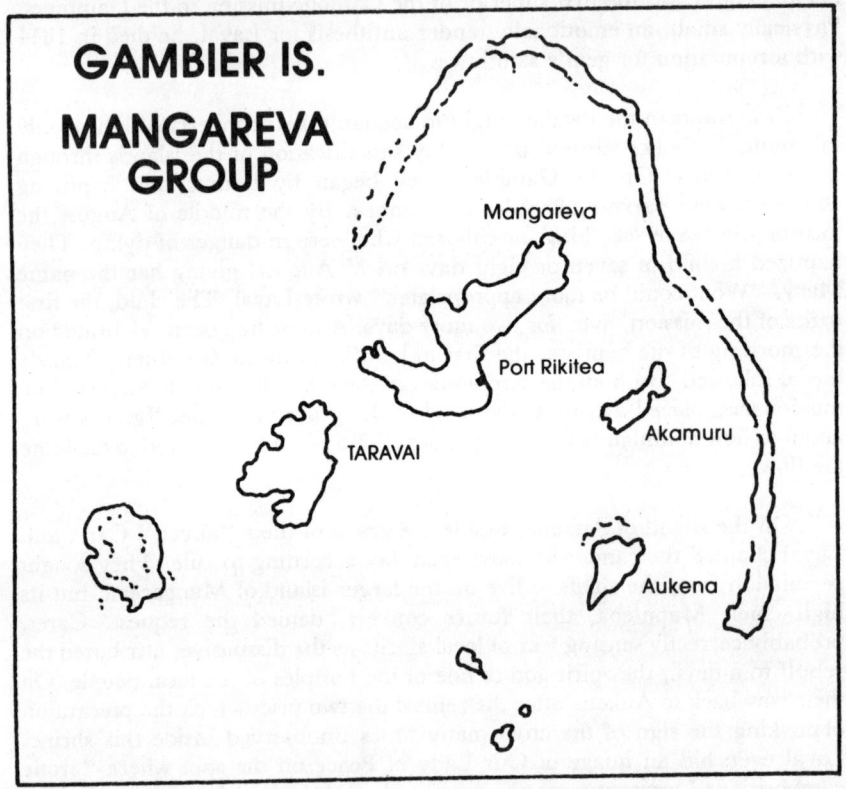

Laval, in his paternalist prose, many years later recalled how he, Caret and Murphy lived in places previously favourable to the Rapa Protestants. The priests had to be content with shabby grass huts. The local population thought, possibly because of their garb, that they were gods. Murphy, true Irishman, succeeded in distilling a liqueur from the *ti* plant; Laval found it consoling as a final flourish at his miserable meals. When Laval and Caret

AVE MARIA OR HALLELUJAH?

visited Mangareva in search of sick children to baptize, Nobbs, according to Laval, told the local people these papists were looking for babies to eat. The aspersion, widely circulated among Pacific island converts, that the Pope ate babies, has been traced to an illustration, in translations of Bunyan's *Pilgrim's Progress,* of one of Christian's grisly allegorical visions.

Caret reduced the language to writing with the aid of a portable notebook. The people regarded this little vocabulary as magic. By Christmas satisfactory versions of the Lord's Prayer, the Ave Maria and the Apostles' Creed had been made. On Akamuru the missionaries singled out likely converts among chiefs to be taught catchy rhymed songs about heaven and the Trinity. At Christmas the midnight mass, using the *Adeste Fideles,* and the new vernacular chants, made a great impression. Shortly beforehand some of the sacred chiefs had asked Laval and Caret to cut their long hair, the sign of their holy power, as testimony to their willingness to renounce the old gods of the islands. Murphy, a melodious singer, led the chanting to the accompaniment of his accordion. This first Christmas, with its fusion of ancient liturgy and local custom, lingered in Laval's memory. He recalled how he thought back to Christmas as celebrated at the Paris mother house of his congregation and cast "a retrospective glance in the direction of the homeland, where all is exquisite civilization," with "many legitimate enjoyments to be savoured."

The whole Gambier group had been visited by February 1835. Murphy, the party's handyman, acquired an ancient whaleboat. Diminutive Caret had trouble mastering the tiller in a strong sea; Laval, physically awkward throughout his life, fell overboard and almost drowned. In spite of this, the progress of the mission was spectacular. Nobbs left on a German vessel to return to Pitcairn, leaving the priests a free hand. They profited by the departure when they pointed to Nobbs' case as a departure from ecclesiastical celibacy. They told the people that God had no wife, Christ had no wife, and they themselves had no wife. Luther, the first Protestant, unable to cope with the divine estate, had taken a wife. So had Nobbs, Luther's spiritual descendant. Their own spiritual genealogy, from Christ through Peter and the Church's bishops, was, moreover, impeccable — a strong argument for a people who admired good lineages.

Caret and Laval gradually gained the interest and support of Matua, a giant among men, who was one of the group's highest chiefs, a priest of the old religion, and the uncle of Maputeoa. Awe before a greater unseen Force evidently swayed Matua's choice. He attached himself to the Catholics, gave them his former temple, and advised them about their approach to Maputeoa. Their work, meanwhile, extended to Taravai, where they instructed the people in the Ten Commandments, cautiously at first, because they believed dogma and the sacraments preceded moral change. By March the young Maputeoa was appearing during mass. He showed curiosity and asked why he could not take communion. Being told he must be instructed, he stationed himself outside Caret's school for children, demanding peremptorily that Caret should come out and teach him. Caret and Laval had already decided to meet such regal orders by asserting their "national superiority" and ecclesiastical authority. Caret told the king to come in and join the children. He was furious, sought out Laval, and insisted on a lesson in how to cross himself.

During Lent, Maputeoa stood by when Matua, on Mangareva, allowed the missionaries, surrounded by the people, to hack down the images of the old deities in the temple he had given the Catholics for their use. On the next day the priests consecrated the shrine as a church dedicated to the Archangel Michael. "Under Constantine and others," Laval observed grandly, "the temples of the false gods were also changed into churches." Matua's protection of the mission continued, against gradually eroding opposition from his younger higher-ranking nephew. Caret and Laval were expecting reinforcements from France; they knew their superior, Jérôme Etienne Rouchouze, titular Bishop of Nilopolis with jurisdiction as Vicar Apostolic of Eastern Oceania, was on his way out to join them. At first they planned to wait for him before pressing on with the baptisms of their 152 catechumens on Akamuru and thirty-five others on Aukena. When he failed to come, they decided to proceed, but providentially Rouchouze appeared in time, on 9 May 1835, with Father Louis Maigret, Hawaii's future bishop (page 54), Father Cyprien Liausu and a group of missionary brothers, destined to be constructors of houses and churches for the islands.

The day after the bishop arrived, when he "came out of our lodgings accompanied by his minor clergy, a general shout of wonder went up at the sight of the mitre and the gilded cross." On 11 May Akamuru witnessed the same spectacle, with the addition of an accolade of crossed spears. The effect was imposing, but odd. Liausu wore dark green sunglasses; he was considered to be a bad god. After watching the episcopal ceremonies, some converts took it upon themselves to go into the churches and conduct their own imitative masses.

In June the bishop celebrated mass baptisms, confirmations and first communions. The *maraes* on the large island were destroyed. The bishop broke the coral idols with a heavy hammer as his followers processed and chanted in his train — a memorable iconoclastic Pentecost, designed to dismay all anthropologists. Baptisms followed fast on Aukena and Taravai. Bishop and priests travelled back and forth. More baptisms on Akamuru paved the way for Christian marriages. The distribution of calico hastily rescued the new Christians from nudity. Laval noted with pleasure that the sign of the cross and the observation of the Angelus were spreading. One of the king's aunts received deathbed baptism and Christian burial, whereupon the king and

AVE MARIA OR HALLELUJAH?

Matua were reconciled. The king agreed to the demolition of the largest temple in the group, at Rikitea on Mangareva, where Liausu, trained under the noted French doctor, Récamier, set up a hospital and treated the sick during a sudden epidemic. Matua, who had postponed the cutting of his hair and submission to baptism, finally accepted both. He was baptized with his family. Maputeoa followed on 25 August 1836, in a church he erected for the occasion. The floor was decorated with white *tapa* cloth. Laval compared it with Gobelin tapestries: "Simple, if you will," he wrote, "yes, it was simple, but it was beautiful." These innovations for the eye went along with Laval's adaptation of local chant to the rites of the Mangareva church — a bold essay in Polynesian plainsong.

The episcopal celebrations gave a somewhat deceptive taste of things to come. After Rouchouze had left for Europe (and his subsequent tragic end) Liausu became head of the group on Mangareva. He worked in good relations with Laval, but was a hard taskmaster for the people. He took in hand the building of churches, the digging of plantations, the sequestration of the young girls who tended the gardens in the convent of Rourou on the slopes of Mount Duff on Mangareva, and the foundation of a community of local sisters there in an ample stone convent. Liausu made himself its chaplain. After his departure without authorization for France in 1855 he left Laval in charge of the mission, but gave authority to run the convent to the superior, Sister Thérèse. The turbulent supremacy of Laval on Mangareva had begun.

He acknowledged that he depended on the special gifts of several of his colleagues for the establishment of his remote theocracy, especially Count Alphonse de Latour de Clamouze, an impoverished aristocrat educated by the Sacred Hearts Fathers, who came with the mission as Brother Urbain. Latour excelled as architect-designer and supervisor of the educational programme, from Latin and French to manual skills. Pierre Adolphe Lesson, a medical doctor who visited the Gambiers on the *Pylade* in 1844, remarked on the contrast between the elevated manners of Latour and the "stereotyped smile" of Laval, who exuded conventional *bonhomie* and maintained in conduct and writing a feeling of over-familiarity with *le Bon Dieu*. This French rural Catholic side of Laval, the son of a day-labourer in a village of the Beauce, near Chartres, appears in the asymmetrical twin towers he bestowed on his modest church on Akamuru beside his simple presbytery. They were almost certainly directly modelled on the great Cathedral dominating the Catholicism of his childhood.

Laval's egregious clericalism successfully controlled, through the practice of private confession, the fewer than three thousand inhabitants of the little kingdom where he was spiritual head. Thousands of post-revolutionary French priests were just like him — wandering about their parishes in flat black hats and stained soutanes, growled at by their parishioners in private, knowing everyone's intimate business, jovial in a stylized way, sure that they had been given authority to use the big stick. Were they not the sacral representatives of the Body of Christ, who gave their trembling flocks the true Body of the Lord in the mystery of the mass?

Unlike many of his fellow priests in the Sacred Hearts mission, who came from the Atlantic seaboard, Laval was no lover of the ocean. He deliberately fashioned his parish into a *petit coin rural,* a sea-surrounded reconstruction of the medieval ideal. Chief priest, king, nobles, commoners, were ringed about by threatening forces, heathenism, heresy, apostasy. Laval incarnated the role of guardian, loved by many of the faithful, loathed by his irate opponents. Etienne Jaussen, his bishop on Tahiti, had to discipline Laval in the end for acting against French traders and administrators as though they were the devil incarnate; yet Jaussen, when he eventually ordered Laval to withdraw into cantankerous retirement in Papeete, called him "large-hearted athlete, first apostle of our mission, oldest surviving veteran, model to all."

The passing years gave Laval full self-assurance as judge of the baptized. His excommunications were summary and severe. He moved abruptly against sailors and traders who sought to inveigle the girls and exploit the local pearls and pearl-shell. Laval's confrontations with them dominate the torrid, slightly tedious, second half of his memoirs. Finally his opposition to French administrators appointed to investigate his curt justice led to his downfall. The French Government decided on a protectorate, then annexation, for Mangareva. Laval's conflict with French troops, a "duel between barracks behaviour and conventual customs," was not, however, merely comic; there is a prophetic pre-echo of anti-colonialism. As early as 1842 Laval protested against French military occupation of the Marquesas. "There are times," he wrote, "when the Catholic priest has a right to say *Caesarem appello;* but to wish to proceed further, to allow bayonets to sponsor both the love of religion and the love of France, no. Never, never."

Laval bears favourable comparison as writer, translator and ethnographer, with the Protestants William Ellis, Wyatt Gill and George Brown. The formidable architecture and massive paved roads still visible among the undergrowth in the run-down and isolated silences of Mangareva stand as monuments to his ill-starred dream. His grammar, dictionary and description of Mangareva's pre-christian culture reveal a classically trained observer affectionately at work.

The Catholics invested Mangareva with the dignity of Christian kingship, a cathedral and a palace; but Maputeoa and the sickly regents who succeeded him offer no parallel to the resourceful Protestant monarchs of Raiatea or Tonga, or to Queen Pomare IV of Tahiti, who had a mind of her

AVE MARIA OR HALLELUJAH?

own (pages 254-6). Laval, as priestly eminence behind the female regent Maria Eutokia, struggled to preserve Mangareva's autonomy against colonists. Fearful tensions were generated in the 1860s over the activities of the pearl trader Jean Pignon, Laval's "nightmare for twenty years."

A succession of French governors in Papeete showed varying degrees of willingness to intervene, but Pignon's punishment by Mangareva's courts led to the sending of a commission of investigation, which foreshadowed reparations. Mangareva's regent, with Laval at her shoulder, appealed to the French Empress Eugénie. The Colonial Office authorized Tahiti's Governor de la Richerie to place a resident above Laval on Mangareva. Under the terms of the French Protectorate Mangareva had no power to expel French nationals. Twenty French soldiers arrived to place the mission in a "state of siege." Laval's Congregation protested in Paris. A compromise was worked out: Bishop Jaussen in Tahiti agreed to pay a fine if the soldiers were withdrawn.

In February 1870 the feeble Prince Regent Arona of Mangareva wrote to the Minister of Marine withdrawing his predecessor's request for a protectorate, which had never been formally ratified in writing by France. The French were reluctant to risk confrontation with the Holy See over the Mangareva question; these were the years of the Infallibility Decree in Rome and the debacle of the Franco-Prussian War. The situation was ultimately sorted out on the spot by a report from the French Commandant de la Motte-Rouge, who convinced both the bishop and the Mangarevan chiefs that proper establishment of the French protectorate was advisable. The report said Laval must leave Mangareva, "the sooner the better." It described him as dominating, explosive, "isolated from the world for thirty-five years and carried away by exaggerated religious ideas." The commandant said Laval wanted "to save souls at all costs, and to that end all means are good." Bishop Jaussen, "to still this storm," recalled Laval to Papeete in March 1871. He maintained Laval's status as Pro-vicar, but the old missionary felt deflated and morose. "How bored I am," he wrote toward the end of his stormy memoirs. "So this is my reward for thirty-six years of mission!" He longed for his beloved corner in Mangareva, but was allowed to revisit it only once, briefly, in 1876. In his lame and lonely old age he pottered in the Papeete Presbytery, played with cats, and bent over a fire in the cool mid-year weather nursing his sadness. One of the cats scratched him. The sore turned septic. Laval died of the poisoning on 1 November 1880. He was buried in the Papeete cemetery.

Ironically, the "Catholic work ethic" on Mangareva seems to have contributed to the decline of the population. An exodus of young men on transient ships and the ravages of introduced epidemics were only part of the story; the other part is attributable to the well-intentioned Catholic diversion of manpower from traditional garden work and fishing into the building of churches, the convent and the roads. Introduced foods replaced the root and fish diet of the people; defective nutrition lowered resistance to disease. Female vows of religious chastity retarded replenishment of the depleted population. The convent of Rourou at the peak of its activity housed between 150 and 200 potential mothers. Old-established modes of alimentation and reproduction were thus disturbed by the attempt to sacralize a Polynesian population on European presuppositions.

Laval's time in the Gambiers was twice, against his natural inclination, broken into by other shorter missions. In November 1836 Rouchouze sent him with Caret to attempt to introduce Catholicism on Tahiti (pages 253-5). Later, in April 1848, Bishop Jaussen sent him to pioneer among the converts of American Mormon missionaries who had begun work in the low-lying coral atolls of the Tuamotus in 1844. There Laval spent three years, "preaching to the Mormons, putting up with their insults, and giving the mission to these arid islets a very gentle start," but he longed for the greener consolations of the Gambiers and was finally allowed by his bishop to go back, though two years later than originally planned. He supervised the building of wattle and daub churches and continued until there were many requests for Catholic baptism. "Now that the Mormons are thrashing around like fish out of water, I think they are on the way out, and the mission is founded," Jaussen told him. Leaving the Tuamotu mission to pass through stormier episodes under the care of his companion there, Father Clair Fouqué, he came home to Akamaru and Mangareva with relief. The priests and brothers who followed up his labours in the scattered Tuamotus, boatmen with legendary patience, contributed a distinctive element to the making of the Roman Catholic Church in French Polynesia (pages 260-2).

WALLIS AND FUTUNA: A MARIST MARTYR

THREE YEARS after the Sacred Hearts (Picpus) Fathers arrived in the Gambiers they were visited for a few idyllic days by Bishop Pompallier and his Marist pioneers on their way to Western Polynesia (pages 68-70). On 13 September 1837 Pompallier made his landfall shortly before midnight, with a bright moon over the islands. Laval thought it all "a beautiful dream." He remembered that "His Lordship and those with him thought our three-year-old Christendom magnificent." St. Pierre Chanel's short account of the joy of the following days confirms the reminiscence. In the presence of the two bishops, the priests and brothers fraternized and celebrated mass on Aukena and Mangareva. Chanel, unawares, was on his way to a martyr's death on the island of Futuna, near Uvea (Wallis) where the Marists made a base as isolated from larger islands as was Mangareva, but placed centrally for

AVE MARIA OR HALLELUJAH?

missionary incursions into the Protestant bastions of Samoa, Tonga and Fiji.

Pompallier skirted these Protestant positions with a sense of frustration on his way to Wallis. On Vava'u in the north of Tonga he met Thomas Boog, a Protestant trader, who told him the culture and language of Tonga were related to those of Wallis, while contact and migration had set up a similar twin relationship between Samoa and Futuna. Boog wanted to go to Wallis; Pompallier took him as his interpreter and guide. Boog went to live on Futuna, shared the last months of trial and danger endured there by Pierre Chanel, and became a Catholic convert.

Pompallier put Father Pierre Bataillon in charge on Wallis, leaving a brother to assist him. Chanel, who was almost sent to Rotuma, went instead to Futuna. Pompallier made off to New Zealand, agreeing to return to Wallis and Futuna within six months — a promise he failed to fulfil. His non-appearance stemmed from problems he could not solve. His finances and manpower were already over-stretched. He went to Sydney and became preoccupied with the beginnings of the mission to New Zealand (page 68). His staff members were Marists; he, though close to the Marist order, had never made his profession. The priests and brothers who served under him acknowledged a line of obedience that ran right through him as their bishop to their superior and founding father, Jean Claude Colin, in France, who corresponded with them direct.

The news from the Pacific nettled Colin sorely. He required his men to go about their apostolic tasks in pairs and to live in community. The priests should, he believed, be able to confess each other and emulate each other in the spiritual life, the quest of sanctity. He learned that they were separated from each other, plagued by local rulers' whims and fears, exposed to theft and famine, victims of fever and dysentery. Those on Wallis fared better than Chanel on Futuna. Pompallier managed to send fathers Joseph Chevron and François Roulleaux as reinforcements. Bataillon reported in January 1841 that every village on Wallis except that of the highest chief, Lavelua, had been converted. But things were otherwise on Futuna. Two rival districts were at war, with possession of the adjacent small food-bearing island of Alofi as a source of contention. Chanel found protection and a sparse lodging in a bamboo hut provided by the high chief of one of the districts, the young "king" Niuliki. He found himself caught in the fortunes of war and exposed to ups and downs as the local estimate of his priestly *mana* rose and fell with the successes and reverses of Niuliki.

Chanel's lucid and uncomplaining journals and letters tell the story of his plight. He learned the language and began to use it within the liturgy. The few catechumens he gathered helped him to supplement his meagre stocks of food, which had been diminished by a hurricane in December 1839 and were replenished sporadically at Niuliki's pleasure. Niuliki's attitude toward him

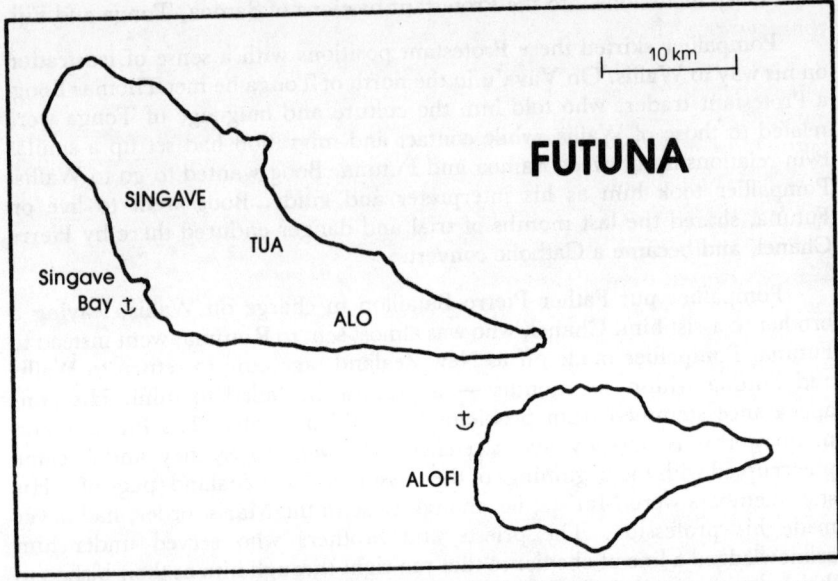

hardened after a bloody battle in August 1839 had been lost. The defeat seemed to point to the displeasure of Niuliki's local spirits about Chanel's presence. The future saint went on patiently with his work. He taught the need to forgive enemies, tended the sick and wounded, and seemed barely aware of the significance of Niuliki's cooling regard. He recorded some baptisms, but in 1840 his journal entries became shorter and less frequent. Hunger, toothache, internal pains and debility racked his body; he became incapable of saying his daily mass. Musumusu, a son-in-law of Niuliki, turned ominously against him. As early as May 1839 he had made a will, sensing where his trials might lead. "I ask nothing for my body," he wrote, "it is too small a thing for me to be concerned about it after I have taken my last breath." In the same month he told Colin, on behalf of himself and his companions in the Futuna mission, "We could well wish our hearts burned as brightly as the climate we live in." His death was hastened by the conversion of Niuliki's son.

On 28 April 1841 Musumusu came to Chanel's hut with a group of people. They said they had come for medicine, but when Chanel turned round to fetch some he was struck by a hatchet. As he bled, some of his converts heard him say that all was well and death was his gain. Then Musumusu picked up Chanel's own axe and killed him by splitting his skull. The assassins buried the body, but the relics were later found, preserved and taken to Rome. In the 1970s they were returned to Futuna. Pierre Chanel was recognized by his Church in 1888 as a martyr, beatified in 1889, and proclaimed Patron

AVE MARIA OR HALLELUJAH?

Saint of Oceania on 12 June 1954. Born at Cuet, in the sumptuous French countryside of Bresse, Chanel was trained in the late medieval architectural splendour of nearby Brou, then went to Belley in the Rhône Valley under the alps of Savoy, where he subsequently taught in the seminary. His life as a missionary links this loved countryside with the tropical rigour he endured on Futuna. In both places his service of his people is explained by his selfless devotion to Christ and His Mother. His simple writings have the spirit of the Beatitudes.

The martyrdom on Futuna symbolized a state of affairs that stirred Jean Claude Colin in France to white heat. He threw himself into the launching of the Oceanian Company, a corporation formed to transport Catholic missionaries and finance the enterprise by trade. Two visionary compatriots supported him, a naval captain, Auguste Marceau, and a Le Havre shipping magnate named Michel-Victor Marziou. Marceau commanded the first vessel, *l'Arche de l'Alliance*. Colin sought big names calculated to offset Pompallier's slow progress. He raised capital in Lyon, the headquarters of the Association for the Propagation of the Faith, then went on in 1842 to Paris and Rome to confer with Cardinal Fransoni of the College of Propaganda.

Fransoni agreed that the policies of Pompallier looked improvident and that his jurisdiction was too wide. Pope Gregory XVI then separated out a new Vicariate of Central Oceania; he made Bataillon its bishop. Colin followed up this elevation of a professed Marist by tightening his own system of communication with his men under both Bataillon and Pompallier. He began by appointing Visitors, to be based in Sydney and inspect the situation of missionaries in the field. The Sydney base, or Procure, established by the first priests to be sent to Australia, Antoine Freydier-Dubreul and Jean Louis Rocher, developed a Marist house, to be called Villa Maria, in the Hunters Hill-Gladesville district near Sydney. This retreat centre and staging point became the nerve centre and headquarters of the Marists' Pacific and Australian work.

At first the Oceanian Company fitted neatly into Colin's enlarged plans. Nobility, businessmen and bishops took up shares in France. Marceau visited Rome in 1845. He made a great impression. His booklet *The Catholic Missions in Oceania* worked wonders in the hands of its author, a naval man of improbably fervent piety. The company set up three branches in Italy. The new Pope, Pius IX, acquired shares with fifteen cardinals, twenty archbishops, thirty-three bishops and the General of the Jesuits. Italian kings, princes and nobles followed. Marceau set out in command of the first ship in 1846 — it was run with "quasi-monastic discipline" and "resembled a Trappist monastery afloat whose captain became its simultaneous father abbot, sacristan and animating spirit." Unfortunately he was also " a very wretched manager."

AVE MARIA OR HALLELUJAH?

Bad management was not the only problem. The company, with a capital of a million French francs, was listed on the Paris exchange. When the revolution of 1848 overthrew the French monarchy the bottom fell out of the market. Marceau, pious and stylish, but lacking the hard-nosed sense of a quick deal, sailed home in 1850 with accumulated debts of 300,000 francs. Despite Marziou's attempt to save the company with fresh capital it was forced to liquidate. The collapse was a bitter sequel to Colin's prayers and labours. He sent 117 missionaries to the Pacific before 1849. He dreamed of creating a flourishing Oceanian Catholicism around their work, injecting an antidote for the poison of heresy, winning the islands for the Church and the Mother of God. Faced with the wreck of his hopes he withdrew in 1854 as head of the Marist Congregation into his final retreat and death. Reluctant to expose his men to further privation, he turned his busy brain to educational and other projects of his Society; Oceania no longer beckoned him.

Bataillon as bishop on Wallis struck out on a line of his own to hold and extend the gains already won. Stubborn, financially extravagant, he nevertheless lived up to his name of battler. His redoubt on Wallis, remote from frequented shipping routes, grew intensely French and Catholic. He instituted schools run by missionary sisters of the Third Order of Mary, and by Marist Brothers of the Schools, founded for this specialized work in 1852 in France. The brothers are now a separate order under their own general. The first brothers had been working alongside the fathers as catechists since 1837.

Bataillon's wider design reached out to commence missions in Tonga, Samoa and Fiji (pp. 77, 129, 286). The Marist fathers he sent out to do the work began with French, but had to acquire English as a further working language in these three island groups where British missionary and mercantile influence dominated the scene. Wallis was too remote ever to become the "Jerusalem of the Pacific" it remained in the imagination of its bishops. As other Marists were named as bishops within Bataillon's jurisdiction of Central Oceania, they turned increasingly to Australia for money and supplies. Their presbyteries and schools, with high shady interiors and wide verandahs, were a mirror of Australian architecture of the period. While Tongan, Samoan and Fijian Catholicism grew, Wallis and Futuna remained wholly Catholic, but relatively static, the proud repository of the heritage of Pierre Chanel. The inaccessibility was dramatized several times on great occasions: representatives of the Australian hierarchy failed to overcome transport problems to attend Pierre Chanel's beatification pilgrimage in 1890, the centenary of the Wallis mission in 1937 and the local celebration of Chanel's canonization in 1955. In 1962, when Bishop Alexandre Poncet, inheritor of Bataillon's out-of-the-way see, took leave of his Wallisians, his parting wish was that they should always remain "Catholic and French."

The Marists' Australian base: old Villa Maria.

TO LIVE AMONG THE STARS
WESLEYANS ENTER FIJI

TONGAN MIGRATION and settlement on Wallis for purposes of family reunion, migration and trade were an aspect of a wider restless movement of canoes from Tonga, along the sides of a triangle with its other two points in northern Tonga and eastern Fiji. From the sixteenth century onward Tongan trading and dynastic connections, formed in the Lau group of Fiji, had opened up a pathway for Tongan rovers through Lomaiviti, central Fiji, to the large and influential islands of Taveuni and Vanua Levu. Taveuni's highest chief, the Tui Cakau, who dominated the Cakaudrove "kingdom" reaching to Vanua Levu, had become traditionally allied with the Tui Nayau, whose ancestors derived their title from the island of Nayau but had come to dominate Lakeba, the main landing point for incoming Tongan canoes. By the early nineteenth century Tongans were familiar infiltrators of Fiji. They traded in canoes and wooden bowls. Tongan names and titles had become joined, through intermarriage, with the family of the Tui Nayau. This Tongan connection aided the coming of Christianity from Tonga to Fiji.

In 1825, at Papara on Tahiti, the LMS missionary John Davies met a Fijian named Takai from Lakeba. He had travelled to Tahiti by way of Sydney, accompanied by a Tongan, Langi, from Tongatapu. Both Davies' visitors had lived in Fiji. They knew Walter Lawry was preaching Christianity on Tongatapu (page 70). Davies taught them to read; he imparted some Tahitian. Takai and Langi "expressed a strong desire that Teachers should be sent to Lageba in the Fijis, saying the chief Tuineau (Tui Nayau) was a friendly peaceable man, and would give the teachers a good reception."

The Tahitian teachers, after being detained on Tongatapu for some time by Aleamotu'a (page 71), reached Lakeba in 1830 — Taharaa from Papara, Faaruea and Hatai from Moorea, all unmarried. Tui Nayau proved to be less ready to receive Christianity than had been expected. In 1832 they moved to Oneata, south of Lakeba, where they succeeded in founding the first place of regular Christian worship on Fijian soil. Though they had problems acquiring the language, they were warmly welcomed. Local tradition still remembers and honours them at Oneata. Hatai and Faaruea co-operated fully with the Wesleyan missionaries when they arrived; the two Tahitians worked on until 1846, when both died. Their helper after the Wesleyans came was a Fijian chief who had been converted in Tonga; Josua Mateinaniu of Fulaga, who accompanied the first Wesleyans to Lakeba in 1835, was a person of far greater importance than most previous accounts allow. His status and his command of both Tongan and Fijian eased the entry of David Cargill and William Cross of the Wesleyan Methodist Missionary Society, whose landfall at Lakeba from Tonga on 12 October 1835 to wait on Tui Nayau is celebrated in Fiji as the true dawn of the church.

AVE MARIA OR HALLELUJAH?

Cargill, who had passed through the great days of the Tongan revival of the preceding year (page 74) was an Aberdeen graduate with considerable linguistic ability. He devised the shortened Fijian alphabet along strictly phonetic lines, laying the foundation for the grammar and dictionary of David Hazlewood, a later missionary. Cargill was a complex mixture of faith, talent and vanity. He could be prickly and disdainful to his less educated co-workers, especially to Cross, who was older than Cargill, but subordinate to him after Cargill became Chairman of the Fiji District in 1838. In the early days of their mission in Lau, while the chiefs played with them by vacillating, they worked in the villages and succeeded in gathering small groups of baptized Christians among the people. The Fijian custom of taking and using their household belongings, in return for hospitalities extended, made life irksome for them; they thought of it as theft. Gradually they became aware that Tui Nayau, who had by this time close associations with Tanoa, the high chief of the rising island fortress of Bau, was not about to embrace Christianity until Tanoa and other great chiefs to westward also moved in that direction.

Bau, near one of the mouths of the Rewa River on the largest island, Viti Levu, was adjacent to another of the most powerful "kingdoms" of Fiji, Rewa. The astute chiefs of Bau had by this time come to play a central part in wars between the chiefs of Viti Levu, Taveuni and Vanua Levu. Naulivou, Tanoa, and his son Seru (the future conqueror who became known as Cakobau, conqueror of Bau) had adopted free-booting beachcombers and castaways, who taught them to use muskets in their battles. The most notorious of these unflattering heralds of European civilization was Charlie Savage, a survivor of the wreck of the brig *Eliza,* adopted by Naulivou of Bau, a callous fighter whose morals, and those of his associates, were "of the poultry yard."

Recognizing that effective Christian mission in Fiji depended to a large extent on the attitude of Bau, Rewa and the Tui Cakau, the Wesleyans sent Josua Mateinaniu westward alone from Lakeba toward the end of 1835 to mingle with the many Tongans who were spread out through the islands and to sound out the situation in the strongholds of the high chiefs. He was a well informed scout who advised on the future course of gospel warfare. By September 1836 he was back at Lakeba. On the Sunday after his return Cargill's small chapel was overflowing with a congregation "of 300 or 400 Tonguese from the Leeward Iss of Feejee." Many of them had

> embraced Christianity through the instrumentality of Joshua, an accredited Preacher whom we sent among them 10 Months ago. He has acted with great zeal and fidelity.

The Wesleyans caught the message of the journey. In June 1838 a large canoe provided by Taufa'ahau of Ha'apai, the future king of all Tonga,

TO LIVE AMONG THE STARS

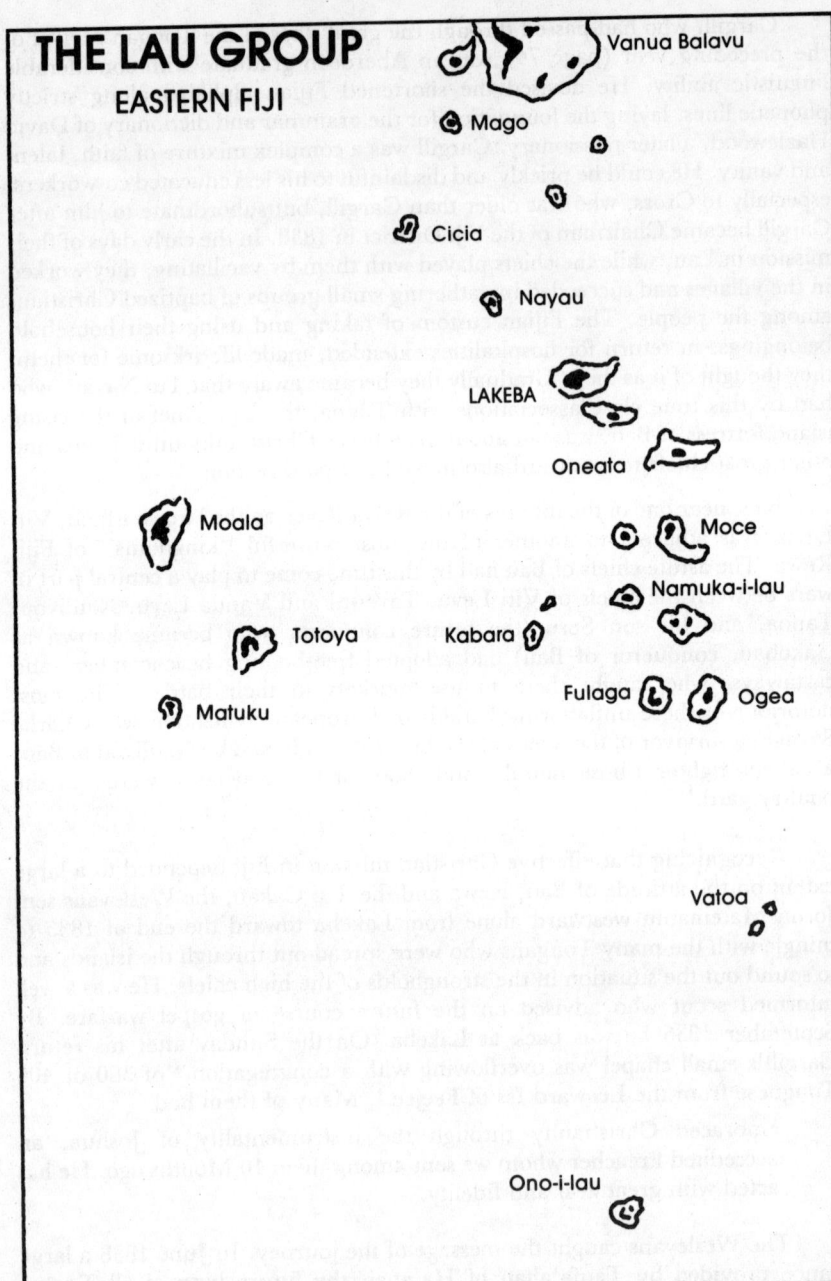

104

AVE MARIA OR HALLELUJAH?

brought to Lakeba six more teachers to serve the Fiji mission: Joeli Pulu (spelt Bulu in Fijian), Sailosi Fa'one, Siuliasi Naulivou, Uesile Langi, Selemaia Latu and Semisi Havea. Guided by Cargill, they acquired the dialect of Lau. Their names, renowned in the annals of Fiji, indicate at this early stage the importance of a long succession of Tongan missionaries who used their country's many contacts in Fiji to introduce their faith. By the time these Tongans arrived Cross had gone on ahead to Bau and Rewa, following Josua Mateinaniu's track. Peter Dillon (page 76), the Irish Roman Catholic mariner, transported him, at a price, to Bau. Unfortunately Tanoa, the highest chief, was found to be not at home. Cross met his son, Seru, the future Cakobau. Young, wild in his appearance, very much in control of the interview, he told Cross he could stay if he wished on Bau, but that his safety was not guaranteed. Cross, with prudence but limited foresight, decided to go on and try Tui Dreketi, the highest chief of nearby Rewa on the Viti Levu mainland, who was at that time allied with Bau. There he was offered the protection he sought and decide to settle.

The meeting between Cross and Cakobau retarded Wesleyan advance in Fiji. Cross, small of stature and sensitive, was no chief. In Fiji men were measured by their physical presence and air of authority. John Hunt, who later earned Cakobau's respect, once observed that one of the pre-christian high chiefs at Rewa feared Hunt as a likely spiritual competitor because Hunt, unlike Cross, was tall. Cakobau, always eager to appropriate white men of any kind for his own advantage, was also piqued because Cross went to Rewa instead of residing on Bau.

Wesleyan reinforcements from Britain came to Lakeba in December 1838, bringing supplies sufficient to compensate Cargill, Cross and their families for the loss of their household goods. The three new missionaries, John Hunt, James Calvert and Thomas Jaggar, all came direct to Fiji in response to appeals in the English religious press. Jaggar, a printer, soon transferred his machinery from Lakeba to Rewa, and later to the island of Viwa near Bau. The mission was deprived of his skill following a sexual encounter with a young Fiji girl on Viwa in 1848. Calvert manned Lakeba for ten years at the beginning of his long service to Fiji; he became an expert on the islands and lived to be present at the celebrations of the mission's first quarter century and half century. Hunt, the other member of the gifted trio, ranks with the most able and dedicated Christian missionaries of any period.

With his wife Hannah, John Hunt followed Cross to Rewa, where he arrived on 7 January 1839. During the next nine years this twenty-seven-year-old former ploughboy from Lincolnshire, ordained in and for Fiji, lived close to the people. He understood them, listened to them, loved them. He lived near the centres of power of the great chiefs — Rewa, Somosomo on Taveuni,

Viwa. His eye for personality traits in Fiji's noblest men was sharp; he measured their quality beneath their outward status. They liked him; his dealings with them were frank, never obsequious. "The fact is," he once wrote, "the favor of a Feejeean chief is rather to be dreaded than courted, and the less a Missionary has of it the better." But the chiefs respected him.

Though not technically trained for linguistic work as Cargill had been, Hunt learned the important Bauan dialect, which was to emerge as the standard of written Fijian. Before he died he had translated the New Testament and begun the Old. He started at Rewa with the Gospels. "I have more help in them than in any other part of the Scriptures," he confided to his journal. He had Cargill's translations in the Lau dialect before him, but wrote, "I don't intend to call any man master but to think for myself." Hunt was as open as any of the missionaries to what he had to learn from the old culture of Fiji; he never "went native," remaining himself, English and a Methodist; but he talked of Christ rather than of European furnishings, clothing to the neck-line and punctual hard work. His readiness to follow the local custom of *kerekere* in giving away his own and his wife's possessions to Fijians exasperated some of his colleagues. This sharing of personal goods in Fiji is customarily reciprocated, without reference to the first appropriation, by later equivalent gifts of food, mats or help in need. John Hunt grasped this aspect of Fiji's social life and reaped its warm rewards. Nor was he easily shockable or prim; his observations of pre-christian religion were acute; he also recognized that some of his own immunity from being killed and eaten was attributable to the special *tabu,* holiness, credited to a "man of God."

From July 1839 Hunt and his family lived at Somosomo on Taveuni, where the Tui Cakau, an elderly warrior and intemperate man-eater, presided over his war-wracked realm of Cakaudrove, where his son, Tui Kilakila, wielded much of the effective military power. Richard Burdsall Lyth, another notable missionary, who was both minister and medical man, lived with Hunt through a period of bloodshed and danger at Somosomo. Lyth's matter-of-fact Yorkshire temperament accorded well with Hunt's. By comparison they found Cargill moody; Cross, who suffered at Rewa from severe dysentery, was relatively weak. Hunt's Somosomo journal astonishes by clear-minded assessments of a world where its author was a stranger. Somosomo gave Hunt the apprenticeship for his later crucially important work on Viwa. He was far from naive about the impression the Methodists created in Fiji:

> The god and the priest are in their opinion so connected as to be one and the same; I asked a person the other day if he knew who Jesus Christ is, and he said yes; I was Jesus Christ and often when we pass the houses the children call after us, Jisu Ruisiti, thinking either that we are pleased when we hear the name or thinking the name belongs to us, most likely both ...

AVE MARIA OR HALLELUJAH?

Cannibal customs, recorded by others in the mission with distraught horror, were to Hunt a matter of calmer consideration; he observed before stepping in to reform. After a battle, he studied the sacrifice of a captured chief, who

> was given to the God, cut up and cooked about three or four yards from our fence; I saw the operation which was performed with a skill and despatch that might be expected from well instructed cannibals. I saw a priest sitting in the door of the temple looking at the men who were employed in cooking, etc.

On another occasion Hunt went into the *bure kalou,* the god's house, to become better acquainted with the religion to which he was presenting an alternative. "We requested permission to go into the temple," he wrote, "which was granted, and we took our seat near the High Priest and the old King." Hunt's journal went on to describe the chief's prayers before a battle, the presentation of highly prized *tabua,* whales' teeth, and coconuts, and the absence of any of the customarily anticipated ecstatic behaviour by the priest. After the war ended he later laconically reported that the women danced to welcome the fighters home and that "the songs on these occasions are very lewd." Hunt, Lyth and Thomas Williams, their successor, were on good terms with the priest of Somosomo's great war god, and visited his temple.

Disease affected the mission seriously during its first period. At Somosomo Hannah Hunt's twelve-day-old baby and one of Mary Anne Lyth's children died. Cargill's wife Margaret bore a child who died at Rewa and herself succumbed afterwards to protracted dysentery and haemorrhage. She had been Cargill's mainstay — one person in Fiji who loved him. Plunged in grief, he sought and gained leave to return to England with his small orphaned girls, against the will of Cross, who thought he should have stayed on. Cross offered to lodge the children in his house if Cargill decided not to go. The two British pioneers of Wesleyan Christianity in Fiji were not easily compatible; there was often friction between them, described ruefully by Hunt: "Our two good brethren soon got warm and we had sad work." Hunt acted as a moderator; he did not conceal his preference for Cross, who died and was buried at Somosomo; he had come from Viwa to seek treatment from Lyth in October 1842. In the swampy Rewa delta Cross suffered from dysentery, typhus and hernia trouble; his transfer to a better climate on Viwa had come too late. Cross would not hear of leaving Fiji for health reasons. Hunt wrote an affectionate memoir of him, but was less devoted to Cargill, whose intended return to Fiji for a second term failed to please him. With characteristic plainness Hunt confided to his journal: "I must object to Mr Cargill as a man and a Christian."

TO LIVE AMONG THE STARS

Cargill, in the event, never reached Fiji a second time. He remarried in England, then came back as far as Vava'u in Tonga, where he died in a state of depression and over-sedation on 24 April 1839, still grieving for his "dear Maggie" for whom he had published a tender tribute. He was dejected over the sagging fervour of the church on Vava'u, where he had lived through the happiness of the revival of 1834. His last pathetic hours were clouded by excessive brandy-drinking, to which he had been long addicted; by a self-administered overdose of laudanum; and by psychotic symptoms, probably brought on as a result of dengue fever. His death could have been suicide, or simply distraught over-dependence on drugs.

From Somosomo Hunt accurately assessed the significance of the presence of Tongan adventurers in Fiji. He noticed how many of them were fighting in the Cakaudrove wars. "Christian men should have something to do besides gossiping about from one Island to another in this way," he wrote as early as September 1839. By 1841 he and Lyth, who had already served in Tonga for a time before coming to Fiji, were trying to minister to the shifting Tongan populace around Tui Kilakila's village. Some of them had been in Wallis and were on their way back to Tonga, including a chief "who appears to have made considerable progress in Popery." Hunt referred to their attendance in the school the missionaries ran at Somosomo. "Many of them attend; some of the party only have actually embraced popery," he wrote,

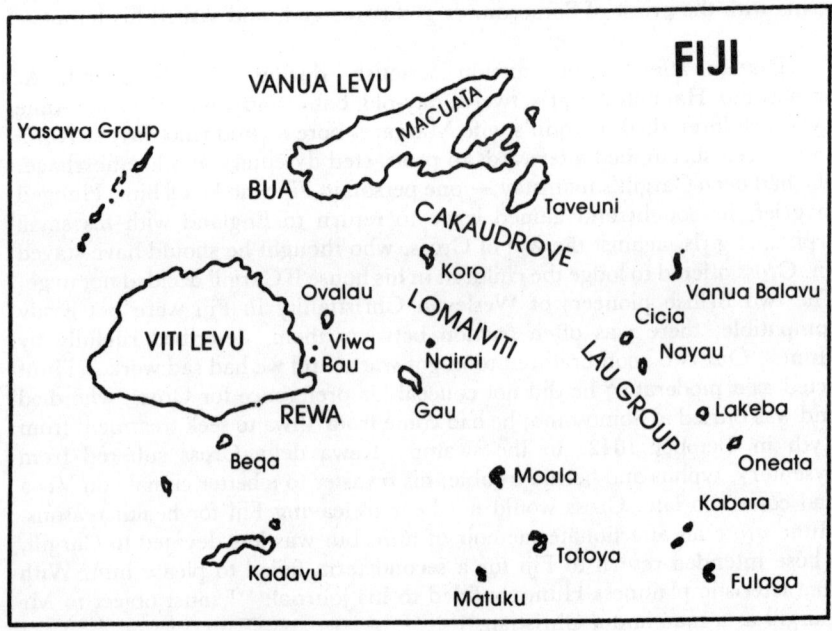

AVE MARIA OR HALLELUJAH?

"and others do not seem to be much attached to it." In fact, neither they nor the Fijians at that stage seemed much attached to anything foreign; Hunt thought they would not "embrace" Christianity "until the king leads the way."

Wesleyan missionaries could not be satisfied until the high chiefs had outgrown their easily recognized longing for the *vavalagis'* knives, cloth and *mana*. They wanted the chiefs to recognize Christ as the God who died as man in love for the world. They were not prepared to instruct and baptize chiefs until they showed "godly sorrow" and made their submission to Christ among their own common people in the church. Though they saw the importance of having the chiefs "turn," the missionaries required evidence of an inner change as prior test; Methodism had itself been born as a protest against merely formal Christian adherence.

There were no obvious results of this kind among the high chiefs at Lakeba, Somosomo, Rewa and Bau when Hunt moved to Viwa in August 1842. Qaraniqio of Rewa was by then a sworn enemy, who had instigated violence against the mission. Cakobau, already prominent as a warlord on Bau, continued hostile toward Hunt and Jaggar's religious claims on nearby Viwa. He knew they had eyes on Bau; when he met them he joked about it. He and the other high chiefs found the pressures mounting within their little cockpits of power. Their wars grew more efficient as they obtained firearms from ships; they lived in fear of reprisals or takeovers by warships of Britain or France. A growing enclave of white traders on the busy beach at Levuka on the island of Ovalau had to be alternatively confronted and placated. The Wesleyans were a partially understood religious complication within this developing dilemma; they seemed to bring a strong *mana*, yet they were peaceful; they condemned many local customs, yet they offered a friendly magic centred in puzzling little books.

On Viwa the conversion of Varani, the nephew of the island's high chief Namosimalua, brought about the decisive break-through. The name Varani (France) was bestowed when its possessor led in looting the French ship *l'Aimable Joséphine* in Bau waters in 1834, murdering its captain and crew. In 1838 the French officer Dumont d'Urville burned the settlements on Viwa. Varani was Cakobau's ally and comrade in arms — famous as a killer and eater of his enemies. To Hunt's surprise, as he was one day reading about the crucifixion from the newly translated Gospel according to St. Matthew, Varani was visibly stirred. When Hunt was teaching him to read he formed the habit of going into the bush to pray in imitation of Hunt. The story of the crucifixion decided him. He told Cakobau he was going to become a Christian. Cakobau, incredulous, threatened to kill and eat him if he did, but never carried out the threat. Varani "publicly bowed the knee to Jehovah" on Good Friday 1845. He married his principal wife and set the others aside when he joined Hunt's Methodist Class Meeting as a candidate for baptism. Hunt's circuit report at the end of June said, "His whole spirit and conduct give the most pleasing evidence of the great change that has taken place in his mind, and the whole so evidently and exclusively the work of God, that we are much, very much, encouraged and strengthened."

Hunt's reports did not usually inflate progress, but Varani's change elated him. Here he had a truly Christian chief. Varani's uncle, Namosimalua, had made a formal submission to Christianity as early as 1839, but Varani's conversion centred in a more fervent attachment to Christ. Hunt located the change in his mind — his thought and his will. Following Varani's experience, in the second half of 1845, Viwa became the scene of emotional revivals comparable with those in Tonga in 1834. Hunt described in October how private houses and the public services of the church reverberated with sobbing, simultaneous prayers and physical convulsions. He did not deprecate them; to him they were signs of a fervour all good Wesleyans longed to see, from the days of John Wesley onward; but behind the excitement he sought a more permanent change of heart and mind. "During the first week of the revival," he wrote, "nearly 100 Persons professed to obtain the forgiveness of sins, through faith in Jesus Christ. Some were exceedingly clear, others not so clear."

Hunt was not blind to the influence external wars and rumours of wars had on the revival. He began his account of what took place by drawing attention to "a great deal of anxiety of mind" over the bloody war impending between Bau and Rewa, two of Viwa's traditional allies. The most extreme emotional seizures occurred in the house of Namosimalua, the high chief. Pre-christian Fijian religion included the ecstatic paroxysms of the *bete*, or priest, who was believed to be possessed by the god of the place when he was consulted about prospect of success in battle, or other grave matters. It seems likely that in the Viwa revival some of this pre-christian conduct transferred itself to the Christian congregation as a whole. All the Lord's people became prophets. J.B. Watsford, the Australian missionary who lived with Hunt through the revival on Viwa noted that "blood and fire and pillars of smoke" (*Joel 2.28-32*) were a classical setting for such Pentecostal behaviour (*Acts 2.17-19*). The war with Rewa, indeed, broke out in December to round out the picture.

Cakobau did not know what to make of the conversion of his great friend Varani, who continued to fight on the side of Bau, but refused to permit the killing and eating of captives. Varani's model was Hunt — forthright and courageous, but a man of peace rather than war. Meanwhile Cakobau passed off his disinclination to have a missionary on Bau with shows of his wit. Hunt told him that the bodies of all he had eaten and killed would rise again at the Last Judgment, and that if Cakobau and his victims did not repent before then

AVE MARIA OR HALLELUJAH?

they would be cast into the fire of hell. Cakobau replied "Ah, well! It is a fine thing to have a fire in cold weather." Hunt told him "I shall still pray for you with a good mind, although you treat the subject so lightly." Cakobau, perhaps revealing a slight chink in his jocular armour, said "Go on with that."

When John Hunt died of dysentery on Viwa on 4 October 1848 at the age of thirty-six, foundations had been laid for the growth of a truly Fijian church. Four Pacific Islander pioneers of the mission were approved to proceed toward ordination to the ministry at the District Meeting a few weeks before Hunt died: Joeli Bulu, Josua Mateinaniu, Uesile Langi and Paula Vea. Hunt and Lyth worked to give the *lotu* in Fiji its own liturgical character, using sonorous local chanting and action songs for canticles of victory like the *Te Deum*. One Fijian who was Hunt's helper on Viwa in translating the New Testament has almost faded from the record; Noa, who "knew his own language better than any other native," was a picturesque and amusing lay preacher, forerunner of many in Fiji. His insanity in later life did not prevent his friend John Watsford, who learned Fijian under him, from paying him tribute.

Hunt and Lyth permitted Christianity to become a spontaneous movement of people and chiefs. Both men belonged to the early Wesleyan tradition; their liturgical forms were derived from the Book of Common Prayer; their doctrine of the sacraments retained Charles Wesley's high doctrine of the Real Presence. Their teaching about practical holiness in everyday life linked up with Fijian ideas of *tabu*, now given moral content within a monotheistic spiritual setting. The missionaries entered Fijian life as new religious persons of high standing. They and their Fijian successors, called *talatala* or ministers, gradually took the social position occupied by the discountenanced priests of the numerous old divinities. In the midst of his healing, translating and preaching on Viwa Hunt found time to write his *Letters on Entire Sanctification*, directly inspired by John Wesley's writings on the same central Methodist theme. "He wrote his own life," Watsford remarked, telling how Hunt, unselfconscious in his longing for the full vision of God, would nevertheless call Watsford away from his language study with the invitation "let's have a run," or "let us do a bit of gardening." Hunt could be heard each morning singing a favourite hymn to the accompaniment of his small accordion. These recollections give clues to Hunt's hold over the affection of Fijians, who like good times and singing and prefer their work to be enjoyable.

Varani prayed memorably at Hunt's deathbed. His eyes met those of Cakobau over the coffin at the funeral on Viwa. The two men, and later chiefs who followed them, knew that Hunt prayed for them while he lived. His life and death had been crucial in leading Cakobau to submit eventually to Christ in 1854, though in Ratu Seru Cakobau, soon to be acknowledged on Bau as *vunivalu*, supreme lord of war, motives were intriguingly mixed. Varani died tragically while endeavouring to reconcile the warring mountain people of Lovoni on Ovalau with those of Levuka. As a Christian he achieved a measure of heroic simplicity.

Not so Cakobau, who was always complicated, even as a genuinely penitent sinner with the new name Apenisa (Ebenezer, *I Samuel 7.12*). The baptismal font in the great church on Bau is made out of the killing stone where Cakobau's victims had their heads clubbed before being sent to the cooking ovens, which were reported "never cold" during the wars with Rewa in the years before his conversion. Those wars, together with the pressure brought to bear on him by incoming white men and unpredictable Tongan soldiers, filled him with forebodings of a change in Fiji, possibly tragic, in any case irreversible. As Cakobau's former world broke up he saw that what could be saved of the past might in part be re-fashioned by the Christian Church. To share in it he must follow the examples of Namosimalua and Varani.

Evidence of the religious changes was on his doorstep. On 30 July 1849, when Lyth and Calvert were absent from Viwa at a District Meeting on Vanua Levu, their wives heard through Namosimalua that Cakobau's father, the old chief Tanoa, was superintending the killing and eating of fifteen female captives. They could hear the great *lali*, the death drum of Bau, beating; they rowed across the small intervening space of water to confront Tanoa in his own house, accompanied by Namosimalua. By the time they entered twelve of the prisoners had already been killed. The women then made offerings of *tabua*, highly prized whales' teeth, to Tanoa, pleading with him to spare the three frightened survivors. Their entreaties were eventually successful. This brave action, revealing the place women could be expected to assume under Christianity, was followed by another in December 1852, when Tanoa died. Six of the chiefly widows were set apart to be strangled according to custom, in the presence of Cakobau. Fijian belief held that they must go to the place of departed spirits, *burotu*, to serve their husband and lord. Watsford went across from Viwa to Bau to intercede for them, this time without success. The gripping pages of his eye-witness account of the silent strangling of the blindfolded women describe the happiness of the victims, "as if going to a dance." Cakobau challenged Watsford. "Are you not afraid to come here to interfere with our customs?" he asked. Watsford said he came out of love for both Cakobau and his victims. "Love," replied Cakobau, "oh, we all love them: we are strangling them because we love them."

Cakobau's awareness of a specifically religious side of the competition between British and French naval power in the Pacific dates from his being informed of Protestant conflict with Catholics in Tahiti. Bataillon on one occasion visited him, travelling on a French warship. He told Cakobau that Bau had been providentially, up to then, preserved from Protestantism by the

AVE MARIA OR HALLELUJAH?

protection of the Virgin. Cakobau fenced with his usual speed; he "told the bishop to leave him and his city to the care of the Virgin, and to come again when the Virgin had converted them." Roman Catholicism never succeeded in establishing itself on Bau. Its representatives, Fathers Jean Baptiste Bréhéret and François Roulleaux came, under Bataillon's instructions, to Lau from Tonga in 1844. After eleven years of frustrating efforts to gain a grip in numerous places in Lau, they settled on Ovalau and Taveuni to nurture a Fijian Roman Catholic Church until it could spread out, and stay (pages 286-8).

In 1853 Cakobau was installed as *vunivalu*, warrior-ruler of Bau; eighteen people were eaten at the traditional feast. In the same year the people of Kaba, an exposed peninsula dominating the delta waterways leading to Rewa, revolted against him in Rewa's favour. He had troubles on Ovalau, associated with more general threats to his authority; in 1853 Varani died in the resulting fight. The instigator of revolt on Kaba and Ovalau was Ratu Mara of Rewa, a defector from Bau. In October Joseph Waterhouse, a resourceful missionary with some of Calvert's tougher qualities, landed to set up house on Bau. Calvert, who had been stationed at Levuka among the fractious whites of the beach community, had prepared the way for Waterhouse; but before he could be sure of a welcome he had to confront Cakobau face-to-face. Cakobau agreed to let him have the house-site of his choice, "on the Bauan summit." The location, in the mind of the missionaries, connoted prestige, though both parties to the agreement were aware at the time that the highest point on the little island had been its rubbish dump. In November a rather more prestigious person appeared on Bau — Taufa'ahau, King George Tupou I of Tonga, at the peak of his power. He came in company with Robert Young, a deputationist from the Wesleyan Methodist Church in Britain, who was surveying the missions in the Pacific preparatory to handing over responsibility for the field to the Australasian Wesleyan Methodists in 1855.

Taufa'ahau urged Cakobau to become a Christian. Cakobau presented him with a large double canoe for ocean sailing, thirty-one metres long, with a beam of of five and a half metres. Young and the missionaries in Fiji were suitably proud and deferential about the visit of the Tongan monarch; their views on monarchy derived from John Wesley, a fervent high church Tory. However, the religious element in the meeting of the two great sea kings was mingled with personal communication between them on matters not directly related to the faith. Waterhouse was present when together they went to look at the military prospects on the Kaba peninsula. "The rebel fortress seems to me to be anything but impregnable," said George. "It was evident," Waterhouse observed, "that each king understood the other."

After he had gone on to Sydney, where he was received in considerable state, Taufa'ahau wrote in February 1854 to Cakobau from Nuku'alofa. He said he intended to come back to Bau, with a gift of a handsome schooner. He said: "I wish, Cakobau, you would *lotu*. When I visit you we will talk about it." But there was no need; on 27 April 1854 Waterhouse "had an unusually long interview in private with the king, entreating him to take up his cross and renounce heathenism." On the following Sunday, 30 April, Cakobau, with his priest, more than forty wives, and his family, attended church on Bau. His submission was made. He cut down a sacred grove of iron-wood (*vesi*) trees, took reading lessons, held family prayers in his house and placed himself under instruction for baptism. He put away all but one of his wives. Three years later, on 11 January 1857, he was baptized.

The conversion of Cakobau did not lead quickly and automatically to acceptance of Christianity by a majority of Fiji's people. On Bau itself other chiefs held out for a short time; then the people came in large numbers to church and were instructed. In Bau's dependencies in Lomaiviti and on Viti Levu the process was slower. Although they loyally followed their chiefs, the people seemed to understand that a fundamental personal decision was also involved in renouncing local and ancestral spirits in favour of Christ. When they did follow, the feeling of the church so formed was overwhelmingly communal. The unity of *vanua*, country, *matanitu*, chiefly authority, and *lotu*, the Christian religion, took on an almost trinitarian solemnity in the inner life of Fijians. The text "Fear God, honour the king" (*I Peter 2.17*) has become part of the heraldic apparatus of Fiji; it stands for a freely honoured union of chiefs and people within the Christian faith. As previously in Tonga, traditional Wesleyans felt no strain over the emergence of a church established within the framework of custom law; John Wesley and his early followers defended and never officially forsook the established Church of England, built on similar assumptions about the sacred and secular.

Cakobau's attempts to storm and recapture Kaba in 1854, the year of his conversion, were repelled. In March 1855 Taufa'ahau arrived in Fiji with a large fleet. He was accompanied by his dashing nephew Ma'afu, who had been securely based as a chief on the island of Vanuabalavu in Lau since 1848, and had been appointed governor over the Tongans in Fiji in 1853. Taufa'ahau stopped to deliver messages at Levuka, en route. There he was provoked by attacks on his troops. The chief at Levuka was in league with Ratu Mara of Rewa, who was defiantly in possession of Kaba. Similar rash shots by Fijians were aimed a little later against the Tongan troops, as they aided the forces of Bau in on-shore preparations at Kaba preparatory to an assault on the fort. Thereupon, without direct orders from their own king, the Tongans took the fight into their hands. With the Fijians, they stormed the position Taufa'ahau had thought "anything but impregnable." Kaba fell and was burned; its defenders fled. Taufa'ahau helped Cakobau to assume Varani's mantle of clemency as together he and Cakobau forbade the

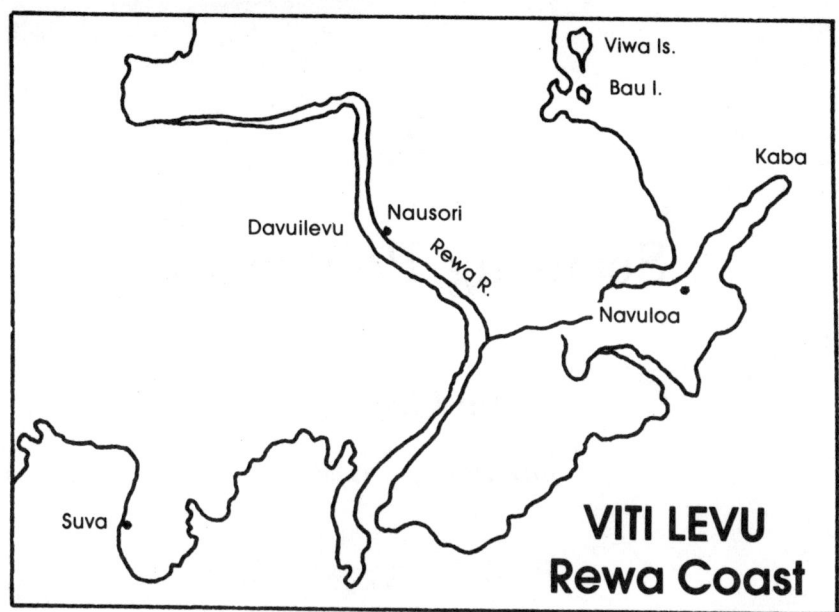

slaughter of prisoners and cannibal feasting. The victory of the *lotu Tonga* and this day of Tongan armed superiority together helped to crown the supremacy of Bau in Fiji. Symbolically, Enele Ma'afu, the Tui Lau, and Joeli Bulu, who ended his days as chaplain to Cakobau on Bau, reaped the fruits of the Tongan intervention in Fiji by the prominent part they played in the country's history in the next twenty years (pages 279ff).

5

Securing Polynesia

The Cooks
Samoa, Niue

WHEN JOHN WILLIAMS sailed in the *Camden* to his death, on the shores of Dillon's Bay on the island of Erromanga in 1839, his colleagues in Samoa and Rarotonga registered their first shock of sorrow on hearing the news by resolutions about the continuation of his work. In the year of Williams' death Buzacott completed the theological institution at Takamoa — the first college building designed to train "native agents." Buzacott's students saw their work as a living memorial to their departed friend and chief, Wiriamu. The walls of Takamoa were solid; they still stand as witness to Buzacott's thoroughness; he was proud when they weathered a bad hurricane in 1846. The Rarotongan church did not call on funds or supplies from London to establish Takamoa; they built it out of coral rock and supported its work by their gifts.

John Williams prepared his Raiatean teachers by example and imitation. As a mobile evangelist he used direct quips and specific points — allowing the encounter to determine his method. The Rarotongans, Mangaians and Aitutakians who endured scholastic disciplines at Takamoa often in practice resorted to Williams' approach once they had begun work in other islands. But Buzacott first gave them a steadying dose of what he himself believed in — the dry Scots divinity lecture notes of David Bogue, the head of the LMS Mission Seminary at Gosport. Though he had not himself passed through Bogue's complete course, Buzacott believed in the Gosport recipe, memorisation of doctrine. He translated Bogue's lectures into Rarotongan, to be copied out by the students. The stress lay on accurate Calvinist catechizing, following the outline of the Creed. In later years pupils of Takamoa became a familiar sight in villages on Niue and Samoa, and across the Western Pacific to Papua, carrying the Bibles they had been taught to expound according to these standards. At the same time they applied what they had learned in terms of local lore and experience. The loaves and fishes of Bogue's lectures were distributed as breadfruit and bonito in countless conversations and sermons adapted to the varied worlds of uninitiated Islanders. *A priori* doctrine, the treasure they shared, was conveyed in home-made earthen vessels, by living conversation, island style.

Buzacott, ever practical, laced his exacting four-year course with useful chores. Subsistence gardening was not enough; Buzacott's interest in technology and teaching methods led him to include "instruction in general knowledge, in the working of day and Sunday schools, in divinity, in preaching, and also in house-building, in the manufacture of chairs, sofas, beds, etc., so that the students may be able to raise the heathen in social life, while they preach unto them the word of eternal life." The "chairs, sofas, beds, etc.," when they became a feature of later family life among distant "heathen," were sometimes considered uppish in Melanesia later on; some of Takamoa's more adaptable ex-students did not bother with them (page 197). Solid house-building in coral lime was accepted more willingly.

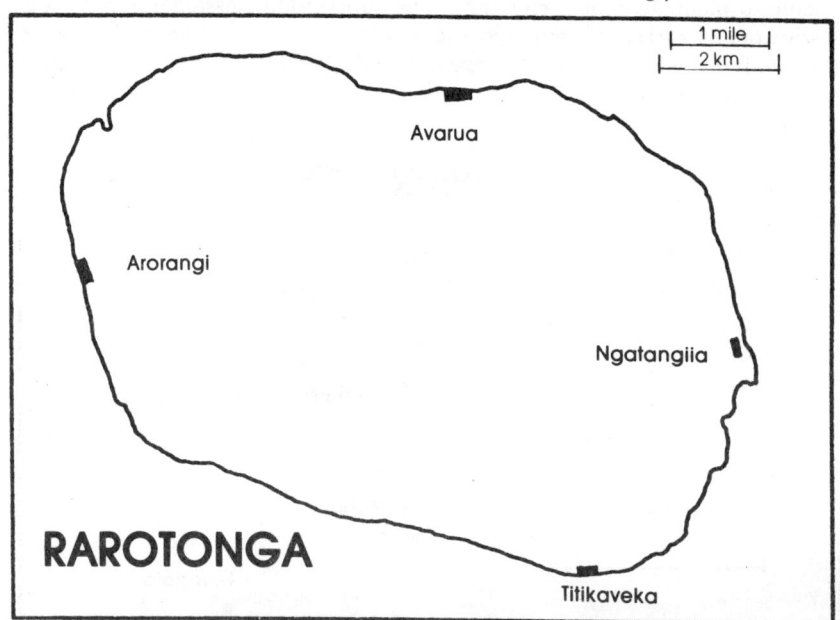

TO LIVE AMONG THE STARS

The Rarotongan type of Christian building was reproduced in many other parts of the Pacific; whitewashed chapels and houses, the best of them made with sturdy simplicity, began to dot the villages. In the plan of evangelization and village uplift, Buzacott and his wife enlisted the wives of the students for a "suitable course of instruction." Men and women gained practical experience in local schools on Rarotonga. The first names of many students can be ferreted out of the printed reminiscences and manuscripts of the British missionaries. Names of wives and children occur more rarely, but their combined presence, brought to bear through family prayer and village conversation in Pacific island societies, became widely influential. At Takamoa each couple lived in a two-roomed stone cottage, a prototype for their later mission houses.

The results were as impressive as the plan. By 1857 Takamoa's roll recorded: "engaged in the mission-fields, sixty-one; superannuated, seven; dead, thirty-six; massacred by the heathen, four men, two women, and one child; widows returned home, four; retired from their work, ten; fallen, twenty-one." Of the "fallen," says the analysis, many had been forgiven and restored to useful service in their home islands. Pupils of the quality of Teava (page 122), who had been left by John Williams to work on the key Samoan islet of Manono in 1832, could at Takamoa be prepared more systematically for regular mid-year posting, in the mission ship, to Samoa and further afield. Seminary, ship, dissemination; the LMS pattern enabled the peoples of the Pacific to plant their own churches. The supervising missionaries were the instigators — catalysts, counsellors and authority figures; the teachers were the cultural mediators; their message and the quality of their altered lives became the means of change, conversion.

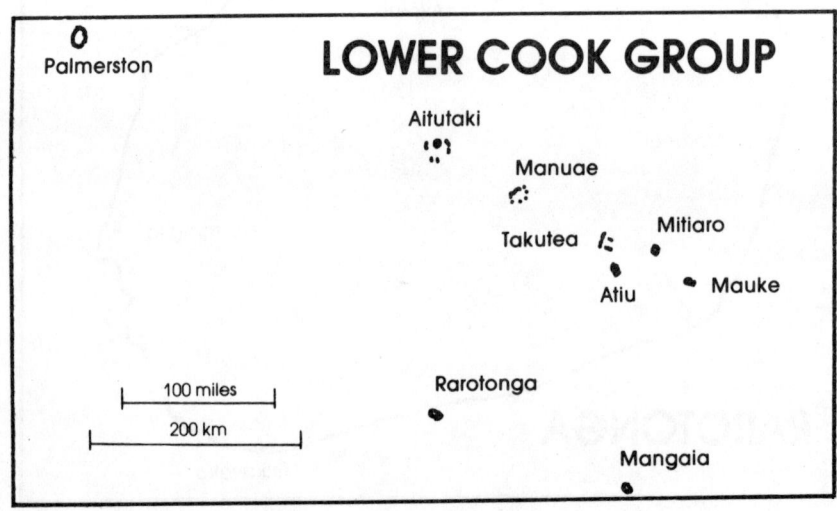

Buzacott's institution was the precursor of a second and more substantial training centre, founded as the church took root in Samoa. George Turner and Charles Hardie, who established Malua in 1844, drew on lessons learned at Takamoa. Hardie and Buzacott had married into the same family; their wives were sisters of a leading English evangelical layman, George Hitchcock. At Malua, under such auspices, training of wives, as at Takamoa, was assured (pages 125-6).

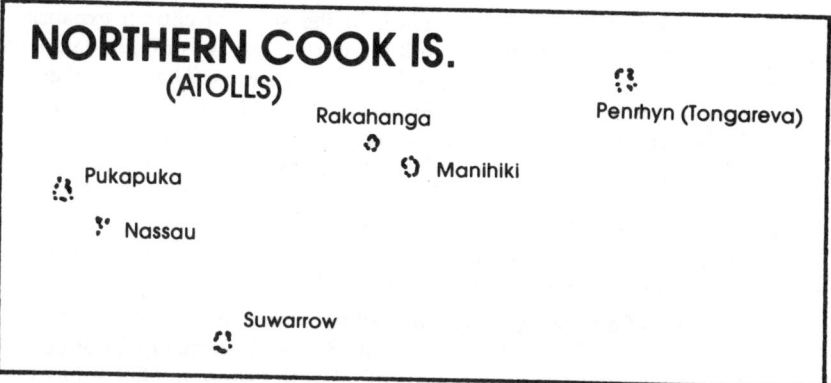

Teava was not the only missionary sent out before the theological institution emerged on Rarotonga in 1839. All Teava's service was given in Samoa. His fellow-trainee, Maretu, went as a missionary to the high island of Mangaia in the Southern Cooks. He was left there in 1839 by John Williams to compose internal dissensions in the young church, caused by two Tahitian missionaries who preceded him. Although he worked in Mangaia only for about three years, Maretu, who left a detailed written account of his missionary work, solved his problems by an ingenious combination of Christian teaching and local custom. He worked, as John Williams often did, from Johannine texts about loving one another. When the quarrels in the church had been settled "they all embraced each other"; Maretu said "stop your weeping and let us pray." Providentially, the event occurred at the home of a man named Havaire, who "had a house full of food, including three pigs." Maretu cheerfully described the climax, island-style: "When we finished praying to God, we ate until our stomachs were full."

In 1854 Pitman and Buzacott sent him on a contrasting assignment — to salvage the mission on the northern atolls of Manihiki and Rakahanga, racked by feuds. Under physically harder conditions, Maretu showed his adaptability; by courage and persuasion he won the confidence of chiefs and people. Vengeance was replaced by peace. The gospel, as in many island situations, was accepted as a novel and welcome relief from the old system's painful logic of honour.

TO LIVE AMONG THE STARS

One of Maretu's Manihiki deacons, Erikana (Elekana in Tuvalu), introduced Christianity to Tuvalu (then called the Ellice Islands by the British), as a result of drifting there in time of storm (page 155). Erikana's son, Tauraki, went as a student to Malua in Samoa; he later served, and was murdered, in Papua. Tauraki's son, Teina Materua, was adopted after the murder by the Cook Island missionary Ruatoka, whose long career in Papua maintained the succession (pages 208-10).

Cook Islanders have a special place in the story of church expansion. Their scattered group, running south to north, has a common language cutting across varied land-forms and subsistence patterns. They are related to the Society Islands and the New Zealand Maoris by close linguistic and cultural associations. The Tahitians brought them Christianity; they in turn carried it further. Maretu conveyed the inimitable feel of their mission — resourceful, optimistic. The flavour is caught in Maretu's dialogue with Tira, the pagan high chief of Mangaia. Maretu could laugh at the chief's annoyance and quick wit at the very moment when the Christian teaching about the equality of all people before God was in question:

> The word of advice I gave to Tira, which made him angry and grab his axe, was this, 'He that believeth in the Son hath eternal life; but he that believeth not the Son shall not see life, but the wrath of God abideth on him.' 'What do you think about life with Jesus and the Kingdom of God?' I asked him 'What is that? If you had said that there was a house of women and some taro swamps there, all right, I'd listen. I don't want all of you to be above me while I'm of lower standing.'

Explaining, cajoling chiefs, coping, serving — these qualities are present in Teava, Ta'unga of Rarotonga, and Paoo of Aitutaki (pages 126f, 190ff, 195ff). Cook Island missionaries tended to be scouts, groundbreakers; the Samoans who came after them were rather different — ample regulators, rulers in newly formed churches. The Cook Islanders' entering wedge prepared a way for Samoan advance on a broad front. Rarotongans and Aitutakians responded instantly to the roving urge of John Williams, to the spirit of "do it yourself" they learned from Buzacott. Samoan style reflected the settled tone of the substantial LMS white missionary establishment in their country — the almost seigneurial rootedness of the Malua institution and the Samoan Missionary Committee.

LMS British missionaries who followed Pitman and Buzacott in the Cooks, by contrast, were prevented by isolation from becoming authority figures over the whole island group. Henry Royle, who arrived on Rarotonga in the year of Williams' death, 1839, served on Aitutaki until 1876 — a Manchester factory worker transformed into the Congregational patriarch of a single island. William Gill and his younger brother George became more closely identified with the pastoral oversight of Mangaia, as did William Wyatt Gill, a London University graduate whose detailed observations of island life were later rewarded with a doctorate.

A more colourful story unrolled on the remote southern Cook island of Palmerston. Uninhabited at the time of European contact, it was populated by an English sailor and his three Polynesian wives, whose descendants now make up the island's three branches. In 1959 the then head of the island, Ned Marsters, recounted in a rambling and salty interview what he recalled of his grandfather, who founded the dynasty's branches through his three wives. He gave the name of the first Rarotongan missionary as Akarongo and described the piety of his father, who always insisted on the observance of Sunday as holy and was convinced that his preaching about manna from heaven one Sabbath in time of drought led directly, on the following Tuesday, to the washing up on the beaches of a cargo of fresh sweet oranges. The unique Marsters family, preserving a distinct Englishness on a remote island, has contributed leaders to the life of the church in the Cooks.

THE LMS ENTERS SAMOA

LMS CALVINIST INDEPENDENCY and Samoan society seemed to have been predestined as partners. The *matai*, or heads of extended families, determined by their alliances and claims the changing structure of such central authority as Samoa was willing to suffer. Virtually autonomous rural villages, linked by obligatory unifying custom, the *fa'a Samoa*, co-existed under agreed *mores* and a single language. The LMS on the Samoan islands ran by a similar consensus between local stations during the heyday of Congregational Independency in Britain. In Samoa, as in the British Isles, ultimate trust lay in the sovereign local congregation ruled by the Spirit and the Word. Samoan Congregationalism grew strong on the basis of a union of social presuppositions.

When the LMS arrived in Samoa in 1830 the people had already heard about the new God, Jesus Christ. Idols and the "high gods" of Polynesia were not widely worshipped among Samoans. The cult of nature spirits in the villages was quickly challenged by Christianity's stronger dogmas and *mana*. Tahitians on passing ships brought news of the *lotu Tahiti* before John Williams came. A Samoan, Sio Vili, had returned home as prophet of a Tahitian-influenced syncretic religion. Samoan chiefs wanted to know what supernatural forces gave the white men their powers in navigation and war. They called the Europeans *Papalagi*, which appears to refer to their bursting through the sky at the horizon. Such thoughts were in the mind of Malietoa

Vai'inupo, holder of one of the country's highest titles, who was involved in fighting on Savai'i and Upolu when the LMS arrived.

Williams and Barff brought six Tahitian teachers and two Aitutakians. Moea, a native of Raiatea from the Huahine church, had previously visited the Marquesas; he was married with three children and served on Savai'i until 1834, then at Falelatai on the south coast of Upolu until 1842. His unmarried companion from Huahine, Boti, was also sent to Upolu in 1834, but was dismissed for immorality. Arue of Raiatea, another single man, had no similar black mark, but Taihaere of Borabora, a married man with five children, was sent home for immorality in 1840. Taatu Ori and Umia, of Raiatea, worked on Savai'i during the 1830s.

The mixed record indicates what happened. Malietoa sent the teachers out into his villages. They became agents of liturgical and religious change, but local custom affected them. When Williams returned in 1832 there were complaints. The teachers had taught the Samoan women to sing hymns; the women took the tunes to the dancing houses and used them for their dances, probably for the explicitly sexual "night dance," afterwards officially outlawed by the LMS.

The placing of the Rarotongan teacher Teava on the fortified strategic islet of Manono on this visit (page 85) underlined a problem. Although Matetau, the chief of Manono, was formally aligned with Malietoa's struggle for supremacy in Samoa, the traditional connections of the island with Tonga, to the south, were also strong. Trade and inter-marriage, by way of the canoe route through the islands of Niua Fo'ou and Niuatoputapu, made Manono a terminus for Tongan voyagers to Samoa. Samoans there knew that the notable Tongan chief, Taufa'ahau, later to become king of Tonga, had married one of Matetau's daughters (page 79). From Satupa'itea, in southern Savai'i, which had been denied a request that Malietoa should allot them one of his teachers, the leading chief, Tuinaula, had visited Tonga and had already, by 1832, as Williams noted, introduced Wesleyan worship, the *lotu Tonga*. John Williams became aware of this on his way southward after his Samoan visit. Possibly he took a mental note at that time to try to fence off denominational competition in Samoa. When he returned to London he hatched a written headquarters compact between the LMS and the WMMS. Consequent pressure from London arrived too late. The Wesleyan missionary on Vava'u, Peter Turner, had gone already in 1835 to reinforce the *lotu Tonga*.

Rivalry between the LMS and the WMMS in Samoa may be viewed in different ways. To the Wesleyan missionaries on Tonga the maintenance of Methodist presence in Samoa was an obligation to the Samoans who asked for it. The LMS missionaries on Samoa resented it as "Wesleyan aggression"; to them it was sheep-stealing. The people of Manono and Satupa'itea saw it as reinforcing contact with the Tongans, their kinsmen and southern neighbours, against the encroachment of Christianity in alien "Tahitian" form. "What do we know of Tahiti?" the Manono leaders asked Peter Turner in 1835. "What communications had the Tahitians with us, or with Tonga? We only heard of Tahiti last night."

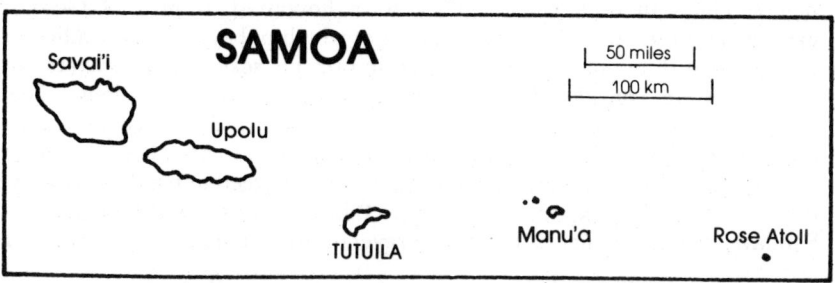

The LMS/WMMS fiat from headquarters was carried out. Peter Turner and his colleague Matthew Wilson were removed by John Williams on the *Camden* in May 1839. The Tongan Wesleyan cause was kept alive by Penisimani Latuselu, the first ordained Tongan, who was addressed by the title Misi usually reserved for white missionaries. Latuselu was sent to Samoa by Taufa'ahau. He was of chiefly rank. Both LMS and Wesleyan observers in Samoa deplored that he mixed his spiritual mission with "politics" and philandering. By the time the Wesleyans re-entered Samoa from an Australian base in 1857 the *lotu Tahiti* had entrenched itself as the majority church. The *lotu Wesele,* however, maintained its cause as a significant minority, oriented toward Tonga and Australia.

An LMS church began almost at once to put down roots and become Samoan. Samoa's villages, around the coasts of the mountainous islands, are the home of a cohesive system centered in the *fono,* or village council, which groups the *matai* — heads of families designated by family·members. These extended families, partly through matrilineal descent, transcend locality and form larger communities under holders of high titles, the *ali'i.* Bestowal of titles within and beyond villages is debated by the orators, who participate in establishing claims when title-holders die or are displaced. The result is a complex society, run with finesse, where office is determined by many considerations more subtle than descent and conquest. A single pyramid under an undisputed king is hard to build and does not endure for long when built. Greater or lesser national, community and village-level pyramids rise and fall unpredictably.

As Samoa's old attachment to natural and totemic spirits waned, the LMS prepared Samoan teachers and pastors to take the place of the older holy men and prophets of the villages and lend Christian sacral sanction to the traditional social order.

The LMS introduced a key figure into the picture — the *faife'au*, pastor, surrounded by his council of influential lay deacons. The pastors took the place of the priests and prophets of ancient Samoan religion as mediators with the unseen world. They were given good houses, inferior only to those of the highest chiefs in each village. They were honoured as men of God; in exchange for their preaching and conduct of worship they received traditional gifts — food, fine mats, cloth — on an impressive scale. Their prayers and presence were considered indispensable on ceremonial occasions. They renounced *matai* status, but exercised special power of their own because of their spiritual authority and social position. They had to be called to a village church, but once there were revered. They were charged to proclaim and live the Word of God, to expound the Samoan Bible, to oversee weekly worship on Sundays and ensure that daily family prayers were offered in each household.

Above them, the LMS British staff supervised the growth and welfare of the church as a whole. In effect, though not in name, the white missionaries were bishops, overseers. They kept a paternal eye on the welding of Christianity into the *fa'a Samoa*. Their skill in the language gave them an understanding of local custom and lore, but not being born into the system they could never integrally participate. In time, under pressure, they conceded ordination to graduates of Malua, thus setting the seal on a process of Samoanization of the church's inner life, distinct from its official mission-dominated structure.

The status of pastors in Samoan villages influenced the bearing of Samoan missionary families in places as different as Tuvalu (the Ellice Islands) and Papua for more than a century. A ministry thought by its missionary mentors to be dependent on them shaped its own style, while showing due respect and gratitude toward the LMS. Evolution of a genuinely Samoan church was compatible with genuine feelings of affection toward resident white missionaries. A bare six years after training of teachers began at Malua, those stationed on Tutuila revolted. They insisted that all local contributions be set aside for their support, not skimmed off for the general work of the LMS. They won the fight. In 1854 it was agreed that two sets of gifts should be presented, one for the pastors, the other for the mission. A pattern was set for future generous Samoan material support of the church.

Christian moral standards were rapidly introduced to regulate Samoan life. Non-Samoan observers interpreted the changeover from old ways to the vigilant policing activities of missionaries and pastors. But local people, logically enough, followed their *matai* in willing acceptance of the new *tapu* system implied by study of the Bible. Restraints were eventually placed on war, following protracted missionary preaching and mediation. Tattooing, long hair, sexually charged night dances, bare breasts and introduced intoxicants were gradually proscribed. Brutal punishments for trifling offences were abandoned, to the relief of hardened sinners under the new order. The loss of old pleasures was thus balanced by greater justice and the curbing of chiefly caprice.

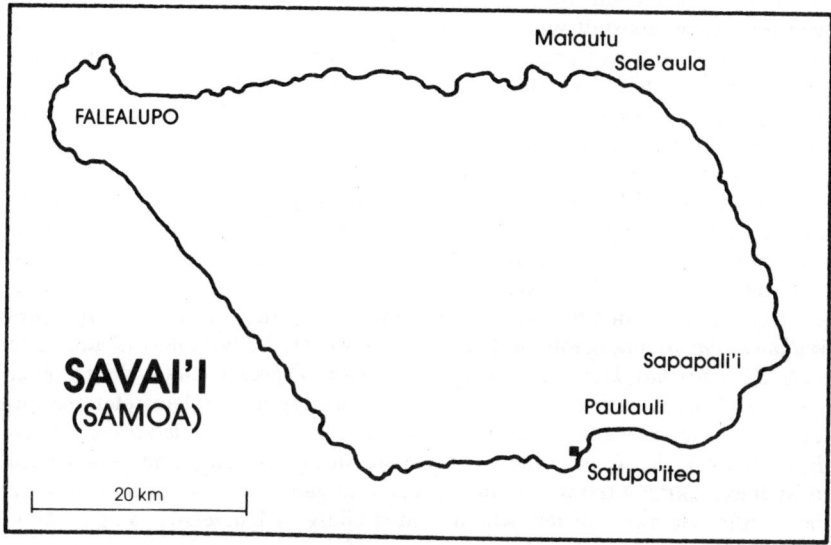

The new laws were based on the Ten Commandments, with sabbath observance as king pin of the system. On Sunday the village people wore white clothes; the women put on straw bonnets. Each evening the sound of singing and prayer was heard in all the family houses. Chapels made of solid stone were built to dominate the villages. The church stood as a sign of the partnership between pastors, the *matai* and God. On Rarotonga the LMS at first brought people in from the villages to be trained in centres surrounding the missionaries' houses. Samoa was different; from the time of Malietoa's dissemination of his teachers Christianity began to take root in existing village life. "I do not know a village in Samoa in which we have not a chapel and a school," wrote Thomas Heath, the LMS missionary on Manono, in 1841. The number under instruction in 1838 had already been estimated as 23,000.

By 1844 the twin stations of Malua and Leulumoega on the northern Upolu coast were beginning to function; the first trained a Samoan ministry, the second became a source of education and of printed matter for the schools. Literacy in Samoa came through the Bible. At his station of Matautu in northern Savai'i, George Pratt, a salty individualist from Portsea in Hampshire, worked steadily at the language. His grammar, dictionary and Samoan Bible took shape. The final form of the Bible, produced under the auspices of the British and Foreign Bible Society, set standards for both written and spoken Samoan. Robert Louis Stevenson thought it "not only a monument of excellent literature, but a desirable piece of typography."

Samoa developed into the pride of the LMS in the Pacific in the nineteenth century. Its staff was steadily reinforced from London. Financial and material provision was generous. Buzacott, with Charles Barff, made an advance guard in 1834. In 1836 Heath, Hardie, William Mills, Alexander Macdonald, A.W. Murray and George Barnden arrived. Murray, a Scots Presbyterian, settled first on Tutuila with Barnden, who was the only unmarried member of the group. Barnden drowned in 1838 under mysterious circumstances, but Murray persevered, to emerge as something of a colossus among his co-workers. Early in his career at Pago Pago he found himself at the centre of a wild series of revivals. From 1854 onward he shifted to Upolu. A "sailing missionary," he was one of the most active directors of mid-year journeys to the "outstations" of the mission on the *Camden* and the *John Williams*. An indefatigable and sententious writer, he became the author of *Forty Years Mission Work* and *Missions in Western Polynesia*, half a dozen other books and many articles for periodicals. Teasingly incomplete references to individual pioneers among the island teachers he superintended are scattered through his works. In later life — he lived to the age of eighty-one — he settled in Sydney, contributed to the daily press, and gained respect as an oracle on the Pacific. George Turner, who attended Glasgow University, was another long-lived Scot who with Murray, placed Malua students in the outstations when the southeast trade winds blew from May to November each year. He wrote *Samoa a Hundred Years Ago and Long Before* and *Nineteen Years in Polynesia* (with a preface by the anthropologist R.B. Tylor). His is one of the best descriptions of the Malua institution and its life.

Tutuila, with the other islands in eastern Samoa, was not unprepared for the settlement of the Murrays there in 1836. "A few rays of light had found their way from the other islands, where teachers had been at work for six years," he wrote, "and especially the visit of Teava." Buzacott's first pupil, left by Williams on Manono (page 85), had exploited his opportunities. He coasted along the southern edge of Upolu and worked at the important villages of Falealili. His travels took him to Tutuilā. In May 1838, following Barnden's death, he was sent to assist Murray, who stationed him at Leone and could count on his help with custom and language. "His knowledge of the Samoan language was accurate and extensive," Murray recalled, and spoke of Teava "and his kind wife" as "our steadfast friends and helpers." They spent thirty years in Samoa, according to Murray, before returning home. The Samoan church owes them more than surviving records disclose. Teava

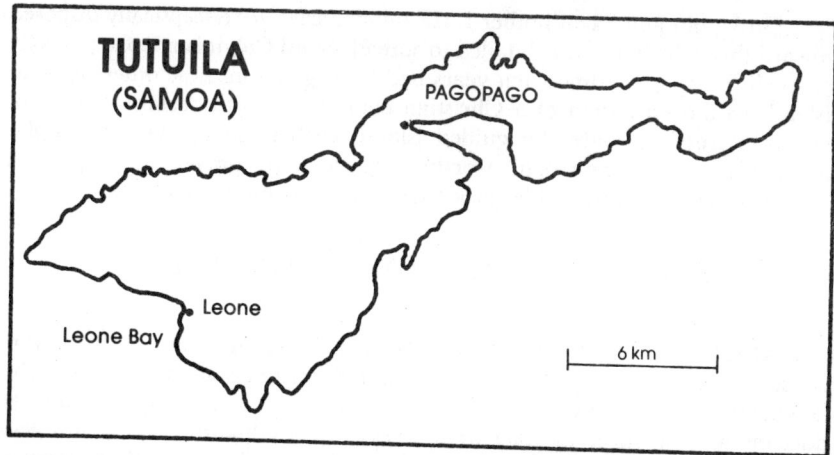

and his friends, from the Cook and Society Islands, belong to the living tradition of the Samoan Congregational community.

Teava lived through the emotional excitement of the Tutuila revival between 1839 and 1842. In Murray's "household," which included many Samoan catechumens and servants, outbursts of violent weeping broke out during the repetition of Bible texts at evening prayers on 4 November 1839. The irruption of this mourning for sin has been traced to guilt feelings over the news of the murder of John Williams, earlier in the year. There were other causes for the awakening; simultaneous revivals broke out in Scotland, in Murray's birthplace, Jedburgh, and in Kelso. Murray and a visiting Scot of evangelical background, George Archibald Lundie, participated in the excitement on Tutuila. Both men were in correspondence with friends in their home towns in Scotland. The Pentecostal fervour "reached its height" during 1840 and gradually subsided during 1841 and 1842. On 1 March 1840 "ten or twelve sank down exhausted, and had to be carried out of the chapel in a state of complete prostration, the whole neighbourhood seemed in a commotion. Nothing was heard on all sides but the sounds of weeping and supplication."

Pent-up shock, involved in rapid transition out of Samoan religion into Christianity, here found release. Convulsive behaviour under spirit possession was familiar among pre-christian prophets in Samoa. Hymn-singing and sober liturgical activity under Murray's moralistic instruction had not as yet provided sufficient outlet for Samoans, who danced ecstatically and wept easily. The recovery of these pre-christian phenomena through the events of the revival is hinted at by Murray himself: "But a short time had passed since we used to be shocked by hearing the coarse and filthy songs of abandoned sailors, and the hellish revelry of the night dance. How changed now!" The revival was partly a sanctified substitute for proscribed forms of entertainment.

On Upolu and Savai'i other LMS missionaries were sceptically disposed toward this behaviour, which failed to spread. Staid Calvinism looked bleakly on such transports. Almost ten years had been given in these other Samoan islands to the formation of a Christian community with decorous forms of group expression. Carefully guided island teachers in the villages implemented a steady transition; worship, instruction, prayer meetings and conversations about the Bible, proceeded busily without explosions.

WESLEYANS AND LMS IN CONFLICT

AFTER THE WITHDRAWAL OF PETER TURNER in 1839 the Wesleyan cause on Manono, and in the Tonga-leaning district of Satupa'itea in Savai'i, languished numerically and became, by mission standards, corrupt in doctrine and practice. In 1855 when Wesleyan Methodism in England was suffering a financial pinch and had handed over direction of its Pacific missions to the Australasian Wesleyan Conference, the veteran Tonga missionary John Thomas persuaded the Methodist churches in the Australian colonies to resume the mission in Samoa. The LMS staff there was aghast. Martin Dyson, the young Yorkshireman sent from the Tonga District to direct the resumption, found his work embarrassing. He clearly liked and respected the LMS, the Methodist remnant appalled him. At first he strove for union of the two missions. In this he was vigorously opposed by his chairman, Thomas, who visited him in 1858 and insisted that there must be no adulteration of Methodist doctrine, liturgy or discipline by compromise with the LMS. Thomas wanted "Methodism in earnest" as in the Tongan revivals. His dream was unrealized. Samoan Methodism proved to be mainly non-ecstatic.

With the coming of George Brown, a brilliant partner from County Durham in England, in 1860, Dyson resigned himself to the task of reconstructing and extending the Wesleyan Church. He was by then, in any case, annoyed by LMS propaganda against "Wesleyan aggression." Intelligent, pertinaceous, a man of wide vision, Brown laid the foundations of a prolonged missionary career in the Pacific by preaching in Samoan within two months of his arrival. He considered the reoccupation of Samoa to have been legitimate, though inexpedient. He decided to push on with it. From his mission station at Satupa'itea on Savai'i he scanned the strategy of the LMS, which had its press and educational headquarters at Leulumoega and its training institution at Malua. Leulumoega's talking chiefs were the most powerful group in Samoa in the determining of who should hold high titles, particularly in the crucially important districts of A'ana in western Upolu and Atua in the east. In 1863 Samoa was constituted a separate district by the Methodists; in that year Brown began to train teachers at Satupa'itea. After Dyson left in 1864, at his own request, to return to Tonga, Brown was made

Chairman of the Samoa District. He and Dyson already had their eyes on the important centre of Lufilufi as a possible station. They knew that Lufilufi's talking chiefs were second in importance only to those of Leulumoega. By 1866 Brown was writing apologetically to Pratt of the LMS about his decision to station two new missionaries, Firth and Austin, at Lufilufi, where the Methodists later trained their teachers and pastors.

Dyson and Brown, two shrewd observers, ensured that the Methodist Church would, in spite of its comparative smallness, have its own strongholds — in southern Savai'i, on Manono (and adjacent Upolu) and at Lufilufi.

Once settled into the country's life, the Methodists maintained their identity. Their church became as genuinely Samoan as its numerically stronger rival. Samoan Congregationalism continued to draw its support in missionary manpower direct from Britain, regarding the colonial Methodists with patronizing disdain. The Samoan Methodists had to be content with a smaller trickle of missionaries, drawn largely from the Australian colonies. Fortunately the lines of battle that raged between high chiefly districts in Samoa between 1840 and the early 1870s never developed into clear alignments on religious lines; family and titular connections shifted too readily across districts. The trend rather led in the direction of leakage by whole villages in and out of LMS and Wesleyan camps, and for non-theological reasons.

MARISTS COME TO SAMOA

A THIRD AND LATE arrival complicated this criss-crossed pattern of co-existing Protestants. In 1845 Roman Catholic Marist missionaries were sent from Uvea (Wallis) in response to repeated requests, addressed by Samoan travellers and converts to Bishop Bataillon. They were, says a Catholic record, "exposed defenceless, in their solitary abodes, to pagan barbarism; nay, more, to persecution from heresy on shore, ahead of them in arrogant possession."

In 1844 an English trader, John Jones, living on the island of Wallis, the mid-Pacific Marist headquarters, was killed when felling a tree for a new schooner. Bishop Bataillon gave him the last rites. Jones willed the schooner, launched in the following year and called *L'Etoile de la Mer* (Star of the Sea), as his deathbed gift to the Catholic mission. On 12 August 1845 the little *Etoile* set out for Samoa with two Samoans, Constantine and Joachim, on board, accompanied by their wives. Father Gilbert Roudaire, from the Diocese of Clermont in France, was head of mission; he withdrew under orders in 1846 because of illness. Father Théodore Violette far outlived him; he stayed on in Samoa without leave until his death in 1887, an inoffensive man with a sense of humour but no great powers as instigator and organizer. Brother Jacques

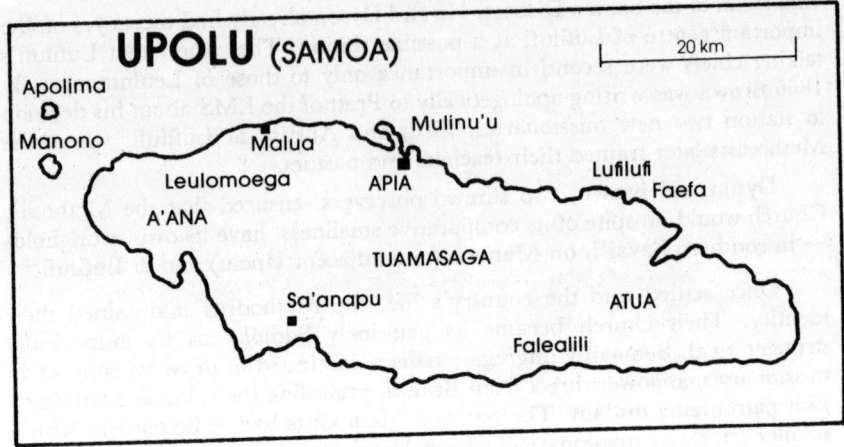

Peloux, a carpenter and mason from the high Beaujolais, north of Lyon, was with them; "I am the only brother within Samoan Christianity," he was to write. "I must put up churches, build houses, ensure such daily bread as God makes for us here; days, weeks, months, flow by rapidly without being noticed."

The *Etoile*, Violette archly observed, was "no shooting star." Her reception, after a stormy passage, was predictable. The Protestants were as anti-papal, and as ill informed about the papacy, as were the Catholics about the heretics they referred to undiscriminatingly as "Methodists," or *"les ministres."* News of their coming had been noised in advance, with normal mid-century Protestant horror stories as lurid as Foxe's Book of Martyrs. The Catholics touched at Falealupo on the western tip of Savai'i; they providentially found a chief who was related to Constantine's wife Amelia. Passing by Matautu, the LMS station of caustic George Pratt, as they coasted northern Savai'i, they collected whiffs of distaste. "Before we had been ashore, in a land that refused to be hospitable to us," Violette wrote, "we were sowing consternation in the Protestant army, composed of sixteen ministers, and several well organized teams of catechists, with powerful chiefs for support! Glory be to Mary!"

They were referred by chiefs in eastern Savai'i to Mata'afa Fagamanu, the high chief of Mulinu'u, near Apia, who later became their most prominent convert, and protector. Mata'afa took them under his wing in recognition of help afforded in 1842 by the Catholics on Wallis to himself and a party of drifters. Mata'afa was by this time a Protestant; Roudaire took up residence with him and succeeded in converting his influential *tulafale* (orator). Meanwhile Violette was sent back to Savai'i to cultivate the two villages of Lealatele and Salelaula in the hostile vicinity of Pratt.

SECURING POLYNESIA

Bishop Pierre Bataillon travelled in 1846 to Samoa on the vessel *l'Arche d'Alliance*, captained by Auguste Marceau and belonging to the newly formed (and ill-fated) French Oceanian Company designed to further missions in the Pacific (page 99). He brought four more priests, two of whom had to leave early on account of bad health. In 1848 the Oceanian Company collapsed on the Paris Bourse. The local Catholic plight in Samoa was worse. "My provisions were giving out," reported Louis Padel, one of the priests set ashore by Bataillon, "and so were my small savings, and with no wine I was on the brink of being unable any longer to offer the Holy Sacrifice, our sole and indispensable solace in the midst of all our sufferings." By the early 1850s the priests on Savai'i in their ill-fitting cassocks and worn shoes found it was painful to walk across the lava floes to other villages. They had no boat to navigate within the lagoon.

In this desperate situation Bataillon provided a stronger person to hold the line. In 1850 he sent Father Antoine Freydier-Dubreul, a Marist with previous experience in the Pacific and at Rome; he made Dubreul his Pro-Vicar in charge of Samoa. Bataillon himself was summoned to France and Rome in 1856 to tidy up his lines of command; Colin, his superior, had retired to prayer and meditation following the trying crises of the preceding seven years. Bataillon found that Father Julien Favre, Colin's successor, had been installed in May 1854. Colin sent no more priests to the Pacific after 1849. Favre named three more for Bataillon. Among them was Louis Elloy, the able future bishop of the Catholic Church in Samoa.

Elloy, in partnership with the Catholic high chief Iosefo Mata'afa, inaugurated a more triumphant era. In the early 1860s he brought splendour into public manifestations of the liturgy. The style of the mission became more princely. Elloy was a diplomat. A German gunboat from Hamburg was in port at Apia for the feast of Corpus Christi on 19 June 1862. Elloy took advantage of glorious weather; he arranged for the ship to fire a twenty-one-gun salute at intervals during the outdoor procession — seven guns when the Blessed Sacrament was carried out of the church, seven more after the sermon and the Benediction of the Blessed Sacrament, and finally seven on the re-entry into the church. Three thousand people attended; the German consul joined the procession and knelt at the exposition of the Host. Elloy, who came from Metz, understood German and Samoan love of ceremony.

Almost a year earlier, on 11 July 1861, Elloy held a formal theological disputation with the Methodists George Brown and Martin Dyson at Lufilufi, home ground of important Samoan orators (page 129). Brown "made a few complimentary remarks with regard to the individual characters of the Priests and disclaimed all personal ill feeling" but thought that Dyson "soft-soaped them rather too much." Elloy's biographer said Lufilufi was the headquarters of the faithful Mata'afa; "the Pro-vicar drew the sword of a victorious word against the aggressors" and the report of the encounter testified to his "eloquent dialectic." Dyson, to the contrary, affirmed that "Popery" at Lufilufi "soon afterwards drooped and withered away." What the Samoan hearers made of it all, and whether the withering away was the result of theological persuasion or subsequent debate among Samoan orators is less clear.

Elloy's other initiatives during his first stay in Samoa in the early 1860s included strengthening a weak mission to the Tokelau Islands and reconnoitring Tutuila, where he spent six weeks. Ten years later his "disciple" Julien Vidal was stationed at Leone, where he won his spurs before going on to become Apostolic Prefect, then Vicar Apostolic and eventually Bishop, in Fiji (pages 288, 298).

On 19 June 1863 Elloy set out for Australia to take charge of one of Bishop Bataillon's visionary projects, the establishment of a theological seminary for island students at Clydesdale, near Richmond, on the Nepean River fifty kilometres west of Sydney. Of twenty-eight uprooted and bewildered candidates for the priesthood under his care, fourteen were Samoans. Isolation, winter cold and floods, summer drought, and a combination of unfamiliar farm labour with scholastic theological education, proved disastrous. Bataillon ran out of money. Elloy himself was removed from the scene fairly early by a summons from the Australian Procurator of the Society of Mary, who took him aside in a farm hut, to his great surprise, and showed him the papal document appointing him titular Bishop of Tipasa with jurisdiction over Samoa. He left the coming melancholy failure at Clydesdale in the hands of a successor and was consecrated at Apia on 30 October 1864.

The material promotion of his episcopal establishment took him back in 1866 on a tour of Australian cities. He raised money and took back prefabricated parts for a wooden episcopal residence at Apia, to serve also as a presbytery, a place for meetings and a retreat centre. He continued his apostolic tours; with Victor (Vitolio) Faleono, a young convert who accompanied him often and had been among his candidates for the priesthood at Clydesdale, he visited Father Marin Breton, the eccentric hermit of Neiafu on Vava'u, who was ill. Vitolio stayed to tend him, but himself died of an incurable illness, to Elloy's loss, some two months later — an early hero for Samoa's infant Catholic church.

In 1868 Elloy visited France to report, then attended the First Vatican Council, where he was "with the Pope" in the voting on the Infallibility

Ill-fated experiment: Clydesdale Seminary building.

Decree. Late in 1868 a destructive *sunami*, a violent wave action caused by a submarine earthquake, struck Upolu; the mission suffered, but for Elloy a greater grief lay in his arriving back in Apia simultaneously with news of the French humiliation by Germany in the Franco-Prussian War of 1870. His landing at Apia coincided with peals of cannon, celebrating the capitulation of his home city of Metz, from vessels of the Hamburg trading house of Godeffroy then in the port. The Samoans thought the salvo was for the bishop; they did not know that Protestants like George Brown were even then congratulating the Germans in Samoa on their victory over a pro-papal power.

In following years Elloy often intervened on behalf of his friend and convert Mata'afa. Albert B. Steinberger, an ingratiating and devious American, came to Samoa with credentials from President Ulysses Grant of the United States. He tried to stabilize a chiefly central government at Apia, with an eye to the advantage of Godeffroy and Company — and his own personal enrichment. Missionaries of all three societies at work in Samoa were at first as much deceived by Steinberger's polished style as were the Samoans. Elloy, being a bishop, made headway with Steinberger and with consular officials at Apia; his prelatical manners and baroque vesture had eye-stopping value for both Samoans and Europeans. Mata'afa sponsored the building of a fine new church at Falefa near Lufilufi; the spectacle moved a Marist historian to observe that "it would be pretentious to recall Constantine here, carrying baskets of earth for the building of the Vatican basilica." Nevertheless he added that "the greatness of his chief is in relative terms to be compared with that of the Emperor vis-à-vis his Romans."

On land made available near Apia, St. Joseph's College was established. The incoming Marist Brothers taught the boys, with hopes of Samoan vocations to the priesthood; sisters laid the foundations of a girls' school, along lines subsequently followed by Marist educators in many parts of the Pacific. As he shaped enduring institutions in the early 1870s Elloy's episcopate reached its peak; with the LMS missionaries, and with George Brown of the Wesleyans, he lent his good offices to compose the strife of titles in Samoa. The attempt to find an acceptable constitution for the whole country caused tension between land-hungry settlers; Americans, Germans and the British played off the great titles against each other. The claims of Malietoa Laupepa were pressed by the Protestants, those of Mata'afa Iosefo by the Catholics. Elloy, a respected negotiator, was widely heeded in the search for a workable compromise government. He retained his prestige even after the hurried departure of Colonel Steinberger under a cloud of scandal. In the weakened position of France in the Pacific after 1870 Elloy was no longer partisan among the powers; the niche of his small Catholic imperium in Samoa was assured. He could speak in favour of "Samoa for the Samoans," as Father in God and *defensor civitatis*. Steinberger is said to have spoken in Catholicism's favour to George Brown "because, more than anywhere else, these peoples need quick thinking, authoritative and precise teaching and living worship, and the Catholic Church alone has them all."

In 1877 Elloy visited Wallis and Futuna, Fiji and Rotuma, all within his jurisdiction. He crossed America, interviewed the United States president about Samoa, and in January 1878 was received in audience by Pope Pius IX, shortly before the Pope's death. In these years Elloy was afflicted with intestinal illness and vomiting. A pilgrimage to Lourdes in search of a miraculous cure was of no avail. He died in a Marist house, not far from the city of the Virgin's shrine, on 22 November 1878 at the age of 49.

NIUE

By comparison with the wide geographical challenge of the Cook Islands and the substantial population of Samoa, Niue, an island with a small population lying between Tonga, Samoa and the Cooks, seemed a small target for missionary effort. From its first contacts with Cook's ships in 1774 it was called Savage Island after a hostile encounter with Cook's landing party. There was no lagoon; to get on to it, mariners had to stand off, put down boats, then scale two terraces of volcanic rock, first twenty metres, then forty. On the plateau above lived the short-statured and independent Niueans. They acknowledged no hereditary chiefs, but only the tenuous supremacy of family heads, who fought for ascendancy among themselves. The population had come in, by drifting and conquest, from Tonga, Samoa and Pukapuka in the northern Cooks, where the people, like the Niueans, are shorter than most Polynesians.

Tongans, Samoans and Cook Islanders had better hope of taking Christianity there than white men; they stood a chance of staying longer on the plateau by pleading traditional rights to hospitality. A landing was no guarantee of general acceptance; the dozen scattered settlements on top were likely to be fighting each other. Tongans, by affinity of language, might have succeeded best, but the Wesleyans were fully occupied elsewhere and had no ships. John Williams and Barff touched Niue gingerly on their way to Samoa in 1830; they landed no one, sensing the problem. Later William Pascoe Crook of the LMS succeeded in 1831 in making contact through Niueans who had themselves done some travelling abroad. One of these was Fanea, who with his wife had been taken off Niue by John Williams. After Crook had taken them back to Niue they were killed. Introduced epidemics, conceivably from mission contact, or alternatively from passing whalers, seem to have increased suspicion of strangers.

Another Niuean who consented to leave with Crook became prominent in the later story; his name was Peniamina. He became a Christian on Savai'i at Palauli under Alexander Macdonald, who was on board the *Camden* when she called at Niue in 1842. So was Buzacott, who had brought three Rarotongans back with Peniamina in hopes of starting a mission. The canoes that came off from Niue at first "gave no encouragement to land teachers among them, as those who had come to see the vessel belonged to the weaker tribes, and they could not protect the missionaries a single day." When canoes came off in the evening representing the "stronger party" they tried to induce the *Camden's* people to land the teachers in their own boat, but refused to stay on board in the meantime or guarantee protection on shore. Next morning they came again and offered to take the teachers ashore with them, but Peniamina's relatives warned that a plot had been made to kill him and the Rarotongans if they came. The warning was accompanied by "a most bitter wail" over Peniamina, one of whose brothers deserted to the ship. Peniamina "gave a faithful address to his countrymen on the guilt of rejecting the messengers of truth; the *Camden* then set sail for Samoa."

After four years the LMS tried again. Peniamina had been at Malua during its beginnings. He was joined in Samoa by another Niuean of some local importance, Fakafitiniu, who had come on a whaler and was willing to go with him. In 1846 the *John Williams* tried to land Rarotongans and Samoans with the Niue men, but the "outsiders" were refused. The LMS had to wait until 1849 to land the real apostle of Niue, Paulo, a Samoan. Peniamina, characterized as "an intelligent man," but "wanting in moral strength" faltered in the process of converting his own people. The LMS deputation found in 1849 that "the conduct of Peniamina had not been altogether consistent." His inconsistencies continued until his death on Niue in 1874, but he acted as a catalyst for the work of Paulo and for later married Samoans from Malua. By 1852, when Murray and James Sunderland visited, they found a group of between two and three hundred people worshipping and learning under Paulo. They brought with them a fresh trio — Laumahina, a Niue chief, and two more Samoans — Paula and Samuela. Laumahina who died in April 1856, played an important part in strengthening the mission. The decade of the 1850s, as yet without any white resident missionary, paved the way, by evangelization, for the conversion of the island. Paula, an effective companion for Paulo, lost his wife in 1859; he was replaced by another Samoan, Elia. In 1861 William George Lawes, a gifted pastor, translator and teacher from Berkshire, arrived as Niue's first English missionary.

Lawes and his wife were accompanied for a settling-in period by George Pratt, the acknowledged language expert among the LMS missionaries in Samoa, who had studied Niuean with students of Malua and was able to preach and converse. Paulo had given the language of Niue written form; in his first year on the island Lawes, according to a British naval visitor, acted as "prime minister, doctor, instructor in divers trades, and religious teacher." It was the beginning of a prolonged affectionate relationship between Niue and the Lawes family. Frank E. Lawes, a younger brother, came to Niue with a printing press on 15 March 1868; he remained as resident missionary until 1910. W.G. Lawes, as first white man to live on the island, faced serious problems. In 1863 ships from Peru took off a hundred young men to labour in the guano mines on the Chincha Islands. Others were recruited, with connivance from leaders of the community, who were paid for it, to work in Samoa on German plantations. The long exodus of migrant workers from among Niue's population of less than 5,000 had begun, under protest from the mission.

W.G. Lawes translated the New Testament; it was revised by Pratt, printed in Sydney, and made available on Niue in 1868. Lawes used it to train local pastors and teachers from among the Niue people. In 1866 he sent two of his students to attend Malua for eventual posting in the remote Tokelau Islands by the Samoan mission. Lawes, the future educator of village teachers in Papua (pages 207ff) learned his skills in Niue's minuscule Polynesian society. The contribution of Niue's own missionaries to the later strategies of W.G. Lawes in Papua went far beyond what could be reasonably expected from its situation and size. Niue's teachers acquired a reputation as comparatively quiet workers, but adaptable and deft.

The relationship between the Lawes brothers and Niue's people was paternal, but not paternalist. They loved and protected many aspects of the local culture against exploitative contact. Old stories, sports and games, songs and dances, were preserved. Fighting between districts faded away; crime became rare. In 1869 the chiefs were persuaded to stop the labour trade; but voluntary selective migration of another kind — mission with the LMS — was imminent. The Presbyterian missionary John Geddie, working in the New Hebrides (pages 168ff) asked for Niue teachers to be sent to help in his work. All Lawes' students volunteered. Two teachers were accepted and sent in 1870. Others followed, and in 1876 the first three recruits accompanied the elder Lawes on his mission to Papua.

When the LMS posted Lawes to Papua, the deacons, members and teachers of the Niue church remonstrated with the Directors of the LMS in London. But Lawes, like James Chalmers, his partner in the New Guinea mission (pages 212ff), was made of visionary stuff. Chalmers was fashioned for hardship, exploring, restless treks for Christ; ten years on Rarotonga sufficed him (pages 270ff) as training for larger populations and harsher landscapes. Lawes gained his teacher's wisdom on Niue, to invest it, with Chalmers, in the strung out villages along Papua's coast.

The London Missionary Society's work thus led to the founding of churches in the Cook Islands, Samoa and Niue. Island teachers under the society's direction were responsible for continuing the conversion and training of their fellow-Polynesians. As they did so, local hands in each island took over the work, using the resources of their own languages and cultures to teach from the Bible and introduce their people to the person of Christ. British customs and attitudes inevitably entered into the resulting mixture, though what emerged was Polynesian with British overtones rather than British Christianity in Polynesian garb.

From Takamoa (Rarotonga), Malua (Samoa) and Alofi (Niue), many volunteered to go as missionaries to Micronesia or Melanesia. They felt they were commissioned by their home churches in the Pacific. The respected white missionaries who gave them directions and provided them with vessels were under orders from London; the Pacific Islander missionaries felt themselves to be sent out, as did the Tahitians before them, by their own young churches at home. They went as islanders to islanders, giving Protestant Christianity in the Pacific a distinctive character beneath the official designation LMS.

Roman Catholic adaptation to the Pacific was slower. Liturgy and teaching assumed a Latin mould. Bataillon's unsuccessful tinkering with training for the priesthood at Clydesdale (and later Rome) inevitably led to alienation for his candidates. Later he established a seminary at Lano on Wallis with only limited success. Cultures clashed within its walls. The French priests in charge believed in disciplined precision and industry, scholastic rationality, individual asceticism. Their pupils' inherited ways were different: insouciance about the keeping of time, exuberance in feasting and dance, enjoyment of sex, pride in male virility and female fertility, full participation in the varied life of the extended family. With few exceptions Polynesian seminarians dropped out. Catholic parish life in the Pacific, already becoming local in quality, depended for sacramental nourishment on a predominantly expatriate priesthood. Rigid scholastic requirements — and the celibacy rule — retarded the growth of a genuinely Oceanian hierarchy.

6

Micronesia: Missions Meet

Carolines, Marshalls, Kiribati Tuvalu

PROTESTANTS WENT FROM HAWAII to northern Micronesia — 2,000 islands scattered over seven million square miles — when two developments interlocked within the young Hawaiian church: American children of missionary parents decided to become missionaries, and trained Hawaiian pastors came forward to serve abroad. Two American missionaries to Hawaii stimulated the expansion. Claudius B. Andrews, a bachelor, and John Paris, a widower, went together to America in 1849 on the ship *Montreal* after completing their first terms of service in Hawaii. Both returned to the islands with wives; at Boston they also busied themselves over Micronesia, having heard from the *Montreal's* mate about the varied peoples and land-forms of the Caroline, Marshall and Gilbertese island chains. Paris wrote passionately to the American Board of Commissioners for Foreign Missions, urging them to begin joint work with the Hawaiian church in Micronesia.

Boston and Honolulu were fired by the thought. Luther Halsey Gulick, one of seven missionary sons of the Rev. Peter Johnson Gulick of the third company of missionaries to Hawaii, had been born in Honolulu in 1828. He went to New York State to be trained in theology and medicine. Just as the call was sent out for volunteers to go to Micronesia, he was completing his studies. He married his wife, Louisa, in New York City in 1851. In November he sailed from Boston with the other pioneers of the Micronesian Mission: Albert A. Sturges with his wife Susan; Benjamin Snow with his wife Lydia.

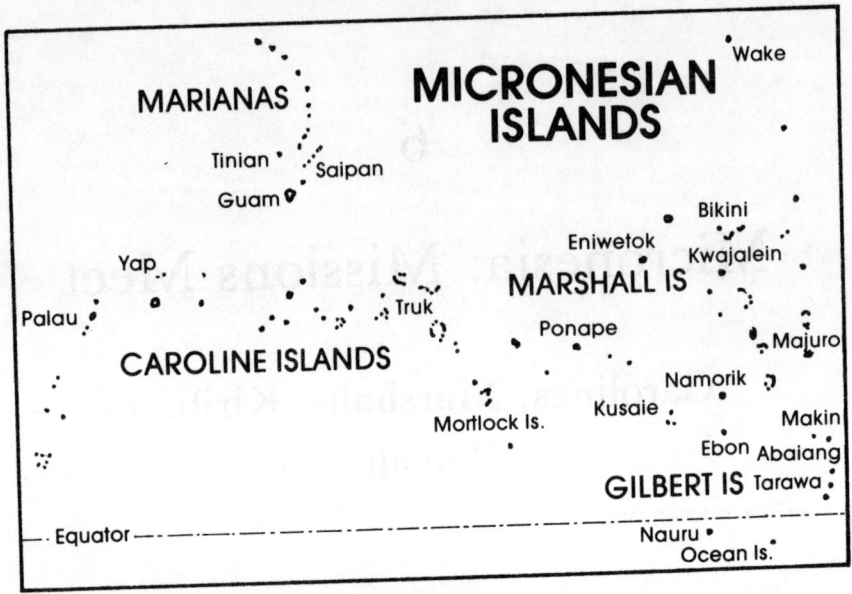

Hearts fluttered in Honolulu on the arrival of "cousin Halsey," with his young wife and impressive education. He became the prime instigator of the Hawaiian Mission Children's Society. In 1852 the children formed themselves into a closely knit body of "cousins," with a pride in their descent reminiscent of the Americans whose ancestors came over the Atlantic in the *Mayflower*. Most of the founders of the Society were talented, well educated, well rooted in Hawaii, and well off. Their enthusiasm and financial commitment to the Micronesian mission became primary sources of their cohesion — though few of them volunteered to forsake Hawaii for tropical rigours along the equator.

More of the work force came out direct from America — and from among the Hawaiians. Since 1843 the high school at Lahainaluna on Maui (page 47) had trained young future pastors. In 1849 James Kekela had been ordained to serve the church at Kahuku, Oahu; other ordinations were pending. The Hawaiians, aware that Tahitians had played an important part in bringing Christianity among them (pages 39-43), responded. The graduates of Lahainaluna provided cultural intermediaries for the missions in the Micronesian, and soon afterward the Marquesas, islands (pages 266ff). Other important changes were taking shape within the Sandwich Islands Mission itself. Twenty-two American missionaries became Hawaiian citizens between 1849 and 1852. Rufus Anderson, the ABCFM's visionary foreign secretary, encouraged the development. He wrote to Ephraim Clark, the secretary of the newly formed Hawaiian Auxiliary Missionary Society, deprecating its name. "The word auxiliary should be dropped," he said, "the years of dependence

MICRONESIA: MISSIONS MEET

are ended." Though he put forward a plan for continued financial aid from the ABCFM, with full reporting on how the money was used, he insisted the two boards were to be regarded as autonomous and equal partners.

When the schooner *Caroline,* fitted out in Honolulu, sailed in 1852 for Micronesia, two Hawaiian couples had joined the group: Daniel Opunui and his wife Doreka; and Berita Kaaikaula (a teacher), with his wife Debora. They had been chosen from fourteen volunteer pairs. The two supervisors of the voyage were also carefully selected; James H. Kekela, soon to become the best known of all Hawaiian missionaries to the Marquesas, accompanied Ephraim Clark in this capacity.

The first four Hawaiians found the going difficult in the Carolines. Their tongues did not adapt easily from flowing Hawaiian to the hard consonants and unfamiliar vowels of Ponape. The missionaries they flanked had slender experience of the Pacific and could hardly avoid condescending to them, which in turn made them subservient. In theory they too were missionaries; in practice they were treated as assistants, their wives as domestics. Anderson's charter — equal partnership — lapsed. Opunui died on Kusaie in 1853, Kaaikaula on Ponape in 1859. The only other Hawaiian to serve the Carolines in the nineteenth century, S. Kamakahiki Kaaha, went to Ponape in 1855, but resigned to resume his ministry in Hawaii in 1857.

The Sturges, Snows and Gulicks, to their credit, quickly applied their skills to acquire local languages. Other problems were not so readily surmounted. New England was in their blood; they saw no reason to examine their faith in the universal validity of their neat *mores* and their judgmental securities by comparing them critically with the standards and assumptions of the cultures they were entering. The assorted whites who preceded them in the islands were fugitives from justice, beachcombers, traders. The morals of these predecessors shocked them. At the same time, they were white; their services had to be used for interpretation until the language came clear. Inevitably the first missionary evaluations of on-shore life, particularly social structure, were influenced by what they heard from the beachcombers. If a chief was called a "king" by bootleggers, whalers and merchants, then "king" it would be; the chiefs too, with some pragmatic knowledge of English, did not hesitate to appropriate the title, though it was a misleading key to the structure of their societies.

Before long the missionaries turned against their white predecessors, as Hawaii's American missionaries had done in the 1820s. The source of strife lay in prostitution on ships and the free use of distilled spirits for barter. The Americans were total abstainers; to them, sex was not for sport or for hire; it had been ordained by God for monogamous marriage. Conflict over these matters alienated them from free living whites and led to ambivalent

MICRONESIA: MISSIONS MEET

relationships with local rulers. As in many parts of the Pacific local people with the inside running on their own territory could play off one group of newcomers against the other for temporary local benefits: friendship with traders gave them the novel solace of binges and orgies; when they sobered up they could lean in the other direction to avail themselves of Christian literacy, clothes of new cut and stronger houses. Eventually, also, in the swaying competition between different sets of white favourites, Christian legislation gave them and their people a much needed antidote to the introduced scourges of drunkenness and venereal disease.

The Gulicks and Sturges on Ponape were good linguists, but not greatly interested in comparative anthropology. It was left to others to explore and explain in careful detail the remains of the ancient rulers of the Saudeleur dynasty who gave substructure to the society they hoped to Christianize, with its high ranks of Nahnken and Namwarkis, and subtler gradations in other relationships between people. They did not visualize an exchange of qualities between such a society and their own, much less any compromise of outward form between their hearty Christian piety and the art forms connected with the local spirits of the island. When they heard music performed on the exotic nose-flute they did not linger to assess its special qualities; they did not think much of it. The first hymn Sturges translated was "There is a happy land, far, far away." Similar "melodious" odds and ends of foreign revivals contributed to early Americanization of the church. The missionaries were eager to push forward, but unable clearly to grasp the essence of old feuds between the rival rulers of Metalanim on the windward eastern side of the island and Kiti to leeward. Even their building labours ran them into minor compromises that grieved them as major capitulations to sin; when Gulick built a house on Shalong Point in Metalanim harbour, and followed it with a seaman's chapel, a school and a hospital, he was forced to pay for the labour in tobacco; no other currency was acceptable.

At that stage Gulick was still young, hopeful, tireless, the energetic and attractive "cousin Halsey." He travelled on foot in Metalanim to meet the people. His wife fell ill; he coped with housekeeping as well as the rest of his work. He felt he must keep up his habits of reading and study; he had 600 books in his house at Shalong. In 1854 smallpox, brought by an infected ship, broke out on Ponape. Gulick found his stocks of vaccine were sub-standard. He took a culture from an infected person, innoculated himself with it, then halted the epidemic by mass administration of the fresh vaccine. On the other side of the island, in what was regarded as a successful display of white magic, Sturges innoculated and saved the high ranking Nahnken. Losses in the epidemic were severe, but the mission, led by Gulick, saved Ponape from worse depopulation.

Old Lahainaluna Seminary: the printing press.

Sturges put equal effort into his work at Ron Kiti. Ponape's pioneers were admirable activists, forging toward goals of conversion and material "uplift." Albert Sturges lasted longer in Micronesia than Gulick. Allowing for furloughs, he persisted there until 1884, dying in the following year when the Caroline Islands came under Spanish rule. He never permitted the relaxed disposition of island-dwellers to erode his convictions about hard work. He wanted a sign that said "WORKERS WANTED" at the entrances to the mission's churches and schools; "it is not passengers to Heaven we want, but workers to make Heaven on earth," he said. The sentiment marks a shift in American theology. Sturges' washed and brushed image of an earthly heaven derived in part from optimism on new American frontiers. The stern biblicist Calvinism of the Sandwich Islands Mission ceded place to no-nonsense hard work as a harbinger of better days for humanity. Cheerful spit and polish were given a place in wiping away sins.

Sturges belonged to a new school of American theology represented by the educator Horace Bushnell. He was an attentive member of Bushnell's public, believers in "reform, self-improvement, and gentility." An optimist, he thought of the old beliefs of Ponape as a crude stepping-stone, rough-hewn signs of a generalized "religious" sensibility. "We gain nothing by weakening the heathen's veneration for deity," he said. "We gain him over for the service of the true God by simply showing who God is and where he can be

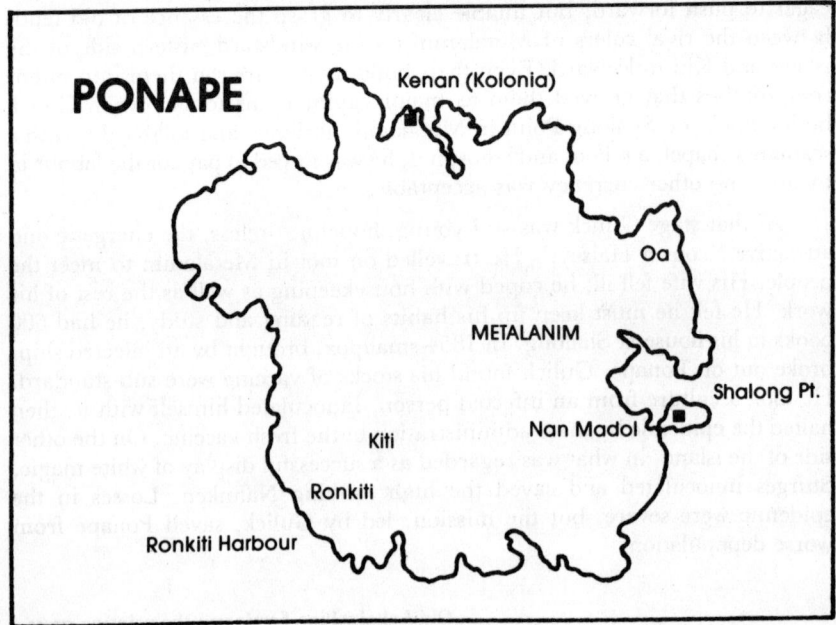

MICRONESIA: MISSIONS MEET

found." His own conviction that God would be more likely to be found in the culture he brought with him from Wabash, Indiana, than newly active in and through the old culture of Ponape is hardly concealed:

> Let us then come to our people and work for them, fully understanding that they are not fools, not even savages nor atheists. Let us treat them politely, and thankfully accept their hospitality. However superior we may feel ourselves to be, let us always see the much that is valuable in them and utilize it in our labors for them.

A succession of vessels called *Morning Star* plied out of Honolulu from 1856 onward to visit and supply Ponape, Kusaie, the Gilbert Islands and the Marshalls. They brought only a slow trickle of missionary reinforcements to Ponape and Kusaie. In 1855 George Pierson, a medical doctor from Illinois, who had worked for a time after 1851 as a missionary among the Choctaw Indians, came with his wife Nancy to Kusaie, where he served until 1857. When the mission extended its work to the Marshall Islands they were sent to Ebon, where ill-health forced them to resign and go back to Honolulu. They never returned. Edward T. Doane, another mid-westerner, also came to Kusaie in 1855. He went as a fellow-pioneer to Ebon with Pierson. His wife Sarah became seriously ill; in 1857 they had to be evacuated to Honolulu, where she died in 1862. Doane, a man of frontier stamina, came back, with his second wife, Clara, in 1865. In 1858 Ephraim P. Roberts and his wife Myra joined the mission. As missionaries on Ponape they were failures; they resigned in 1861.

In these years of expansion into the Marshall Islands the problems were acute. Gulick, whose hope from the time of going out to Micronesia was that he should serve eventually in the Gilbert Islands, which he had seen with great fascination during the *Caroline's* visit in 1852, was forced by events to accept instead a posting to Ebon in the Marshalls, following a meeting of missionaries on Kusaie in 1858. By then the work at Abaiang in the Gilberts had been begun in the previous year by another member of the second generation of Sandwich Islands missionaries — Hiram Bingham, Junior. On Ebon, Gulick and his wife, already taxed by over-exertion on Ponape, suffered from exposure to the hard diet and atoll climate of the Marshalls. In 1860 they were forced to retire to Honolulu, broken in health and prematurely aged; but the relapse, true to the traditions of his family, was not permanent. He recovered, visited the Hawaiian missionaries in the Marquesas, made inspiring speeches in the United States to raise funds and settled in Honolulu as secretary to the Hawaiian Evangelical Association in 1864. His later career in mission took him to Spain, Italy, Japan and China. He continued to translate into the language of Ponape.

Reverses for the ABCFM in North America coincided with all the adversities in the Micronesian field. Civil war broke out in 1861. Financial retrenchment lay in the background of Rufus Anderson's visit to Hawaii in 1863 and the subsequent detachment of the Micronesian work from Boston in 1865, when the Hawaiian Board of Missions became fully and solely responsible for continuing oversight. Unhappily, the original dream of sending children of the Hawaiian missionaries in force to work alongside Hawaiians also languished. Apart from the service rendered by Orramel Gulick, Luther Halsey's younger brother, as an officer on the *Morning Star* from 1857 to 1862, there were no more. Orramel and his wife Ann Eliza, however, later proved their mettle as missionaries in both Hawaii and Japan. He lived to age 92, she to 105.

Sturges on Ponape and Snow on Kusaie established themselves in this troublesome early period as the twin pillars of the future enterprise. Sturges, after eight years, baptized three people in 1860; the numbers grew to 154 by 1864. The church on Ponape advanced steadily, but its consolidation depended on the variable whim of local rulers. Doane's return strengthened the mission's hold. His second wife, Clara, had to be taken back to Honolulu because of ill-health. When Sturges and his wife took their first home leave in 1869 Doane worked on by himself on Ponape. He outlived both Sturges and Snow, served later in Japan from 1877 to 1885, and returned to become a participant in dramatic confrontations with the Spanish when they occupied the Carolines in 1886.

From 1860 onward Snow was obliged, through lack of other ready manpower, to turn eastward to the Marshall Islands, where he spent a large part of his time. The atoll of Ebon, southern-most of the Marshall chain, came to the attention of the church on Kusaie through a party of Marshallese drifters. Pierson and Doane went in response to their request for missionaries. From the high and luxuriant island of Kusaie the mission moved to a more testing physical environment, low rims of sandy coral around circular lagoons, hardy people accustomed to both drought and storm, using fish and the coconut palm as staples for survival. Beginning in 1860, Snow superintended the growth of Christianity in the Marshalls, travelling to and from Ebon, or to Honolulu. Following the withdrawal of American missionaries from the atolls he was away from Kusaie for long periods. The young church there, small in numbers, for seventeen years, during his absences, evolved its own style and leadership under Kaluka (Luke) and other local deacons. One of Snow's aims when he went to Hawaii was to recruit the effective Hawaiians who now carried on the work in the Marshalls.

The first of them was the most remarkable — Hezekiah Aea, a young graduate of the Lahainaluna Seminary, who was assisting Titus Coan at Hilo (pages 55-57) when he volunteered, in 1860, to go to Micronesia. Before he went he married Debora, the widow of Berita Kaaikaula, who died on Ponape

MICRONESIA: MISSIONS MEET

in January 1859. Aea was the outstanding missionary builder of the Marshallese church. He had dedication and verve; the local people accepted him. He and his wife were followed by six other Hawaiian couples; together they used the methods of their Hawaiian home churches to train local deacons, compose chants to local words and music and recruit the people of the lonely and thinly peopled atolls into churches. They used pre-christian forms of social organization and festivity, giving local custom a fresh Christian meaning. In 1869 Aea moved from Ebon to Majuro; in 1872, still in his early thirties, he died on a visit to Honolulu. He and his Hawaiian colleagues did some of their finest work in the Marshall Islands, allowing a local church to evolve along its own lines, without over-supervision. Each year they accustomed themselves to a seasonal rhythm of travel and festival up and down the twin island chains of the Marshalls, running south to north. Visitation by the mission ship revealed small communities eager to emulate each other in zeal and the practice of the new faith. Aea's model was followed, with varying degrees of fidelity, by his successors: David Kapali and his wife Tamara on Namorik and Jaluit; J.W. Kaelemakule and his wife on Namorik; Solomon P. Kaaia and his wife Kanoho on Namorik and Arno; Samuel Kahelemauna and his wife on Mille; Samuel W. Kekuewa and his wife Miriama on Majuro; and S.P.K. Nawaa and his wife Mary on Mille.

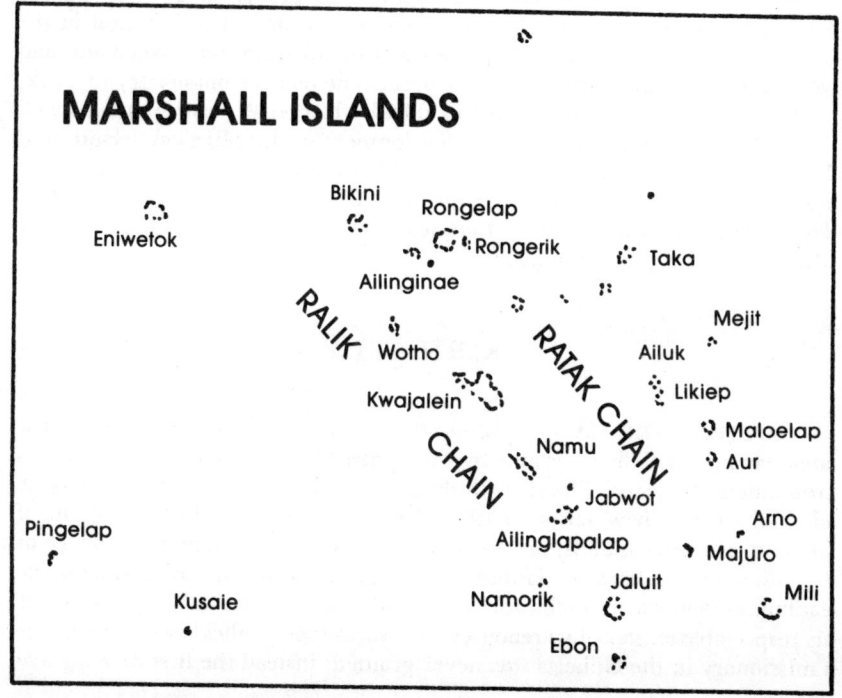

Marshallese were taken for training on Kusaie as pastors; as they returned to their own islands they gradually took over direction of their own church from Hawaiians who returned home. Offerings for the church and for the support of the *Morning Star* took the form of coconut oil, brought willingly to monthly "concerts of prayer." These New England social festivals came through Hawaiian intermediaries to tiny islands; the recurrent solace brought spiritual joy into the predictable round of daily life. Marshallese forms and traditions were without effort infused into these eagerly awaited meetings, out of which came the strong affirmation of self-support of the church of the Marshall Islands, preserved under successive political occupations by Germany, Japan and the United States.

As Kusaie had acted as base for eastward expansion, Ponape's young church turned westward to strike new roots in another atoll setting, the Mortlock Islands. Sturges visited the group in the *Morning Star* in 1873, accompanied by Doane and Snow. They found the people aware of the mission's work and eager for missionaries. The church on Ponape sent three couples in January 1874, led by Opatinia, a woman of high rank, and her husband Obediah. They began on Satawan and Lukunor. More teachers joined them; Snow recruited new Christians from the Mortlocks to be trained on Ponape at Oa (Oua, Owha) alongside Ponapeans. In 1878 he settled Moses, a teacher of mixed Gilbertese and Ponapean origin, on Etal in the Mortlocks. Two years later he picked Moses up from Etal, where he had worked well, ordained him, and took him as the pioneer missionary to Truk, further north. There he was joined in 1884 by Robert W. Logan and his wife Mary from the United States. The development in the Mortlock Islands and Truk took place under the guidance of Micronesians themselves. When he launched it in 1874, Sturges, with his normal exuberance, hailed it as a new day; "Hawaii, the child, Micronesia, the grandchild, and Interior Micronesia, the great-grandchild!"

KIRIBATI

SOUTH OF THE MARSHALLS lay the chain of atolls known as Tungaru, later named the Gilbert Islands by the British. The Tungaru people always pronounced the word Gilberts with their own inflection as Kiribati, the name adopted for their new nation in 1978. The *Caroline* touched Butaritari, one of the most northerly islands, on 8 August 1852, during the inaugural voyage of the Micronesian Mission. Gulick made contact with Richard Randell, the leading resident coconut oil trader in the Gilberts, who flew a Union Jack over his respectable cluster of warehouses and workshops. Gulick's wish to become a missionary in the Gilberts was never granted; instead the first *Morning Star*

MICRONESIA: MISSIONS MEET

brought Hiram Bingham II and his wife Minerva Clarissa, with the Hawaiians J.W. Kanoa and his wife, Kaholo.

Hiram Bingham, Junior, gentle son of a dominating father (pages 37-48) came out to the Pacific fresh from Yale. He touchingly venerated his father's piety and theology. A good boatman, he was qualified to sail the *Morning Star;* he needed all his New Englander seaman's lore when a smaller vessel called *The Star of Peace* was made available to enable him to thread his way down as far as the southern Gilberts. In other ways he was sorely tested; the atoll climate and diet plagued his weak eyes and weaker digestion. His throat and voice suffered under the strain of frequent public speaking.

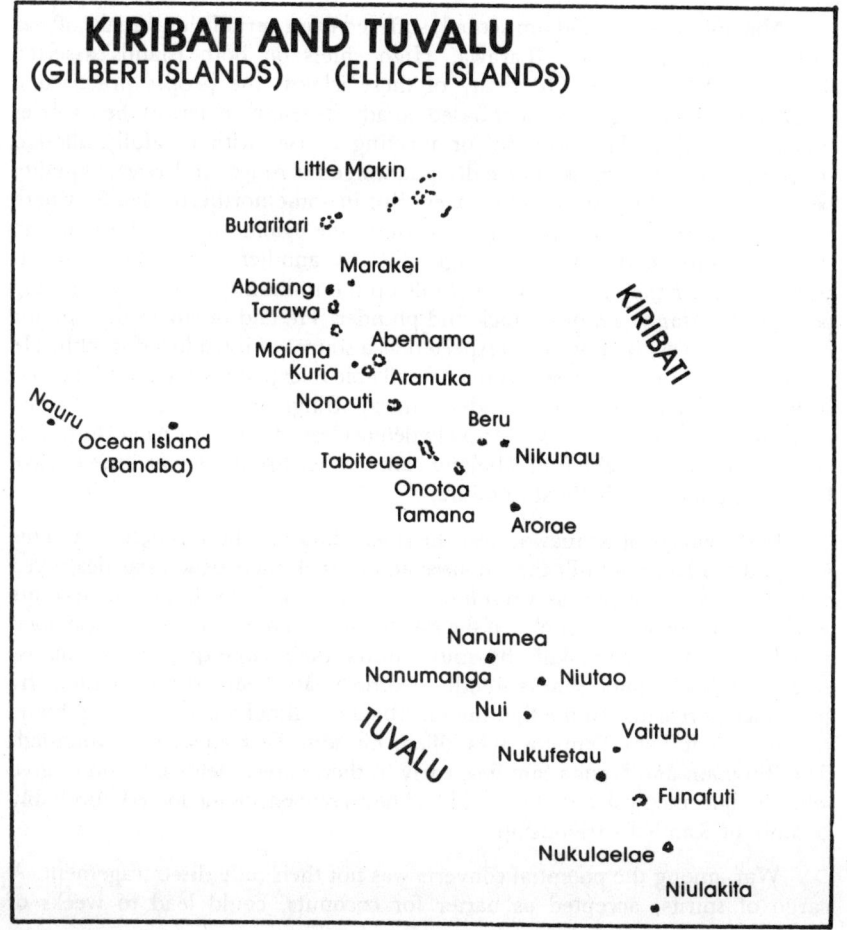

TO LIVE AMONG THE STARS

Within the limitations of these physical disabilities Bingham's work took on a special mould. He deputed much hard toil to his Hawaiian associates, while he translated, planned and supervised from Banner Cottage, the little house on Abaiang he and his wife artlessly called "Happy Home." He built it with timber brought on the *Star*. Within its walls he reduced Gilbertese to writing and embarked on his translation of the Bible. Randell liked him; they became and remained friends. From Randell, Bingham derived valuable information about the Gilberts; as a pastor he discussed the moral aspects of Randell's colourful domestic life, inducing him eventually to trim his menage of four Gilbertese wives down to one. At one stage he felt Randell's sound conversion was imminent. The two men enjoyed their unlikely Anglo-American mutual regard at the world's end.

Abaiang, where Bingham settled, suffered from periodic outbreaks of war with its near neighbour, Tarawa. High chiefs on both islands asserted themselves by feuding. On many of these islands the people practised a deliberative form of government based on adjustment by elders of the rivalries between families. The *maneaba*, or meeting house, with carefully allotted seating according to rank, normally guaranteed a rough and ready equality between all social classes except slaves. But in some northern islands, where higher chiefs tried to dominate permanently, the egalitarian spirit was not so strong. Insults rendered to one high chief by another had to be avenged. Randell, under the circumstances, built up the immunity of his own trading posts in the islands against attack and plunder. He laid in stocks of superior arms — and was, in any case, respected as a source of introduced wealth. He was also fluent in Gilbertese, therefore well able to explain what would happen if his establishments came under attack. Bingham, as the only white missionary, was known to be relatively defenceless, despite his friendship with Randell. If the high chief on Abaiang came under fire there was little to save him from pillage in the heat of battle.

In the village of Koinawa, near the chief's house, where Bingham and his wife and the Kanoas built their houses and chapel, their peace was destroyed in this way within a year as a result of invasion from Tarawa. The inhabitants were among the heroic peoples of the Pacific; their canoes, laden with warriors, sailed with impressive skill. By mid-century their close-quarters weapons, serrated spears and sharks'-tooth swords, had been supplemented by introduced firearms. In the fighting on Abaiang, Bingham's near neighbour, the high chief Tem Temaua, was killed; his son, Te Kauea, was wounded. The Bingham and Kanoa families, early in their career, felt called on to give what simple medical aid they could. They escaped being looted, probably because of Randell's friendship.

War among the potential converts was not their only discouragement. A cargo of spirits, accepted as barter for coconuts, could lead to weeks of intoxication, with no hope of evangelizing anyone. White men had also taught the Gilbertese how to brew and distil sour toddy from the juice of the coconut palm. Singing and dancing under these conditions led to breaches of local chastity codes, previously respected, except with women of lower slave status and among polygamous high chiefs. Bingham's disapproval of these social convulsions does not appear to have led him to point the finger over-much at the goings-on of his as yet non-christian neighbours. He lived and let live until he made converts who came slowly and in small numbers. In hopes, he built his chapel too big for his congregation. He and his adoring wife — she referred to him in her journal as "darling" rather than Hiram or "my husband" — cut an exotic tropical figure on Sundays in their sober hats and outfits. They induced churchgoers to turn out to match them. Bingham never became acculturated, yet most of the people learned to like him as he was.

The Binghams' offer of reading, writing and arithmetic failed at first to hold the attention of the people of Abaiang. The traditional occupations of the people — tending palms, weaving, sailing, fishing, dancing, sleeping — seemed more pleasant, and in some senses more rational, than toiling over writing. The pre-christian religion lacked the idolatry and pomp attached to highly personified marine or rural deities. Legendary creators and heroic ancestors were venerated in story, but busier daily rites were associated with the cultivation and placation, through priestly mediums, of omnipresent and numerous *anti*, haunting spirits, whose influence is still sometimes feared today.

In the approach to this world, Bingham's attitude to his Hawaiian helpers, who were often left to minister alone when he was travelling, was free of excessive paternalism. He spoke gratefully of their contribution to the task. He called J.W. Kanoa, his first colleague on Abaiang — underlining the tribute — *"a humble, faithful, patient, persevering, devoted missionary. Oh for many more like him.* We ask not for 'domestics' but for missionaries like Kanoa." For thirty-eight years Bingham's early judgement did not waver. When Kanoa died on Butaritari on 30 June 1896 Bingham wrote his obituary.

> The memory of my dear friend and fellow-laborer is very sweet ... In the rough work of touring without beasts of burden from village to village, and in sailing from island to island in our open boat, he did not shrink. Self-collected, cautious, kind, observant, courageous, industrious, active, he was ever a comfort to us, in perils among warlike people and often drunken savages, in perils on the deep, and in the loneliness of defenseless extreme isolation.

As the mission spread southward other Hawaiians were placed; the roll is longer than that of the Marshalls. J.H. Mahoe was shot in the arm and seriously wounded during ten threatening weeks of internal revolt on Abaiang in 1869, when the Bingham's house was entered and rifled. George Haina, who went out in 1860, was drowned. Robert Louis Stevenson met the less heroic missionary Robert Maka on Butaritari in 1889. Maka was then in his second term of service. "I have never known a more engaging creature than this parson of Butaritari," he wrote, describing their friendly drolleries. Stevenson went on to describe the cultural melange beneath the surface of the Hawaiian missionary — Polynesian vivacity poking through a New England Calvinist overlay. Hawaiian speaking people contributed to an emerging style in the emerging Kiribati church. They were homesick, but devoted. There were lapses from required standards of chastity and industry, but the Hawaiians carried and explained the Bible and hymn book among the people as Bingham translated. Their life and preaching mediated Christ to another Pacific people in terms that could be grasped. Through the Hawaiian presence and example Gilbertese Christianity would early aspire to an identity of its own.

Hiram and Clarissa Bingham persisted through ill health and frustrations. Bingham twice refused an invitation to become the pastor of his revered father's Kawaiahao church in Honolulu, a call that came relatively early in his time in Kiribati. "I have great compassion for the poor people of the Gilbert Islands and find it difficult to leave them," he told Ephraim Clark, the secretary of the Micronesian Mission, then pastor at Kawaiahao. He said his health, his voice and his eyes were weak, describing himself as "only about *half* a missionary." The self-estimate was modest; Bingham made the most of what he had. He went on placing his Hawaiian colleagues on new islands, visited on the *Morning Star*, and continued throughout his somewhat interrupted whole period of service, from 1857 to 1875, to work with his wife on the translation of the New Testament. His reports paint a picture of shadow-crossed success: "the Rev. Messrs. Kapu and Leleo" at work on Tabiteuea; Mahoe lying in a pool of blood and their own Happy Home "a complete wreck" after the fighting on Abaiang in 1869; his own surprise and pleasure when he visited southern Kiribati and Tuvalu on board a new *Morning Star* in 1867.

"We shall not soon forget this delightful visit," he wrote. He had found Samoan missionaries of the LMS already working in Tuvalu, where the people and language were Polynesian and related to Samoan. On Nui, in the north of Tuvalu, they nevertheless discovered that Gilbertese was spoken. Their contacts with two Samoan teachers, Peu on Vaitupu and Kirisome on Nui, impressed them. The Binghams had been in correspondence previously with A.W. Murray of the LMS Samoan Mission (pages 126-128) and had made available their Gilbertese hymn book to be "done at Samoa for the benefit of the Nui people" by the LMS. On Vaitupu they had the pleasure of finding "one of the sixty-four original copies of the Gospel of John printed on letter paper on our little press at Apaiang in 1864." Clarissa Bingham, said her husband, found two Nui women who were "able to read fluently in our new books." They "had been instructed by two of her own pupils."

Bingham, observing the early successes of the LMS in the south, commented wistfully: "The contrast of one year and eight months' missionary labor here with those of six years and a half at Apaiang could not be otherwise than — I had almost said — painful." S.J. Whitmee of the LMS wrote from Sydney to Honolulu to inform the Hawaiian church that Samoan missionaries were moving north from Tuvalu into southern Kiribati, following an understanding between the British and Hawaiian boards that they should respectively evangelize south and north of the equator. Gradually the way was prepared for the entry of more Samoans to the Gilberts, the gradual withdrawal of Hawaiians, and the handing over of direction to the LMS on the outbreak of World War I.

The delineation of the equator as a frontier between the missions left Bingham free to cultivate Abemama, just north of the line. Since 1851 Abemama in central Kiribati, with its nearby subject islets of Kuria and Aranuka, had been a tiny absolute monarchy under an astute ruler, Tem Baiteke, who traded in coconut oil with Randell and his partners, but denied all outsiders the right to reside. In 1851 Baiteke coolly wiped out nine foreign adventurers residing on Abemama, and another twenty-five on Kuria and Aranuka. Thereafter he ran his sealed-off realm efficiently through a self-appointed hierarchy of chiefs. He encouraged trade, but only through a tiny island at the entrance to his lagoon, where he imported the goods and ideas he wanted in return for his valuable coconut surplus. The ingenious social arrangements were policed by the ultimate sanction of imported muskets. Missionaries were included among the prohibited imports.

The mission made several contacts with Abemama, probably through Randell. In 1867 Bingham asked for an interview with Baiteke, but received "a very short but decisive" reply that declined to "have anything to do with the missionary business." In 1873, when he visited again, Bingham had the satisfaction of becoming the first foreigner since 1851 to be allowed to sail a ship into the Abemama lagoon. On 5 July Binoka, Baiteke's degenerate son and successor, met the *Morning Star* at the entrance. He was observed to be "a short thick-set corpulent man of twenty-five or thirty years, dressed in hat, shirt, & pants, and sporting a red handkerchief. As he drew near," Bingham wrote, "I saluted him in English with 'Good morning Binoka.' He at once replied with remarkably good accent and a pleasant smile, 'Good morning Mr Bingham.'"

The visitors were escorted to interview Baiteke, "one of the most famous of the Gilbert Islands kings," who commanded respect, with "a mild face, fine head, a good figure," and an unexpectedly positive welcome. The missionaries reminded him of his previous negative decision; they told him they would not try to stay if he was still of that mind. Baiteke replied, "We will not send you away." He gave permission "to land one or more American or Hawaiian or Gilbertese Island missionaries at once, if any could be spared." Bingham was elated. "Bless the Lord!" he said, "the point is gained." He gave Baiteke a copy of his own recently printed translation of the New Testament and was permitted to beat up the lagoon and anchor directly opposite Baiteke's "capitol." In September he returned, to leave a Gilbertese preacher, Moses Kanoaro, who was not a great success. Kanoaro found the sexual promiscuity on Abemama hard to resist; he became abjectly subservient to Binoka, in whose favour Baiteke abdicated in 1878. Although Binoka made some show of becoming Christian, he was not deterred from maintaining his tyrannical despotism over his subjects, including the pastor, whom he ultimately deported for dabbling in the copra trade. Binoka refused to proscribe polygamy; he retained his own sycophantic harem, though he was reported to be impotent. Toward the end of his reign he tried to foster a syncretic religion of his own. When Roman Catholic missionaries arrived in 1891 he encouraged them, thereby following his characteristic policy of divide and rule.

Toward the close of 1874 Bingham suffered from bouts of recurrent dysentery and debility. His fragile health gave warning of the end of his time in the Gilberts. Clarissa Bingham became pregnant in the following May; her only previous recorded pregnancy had miscarried. Together they took the needed drastic decisions — to leave their Happy Home on Abaiang and board a passing ship for Apia, Samoa. Bingham was treated by a doctor; he was allowed to go on, still in a critical state, to Levuka, Fiji, and from there to Auckland, New Zealand. Finally, the long way round, they arrived in Honolulu on 8 November, in time for Hiram Bingham III to be born in that same month. Bingham's health was restored. They settled down in a house in suburban Punahou, called it *Gilbertinia,* and began the two major labours of their later years — the pastoral care of Gilbertese migrants in Hawaii, and the completion of their Bible translation. The revision of the New Testament and the translation of the Old became a tribute, rendered *in absentia* and with love, to the people of the Gilberts.

On 11 April 1893, in the presence of numerous high toned Honolulu Christian witnesses, Bingham dictated the last verse of the Book of Malachi to Moses Kaure, one of his converts from Abaiang, who had come from his work as catechist in the Gilberts to be adviser and amanuensis — a current account of the event calls him Bingham's "native pundit." Often credited with being one of the few people ever to translate the Bible single handed, Bingham was in fact materially helped by his wife, who knew Greek and was called a "born linguist" by her husband. This accomplished woman from the intelligent community of Northampton, Massachusetts, while playing the part of a conventional helpmeet discussed the rendering of every verse with her husband, who resurrected his Hebrew before setting out on the Old Testament.

A photographer attended at the translation of the final verse in the cosy context of the Punahou living room. The godly faces in the picture were a "pleasant perpetuation of the scene of the great undertaking." Bingham presented the Hawaiian Board with a Hawaiian Government Bond for $1,000 so that the interest could be used for circulation of the Bible among the Gilbertese; the sum represented the accumulated savings bank interest on $200 given twenty years earlier to the Binghams by grateful English traders in the Gilberts, Randell and friends, who had the good fortune to marry Gilbertese girls trained in the missionaries' home. Bingham was presented with a gold watch, Clarissa with "a brooch with gold bible pendant," and Mr and Mrs Kaure with "a small purse of gold."

Unfortunately Moses Kaure disappointed his mentors by relapsing into wild pre-christian customs after he returned home to Abaiang. He took the lead in closing the schools and urging people to go back to their old dances. Had the years of living in a black suit and conforming to Honolulu church custom been too much for him? The impassive face of his tightly buttoned-up wife and the correct jacket on his young son, cutely called Morning Star, suggest some of the tensions generated by their exile. Later Kaure wrote penitently to the Binghams, regretting the excesses of his homecoming. Bingham continued his own work among the community of Gilbertese plantation labourers in Hawaii. He compiled a dictionary, outlived Clarissa by five years, and died in Baltimore, Maryland, in 1908 at the age of 77.

In Kiribati, as Hawaiian teachers were gradually eased out, a new form of Christianity would appear in 1888 — Roman Catholicism, brought by the French Missionaries of the Sacred Heart (MSC) (pages 288ff).

TUVALU — POLYNESIAN BRIDGE

THE LONDON MISSIONARY SOCIETY followed a northwesterly track from Samoa to the Gilberts. A man from Manihiki in the Cooks, Erikana, who is called Elekana in Tuvalu (formerly the Ellice Islands) provided the stimulus for the LMS to include the Ellice group in its annual missionary cruises from Samoa (page 118). Elekana landed on the most southerly atoll of Tuvalu, Nukulaelae, in 1861, one of a group of storm-blown drifters. They found the culture and language closely related to their own, and to Samoan.

TO LIVE AMONG THE STARS

Elekana found one Cook Island woman present who could interpret for him. Elekana, a deacon of the church on Manihiki, where the Rarotongan missionary Maretu had worked for almost two years, had trained for three years at Malua and was placed on Nukufetau, Tuvalu, in 1865. Two Samoans and their wives accompanied him; Matatia was set to work on Funafuti, where Elekana had influenced the chief, Kaitu, as he returned from his earlier stay on Nukulaelae; Ioane followed up Elekena's contacts on Nukulaelae itself.

Murray noted features favouring the work of his Samoans in the group. Already on Nui, where a form of Gilbertese was spoken and on Vaitupu, there were signs of the influence of the Hawaiian mission (page 152). Co-ordination of effort and aim between the LMS and ABCFM followed; for the LMS, experience in Tuvalu became a stepping-stone to the southern Gilberts. Several resident traders on the scattered atolls of Tuvalu were open to Christian penetration as favouring contact and trade, particularly Jack O'Brien of Funafuti, who was resident there for more than forty years, advised the chiefs, married a local woman, aided the mission and played a part in resisting Peruvian slavers. These traders supplied copra to the visiting ships of Godeffroys, a German trading house operating out of Samoa, and to Sydney-based traders. In the ocean-bound rhythm of their lives it became obvious that ships from Apia appeared either to drop missionaries or pick up copra; some did both. Trade and mission were two aspects of continuing contact and goodwill; at times the two became so intertwined, as the number of Samoan pastors pastors multiplied, that trader and missionary became partners dominating a single island, occasionally to the detriment of a local chief.

The LMS generally worked first with the chiefs on the atolls, since their goodwill was essential for the settlement of a pastor. In all thirty-six Samoans, all married, served in Tuvalu. Their task was made smoother by the close relationship between Samoan and the language of Tuvalu; climatically, the life on the atolls was subject to drought and storm, but not unhealthy; the total population was fewer than 2,400, giving each well trained Samoan scope to convert and nurture the few hundred people on his appointed speck of land. Roman Catholics and other missions did not appear until the middle of the twentieth century, with the exception of a single Roman Catholic Tokelauan catechist on Funafuti, who was not accepted by the island. Tuvalu, now the world's second smallest sovereign nation, is overwhelmingly Congregational in religious composition.

The years 1864 to 1869 made transport difficult for the LMS in Tuvalu. *John Williams I,* launched in Britain in 1844 to take the place of John Williams' *Camden,* was wrecked on Pukapuka in the Cooks in 1864 and replaced by *John Williams II,* which was in turn wrecked in 1867 on Niue. *John Williams III* came into service in 1869. She never returned to England, but was serviced within the Pacific. Before she was sold and replaced by *John Williams IV* in 1894 she had become the lifeline for the Samoan outstations in Tuvalu and Kiribati. All these "little ships" of the LMS were paid for by the pennies of children in Sunday Schools; they fired the children's imaginations with missionary concern and made their prayers vivid with tales of islanders who carried the gospel across their own ocean.

When Murray revisited in November 1866 on the Samoan-based Hamburg trader *Susanne* he was on the look-out for two other Samoan couples who had been brought by the *Dayspring*, the vessel of the New Hebrides Presbyterian Mission, to join the three pioneers; Kirisome had been placed on Nui, where there was already a worshipping group, thanks to Hawaiian infiltration; Peni had been sent to Vaitupu. Murray commented on the symptomatic changes already taking place. Kirisome on Nui had established his ascendancy in a conflict with a local resident trader, Robert Waters, known as Bob, who was eventually forced off the island along with his three wives. Gradually, over the next twenty-five years, coconut and cash were contributed to the mission by worshipping converts, to cover expenses and make the pastors self-supporting. Inevitably the process meant that the resident traders had leaner pickings, though they tried to compensate by importing building materials — even "French windows" — for the pastors. By 1872 full self-support had been achieved by the churches; in 1892, when Britain declared a protectorate and began to collect taxes, the heyday of the traders was over. The church's role in the change was important, but its climb to a position of decisive influence was also favoured by the withdrawal of Godeffroys from the Tuvalu trade, their gradual replacement by the Australian-based firm of Henderson & Macfarlane and a recession in the copra business in the 1890s.

When Whitmee visited again in 1870 on the new *John Williams* he found Elekana, the nominal hero-pioneer of the Tuvalu church, going about the game of king-making and trade on Nukufetau. The LMS, by a long-standing rule, forbade direct trading by pastors, as distinct from exhortation to free-will offering for the benefit of the church. Elekana had engineered the deposition of the chief and set up his own puppet. Whitmee had to move him. Peni, who had made considerable progress on Vaitupu, was ill; he too had to be taken back to Samoa, to the distress of the weeping local people.

Samoan clerical ascendancy had begun to establish itself. The pastors used the Samoan Bible and hymn book, creating a specialized language for religion, though the local vernacular prevailed in conversation and all other matters. The Tuvalu people accepted what occurred as an aspect of the new *tapu* associated with Christianity. Two forms of Tuvalu community discourse were in the making — one in the church, the other outside it. Samoan pastors and their wives and children, practising family prayer each day and gathering converts into a new charmed circle of literacy, music and prayer, established the right of their monotheistic faith over the older totemic, ghostly and fetishistic cults of the atolls. The church's presence brought about a further social change: on most islands scattered hamlets coalesced into villages under the Samoans, partly from fear of local spirits.

The magisterial, and usually iconoclastic progress of the Samoans was dramatized by the unusually swift success of one of them, Ioane of Nanumanga, "the most remarkable pastor ever to come to Tuvalu." On the first Sunday he spent ashore in September 1875, Ioane, who came from Sa'anapu on Upolu, preached to twenty-four people. He induced his congregation to give up Sunday work on the second Sunday; then, on the following Friday, he talked to the people of the island about their gods, persuading them that the Christian God, as the imperishable creator, made and controlled their sacred pillar, their fish totems and sacred cuckoo, and the shooting star in the night. Later the chiefs, who were already wavering, took him into the bush to share their fear of actually destroying the sacred objects of the old religion.

Ioane said he would do it himself. Next day he summoned everyone and solemnly removed and broke the sacred necklets of five chiefs, their symbolic link with ancestor gods. Spared from annihilation and encouraged, the chiefs told him he could go ahead and strip the god-houses of skulls, sacred stones, clubs and spears, together with wooden images dedicated to the feared shooting star. He reverently arranged for the care and burial of the skulls beneath the *malae* and turned the clubs and spears into a railing round the court house, the meeting place of the people. He did the same with skulls and sacred objects sacred to each extended family, suggesting that one of the god-houses be used for Christian worship on the third Sunday of his stay among them. They declined, deciding prudently instead to use their court house, a less spiritually awesome site, as a "temporary chapel." On that day ninety-eight people attended worship. The transformation of Nanumanga had begun with a dramatic sequence of persuasion and overthrow. Significantly, the chiefs — living to north of Nui and Vaitupu, and exposed before Ioane's arrival to Hawaiian influence from the adjacent Gilberts — were ripe for the change.

Ioane's initial steps indicate that he began by pleading the incontrovertibly superior *mana* of the all-creating and all-ruling Father God of the Christians. His prophetic symbolism conveyed a riveting sense of awe; it appeared to be a contest between rival spiritual powers. Afterwards, Bible in hand, using pulpit and school, he spent ten years on Nanumanga, acquainting the people in more detail with the person of Christ and the doctrines of the Incarnation and Atonement. What commenced in Tuvalu as substitution of a single omnipotent power for a multitude of previously revered spirit forces focussed, in time, in forms of regular worship and prayer in the home and village — the steady explanation of the Sermon on the Mount, teaching about the Kingdom of God. At the heart of the transition from the old religion to the new stood the influence of Christ, shaping in the lingering atmosphere of the old beliefs new ethical demands and resources, contributing in the Tuvalu Islands, as in Kiribati, to eventual definitions of national character.

Ioane's work "received unanimous praise from a succession of visiting missionaries." The same could hardly be said of every one of the Samoan pastors, who were visited forty-five times by deputations from Samoa in the years up to 1906; the work done in that period bound the Tuvalu and Samoan people together in a fluctuating relationship. As Tuvalu produced its own pastors they were sent to Malua for training. The Ellice Islands became a district of the Samoan mission. Both peoples had Polynesian ancestors. At the same time, because the logic of mission geography and British administration conspired at the end of the nineteenth century to make Tuvalu part of the British Gilbert and Ellice Islands Colony, with its churches, they were also exposed to Gilbertese influences from the north calculated to estrange them further from the tradition represented by the buried skulls of their ancestors. Their everyday language, related to Samoan, but distinct, became a repository of their special identity. The first hundred years of Tuvalu's Christian history contain an undercurrent: ministers and laity, many of whom went for more advanced education in Samoa, retained a strong sense of the family unity of their atolls, culminating in final re-assertions of independence by both church and people.

Perhaps the most remarkable enterprise of the Tuvalu church has been the part played by Tuvaluans in "evangelization of the world." Atoll dwellers, feeling the fascination of visiting ships, tend to leave home for various reasons as sea rovers. In the church a sense of obligation to share the message of revelation and atonement accounts more largely for the foreign service rendered by at least seventy-nine Tuvaluan missionaries, probably many more, in eight different regions of the Pacific. In most cases only the Christian first name has been recorded; wives and children remain nameless, except in folk memory. Today, as in other parts of the Pacific, students and families are piecing together and checking what they can disinter or remember of the lives of those who contributed to the day-to-day work and decision-making involved in spreading Christianity in distant villages in places as remote from each other as the Tokelau Islands and Papua.

The church in Tuvalu owed its spirit and form mainly to the labours of Samoans and Tuvaluans themselves; white resident educational missionaries came only for limited intervals before 1958, when Samoan district status was finally dropped; a permanent LMS missionary was stationed at Funafuti to prepare for full autonomy under local leadership, which came in 1969.

TO LIVE AMONG THE STARS

EVANGELIZATION IN MICRONESIA was a convergence of several missionary movements. The first, directed and staffed in Hawaii, continued to be morally and materially supported from Boston. The second arose out of partnership between Samoans and the LMS, with a chain of command extending to London. A third line of partial dependence for the LMS extended to the Australian colonies. By mid-century Dr Robert Ross, the formidable old school Calvinist minister of Sydney's influential Pitt Street Independent Church, had become the colonial agent of the LMS. Other Congregational Independents in Hobart, South Australia and Melbourne exercised the nonconformist conscience in the Pacific through missions; some merchants among them also sniffed out possible trade routes. British missionaries from Samoa tended to retire to Australia; their presence and writings kept the Australian public informed about the islands. Ships in and out of Australian ports brought copra — and sometimes fresh word of the "glorious Gospel of the blessed God."

As Polynesian missionaries entered Micronesia they gave local churches a flavour partly derived from their own origins. The Christians of Ponape, Kusaie, the Mortlock Islands and Truk were proud of their Hawaiian and American connections long before the modern political era of atomic bases and economic dependence. The Marshallese never forget their Hawaiian pioneers. In Kiribati, Hawaiian humour and the American accent were later modified by incoming British stoicism and reserve; these qualities found an answering strain in the silent side of the Gilbertese, who have always known how to endure. The Gilbertese absorbed the Samoan Christian occupation as they had once previously evaluated and absorbed Samoan invaders, assimilating what they prized, but waiting for pastors and deacons of their own to put an independent stamp on their church. The people of Tuvalu, a largely Polynesian diaspora long exposed to a Micronesian environment, lay at the point where the converging missions met. They too gathered Christianity, along with a touch of British capacity to adapt and "muddle through," into the formation of an independent church that is now directed — under God — by them alone.

7

Melanesian Footholds I

Vanuatu

WHEN JOHN WILLIAMS was clubbed to death in the waves at Dillon's Bay, Erromanga, on 20 November 1839, as he tried to struggle back to the *Camden's* waiting boat, a shudder from unfamiliar shores passed through the English-speaking Protestant world. One of its heroes had fallen in crossing an unknown religious frontier into the western Pacific. The very name Melanesia, distinct from Polynesia, had yet to be coined. Few white men knew the inhabitants of the islands between Vanuatu and New Guinea. A few explorers, whalers, seekers of bêche-de-mer and sandalwood traders, together with an assortment of deserters from ships and fugitives from justice, had made contact. They found the populations blacker than the Polynesians; hence they eventually called the area Melanesia, with a hint that black must be dark, threatening, unlovely.

The Melanesian world did indeed differ from both Polynesia and Micronesia in many ways, though on its eastern rim it had been modified by the influence of other parts of Oceania. Old migrations of Polynesian drifters and adventurers had established various pockets by voyaging, battle and intermarriage. The Polynesian outlier islands, such as the Loyalty group off New Caledonia's mainland, Futuna and Emae in Vanuatu, Sikaiana and Vanikoro in the Solomons, influenced custom and social structure in some coastal areas of the larger islands, bringing with them hereditary forms of high chiefly authority.

TO LIVE AMONG THE STARS

In most parts of Melanesia social rank depended to a greater extent on individual initiative and talent. A person could become an acknowledged Big Man in his own lifetime by prowess in war, or he could amass wealth, measured in pigs, women, shell money or human skulls. The ingenuity he showed was normally mingled with magic. Men, once initiated into adult life, could blaze their own trails to higher social status. Local Big Men in most cases stayed within their own terrain except in times of active trading and of war. Few islands had been unified under single dynasties or horizontally stratified into rigid social classes as in many parts of Polynesia.

Patterns of early immigration and the influence of geography compartmentalized neighbouring societies in other ways. Bush people were separated from sea people, except during warlike forays and trading; occupants of one inland valley were often separated from those in other adjacent valleys. Hundreds of barely related languages, scattered across the whole region, accentuated unfamiliarity and a competitive spirit. The question "war or trade?" arose when separated groups met through their cautious representatives, frequently women sent as go-betweens. As a result, both feuds and trading flourished. The Melanesians used pierced and finely polished shell money, suspended on necklets, to carry on trade; they were thus psychologically able to comprehend would-be tycoons from white society when these arrived. The habit of shrewd bargaining long preceded the appearance of gun-toting whites, with their new tools and skills.

When these white men arrived in larger numbers to settle down they imported rifles, liquor, tobacco and trade goods — metal tools and cloth. Whalers, the bêche-de-mer fishermen and sandalwood cutters were followed by Christian missions. In some places the missions depended on the experience of sandalwooders who preceded them; they were, however, affronted by the sandalwooders' business practices, their morals and their profane language. Nevertheless, many Melanesians were as frontal in method as their white trading partners. Missionaries, both white and Polynesian, adapted to these quicker eyeball-to-eyeball transactions as contact proceeded.

Melanesian artifacts used in fishing, hunting, gardening, house-building, war and religious ceremonies reflected the dynamism of the people. Their food dishes of polished wood, the gleaming pearl-shell eyes of their totems and ancestor figures, the imagery of their carved log drums, expressed the religio-magical belief systems underlying their work, whether at sea, in their gardens or in the village. Priests, who were often Big Men in their own right, guarded the rites and spells uniting the people with productive nature. Sorcerers, on the other hand, through incantation and spell, regulated the malign activities of the omnipresent manifold spirits and ghosts of the dead. Reverence and fear before the supernatural penetrated all aspects of life. The spirits of nature and the souls of the departed were believed to be alive with *mana*, power, working

MELANESIAN FOOTHOLDS I

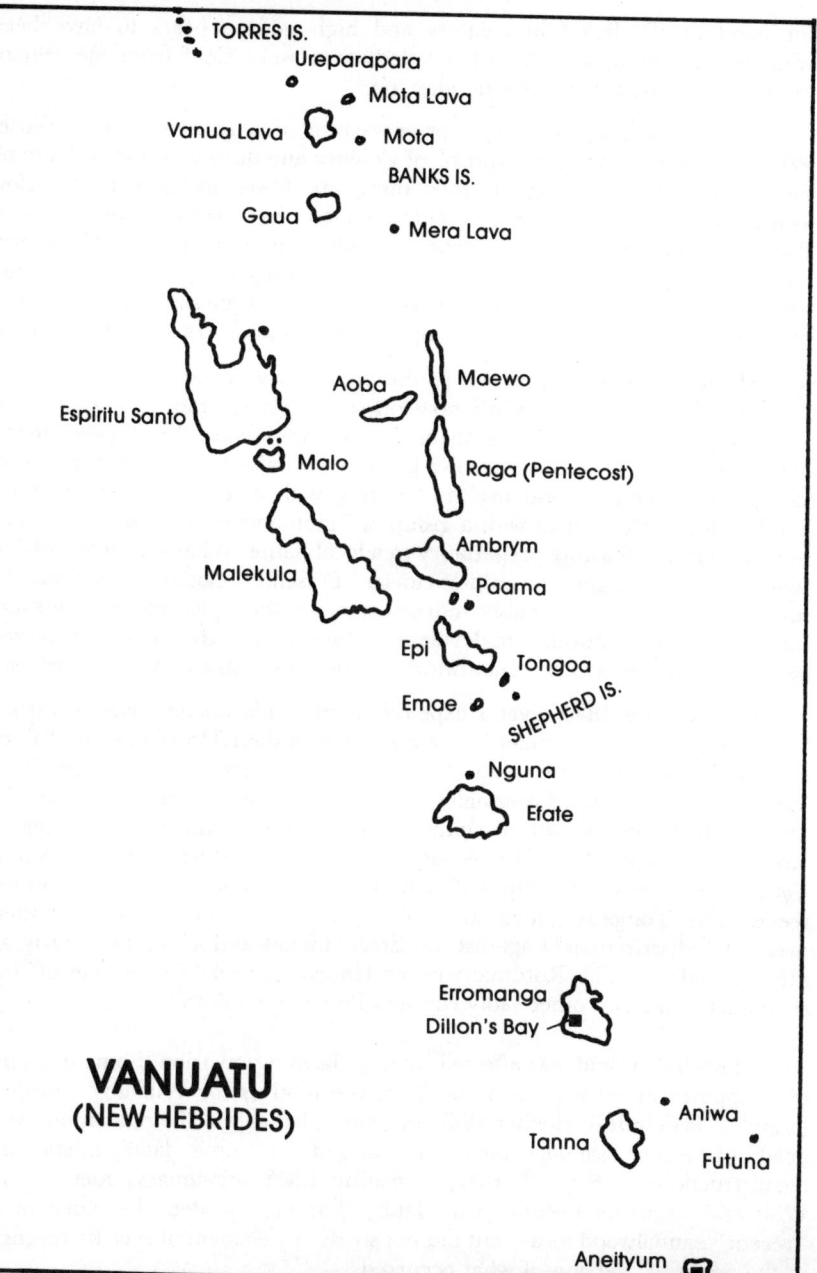

for good or ill. Belief in creators and high gods appears to have been widespread, but they were not invoked; they were aloof from the religio-magical complex governing everyday life.

Melanesian peoples had little prior warning of Christianity's appearance. White men who survived the threats of violence and disease and settled among them did not teach religion; thus there are fewer parallels to the slow awareness of the coming of a new religion that created expectancy in Polynesia. Traders brought wealth; preachers were suspected of sorcery, particularly if they unknowingly brought fatal influenza or measles epidemics with them. In the smaller and more bellicose Melanesian societies quick murder was an accepted way of giving notice to newcomers not to stay longer.

Most of this was unknown to the people who stood anxiously on the *Camden's* deck, or in the ship's boat off-shore, on the morning when John Williams landed. He was accompanied by Cunningham, the *Camden's* mate, and James Harris, an unsuspecting layman who was cruising on the *Camden* for his enlightenment and health. Landing with a few small gifts in their hands, they made contact with a group of Erromangans at a time when they were engaged in feasting preparatory to a local battle. What they made of two solidly built strangers in mid-Victorian Dissenter clothing can only be surmised; they were probably more suspicious than pleased; such visitors might be supernaturally malevolent. They found themselves squeezed between a known enemy to landward and unknown strangers from the sea.

In 1829 and 1830 several expeditions of sandalwooders had disturbed Erromanga. Captain Samuel P. Henry, a son of the LMS pioneer to Tahiti, had led one of them, bringing a labour force of aggressive Tongans. Two other ships, commanded originally by High Chief Boki of Hawaii (page 52), carried Hawaiians aiming at conquest. Boki's own ship, after touching at Rotuma, was lost at sea. His second vessel arrived and its crew set to work. Yet another competitive ship, with 200 Rotumans on board, appeared on the scene. The Tongans joined in local conflicts; the Hawaiians used their firearms indiscriminately against the Erromangans and Tongans. Nearly all died of malaria. The Rotumans never landed; they helped to take off the remnants of the two other sadly ravaged Polynesian crews.

The whole island was affected by this alarming invasion. Some memory of it appears in subsequent accounts of the motives for Williams' murder, though it is doubtful whether Williams was killed as specific retaliation for a deed of recent sandalwooders as alleged in some later missionary reconstructions. George Turner, a visiting LMS missionary, met two of Williams' assassins twenty years later; Turner repeated the story of a "recent" sandalwood foray, but did not stress any element of specific revenge in the assassins' version of what occurred.

MELANESIAN FOOTHOLDS I

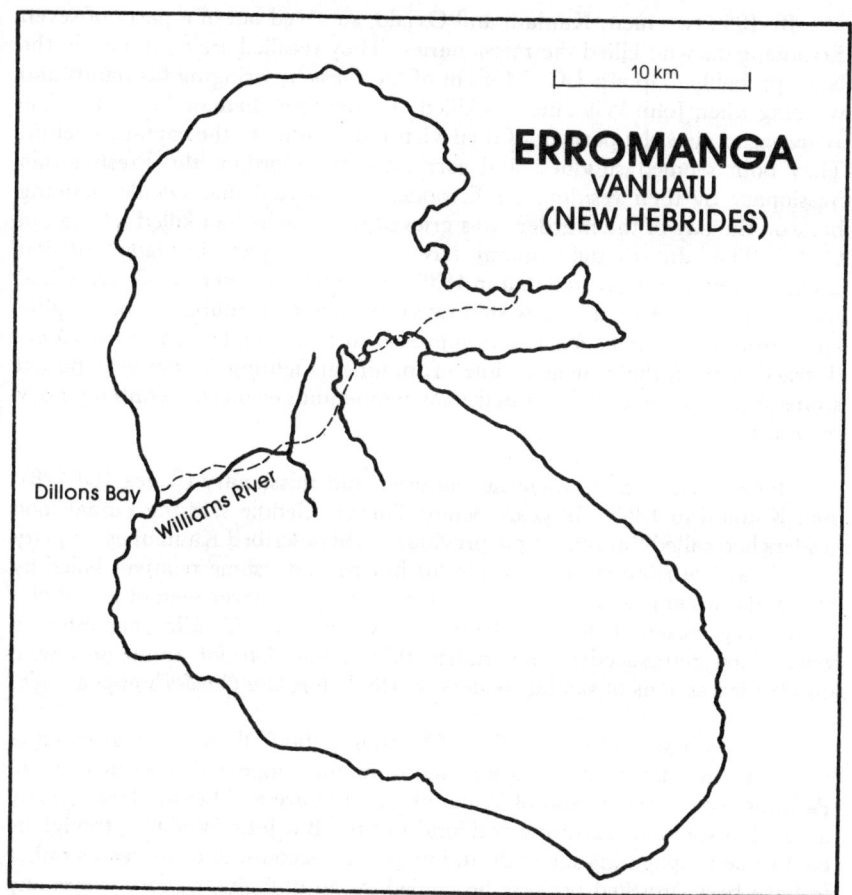

Williams, Harris and Cunningham went inland along a small stream. The Erromangans who approached them seemed uncertain how to act. Turner reported that some of them wanted to attack the missionaries, others did not. When Williams and Harris approached the spot where taro and yams had been piled ready for their feast, they retreated and hid. The men from the *Camden* were probably violating a taboo by approaching the food. On a signal from a conch-shell trumpet, their assailants came out from the bush. All ran for their lives. Cunningham regained the boat. The Erromangans first struck and killed Harris, beside the stream. Williams hurried back to the beach; he was clubbed on the head and pierced by arrows as he tried to wade back to the ship's boat. Both men were eaten.

TO LIVE AMONG THE STARS

By 1859 two men, Kauiaui and Ovialo, survived out of a party of seven Erromangans who killed the missionaries. They recalled seeing a man in the boat, probably Captain J.C. Morgan of the *Camden*, wringing his hands and weeping when John Williams was killed. Turner took them on board the *John Williams* to view the portrait of their victim that hung in the captain's cabin. They both seemed subdued and sorry. George Gordon, the Presbyterian missionary by then residing on Erromanga, reported that Ovialo, looking back on the day of the murder, was grieved to know he had killed a "man of God." The after-thought might have been prompted by later mission teaching, but also suggested that in 1839, only ten years after the Tongans had come to Dillon's Bay, any new ship raised suspicion of trouble to come, quite apart from the anxiety felt about approach to food supplies and unwelcome distraction from the rear at a time of imminent fighting. A ten-year period seems short to people who can make any momentous events feel contemporary by oral recall.

John Geddie, a Presbyterian minister and missionary (pages 168-178), met Kauiaui in 1853, six years before Turner. Geddie said the sandalwood traders had called "at some time previous." He described Kauiaui as "a petty chief," who attributed his action to his having had "some relatives killed by the sandal wood traders," and said "the natives had never seen or heard of a missionary vessel before." Kauiaui's account to Geddie suggested a generalized retrospective fear rather than retaliation for some otherwise unrecorded actions of sandalwooders shortly before the *Camden's* appearance.

Was Williams a martyr? The "Christian public" thought so, grieving as they read the flood of eulogistic literature that appeared after his death. Paintings of the event, and of Williams' stout figure and benign face, greatly assisted missionary recruiting and fund-raising. But John Williams, though he died while propagating his faith, did not die on account of it; he seems rather to have been attacked because he landed on an unfamiliar shore where any ship spelt suspicion. If a more general sense is given to the term "martyr," Williams' restless explorations and dangers, including the landing at Dillon's Bay, were part of his dedicated obedience — the service of the Word on behalf of the peoples of the Pacific. At the close of his career Williams was already "weary in well-doing." When he crossed over to Melanesia he was face-to-face with presentiments of premature age, failing powers and the possibility of a violent end.

Two days before he died, as the *Camden* approached Erromanga, Williams wrote in his journal:

> This is a memorable day, a day which will be transmitted to posterity and the record of the events which have this day transpired will exist

after those who have taken an active part in them have returned into the shades of oblivion, and the results of this day will be ...

No more follows. In the events at Dillon's Bay an inwardly complicated man gave himself in a cause that claimed him in and through his compulsive drive and ambition. John Williams was not a saint; he saw himself as a forgiven sinner whose aim was to share what he had received. For many Pacific peoples his life's passion was symbolically passed on by the way he died. A long succession of Islander missionaries followed in the wake of the *Camden*. A.W. Murray wrote:

> At a meeting of the missionaries of the Samoan mission held on the arrival of the *Camden* with the stunning intelligence that the first mover in the work of evangelizing Western Polynesia had fallen it was resolved to take up the work at once.

In the following nine years Cook Islanders and Samoans were taken by the *John Williams* to settle, mostly in pairs, on the islands of Aniwa, Futuna, Aneityum, Tanna and Efate. They were exposed to violence and disease, baffled by language problems and culture shock. Sometimes they introduced infections that ravaged the local people. The epidemics were attributed to local *natmasses*, spirit forces, who were considered to be angered by the new religion. But the most deadly enemy of the LMS teachers was the unsuspected *Anopheles* mosquito; from unaffected Polynesia the missionaries migrated to malarial islands. The most common cause of removal and death was listed as "fever and ague," then believed to be caused directly by living on low-lying land. John Williams left three Samoans, Lalolangi, Salomea and Mose, on Tanna in 1839. Salomea died; the others had to be returned after a few years to Samoa. Thomas Heath reinforced the group in 1840, taking Pomare and Vaiofanga. All the teachers were ill that year; Pomare died.

In May 1840 Lasalo and Taniela were left on Erromanga, though prudently not at Dillon's Bay. They were maltreated, starved out and withdrawn. The LMS tried a new approach on Erromanga in 1849, when four Erromangans — Joe, Mana, Nivavave and Nebore — were taken off to be trained at Malua for three years. Nivavave died on the return voyage in 1852; Mana, returning home, commended Christianity to the Dillon's Bay people. We have a glimpse of him on 22 May, "standing on the deck with his countrymen, to whom he was reading and speaking about Jesus. He was reading about His advent in the flesh, and pointing to his own hands and feet to convey an idea of the crucifixion — and to heaven, where Christ now is." On Erromanga he was joined by two Rarotongans and their wives, Vaa and Akatangi; he "continued steadfast" until we lose sight of him in 1860.

Progress before 1848 proved intolerably slow. Each annual visit added to the roll of losses. The LMS changed its policy by recruiting, locally, people who were relatively accustomed to malaria and could use family, culture and language as effective points of contact. They continued to be accompanied by Polynesians. The new policy coincided with the beginning of an LMS partnership with the newly launched Presbyterian mission to the New Hebrides. The first Presbyterian missionary, John Geddie from Nova Scotia, began his work on Aneityum with LMS support.

Geddie, a colonial Scot, was born in Banff, Scotland, and brought up in Nova Scotia. His evangelical and missionary enthusiasms grew in the atmosphere of revival generated in Scotland by the work of Robert and James Haldane. The Secession and Relief Churches and the Scottish Congregationalists participated in the fervour, to the benefit of the LMS. The Presbyterian Synod of Nova Scotia, within which Geddie came forward for the ministry, was connected with the Secession churches in Scotland.

The theology and teaching method of the New Hebrides Presbyterian Mission reflected the emotionally warm Calvinism of the late Evangelical Revivals in Scotland. The early missionaries were loyal, doctrinally, to the Scots and Westminster Confessions and the Shorter Catechism, but they were stronger on unction than precision; the head had become captive to the swelling heart. Their cultural presuppositions were thoroughly Scots. The names New Caledonia and New Hebrides acted on them like magnets. Their concern was first to convert, then educate; to "raise" the converts by schooling them and forming them into churches governed by properly "erected" Kirk Sessions, with clear disciplinary procedures. Being primarily busy with this process, the mission did not give much time to ethnology. Students of the order of William Ellis, W.W. Gill or R.H. Codrington (pages 28, 121, 185) did not emerge.

Though in co-operation with the LMS, the Presbyterian Mission was distinct. It was born and bred in a church mould, not as a trans-denominational "society." Geddie came as the envoy of the Presbyterian Church in Nova Scotia. Against advice he sailed with his wife precariously round the Horn to Honolulu in an unsuitable ship; thence he joined the LMS in Samoa; he found a nest of Scots missionaries with the same religious background as himself. Archibald Murray, on Tutuila, with whom he resided, gave him orientation and several months of virtual in-service training. He learned to speak Samoan. His fellow countrymen of the LMS in Samoa were George Turner, Henry Nisbet, Alexander Macdonald, William Mills, Charles Hardie, George Drummond and Ebenezer Buchanan. Most of them visited him at some stage during his time on Aneityum.

The annual cruises of the LMS ships brought Rarotongan and Samoan teachers and their wives to be stationed in the villages on Aneityum, or on Erromanga, Futuna, Tanna, Aniwa and Efate. Later Geddie and his wife

Charlotte travelled occasionally with the *John Williams* as far afield as the Loyalty Islands, further south, partly for the benefit of their health. The *John Williams* was often in the port of Sydney to be fitted and supplied, and to drop and pick up missionaries in transit. Sydney soon became a source of supply and support for the Presbyterians in the New Hebrides. Dr Robert Ross, of Pitt Street Independent Church, the colonial agent of the LMS and a former minister of the Church of Scotland and a missionary to Russia, also served the New Hebrides Presbyterians as agent for eleven years, to 1859, without charge. Geddie stayed with him in 1856; when Ross resigned from his service to them the mission thanked him for his interest and his "eminently correct business habits."

In July 1848 Geddie, his wife, and Isaac Archibald (a Nova Scotia lay teacher) and his wife, with Thomas Powell and his wife of the LMS, settled on Aneityum. Powell contracted bad malaria; he wanted to move from the south to the north of the island, but was overruled by the majority. Other tensions developed; Powell withdrew to Samoa at his own request in September 1849, contrary to the advice of Geddie and his colleagues of the LMS. Geddie bluntly "told him that if he left the work under present circumstances he would never look back on the step with comfort." Archibald was another who gave trouble; he was stationed at Ipece on the north coast, where he committed adultery with a local woman, was censured and admonished by Geddie, and "withdrew" to join the sandalwood trading establishment directed by Captain James Paddon.

Charlotte Geddie recorded that Paddon had shown "the greatest kindness ever since our arrival; he is very kind to the natives, and they are very fond of him." She added that he was "engaged in the sandalwood trade, which of course we do not approve of, but I wish that all engaged in the trade would act as humanely as Captain Paddon." The mission received a frame for their house from Paddon, but the relationship soured when Geddie, who was more ready to tolerate the sexual customs of Aneityumese than the diversions of Europeans, took a stand against the acquisition of local women for trifles; he condemned the sandalwooders to their faces among the people of Anelgauhat, where they had their base alongside the mission. Paddon, on his part, refused to discourage widow strangling, thereby further alienating the Presbyterians. By the end of 1851 the opposed goals of the two settlements brought about "a malignant state of feeling" between Geddie and Paddon (with his assistants Edward Rodd and William Underwood). In March 1851 Geddie attributed threats that his house would be burned to behind-scenes hostile activity of the traders. Paddon, whose business was indeed being hindered by Geddie's preaching having drawn off part of his labour force to the mission, confronted the missionaries and lost his temper in a "torrent of abuse."

Archibald, after his misdemeanour, had become Paddon's employee. Geddie refused baptism to Archibald's child, thereby following a Presbyterian rule of order that the sacrament is administered only to the children of believing parents in good standing with the church. Further embarrassment followed when the Anglican Bishop of New Zealand, George Augustus Selwyn, who had already made two visits to Aneityum and formed good relationships with Geddie, explained to him that Anglican discipline permitted baptism irrespective of the sins of the fathers. He baptized the child, after conferring with Geddie and obtaining a regretful Presbyterian *nihil obstat*. A triangular tension between the traders, Selwyn and the Presbyterian Mission emerged. The traders thought of Anglicans as pleasant and accommodating; they called John Geddie "blue Nose."

Ill feeling came to a head on 24 November 1851 when the mission house at Anelgauhat was set on fire by an incendiary named Thero. The motives were obscure. A high local chief, Nohoat, who possessed the *mana* and sacred functions of his rank, had by then attached himself as a protector to the Geddies. The situation was further polarized by the threat of the new religion to the old. The missionaries were observed to be estranged from the sandalwooders — and trading accusations with them; local people suspected of arson could thus transfer responsibility back, by gossip, to rest on Paddon and Underwood. In the aftermath of the fire Thero was seized and accused in the presence of the Geddies by Waihit, another of their catechumens, who had already shown his allegiance to the mission by the symbolic act of cutting his long hair, the "dwelling place" of his *mana*. Two powerfully built Samoan teachers, Munumunu and Sakaio, were present. They seized Thero in an "iron grasp," but were dissuaded from taking more violent reprisals by Geddie, whose constant rule was to avoid evil for evil.

Shortly afterwards Paddon and Underwood appeared, Paddon carrying a large pistol. "I thought the pistol was brought to intimidate the natives," Geddie wrote, "and they thought it was intended for me." Paddon and Underwood swore volubly in the shocked hearing of Charlotte Geddie. "They were both at home in the language of Billingsgate and they added to this much Botany Bay slang which I have not heard elsewhere," wrote Geddie, who thought of the crisis as a turning point in the mission's progress. Paddon said he would leave Aneityum; he eventually did in early 1853, only to be replaced in September of the same year by another trader. The day after his heated encounter with Paddon, Geddie had the satisfaction of dissuading the opposing heathen and Christian groups from fighting about religion. Geddie learned from them that "the cause of the late excitement" over the burning of the house had been a warning Paddon issued to the local people that he intended to quit because of Geddie. "They will have no more tobacco," Geddie wrote, "to the use of which they are slaves."

MELANESIAN FOOTHOLDS I

The involvement of the two brawny Samoan teachers in the crisis points to the importance of the LMS Samoans in the early progress of Christianity in the New Hebrides. They had the status of "assistants." Charlotte Geddie, when she released Samoan wives from household chores to help the men with thatching, said "our servants are Samoans." As Pacific Islanders, the part they played was of greater importance than the status they were assigned. Simeona, a resourceful Samoan who had been on Aneityum since 1842, well in advance of the Geddies, was one of many who lived close to the people in the villages. When the LMS or the Presbyterians visited them they were reported usually as either "doing well" or "fallen away." Details are missing — there are few second names, home villages in Samoa, evaluations of character. Pita (Peter) for instance, recurs in the narrative, but there is more than one Pita; which is which? With Simeona we are on surer ground; he was the early interpreter and guide on Aneityum for Geddie and Powell; he and his companion Pita knew the local language; when Geddie found himself in danger Simeona advised him what to do. There is no way of discovering what contacts in many villages made Simeona acceptable to the people, but his oral transmission of the Christian faith preceded Geddie's acquisition of the language and its assumption of written form. Samoans and Rarotongans prepared the way by unrecorded conversational work; later, when reading and

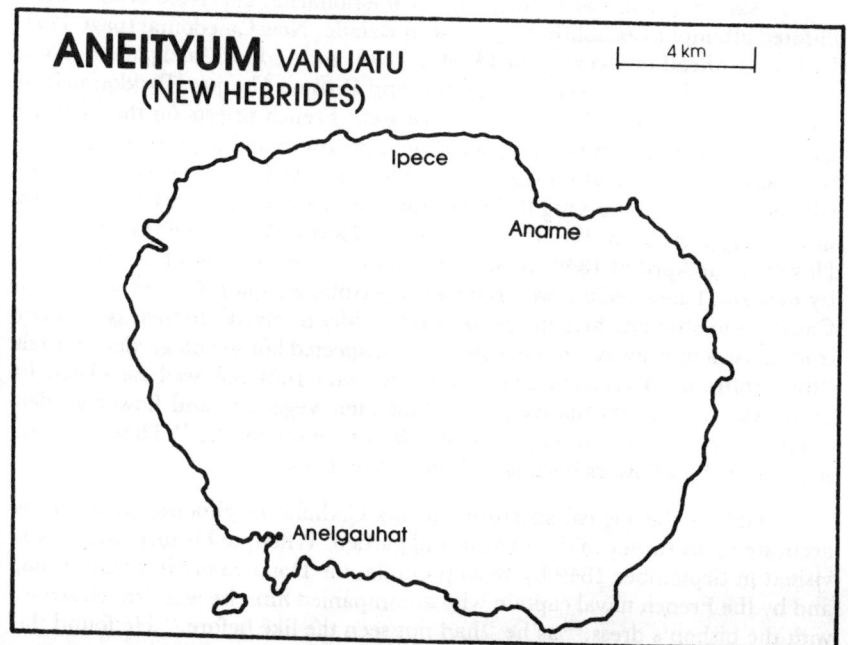

writing followed, the written materials created processes of protracted discussion and evaluation between New Hebrideans and Polynesians. In an oral culture these hidden personal transactions were integral to the growth of the church from within. What they conveyed has to be weighed carefully against the written accounts of white missionary "superiors," whose customs and modes of communication were less readily assimilated.

When Simeona died in a disastrous measles epidemic that broke out in December 1860 he had worked willingly along these lines for eighteen years. "His life was that of a Christian, and his latter end was peace," Geddie wrote. "I feel his loss very much. He gave me much valuable assistance. I was much attached to him, as he shared with us many of the early trials of the Mission." Many of Simeona's colleagues and their often nameless wives shared in similar service — on Erromanga, Tanna, Futuna, Aniwa and Efate. We catch occasional — and sometimes patronizing — references to them in the journals and printed books of the missionaries who nevertheless depended on their endurance and their locally acquired skills.

ENCOUNTER WITH CATHOLICS

A SMALL GROUP of French Marist missionaries, survivors of an earlier ill-fated attempt to establish their cause at Balade, New Caledonia (page 192), had come ahead of Geddie, on 14 May 1848, to reside at Anelgauhat. Their leaders were Fathers Pierre Rougeyron and Prosper Goujon. Paddon helped them to find land and build. "As there were French priests on the island," Geddie wrote, "we felt that no time should be lost in taking possession of it in the name of Reformed Christianity." He remarked that the Aneityumese, who were already observing the Scots Sabbath and the Samoan Christian *tapu* day, disapproved of the Catholics for "sporting" on the Lord's Day. However, in April of 1849, when both missions were hit by a hurricane, and by malaria, fellow-feeling won out over doctrinal scruples. Geddie visited the Catholics to offer any help he could, was "kindly received" in their two-storey iron house a mile away from his own, and inspected house and garden. He felt "the profusion of crimson cloth about the alter [sic] was well calculated to please the taste of the natives" and that their vegetable and flower garden "certainly does credit to the industry and taste of the priests." They, in turn, sent a bunch of flowers back with him to Mrs Geddie.

Geddie's theological strictures on his Catholic neighbours were not as accurate as his survey of their house and garden. When, to his surprise, he was visited in September 1849 by Bishop Guillaume Douarre of New Caledonia, and by the French naval captain who accompanied him, he was "much struck with the bishop's dress," as he "had not seen the like before." He found the bishop "pleasant," though unable to speak English, accepted a bottle of Madeira, and confided with regret to his diary that he had heard "the French priests on this island are Jesuits. This class of Papists," he mused, "are to be dreaded wherever they go. May God preserve these poor islanders from the delusion of popery." The misinformation about the Marists probably came through the LMS, a body of missionaries the Marists called "Methodists" with equal inaccuracy. By July of 1850 Douarre had withdrawn his men from Aneityum. They had "uniformly manifested a friendly disposition"; when they left they invited Mrs Geddie to take what she wanted from their garden. The Catholic attempt "to win the unbelievers through Mary" was not renewed in the New Hebrides until 1887 (page 293).

John Inglis and his wife joined the Geddies on Aneityum on 1 July 1852. Between them, the two men during the next eleven years set a special stamp on the style and method of the Presbyterian Church in the New Hebrides. Inglis had cruised previously to Aneityum and other places in Melanesia with Captain John Erskine of HMS *Havannah*. He came from the Free Church of Scotland by way of New Zealand, where he wanted to be a missionary to the Maoris and chafed at having instead to minister among the settlers of Otago and Southland. John Geddie welcomed him. However, with the punctilio due to the laws of two separated Reformed churches, he delimited their spheres of ministry. Inglis was from the Free Church; Geddie belonged to the earlier Secession Church. Inglis agreed to be stationed at Aname in the north of the island. These niceties between different jurisdictions were softened by the affection the missionaries felt for each other and by their commitment to mission. They agreed about strategy; both men travelled round the coast, visited their inland villages and availed themselves of the *John Williams* and other vessels to go to other islands as opportunity arose. They supervised the Samoan and Rarotongan teachers, studied the language, began translation, founded schools, built neat white houses and churches, and thought little of hardy journeys on Aneityum, along rough tracks in the mountains, up stream beds and in small open boats along the coast.

The white missionaries who served the Presbyterian Church in Vanuatu in the period of its formation established a tradition — ready acceptance of recurrent fever and of perils at sea. The advance of their cause depended also on the sympathy of sacred chiefs — especially Noahat, who had high born relations among the people on Tanna, and Waihit. Womra, a lesser chief from the northern part of the island, befriended Geddie. He helped the missionaries to learn the language, having been sent to Samoa by the LMS before Geddie's arrival to be trained as a Christian teacher; he returned, only to die in February 1851. Womra was "one of the first converts." He had been deeply influenced by Samoan teachers of his own district of Ipece. Geddie, observing him, resolved on a policy of replacing Polynesian teachers with New Hebrideans as soon as possible.

Geddie consistently delegated responsibility to his converts. He believed in the early erection of self-governing presbyteries at the earliest opportunity, unlike many of his successors, who held control in their own hands. As early as February 1852 Geddie commissioned Nakoai as the first Aneityumese teacher in the village of Anniblidai. "I hope to see the day when every village will have its own native teachers," he wrote. On 13 May, when Murray and Sunderland of the LMS visited Aneityum, thirteen persons were baptized and given Holy Communion, six men and seven women, "the first Church that has been formed in Western Polynesia." In March 1853 another church was constituted at Inglis' station, Aname, in the presence of 1,000 people. In the meantime Waihit, Geddie's influential convert, had gone, with Josefa, another man from Aneityum, on a mission to Futuna.

In 1855 Geddie began to ordain deacons, church officers charged, in Presbyterian polity, with practical "temporal" tasks assigned to them by elders and ministers within the "church session." These deacons of Anelgauhat were Simiona, Karaheth, Topoe, Navalak and Neiken — "trustworthy men to attend to the temporalities of the Church." The higher "spiritual" level of the church structure, composed of ruling elders, was not completed by further ordinations until Geddie and Inglis thought the people knew enough of the Bible; only in April 1860, when a large new church building had been completed at Anelgauhat, was the full polity of the church put into effect by the appointment of seven elders, each with a pastoral district of his own. Elders in the Presbyterian Church of the New Hebrides have since that time played an important part in its life; their experience of church government has schooled them for participation in wider social and political contexts.

Charlotte Geddie and Jessie Inglis developed into busy educators of women. They gave time to sewing classes — and the clothing of the previously near-naked. Calico and catechism were complementary; the dubious benefits of sweaty garments in a steamy climate were offset by gains in the status of women. The wives of the missionaries fought to stem the sale of women by chiefs; they opposed wife-beating. "The tables are now turning," Geddie remarked in 1851; "those men who embrace Christianity must give up their barbarous practises and treat their wives with humanity and kindness. Some of the women begin to take advantage of the altered state of things and to retaliate on their husbands."

Geddie was not blind to the effect of the Christian abandonment of polygamy on the cast-off wives; he did his best to arrange marriages for them with other men. Though not a collector of scientific information about the society where he worked, this single-minded Scot, firmly persevering in the faith he had received, evoked loyalty from his new Christians; he "possessed a kind of intuitive sagacity for treating them so as to gain their confidence." He brought the same intuition to his translation work, but Inglis showed greater editorial skill and was chosen to visit England to see the New Testament in Aneityumese through the press in 1859. Both men received honorary doctorates — Inglis from Glasgow, Geddie from Queen's College, Kingston, Ontario. On hearing about his, Geddie declined to make use of it, as being "unsought, undesired, and undeserved."

In 1860, when the conversion of most of Aneityum's estimated population of 4,000 seemed complete, Geddie planned northward expansion through the rest of Vanuatu, using teachers he trained on Aneityum. Presbyterian missionary reinforcements had arrived: George N. Gordon and his wife Ellen for Erromanga; John G. Paton, his wife Mary, Joseph Copeland, John W. Matheson and his wife Mary (Geddie's niece) — all for Tanna. Of these, Paton, energetic and voluble, had most to do with the next phase of the mission's development. He came from the Reformed Presbyterian Church in Scotland. More than any other member of the mission he strove to root its support in Australia. The other new recruits maintained the sending tradition of the Canadian churches.

Geddie contemplated many exploratory voyages northward from Aneityum, to Efate, Epi, Ambrym and Malekula; at first he retained the services of Polynesians from the LMS, but built a training school to equip Aneityumese and other southern New Hebridean teachers. He planned to bring people from further north in the group to be trained there for eventual service in their own islands. To Geddie's delight, a schooner, the *John Knox*, had arrived in 1857 from Glasgow; he would become a "sailing missionary"; the title fitted many of his LMS predecessors and Presbyterian successors in this region of scattered high islands and changeable tropical weather.

Ironically, in 1861, when the future seemed clear, disasters disturbed the far-sighted dream of the mission's founder. A measles epidemic, introduced by a sandalwood vessel, carried off an estimated one-third of the population of Aneityum. The infection began in December 1860 and spread rapidly in the wet, hot season. Conditions favouring its transmission were created among unusually large crowds of people gathered in the recently built schools and churches of the mission, who wore obligatory moist clothing on the upper body — a harbouring place for droplet infection. Many of the most active converts died. A latent streak of melancholy in Geddie's personality was intensified by these events; he admitted he suffered from "much languor of body and much spiritual deadness ... partly caused from climate and the depressing effects of fever and ague."

More reverses followed. Early in March a man named Nihiang was accused of burning down the large new church and school house at Anelgauhat. He and his companions, still attached to the old religious beliefs, thought of the measles epidemic as retaliation by local spirits for the adoption of Christianity. The Christians' faith was tested further when within a week a hurricane followed the fire. Later, on Erromanga, where G.N. Gordon and his wife Ellen had begun work, another devastating epidemic of measles was introduced by the crew of the sandalwood ship *Blue Bell*. On 20 May Gordon and his wife were attacked with tomahawks and murdered. A resident sandalwood trader, Rangi, was accused of having incited the attack. Geddie said Rangi was "a native of India," Inglis said that he had been born in Singapore; both missionaries described him as a Muslim with several wives, hostile to the mission.

Recently questions have been raised about Rangi and his origins. His full name was Toriki Rangi; his descendants on Erromanga are confident that he was a Polynesian, possibly a Tongan. He might at some stage have visited Singapore as a seaman. Even if he had become a Muslim, or had sympathies in that direction, his dislike of the Gordons' religion could have done little more than add to local resentments already felt by the people. Gordon had himself preached that the measles had come as God's "terrible judgement" upon the "catalogue of crimes" of the Erromangans. Gordon estimated that in many places two-thirds of the people had been "cut off." The Erromangans, attributing the scourges to Gordon's God, took desperate action against that God's messengers. Geddie believed Gordon had been unwise to preach as he did about measles epidemics. A lone wolf in the mission, Gordon had declined to be posted on Tanna. His brother James, another east Canadian who had trouble working amicably with his colleagues, also died by violence at Dillon's Bay on Erromanga on 7 March 1872, a fifth victim of fatal encounters on Erromanga between local fears and missionary mistakes.

John G. Paton, another recruit to the mission who suffered early from violent local opposition and diseases, lost his young wife and child on Tanna in 1859. His harrowing account of the dangers leading to his subsequent withdrawal to Aneityum in February 1862 was recorded in his memoirs, an end-of-century missionary best seller. Except for a relatively brief later term on Aniwa, the rest of his career in the cause of the mission was spent mainly as promoter and fund-raiser. He whipped up passionate indignation in Australia about the Melanesian labour trade. His hearty evangelical piety — marked by a surprising certainty (for a Calvinist) about the precise activities of God in his vicinity at given moments — was expressed in a combination of British imperial assurance and paternalist concern for the peoples of the western Pacific.

His later protective solicitude over the mission's converts and potential converts stood in contrast with his acquiescence — to Geddie's undisguised dismay — when punishment was meted out to the "savages" on Tanna who had made his own stay there so unbearable. Geddie, dogged but modest, was against any use of gunboats to teach lessons to the people who had used violence against British nationals on Tanna and Erromanga. While Geddie was away in Canada on his first leave, Inglis, the younger Gordon and Paton all sailed in the *Dayspring* to accompany the British naval vessel *Curacoa* on the occasion of the punitive shelling of a group of Tanna villages. They maintained they did not advocate or urge the action — that they were there as interpreters and guides. But the mission had previously requested an inquiry by the Governor of New South Wales. The visit of the warship was the result. Geddie was affronted by what happened; it ran contrary to his rules of mercy and forgiveness. He and Paton confronted each other angrily before the Presbytery of Sydney. For the mission, the episode marked a turning point in the direction of a "theology of imperialism"; a semi-religious conviction of national destiny and duty was superadded to obedience to the gospel. Paton later summoned the militant imperialist Protestantism of the Australian and New Zealand colonies to a paternal crusade on behalf of the peoples of Vanuatu against encroaching French Roman Catholics and labour traders. Against this background Paton's speeches and journeys on behalf of the mission brought astonishing results in Scotland and Australia. In Australia the new wealth of the gold rush era, flowing into the churches, helped to provide funds for a new *Dayspring,* a symbol of Paton's vigorous approach.

Geddie, who advocated the earliest possible transfer of direction of the mission to the local people, received a further setback toward the end of his service. In 1860 he had asked the Scottish and Nova Scotian churches for advice about completing the local pattern of deacons and elders by the formation of presbyteries, as a step toward full internal self-government for the church. The reply ruled that "the step proposed is in the circumstances premature." The decision left the way open for many years for white missionaries to dominate the proceedings of the developing church by reference to the superior jurisdictions of their sending agencies. Local internal self-government had to wait.

The shadows of failing health and of dissent from the policies of his younger colleagues fell over Geddie's last years. He remained as missionary in charge of the Anelgauhat station, but made journeys to Britain, Canada and the Australian colonies to arrange future use of the *Dayspring,* the printing of the Old Testament and the promotion of the mission's cause. By 1870, when he returned, a new form of trade had appeared in the islands.

Ships in search of labour, for cotton plantations in Fiji and sugar plantations in Australia, had begun to recruit. Serious abuses — specious inducements and outright kidnapping — became common, but for the most part young men migrated willingly, either on their own initiative for the sake of wages, or at the bidding of local chiefs who acted as recruiters. The mission, reacting to abuses, began to call the business "the slave trade," a striking label, but scarcely accurate. Alarm over the morality of the labour traders was mixed with distress over the exodus of recent converts. Many joined the recruiters of their own free will; they longed for more money, for experience of a wider world and for the technology of the white man. The missionaries sought to protect their new Christians against the drinking, swearing ways of their colonial countrymen; in doing so they inevitably suppressed understandable local desires to be free to travel and learn. In the midst of this development, disquieted by the many obstacles in the way of his earlier visions, John Geddie, during a meeting of missionaries at Anelgauhat in June 1872, suffered a partial stroke. He was invalided to Australia and died on 14 December at Geelong, Victoria. His candour, perseverance, orderly methods, unshakable faith in Christ — qualities both Scots and Reformed — remain imprinted in the characters of many of the people in the church he pioneered.

8

Melanesian Footholds II

Solomon Islands
New Caledonia

MENDAÑA AND QUIROS, the Spanish navigators who touched the Solomon Islands in 1595, had priests on board their ships. Mendaña was drawn by the hope of finding the legendary isles of gold, the source of King Solomon's wealth. His landings, disillusioning and ill-fated, on the forbidding coasts of Isabel, among strange people, appeared to Quiros to have been "the tragedy of the islands where Solomon was wanting." When the French came, missionaries of the Society of Mary, drawn to an area where Catholic Spain had at least landed, they showed little of the wisdom of Solomon in planning and carrying through the expedition. Two young bishops and eight priests and brothers died before they were finally forced to withdraw altogether.

When in 1844, with the assent of Rome, Jean Claude Colin, the superior of the Marists, carved several new vicariates out of the former mission territory of Western Oceania, Jean Baptiste Epalle, an ardent young Marist from the Diocese of Lyon, was appointed Vicar Apostolic and Bishop for Melanesia. The map of the Solomons and such information as had come through Sydney suggested an enticing prospect for a mission — seemingly thickly peopled islands untouched as yet by Protestants. Further west, New Guinea beckoned; the Solomon Islands would surely be suitable advanced stations for its future conquest? As yet only fragments of news had arrived in Europe about the Marists' discouragements in Polynesia; the tendency was to

179

attribute failure to an imperfect adherence to the religious rule of life of the Society rather than peculiar obstacles presented by geography and culture contact. The Marists were slow to recognize that though God might be for them, these were against them. They held out unrealistic hopes of planting religious communities calculated, by their devout life, to attract — with divine approval — the admiration and adhesion of the indigenous people. The well equipped party of seven priests and six lay brothers who went to the Solomons on the Sydney-based sandalwood vessel *Marian Watson* ran head-on into fighting between closely adjacent populations, fever and little local belief that the Christians' God could work any strong magic.

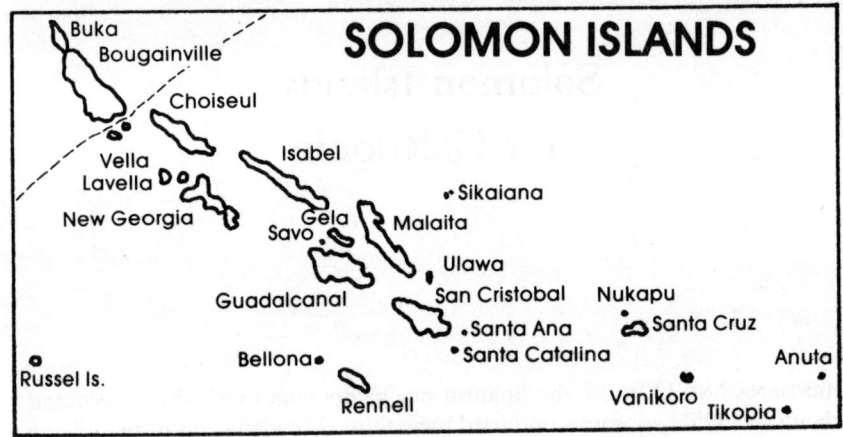

Epalle was first to die. His thirty-six years had been mostly lived in the mental securities of a bourgeois and rural Catholic environment. A brief experience in New Zealand among Polynesian Maori people probably misled him into failing to recognize how much more dangerous Melanesia was at that time. He and his companions spent a few days making first contacts on San Cristobal without any warning incident. On 10 December 1845 they landed at Astrolabe Harbour on Thousand Ships' Bay, Isabel. Again their initial welcome from the people lulled them into feeling secure. Epalle was told by his local informants that it would be dangerous for him to venture among the people's nearest neighbours, who were hostile to them. He dismissed the warning and went. He and his companions were attacked. Axe blows were rained on his head. Three days later, on 19 December he died from the wounds.

The surviving members of the group, including some who had been injured in the attack, withdrew on the *Marian Watson* in March 1846 under the leadership of Jean-Pierre Frémont to Makira Bay on San Cristobal, their first landing place. They were welcomed by Maimara, chief of the village of One, but decided not to reside there; nudity and local customs offended them; they felt they needed to build away from the village where they could attend to their regular hours of prayer in a compound and garden, protected if necessary by their firearms. Before they could complete this bastion, one of them, Xavier Montrouzier, an intellectually gifted and spiritually rigid missionary who stood at the beginning of a long and frustrating career in Melanesia, was speared in the back in retaliation for an attempt by one of the *Marian Watson's* crew to molest a local woman. The vessel left when the missionaries' house was finished. Montrouzier, not wounded seriously enough to earn the martyr's crown he coveted, was taken off with two other missionaries to a dangerous convalescence at Balade in New Caledonia (page 192) with another group of beleaguered Marists.

Jean-Georges Collomb, Epalle's coadjutor who had been intended as bishop of a future Vicariate of Micronesia, was named instead to succeed Epalle. He came to inspect the progress of the mission in February 1847, accompanied by Montrouzier, who had meanwhile recovered. They found that some progress had been made. Living and working conditions in the Solomons were better in the cooler mid-year weather. By the time the bishop-designate arrived malaria, with the onset of hot and moist weather, had badly affected the group. Frémont had acquired a second house at Pia, to the north of the One, still not grasping clearly that sending missionaries among a rival tribe would excite resentment and an ugly tug-of-war over possession of the mission. Collomb, who had still not been consecrated as bishop, nevertheless advised some of his men to occupy the house. He then left them for New Zealand to be made bishop. While he was away their situation deteriorated as a result of the policy of limited diffusion he had laid down. The One became hostile at the loss of part of their source of iron and trinkets when some of the Marists moved to Pia. Father Cyprien Crey died there of malaria and dysentery in March 1847. In April Father Jean Paget and Claude Jacquet, with Brother Hyacinthe set out to cross the island in search of a new and better place to build a house. All three were murdered by the inland Toro people, enemies of the One.

The One people, who knew the Marists were armed, tried to induce them to join in a war of retribution. The approach was declined. The missionaries' reputation with both the Toro and the One deteriorated. The seven survivors of the mission were living in fear, sealed into their Makira Bay house at night in expectation of attacks. Collomb returned at the end of August. He had already decided to revert if possible to the mission's earlier plan of moving closer to New Guinea, its eventual goal. The vessel *Anonyme* which brought him removed the survivors with the bishop on 3 September to pursue their ill-fated work on the island of Murua (Woodlark), then later on Umboi, west of New Britain and still closer to New Guinea. The Marists' withdrawal from the

Solomons was a prelude to further untoward frustration and withdrawal. Collomb died of fever on Umboi on 16 July 1848. The surviving Marists were removed. Milan Fathers, who replaced them, also left, equally frustrated, in 1855. Catholic missionaries did not re-enter the Solomons until 1898.

THE ANGLICAN MELANESIAN MISSION

BISHOP GEORGE AUGUSTUS SELWYN of New Zealand, the founder of the Anglican Melanesian Mission, ventured with more prudence into the prickly area of the Solomon Islands. When he arrived in Auckland in 1842 he brought a High Church tradition, the ideals of the early Oxford Movement, into his predominantly CMS, Low Church Evangelical, diocese. He stood for a sacramental view of the Church, for sound life-long teaching rather than sudden conversion, for the historic episcopate in continuous succession from the Primitive Church. The atmosphere of Cambridge, Eton and Windsor made Selwyn an easy associate of politicians, soldiers and colonial administrators. He was courteous, but not condescending, in his contacts with non-Anglicans; he firmly believed that mission was not a matter for societies of enthusiasts (whether CMS, LMS or Marist) but for the Church as such.

All this fitted in neatly with a deliberately uncorrected error in the legal documents defining the limits of his New Zealand jurisdiction — 34 degrees and 30 minutes north of the equator instead of south. He saw his commission to Maoris and Melanesians in much the same light: the Church was to be planted among them in a way suitable to their customs and culture, as it had once been planted among the English, bearing the apostolic marks of early creeds, Prayer Book worship and episcopal government in apostolic succession. Such a programme did not call for haste. Selwyn used the services of British naval ships to reconnoitre Melanesia. In the cooler sailing season he made contact in Vanuatu, the Loyalties, New Caledonia and the Solomons. He became aware of the toll of disease and suffering among the Marists and the LMS Polynesian teachers. He offered help in the field to the Nonconformists, regarding what they were doing as not incompatible with later introduction of Anglicanism. He eventually reached agreement with them on missionary comity: the Loyalty Islands were conceded to the LMS, southern Vanuatu to the Presbyterians; the Solomons and northern Vanuatu could thus be entered without offence to other Christians.

Selwyn's policies were extended and made more precise by John Coleridge Patteson, who came as his chaplain to New Zealand in 1855 and was consecrated in 1861 as Bishop of Melanesia. Patteson cruised with Selwyn and took control of the mission. Young men were recruited, with the consent of their families, from the Banks Group, north of the New Hebrides, the

MELANESIAN FOOTHOLDS II

Loyalties, and parts of the Solomons, to be trained as "scholars" in Auckland and sent back to teach Christianity to their own people. At first they attended a "winter school" on Lifou, then a Melanesian school at Selwyn's foundation, St. John's College, Auckland. During the summer months they were taught English, Prayer Book worship, and the essentials of Christian faith; the "winter cruise" of a new mission schooner, *Southern Cross*, returned them to their islands. Though they were to some extent anglicized by their experience, Selwyn and Patteson did not intend it. Both bishops studied Melanesian languages and took pains to relate their observations of local pre-christian religions to the developing study of comparative religion. Patteson, a gifted linguist, had learned Maori on the voyage out to New Zealand; he followed up the achievement by acquiring a speaking acquaintance with as many Melanesian tongues as he could, classifying cognate features and beginning lexicons and grammars.

In 1859 funds arrived to enable the Melanesian Mission to re-locate its Auckland school in new buildings at St. Andrew's College, Kohimarama, beside the harbour. Charlotte Yonge, the novelist, who was a cousin of Patteson, contributed substantially to its building out of royalties from her books. The biography she later wrote of her admired relative — Etonian, Oxonian, athlete, scholar, bishop, winsome friend of his converts — was devotedly documented and came close to the reality of the man. Selwyn ruled; Patteson befriended. Though he never lost the endearing English patina of his upbringing and his Devonshire home, his understanding of the spirit of the *Acts of the Apostles* helped him to treat non-whites as brothers and potential equals, to look forward to a day when Melanesians of varied backgrounds would shape a church in their way, not his. At these points Patteson transcended prelatical, imperial and racist assumptions and attitudes.

His stance emerged in an instructive episode early in his career in New Zealand, when he had learned Maori and was on good terms with the New Zealand Anglican clergy of the CMS Mission. His time as Selwyn's chaplain coincided with Maori-settler disputes over land, leading up to the tragic Maori wars. Patteson was in Auckland in 1859, in contact with Selwyn and Colonel Gore Browne, the Governor of New Zealand and an ex-Indian Army officer. Gore Browne took a repressive stand against Wiremu Kingi, a Maori chief whose land at Waitara had been alienated by land agents and settlers in contravention of the Maori understanding of the Treaty of Waitangi between the Maoris and the British (page 65). A CMS missionary, Archdeacon Octavius Hadfield, who had baptized Kingi, reacted to Gore Browne's policy with a trio of blazing denunciatory tracts, published in Britain. Gore Browne, in conversation with Patteson, furiously accused Hadfield of treason. Thus Selwyn, who was himself not Erastian and saw the justice in the Maori case, found himself caught in an embarrassing situation between Hadfield's "unwise and intemperate" language and the governor's wrath.

Selwyn's friends William Ewart Gladstone and the Duke of Newcastle were members of the British cabinet at the time. He did not feel free to intercede with them himself on behalf of the Maoris; such action would have gone behind the back of the governor; but Selwyn asked Patteson to keep his father, Sir John Patteson, informed of what was going on, knowing that the Patteson family had private access to members of the cabinet. Patteson's letters on the subject, to his father and others, up to and beyond his consecration as bishop, rival Hadfield in the severity of their criticism of settler tactics and the governor's military measures. He carefully explained to his father the Maori understanding of land, as being a sacred inalienable trust from ancestors, open to temporary cession, but not permanent surrender. "Between the mass of the English and the mass of the native population," he wrote, "there is a bad feeling; owing I verily believe, almost exclusively to the intolerable Pride of Race & covetousness of the white man." Elsewhere in the correspondence he asserted that the "intolerable pride of race on the part of the white man has not been humbled by the thought of our sins in India, Africa & elsewhere." He urged his father to use his influence in London to have the governor recalled: "offer terms of peace — investigate the whole question openly and honestly — do not be so cowardly as to be ashamed to confess that we are in the wrong."

In the same series of letters Patteson directed his father's thinking to his work among his Melanesian pupils at Kohimarama, his future plans for the islands, and his consecration as (his own style as signatory) "Missionary Bishop." His prophetic words about the war with the Maoris looked forward to the tone of his later critique of the labour trade in the Banks and Solomon Islands. Patteson did not seek abolition of the trade, but regulation. He himself used trade goods as an inducement to good relations with the young men he took away from their homes to become his pupils. His objection was not to their emigration, but to treating people as exploitable and inferior.

In a later letter, written in 1866, he carefully explained the policy of the mission:

> we start with the fullest belief in the capacity of these races; & with a very strong conviction that we must by our treatment of them & life with them prevent their acquiescing in the idea of their inferiority, inability to help themselves etc... I always regard *them* as the permanent, ourselves as the transient element in the mission, & try to raise them to the consciousness of their being called and intended by God to be the evangelists of their own people. We aim at a practical teaching of the truth "God hath made of one blood, etc." And this is done by making no distinction whatever between whites and blacks as such; by eliminating all that is conventional etc in us & does not belong to us as Christians but *qua* Englismen with English notions of civilisation etc. We don't aim at making Melanesians Englishmen but Christians; & we try

to think out the meaning and attitude of the Melanesian mind & character — not to suppress but to educate it.

In 1866 Patteson moved the base of the mission further north. New Zealand was cold; it was also desirable to take the school nearer to the mission field. He chose Norfolk Island for his new headquarters and school, adopting Mota, a language of the Banks Group, in place of English. The staff he assembled to oversee the work of St. Barnabas' College on Norfolk Island took Thomas Arnold's method at Rugby School as a model. R.H. Codrington, an English priest with experience in New Zealand, ran things with cool Anglican benevolence. His Oxford background equipped him to write a standard work on Melanesian peoples. His staff reinforcements almost all came direct from England, partly on account of Patteson's preference for missionaries educated in English Public Schools, but also because Patteson never succeeded in finding much money or many recruits in New Zealand and Australia. Colonial Anglicans were preoccupied with their own problems, and too far from Norfolk Island to be greatly concerned. During Patteson's lifetime his personal fortune and the support of his influential English friends kept the mission solvent; after his death alternative resources proved hard to tap.

Until 1920 Norfolk Island — not quite Australia, not quite New Zealand — formed the character of many of "Patteson's boys," for whom it became a nostalgic memory. Its corporate Old Tractarian life and atmosphere, moulded by the Anglican ecclesiastical calendar, yielded only slowly to the Romanizing ritualism of the later Oxford and Cambridge movements within Anglicanism. In the middle months of each year members of the mission staff travelled with the bishop in the *Southern Cross,* spending time with their former pupils and making contact with new villages. White members of staff did not settle permanently in the enervating northern climates, on the theory that their scholars, not they, should build churches among their own people. Villages on Mota, Mota Lava and Vanua Lava in the Banks Islands developed a northerly sub-base of the mission. From there it moved slowly into the south Solomons and central Solomons, where the future heart of a more populous Melanesian Church was in the making. The slow pace was partly attributable to the fragmentation of Solomon Islands society. Gifted and dedicated Melanesian protégés of Norfolk Island found it hard, when they returned home, to resist the influence of local Big Men, the power of secret societies, and traditional local systems of amassing wealth. These were all connected with the world of pre-christian spirits. Two trusted early pupils of the mission succumbed to these influences — George Sarawia and Clement Marau.

Sarawia was a boy of fifteen when he saw Selwyn and Patteson arrive together at Vanua Lava, his island in the Banks. They and their ship seemed to him to be spirit manifestations. Patteson took him to be trained at his school on Lifou in the Loyalty Islands; from there he went to Norfolk Island, where the course (at least eighteen months) was more intensive. Sarawia was baptized with Selwyn's first name in 1863. He was confirmed in 1865 and returned to Mota, in the Banks. His school and village were visited by John Palmer, a New Zealand trained clergyman of the mission, who worked closely with Sarawia. In 1870 and 1871, as the work on Mota flourished, some dreamed that the Mota community would become, under its new name, Kohimarama, a model of sound teaching and liturgical life. The hopes were dimmed when a bad hurricane in 1872 spread fear among the people that their old spirits were displeased with the Christians and their God.

Despite the setback, Sarawia was ordained at Auckland in 1873 — the first Melanesian priest. He returned to Mota, where he ministered for the rest of his life, believed by the mission to be a true father to his people and their respected spiritual guide. After his death in 1901, the received version of his work and stature persisted until 1910, when it was revealed that Sarawia's hold over the people had been in fact due to his having secretly continued to hold the rank of Head Man in the *sukwe,* a Motà pre-christian ceremonial society of rank and status intermeshed with traditional amassing of wealth and prestige by spells. The *sukwe* was officially proscribed by the mission. Sarawia's Christian priestly role, the pleading of the Supreme Sacrifice, had been neatly tied in with non-christian sources of possessions and power. This sobering information came through deathbed revelations of an Anglican deacon, Robert Pantutun, who had been his assistant.

The name of a second lapsed leader among Melanesian priests, Clement Marau, spread beyond the Solomons through R.H. Codrington's translation of his autobiography from the Mota language. Marau came at the age of twelve from Mere Lava in the Banks in 1869. He was made deacon in 1881, and sent as resident teacher to the small island of Ulawa in the Solomons, south east of Malaita. Having mastered the language, he brought about great religious and social changes by astute use of family groups. He personally exposed the impotence of greatly feared local spirits by joining in the cutting down of a sacred grove. He built a large church to dominate the community — a symbol of the changes, acting among his people with many of the marks of traditional Big Men. In 1903 he was belatedly ordained to the priesthood. The sound of the bell in his parish punctuated daily life; he had become an unquestioned ruler; but in 1907 it was discovered that a curfew he imposed had been used by him to cloak his own surreptitious adulteries. These were kept secret by threats of reprisal against any who divulged them. The mission suspended his priestly functions. After penance, he was later reinstated, but he was sent away from Ulawa to spend his last days on Mere Lava; the Ulawa people did not want him back. His son Martin Marau subsequently, however, carried on his work on Ulawa. It is possible that the father's abuse of power and fall from grace were in part results of his frustrations — the retarding of his advance in status as a result of geographical isolation, and the reluctance of white missionaries to devolve wider power over the church as a whole by promoting able Islanders.

Personal disgrace was not confined to Melanesian converts. Charles Brooke, an Irishman, after years of hard work establishing Christianity on Gela (Florida), a future strong base of the mission in the central Solomons, was withdrawn in 1874 on account of overt homosexuality. Others had by then begun, like Brooke, to forego the annual residence on Norfolk Island for the sake of living for more extended periods in the islands among the people. One of these, Joseph Atkin, a New Zealander, died tragically, with Patteson, in 1871.

Before his death Melanesia's first bishop went through a period of foreboding. New sources of hatred were being sown in the islands by unscrupulous labour traders who resorted to forcible abduction. Patteson found the English world of his past seemed increasingly remote from the Pauline simplicities he shared with Melanesians during his long journeys. He felt pained by his countrymen's commercial exploitation of island peoples. As he contemplated the size of the remaining missionary task in Melanesia and the fragmentary successes of twenty years' work his health began to fail. In 1870 he went to Auckland for medical treatment, but refused to consider leave in England. His friends thought he should marry; he rejected the idea, not wishing to expose a wife to the conditions of service in Melanesia. To his friends he seemed withdrawn; the early vivacity had diminished; he was greyer, stooped and prematurely aged.

Patteson landed, by himself, on 20 September 1871 on the atoll of Nukapu to the north of the Santa Cruz group, as advance guard for the members of his party on board the *Southern Cross*. He had twice before visited Nukapu; but this time, within an hour of his going ashore, the ship's boat's company, anxiously awaiting him in the lagoon, was attacked by a rain of arrows from the beach. Joseph Atkin, and Stephen Taroaniara, a young man from the village of Tawatana on the north coast of San Cristobal, were wounded. Atkin at once returned to the *Southern Cross*. Soon afterwards he led a party back in the boat toward the village on shore. They found the bishop's body floating in a canoe on the water of the lagoon; the head had been beaten in by a blow from a club. Patteson's assailants had covered it with a palm branch knotted in five places. A week later both Atkin and Taroaniara died in agony of tetanus.

Various significances were later given to the five knots in the palm frond. Some thought they were meant to convey retribution for the abduction of five young men from Nukapu on a labour recruiting vessel from Fiji, the *Emma*

Bell. Soon pious reflection embroidered the accounts with allusions to the five wounds of Christ. An aura of martyrdom began to gather as Charlotte Yonge's moving biography spread Patteson's name and fame in Anglican circles and further afield.

In Britain, Australia and New Zealand, the "missionary public" joined in sorrow for Patteson as victim and praised him as a Christian. Presbyterians and supporters of the London Missionary Society believed his murder had been an act of ill-directed revenge for the excesses of the labour traffic. Careful sifting of the testimony of Nukapu people and missionaries has been inconclusive about the motives for the deed. However, Patteson's death increased public outrage over kidnapping. Governments legislated to control the trade; High Church Tories made common cause for once with the British Nonconformist missionary societies of Exeter Hall and vociferous Protestant opinion in Australia and New Zealand.

Within the Melanesian Mission itself the shock of the bishop's death was not sufficient to produce permanent giving and recruiting for the continuance of his work. His successor was not appointed for seven years, partly because nominees were reluctant to follow so remarkable and saintly a man; Codrington was among those who declined to be nominated. Patteson had been a father in God to Melanesians; he evoked spontaneous love from those he served. Toward the end of his fatiguing career among Melanesian peoples he had identified deeply with them: "White folks," he wrote, "look as if they were bleached and had all the colour washed out of them."

A satisfactory successor would have had to accept the physical burdens of Patteson's style of mission; he would also have had to raise enough money to maintain the mission ship and the school on Norfolk Island. Patteson had paid out of independent means and special gifts. Problems were inherent in the method itself; the seductively English atmosphere of St. Barnabas' Chapel and school on Norfolk Island estranged trainees and made their return to their own islands difficult. White dominance and black subservience, whatever Patteson's own beliefs and intentions, affected relationships between staff and scholars. Anglo-Catholics, proud of the mission, liked to compare it with Anglo-Saxon medieval missions to Germany and the Low Countries. The baptismal names of converts display a tendency to interpret the work in this light within the Norfolk Island community; it was believed Melanesians were being trained as missionaries had once been trained at Whitby and Lindisfarne. The historical parallel was appealing but defective. Medieval Britain was related closely by language and culture to Germanic peoples; not so the regime on Norfolk Island when its ways were transplanted into the vastly different cultural world of Melanesian villages.

The bishops and missionaries who came after Patteson faced the problems bravely, but with limited success. The heart of the mission shifted gradually to the central Solomons. As it did so in the last quarter of the nineteenth century other forces appeared alongside the church — planters, traders, administrators, non-Anglican Christian missions. The Melanesian Mission had preceded its new neighbours. Its way of life in many villages, large and small, gave meaning and purpose in religious terms long understood and valued, altruism and peace-making. Its sacramental life preserved spiritual significance and meaning for the daily round of fishing and gardening; the mysteries of birth, death and generation were illumined by the doctrines of the Church. The mission itself gave access to a wider world; its standards of conduct and its goals gave it advantages in the affections of its adherents over other white men who came merely to police, to tax, or to trade. Melanesian resident clergy at their best accommodated their material way of life to the old ways of the villages; their Christian teaching at the same time offered an innovative challenge to the old order's sorceries and acts of violence.

Inland from the coastal strongholds of earlier days much remained to be done. In larger and more mountainous islands Melanesian missionaries began to share the work of evangelizing the interior populations in the bush. Mota gave way to English as the *lingua franca* of the mission. Later on, racy and flexible forms of Solomon Islands *Pidgin,* the future tongue of local administration and trade, were adopted in the teeth of English Public School prejudice against them. The Word was made increasingly Melanesian, released from British leading strings.

THE LMS: NEW CALEDONIA

NEW CALEDONIA and the Loyalty Islands, furthest south in Melanesia, were immune from malaria. Polynesian teachers of the LMS brought the first Christian presence of any size. Subsequently the Loyalties became a cockpit of missionary rivalries, then the scene of theatrical political interventions from Britain, France and the Australian colonies. Soon after the LMS landed the first four Samoan teachers in 1840, on the Isle of Pines and on Mare, sandalwooders arrived. On the Isle of Pines a high chief of Tongan descent ruled effectively; on the nearby mainland missionaries and sandalwooders found their dealings with local groups complicated by wars between adjacent tribes. The LMS and the Marists tended to blame sandalwooders for stirring up trouble by their godless activities. Local leaders, used to frequent minor fights, took a different view. Any kind of Europeans were to them a likely source of firearms and iron implements; competition to get them was keen; sometimes whole boats' crews were slaughtered in the cause.

TO LIVE AMONG THE STARS

The *John Williams* visited the LMS teachers on the Isle of Pines in 1841. A member of her crew, Edward Foxall, saw sandalwood there. He sold the information in Sydney to the first sandalwooders, who sailed secretly at short notice to capitalize on his tip, thus setting the scene for later violence. Two other Samoans were landed by the *John Williams,* with Rangi, a Rarotongan. In the following year Ta'unga from Rarotonga was stationed at Tuauru on the New Caledonian mainland together with two Samoans — Taniela and Noa from Manono. More than twenty-five such Polynesians, mostly married, laid the groundwork in New Caledonia and the Loyalties before the coming of white resident missionaries. They were ground-breakers who worked often in areas where Polynesian speech had affected local languages. Since the eighteenth century Tongans, compulsive voyagers, had been blown or had navigated to these shores. One writer speaks of a Tongan empire in the western islands. Ouvea in the Loyalties derived its name, culture and speech in part from Tongan-influenced Uvea (Wallis) whose people had colonized it. LMS teachers therefore did not feel they were among total strangers. They lived with the people, accepted their diet, responded quickly to their customs, and were received as distant cousins bearing a religion of which advance notice had been received through previous Polynesian visitors and settlers. The terms of their welcome gave scope for religious dialogue.

Ta'unga, a discerning Rarotongan, left a first-hand account of his work among the Tuauru people and on the Isle of Pines, where the powerful chief Touru acted threateningly toward Tuauru and its chief, Wadoka. Ta'unga's stories of southern and eastern New Caledonia bristle with vivid detail. He and Noa learned the Tuauru language. He was welcomed with gifts by local chiefs, investigated the people's beliefs about the spirits and relics of the dead, and instituted the Sabbath as a holy day, an easily accepted Christian addition to local taboos.

The three teachers treated Tuauru as a centre for visits to other southern areas on the mainland. Taniela went overland to Noumea to attend a local feast and meet the chief. Some of the methods of the Samoans were too severe for Ta'unga. He took Noa aside to plead with him, urging him to emphasise love, compassion and the selfless death of Christ for others. Ta'unga impressed many of his hearers, including chiefs, by setting the Christian creation story in contrast with the partial cosmologies surrounding local divinities. Some chiefs showered gifts on him; they voluntarily surrendered their former cult objects and brought them to Ta'unga for disposal. Noa and Taniela, according to Ta'unga, were jealous of his successes; they accused him of alienating the people from them. Ta'unga denied it; he said the Samoans "were bad tempered and the people were not attracted to them." He argued the point with his two colleagues, telling them to "go and ask the people about it." Ta'unga, in his conversations, as he has recorded them, understood feelings and went to the point. His approach to chiefs was similarly.

direct, in keeping with his descent from a line of high-ranking Rarotongan priests.

Ta'unga referred to Touru of the Isle of Pines by his title of address, Matuku. Touru threatened the LMS teachers at Tuauru; he blamed the Polynesian teachers on the Isle of Pines for provoking, by their supernatural influence, insensitive conduct by sandalwooders and introduced epidemics. Rangi the Rarotongan and two Samoans — Taniela from Tutuila and Lasalo of Tufulele — died in a fight when Isle of Pines people massacred the crew of the brig *Star* at the Isle in November 1842. In 1843 Touru himself came to Tuauru with twenty canoes. He vowed to kill Ta'unga and his companions. After landing with his armed men, Touru, shouting obscenities, summoned the teachers by calling out their names. Ta'unga's courage and capacity to deal with big chiefs saved them. Noa and the other LMS teachers were terrified. Ta'unga deliberately went out to meet Touru, who carried an axe and a spear. Ta'unga — his name means "priest" — walked out with the assurance of a man of God facing a monarch. "Greetings," he said. Touru extended his hand, put a hat on Ta'unga's head, gave him a shirt and told him he was safe. The chief then presented gifts to the other teachers and arranged a feast. He had been touched by Ta'unga's courage. "This was similar," Ta'unga said, "to their customary way of behaving towards their own priests. That was the way they intended it."

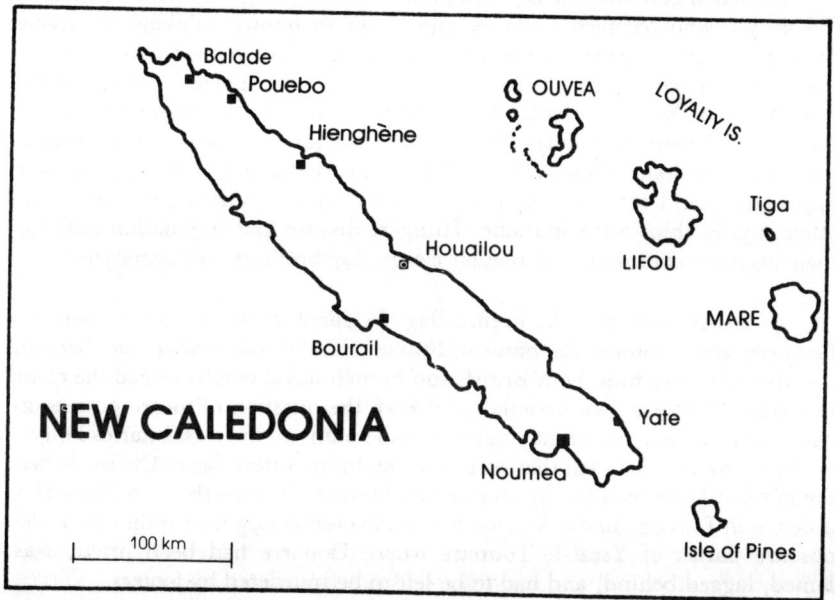

Murray and Turner of the LMS nevertheless feared for the safety of the Polynesians. In 1845 they decided to withdraw them. Touru, who had been vexed when they refused his invitation to come to the Isle of Pines as his personal teachers, was again threatening their lives. Ta'unga was reluctant to leave; he said he was willing to remain, and if necessary to die. He did not doubt he could face Touru again; but Murray and Turner persuaded him to leave, pointing out that he was under authority.

MARIST ENTRY

ADAPTATION AND SETTLEMENT were more complicated for the French Roman Catholic Marists who came to Balade in the north of the New Caledonian mainland in 1843. Their leader, Bishop Guillaume Douarre, an early Marist from the vicinity of Puy-de-Dôme in the Auvergne, was shaken when appointed as bishop for New Caledonia and coadjutor to Bishop Bataillon of Central Oceania in 1842. A little over a year later, self-effacing and gentle, he arrived in New Caledonia. For the next ten years his missionaries laboured under adversities they could not control. Douarre, who had many of the qualities of saints, by his own admission lacked power to command.

A French gunboat, the *Bucéphale,* landed the missionaries. In the minds of the people who received them — indeed, in their own thinking — divine protection and fire power were somehow related. Their strict observance of their religious community rule shut them up in their house for much of the time. Curious New Caledonian tribes sought to acquire the possessions inside the walls of their enclosure. Their stores, so long as they lasted, were a temptation to loot. They were armed; a surprise attack might mean their opponents could get the weapons for their own use. Visits from French or other supply ships were sporadic. Hunger, disease and trepidation afflicted their ingrown community of regular clergy, lay brothers and neophytes.

At Balade they flew the French flag. Douarre, at the time of his arrival, favoured annexation in the name of France. Sandalwood traders had been in the district before him; both British and French naval vessels visited the coast to watch over their own nationals and keep the question of future possession open. Under their recurrent trials at Balade many of the missionaries longed for martyrdom. They felt they were sharing in the sufferings of Christ. When the mission house was finally attacked and burned in July 1847, in Douarre's absence in Europe, Blaise Marmoiton, a devoted young lay brother from the obscure parish of Yssac-la-Tourette where Douarre had been priest, was lamed, lagged behind, and had to be left to be murdered by looters.

MELANESIAN FOOTHOLDS II

Those who escaped took refuge further south at Pouebo, then Hienghène. Bwaxat, the powerful chief of Hienghène, favoured the British. He made life hard for the Marists. They moved on, further southward; after a short stay at Yate they were forced by local hostility to take refuge on the Isle of Pines, which became one of their future strongholds. During the period of uncertainty about the mission's future, Father Pierre Rougeyron was compelled to withdraw, with a nucleus of converts, to Futuna. He returned later to the New Caledonian mainland to stay on and consolidate the mission. Douarre's sense of obligation to his companions and converts conflicted with his obligation to report to his superiors; he visited Sydney; afterwards he returned for instructions to France and Rome. On his voyage to Europe he urged annexation of New Caledonia by France, lived through the demise of the Oceanian Company in 1848 (page 101) and visited Pope Pius IX. He arrived back in time to give bewildered sanction to the southward flight and the final temporary evacuation of the Marists from the Isle of Pines to Wallis and Futuna, and for a time to Aneityum in the New Hebrides (pages 172-3). After they and he returned to New Caledonia to face further hardship he died of wracking illness at Pouebo in April 1853, plagued by feelings of acute unworthiness. His end was recorded in pious detail by Xavier Montrouzier, who had come to join the New Caledonian Marists permanently in 1851 after passing through the trials of a Marist mission to the Solomons and Murua (pages 179-181). Montrouzier persuaded the French admiral, Febvrier-Despointes, to annex New Caledonia a few months after the bishop's death. The work Douarre had begun was carried forward from another site, the Bay of Bourail, northwest of Noumea, by Rougeyron, his long-suffering lieutenant.

THE LOYALTIES: MARISTS MEET THE LMS

MONTROUZIER WAS SENT in 1858 to Lifou in the Loyalty Islands. He came late upon a scene where the main parts since the early 1840s had been played by LMS teachers from the Cook Islands and Samoa. The islands of Mare and Lifou offered a field more outwardly inviting than the malarial Solomons and New Hebrides. The Presbyterians visited them for the sake of a breezy respite from their work on Aneityum. They were passengers on LMS vessels; the prior right to evangelize belonged to the LMS as first arrivals. Selwyn called there; later Patteson used Lifou for annual schooling of Melanesian future teachers. He met and conversed with Montrouzier. By the time of their meeting, however, the responsibility of sending white missionaries permanently to the Loyalties had been resolved by gentleman's agreement in favour of the LMS. The Samoan LMS Missionary Committee held Selwyn and Patteson in high personal regard, but lamented their

"Puseyite" high church opinions. They were willing to concede the Loyalties to Anglican Evangelicals of the CMS, but rather than have their teachers' work overlaid with Selwyn's Tractarianism or supplanted by the "Romanism" of the Marists, they moved in themselves.

A firm groundwork had been laid by their Polynesian forerunners. Beginning on Mare in 1841 LMS teachers lived with the local people, who were used to Polynesian infiltrations and aware through Tongan contact of the coming of Christianity to the Pacific. The ships of the LMS were sailed by white men; when they set teachers ashore they raised hopes of further contact — material and spiritual. Local chiefs adopted and used their Polynesian Christian visitors with hopes of future white resident missionaries in the back of their minds; but Pacific Islander missionaries were in a different category from beachcombers, escaped convicts, sandalwooders or naval officers. Curiosity about them was more explicitly religious, for it was on religious terms they presented themselves. In language and custom they fitted into Loyalty Islands society far more readily — and cleverly. Most were Samoans; their record was mixed. Acculturation led to compromises in sexual behaviour and the acquisition of wealth and power. Most stayed for several years, some longer. Solia, who began on Mare in 1846, went from there to the minuscule island of Tiga, which produced important leaders in the future church, despite its size. He worked there for seven years before returning to Samoa.

A minority of Cook Islanders played a resourceful role alongside the Samoans. Ta'unga, after being withdrawn in 1846 from the New Caledonian mainland against his inclination, spent more than a year working on Mare and Lifou. Mare proved frustrating: Ta'unga repeated his gadfly treatment on his two Samoan co-workers, Tataio and Iakopo. He accused them of being gluttonous and lazy, but subsequently found he was himself unable to make much headway as a missionary with Yiewene Naisiline, the chief who was their host and protector. However, under Ta'unga's influence the chief's son, Wanakam, and a family of immigrant Tongans became Christian. Taufa, from Niuatoputapu in northern Tonga, had settled as the *enehmu* (protected guest) of Yiewene, among the powerful Si Gwahma tribe. Used to cannibal societies from childhood, Ta'unga observed the murder and eating of seamen, and of escaped convicts from Botany Bay, with accurate apparent calm. His accounts of man-eating in New Caledonia are among the most detailed on record. Again Ta'unga displayed his no-nonsense manner of dealing with chiefs; when Yiewene was inclined to believe that bad epidemics on Lifou, not far away, had been caused by Jehovah, Ta'unga stood up to him. "Don't you listen to that talk, it is absolutely untrue," he said. Yiewene, though not converted, was impressed by this resident "priest" of the Christian God.

MELANESIAN FOOTHOLDS II

In September 1846 Ta'unga accompanied Yiewene on a visit to Lifou. There he worked for some months alongside Paoo (called Fao on Lifou), an ingenious Aitutakian, one of the most dedicated of South Sea Island Christian missionaries, and one of the most successful. Ta'unga found on Lifou that not all the unsatisfactory LMS teachers were from Samoa; Paoo was having trouble with a Rarotongan, Zekaraia from the village of Arorangi, "a bad example of a man." Ta'unga's reminiscences dealt curtly with his sexual misdemeanours, naming the wives of one of the chiefs, with whom he had misbehaved. During a busy month together Paoo and Ta'unga had long religious conversations with one of the Lifou chiefs, and with Whenegay, a high chief from southern Ouvea, who was then on a visit to Lifou. Whenegay subsequently became attached to the LMS; his people provided a nucleus of the Protestant minority on Ouvea when it later became predominantly Catholic.

At the end of September the *John Williams* collected Ta'unga and took him back to resume his interrupted work at Tuauru on the mainland. He found the district had been laid waste by warriors from the Isle of Pines. Rather than try to remain, he returned in December to Rarotonga, accompanied by a New Caledonian, Navie, who had become his inseparable companion and servant — a startling living exhibit to accompany Ta'unga's stories of life in the western Pacific. Navie had been involved at Yate in an attempt on Ta'unga's life. Some of Ta'unga's local friends and protectors threatened to kill and eat Navie as a reprisal, but Ta'unga pleaded successfully for his life. Navie attached himself permanently to Ta'unga in gratitude — an acted parable of the theme of salvation by unmerited grace. Navie died after a few years of exile on Rarotonga; Ta'unga lived on until 1898, completing his varied career as a missionary on Manu'a in Samoa and Mauke in the southern Cooks.

Paoo, a second Cook Islander, the apostle of Lifou, was motivated and adaptable. As a young man he had travelled about on ships. He spoke Samoan and soon acquired the languages of the Loyalties. He appears to have been as happy in a canoe as on shore. From Mare he evangelized Lifou, where blind Bula, a local high chief of the southern district, Losi, adopted Paoo as his *enehmu*. Bula never adopted Christianity, but he favoured and protected Paoo and his work. Bula's rival, Ukeneso, the chief of the northern region of Wet, resented Bula's appropriation of Polynesian teachers. He looked about to find a counterbalancing force, turning hopefully toward the Marists on the mainland. A prophet of the old religion in the district of Wet, Upinu Walewen, made difficulties for Ukeneso by oracles encouraging the people of the north of Lifou to accept messengers from the east and reject those from the west. The pronouncements were in line with older tendencies on Lifou, where the population had been supplemented by Polynesian arrivals for generations.

TO LIVE AMONG THE STARS

Paoo, eager to take advantage of the situation for Christianity, sent his Samoan teachers into the north of the island to Ukeneso's lesser vassal chiefs in Wet. They succeeded in converting one of them, Wainya, the young chief of Chépénéhé. Before long Chépénéhé developed into the most important Protestant centre on the island.

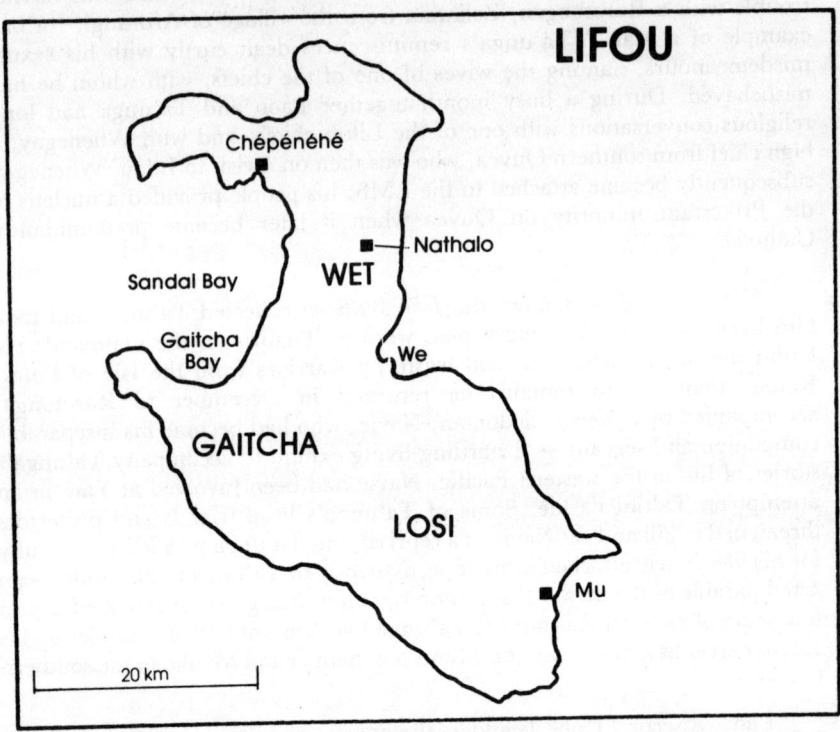

Paoo shaped his missionary approach against the political background, but made it plain that he came as the messenger of Christ and was not a political pawn of his friend Bula. He shifted his headquarters from the southern centres of Mu and Amelewet, where he had worked at first, to a site at We, on the east coast, where his teachers could be conveniently sent into all three large districts of Wet, Losi and Gaitcha, without acting explicitly as representatives of any of the warring high chiefs of the island. At We, Paoo built neatly spaced houses of whitewashed coral lime in the Rarotongan-LMS style. He dug orderly gardens, instituted worship that included hymns translated by Ta'unga, and was visited by both the Marists and Anglicans, who acknowledged him as moving force behind the Polynesian missionaries on Lifou for a period of eighteen years before the arrival of his white successors. By the time of Patteson's visits to We in 1857 Paoo had built houses to receive white LMS missionaries at Mu in the south and Chépénéhé in the north. At Mu, blind Bula's son and successor of the same name, had become a Christian. Patteson helped Paoo with his school programme. He presented him with Mark's Gospel printed in the language of Lifou. He even took off seven young Loyalty Islanders to Auckland to be trained, but withdrew all claim to Lifou after corresponding with the LMS about their future plans.

During the second half of 1859 Paoo was also visited at We by Fathers François Palazy and Laurent Fabvre of the Marists. Palazy called Paoo "a serious and elderly man of whose good faith I have no doubt whatever." He spoke Samoan with Paoo, who served his visitors roast turkey. While they sat at table, Paoo took his meal in his own fashion, from banana leaves on the floor. Palazy called the We station "a veritable Roman building feat." He found Paoo and his colleagues courteous, describing how the LMS teachers had been critical of the Marists before they arrived because they had identified them with French gunboats, but had changed when they talked with the Catholics and found the Catholic religion was good and the same as theirs. Palazy vehemently protested about this equation. He and Fabvre made it known that Luther, a "libertine, a cad," had given birth to Protestantism, whereupon the people of Lifou laughed and called the Protestants "sons of Luther." This did not seem to interfere with Palazy's warm feeling toward Paoo. "We never heard he had spoken against us or our religion," he said.

Ukeneso, thwarted in attempts to persuade John Jones of the LMS, who had arrived on Mare to reside in 1854, to send him teachers of his own, seized on the presence of the Marists. He was helped by two dissolute beachcombers who were *enehmu* to him. When Palazy and Fabvre, who had already been to Ouvea in the preceding year, came to Wet on 11 April 1858, accompanied by Father Jean Bernard and the French New Caledonian military commandant Jules Testard, they brought a gift of cattle for Ukeneso. The Marists came to bring their faith, which recognized no barriers of missionary comity; their government, already in possession on the New Caledonian mainland, came to assert its right over the Loyalties and mistrust of British pretensions, naval and missionary. The Roman Catholics arrived on Lifou shortly ahead of Samuel McFarlane of the LMS, a busy and pernickety Scotsman with a neat little wife. McFarlane's twelve years of confrontations with the French further complicated Lifou's local wars; the small island turned into a cauldron of Franco-British and Catholic-Protestant recriminations. A wider world heard about the Loyalties — as never before or since.

Before Samuel McFarlane arrived on Lifou in 1859 Bula and Wainya had unashamedly used the LMS Polynesian missionaries to further their power on the island against Ukeneso, who resented it. Ukeneso's dominance

over Wet was traditionally from the inland centre of Nasalo (Nathalo); he was frustrated by Wainya's relative ease of access to shipping and foreign influence at Chépénéhé on Sandalwood Bay. McFarlane's presence at Chépénéhé shifted the focus of LMS effectiveness away from Mu in Losi — where McFarlane's fellow missionary William Baker resided. Ukeneso's irritation increased because the Marist missionaries at Eacho, close to Chépénéhé, were ill supplied, badly housed and in wretched contrast with the solid establishment and humming programmes of the LMS. McFarlane asserted that Wainya and Bula were constituted secular powers; he supported the summary and sometimes violent methods of their "police" in imposing his new Christian laws on the subjects of Ukeneso, and those of Zeula, the ruler of neighbouring Gaitcha. It was easy for McFarlane to believe that Christian-inspired laws were for the benefit of all when hearing about their enforcement from Wainya and the younger Bula, in conferences with his converts in the mission house. The enforcements were harder to bear for those who suffered under them in the scattered settlements where most of the people lived.

Ukeneso and the Marist missionaries had at first agreed with the drawing up of a law code; their objection was to over-zealous enforcement by Wainya's agents when dealing with his traditional local enemies, many of whom were Catholic converts. His resentment of the LMS for its part in this business found an echo in the attitudes of Charles Guillain, the French Governor of New Caledonia, whose reasons for disquiet about McFarlane's prospering mission were different. Guillain's interest was strong French administration over New Caledonia and its "dependencies," as vaguely proclaimed when the mainland was annexed in 1853. A secularist and anti-clerical, in his social ideas a "passionate follower of Fourier," he resisted what he saw as a British *imperium in imperio* where his own writ was meant to run. From his point of view McFarlane's efficient theocratic methods, pressed against Ukeneso's people and the French Marists with discriminatory severity, had to be stopped.

When Guillain declared Lifou a military district in May 1864 and sent in a detachment of twenty-five soldiers to occupy Chépénéhé, both the LMS and the Marists were appalled. The soldiers banned English and the local languages in the schools and prohibited McFarlane from engaging in religious activity, though they did not expel him. McFarlane, true to his British Nonconformist liberal convictions, fired the first salvo in a long barrage of formal written protests at Noumea. He did not stop there. Sensing a chance to turn these little outrages in the Loyalties into a larger test of "religious liberty" against the background of Franco-British relations during the sensitive period of the late French Second Empire, he embarked on his "successful paper

Samuel McFarlane's house, Chépénéhé.

war," waged through Sydney, London and Paris. His skill in framing accurate and pompous letters to the local governor and the Emperor Napoleon III proved his training at the Bedford Missionary College had not been time wasted. The spectacle of McFarlane, a former railway mechanic, successfully appealing to the French Emperor over the head of his tormentors on the remote coral outposts of the Loyalties, tickles the imagination. In Sydney he counted on the weighty support of socially eminent Pitt Street Congregational laymen, who had a straight line through the proprietor of the *Sydney Morning Herald,* John Fairfax, to the Rev. John West, the editor of the paper (and a Congregational minister). West's news and editorial columns, his correspondence pages, and articles written in Sydney by A.W. Murray on the progress of Christianity in the islands of Melanesia, turned the attention of the Australian colonies to the events on Lifou, Mare and Ouvea.

A month after the appearance of the first small group of French troops at Chépénéhé, Guillain, exasperated as much by McFarlane's stubbornness as by the tactics of the Samoan teachers and Wainya's police, moved in a much larger force of 300 men. His forces made a military pincer sweep from east to west across the island to join forces with soldiers landed at Wide Bay, retaliated brusquely at Chépénéhé against provocative defensive acts by Lifou Protestants, and finally interrupted a church service, burned the village, took up quarters in the chapel, and rounded up all the LMS teachers and their wives on ships in the harbour. McFarlane, unharmed in his house, bristled with the passion of a Cromwellian Independent before this display of absolutism. In the interval granted by the suspension of his missionary duties he put his complaints in writing for his Sydney friends, then through them direct to the LMS in London. The incidents were reported to the mission boards and their secretaries, working together as Liberals at prayer in the atmosphere surrounding the annual May Meetings of the missionary societies at Exeter Hall in the Strand. On 13 January 1865 they mustered an impressive list of signatures in an appeal, over the head of Governor Guillain, to the Emperor Napoleon III. The signatories were Lord Shaftesbury, the Bishops of Chichester and London, the Dean of Westminster, the Lord Mayor of London, three sherrifs, and officers of the London Missionary Society, the Baptist Missionary Society, the Church Missionary Society and the Wesleyan Missionary Society.

Following a flurry of manoeuvres in the British Foreign Office and the French Department of the Marine and the Colonies, Guillain was instructed from Paris to tell McFarlane that he could reopen schools and resume his missionary work. Napoleon wrote on 24 January to his petitioners in London to let them know what he had done. In the months that followed the exchange, Guillain, whom McFarlane found "a very agreeable fatherly old gentleman in private," received McFarlane at Noumea — then called Port-de-France. On the basis of the Emperor's assurance they worked out a compromise. The Bible was allowed to circulate in the vernacular. McFarlane succeeded in getting relief from grievances against French troops billetted on Lifou. The Protestant and Catholic Lifouans were deterred by the forces of occupation from pursuing their district wars. Chépénéhé became a centre for training Loyalty Islanders as their own religious teachers and evangelists; McFarlane from his seminary began to look outward toward the possibility of sending Loyalty Islander missionaries to other places. The Marists and the LMS worked alongside each other; both groups showed distaste for the non-religious ideological preferences of Guillain and his studied indifference to what they believed in most. The Marists were peeved at his non-support and critical of the behaviour of his soldiers. Nevertheless they tried to consolidate themselves by building an impressive stone church in the style of nineteenth century Lyon at Ukeneso's centre of Nathalo.

Curiosity about this church overcame McFarlane and his wife when they passed one day in 1865 as they crossed the island. Elizabeth McFarlane, who was unfamiliar with Catholic worship, asked an attendant about a "statue of the Lord" inside. By a confusion of language — she probably asked after "the body of Christ" — she found herself directed to the tabernacle on the altar normally containing the consecrated Host. Taking this as an invitation to inspect what was inside, she opened it. Catholic sentiment was understandably horrified by the *faux pas*. Cries of sacrilege were raised in Noumea, Paris, then finally London. The French ambassador in London, De la Tour d'Auvergne, asked the British to have McFarlane withdrawn. The LMS, embarrassed, apologized for the unintentional sacrilege, but drew attention to the fact that Guillain's troops were active on Ouvea, repeating their earlier performance on Lifou. A commission of inquiry sent from France reported unfavourably on the behaviour of the Marists on Ouvea and the conduct of Guillain and the troops. Guillain was withdrawn as governor and replaced. The LMS, as a diplomatic *quid pro quo,* then honourably withdrew McFarlane and sent him with Murray to survey the prospect of a mission for his Chépénéhé Loyalty Island students along the southern coasts of the New Guinea mainland (pages 206ff).

Minor dramas between Catholics and Protestants, though not of comparable proportions, unfolded on Ouvea and Mare. Samuel Ella from Samoa, who had gone to Sydney for the sake of his wife's health, was sent to Ouvea's recuperative seascapes as resident white missionary, there to be embroiled between 1864 and 1875 in local wars fought on religious pretexts. Ouvea's divided tribes had been separately cultivated by the LMS and Marist missions. The northern chief, Bazit of Ohwen, ruled over tribes extensively infiltrated for many years by immigrants from Wallis (Uvea). In 1857 he

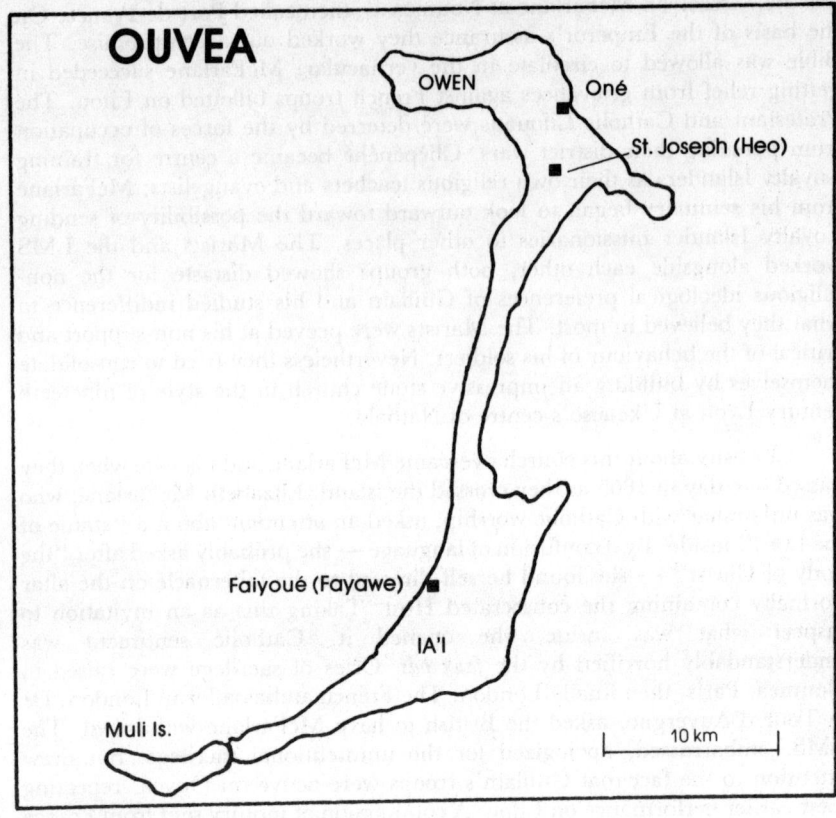

invited Jean Bernard and François Palazy to live at Heo, thus countering the influence of two Mare-born LMS teachers who had been sent to Ouvea by John Jones, the missionary on Mare, at the request of Bazit's rival Whenegay, the chief of Fayawe. Both missions were progressively reinforced. Bazit consolidated his position against Whenegay by alliance with the southern islet of Muli.

In 1864, after the arrival of Ella as the first white LMS resident missionary, French soldiers moved in under Guillain's orders to curb Whenegay's warlike activities and support the Marists against British influence. Ella, with help from McFarlane, was then drawn into the international "paper war." His station at Fayawe was subjected to French military intervention; he joined the chorus of protests over Guillain's head to the French Emperor. Commissions of inquiry censured the Draconian behaviour of Governor Guillain in 1869 and 1873; they found that Jean

Bernard and his associate Eugène Barriol had actively urged Bazit and the Catholics to attack Protestants. Both Marists were withdrawn, but the balance of power on Ouvea had by then been laid down for the future. Catholics had become, and remained, the majority. The Protestant minority, centred in Fayawe, was consolidated by James Hadfield of the LMS for seven years from 1879, then tended by him sporadically from Lifou until 1920.

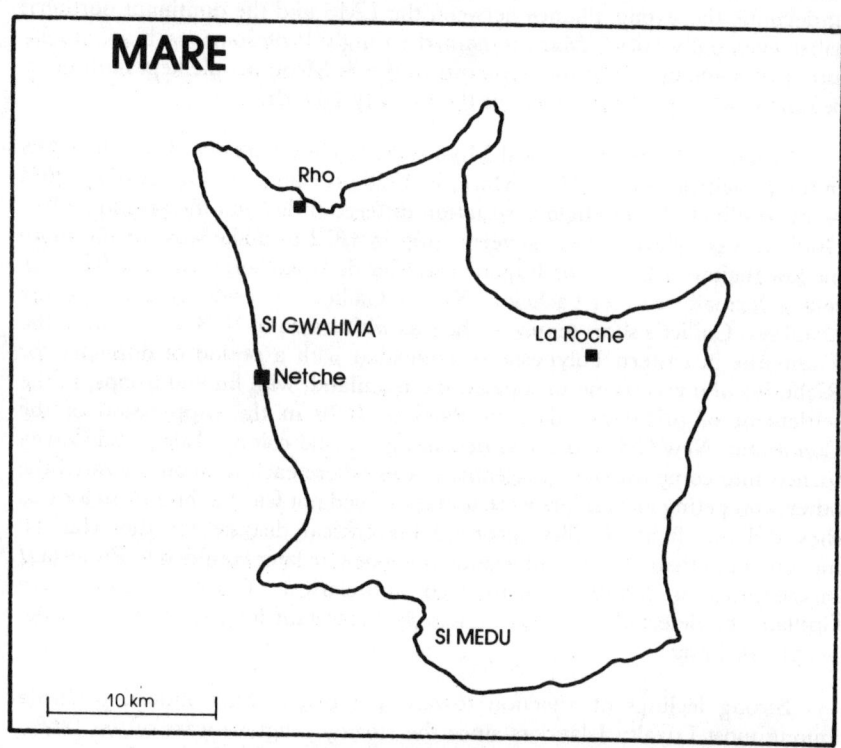

On Mare the balance of power swung the other way. Early LMS Polynesian teachers were under the protection of the high chiefs of the Naisiline family of the northern district of Si Gwahma, at Netche and Rho. The Naisilines' wars against the southern tribes then began to be waged under the banner of Jehovah, the new God proclaimed by the LMS and gradually accepted by chiefs and people. To the south, the main core of resistance gathered in the Si Medu district; Si Medu refugees from the campaigns of Nidoish Naisiline went in large numbers to the Isle of Pines, where the population had become Catholic. Marist missionaries, Jérôme Guitta and François Beaulieu, advised and helped the Si Medu people against their northern Protestant assailants. The Protestants were similarly helped and encouraged by John Jones, who saw in the wars of the Naisilines a just and necessary defence of Protestantism against popery. Jones of the LMS consistently endorsed the claims of the Naisilines to be kings by right over the whole of Mare. Guillain's French troops, never much of a garrison for the Loyalties as a whole, could not cope with the deterioration of public order on Mare as they did on Lifou and Ouvea. All subsequent French attempts to undermine the strong alliance between the LMS and the dominant northern tribes eventually failed. Mare remained strongly Protestant, with a Catholic minority made up out of the remnants of the Si Medu people kept faithful by Beaulieu, who spent fifty years in the Loyalty Islands.

When the Paris Evangelical Missionary Society took over from the LMS in the Loyalties — in 1898 on Mare, in 1920 on Lifou and Ouvea (page 294) — the outlines of the religious situation differed little from the position when Guillain was relieved of his governorship in 1872 to make way for the more mellow regime of Governor Eugène Gaultier de la Richerie. In 1871 Richerie sent a formally correct bachelor, Xavier Caillet to reside on Lifou in the Loyalties. Caillet's short tenure — he was withdrawn in 1874 to be sent to the Tuamotus in eastern Polynesia — coincided with a period of difficulty for Richerie, who was trying to cope on the mainland, with limited troops, in the settlement of prisoners taken in Paris in 1870 in the suppression of the Commune. New Caledonia was becoming a penal colony. Lifou and Ouvea turned into comparatively peaceable places where each mission tolerated the other; competing local rulers were told they need not fear the French so long as they did not fight. Caillet recorded his critical distaste for the Marists' incitement of their converts in a small notebook he later confided to Protestant missionaries in Tahiti. A convinced anti-clerical of milder stamp than Guillain, he detected the overwhelmingly Protestant loyalties of most of the people on Lifou.

Strong feelings of affection toward the British have indeed persisted among most Loyalty Islanders since the stormy religious wars of the 1860s. The condition of mind has been called Anglophilia; for the people of many tribes it was mixed up with Francophobia. The Marists too, did not always approve of the sterner measures of their own government; they found they were suspected by many because the soldiers were their countrymen. On Ouvea, where Catholicism eventually prevailed, the preferences of most of the common people are partly accounted for by the island's close ties, through language and culture, with the island of Wallis, which had already become Catholic (page 96). Similarly, Protestant preference for British white missionaries did not imply a desire for British annexation. In forming themselves into singing, praying and self-governing Christian congregations, they followed their first missionaries, Cook Islanders and Samoans. Protestantism took hold among them because they fused it with many of the religious attitudes of their ancestors, accommodating its cosmology and sacred history to their traditional beliefs. The missionary training school McFarlane built at Chépénéhé was regarded as continuing, in the direction of New Guinea, the transmission of a faith originally brought to the Loyalty Group by Pacific Islander migrant peoples related to them by marriage. Local belief in the powers behind nature and their own origins merged in their thinking with worship of Christ as Saviour and Word of God. The gospel became incorporated functionally into their supportive mythology.

What began for the high chiefs of the Loyalties as manipulation of incoming Christianity in the interests of gaining more power developed into adoption of Christianity in defence of their culture against encroachment by colonizers. Thus in 1883, when the French government introduced Jean-Pierre Cru, a Protestant missionary who was not acceptable to the LMS, the ambitious high chief Yiewene, a member of the Naisiline line, accepted and protected Cru. He formed a church to offset the power of Jones — always a dominant and assertive personality — and the LMS. Rather than follow Yiewene many rank and file LMS deacons and adherents among his people took to the bush to defend their church against the usurpation. The struggle between the Christian factions lasted until 1898, when they were reunited on condition that the Paris Evangelical Mission, with LMS support, should take over the direction of all church work.

The Catholics of the Loyalties, more contentedly aligned with the French mission and government, found some refuge for old ways and beliefs in the sacramental life of the parishes. As in many parts of the Pacific, the use of Latin, as an esoteric third language for the liturgy, preserved a sensation of the supernatural alongside the French language imparted by the government for daily use; but the absence of a vernacular Bible in the hands of the people made them less assertive of their own cultural heritage. Since the Second Vatican Council of the 1960s their descendants, many of whom work in Noumea or the mines of New Caledonia, have drawn nearer to the Protestants in the attempt of post-colonial Pacific Islanders to recover and conserve their past (page 296).

9

The Lure of New Guinea

The LMS in Papua
Wesleyans in New Britain

THE LURE OF NEW GUINEA, a heavily populated and mysterious island, affected the imaginations of LMS workers in other parts of the Pacific — Samuel McFarlane of Lifou, William Lawes of Niue, James Chalmers of Rarotonga. Each of them came further west accompanied by Islander missionaries. McFarlane, with A.W. Murray, formerly of Samoa, went in 1871 with a group of eight students from his mission seminary on Lifou to survey prospects among the Torres Strait Islands and on the southern coasts of the New Guinea mainland. Murray had engaged his brain and pen as a publicist for missions in the western Pacific from the time of his first journeys to the New Hebridean LMS outstations on the *Camden* and *John Williams*. His reminiscences, spiced with theological interpretation, promoted a cause he endorsed with his life. His books contained much that appeared first in British and Australian newspaper articles, making it plain that forces other than the British navy had a vital interest in the future of Melanesia.

McFarlane saw himself as the main pioneer in New Guinea. Murray received small notice in McFarlane's account of their joint cruise. Looking back in 1888 on their cautious contacts on Darnley and Murray Islands, on Dauan Island and around Milne Bay, McFarlane glamourized his first impressions in a book written for British Sunday School children. The wild people of the mainland repelled him; he rationalized his preference for

THE LURE OF NEW GUINEA

establishing a relatively secure base in the strait as due to his "common sense, without which a man may be ever so pious and clever, and self-sacrificing, and kindly disposed toward the natives, and yet fail in his mission." His strategy from the beginning was to avoid prolonged residence among the mangroves and fever-stricken wastes of the coast, but to place his Loyalty Islander missionaries there and visit them from time to time; to bring young Papuans for Christian teaching to his "central station"; to teach them English and useful industrial skills; then to send them back as founders of churches among their own people. A Scot, he thought of Darnley Island, where he wanted to settle first, as his Iona. His future colleagues of the LMS intended to live on the mainland. They did not consider McFarlane a latter-day St. Columba; they were convinced his approach was wrong.

Lawes arrived in 1873; Chalmers joined him in 1877. Both men disliked McFarlane's treating his Loyalty Islander companions "as servants." Gucheng, their leader, had been McFarlane's house-boy on Lifou. Lawes was at first linked with McFarlane and Murray in planning the New Guinea mission; both were away together on furlough in England in 1871. While they were there, Murray, from his base at Somerset on Cape York, had coordinated the placement of new Islander missionaries — five Rarotongans with their wives, and seven additional Loyalty Islanders, Between 1872 and 1874 he made five voyages on the *John Williams*. On the first of these William Wyatt Gill of Mangaia, who recruited the Rarotongans with later help from James Chalmers, accompanied him. Chalmers had spent ten years consolidating the church on Rarotonga where he involved himself enthusiastically in the island's daily life (page 270). The LMS appointed him, with Lawes, to work among the Papuans of the southeast New Guinea coast, who had some cultural affinities with Polynesians; McFarlane's major responsibility rested with Melanesians, in the western part of the LMS area.

McFarlane went to England before setting out on his new work, still glowing with the fame of his "paper war" with the French (pages 199-201). He published *The Story of the Lifu Mission,* then returned to Torres Strait. The *Ellangowan,* a thirty-six ton vessel, had been given by Miss Baxter of Dundee, who was impressed by his plans. McFarlane took his seniority for granted. He called Lawes "an able, plodding, cautious, conscientious, kind, and gentlemanly man, who had been to Savage Island pretty much what I had been to Lifu." Lawes' subsequent career proceeded to outstrip these adjectives. McFarlane, by his own account, used South Sea Island teachers to "get at" the "cannibals." Chalmers wrote of him: "You know that Mac stands at the portals and only occasionally looks in." He and Lawes, by contrast, determined to work on the mainland alongside the Islanders they brought with them, sharing as far as possible in trials and crises and gaining first-hand knowledge of Papuans in their home setting.

Lawes and Chalmers thus called the tune of advance; McFarlane grumbled in the rear. Chalmers was the inventive pioneer, Lawes the wise builder-teacher. Chalmers' inner life depended on close communion with Christ; outwardly he was gregarious, his moods alternating between rowdy courage and tender friendship. His intense eyes seemed fixed on unvisited places. Patient cultivation of a single post soon irked him. On deputation during furlough — which he disliked — he could be eloquent and visionary about missions, in the grand manner of the orator Peter Taylor Forsyth. In the Pacific he felt at home in the company of freebooters such as the pirate Bully Hayes, and of bohemians. Robert Louis Stevenson knew and admired him as being free of "the grimace." Chalmers enjoyed his pipe; his fondness for whisky provoked McFarlane's distaste. His stricter LMS colleagues deplored his affection for Pacific Island "old hands," who seemed to them to be worldly and immoral. Lawes, more formal and abstemious, did not fuss over these aspects of Chalmers' behaviour. He held the line between Chalmers' unconventionality and McFarlane's tendency to daintiness.

Lawes and Chalmers needed each other's talents. Lawes wasted no time in moving in November 1874 from the Torres Strait, to take up residence as first white man on the mainland of New Guinea, at Port Moresby. He had been preceded on Papua's coast by a group of Cook Islanders landed by Gill and Murray on 25 November 1873 at Manumanu, west of Port Moresby. At Manumanu Ruatoka, Rau, Piri, Adamu, Anederea, Heneri, their wives and one child settled for a short time among a people whose language was marginally related to their own. Attacks of malaria, and serious food shortages in the dry season, forced their evacuation to Somerset. Murray returned those who survived to settle at Hanuabada village, Port Moresby, in November 1874. In the following months they moved slightly inland, preferring dry land to the houses built out over the water by Hanuabada's fishermen and traders. Their good welcome at Hanuabada however prepared the way for later contact in Motu-speaking coastal villages along trade routes used by canoes bearing food and artifacts. When Lawes arrived in Port Moresby he depended on their prior knowledge; Ruatoka, their spokesman, guided his first contacts with Papuans.

Ruatoka's name is widely known in Papua New Guinea; he stands high within a succession of ground-breaking Islander missionaries trained in the Cooks. Slight of build, but strong, he stood alongside Chalmers; they had been friends already on Rarotonga. Ruatoka could cope, in boats, in the bush, with his hands; he had Chalmers' aptitude for trustworthy first contacts; as a missionary on a station he was more at home with carpentry than school-teaching. His first wife, Tungane, who died in 1885, was a better teacher; she

Ruatoka, Cook Islander missionary to Papua.

won her place among Motu women by teaching them how to keep house and to read and write. Ruatoka's relationship with white missionaries was not uncritically subservient; when his fellow-Islanders felt they were underpaid he stood up for their cause against Lawes. He knew villagers around Port Moresby well — and soon made friends along the coast and inland. Papuans accepted him as one among them. He and Chalmers often worked together; Chalmers called him Rua. Motu people accepted Ruatoka as a leader; they virtually adopted him. His second wife, a Papuan from Hula, co-operated with him in introducing Polynesian singing, dancing and *peroveta* (prophet) songs into the diversions and worship of Motu-speaking people.

White men who arrived in Port Moresby and its hinterland in the first New Guinea gold rush of 1878 were grateful to Ruatoka. He carried some of them who became critically ill out of the bush on his back; local people would not touch them for fear of being haunted by their ghosts. The miners presented him with a testimonial; the Queensland government sent him an inscribed fowling gun in recognition of the service he rendered. He lived in Papua for thirty-one years. In 1893 he declined to revisit his native island of Mangaia; he felt Papua had become his home. The reasons for the feeling were many. Aruadera, the first Papuan baptized convert, had turned to Christ at a Sunday service addressed by Tungane, Ruatoka's first wife. When Ruatoka's able colleague Tauraki, the son of Elekana of Manihiki and Tuvalu (page 155) was murdered at Toaripi in the Papuan Gulf in 1887, Ruatoka adopted his son, Teina Materua, who grew up in Port Moresby with a reputation for being wild. In a dream Teina Materua saw Ruatoka rebuking him. Teina Materua turned to Christ; he became influential in appealing to Papuans to enter the ministry; he himself became the first non-European civil servant in the British administration. When James Chalmers was murdered at Goaribari in 1901 Ruatoka was deeply grieved. He volunteered to go as a missionary to those who had killed his friend, but was by then too old. He died in 1906 and was buried with honour at Port Moresby.

Chalmers, in working with Ruatoka, used Rarotongan. Lawes conversed with missionaries from Niue in their own language, McFarlane with his recruits in a Lifouan language, Murray and Albert Pearse with Samoans in Samoan. Pearse came to Papua after seventeen years spent in training pastors in the Leeward Islands of Tahiti, followed by two years in Samoa. The Samoan names in Papua do not stand out so boldly as those of the Cook Islanders, but they made a substantial contribution to the growth and customs of the church. They brought to the villages the relaxed and integrated feel of the *fa'a Samoa*. Their houses were often made with rounded ends and open sides, as in their homeland. They kept regular hours of family prayer, maintained the support of themselves and their families by regular gifts of mats and food, introduced Samoan hymns, new ways of weaving, dance-drama and festive songs. LMS white missionaries and Papuans sometimes objected to their lordly expectations and conduct. They dominated many villages by their physical size; the church buildings and elementary schools they founded were firmly at the heart of village life. The impact of these Samoan missionaries continues to be gratefully recognized whenever their descendants visit the scene of their achievements. Cook Islanders, as elsewhere in the Pacific, tended to be shock troops of the Christian warfare, Samoans the occupiers and stabilizers.

Working from such beginnings, Lawes conceived his task, when the nucleus of a church had been baptized, as the preparation of Papuan teacher-evangelists for the south coast, beginning in the Eastern District. Methods he had tested on Niue were adapted to fit the needs of many tribes living in uneasy relationships with each other to eastward and westward of his headquarters. They were often held together by canoe trade routes, but strife-ridden as a result of feuding among them within the code of honour called "pay-back." Lawes founded his training school at Port Moresby. He adopted Motu as the language of the mission. Chalmers questioned whether this was wise, favouring English, as better preparation for the inevitable opening up of New Guinea to a wider world, and as a more neutral and therefore acceptable *lingua franca* when entering the strife of tongues further inland. In 1894 Lawes moved his training institution further east to Vatorata. His policy was in contrast with McFarlane's, whose industrial school on Murray Island lay out of the stream of exploration and colonization on the mainland.

McFarlane tended a cluster of small LMS congregations among the polygot and widely intermarried inhabitants of the strait — migrant Polynesian sailors, Filipino pearlers, small traders and the aboriginal islanders. Their external orientation was toward North Queensland, their main source of supplies and place of employment for emigrant labourers. The Papuan Western District mission, also officially under McFarlane, languished. The teachers he placed there were ill-supported and dispirited. In 1887 he retired to England to join the home staff of the LMS. St. Andrews University made him an honorary LL.D. The growing attention paid to the achievements of Chalmers and Lawes did not please him; he blamed them for not responding to his own view of what should have been done. McFarlane was a mixture of progressive notions and cautious action. He held liberal views on sabbath observance, the use of yams and coconut milk for Holy Communion services, and early baptism for people under instruction. Lawes and Chalmers delayed baptism until they were satisfied with candidates' doctrinal and moral progress. McFarlane deprecated preaching on the perils of hell. He believed in elevating the heathen in the social scale by imparting honesty, cleanliness and hard work. John Howard Angas of South Australia, a wealthy Congregational philanthropist, donated liberally for the industrial training school he built on Murray Island. Nor was McFarlane a sympathetic ally of neutral anthropological science; one of his beliefs did not falter — that British Nonconformist customs and comforts were also Christian and should prevail.

Other exotic worlds appealed more to Chalmers, who was elated when able to travel on the beaches and in the bush. Village headmen along the shore took him into the great houses of the men in many places and showed him the rituals. He prized the camaraderie of warriors and was abrupt about attempts to Europeanize them prematurely. In 1885 he wrote:

> A great mistake has hitherto been made in missionary work; the missionaries have reported 'respectably clothed natives who once were naked savages,' and the churches have applauded the conversion of the savages. These clothed natives are, I believe, only hurrying along a respectable and easy road to the grave. To swathe their limbs in European clothing spoils them, and, I fear, hurries them to premature death. Put excessive clothing with syphilis and strong drink, and, I think, we shall be nearer the truth.

At the same time his admiration for aspects of Papuan life did not make him a relativist any more than McFarlane. He recognized that people wanted beads, cloth and tobacco; he used these as ways to catch their interest in simple teaching about God's love in Christ. He believed faith in God's love would help them question their fear of local spirits and ghosts. He had been trained at Cheshunt College at a time when the doctrinal system of Calvinism was being softened by simple assurance of the presence of Christ in the life of the believer. "Our trust is in Him;" he told his wife in 1878; "nearer still to our adorable Lord Jesus, to live His life and to be filled with His love, to be lost to self; His alone, safe in His arms; rest!" This warmly Arminian note was first struck in Chalmers as a boy by Gilbert Meikle, the minister of his Scottish Presbyterian parish church. In deciding as a young man to become a Congregational minister he accepted the doctrine of free universal grace then flowing into many Congregational churches as a result of their theological accommodation to Wesleyan influences.

Four stages succeeded each other in Chalmers' Papuan career as he advanced from east to west along the coast. He began, after a short initiation under Lawes at Port Moresby, in the Eastern District, where he settled with his first wife, Jane, on Suau Island off South Cape. The Islander missionaries who accompanied them were harassed by the acquisitive Suau people and by the attacks of their jealous neighbours. Eventually, after violence had spread to the mission's schooner *Mayri*, anchored off-shore, a Suau man was killed on board. The *Mayri* cast off to obtain refuge and help at Port Moresby. In the three weeks of acute emergency that followed Chalmers proved his ability to live among the people without firearms. His courage and authority in the emergency established his standing among Papuans, then and in the future.

THE LURE OF NEW GUINEA

When the situation at Suau settled he entrusted much of his task to Pi, the leader of his Rarotongan missionary associates, and began his journeys into the villages between East Cape, where Polynesian teachers were stationed, and Orangerie Bay. He often left his wife alone at Suau. She had shared Chalmers' life in Rarotonga and now endured malaria, dysentery and loneliness with cheerful patience. In 1878 her health broke down; she had to be sent to Sydney, where she died in February 1879. In July Chalmers, after returning from visiting Australia, moved to Port Moresby.

For almost four years, when Lawes was away on furlough in England, Chalmers was in charge there. This second phase of his service coincided with crucial changes in the government and the mission. The gold rush of the late 1870s had opened the way for prospectors and traders. Land-hungry men coveted the wealth of New Guinea. Australians, particularly in Queensland, became touchy about German colonizing activity in the north. Patrolling British warships of the Australian station were called to intervene when LMS Polynesian missionaries were violently treated in Papua. At Kalo in March 1881 four Rarotongans, their wives and four children were murdered. When the warship *Wolverene* went to punish the Kalo people in the following August, Chalmers was on board. He and Lawes, like Inglis and Paton in the New Hebrides (page 177), believed such prompt action was familiar under the customary codes of the peoples of Papua and would help in eventual pacification of the region. They also thought a British protectorate was needed to police the conduct of land-hungry white men and would-be labour recruiters, mostly from Queensland. Lawes lobbied the imperial government; he sought a British protectorate, as preferable to annexation by Queensland.

When Queensland did annex the territory in 1883, the LMS made representations in London in favour of a wider British protectorate. The plea was heard; Commodore Erskine of the Australian Naval Station brought a force of blue-jackets to declare the protectorate on 4 November 1884; the first ceremony took place on the steps of the LMS Port Moresby mission house. Chalmers was away at the time; when he returned he accompanied Erskine along the coast as intermediary with the villagers when the flag was hoisted wider afield. The LMS had already been through this symbol of pomp when Queensland stepped in. "Flag-hoisting," Lawes observed wryly to Wardlaw Thompson, the LMS Secretary, "must seem to the natives to be a white man's amusement." To Lawes and Chalmers a protectorate seemed sufficient; they feared an influx of settlers would follow proclamation of the territory as a colony and lead to alienation of Papuan land on a large scale. But naval patrols could not control disorders when these developed inland. In 1888 British New Guinea was made a colony. Sir William MacGregor, the first governor, had been in Fiji as Chief Medical Officer and had acted there temporarily as Governor and High Commissioner for the Western Pacific. A

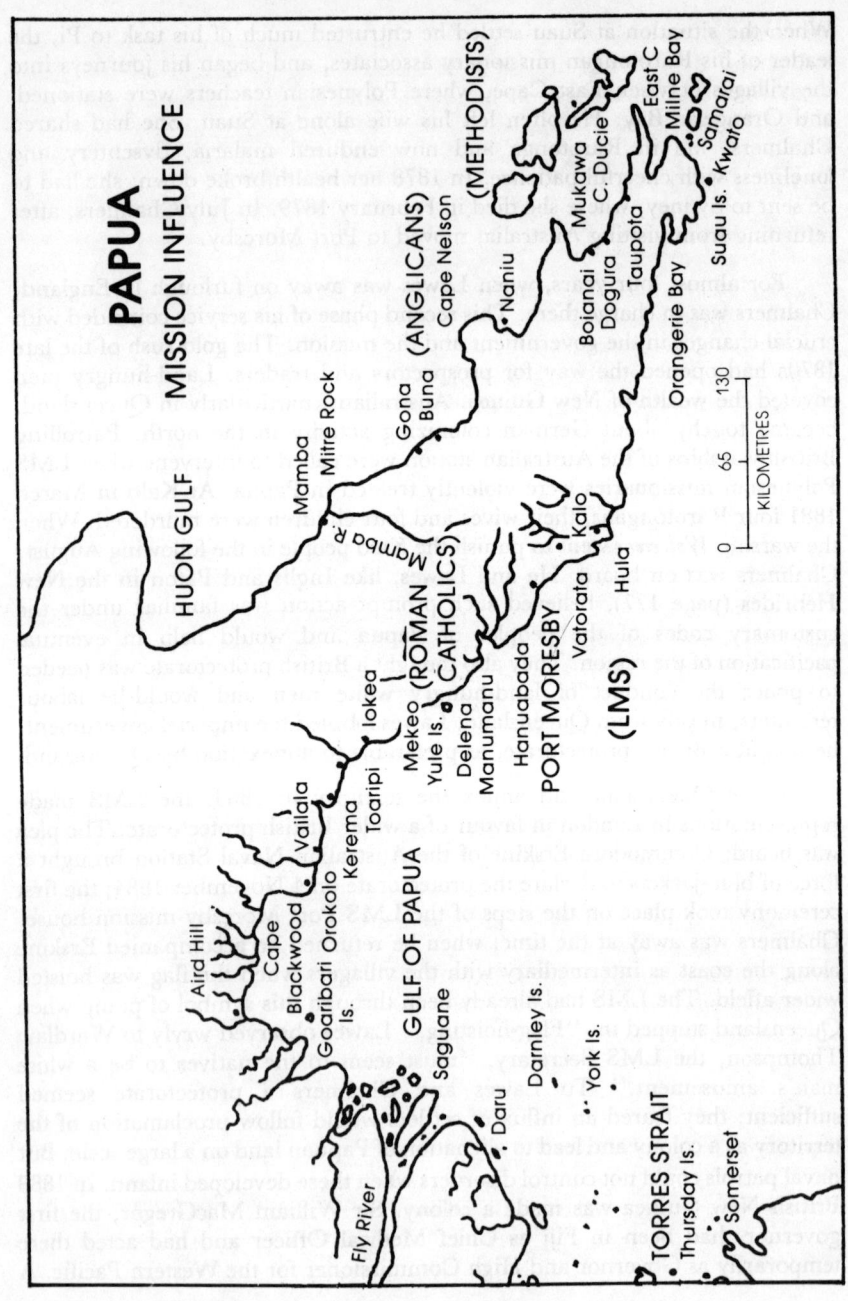

THE LURE OF NEW GUINEA

Presbyterian, he supported missions within his jurisdiction as promoting order and peace. He worked amicably in Papua with the LMS — and later encouraged Methodists and Anglicans to enter parts of the colony the LMS was unable to consider because of limited resources.

During Chalmers' time at Port Moresby his friendship with Lawes ripened. His flamboyance was a foil to Lawes' patience and system. In his tropical whites and scarlet cummerbund James Chalmers was an unconformable servant of the Word who spent free hours over a glass in the company of traders and government officials. Lawes, working on the Motu New Testament, knew that Chalmers was the man who would help him disseminate it in the villages. Chalmers depended on Lawes and his wife to provide him with a fixed centre — their home — which was his restorative oasis in his time as a widower. Wardlaw Thompson and his colleagues in the LMS District Committee urged Chalmers to take the furlough owing to him. He recoiled from the thought:

> Rather than go home engaged to do deputation work I would risk climate, savages, and sea and land travelling; the former in open boats, and the latter carrying my own swag on New Guinea.

When he finally yielded, in 1886, he achieved celebrity in British missionary circles. His flair for oratory and his leonine appearance set him alongside another LMS veteran, Robert Moffat of Matabeleland — as an evangelical explorer at an outpost of the Empire. He acquired a new bride, Sarah Elizabeth (Lizzie) Harrison, a widow who had been a close friend of his first wife. She came out to marry him at Cooktown in October 1888.

His journeys during his stay at Port Moresby had opened the way for new stations in the Gulf of Papua, at Iokea, Toaripi, Kerema, Vailala and Orokolo. In 1887 Chalmers was saddened by the murder of his friend and former pupil, Tauraki of Mangaia, at Toaripi. The people of neighbouring Moveave killed Tauraki and five Toaripi villagers. A British "eye for an eye" reprisal in which five Moveave were killed shocked Chalmers by its brutality. Early in 1888 he settled with his new wife at Toaripi in a solid cedar house he thought palatial. His wife, loyal, but not accustomed to missionary austerity, was less entranced, but set her hand to turning the place into a more inviting home.

From Toaripi Chalmers strengthened the LMS presence in the villages of the gulf. He placed and supervised Cook Islanders, leaving his wife for long periods at home alone. She did not protest. The Toaripi villagers were considerate and kind, but she was lonely. Malaria undermined her strength. Chalmers took her with him in 1890 to visit LMS churches in Samoa and Rarotonga, partly as convalescence for her, partly to recruit new Islander missionaries. On the way from Sydney to Samoa they were fellow passengers with Robert Louis Stevenson, and with George Brown of the Wesleyan Missionary Society, another Pacific old timer (page 128). The three men shared many qualities — wide-ranging imagination, love of a telling phrase, a taste for colourful company, antipathy to religiosity. Brown and Chalmers, said Stevenson, were "pioneer missionaries, splendid men, with no humbug, plenty courage, and the love of adventure." After visiting Samoa Chalmers went on to Rarotonga where he had learned how to be a missionary (pages 270-1).

His wife returned refreshed to Papua, but the improvement did not last. In 1891 recurrent malaria nearly killed her; she and Chalmers agreed she must return to England to recuperate. For five years after her departure in March 1892 Chalmers was left to restore the dilapidated LMS work in the Western District. Chalmers and Lawes lamented its collapse after McFarlane's departure in 1887. From 1891 onward Chalmers, pained by what he considered wrong previous strategy, tried to mend the situation by sailing repeatedly between Murray Island and the run-down western mainland stations, to the detriment of the work in the gulf and the concern of his fellow-missionaries. After his wife left he threw himself uninterruptedly into the tasks of setting right the situation in the strait and the west, with one break for home furlough in Britain in 1894.

While Chalmers was away in England, Robert Bruce, his down-to-earth but free-living lay assistant and crony in the Strait Mission, scandalized the other LMS missionaries in Papua by his drinking habits and his liaisons with women. Frederick Walker of the Western Division, who had been inspired by Chalmers to become a missionary, broke with him during the resulting crisis. Chalmers, in England, defended Bruce; he portrayed his colleague as an occasional sinner and deprecated the condemnatory attitudes of his brother missionaries. Chalmers tolerated Bruce's vagaries, as one among many Pacific characters, in return for his usefulness and companionship. Lawes, uncomfortable, tended to sit on the fence until the problem resolved itself; Walker asked to be transferred to the Eastern Division away from the unsavoury debate; Bruce resigned.

For the limited remainder of his life Chalmers' relationship with most of his younger co-workers was strained. He buried himself in toil beyond his strength. When his house at Toaripi was threatened by the encroaching sea he moved to Iokea in the gulf. In developing village churches around the mouth of the Fly he often acted independently of the District Committee, suggesting to the other missionaries that Wardlaw Thompson as Foreign Secretary of the LMS had given him direct authority to proceed. Thompson, when he heard of it, was surprised to find how much rope Chalmers had taken; he took steps to rein him in. By then Chalmers had brought better order to the situation on Murray and Darnley; he then fixed his eye on building a permanent station for himself at Saguane, situated handily between villages of the Kiwai people to north and south of the Fly estuary. His wife joined him in the newly built house in 1897, bringing with her the haven he needed in his travels. Together they began to revive Christianity among the Saguane people, assisted by the Rarotongan teacher Hiro. From 1898 Chalmers had the close friendship of a fellow-individualist, John Henry Holmes of Orokolo. Oliver Tomkins, an earnest young Congregational minister fresh out of Cheshunt College, came to join Chalmers in February 1900. Tomkins was put in charge of work in the strait, where his grave and eager piety found a good welcome.

The lately won consolations of Chalmers' renewed married life at Saguane did not endure. In 1900 Lizzie Chalmers' health failed again. Her recurrent tropical illnesses, including heat-rash and boils, became complicated by more serious weakness, believed by Chalmers to have been cancer. He nursed her gently through her bed-ridden months; finally he moved her at her own wish to die and be buried on Daru, the government station of the Western Division. Hard work followed — Chalmers' antidote to grief. He removed his headquarters from Saguane, where the tide threatened yet another of his Papuan homes, to Daru. The last months he spent there were darkened by depression he could not permanently shake off. Before his wife died, he had suffered a serious fall. Rheumatism and headaches troubled him. He reflected sadly on his childlessness, easing the pain of his mourning with whisky, which had long been his private pleasure. Tomkins, probably affected by Chalmers' mood, mused on the meaning of Christian death and martyrdom. Both men had private presentiments of heaven. News of Queen Victoria's death sharpened Chalmers' foreboding; an era seemed to be ending. But he continued with his old courage to plan for work ahead. He used some of his time in setting down reminiscences; they contained sharp asides on the LMS and on his Papuan associates in particular. He believed, as did Holmes, that the members of the District Committee were too willing to defer humbly to government people with whom they fraternized. When his colleagues went through his papers after his death they were stung by what he wrote. They destroyed the papers, but some of the content has survived by report.

A.H. Jiear, the acting government administrator on Daru, irritated Chalmers by accusing him of moving from Saguane to take shelter under the government's wing. After Lizzie Chalmers' death, Jiear hurt Chalmers by shooting his wife's pet collie dog under circumstances that are unclear. The episode preceded Chalmers' setting out in April 1901 on his final mission to Goaribari. In March the Papua District Committee had met at Daru. The good company revived him. It seems likely that he chose to set out for the as yet unevangelized coasts of the Gulf between Cape Blackwood and the Fly as a way of linking the LMS work in the Gulf with what he had achieved in the west. His altercation with Jiear might also have affected his choice of

Goaribari as destination. By going unprotected among its fierce and suspicious people he freed himself from any thought of working under governmental shelter.

On Easter Sunday, 7 April, the drama reached its peak when Chalmers, with Tomkins, nine Kiwai students from his training school at Daru and two others, went ashore from the mission vessel *Niue* among the little known warriors of Goaribari Island; they were all killed and eaten. The exact details of the killings and the motives have to be conjecturally reconstructed from a variety of subsequent accounts. When news of the tragedy reached Australia and Britain a wave of sorrow was succeeded by many eulogies. In New Guinea, among his colleagues, the tributes were muted. They had loved the great missionary but witnessed his powers failing as he drew near the end they long feared. The Rarotongan missionaries, led by Ruatoka, were inconsolable. To them he had been both father in God and a brother. Grim sequels marred the record and alienated the Goaribari people. The government, against the better judgment of the LMS, sent three punitive expeditions to Goaribari. The third, led by an inexperienced young administrator from Australia, C.S. Robinson, led to clashes, then slaughter. Protests in Australia forced the setting up of a Royal Commission to inquire into what occurred. Robinson, badly shaken by public reaction to his handling of the situation, defended his actions in written depositions, then dramatically shot himself, standing in the early morning light beside the government flagstaff at Port Moresby.

The successive stages of Chalmers' career chart the expanding map of the LMS Papuan field, but other resourceful missionaries reaped patiently where he sowed. Harry M. Dauncey, who came with Frederick W. Walker in response to Chalmers' appeals in England, stayed for forty years, spent mainly at the "delectable" Delena station. Walker, after his breach with Chalmers, became co-founder, with Charles W. Abel, a masterful personality, of prosperous industrial missions and plantations; their distinctive approach led to controversy with the LMS and to the secession of the Kwato Evangelical Association from affiliation to the LMS. Holmes of Iokea, a skilled observer of the cultures of the gulf, and William James Saville on the island of Mailu, were valued informants of the anthropologists Haddon and Malinowski. Benjamin T. Butcher, a lovable man of powerful physique, able to lead Papuans in building and bush-craft, came out as a young man to the strait when he heard of Chalmers' death. He was the first to succeed in reopening relationships with the embittered Goaribari people. From his Aird Hill station he travelled inland and along the shore, gentle in his personal relationships. He served in Papua for thirty-six years, defending his simplified liberal modernist theology in Australia in the course of a long retirement.

W.G. Lawes, LMS pioneer in Papua.

These and others who followed, the "bishops" in the Papuan structure of the London Missionary Society, pledged, often against the grain of their prevailingly Congregational Independent personal convictions, to doing as the Directors in London told them. In the local churches of the Papuan villages, once established, they encouraged elected Papuan deacons to take local initiative. The primary schools they founded in many villages laid foundations for unification of a culturally fragmented littoral. Motu, used by the police and in the church, helped shape a Papuan identity. As MacGregor had hoped and urged, village leadership underlined the harmony of law and gospel, police and deacons. The white dove on a blue ground, banner of the LMS, still flutters on important occasions over many villages. The acquisition of English and experience of governing on a small scale have contributed to the Papuan share in forming the modern state of Papua New Guinea. Hymns and forms of worship evolved out of the fusion of Samoan, Rarotongan, British and local elements. The Motu Bible edited by Lawes, in the hands of the pastors trained in a succession of schools he pioneered, has given the person of Christ a controlling place within the context of widely held belief in the power of nature and ancestor spirits. As in all Christian churches of any size, popular conceptions and resort to magic mingle in a religious amalgam with the "deposit of faith" expressed in catechisms, preaching and creeds. The LMS church in Papua was the first to emerge from the Stone Age as a literate society formed by contact.

NEW BRITAIN: METHODISM

THE AUSTRALASIAN WESLEYAN METHODISTS entered the islands around New Britain after George Brown, who had served for eight years in Samoa, expressed his wish to go to Melanesia (pages 128-132). In August 1868 he told his general secretary in Australia he was ready for bigger things:

> Don't forget that whenever our people wake up to a sense of their duty and resolve to send the Gospel to New Guinea & the densely populated Islands on the Line that I claim to have a share in it. I do wish that we could extend. Our brethren of the L.M.S. are extending their operations...

Brown's angling bore fruit, but not for six years. When he left Samoa he went on deputation to New South Wales, Tasmania, Victoria and New Zealand, canvassing the prospect of a mission to the large island of New Britain, northeast of Papua. He impressed Henry Reed, a Wesleyan Methodist merchant and shipowner of Launceston, Tasmania, who supported his project and gave a steam launch, the *Henry Reed*. The Australasian

THE LURE OF NEW GUINEA

Wesleyan General Conference authorized Brown to go to Levuka, the capital of the then recently ceded British Colony of Fiji, and to Samoa. He was charged to follow LMS precedent by recruiting locally prepared assistant missionaries as teachers and pastors for New Britain. In Samoa he had often advocated handing over more control in the mission to Islanders. Before going to Samoa to pick up two of his own "old boys" he visited Fiji to recruit the larger part of his future contingent.

At Levuka there were problems. The Wesleyan missionaries had been preparing a group of Islanders for Melanesia; many of these died in a catastrophic measles epidemic in Fiji just before Brown arrived; others were no longer available. With help from three missionaries — Lorimer Fison, Jesse Carey and Joseph Waterhouse — Brown visited Rewa, Bau and finally Navuloa, near one of the mouths of the Rewa River, where Waterhouse was in charge of an institution for training Fijian pastors. On the night of 1 June 1875 Waterhouse assembled eighty-three students at Navuloa in a dimly lit hall. Brown addressed them and called for volunteers. He gave a deliberately sober picture of New Britain — of "the ferocity of the natives; of the unhealthy character of the climate"; he said "that they would be exposed to dangers on every hand; that in all probability many of them would never see their own Fijian homes again." He asked the students to think it over during the night before giving their answer. Waterhouse told them to pray and to consult their families.

Next morning all eighty-three volunteered. Six married and three single men were chosen. Joeli Bulu, the patriarch among Tongan Wesleyan missionaries to Fiji (pages 281ff) "gave them a very stirring address." During the following ten days, as the expedition prepared to sail, the British government officials at Levuka grew apprehensive, especially the Administrator, Edgar Layard, who thought the nine teachers, now protected British subjects, might be persuaded against their (and his) judgment to go to New Britain. Government officials began privately to interview the volunteers. Brown then sought an interview with Layard in the presence of the students who had been chosen and of other officials, including John Bates Thurston, who was experienced in Fiji and informed about the Western Pacific. Layard was anxious not to be suspected of conniving at transporting a labour force out of Fiji so soon after cession, even for religious reasons; he painted a gloomier picture of New Britain than Brown had already done. The leader of the group, Aminio Baledrokadroka, was then given leave to reply on behalf of all nine. In a speech that became classic as expressing the mind of hundreds of missionaries who followed him then and afterwards to Melanesia, Aminio assured Layard that they understood the dangers involved, were grateful to Britain for its concern, and had not been coerced, but had volunteered:

Sir, we have fully considered this matter in our hearts; no one has pressed us in any way; we have given ourselves up to do God's work, and our mind today, sir, is to go with Mr Brown. If we die, we die; if we live, we live.

Layard, still not satisfied, tried again to warn them; he quoted grim accounts of violent incidents in New Guinea. Thurston then asked permission to speak. With Brown's aid he respectfully corrected some parts of Layard's Jeremiad, adding that Layard wished each man to speak for himself. The volunteers thereupon individually "in loud tones" said, "It is all perfectly clear to us. *Sa macala saka.*" All signed a written declaration that they accepted freely.

Brown and the Polynesian teachers with him reached the strategically chosen first base at Port Hunter on Duke of York Island in St. George's Channel between the larger islands of New Britain and New Ireland on 15 August 1875. No invading government authority had as yet been proclaimed over New Britain. Occasional cruising warships watched over the safety of their own nationals. Hernsheims, a German trading firm, was setting up stations and plantations. Brown's advance information about New Britain came partly from his contacts with German commercial representatives he had known during his years in Samoa. Melanesia appealed to his adventurous side. He liked the feeling of conquering untamed country. Crocodiles and birds abounded for shooting and stuffing; new tribes and tongues opened up for the observer and linguist in him. A missionary in such a spot could run his own outfit, nurturing churches among man-eating populations to whom he would be the first preacher.

The composite role suited Brown. A true Wesleyan, with a high regard for the Anglican Prayer Book religion out of which the Wesleys came, his style made him readily acceptable to colonial administrators and traders; a glass of wine at dinner did not go amiss with Brown, whose convictions pre-dated the total abstinence movement in Methodism and linked him with the old fashioned Wesleyans around Jabez Bunting, Britain's mid-century Methodist giant, whom he revered. Brown was brisk; he had grit, despatch. His tropical whites, pith helmet and trim goatee were late Victorian frontier symbols. Melanesians, shorter in average physique than Polynesians, fell into scale alongside his wiry frame. Wherever he went he wrote diligently for posterity. He outshone most of his Methodist contemporaries in Australia and New Zealand in mental grasp, but he was proud of being a Wesleyan and a missionary. Nothing diverted him from that principal calling. He had instant bonds of union with the Samoans and Fijians he supervised. He learned Fijian before he left for New Britain and was later proud to have baptized people at various times using six different languages. On the voyage from Fiji he decided he would stay on with the teachers in New Britain, even though his wife and children in Auckland expected him back. He was deeply moved by sermons in Fijian from Fiji's Elimotama Ravono and Ratu Livai Volavola. He never doubted the wisdom of working through them in the villages; he reported that the teachers told him "the natives often considered them as belonging to them, and forming part of their community." The inner process of growth in the churches of the New Guinea islands came largely as the result of a substantial missionary migration of Fijians and Samoans bearing a new religion in terms that could be understood more readily because there were cultural affinities between teacher and taught.

Within a week of arriving Brown had supervised the building of a rough house on Duke of York; he made his first excursion to the fearsome people on Matupit, close to the Gazelle Peninsula, the future main centre of the mission's work. He noted that the Duke of York people, unlike Polynesians, were "inveterate traders and pedlars." Trading routes among the diverse language groups of the area were traversed by the mission as it offered a new religion in place of the old — a message of peace that was attractive to headmen when it was seen to lessen feuds and facilitate trade. Development concentrated among the Kiwai people of the Gazelle and on the western New Ireland coast. Brown's hopes were high. He used the *Henry Reed* to make contacts with chiefs, remaining for a first spell of fourteen months. As expected, he and the teachers suffered from malaria. At the end of November Timoci, one of the Fijians, died. All the women of the pioneer group of Pacific Islanders, except one Samoan, died in New Britain. Seven more Fijians came as reinforcements in 1876. Brown stationed them provisionally in places he had visited, then left for Australia to report, to improve finances and supplies, to bring his wife and two children from Auckland to join him and to arrange for the schooling of his other children. When he came back he was displeased to find the teachers had made no move to leave the Duke of York group for the stations he had assigned to them. Probably at that stage he could not sense the advantages — in terms of personal security — his presence, as a white man, gave him, especially as he was known to be a good friend of well armed resident traders. Eduard Hernsheim had personally greeted Brown when he first arrived.

When he returned in July 1877 Brown concentrated on improving the situation, through seven stations in the Duke of York islands and eleven on New Britain. By October he was on New Ireland, where Le Bera, the chief at Kalil, was friendly. Five stations were set up there, under six teachers. In the following January and February volcanoes on the shores of Blanche Bay erupted; an island was thrown up in the bay, though the Duke of Yorks were not seriously affected. Brown's powers as observer took over as he vividly recorded details — a boiling crater filled with water, rafts of pumice in the sea.

TO LIVE AMONG THE STARS

This apocalyptic opening of what was to be one of the most traumatic years of his life was succeeded in March and April by outbreaks of malaria among the mission's staff and traders in the district. Hernsheim's resident trader, Hans Blohm, took refuge when ill in the Port Hunter mission house. Outbreaks of violence against white traders in isolated places gave warning of more to come. Brown was distressed when two children of his old Samoan friends Misieli and Paseta died. He himself suffered from the filariasis he had contracted in Samoa and from fever, but treated himself with his usual remedy, work, which he pronounced "in some respects more beneficial than any medicine I could have taken."

On 8 April he heard that the Rev. Sailasa Naucukidi of Fiji and three other Fijians had been murdered while crossing the Gazelle Peninsula on mission south of Kabakada. Talili, a powerful trading chief who lived not far from Kabakada, had for some time been angry over the disruption of his coastal and bush trading by white traders and the missionaries. His men waylaid and gruesomely killed Sailasa, Livai Naboro and Timoci Barave (a

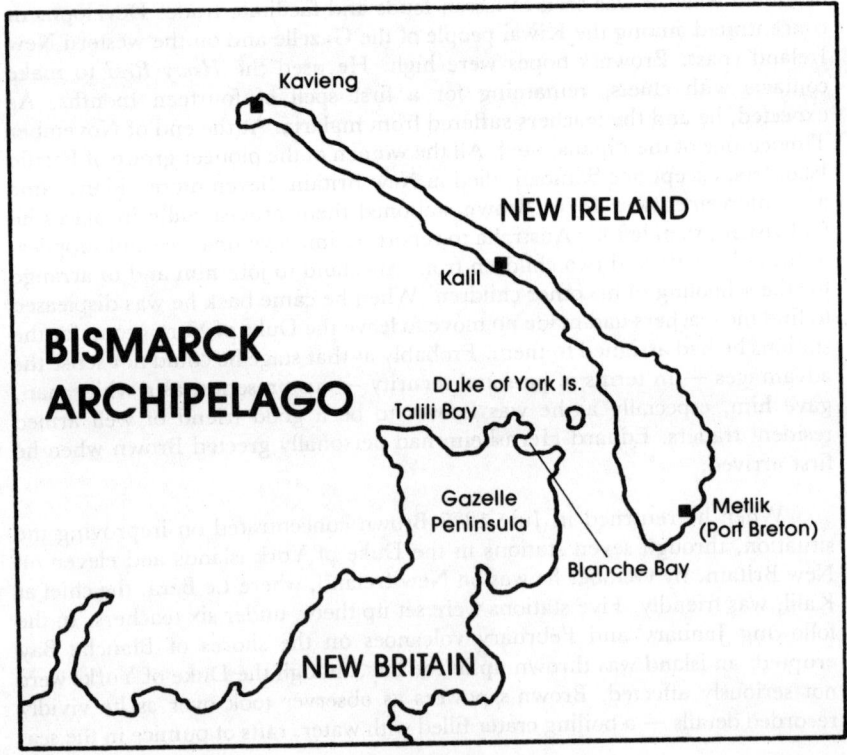

lay helper). Peni Luvu, a big man, broke loose from the ambush in long grass and fled exhausted for refuge to Talili's village, not knowing who had directed the attack; he accepted a coconut and threw back his head to drink the milk; as he did so Talili savagely cut off his head with a scrub knife. All the victims of the attacks were eaten. Brown hurried to Kabakada as soon as he heard the news to find his teachers and other local white men already planning punitive action. The Fijians and Samoans believed it was their duty to their kinsmen and friends to retrieve any remains of the dead and demand satisfaction from Talili. The white men, in the absence of a police force, were resolved on prompt frontier justice. Sir Arthur Gordon, the Governor of Fiji, was to become High Commissioner for the Western Pacific during the year; his future powers were as yet undefined. News of his pending appointment came too late to be taken into account. Brown, after unsuccessfully putting out feelers for Talili to come and negotiate with him, conferred with traders and missionaries; they agreed on an armed expedition. News came through that Talili defiantly announced he had prepared local vegetables as a "relish" to eat with Brown. All thought the lives of teachers and traders were in further danger; the Fijians, who knew Talili already, insisted that only a show of force could restrain him under the code he lived by.

Eight days after the murders two parties moved from different directions to attack Talili and the inland settlements of his accomplices. The northern avenging party of residents and sailors, led by Brown, stood off shore from Talili's village in boats. The other party landed from Blanche Bay and worked northward across the interior, doing most of the damage. Aminio Baledrokadroka warned Brown that villagers friendly to the mission would not hesitate to turn over to Talili if attacks on his village did not succeed. This was confirmed when Brown found his two whaleboats ringed around by the canoes of these supposedly friendly allies, ready to move in for a share of the loot if Brown's measures against Talili failed. Brown ordered shots to be fired to disperse the canoes; one or two people in them were lightly wounded. After talking to the occupants of the dispersed canoes and paying them off appropriately, Brown's raiders landed; they burned Talili's house and smashed his canoe. After this the bought-off allies co-operated to join the southern party in forays inland; bones of the dead teachers were recovered; shell-money, betel, coconuts and bananas were sent by most chiefs as a sign of capitulation; finally Brown personally went inland to seal the peace, offering forgiveness in return for a pledge that there would be no repetition of hostilities. He eventually met Talili, who became his friend. Brown regarded him as a touching old rogue, whose "natural force of character and intelligence" he savoured with a victor's satisfaction.

George Brown knew at once his actions were controversial. He covered his tracks by writing to the newly installed Sir Arthur Gordon. "We only heard of the appointment being made long after we were friends again with the people," he said. The white sailors and resident traders who had joined in the expedition furnished him in May with a letter approving his support in the joint action they took against the chief referred to comically by one of them as "Tarlily." Australians soon heard what had happened. Imperial watchdogs approved; outraged liberals were dismayed. The Melbourne *Age* thundered in its editorial columns against Brown: "If Wesleyan Christianity obtains a foothold in New Britain it will have been by the means introduced by Mohammed — the sword in one hand, the book in the other — baptism or butchery, the only alternative of the people." Wilfrid Powell, master of the ketch *Star of the East,* who had joined in the raids, defended Brown manfully. British naval commanders on *Beagle* and *Sandfly* joined chorus with Captain von Werner of the German gunboat *Ariadne* and Theodore Weber, the German consul in Samoa, to rally to his side. Munster, the German Ambassador in London, commended him to Lord Salisbury. "There is not a native in the group," wrote Brown in his own defence, "who does not acknowledge that we did right." Within the Wesleyan Church in Australia, where some hesitations were felt at first, support stiffened and was finally confirmed in the Australasian Conference, where John Watsford, formerly of Fiji (page 110), who had been Brown's ally in promoting the New Britain mission, upheld his cause.

Watsford was father-in-law to Benjamin Danks, who joined Brown in New Britain in December 1878, accompanied by his wife Emma and eight more Fijian missionaries, seven of whom were married. Watsford came with them on a visit. They were in time to see Brown perform the first baptisms, for five young men from Duke of York Island and two from Kalil. Danks came from a family of engineers; he "succeeded in effecting some very necessary repairs" to the steam launch *Henry Reed.* The mission board had instructed him to live near Brown at Kinavanua on Duke of York, but with Brown's endorsement he sought and gained permission to go instead as the first white resident missionary at Kabakada on New Britain, which he described as "a land, to me, full of glorious missionary possibilities and lurking dangers." Danks was a simpler person than Brown. His uncle and cousin, stalwarts of the Methodist Church in Melbourne, were successful mechanics and hardware merchants. His career in New Britain ended in 1886, to his disappointment, when his wife's health gave cause for alarm and plans for him to become principal of a school on New Ireland for local pastors fell through. But in the years between he collaborated effectively in the work of "the first quartette of New Britain missionaries: Brown, Danks, Rooney and Rickard." Isaac Rooney had spent fourteen years in Fiji before coming to New Britain; he and R. Heath Rickard, who compiled a dictionary and grammar of New Britain languages, gave the local dialects written form with Danks and began Bible translation. In the villages the work of the mission was chiefly carried on

THE LURE OF NEW GUINEA

by the large staff of Fijian and Samoan teacher-pastors, whose names outnumber those of the Australians and Germans in the list of serving missionaries to the close of the nineteenth century.

George Brown's troubles of 1878 continued. In May 1879 he was evacuated to Queensland on Hernsheim's steam launch *Alice* following the breakdown of his health, leaving behind his wife and three children, including one born in New Britain. In Sydney Benjamin Chapman and William Fletcher of the mission board gravely told him doctors had given up hope of his survival and he should prepare calmly for death. Brown declined their advice. Dragging himself from what was considered to be his deathbed, he sailed to Auckland to visit his other children. The controversy over his participation in the punishment of Talili was at its height. With a combination of stubbornness and adroit manoeuvre, he decided, as his health revived, to go on the *John Wesley* to Levuka and put himself within the jurisdiction of the Western Pacific High Commission, where the Honourable John Gorrie was preparing, as Chief Justice of Fiji and Acting High Commissioner, to hear a charge of manslaughter against him on account of his impromptu police activity in New Britain. He arrived at Levuka on 3 November to find that Sir Arthur Gordon was back in Fiji after visiting England.

Gorrie and Gordon disliked each other. Gorrie had been praised by the Aborigines' Protection Society, a humanitarian organisation in close touch with Exeter Hall, on account of his share as a barrister in prosecuting Governor Edward John Eyre for his conduct in suppressing the Jamaica Rebellion. Gordon, in private, had a low opinion of Gorrie's legal abilities. When Brown appeared Gordon invited him to dine at Government House, explaining that proceedings in court would be deferred until Gorrie, who had been acting for him at the time when the events in New Britain took place, returned. Meanwhile Brown went visiting mission stations elsewhere in Fiji, receiving assurances on the way from Levuka that reports of an investigation made in New Britain by Captain Purvis of H.M.S. *Danae* were encouraging. A week later, when Brown returned to Levuka, Gordon informed the Wesleyans he was surprised to find a criminal summons had nevertheless been issued against Brown in Gorrie's court. Gordon proceeded to up-stage his resident judge by receiving Brown in audience, dressed in robes that appeared to Brown to be those of his honorary Doctorate of Civil Law. J.B. Thurston, one of Brown's friends in Fiji, was present as secretary to the governor.

Gordon formally addressed Brown; he said no evidence in his possession suggested a crime had been committed — and he hoped none would come before the court when it convened next day. Overnight, on Gordon's instructions, the prosecution was withdrawn in view of insufficient conclusive evidence. Thus, when Gorrie convened the court he found proceedings stalled by two technicalities — the withdrawal of the expected prosecution, and a prior opinion expressed by the High Commissioner for the Western Pacific, as "head" over the court. Brown considered that Gordon's address to him, of which he received a copy, was equivalent to the findings of a Grand Jury. Gorrie was obliged to dismiss the case; he was chagrined by the colonial comedy that had left Brown free to depart out of his jurisdiction. The settlers on the beach at Levuka — champions of rough frontier justice — were jubilant; they offered Brown a celebratory dinner, which he declined with thanks. He had put his head in a noose that never tightened. "Here we are distressing ourselves with anxiety and fear," wrote Langham, the formidable chairman of the Fiji Mission, "and he is quite unconcerned." The outcome of the non-trial provided Brown with ammunition in London against mission administrators and philanthropists who were still stirring indignantly at Exeter Hall. "I have yet borne a great deal of unmerited obloquy and suffering from the few, especially from one or two in England who know least about the matter," Brown wrote to the editor of *The Australasian*.

Sailing back toward New Britain on the *John Wesley* he felt he was being pursued by Gorrie's lingering venom as a bad hurricane threatened the ship's company with what looked like death at sea. His indignation when the captain of the limping *Wesley* put back to Sydney instead of heading to the nearby Solomons for repairs verged on fury. He knew his waiting family would be anxious for him; they had indeed been desperately ill; a son and daughter had died. After he rejoined his wife he was still emotionally wrought; he climbed back to his old equanimity only gradually during his short third term of service between March 1880 and the following January. Resuming his toil in caring for about thirty mission stations in the group, he supervised the work of the first local preachers, including Peni Lelei of Duke of York, who became his "best pundit"; later Peni visited Australia to help with translation before going back as a missionary among his own people.

The activities of labour traders, who appeared in the area in increasing numbers to recruit men from the islands for plantation work in Queensland, provoked Brown and Danks to strong protest. When the German Government occupied New Britain in 1884, Danks applauded its action in stopping the traffic. Other newcomers, victims of Charles de Breil, Marquis de Rays, a French swindler, founded the bizarre colony of New France at Port Breton (Likiliki, Metlik) on the coast of New Ireland in 1879. In response to appeals from ragged refugees who landed on their doorsteps, the missionaries rescued fifty survivors of the Marquis' elaborate fraud in March 1881 and brought them to Port Hunter. Brown found them starving and shivering with malaria at Port Breton. They showed him the Marquis' plans for a cathedral; the layout of the future city included a "suburb for the nobility." Surveying the survivors in the desolate jungle, Brown whimsically asked the leader to reserve a lot for him in this section; the leader said he would.

THE LURE OF NEW GUINEA

A medical man from the colony, Dr Goyon, returned the mission's favour when Brown and Danks sent from Port Hunter to Metlik to bring him to help in the difficult birth of a son to Emma Danks in December 1880. The Roman Catholic chaplain of New France, the Abbé René-Marie de Lannuzel, also made himself known courteously to the Wesleyans; de Lannuzel, disillusioned, became the forerunner of a substantial Roman Catholic Mission to New Britain (pages 237-245). After the departure of Brown, German influence in the area increased. In 1884, when Germany annexed New Britain, an outcry in Australia failed to prevent the Methodists from rendering due respect to the incoming Caesar. They wrote to obtain missionaries from the tiny Methodist Church in Germany; the most eminent of them, Heinrich Fellmann, came in 1897; he remained to serve the church in various ways until 1919 and was permitted to spend the war years quietly translating and advising in Australia.

10

Partitioning Papua

Wesleyans, Roman Catholics Anglicans

THE NEW SOUTH WALES AND QUEENSLAND Wesleyan Conferences appointed George Brown to take up the post of general secretary of their mission board early in 1887. After returning from New Britain he had travelled extensively in Australia to tell his story. His ruffled feathers had been smoothed when in 1881 the General Conference of his church, without endorsing all his para-military exploits in New Britain, assured him of its "full confidence" in him. He acted for a time as a missionary secretary in the office, became minister for three years in the "large and important" Bourke Street circuit in Sydney, then in 1886 travelled widely in North America and Britain. He assumed his new responsibilities in his early fifties, well seasoned by previous experience. The fortunes of Australian Methodism, enjoying the benefits of merchant wealth generated by the gold rushes of the 1860s, and expanding in country districts, favoured him as the right man in the right place at the right time.

In 1890 he went to New Guinea in response to a request from Governor William MacGregor, who had indicated he would be happy to have the Wesleyans, whom he had admired when he was serving in Fiji, as missionaries somewhere in Papua. MacGregor liked traditional Wesleyan attitudes of studied deference to the Crown. They transformed violent "natives" into milder subjects; their influence admirably complemented the beneficent advance of the Pax Britannica, his own first concern. Missions helped him; he helped missions. On tour he carried a Greek Testament, provided transport and escort for missionaries, dined happily in their houses, and did not serve alcohol at his own table because he considered the colony was better without it. Soon after he arrived in British New Guinea MacGregor saw that the LMS needed help if the whole territory was to receive Christianity. Who better to move in than the efficient and loyal Wesleyans he had known in Fiji?

MacGregor thought the eastern Papuan islands region was worth considering as future Wesleyan ground. George Brown received the news with personal delight, but decided to walk circumspectly with the LMS, already in occupation of much of Papua. Ten years of "scratching old sores" in Samoa, where he had been an actor in a melancholy drama between his own society and the LMS (pages 128-9), led him to seek out William Lawes, an old acquaintance, at Port Moresby before surveying his mission's prospective assignment. Declining MacGregor's invitation to stay at Government House, he was Lawes' guest. He complimented Mrs Lawes on the provision she made for him and visited LMS stations. At the time of his visit some Australian Anglicans were also beginning to plan a mission somewhere in New Guinea. Already, elsewhere in the Pacific, competition and overlap had been avoided by clear comity agreements.

At Port Moresby on 17 June 1890, after conferring with MacGregor, Lawes, Brown and Albert Maclaren — who had come to seek the right place for an Anglican mission — formulated a set of resolutions agreeing provisionally to the future boundaries between their missions. Anglicans were to occupy the northern coast and its hinterland from Cape Ducie to Mitre Rock, Wesleyans the eastern Papuan islands, except what fell within the existing work of the LMS based at Kwato. Mission boards in Australia endorsed the gentlemen's agreement, with one variation, giving the Wesleyans a small strip of eastern mainland shore for a station. MacGregor, duly informed, never wrote this parcelling out of territory into government regulations; he and his successors simply respected it by refusing to cede land anywhere round the coast to missions other than the parties to the compact. The Roman Catholics of the Sacred Heart Mission who arrived on Yule Island contrary to the wishes of the government in 1885 consistently denounced the arrangement; it ran contrary to their mandate to bring their church to all humanity. They attacked what they saw as its iniquitous interference with religious liberty, later pressing defiantly inland to the mountains where government interest in policing them was minimal — a bold reply to the implication that they were not wanted (pages 243-4).

Carrying the draft agreement, Brown sailed with MacGregor on the government vessel *Merrie England* to investigate the Louisiade and Calvados Islands groups, Murua (Woodlark), the Trobriands and finally the d'Entrecasteaux, where he located the future headquarters of the Methodist mission. The small island of Dobu, situated conveniently for approach to larger populations on adjacent Goodenough, Fergusson and Normanby, seemed to him to be what was needed. Possibly he looked back with assurance to his previous selection of the Duke of York group as springboard to New Britain and New Ireland. His choice over-rode Macgregor's prior warnings about the fighting men of Dobu. "Now, Brown," MacGregor said, as they parted temporarily on the mainland before Brown first went there, "take care of yourself at Dobu, or they will knock you on the head. They are about the worst natives I know in New Guinea." Brown remained undeterred; he liked contact with warriors, being temperamentally one of them; he also quickly saw that the Dobu belligerents were aware of the government's superior avenging fire-power. The Wesleyans availed themselves gratefully of MacGregor's auspices when they moved into Dobu in the following year. Providentially, Dobu also proved to be influential among the Massim peoples of the surrounding islands through the working of the Kula ring, a canoe-trading circuit for the regular exchange of prized artifacts. Brown conducted a large party of missionaries to Dobu in the middle months of 1891, on board the *Lord of the Isles*.

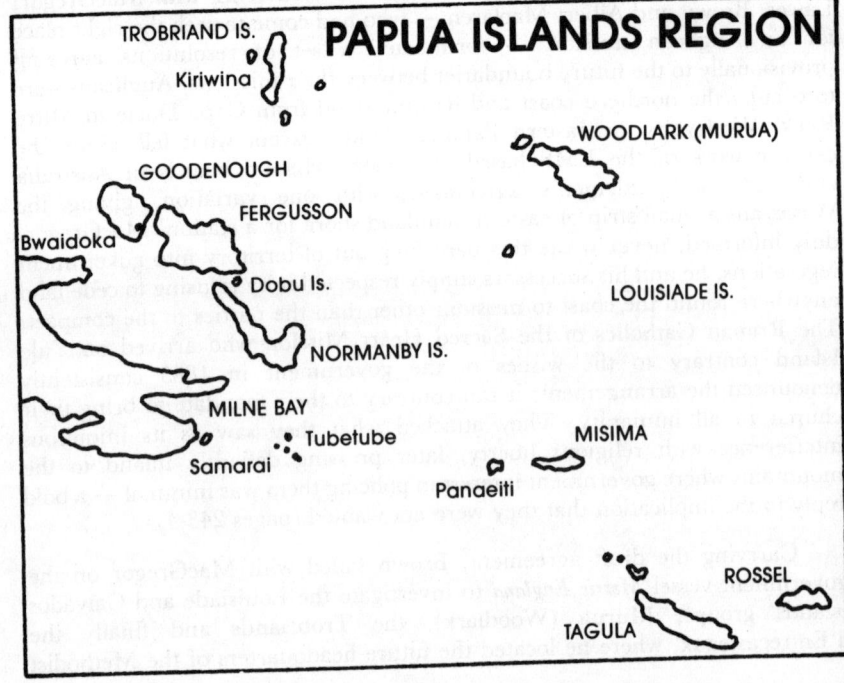

PARTITIONING PAPUA

The expedition out-did the *Duff* (page 12). Contemplating its provisioning and sailing from Sydney on 27 May Brown thought it "the largest party that ever left any port to establish a new mission" — over seventy people. After arriving at Samarai on 13 June they were becalmed en route to Dobu. The *Merrie England,* following watchfully, towed them in under steam power. The sight gave second thoughts to Dobu chiefs who eyed the fleshy frame of William E. Bromilow, the head of the mission, considering him to be good for eating. The *Lord of the Isles* was loaded with equipment: timber, tools, supplies, firearms. The large mission house could be fortified and defended in case of need. In three weeks, under the guidance of J.T. Field and R. Heath Rickard (who were both builders) twenty-two Islander missionaries, mostly Fijian, helped build it. When MacGregor looked in again at Dobu on 13 July he pronounced it "the finest house in New Guinea, a far better one indeed than he had himself in Port Moresby." The Governor then towed out the *Lord of the Isles* as she had come in, taking Brown and Rickard further north to the New Britain mission and leaving Bromilow in charge.

William Bromilow had served in Fiji for ten years. The Fijian contingent he brought with him to Papua introduced customs among the Massim that permanently affected social life in the Papuan islands. The gospel was presented as *tapwaroro,* a local word meaning the bending of the knee; the word for church was Tongan (and Fijian by adoption), the *lotu.* Bromilow's lively American-born wife Lilly was addressed in Fijian style as *marama,* ma'am. The mission's canoe was given the same name, denoting a lady demanding respect. In Dobuan society women were accorded special status and privileges by virtue of matriarchal descent patterns in some ways reminiscent of the Fijian *vasu* relationship; women on Dobu even had the right at cannibal feasts to drink the blood of their warriors' victims. Bromilow, his wife and his daughter were adopted into the powerful Edugaula tribe with honorific rank. "We three," he roundly asserted, "were Dobuans." Some of his Fijian and Tongan associates married local women and were thus absorbed into the extended families of their wives, with access to local worlds white missionaries could not enter. Bromilow's bluff and physically imposing figure dominated the mission and the young church. Gagunamore, the most widely feared Dobuan chief, adopted him as a protected friend. When Bromilow took out his dentures the Dobuans referred to him as *Saragigi,* man with removable teeth — a sorcerer with supernatural power indeed. The Kula ring accepted him as a member, with rights to accompany the canoes seasonally to other islands. In time of war, as at Bwaidoka on Goodenough Island, his advent as bearer of peace was congruent with old local customs governing acceptance and reconciliation. In the background of his extroverted presence the remembered forcefulness of the government stood like a guardian angel.

Bromilow's tributes to his Fijian and Tongan subordinates read like a field officer's appreciation of his NCOs. In reality they were the commando element in the mission, he the base officer who was not averse to some action. With his colleagues S.B. Fellows, J.T. Field, Ambrose Fletcher — and later M.K. Gilmour, his gifted successor — he planned and participated. Inevitably the Fijian and Tongan teachers, and the less numerous Samoans, had partly hidden advantages in their ability to impart Christianity to other Pacific Islanders. They lived in the villages as villagers. Their temptations, to dominate, or alternatively to conform, in such an atmosphere, were many; but their conventions in conversation, their idiom in teaching and their dark skins commended their message. The churches from which they came had been formed in a similar way, by reinterpretation of the Incarnation in Tongan and Fijian categories. Bromilow knew this was the case and described part of the process:

> It was easiest and most natural for a people at the Dobuan level to adopt first some of the external forms of the new religion, such as the observance of Sunday, attendance at the services, and a readiness in some other ways to please the missionary. Meanwhile, there was gathering and forming out of sight a deeper, more spiritual movement.

Dobuans were confused as to what it all meant in terms of sorcery and magic. "Is this house of yours the house of Jesus Christ?" they asked Bromilow. "Where is He? We cannot see Him or hear Him. Are you Jesus Christ?" Three years passed before the first three church members were baptized in July 1894; thereafter for many years, until locally trained Papuan teachers and pastors began work, the "deeper" movement involved contact between Fijian and Tongan teaching and slowly forming Papuan Christianity — a recognition and absorption of island faith by island faith. Fijian teachers, *vakavuvuli*, were largely responsible. Seventy-seven came before Bromilow left in 1908; twenty-seven died, many settled permanently. The part played by their wives, most of whom, with male insouciance, were left unlisted, has to be surmised. The most vividly remembered of the Fijians, Simioni Momoivalu, was born in the Yasawas and spent twenty-five years in the islands, where he was influential in converting the people of the mission's second station, Panaeiti. He played various parts in doing so, negotiating with the government when police action for local disorders threatened, using the Methodist institution of the lovefeast and supplementing its observance with the prestigious practice of pig-slaughter, marrying men to their favourite wives while arranging suitable partners for the forlorn rejects, adapting the Methodist practice of individual testimony to local conventions of oratory. By these contagious methods he came to seem more in charge than the white missionaries in charge of him. Oral history and missionary correspondence show similar activities of his less prominent companions.

PARTITIONING PAPUA

A Tongan, Joni Kuli, navigator-missionary from among a people known for seamanship, steered the mission's ketch *Dove* and its whaleboats. He saw his work as service of the gospel. When Bromilow took him to Australia he addressed a congregation in a Sydney suburban church illuminated by gas chandeliers, one of which was not working. Kuli pointed to them, impressed by the fact that the gas came from one centre, which he compared with England as the source of Christianity for the Pacific.

Then with a fine sweep he pointed to one gleaming chandelier after another, 'That is Tonga. That is Samoa. That is Fiji. How brightly they shine!' Then again, dramatically pointing to an unlighted chandelier at the back of the church, he cried, 'But what is that? Dark! Dark! That is poor dark New Guinea. But we go to light up dark New Guinea, also, with the gospel of Jesus Christ, and it, too, will shine bright with the love of God.'

Kuli, to the Papuans, Bromilow thought, "was the embodiment of leadership, and they gazed at him with unconsciously admiring eyes," with his "towering shock of black hair," his "natty trimmed beard," his "easy athletic pose," his "majestic and unstudied" stride, and his laugh "of a happy child." Kuli came with Bromilow's first group, stayed ten years and wanted to go back again in his old age.

Gagunamore, Dobu's colourful head-hunting protector of Bromilow, responded to the mission warmly. Modern critics, armed with the findings of anthropology, tend to blame the mission for destroying Massim culture by its moral strictures. Bromilow in this respect was less destructive than government and traders. He was among missionary champions of grass skirts and was not put off by comfortable toplessness. He saw no harm in dancing if it did not lead to orgies; he withdrew his membership in the Kula ring in protest when coin supplanted the red shell discs and armlets of the old trade circuits. He could be blunt with white supremacists; he gave some a piece of his mind when travelling with them on board ship in 1920. "The idea that these brown natives are not as other men are dies hard," he said, "even among those who are willing to 'give the beggar a chance.'" Gagunamore's contacts in trade and war had made it possible for Bromilow "to know more of them than those who knew them chiefly as 'labour,' only to be duly fed and paid." On the other hand Bromilow did not pretend to be a detached observer, preserving a living museum; the definition of his presence in the islands involved deliberate choices as to the direction of religious and cultural change. MacGregor's patrols, or busy trader-exploiters, such as "Nicholas the Greek" on Kiriwina in the Trobriands, were in any case disrupting and altering societies in their own ways. Local people on the whole preferred missionaries to administrators and businessmen. Most of them, given options, chose

Bromilow as friend. Gagunamore died convinced of Christianity's truth, under instruction, but not baptized.

Dobuan was used as the mission's normal language in the extension of the message, but the importance of other distinct cultures and languages came to be recognized. J.T. Field and his wife went to Tubetube, Fellows (with Watson, who had to be invalided out early with malaria), to Panaeiti. After about two years Fellows, who became an accurate observer of Trobriand culture, settled at Kiriwina. E.J. Glew, a lay missionary who worked among miners during a gold rush on Woodlark (Murua) in 1894, was forerunner of many laymen who brought new interests in medical missions and training for trades. In 1897 Bromilow paid his first visit to Bwaidoka on Goodenough Island, where Ambrose Fletcher and his wife took up residence in 1900. The names of these early stations came later to apply to the circuits of the developed church. Bromilow approached them with guarantees of hospitality and protection through the avenues of the Kula ring. The pre-christian trading relationships, based on the love of exchange, with its multifarious psychological, social and political ramifications, also met a theological echo in the Methodist preaching of free grace, "without money and without price" *(Revelation 21.6; Isaiah 55.1).*

Lilly Bromilow's influence rested in part on high pre-christian status accorded to some women in the society; institutions for girls saved from infanticide were accepted, as were the mission sisters in charge of them who came from Australia as persons of prestige to emulate the "mother of the mission." Medical work seemed an agreeable alternative to sorcery; industrial training inevitably drove out old craft skills by much coveted technology. What was offered as part of the Christian package was only partly imposed from above; it was also adopted because it was wanted. The same may be said of the progress of Christian worship and teaching; the people of the islands wished to make Christianity their own and practise it themselves. When Lilly Bromilow's weakened health obliged her to return to Australia in 1908 the training institution on Dobu had already produced the first local pastors — Sailosi and Lasaro Banobano. M.K. Gilmour, Bromilow's successor as head of the mission, was given the anthropologist Malinowski's accolade as "distinguished." Gilmour consolidated at all points; at Salamo, where the children's home and training centre were located, he built a fulcrum for self-propagating churches. After Bromilow left to take up circuit work in New South Wales he went on with his revision and translation of the whole Bible in a Dobu dialect, aided by Lemeki Muiowei, a local informant who accompanied him. During World I, when manpower was short in the islands, Bromilow came back to help; he was received as though some returned ancestor, having become in his lifetime part of the mythology of the people he served.

PARTITIONING PAPUA
THE SACRED HEART MISSION IN PAPUA

ROMAN CATHOLIC MISSIONARIES OF THE SACRED HEART (MSC) came to mainland Papua after five years of feverish fits and starts. Their congregation was founded in 1856 at Issoudun by Father Jules Chevalier. Its missionary vocation emerged during years of crisis for French Catholics under the early French Third Republic. Its members concentrated their devotion on the passion and wounds of Christ, stressing the cult of Our Lady of the Sacred Heart, initiated in the parish church of Issoudun. Their experiences of suppression and exile under the anticlerical Ferry Laws of 1880 reinforced their conception of their calling as reparation for the sufferings of the world. When they were dispersed in Spain and the Netherlands in 1881, Pope Leo XIII appealed to them to provide missionaries for the temporarily unoccupied vicariates-apostolic of Melanesia and Micronesia.

The background against which they responded to the summons was odd. The two vicariates had remained untended for a quarter of a century after the Marist and Milan Societies were forced off Murua and Umboi in 1855 because of malaria and the hostility of the inhabitants (page 181). The decision to reopen New Guinea came from the College of Propaganda in Rome in response to a set of roseate false reports. The fraudulent — and possibly self-deceiving — Marquis de Rays, absentee-founder of the pathetic colony of New France in southern New Ireland (pages 228-9) said he wished to supplement the presence of the colony's chaplain, the Abbé René-Marie de Lannuzel, by arranging for a mission to the native people. His overtures to Rome were successful. By a decree of 24 June 1881 the Pope confided the Vicariate of Melanesia to Missionaries of the Sacred Heart as de Lannuzel was enduring disillusionment among the tattered and diseased survivors at Port Breton. Chevalier accepted the task assigned. He sent the first group intended for New France — Father Joseph Durin and Father André-Louis Navarre, accompanied by three others — to receive the blessing of the Pope. They then returned to their house of exile in Barcelona and embarked for the Pacific by way of the Philippines. At Manila they found that de Rays had, without their knowledge, falsely certified they were Spanish. The Jesuits in the Philippines retrieved them from being detained on this account. They then heard with pain that New France had proved a cruel misrepresentation and was collapsing.

At first Durin, as head of the mission, thought it best to proceed to some other part of the vicariate. The Holy See, vague in its information about what constituted Melanesia, had included the Indonesian island of Ambon within its boundaries. Durin decided to go to Ambon. When he stopped, on the way, at Macassar, startled Dutch colonists directed him to Batavia to the colonial government, to become better informed. Unable to determine where in the world he ought to turn next, Durin suffered a seizure. He decided to go back to Europe, where he eventually died of cancer. Navarre, with Father Théophile Cramaille and Brother Mesmin Fromm, stayed on to await definite instructions from Chevalier; when these arrived they required Navarre to join de Lannuzel as originally planned. However, when the group reached Cooktown in Queensland they heard the disenchanted chaplain had gone back to Europe. Navarre and his men then went south for the time being to Sydney; they were lodged and counselled at Villa Maria, the Marists' Pacific headquarters, then set off doggedly north again to do as they were told. When they reached Port Breton they found it deserted. They decided to move closer to white habitation, on the Gazelle Peninsula of New Britain, where they set up a house and chapel. Life there was unpleasant for them; Fromm became seriously ill, the Methodists nearby were not unfriendly, but galled by this overlapping Catholic invasion of their field of work. Local people, probably sensing Methodist disapproval, burned down the Catholics' buildings. They were forced to take refuge in one of Hernsheim's trading posts. From there they wearily regrouped in Sydney at Villa Maria.

It became clear that sustained missionary activity in Melanesia would depend on acquiring a solid sub-base in Australia. They found an ally, Patrick Francis Moran, the newly arrived Irish Archbishop of Sydney. Moran deeply believed in the divine mission of Catholicism throughout the Melanesian region, which he knew had been placed under the protection of the Holy Virgin by the ships of Quiros in 1606 and prophetically named "The Austral Land of the Holy Ghost." Beginning in 1884, the Fathers of the Sacred Heart founded their Procure, following Marist example, working in the growing Sydney suburbs of Randwick, Kensington and Botany. Their outstanding planner was Louis Couppé from the Diocese of Blois, the future bishop of temporarily deserted New Britain. Couppé organized parishes and schools. The teachers were Daughters of Our Lady of the Sacred Heart, destined in time also to go as missionaries to educate children in Melanesia and introduce order into the chaotic housekeeping of clerical celibates in the tropics. Couppé was accompanied on part of the voyage out by Henri Stanislas Verjus, a young and eager zealot who goaded his more cautious *confrères* to undertake a direct assault on the Protestant-occupied Papuan mainland. Moran, irritated that heresy should steal an advance on the Church, supported Verjus' impatience. Navarre took up residence on Thursday Island with a view to attacking Papua. He was hesitant about the next steps; not so Verjus, "avid for martyrdom" and eager to be in the front line in the strife with whatever demons were about to bar the way to New Guinea.

Verjus came of mixed Savoyard and Italian parentage. His passionate commitment to missions began when he was three years old. He never looked back. His mind, "more intuitive than dialectical," was formed as a schoolboy and student for the priesthood by the visions and sufferings surrounding the cult of Issoudun. A Josephite nun, Sister Flavia, praying and knitting in Verjus' boyhood town of Annecy, influenced him on his chosen path. In October 1884 Verjus arrived at Thursday Island to join Navarre's group. He found Navarre pleading unavailingly with Henry Chester, the resident magistrate who had annexed New Guinea — temporarily, as it proved — for Queensland, for the mission's right to enter Papua. Verjus, especially after an inconclusive meeting with Samuel McFarlane of the LMS in March 1885, chafed at this irresolute lingering. His ingenuous manly exterior, which appealed even to Protestants such as Lawes and Brown, concealed a burning impatience bordering on masochism. "Deep in my heart," he wrote, "I have the conviction that the first missionary to New Guinea must be ground up, pulverized, to make the mission succeed. As that's all I'm good for I should be in my element."

Navarre was not so sure. An unlikely apparition — a swashbuckler with a boat — was required to persuade him. Edward Mosby, otherwise known as Yankee Ned, appeared on the priests' doorstep at Thursday Island just after they had said a mass with the special intention of being granted a way out of their "Thursday Island cage." Mosby, "an old man in shirtsleeves with bare feet, a grog-blossom complexion and a bushy beard," told them his story through whiffs of stale whisky. He had come from the Catholic bishop in Cooktown, who had visited him when he was ill; he offered his lugger as transport to Yule Island for the missionaries. Verjus, with Brothers Salvatore Gasbara and Nicola Marconi accepted the offer. On 19 June 1885 Mosby's boat slipped out of Thursday Island quietly late at night, leaving Navarre waving his lamp disconsolately from the mission house verandah where he stayed to hold the fort. From York Island, where Mosby was based, the group sailed on the small fishing boat *Gordon* to Yule Island. At the last moment Mosby said he could not provide a master for the voyage. Verjus put a small bronze statue of the Virgin — Our Lady of the Sacred Heart — on the bridge as official pilot, whereupon one of Mosby's men, almost superannuated, volunteered after all to go as captain. On the way they ran into a vicious storm with mountainous seas. A Catholic historian described the journey as

> the last episode in the long struggle to force entry into Papua. 'The Angel's wrestle against Lucifer reached its paroxysm. Mary sustained the Angel, and Lucifer defended the last province of his empire. This sea in agony was the last twist of the prodigal serpent under the Virgin's heel.'

The apocalyptic symbolism *(Revelation 12.1,9)* reveals the scale on which the members of the mission viewed their raid into one of the world's last unknowns. The *Gordon* reached Yule Sound on 30 June. Verjus bought land on the island for "three shirts, three pocket-knives, three necklaces, three mirrors, and two small music boxes, with a bit of tobacco." The missionaries built a hut; they said their first mass in New Guinea on 4 July. Brother Salvatore — later to win acclaim among Papuan converts as the bluff woodsman "Kala" (a diminutive corruption of the first part of his name), knocked over Verjus' portable altar just after the consecration in an effort to chase off a prowling wild dog, "image of the Infernal Prince." The chalice overturned and "the precious blood was spread on the soil of Papua, which eagerly drank it up."

In accordance with his wish Verjus became the leading pioneer among the Oro people of Yule Island and its nearby shore. Hunger, fever, illness, the failure of the *Gordon* to return with supplies; none of this discouraged a would-be martyr. When some relief appeared in the form of the LMS' *Ellangowan*, it was accompanied by an irritating message from the government at Port Moresby that Yule was needed for a government station and the missionaries must leave. They were told to try Papua's northeast coast, where no mission had yet appeared. Verjus declined; he said he needed orders from Navarre. On a second visit Sir Peter Scratchley, Her Majesty's Commissioner for the New Guinea Protectorate, took the group off to Thursday Island for consultations with Navarre, who again dawdled while Verjus fumed. Scratchley died in December. By then Verjus could stand the delay no longer; he finished his filial debate with Navarre, the *Gordon* was re-christened *Pius* after the late Pope Pius IX, and in January Verjus left again, encountering another big storm at sea.

Navarre finally joined him on Yule Island in April, to find a school had been founded. Verjus was studying the Oro language and sounding out prospects on the mainland. The LMS, finding its teachers in the Delena sub-district challenged by the Catholic presence, asserted its rights to the area and the island by landing two teachers on Yule in July. The government then called Verjus to Port Moresby for more consultations, this time with Scratchley's successor John Douglas, who declined to take sides. Verjus profited by the uncertain situation. He made a show of *de facto* strength. The narrow bridgehead to Papua was gained, even though expansion eastward and westward proved impossible on any large scale under the government's tacit support of the comity agreement of 1891 (page 231). The Roman Catholic mission was obliged to push gingerly inland, among the Mekeo people along the river it named the St. Joseph, and from there upward to forbidding mountains behind these first conquests.

In November Verjus, joined by Couppé, prepared the way for Brother

PARTITIONING PAPUA

Salvatore (Kala) to explore Mekeo by river; Kala lived up to his title of "Brother" among the Papuans, with whose "wild" simplicities he identified, a forerunner of many members of the mission who lasted out on precipitous trails and took along builders' tools to erect new stations. Two Dutch brothers, equally original in their own ways, shared with Salvatore in the labours of the early years. Brother Hendrik (Rick), a carpenter, arrived at Yule Island in the late 1880s when he was twenty-eight. He lived on in Papua until 1931. His unspoken comment when newcomers reached Yule Island was to measure them silently for their coffins as they stepped ashore. Brother Stanislas Van Rooij, called Tani, a jack-of-all-trades, drowned in 1917. Younger and fitter men inevitably took over initiative from Navarre; in 1887, already set in his ways, he was made a bishop. He went to France in 1887 to be consecrated as Vicar Apostolic for Melanesia and Micronesia. In August he was elevated to Archbishop, was received in papal audience at Rome, and returned with reinforcements for Sydney and his twin vicariates.

Navarre reigned in the background, bearded and dignified, overseeing logistics, but outrun by the tactical abilities and improvisatory daring of Verjus, Couppé and later Alain de Boismenu, his eventual successor. Navarre tended to give the *nihil obstat* from his comparative backwater on Thursday Island, where he lived, as head over the mission and father-in-God to the scattered and culturally mixed Roman Catholics of the Torres Strait, until 1912. From 1889 onward Verjus and Couppé, who were named bishops, assumed the bulk of the work in New Guinea. The unwieldy vicariate was divided into three parts. Couppé went to New Britain. Micronesia was placed in the care of Father Edouard Bontemps. Navarre consecrated Verjus as his coadjutor in British New Guinea and the Torres Strait.

In the next three years Verjus burned himself out. Couppé, who was beside him for a time in New Guinea, told Navarre in 1887 that he was "a good religious and zealous missionary, in spite of a certain hastiness and a tendency to exaggeration in his ministry and varied tasks." In fact he was precipitate and authoritarian, his manner redeemed by his infectious enthusiasms. His inner life revealed partly concealed self-mortifications comparable with the excesses of fourteenth century flagellants. As he pushed his fever-ridden body to its limits in the Papuan bush he kept in touch with a circle of corespondents in Europe — Carmelites, Poor Clares, religious, priests and laity — who practised similar austerities as a means (they believed) of obtaining graces for Papuans. Verjus' intimate journal tells how he progressively "victimized" himself by wearing chains on his legs under his robe, putting on a hair shirt, then an iron belt "to obtain the conversion of the Roro." He beat his body with a whip covered with iron and lead bristles. On 19 October 1891 he lashed himself with thorns, alone in the bush, then rubbed vinegar and salt into the cuts. He etched symbols of the stations of the cross on many parts of his body, rubbing salt into the open sores. When the wounds healed he reopened them with a surgeon's lancet. He induced some of his fellow-workers in the mission to join him in these "holy follies." Navarre inspected and approved a manual for Verjus' New Guinea Victims of the Sacred Heart. The founder's act of consecration was written with his own blood and signed "Stanislas Henri Verjus, Slave of Mary, Victim of the Sacred Heart."

A psychologist might see all this as ornate death-wish. Verjus' outward circumstances, interpreted in terms of theologies of strife against demon-possession, voluntary stigmatization and persecution, contributed to his state of mind, however categorized. A monopoly enforced by the trading company Burns Philp, whose chief executive did not approve of Roman Catholics, led to severe want in the mission. Loneliness and tropical disease heightened the stress. Sir William MacGregor, after he arrived as Governor of British New Guinea, questioned the mission's right to own its Yule Island land. Navarre and Verjus, both ill, were summoned to Europe on account of a crisis in the affairs of their congregation. Verjus left first, in April 1892. Chevalier, the head of the order, noticed (not surprisingly) that he was anaemic. Pope Leo XIII, to whom he presented a crown of Bird of Paradise feathers from Yule Island chiefs, received him in audience and sanctioned sending thirty more missionaries to Papua. On 30 November 1892, Verjus died at the age of thirty-two, at Ollegio, Italy, his birthplace; not, as he had wished, in Papua.

Navarre heard of Verjus' death as he was about to follow him to Europe. He proceeded to recruit the new workers approved by the Pope. Their coming corrected lack of academic distinction among early members of the mission. Father Jean Genocchi, an Italian priest who had worked for the order in Beirut and Constantinople, arrived in 1893 as superior of the New Guinea mission and professor for other recruits whose seminary training was incomplete. He clashed with Navarre, succumbed to malaria, and in 1896 was invalided back to Europe for a subsequent distinguished career at Rome. His successor as superior, André Jullien, ushered in a new style and era, combining French bourgeois felicity with theological acuteness and artless enjoyment of untamed peoples. "Comically lost in the midst of the amenities provided by civilization," he became "the intrepid discoverer of wild country." The connections of his wealthy Marseillais family later drew to the mission Mother Marie-Thérèse Noblet, the founder of an order of Papuan sisters whose practice combined a local Papuan ascetic style with the insights of French Ultramontane neo-scholasticism and the piety of the *dévotions particulières*. Other priests of the high Papuan mountain country, such as Fathers Joseph Chabot and Gustave Desnoes, became members of the advisory council of their bishop. The whole close-knit community reflected the early twentieth century renaissance of French Catholicism — and the restoration of Catholic mission exemplified in the careers of Cardinal Charles de Lavigerie and Charles de Foucauld.

Their leader — one of the most resourceful and versatile of missionaries in the Pacific — was Alain Marie Guynot de Boismenu (1870-1953). De Boismenu was the twelfth child of a noble Breton family. His schooling, profession in the order of the Sacred Heart and advance when aged twenty-seven to the priesthood and a theological professorship, gave little hint of his future at the other end of the earth. In 1897 he was sent to Papua by Chevalier; he arrived at Yule Island in January 1898, was made adviser to the bishop two weeks later, reorganized the mission during his own initiation as a missionary and was rapidly advanced to Bishop Coadjutor with right of succession to Navarre. De Boismenu vigorously supported Jullien's adventurous policy of exploration in the mountains behind the mission's small coastal enclaves. His own first expedition into the ranges ended in near-tragedy; its members were deserted and pillaged by Papuan porters and had to come out by forced marches. After the ordeal de Boismenu sank into eight days of semi-comatose sleep. When he woke he heard that he had been named a bishop. His restructuring of the mission provided for a fluid programme of expansion from seven head stations; the old European parish system, dear to the heart of Navarre, was abandoned as inapplicable. On 29 November 1900 de Boismenu was consecrated in the basilica of Sacré Coeur, Paris. He returned to Papua at the head of a new group of four priests, three priests-in-training and six sisters (including now some Australians).

With help from Australian bishops de Boismenu strove to consolidate the Australian connections of the mission throughout his long period of office as bishop and later archbishop. He took issue with MacGregor and later with Governor Sir Hubert Murray (a Roman Catholic who walked wary of the charge of favouring his own church) over the boxing-in of the Sacred Heart Mission under the debatable "spheres of influence" policy flowing from the comity agreement of 1891 (page 231). The administration accepted in principle the idea that there should be a single church in any one village; de Boismenu and the Australian bishops attacked the principle as denying "liberty to work for missionaries and religious liberty for the natives."

De Boismenu looked like some upright French provincial official, with round face and beard, his eyes contemplating the world sharply like an owl through close-fitting spectacles. His identification, as an intellectual, with the exotic stone age world of the Papuans, had an air of surprise about it. In 1900 he and Father Chabot opened up the first range of mountains. The first church in a further central range was built at Mafolo in 1905. In 1913 the high mountains around Fuyuge had been entered. Gradually the mission breached the barriers of the hated "spheres" by unrelaxed pressure on the administration and through donations of land by Catholic laity within the territory of other missions. In 1915 the parish of Our Lady of the Rosary was founded at Port Moresby, "the headquarters of heresy." Chalmers' old station at Toaripi in the gulf became an established parish in 1927; Samarai's parish was dedicated as headquarters for the Papuan Islands district in 1932. By that time the Papuan Roman Catholic laity had begun to move more freely beyond their home districts; the mission could argue that it must expand in order to care for its own.

Navarre handed over all his powers to de Boismenu in December 1907. In the following five years the mission succeeded in reducing its debt and balancing its budget. De Boismenu's annual reports and pastoral letters laid down exacting standards — one year's catechumenate for adults before baptism; translation of elements of the liturgy into local languages; planned monthly visitation of all outstations; more frequent communions for converts as necessary for the building up of a genuinely Papuan Catholicism. He counselled his clergy against transferring European individualist presuppositions into this vastly different world:

> The spontaneity we might like to see among our people will never be like our own; we are by nature much more individual, personal, than our people; they for their part, are 'tribal.'

De Boismenu tried to balance out his staff, top-heavy with French and Dutch priests and brothers, by using catechists from the Torres Strait island churches, then from parish schools. They were married, and acted in the local Catholic communities as "eyes and ears of the priests." Their record was uneven; vocations to the priesthood, at the same period, came slowly. The first to come forward, Joseph Taurino, was part-Rotuman; his training in France and Switzerland was cut short when he died of tuberculosis. Louis Vangeke, from Mekeo, who followed in 1925, persevered to become priest, bishop and finally archbishop. But most, as in other parts of the Pacific, found the celibacy rule and the ideal of individual asceticism to be impassable cultural barriers on the road to the priesthood.

In the face of other obstacles de Boismenu prevailed. The "mountain road" to the interior, opened up and maintained by the mission staff and Papuans, became for him a symbol of his life's work — the nurture of a church remarkable for its surmounting of suffering and isolation. The priests, brothers and sisters who traversed streams, jungles and spurs to teach and serve felt that what they were doing began to reap its spiritual reward with the arrival in Papua of a new priest, the decorated flying ace Léon Bourjade, and an extraordinary mystic and stigmatic nun, Marie-Thérèse Noblet. These two became linked with de Boismenu in new departures. His friend, Couppé, developed meanwhile in New Britain, New Ireland and the Admiralties a parallel Roman Catholic community — more than half the population of the area.

PAPUAN ANGLICANISM

AN IMPROBABLE PARTNERSHIP formed in the course of an Australian railway journey launched the Anglican Mission to British New Guinea. In 1890 Albert Maclaren, an Anglo-Catholic bachelor priest who had served a parish at Mackay in Queensland, was travelling in eastern Australia to raise money and support for missionary work on the northeastern coast of Papua. Earlier in the year he had been promised moral support from Sir William MacGregor, who suggested to the Anglicans that they should take up the coastline between Cape Ducie and the border with German New Guinea as their area (page 231). Maclaren sought to go under the auspices of the Society for the Propagation of the Gospel in Foreign Parts (SPG). The SPG gave him £1,000 but declined to sponsor the mission. The Australian Board of Missions (ABM), a body broadly representing the missionary concerns of the Australian bishops, then gave a general blessing and encouraged him to solicit funds. They appointed him in 1890 as head of the mission under the "episcopal superintendence" of the Primate, Archbishop William Saumarez Smith of the low church evangelical diocese of Sydney.

By chance, on a train in New South Wales, he met Copland King, evangelical son of an evangelical Sydney clergyman, a fellow-bachelor who was also dreaming of a mission to New Guinea. The two men differed in temperament and theology; they were reconciled by their single aim and able to work together on account of the comprehensive nature of the Anglican Communion. Maclaren, who had earlier offered unsuccessfully to serve the Universities Mission to Central Africa (UMCA), imparted an early Anglo-Catholic flavour to the New Guinea Mission. Its origins and development recalled aspects of the UMCA; both were epic (and romantic) improvisations in tropical landscapes. Both missions were inspired by the theological ideas of the Oxford Movement.

William MacGregor's cordial attitude as administrator seemed to favour an Erastian relationship. But it was not to be, the Oxford Reformers had been wary of state control; they regarded the church's ills as being partly due to Establishment. The remote Papuan region gave promise of freedom — to experiment liturgically and to attach a Catholic sense to the Articles of Religion of the Church of England without interference from secular courts. Anglican churchmanship in Queensland was high; the further north the diocese the higher it seemed to get. Where better than further north still could virgin ground be found for recovering the order and worship of the medieval *Ecclesia Anglicana,* successor to the "ancient undivided church" of the Fathers? Unspoiled primitives, once converted, would be the members of the church, which would be without taint from Geneva or Rome.

TO LIVE AMONG THE STARS

The vision was shaped by the thought of Edward Pusey and John Mason Neale rather than Rousseau or social Darwinism. There was a hint of the semi-Pelagian hope that if the gospel and the Church, in what was believed to be restored Catholic fulness, could take root in the Papuan tribes, the overlaid *anima naturaliter christiana,* some spark of latent grace in primitives, would be re-illuminated by the operation of the catechism and the sacraments; grace would elevate and redeem unsophisticated nature. The assumptions belong to the late Victorian English Catholic revival: they trust in a new springtime for the spiritual children of Canterbury. In other ways too, the mission was unmistakably English. Its leaders had upper class manners. Its English-educated bishops and clergy felt on good terms with cool, classically trained colonial administrators. At a deeper level Australian elements nicely balanced this Englishness. Many clergy, teachers, mission sisters and laity added Australian content. Maclaren had worked in Queensland among Melanesian labourers from the Pacific islands on the sugar plantations. In the mission's earlier period he therefore planned to bring these Australian-influenced Melanesians as assistant missionaries among their western kin, the Massim of Papua. This decision contributed a final ingredient for the ethos of the emerging church.

In villages, the imparting of Christianity came frequently to depend on intuitive understanding between Melanesian and Melanesian. Curiously, when Maclaren and King landed on 10 August 1891 on Kaieta beach below Dogura in Bartle Bay, their Papuan interpreter, Abrieka Dipa, was a local man, recruited in his home village of Taupota a few days before. Dipa had learned some English in Queensland, where he had been a plantation worker. Returning home, he brought scraps of Christianity. His English, his material possessions, his knowledge of white men, helped him to acquire chiefly status at Taupota. Others who wanted to acquire similar advantages were told by Dipa how to get them. Maclaren was pleased to see him holding a Christian service among the Wedauan people near their landing place. When they ascended the Dogura plateau to establish the mission's mother-station by buying land Dipa acted as negotiator with Gaireka, the local chief; Maclaren bought Dogura in return for two tomahawks, about fifty kilograms of trade tobacco, twenty knives, twenty-five pipes, twenty-four mirrors, a piece of red cloth and boxes of matches. But when he heard Dipa had exacted a share of the barter from Gaireka he dismissed him. Returning home to Taupota, Dipa persevered. He ran a small cult of his own until Harry Mark, a Melanesian missionary, steered its adherents into Anglicanism.

Close understanding of the importance of prestige, possessions and trade was one among many aspects of contact between Papuan pupils and Islander missionaries. Maclaren and King, unlike the early Melanesian teachers, had poor resistance to malaria. King became ill in the first few months; Maclaren sent him to Sydney to recover. After four and a half months of exhausting work Maclaren himself died, on the way south for treatment, on the government vessel *Merrie England*. His remains, exhumed from his grave at Cooktown, were afterwards placed in Dogura Cathedral. In 1892 the Archbishop of Sydney, acting as Australian Primate, appointed King as head of mission in his place. In the following year the first of a line of forty-five Melanesian missionaries arrived.

Many who responded to the mission's appeal were attracted by secure status. Their surface europeanization gave them leverage as leaders in Papuan settings. Silent and polite (except when they exploded) before their clerical superiors, among the people they went to evangelize they could use pre-literate modes of personal communication common to many Melanesian cultures, a power their literate leaders acquired with difficulty. Until 1915 they were often the first people to share Christianity by day-by-day life in among the Massim people of the south of the Anglican field and the Binandere tribes of the north. They ensured that Anglican Christianity did not seem to be simply the religion of the *dimdim* (whites). Abrupt rebellion against the foreignness of the white missionaries, breaking through normally submissive behaviour, sometimes showed what smouldered in the attitudes of both the Melanesian missionaries and Papuans aspiring to become clergy. The impatience of a Melanesian church in formation, waiting to be let out of school, came through strongly in such incidents.

James Nogar, one of the missionaries, who had been a Presbyterian on Tanna in Vanuatu as a boy, made the point. Tanna men are known in the New Hebrides for their independence. Nogar had been an Anglican schoolteacher in northern New South Wales. He proposed to a white girl who sang with him in a rural church choir — and was predictably ostracized by the white people of the parish. He went to Brisbane, where Montagu Stone-Wigg, the first Bishop of New Guinea, selected him to accompany him in 1898 to Papua. Nogar worked at Wanigela alongside Wilfred Abbot, a dauntingly authoritarian English priest, to mould the people with an iron hand. When Abbot left in 1901 Nogar was put in charge. As a lay reader he combined ecclesiastical regimentation with village improvements inspired by his exposure to Australian technology. His career gave him the kudos of a sacred Big Man. He married a local woman, demonstrated his control over local evil spirits and stopped clan fighting by his fearless personal interventions. When he died of fever in 1908 his bishop and the Wanigela people praised him. Although the Anglican churches in the Solomons and Vanuatu did little as churches to help the Anglican mission in Papua, men like Nogar, who came indirectly from the islands through Queensland, contributed seeds of growing Melanesian Christian solidarity for the second half of the twentieth century.

TO LIVE AMONG THE STARS

Copland King, an evangelical among Anglo-Catholics, stayed on for twenty-seven years and died in Papua. When a bishop for the mission was proposed in 1896 Archbishop Saumarez Smith urged King, as an evangelical, to accept nomination. He declined. When Stone-Wigg arrived as first bishop at Dogura in 1898 King helped to break him in. He then asked to be sent north among the warrior people on the Mamba River, where there was as yet no permanent missionary. The schooner *Albert Maclaren* arrived to improve coastal communication. Work had also to be done in the country of the Binandere, or Orokaiva, people, among white miners who went there in 1895. In the north King mediated between the fighting tribesmen — the Binandere — and the Massim. He prepared aids and translations for the Wedau-speaking portion of the church around Dogura. In the mountains of the north he began his translation into Binandere. He also pursued his favourite botanical studies. In his Ave station, the first on the Mamba, he was physically separated from high church practices he did not fully approve, but remained loyal to episcopal authority — a lonely pioneer. A pittance was enough for his salary; his family in New South Wales had private means. Other spartan celibates, single by Anglo-Catholic conviction, swelled the staff. Their image in the bush fitted their Catholic frame of reference; they were also content to be badly paid within a budget that was pinched to a minimum.

Such isolation and asceticism were cheerfully accepted as marks of their calling by the first three bishops in New Guinea and by the priests who served under them. Bishop Montagu Stone-Wigg had upper class assurance, a record of involvement with the English urban poor and a love of full liturgical ceremony. In Australia he had worked as canon of the pro-cathedral in Brisbane. His appointment followed testy exchanges between the Bishop of Brisbane and Saumarez Smith of Sydney, who wanted an evangelical. The bishops, acting through the Australian Board of Missions, could offer little financial assistance out of church funds. They encouraged Stone-Wigg to stump the country for donations. This he did, in England, then Australia. Most of the money came from individual well-wishers. His personal income could meet his own needs. In England he found others, gentlemen priests, in the same situation. His fatherly manner as bishop in Papua was accompanied by spasms of self-doubt. He genuinely admired and loved many aspects of his Papuan converts. To him they were not savages sunk in satanic darkness, but appealing children of God. He took their silences to indicate teachability. They on their side enjoyed the vestments, candles, altar lights, processions and sense of awe before the spiritual, in the kind of liturgy he favoured. The rituals of the seven sacraments were zestfully absorbed and imitated. Dogura, as mother church of the mission, set standards of beauty and dignity, contrasting with the comparative formlessness and raw vigour of Methodism and the LMS. Literacy, on the other hand, was lower. Anglicans spurned racy New Guinea Pidgin for many years as an abomination; pure English, on the other hand, made slow progress. Advanced written English, as distinct from spoken, was not in any case essential in a rural church; the Dogura schools, where English was good, were for elites. The catechism, Bible and liturgy were promoted in local languages. Papuan Anglicanism acquired "peasant" simplicity; the bishop and his clergy guarded a people who were warriors, subsistence gardeners, hunters and fisherfolk, far from the pollution of towns.

The approach was confirmed in 1908. Stone-Wigg resigned and was succeeded by another Anglo-Catholic, an organizer with great patience, Gerald Sharp. Many adults were by then accepting baptism, frequently administered in rivers. Christian beliefs in resurrection and an after-life began to supplement and challenge previous attitudes of respect and fear surrounding the haunting spirits of ancestors. Cults seeking to obtain material goods and fertile crops sprang up while Sharp was bishop; his attitude to the Baigona and Taro religions in northern Papua, both combining aspects of Anglican practice with older ceremony and beliefs, was wise — tolerant and attentive. Most of the excitement was thus eventually channeled into the life of the church. Sharp kept in touch with his white clergy and with emerging Papuan leadership. In his pastoral office he was flexible in dealings with local people and his staff. Papuan clergy were trained. In 1917 Peter Rautamara, a vivid preacher who had a mind of his own when dealing with white people, was ordained as the first Papuan Anglican priest. Others, some after long probation, followed.

Their preparation was at first entrusted to Henry Newton, who came to Dogura in 1904. Originally from Sydney, Newton was a student at Oxford and worked in Brisbane before going to New Guinea. He spent almost half a century in the tropics and died there. Newton brought the no-nonsense approach of a burly footballer into his chosen world of mitres and birettas. Stone-Wigg put him in charge of confirmation classes. He sifted out candidates for ordination. His unashamed love of one-man rule was reminiscent of many of his contemporaries in Australia in the Bush Brotherhood. Since divine authority was committed to the priesthood, what more simple than to use it and to see that it was obeyed, with due provision for good humour and the disparagement of doubts? Many of his colleagues, inclined to soften this doctrine with some concessions to consensus, were not so sure, though his ability to give and take hard knocks appealed to them. When Stone-Wigg resigned in 1908 Newton's name came forward as a possible bishop. Other missionary clergy were not willing at that stage to have him.

In 1915 Newton left to spend six years on Thursday Island as the second Bishop of Carpentaria. He took over the fragmented churches of the LMS in the strait by agreement and incorporated them, with a different authority and liturgy, into his diocese. When Sharp resigned in 1921 to become Archbishop

of Brisbane Newton returned to New Guinea, this time as bishop. Clergy he had trained were being ordained. They responded to the cheerful warrior in his monarchical rule; he understood much about Papuans; they in turn absorbed aspects of his behaviour and followed him. After he retired in 1936 he elected to stay on at Dogura, watching with satisfaction the further progress of his former confirmands and ordinands in their own church. When he died in 1947 his teaching and personality had fashioned, though not permanently fixed, a style for Papuan clergy.

Within the system he established individualists flourished, including Newton himself. Francis de Sales Buchanan, shaggy eremitical incumbent of Boianai, a former Roman Catholic, had once been a Benedictine oblate and librarian at the great Italian monastery of Monte Cassino. Stephen Romney Gill's English family's pilgrimage more or less Romeward out of lower middle class nonconformity led him to a talented and eccentric life of devoted service, first at Boianai, then as Archdeacon of the Mamba. Exhilarating Nellie Hullett was the physically huge missionary of the tiny island of Naniu for nearly twenty cheerful years. A white Big Woman, respected as an authority among the clans in her vicinity, she died in Papua in 1937. The longest record belonged to a Melbourne couple who arrived in 1891. Samuel Tomlinson and his wife Elizabeth — "Tama" (elder) and "Sina" (woman) — became acknowledged as parents of the community. Tomlinson came as a lay builder. Later made priest, he spent thirty years at Mukawa near Cape Vogel, speaking the local Are language as though he were one of the people. He translated the whole Bible and many liturgical texts. His wife was the first white woman to live in northeast Papua. She did her work with women without oddity or flourish. Both became expert missionaries with no undue airs. They finished their lives at Dogura as guides for newcomers, unpretentious agents of profound religious change.

Although it was close to the Kwato Mission of the LMS and to the prosperous Methodist work on the Papuan islands and mainland, the Anglican Church in Papua grew up in relative geographical and ecclesiastical isolation. Visiting anthropologists could marvel at the remote, almost sealed off, existence of the Dogura community. Papuan Anglicans, in the years after World War I, migrated to work in other parts of New Guinea. They were surprised to find themselves deprived of sacraments and pastoral care. Roman Catholics regarded them as heretical. Their own church authorities considered Protestant churches, in the majority elsewhere in New Guinea, as schismatic. The tensions produced by this state of affairs, by growing mobility after World War I within the more closely integrated Australian Territory of Papua and the Mandated Territory of New Guinea, and by the development of the ecumenical movement, led at a later date, to the Australian Proposals for

Peter Rautamara: first Papuan Anglican priest.

Intercommunion. These suggested, in Australia as well as New Guinea, mutual commissioning of ministries by the laying on of hands to facilitate unity and sacramental sharing.

At at time when social changes raised questions about aspects of the inner workings of the Anglican Church, its pastoral care had to be expanded to serve growing towns. White settlers, with Papuan Anglicans who went to work in urban centres, formed a nucleus in Port Moresby. As horizons widened Anglicans who had been in Dogura schools entered colonial government service as administrators and teachers. The best known among them was John (later Sir John) Guise, a Papuan of part European parentage, who became Governor General of the independent nation of Papua New Guinea. His career included commercial experience with Burns Philp at Samarai and Port Moresby. He joined the Royal Papuan Constabulary, was a local government officer, then a member — and later Speaker — of the Legislative Council. He saw war service against the Japanese and was a member of the Australian delegation to the United Nations in 1962. He was also a member of the Australian Anglican General Synod. His recreations were gardening, cricket and football. His biographical data show how Anglican Christianity in Papua, and later New Guinea as a whole, could facilitate authentic *via media,* a pathway between cultures, while affirming both local identity and a Christian faith with claims to catholic breadth.

11

Each Church Distinct I

The Societies, Hawaii
Cooks, Tonga, Samoa

THE PEOPLES OF THE PACIFIC, as they adopted Christianity, also adapted it. The transmutations were not easily detected by white missionaries. Island societies take what they approve and shape it to fit their own cultures. They are polite and grateful toward the importers; among themselves they test and sift introduced goods and ideas. Inherited wisdom has taught island peoples to anticipate that those newcomers who do not depart will stay on and be slowly acculturated. The processes of change within the emerging churches of Oceania up to the end of the nineteenth century therefore disclose an exceptional variety in local and denominational forms, accompanied in most places by acceptance of the substance of the Apostles' and Nicene Creeds and of a growing sense of regional identity based on inter-island contacts and common oceanic environment.

In the Society Islands in 1836 the Roman Catholic missionaries Laval and Caret (page 96) set up a tension between two forms of Christianity when they landed at Tautira on Tahiti and walked to Papeete to commend Catholicism to the Protestant queen, Pomare IV. They presented themselves to Jacques Antoine Moerenhout, a Belgian adventurer who had French sympathies, a devoutly Catholic Spanish wife, and no particularly ardent religion of his own. When Moerenhout had arrived in Papeete two years earlier he lodged with George Pritchard, the LMS missionary in charge at Papeete's main church. Moerenhout, after sounding out the situation on

Tahiti, visited the United States and succeeded in having himself appointed as American consul. When he gave hospitality to the French priests a crisis erupted. The church founded by the LMS was at that time in a state of internal controversy. The Mamaia cult, a visionary and millenarian reaction against the dominant LMS Anglo-Saxon church, had broken out in 1826 on Tahiti under the leadership of two dissident prophets, Teao and Hue. The Mamaia's adherents revived ecstatic behaviour associated with the pre-christian religion of Raiatea, combining this with wild sexual conduct, drinking and belief in the imminent return of Christ to endorse their cause. This reaction against the LMS, with its expectations of "cargo from heaven," was possibly most acute on the remote Leeward island of Maupiti. In the 1830s the movement spread widely on the Leewards and Tahiti; some of the great chiefs of Pomare II who had adopted Christianity veered toward the Mamaia, others opposed it by personal intervention and arms. The cult continued active until it finally died out in 1841. Thus, when Laval and Caret appeared on Tahiti with a new and alternative form of Christianity, they presented fresh elements of possible dissension in an already delicate situation. Queen Pomare, officially the guardian of a national and monolithic Protestant church, was young and impressionable. High chiefs related to her were vacillating between the LMS and the Mamaia. Pritchard, who was prejudiced against papal agents as were all LMS missionaries, also resisted the entry of the priests as an undesirable further complication in a troubled scene. Disaffected chiefs could use Roman Catholic and French influence to undermine the authority of the LMS, further unsettle the notoriously unstable and inexperienced queen, and revert to the rivalries that divided the country before the unification under Pomare II.

Moerenhout arranged an audience with the queen for Laval and Caret. They gave her gold coins and a shawl and asked for the right to reside and teach. Within a few days the combined pressure upon her of Pritchard and a majority of the high chiefs, who were anxious to maintain British influence and Protestant monopoly, led to the summary deportation of the two priests. Moerenhout saw his chance; he protested the right of the Catholics to religious liberty and communicated his case to the French government. Caret tried to land again, this time accompanied by Father Louis Maigret, the future bishop in Hawaii (page 54). In June 1838 Moerenhout's activity led to the arrival of the French gunboat *Vénus* commanded by Du Petit-Thouars, who had instructions to demand indemnity on account of the treatment of the Sacred Hearts priests, with an apology and an honorific twenty-one-gun salute to the French flag. Thouars threatened bombardment if his conditions were not met. The queen apologized; Pritchard raised the money from Papeete's frightened white citizenry; the French provided the gunpowder for the salute. This salvo inaugurated a parade of naval power; France and

England asserted their vital interests in the Society Islands. French and English gunboats visited in turn, while diplomatic exchanges on the issue took place between London and Paris. In spite of steady intercessions by the LMS, London eventually conceded France's claim to exercise its "protection" over Tahiti. Palmerston and Aberdeen, successive British foreign secretaries, cynically traded recognition of French influence in Tahiti in return for French acceptance of British rights over New Zealand. The British Foreign Office more or less politely declined the pleas of the LMS and of Queen Pomare for continuing unprotected and independent Tahitian sovereignty.

Pritchard, the focus of contending religious and political rivalries, travelled to Britain to plead the case of queen and chiefs. While there he was made British consul, though he did not surrender his office as a missionary and Christian minister at Papeete. His intransigence in dealing with the Catholic missionaries and French naval officers was based on the expectation that the British government would eventually support Pomare IV. When he returned to Tahiti a French protectorate had been proclaimed. In 1843 the British acquiesced in the new state of affairs and accepted French insistence on full religious liberty for Roman Catholic missionaries. Pritchard had fallen unhappily behind the development of his own country's compromising policies. In 1844 the French arrested, incarcerated and deported him. Queen Pomare, acting on his advice, had addressed a succession of sisterly appeals for help direct to Queen Victoria. There was no reply. Baffled by the sudden switches of diplomatic position in Europe, Pomare crossed the water to internal exile on Moorea, then on Raiatea. The great chiefs who had supported her claim to complete independence of foreign domination felt exposed and perplexed by developments. In 1838 four of them — Utami, Tati, Hitoti and Paofai — wrote jointly to Queen Victoria seeking her aid against threats to "what is dear to Tahitian hearts: the Protestant faith and our nationality." All four had been active in the wars of Pomare II and had adopted Christianity under the LMS. Utami, Paofai and Hitoti (Paofai's half-brother) were among the early pupils and converts of Davies on Moorea (page 22). Paofai died in 1842 before the outbreak of the full conflict surrounding Pritchard. The other three, eventually, submitted to French authority, convinced that acceptance of a *fait accompli* was preferable to comparative anarchy.

Between 1844 and 1846 the queen herself and the chiefs were warned, cajoled and offered bribes by French officials who were trying to consolidate the protectorate. Pomare for a time remained defiant in her refuge on Raiatea, the symbolic focus of Tahitian unity and resolve. She issued commands to resist. The chiefs on Tahiti differed in their responses. Some rebelled with their followers; they took to the interior of the island, set up camp and waged a war of resistance against the French. In June 1844, on the outskirts of Papeete, Thomas McKean, an LMS missionary, was caught in crossfire and fatally shot. Hitoti, persuaded that Tahitian resistance would be folly, fought with the French and was killed in 1846. Tati opposed the revolt. Utami, whose hereditary links with Raiatea and its adjacent island of Tahaa were strongest, personified the strife of loyalties that racked many of the Protestant chiefs. At first, in 1844, he came out in favour of the French protectorate; he told his people of Atehuru, where Pomare II had made him high chief, not to join the revolt. Later, convinced that he had been mistaken, he joined the rebels and sent messages to the queen on Raiatea that she must hold out in hope of British support. But in 1846, all hope of further effective resistance having gone, he despondently surrendered to the French. The queen, sheltering in the Leewards with her high-ranking relatives, also returned to accept French rule, thus retaining her line and throne. "My government is taken from me by my enemies, Paraita [her regent on Tahiti], Hitoti, Tati, and others connected with them," she had complained in 1843 to Queen Victoria. The simplification of her plight was easier for her than for her chiefs, who became disturbed and ambivalent over the alienation of their lands by French soldiers and settlers in 1844. Before and during the revolt the French authorities exploited the rival chiefly lineages against each other in order to divide and rule. The wound thus opened did not heal for the chiefs. When the revolt was quelled, largely because of the despair of the resistance forces and their leaders, national sentiment took refuge in adherence to the Protestant church, which became a kind of hiding place — a Maccabean lair — for the Tahitian personality and language the British had discreetly declined to champion by armed intervention.

After the collapse of the revolt the continued presence of English-speaking missionaries of the LMS became anomalous. Those who stayed on went in two separate directions. John Muggridge Orsmond (page 25), acute, peppery, reflective, preserved the distance he had established from the Directors of the LMS since the supercilious period of his first arrival in Tahiti. He left the Society and took service under the French to supervise the Protestant church they subsidised and sought to domesticate. Orsmond had a close and intellectually curious acquaintance with things Tahitian, but he kept for Tahitians, as for the LMS, his independent Dissenter's waspish standards of criticism. To him the church of Pomare II had been from the beginning a diluted and morally corrupt compromise. By buttressing it under the French he came to terms with it — and with the realities of French administration — indulging as he did so in withering judgments of its foibles and failings. By contrast, William Howe, an Irishman who arrived to serve the LMS in Tahiti in 1839 after being a pastor in Lancashire, distanced himself from the French; he supported Tahitian pastors and lay deacons in maintaining a genuinely

EACH CHURCH DISTINCT I

Tahitian tradition of worship and church government left in disarray by the troubles of Pritchard's time. In 1844, when the French took over, he went to London to revise Henry Nott's Tahitian Bible and confer with the LMS about future policy. In 1847 he returned and began to use the pulpit openly in both English and Tahitian to oppose government control of the local churches, where the pastors were paid by the French. He was strident against Catholicism — as only Irish Protestants know how. He advocated the withdrawal of English LMS influence in the church and the introduction of French-speaking Protestant missionaries.

The Tahitian legislature, as a result of his promptings, requested the Paris Evangelical Missionary Society, founded in 1822 in Paris, to send French pastors as missionaries. The LMS co-operated in the transfer. The Paris Mission, a voluntary interdenominational and international enterprise, was formed partly through the initiative of Swiss, South German, British and American Protestants who sympathized with the efforts of beleaguered French Protestants in their struggle for the right to evangelize in France and abroad. Government restrictions in France, throughout the nineteenth century, prevented the emergence of a national Protestant church with an authoritative supreme synod. A voluntary missionary society was permissible, but not a nationally organized church. The first missionaries sent to take over from the LMS were thus accustomed to working within their own national setting to safeguard the integrity of the churches against disabilities and state controls. Thomas Arbousset, the Paris Mission's pioneer in Tahiti, was inducted by Howe in 1863. Arbousset had spent twenty years as a missionary in Basutoland. His instructions were to assess the situation and build on Howe's foundation. He acted as chaplain to the queen, visited churches on Moorea, in the Australs, Tuamotus and Leewards and prepared the way for his son-in-law Emile Atger, who founded the first Protestant school in Papeete. Atger was joined by Charles Viénot, who arrived in 1866 and died in Tahiti in 1903. Viénot, in a long and combative missionary career, helped to give a national structure to the Tahitian church. He drafted its constitution and established its governing council, the *Conseil Supérieur*. Viénot's anti-catholicism reflected the bitterness of his era — and communicated itself to many Protestant Tahitians.

The efforts of the French evangelical missionaries in Tahiti imparted a special flavour to the church they tended. Unexceptionable as loyal French patriots, they nevertheless mastered the Tahitian language; they encouraged the Christians of the Leewards, Australs and Tuamotus into a sense of belonging together. Tahitian Protestantism under their care was biblical in its narrow piety, tenaciously Tahitian in conserving many of the manners and values of the Christian chiefs of the time of Pomare II, exemplary in avoiding implication in secular politics.

TO LIVE AMONG THE STARS

The Vernier family, inheritors of a prudent but rugged Reformation tradition in the sub-alpine Drôme department of France, contributed a striking missionary succession to the Society Islands' churches under French rule. Jean-Frédéric came in 1868; he acted as chaplain to an older and wiser Pomare IV until her death in 1877. He spent forty years, punctuated by a single furlough, cooperating with Viénot in giving shape to the church, mastering Tahiti's elegant language, and encouraging pastors and people not to lose, but to conserve it, as expressing their distinctive personality. His son Charles, born at Papeete, returned to Uturoa, Raiatea, as a missionary, after his education in France. Charles Vernier's understanding of Tahitian aspirations and tradition — he occupied a chair of Tahitian at the School of Living Oriental Languages in Paris — did not dim his patriotic love of France. Significantly, when he stood after World War II as a candidate for the French National Assembly, he was beaten in the elections by Pouvanaa a Oopa, a Tahitian local patriot whose biblical eloquence told of the religious background of his life's work. Charles Vernier's older brother Paul spent thirteen years from 1897 as a missionary pastor on Hivaoa in the Marquesas. Trained in medicine, he visited and treated the painter Paul Gauguin when he was dying of syphilis. One of Paul Vernier's deacons, Tioka, was Gauguin's friend. His nephew Henri Vernier, son of Charles, grew up on Raiatea speaking Tahitian. He now directs the Pastoral School of Hermon, in the foothills above Papeete, at times sharing "his disquiet over the danger the Tahitian people feel that they may be losing what lies in the depth of their soul."

Tahitian culture and identity have been more closely guarded in the Leeward and Austral islands than on Tahiti itself. France annexed Tahiti, the Marquesas and the Australs; the Leewards continued longer as an independent kingdom in decline; the influence of the LMS and of Britain remained strong. Between 1887 and 1897 a military revolt against France on Raiatea was led by a vigorous chief, Teraupoo. Frédéric Vernier offered to mediate; when he arrived, Teraupoo told him that if he came as chaplain to the rebel troops he was welcome, but if he came on behalf of France he would be arrested. After the quelling of the revolt and acceptance of French rule the churches of Raiatea, Bora Bora, Huahine and remote Maupiti continued to maintain many of the old traditions of the LMS. To Protestants in the rest of the group, frequently linked by family ties and kept in touch by the movement of pastors and their families, the Leeward Islands, as in Pomare II's heyday, became a reminder of origins and a repository of treasured custom. Meetings of all kinds in the Society Islands were prefaced by biblical oratory and long prayers. Though tedious to expatriate observers, these usages, keeping the

Pastor Henri Vernier at the Pastoral School, Hermon.

regal language of the Tahitian Bible, embody a social code that might otherwise be lost; they assert an underlying identity suppressed by omnipresent French culture. The annual *Me,* festivals of giving for mission, are even in name a Tahitian version of the London May Meetings of the British missionary societies at Exeter Hall during the nineteenth century. The office of deacon, a Congregational expression of lay responsibility in church discipline and government, was retained after the eclipse of all chiefly authority. Many active politicians are today also church deacons. The *Conseil Supérieur* of the Evangelical Church of French Polynesia is a focus of Tahitian solidarity; its business is done in the Tahitian language. The *himene,* songs of faith, the Bible and the ancestors, incorporate Polynesian intervals and rhythms pre-dating Christianity; the bodily attitudes of the singers express an ecstasy and dynamism anterior to the arrival of Christian faith. Old matriarchal and matrilineal ways reappear in the discreetly run but influential women's groups of the church. The *tuaroi,* prolonged community exchanges of "spirit guided" insight on chosen biblical texts, are oral jousts treasured within Tahitian evangelical Christianity. They are conducted in "parish houses" erected alongside the Protestant "temples." People who otherwise seem to be lapsed and secularized citizens may be seen participating with old and young church members in these affairs.

THE ROMAN CATHOLIC CHURCH'S VERSION of Tahitian Christianity assumed its own local colour. The earliest missionaries of the Sacred Hearts were committed for life to their work; their converts slowly put down deep Catholic roots on Tahiti. Priests ministered to small minority parishes. No high chief on Tahiti became Catholic until 1856. Bishop Etienne Jaussen, the first Vicar Apostolic of Tahiti, came from the Ardèche; his hobby was botanical cultivation, an activity symbolic of his pastoral patience. At Papeete he acquired and tilled land in the "valley of the Church," introduced the teaching Brothers of Ploërmel and the Sisters of St. Joseph of Cluny to found excellent schools, and built a cathedral. Meanwhile, in the Tuamotus and Marquesas other fathers and brothers of his order, many of them from seaboard departments of western and northern France, "integrated perfectly into the décor." Father Albert Montiton went in 1852 to Anaa in the flat and scattered sea-wilderness of the Tuamotu atolls. He converted Anaa to the accompaniment of his accordion and clarinet, devoting his missionary career to wanderings, on small schooners and locally built canoes, among the tiny populations of the coral platforms. Many people who entered the Catholic Church on these outer islands later migrated to swell the church's numbers on Tahiti. Some weather-beaten priests and bishops also settled in later life at

Papeete's new Polynesian-style Roman Catholic cathedral.

Papeete. By then they were masters of the dialects and ways of the islands. Chinese migrant workers came in 1865 to work on plantations in Tahiti. Many later moved into business. They and their children became a special concern of the Catholic mission. By the close of the nineteenth century the Catholics, tended by impecunious and often eccentric celibates who gave off a marked local "cachet," could no longer accurately be derided as merely promoting "the religion of the French."

The French administration in practice, however, often gave Catholics the inside running; the Protestant majority suffered disabilities. Catholic schools, run to foster elites, with the aristocratic flavour of episcopal patronage as common ground with colonial administrators, educated many community leaders who looked naturally toward Paris. Catholicism catered especially to a large non-Tahitian and mixed population. Two problems retarded the rooting of the Roman Catholic Church in local Tahitian culture. The first of these was the dominating influence of strongly French (and, among teaching sisters, French Canadian) missionaries in decision-making at local level. Nor did any structures of government in the church emerge, comparable with those the Protestants evolved in the 1880s. Lay participation was largely confined to voluntary organizations for piety and works of charity. The second problem lay in the absence of a Polynesian priesthood. Both these problems were, however, balanced to some extent by an advantage of the Catholic system within its Tahitian setting; its pageantry and finesse in the liturgy appealed to Tahitian love of the festive arts.

HAWAII

MANY ASPECTS OF THE PROTESTANT-CATHOLIC contrast in Tahiti also applied to church life in Hawaii, where Protestantism had been shaped by American democratic individualists. The early American missionaries nevertheless deferred to Caesar, to Hawaiian royalty and to the high chiefs, thus identifying Protestantism with the social structures and old customs of the islands. After the great revival (page 55) Protestantism became a mass popular faith, embodying many of the cultural observances and mannerisms of traditional Hawaii in an altered religious context. Gradually such *mores* became submerged — but never wholly obliterated — under waves of new influence — alienation of the land from its native owners, dissolution of the royal and chiefly prerogatives, influx of newcomers from the Pacific islands, Asia, Portugal and America. After the death of Kaahumanu, the powerful queen mother, who was a devoted patron of the mission, Hawaiian royalty grew tepid in its Christian piety. Sometimes, as in the case of King Kalakaua, royal persons openly encouraged the performance of erotic hulas in celebration of royal sexual prowess. Before Kalakaua's defections evangelical upbringing had jaded the Christian fervour of Kamehameha III and Kamehameha IV (Alexander), who with his brother Lot, the future Kamehameha V, had been impressed by the Church of England when they visited London in 1849. Anglican ceremony and deference to royalty appealed to them. When Lot came to the throne his Scots adviser, Robert Crichton Wyllie, a convert to high church Anglicanism, steered the king in that direction. When a young prince was born Wyllie, with the largesse of a medieval vassal, set aside his bachelor's estate at beautiful Hanalei on the island of Kauai for the use of the successor to the throne, suggesting the little boy should assume possession of the domain as "Baron de Princeville." The gothic fancy was endorsed by Manley Hopkins, the Hawaiian consul in London, who shared Wyllie's enthusiasms. Hopkins published an effusive book on Hawaii, written at short notice and concluding with the information that Hawaii was about to receive, with royal assent, a form of Anglicanism to be known as The Reformed Catholic Church of Hawaii. The preface to the book, written by Samuel Wilberforce, Bishop of Oxford, announced that an Englishman, Thomas Nettleship Staley, had been named as the first bishop. Wilberforce, elevated by the prospects, predicted that Staley would before long co-operate with Patteson of Melanesia (who was probably unaware of this dream) to inaugurate a single Anglican church in the Pacific:

> Southward, on his way of benediction, may the Bishop of Honolulu speed, until the two advancing currents of the living Gospel of our Lord knit in one long grasp the hands of the two Island Prelates; and they kneel together on the shore of some jointly conquered island, to exclaim in grateful adoration, THIS HATH GOD DONE!

Queen Victoria agreed to be godmother *in absentia* at the delayed baptism of the young prince, to be called Albert Edward. Unhappily, before Staley arrived to preside at the sacrament the boy became ill. In 1862 he had to be hastily baptized with English Prayer Book rites by Ephraim Clark, the Congregational pastor of Kawaiahao church. Clark's church, Manley Hopkins had written, suffered from "a 'hidden want,' which shows that vital power is lacking." Hopkins' book was also unflattering toward the Roman Catholics in Hawaii; he called their local church "a religious clique, differing somewhat in form under the atmospheric pressure of Protestant opinion, from the perfect development she exhibits in lands which she calls her own."

This Protestant "pressure" in Hawaii, Boston and London was soon making accusations of proselytism against the Church of England for sending Staley. Rufus Anderson of the American Board and William Ellis of the LMS — formerly in Hawaii (pages 25, 47) — wrote and lobbied vigorously in Anglican circles to obtain at least a Protestant-minded Anglican bishop and prevent the sending of a "Puseyite." They were at first fobbed off by affable temporising, then faced with Bishop Staley. When Staley finally reached

TO LIVE AMONG THE STARS

Honolulu, his reception by the Congregationalists was civil but stiff. When in 1867 he brought out Miss Priscilla Lydia Sellon, Abbess of the new-fangled Anglican sisterhood of the Society of the Most Holy Trinity, who introduced some of her nuns to Hawaii, local Protestant sentiment was irritated. Miss Isabella Bird, an observant British visitor, wrote after her travels in Hawaii in 1873 that Staley's church was "a pining and sickly exotic." By then Staley had gone. He had resigned in 1870 to make way for his successor, another Englishman, Alfred Willis. The new bishop, patient and dedicated, stayed for thirty years. "The ritual is high," wrote Miss Bird; "I am told that it is above the desires of most of the island Episcopalians, but the zeal and disinterestedness of Bishop Willis will, in time, I doubt not, win upon those who prize such qualities." Willis' ultimate departure at the close of the century was logical enough from his standpoint. American annexation was uncongenial to him. He had striven to preserve what he believed in — royalism in politics, ritualism in worship. When the decision was made within the Anglican Communion to hand over responsibility for Hawaii to America's Protestant Episcopal Church Willis saw the time had come for him to move elsewhere in Polynesia to continue to promote what he held dear. In Tonga, a surviving sacral island kingdom modelled on Tory principles, he found a small community disaffected from Methodism and ready to receive him as its father-in-God. There he remained for a further eighteen years, a lonely forerunner of the future Anglican Diocese of Polynesia, which was to emerge as a small flock in a vast watery fold (page 285).

ROMAN CATHOLICISM IN HAWAII kept the flavour of its French origins until the end of the nineteenth century. At parish level and in the schools among the Hawaiian faithful the church took on its own local character. Incoming populations of Catholics from the Philippines, from Madeira and the Azores, and from the United States, diversified the heritage. The brothers and fathers of the Sacred Hearts tended seaside and mountain parishes through uninterrupted spells of duty. On foot or horseback they became intimately bound to Hawaii's life through the sacraments, especially confession and penance. Their most famous son, Father Joseph Damien de Veuster, resembled many saints by not pleasing those in authority so much by his life as by the manner of his dying. This gruff and earthy son of Belgian peasant stock brought the attention of the world to Hawaii by the prolonged calvary of his ministry among leprosy sufferers at Kalawao on Molokai. "Father Damien's *humaniora* and his ecclesiastical studies were sadly lacking in completeness," wrote one of his colleagues, who did not approve of Damien's tendency to baptize indiscriminately, calling him "a great baptist." Damien spent sixteen selfless years on Molokai, emulated his Lord by touching the lepers,

Wailuku church, Maui, symbol of original Hawaiian Protestantism.

contracted leprosy and died of the disease in 1889. Many Catholic priests and sisters were terrified by the look of him and repelled by his rough and insanitary appearance and ways. They declined to take communion from him; on his visits to Honolulu they elaborately disinfected the rooms he had used.

After Damien died his fame was guaranteed by a mildly bohemian Protestant — Robert Louis Stevenson. The novelist had visited Molokai not long after Damien's death to see the site of Damien's self-immolation. He had been deeply stirred. When Stevenson read a private letter of the Rev. Dr Charles McEwen Hyde, an eminent Honolulu Protestant, deprecating Damien as dirty and "immoral," he was furious. Hyde's letter had been sent to an American clergyman but had found its way into the hands of the editor of a Presbyterian paper in Sydney, who published it. Stevenson was stung into penning one of his most eloquent and withering pieces, his open letter to Hyde, defending Damien's Christ-like identification with outcasts against what he considered to be the smug censure of his Protestant critics, living in hygienic prosperity in Honolulu. Hyde was deeply hurt; the world sat up and attended. Damien's work among the "untouchables" was matched at Kalawao after his death by Mother Marianne Kopp, the Provincial of the Franciscan Sisters of St. Joseph of Syracuse, an American nun. Damien called the arrival of the sisters, who came especially to care for women and girls in 1888, a year before his death, his Nunc Dimittis. Mother Marianne remained in Hawaii until her own death in 1918 at the age of eighty-one.

THE MARQUESAS

CHRISTIANITY IN THE MARQUESAS ISLANDS was linked in its origins with both Tahiti and Hawaii. LMS missionaries sent teachers from the Leeward Islands and from Tahiti between 1825 and 1831. The Tahitians worked with the sanction of local chiefs on Fatuhiva, Tahuata and Uapou. William Pascoe Crook, one of the two earliest Christian missionaries to the Marquesas (page 15), spoke the language and assisted these new attempts. In the green Marquesan valleys war was a way of life. The polyandrous societies and unabashed sexuality of Marquesan women captivated visiting sailors and raised immediate barriers against Christian moral instruction. The Tahitian teachers tried, but asked to be withdrawn or had to be taken off the islands. In 1832 the LMS and ABCFM agreed to unite forces and divide the Marquesas geographically between their two societies. The LMS took Nukuhiva, Uapou and Uahaka; the ABCFM was assigned Fatuhiva, Tahuata, Hivaoa and Fatuuku. This division was only approximately observed. In the 1830s David Darling, George Stallworthy, John Rodgerson and Robert Thomson of the LMS tried to preach and teach with little success. William Patterson

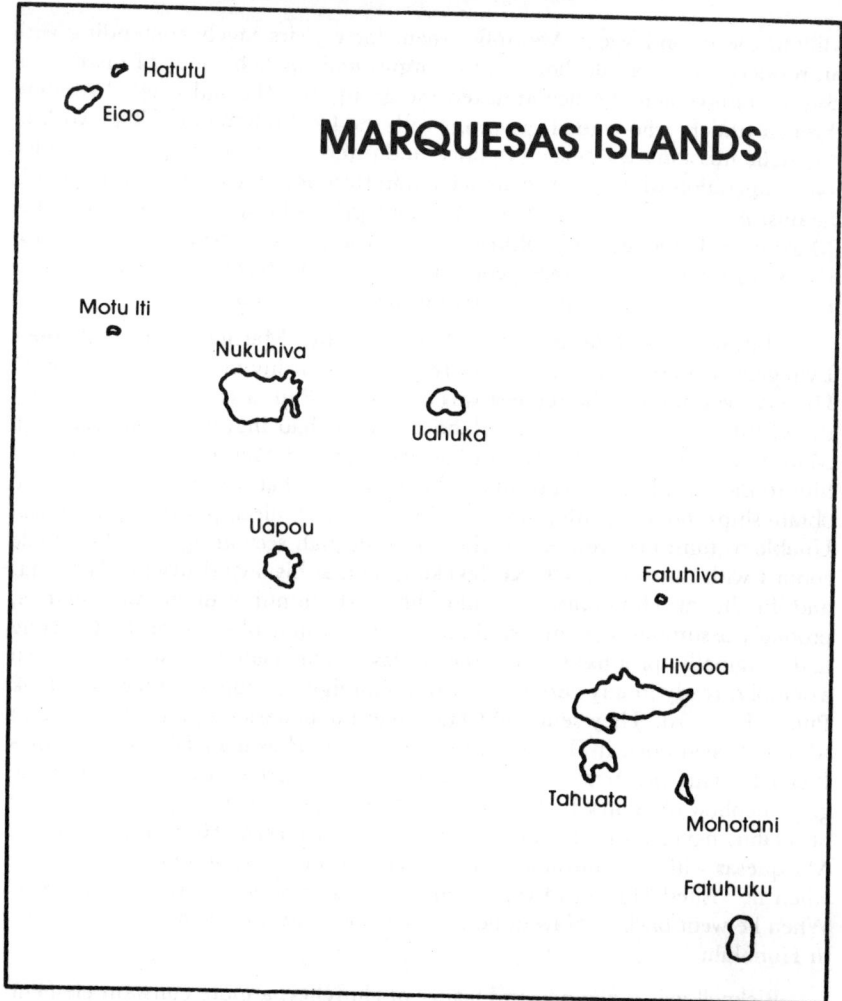

Alexander, Richard Armstrong and Benjamin Parker of the ABCFM, who stayed for a little over a year, similarly failed on Nukuhiva in 1833.

ROMAN CATHOLICS WERE MORE PERSISTENT. Joseph-Paul Baudichon, the first Sacred Hearts bishop in the Marquesas, came to Vaituhu in 1839 with Bishop Rouchouze (page 92). He later settled on Nukuhiva, where he was received by Iotete, a chief who had already shrewdly welcomed Protestants for what he could get out of them. Monseigneur René Ildefonse Dordillon, the second Vicar Apostolic, spent forty years sagely contending with introduced diseases, alcohol, opium, orgies and the behaviour of his French fellow-countrymen. France annexed the group in 1842 and abetted resident French traders who traded in opium with the local inhabitants. The work of Catholic missionaries in such isolated and unfavourable conditions depended on co-operation with a seedy colonial administration; they fought a losing battle against population decline. Many Catholic priests became authorities on the Marquesan language and culture. To a greater extent than their Protestant rivals, with whom they were generally on amicable terms, they blended into their remote environment and took on the slow rhythms of its life.

Hawaiian Protestants resumed work in the Marquesas through their Evangelical Association in 1853 in response to an invitation from a chief of Hivaoa, Matuunui. The request was equivocal; Puu, a Hawaiian sailor from the vicinity of Lahaina on the island of Maui, had ingratiated himself with Matuunui and become his son-in-law. He induced Matuunui to accompany him to the big island of Hawaii on the assurance that it would be possible to obtain ships, horses, cattle, money, houses, guns, bullets, powder and canoes. Unable to fulfil his promise to Matuunui through secular agents, Puu made contact with missionaries at Kealakekua, then at his own district of Lahaina, and finally at Honolulu. He told them Matuunui wanted missionaries, probably assuming that this would also create a flow of some of the items he had originally promised his father-in-law. The elated Hawaiian church assembly, ready in any case to embark on foreign missionary enterprise, took Puu at his word. They sent eight Hawaiian missionaries and a white layman who had been born in Tahiti and settled in the Hawaiian Islands — James Bicknell. This practical — and largely unacclaimed — carpenter, was the grandnephew of Henry Bicknell of the LMS (pages 21ff.). He made his home on Oahu, never losing his family's missionary concern. He remained in the Marquesas with the Hawaiians until 1861, except for an absence of one year, when he visited Hawaii to report and to see translations through the press. When he went back to Hawaii he was ordained and became a city missionary in Honolulu.

Bicknell was a planner and leader of churches; a more constant element in daily contact and teaching was provided by Pacific Islanders, as in many parts of the Pacific. Of the Hawaiians two of the pioneer ordained preachers, James Hunewell Kekela and Samuel Kauwealoha, were the best known. Kauwealoha never returned to Hawaii. Kekela was forced to retire to Honolulu after forty-six years on account of ill health and bad eyesight. His integrity passed into legend when he rescued an American seaman, Francis Whalon, from being killed and eaten by a Hivaoa chief who had become enraged by the activity of Peruvian slavers and intended revenge on foreigners. In return for his action — his own account of the episode showed his mastery of local forms of bargaining — Kekela received an inscribed gold watch and a letter of thanks from President Abraham Lincoln. Kauwealoha's and Kekela's children married Marquesans; they have living descendants there. In 1897, by agreement between the Hawaiian Protestants and the Paris Mission, Pastor Paul Vernier from France (page 258) was sent to carry forward the work of the Hawaiian mission. Protestant co-operation in the Marquesas between the peoples of Hawaii and Tahiti thus came full circle. Former Tahitian missionaries retired in the Leewards can today still tell of Kekela and his descendants, whose friends and associates they became in a continuing twentieth century endeavour to aid and christianize the depleted Marquesan people. Protestant and Catholic missions, located within Marquesan societies, were appreciated rather than imitated; Marquesans have not become noted either for Catholic sanctity or biblical rectitude. The impact of European administrators and traders, the devastating inroads of Peruvian labour ships, and damaging epidemics also destroyed many of the colourful and intricate patterns of life that sustained an estimated population of 50,000 early in the nineteenth century. By 1911 the number had fallen to 3,116 after a century of "tragic and sordid history." In 1971 the population was 5,593.

Some Tahitians remember Kekela as a person of language and outlook similar to their own. Fewer Hawaiians know that a Tahitian, Tute Tehuiarii of Moorea, who went as a missionary to their people in 1826, was a chaplain to Hawaiian royalty until his death in 1858. Tute was one of the first Tahitians inscribed by Davies among the "praying people." He accompanied Pomare II and the LMS missionaries to the Leewards and was baptized on Huahine. Tute was of chiefly build — 183 centimetres high. Pomare I, Pomare II's father, adopted him and gave him his name Tute, in honour of Captain Cook. William Ellis, the LMS missionary who helped the ABCFM in Hawaii (pages 39ff.), commended Tute to the Hawaiian royal line. When his friend Auna (pages 39ff.) returned in 1824 to Huahine Tute was chosen to succeed him in Hawaii. When Samuel Whitney, Reuben Tinker and William Alexander of the Sandwich Islands Mission visited Huahine and the Marquesas to plan for the Marquesan mission with the LMS Tute accompanied them. He served the Hawaiian kings Kamehameha III and Kamehameha IV. Tute's daughter married William Sumner, a ship's captain, who was master of the Hawaiian government schooner *Waverley*. He was granted a landed estate on Oahu. After he died, the parallel decline of the Tahitian and Hawaiian monarchies and chiefly systems removed the cultural context in which this kind of Christian co-operation between the two groups had been inaugurated.

THE COOK ISLANDS

WHILE THE CHURCH IN THE COOK ISLANDS was sending some of its best representatives as missionaries to other parts of the Pacific, at home the LMS lamented a moral and spiritual decline among second and third generation Christians. The first novelty wore off; old aspects of local culture entered into an easier alliance with the new religion. Common elements of language, dance, song and mythology extended from Tahiti through the Austral Islands and the Cooks to New Zealand. By the close of the century, to be Christian and to be Maori meant sharing in this christianized common heritage. The five small Austral islands had acted as a trial bridge for the LMS in approaching the Cooks. Tahitians and Leeward Islanders were sent to preach and teach on Rimatara, Rurutu, Raivavae, Rapa and Tubuai from 1821 onward; they were sporadically visited by European missionaries who checked on the slow growth of the churches. Davies, Nott, Pritchard and Simpson shared in making the early contacts. David Darling administered the first baptisms on any scale in 1831 on Raivavae, Rapa and Tubuai. Rimatara and Rurutu had earlier been evangelized from the Leewards Mission. The isolation of the Australs and their partial conservation of their own music and customs in a new Christian framework have saved into the twentieth century folkways the modern world now threatens to efface; in this respect they also resemble the least easily accessible of the Leeward Islands, Maupiti.

In the Cooks, on Rarotonga, where Pitman and Buzacott (pages 83, 116) had become in their lifetimes "the Rarotongan standards next to the Bible," James Chalmers served his Polynesian apprenticeship; his was a refreshing change of approach to chiefs and people. Chalmers was young; he brought love of adventure and a taste for off-beat company. He arrived on a ship captained by Bully Hayes, the south-sea trader-buccaneer; he reported that Hayes had been "a perfect host and a thorough gentleman" on the voyage. Hayes told Chalmers "If you were near me, I should certainly become a new man and lead a different life." Chalmers was carried ashore at Avarua by a Rarotongan on 20 May 1867. The man asked his name. Told it was Chalmers, the man "roared out, 'Tamate'; hence the name." In Rarotongan "Tamate" means "kill"; it was the closest known sound to what the man thought he heard — and it stuck to Chalmers for the rest of his life. Throughout his time on Rarotonga Tamate had his eyes on Melanesia and said so to the directors of the LMS. He chafed at the chore of superintending ready-made Christians. He and Henry Royle, the veteran missionary on Aitututaki, had frequently to agree to differ. Royle thought Chalmers was permissive and that he gave a bad example by his visits into the bush to seek out young men and women who brewed and distilled potent liquor from the island's sweet oranges. Chalmers never cared about accusations that he kept bad company; he thought that was the first part of a missionary's job. He refused to inform on the bush revellers or to fine them, though he admitted he was shaken by some of the nocturnal fighting, swearing and lechery he uncovered. Chalmers' aim was reclamation rather than censure. He discovered gangs of young Rarotongans reasserting their warlike heritage by clandestine military drilling in secret rendezvous. Chalmers seized on the para-military formula; he persuaded them to keep it up, to march to church and do their bit for God. Unconventional sinners of all kinds loved and admired him; many were willing to follow him. Royle was horrified by his colleague's use of "the medium of military evolutions." He remonstrated in writing to Chalmers, who calmly returned his letter; Royle took the matter up with the LMS in London. The old and the new approaches proved incompatible, but Royle retired in 1876.

Chalmers trained local pastors and missionaries at Takamoa (pages 116-119). He formed close links with some of the most effective Islander missionaries, including the veterans Teava (pages 119, 126) and Maretu (pages 119-120). Maretu he called "a prince of men, and one of the finest men I have ever known, white or coloured." He farewelled Ruatoka, Ananderea, Adamu, Henere, Rau and Piri, the first five missionaries to settle on the Papuan mainland (page 208). Before Chalmers' arrival on Rarotonga, Piri, who towered over Papuans — he stood 188 centimetres high — had turned back to the church after a period of addiction to bush beer. Chalmers, among these men and their wives, early reached opinions ahead of his time concerning the need to advance local Pacific Island churches to self-government and self-support; he thought it a logical consequence of their will to self-propagation. His views on the need for this in the Cooks were received in London with bemused coolness. He wrote:

> I think it is time these churches were left to their own resources, under the superintendence of one foreign missionary, who could take charge of the Institution. So long as the native churches have foreign pastors so long will they remain weak and dependent ... I assert that there is no mission in the Pacific under the control of a white missionary which surpasses the stations that are under native pastors superintended by a European missionary.

Chalmers worked hard. "I have been on every mountain-top in Rarotonga," he wrote, "and there are few valleys I have not explored." His approach had more in common with William Wyatt Gill's curiosity about local custom and story during his years on Mangaia than with Royle's type of tutelage on Aitutaki. Chalmers printed a small newspaper in Rarotongan. He discontinued the mixing of "foreign wine" with coconut milk at Holy Communion, using coconut milk only; he discovered that wine, like all other forms of alcohol, tended to set up irresistible cravings among the people. His most telling innovation was to give full responsibility for the ordained ministry of the church into the hands of local pastors. They were paid out of local church funds, not by the LMS. "Of course," he wrote, "subscriptions to the London Missionary Society declined, but that was to be expected, and had been used as an argument against the change."

These measures affected the church's capacity to impart a sense of unity to the scattered and diverse Cook Islands. Chiefs, pastors, deacons and people, irrespective of their checkered record in deviating from sanctioned church behaviour, treated the church as their own. The celebration of Sunday in the white coral-lime or weatherboard chapels developed into a treasured festival; the women put on woven local hats of bleached pandanus fibre and wore immaculate dresses; the men dressed smartly; plenty of food followed the services. The work ethic in Polynesia was of less consequence than to European missionaries. Abstention from work, the sabbath rule, was therefore a cheerful ordinance, relatively free from the dull sobriety of mid-Victorian English sabbatarianism. The institution of the church picnic, a quickly adapted group ritual consonant with pre-christian lighthearted peace-time journeys between villages, helped to gather up old ways into Christianity. Dances of battle and sexual delight on the other hand were officially banished by the church; the battle dances — of great power and elegance — could still be enacted as a secular diversion, but those portraying erotic love had to be danced secretly, beyond clerical gaze. To compensate to some extent for this deprivation Bible dramas were enacted on the mown grassy spaces outside the church buildings. They depicted the coming of Christianity to the islands and further contributed to a sense of Christian unity for the people of each island and of all the islands. Cook Islanders who migrated to New Zealand in the twentieth century in large numbers thus sought each other out at week-ends within the life of the church, since worship expressed their collective integrity and guarded them against the uprootedness of industrial life in a distant land. The Cooks remained an LMS preserve until 1895, when Roman Catholic sisters arrived from Tahiti to commence schools. Before that date 500 students had been trained at the Takamoa Institution for varied tasks within the group and as missionaries to the Pacific. The Cooks inherited a missionary tradition from Tahiti; in turn they transmitted it to Samoa and Niue.

TONGA

THE TIES BETWEEN the British Wesleyan Conference and Tonga were severed in 1855 when direction of the mission in the Pacific passed from London to the colonial Wesleyans in Australia. John Thomas, the mentor of King George Tupou I (pages 71-74) promoted the change, correctly anticipating that it would also favour re-entry of Methodism into Samoa through Tonga. He could not foresee that the Tongan king, who had tasted conquest in Fiji and the delights of international deference in Sydney, would shortly cast off Thomas himself as adviser and take more effective control in church and kingdom with help from a new counsellor. Thomas' disconsolate exit from Tonga in 1859 preceded the arrival of the Rev. Shirley Waldemar

EACH CHURCH DISTINCT I

Baker from Australia in 1860. Thomas was always afflicted by a sense of his own inadequacy; not so Baker, who brought the self-confidence of a bustling local preacher on the Victorian goldfields to his work as a missionary. Baker ingratiated himself with the king; in 1862 he helped to frame the first Tongan constitution. He brought a new atmosphere into the kingdom — colonial brashness without undue subservience to British influence. The British missionaries, from Thomas onward, were mostly British patriots and Tories; Baker belonged to a more brisk and precipitate breed; he carried out his policy in his own way. His quick grasp of the Tongan language and his relative distance from the British Wesleyans appealed to the king, who was also determined to act as his own man in church and state.

Energetic, fond of money, eager to build up a flattering picture of his own ancestry and abilities, Baker plastered over gaps in his formal education by his skills as promoter and negotiator. With great energy, he used the Tongan love of presenting crops in kind to make the church self-supporting. When he went to Australia the colonial Wesleyans were impressed by his standing with the king, and by his oratory. In 1869 they elected him as Chairman of the Tonga District, thus passing over James Egan Moulton, the gifted founder-headmaster of Tupou College, who went to Tonga in 1865. Baker's subsequent bitter rivalry with Moulton, who was as proud and English as Baker was ambitious and "colonial," grew to be the eye at the centre of the storm during the subsequent thirty-five years in the Tongan church.

Baker shrewdly sensed that power in the church in Tonga rested with the support of the king and the high chiefs; the people would follow. John Thomas had reinforced the pre-christian hallowed status of the chiefly society by stressing that the king was God's anointed. Baker's intuitive grasp of this point — at once cultural and theological — enabled him to outmanoeuvre others. He also quickly observed the anxiety of the masterful king to keep foreign powers from taking over Tonga. He was well aware of the imperial game played by Britain, France and the United States in mid-century Oceania. Baker's personal lines of communication with the German trading house of Godeffroy were laid so as to create a counterbalance to British imperial interest; they were not there purely for reasons of personal greed and advantage. Living close to the royal palace in the rambling chairman's house in Nuku'alofa, Baker, like the king, was a politician by temperament. Moulton, in contrast, defended the majesty of the Church, if necessary over against the rulers of this world. Moulton's style reflected his study and love of the great Old Testament prophets. He was a scholar, teacher, translator of the whole Bible into elegant Tongan, and the author of grand Tongan hymns. Moulton's attachment to the essence of Wesleyanism was constant; Baker's had a flavour of opportunism; he prided himself on being, he said, the son of a clergyman of the Church of England; when he fell from power in Tonga at the close of his career he flirted desperately with Anglicanism in the hope of keeping some standing ground in Tonga. Baker was too astute to thunder for long at moral lapses among high-born Tongans; Moulton, who was dedicated to the higher intellectual and moral education of Tongan chiefly persons, was far less hesitant in denouncing sexual or other peccadilloes, inside or outside his college.

The strains set up within the Australasian Wesleyan Mission Board and Conference, as the king of Tonga became estranged from Moulton and more attached to Baker, created uncertainty and stormy debate. Moulton criticized Baker; he considered that his fundraising methods and personal financial aggrandizement were shabby and incompatible with the calling of a preacher. Baker responded by accusing Moulton of trying to steer Tonga into the arms of England. When the king gave a second and more elaborate constitution to Tonga in 1875, Baker helped, this time substantially, in drafting it. Henry Parkes, the stormy and politically wily New South Wales politician, responded to Baker's appeal for advice. Royal pre-eminence was assured; commoners and nobles were balanced against each other. Baker also designed the Tongan flag. His advisory activity was criticized by his fellow missionaries as out of place; their chairman, they believed, should be a man of God with a spiritual task. The Australasian Conference instituted a prolonged inquiry into accusations against Baker. He defiantly justified his actions. The Conference finally found against him. He was recalled in 1879 from Tonga and displaced as chairman.

The king, offended by this treatment of a man he trusted — and used — recalled Baker to Tonga in 1880 and made him his Premier. The Australian Conferences told Baker acceptance of political office by a minister of the church was contrary to Wesleyan law. They appointed Jabez Bunting Watkin as Chairman of the Tonga District for 1880, then in 1881 replaced him and chose Moulton. Baker, who had resigned as a Wesleyan minister, was determined in his new capacity to retain the power he needed within the Tongan church. In 1885, when a split occurred in the church at Ha'apai, the king's ancestral home, Baker, with royal support proclaimed the split-off section as the nucleus of a new church — the Free Church of Tonga. This secession from Australasian Wesleyanism spread throughout the group rapidly and became the Tongan establishment. Moulton, his Australian superiors and a loyal remnant of Wesleyans resisted the king's call for all to submit to the newly proclaimed Free Church.

In 1887 the king used soldiers to enforce his will. The Wesleyan remnant was severely persecuted; some of them, including a few of chiefly rank who were loyal to Moulton, were exiled to the island of Koro in Fiji. Moulton and other white missionaries, who could claim the protection of the British High Commissioner for the Western Pacific, were untouched by the violence. J.B. Watkin sympathised with Tongan aspirations to have an independent church;

he had been hurt when Moulton took his place as chairman. He was made Chairman of the Free Church and held the position until it was reunited with the Wesleyans in 1924. Baker, alarmed by the intervention in 1886 of the British Western Pacific High Commission on behalf of its nationals in Tonga, played off his German connections against the British, even unsuccessfully proposing that a German gunboat should be sent. In January 1887, at the clamour's height, a group of Tongans tried to assassinate Baker. Their motives arose from local resentment and hatred of Baker at Mu'a on Tongatapu; they were not directly inspired by Wesleyan sentiment. The aged king — he was ninety — was furious. He blamed the Wesleyans for the outrage, treated it as rebellion and had many Wesleyans savagely flogged.

Baker had overreached himself. His erratic administration was criticized by J.B. Thurston, who was appointed High Commissioner for the Western Pacific in 1888. Baker's relationship with the Wesleyan and Free Churches was subjected to the careful, and finally terse, scrutiny of George Brown, who led an Australian Wesleyan Deputation to report and advise on the possibility of reconciling and reuniting the two churches. Brown suggested Moulton's withdrawal from Tonga, which was arranged in 1888 at Moulton's own request as a prelude to further conciliatory efforts by Brown as special commissioner of the Wesleyans' Australasian General Conference. He tried to arrange reunion and to renew, for the Free Church, links with Australasian Wesleyanism. Baker wriggled evasively against the second of these proposals; he said it would frustrate the first. The ear of the king was still open to him. "The King is Mr Baker in these matters, and Mr Baker is King," Brown wrote in 1889 to the President of the Australasian Conference. Opposition to Baker's autocratic ascendancy increased in Tonga itself. "These poor people have suffered enough from the man," Brown confidentially told Thurston. "I most firmly believe that the old King himself would not be sorry to see him taken away." In July 1890, Thurston had Baker removed from Tonga for two years, under a High Commission Order in Council, as a British subject who endangered good order in the Kingdom.

King George Tupou I died in 1893. He had allowed the recall of the Wesleyan exiles from Fiji. Moulton returned to Tonga in 1895 and served as Wesleyan chairman for a further ten years. The majority Free Church continued its separate existence under royal patronage until 1924. In that year reunion was achieved, largely through the combined efforts of Queen Salote, newly on the throne, and Rodger Page, the Australian Chairman of the Wesleyan Church in Tonga. Under the settlement Page became chairman of the reunited church, the Free Wesleyan Church of Tonga. The aged J.B. Watkin, with support from a high chief, Finau Ulukalala, seceded from the union. Watkin died in 1925; his continuing Free Church, with 4,000 members, unsuccessfully contested the validity of the union in the Tongan law courts. In 1928 they were further split by Finau's establishment, from within their ranks, of yet another church known as the Church of Tonga. Shirley Baker's embattled career, trading on his access to the king in his prime and his old age, interwoven with Tongan chiefly and family rivalries, helped to create three separate churches, all more or less Wesleyan in doctrine. All still exist. Baker retired to Auckland, where he lost money. He returned in 1897 to settle on Ha'apai, was refused status as a minister in the Free Church, then sought orders in the Church of England. The occasion of this unexpected turn of events was non-theological.

Taufa'ahau's successor, Tupou II, offended some of his subjects by jilting the chiefess 'Ofa, to whom he was betrothed. He broke the engagement in order to marry the chiefess Lavinia instead. Prominent families related to 'Ofa felt alienated and disgruntled. Baker, with his customary sharp ability to capitalize on dissension, cultivated the protesters. He assembled them into a church that broke away from the royal Free Church, calling it the *Siasia a Vika*, the church of Queen Victoria. He then put out feelers toward the Anglican Communion, claiming that he was himself an Anglican by breeding and inclination, and seeking regularization through Anglican orders. The Bishop of Dunedin in New Zealand, impressed, corresponded favourably with Baker and attempted to persuade his brother bishops in New Zealand (and the Archbishop of Canterbury) that Baker's flock should be recognized and Baker endorsed by the laying-on-of-hands.

Other bishops in New Zealand looked coldly on Baker's approaches. A person with better claims then appeared. Bishop Alfred Willis of Honolulu (page 264) was at that time regretfully making way in Honolulu for his American successor. Willis already had contacts in Tonga; he had been there in 1897 to conduct confirmation services for expatriates. The marooned members of Baker's little church petitioned him for help. On his personal initiative he went to Tonga in 1902 to shepherd them. He called himself simply Missionary Bishop of Tonga. His canonical status as a bishop was unimpeachable; his claim to jurisdiction within the Anglican Communion remained discussable. As a detached episcopal bird of passage he created lengthy debate among Anglican bishops as to his authority and status. The subsequent negotiations led in 1908 to the setting up of the Diocese of Polynesia, grouping together Anglicans in Fiji and small chaplaincies further afield with the small church Willis tended in Tonga. Willis became assistant bishop for Tonga within the structure. Earlier, Baker, bereft of political and religious options and practically indigent, had died disconsolate at Ha'apai in 1903. A travelling Seventh-day Adventist missionary buried him; his daughters could find no other ministers or clergy willing to officiate.

EACH CHURCH DISTINCT I
SAMOA

IN SAMOA the church of the LMS settled down as the dominant religious force in most areas. By 1900 the close relationship between *matai* and pastors had been supplemented at a higher level by governing bodies for the church as a whole — the Council of the Elders *(Au Toeaina)* and the wider representative *Fono Tele* or Great Assembly, which by 1893 included laity as well as pastors. Characteristic local patterns of deliberation thus coexisted alongside the supervisory District Committee of LMS missionaries. The subsistence wealth of Samoan villages ensured local self-support for pastors. Retention within the system of the District Committee meant, from the Samoan point of view, that not too much permanent centralized power fell into the hands of particular Samoan local leaders; the white missionary could thus be opposed in the church when he over-dominated, praised when he checked untoward local monarchical urges.

The novelist Robert Louis Stevenson, who settled in Samoa in the 1890s, assessed the significance of the church in Samoan life more sympathetically than the administrators and store-keepers on the beach at Apia. He called himself "a great missionaryite." His estimates of LMS missionaries were mostly friendly. He once wrote that he preferred "the excellent William Clarke to anyone in Samoa, and to most people in the world." He called Clarke "a real good missionary with the inestimable advantage of having grown up a layman." Clarke, who presided at Stevenson's burial service, worked with John Marriott and James E. Newell to carry forward the tradition of the Malua Institution, "Christianizing but not Anglicizing" Samoan society through the training of the ministry. The policy was probably a product of Samoan insistence rather than a solicitous invention of the mission. On the other side of Apia from Malua — and run with similar respect for Samoan custom — the Papauta institution developed as a school for girls and became another of the country's formative institutions. Founded by the LMS in 1890 at the outset of German political influence and rule in Samoa, Papauta was put under the joint care of Valesca Schultze from aristocratic Brandenburg in Germany, and Elizabeth Moore. The partnership was functional. Priority in entry to Papauta was given to the daughters of the *matai*. Many young women who attended subsequently married pastors trained at Malua. A strong sense of Samoan order, grace and group creativity prevailed. Miss Schultze was a natural contact with German colonizers, Miss Moore with the British.

In the Samoan villages two signs of prevailing English Protestant addictions of the period appeared — large mock-Gothic church buildings and the arcane rituals of cricket, adapted to Samoan inclinations. Samoans are builders and athletes. Their desire to emulate the late Victorian zions of sunny

TO LIVE AMONG THE STARS

Sydney or smoky Birmingham seems to have found a response in design advice from missionaries. The idiom persists in the cavernous cement structures still being built, contrasting with the local materials and designs of the surrounding Samoan *fale,* houses and meeting houses with open apertures and rounded roofs. Cricket, the secular amusement of the reserved English, by contrast changed profoundly when adopted by the Samoans. Games went on for weeks, involved whole villages, and had to be curtailed by mission regulations. The bats looked like battle clubs, the size of the team and the length of the match were in principle limitless, the spirit of group abandon unrelated to the teacups and cucumber sandwiches of the Marylebone Cricket Club. In Samoa Christianity and culture became closely knit together. Steadily and for the most part courteously the Samoan people selected what they wanted from foreign governments and missions. Standards of faith and morals were taken over from Congregational, Methodist and Roman Catholic sources; the inner life of the churches was increasingly of Samoa for Samoans.

12

Each Church Distinct II

Fiji, Kiribati, Vanuatu
New Caledonia, Solomons

FIJIAN METHODISM at the same period evolved without passing through the divisive crises of its mother church in Tonga under Baker, Moulton and King George Tupou I. In Fiji the excitement of the first conversion of the islands tended to subside into staid consolidation, moralism and uneasy partnership between dominant white missionaries and restive high chiefs. The fortunes of the Wesleyan Mission had been affected by the wars and ultimate victory of Cakobau (pages 113-115). For a few years after Cakobau's conversion the influence of the church on other parts of the group, beyond Bau and Rewa, assumed a Bauan complexion as the Cakobau government unsuccessfully tried to run Fiji as an independent monarchy. When the attempt foundered, Cakobau and a group of the highest chiefs ceded supreme authority to Queen Victoria in 1874 with the understanding that there was a general desire "of securing the promotion of civilization and Christianity and of increasing trade and industry." Joseph Waterhouse, Cakobau's guide at the time of his conversion, was a blunt and able Yorkshireman who believed in helping Fijians toward full equality with missionaries in a church of their own. After direction of the mission passed in 1855 from the British to the Australasian Wesleyan Mission Board, Waterhouse fell out of sympathy with an incoming breed of colonially trained missionaries whose authoritarian approach did not show his own confidence in the capacities of Fijian ministers and Tongan missionaries to take fuller responsibility for running the church.

TO LIVE AMONG THE STARS

Frederick Langham, born in Tasmania, became the strong man of the mission as its chairman for the last quarter of the nineteenth century. Unlike Waterhouse, who was born in a parsonage, Langham was a builder's son. He visited England when still young and was a schoolmaster at Castlemaine in Victoria before proceeding to Fiji and ordination. Sir Arthur Gordon, Fiji's patrician first governor, who resented Langham's great influence in Fiji, called him "the Cardinal." Gordon, who idealized Fijian chiefs as analogues of Scottish highland clan leaders and noble families, strove to cultivate them in spirit; Langham knew them more intimately through the church. He could count on immediate contacts in the villages and with great chiefly families. His influence on Bau was strong. Langham's career was marked by a contest of authority between the church and the Fijian administration instituted by the colonial government. His colleague Lorimer Fison, better educated than Langham, stood on middle ground between Langham and Waterhouse in a bitter conflict. Waterhouse supported Fijians and Tongans in their claim to equal representation with European missionaries in the governing bodies of the church; Langham resisted him. Fison, a gradualist, mediated by advocating movement toward full equality in stages. His training at Cambridge gave him criteria for the study of Fijian social structure and land ownership. Fison's observations and learned papers laid foundations for a governmentally received version of the collective rights of the owners of the land — an inalienable endowment through the ancestors. As a disciple of the American anthropologist Lewis Henry Morgan, he interpreted what he found in Fiji as a variety of primitive communism, with patterns of descent he believed to be universally present in the "ascending scale" of human societies. Notions used by Darwin and Engels thus became associated with a "socially concerned" Christian theology — broader than the classic Wesleyanism of Fison's forerunners in the mission — while preserving the quest for personal holiness and perfection.

The conflict between Waterhouse and Langham ended when Waterhouse was drowned in a shipwreck off New Zealand in 1881. The death of the author of *The King and People of Fiji*, whose work had culminated in Cakobau's acceptance of Christ, marked a transition to different leadership from the Australian colonies. Both Langham and Fison were ordained within the new order of things; they ceased to look back to London; their marching orders came from Sydney and Melbourne. Langham had a raw streak within his masterful personality; he was solid, dogmatic, anti-papalist, tough in a fight. Wesleyan brushes with the administration were often based on fuller knowledge of things Fijian within the church, but the thrusting middle-class style of many of the new missionaries from the Australian colonies in time came to contrast unfavourably in the eyes of Fijian chiefs with the assured urbanity of British administrators — and with the selfless devotion of earlier missionaries of the quality of Calvert, Lyth and Hunt. Under Langham's chairmanship evangelism — centred on the person of Christ and communion with God — was succeeded to a great extent by moralism, with rigid enforcement of penalties for drinking and sexual offences. Many Fijian chiefs felt and resented the change; though most adhered to the church of Cakobau, their English accents and social preferences testified to the influence of Sir Arthur Gordon and his successors. By the early twentieth century, in the era of Edwardian imperialism, the colonial government had more power among chiefs and in the villages; white Australian missionaries also deferred more readily to Government House, in uncritically patriotic adulation of their empire, on which the sun was not expected to set.

A deeper continuity in the life of the Fijian Wesleyan Church lay at the level of the circuits and villages. Lorimer Fison's translation of the *Autobiography* of Joeli Bulu conveys this continuity in Bulu's own dictated memories. Born in Vava'u, Tonga, in about 1810, Bulu became a Christian through the preaching of Peter Turner in 1833. He recorded the shattering experience of the great revival of 1834 in northern Tonga. Of his own acceptance of Christianity he said:

> I went forth with the lads of our town. It was a fine night; and looking up to the heavens where the stars were shining, this thought suddenly smote me: 'Oh the beautiful land! If the words be true which were told us today, then are these *lotu* people happy indeed;' for I saw that the earth was dark and gloomy, while the heavens were clear, and bright with many stars; and my soul longed with a great longing to reach that beautiful land. 'I will *lotu*,' said I, 'that I may live among the stars.'

Bulu came to Fiji with Calvert. He was with John Hunt at Rewa, and later on Viwa at the time of the revival and the conversion of Varani (page 109). He spent eight years on the small island of Ono in Lau where he was ordained and put in charge. "I used to think Ono was a little heaven," he said. He served twice at Nadi in western Vanua Levu, where his dual allegiance — to his own Tongan chiefs and to the mission — made it hard for him to avoid suspicion of entanglement in the wars of Ma'afu's ruthless Tongan henchman Wainiqolo. Between 1863 and 1866, following the death of his first wife, he was in charge of a training institution for Fijian pastors and evangelists at Waikava (Fawn Harbour) on Vanua Levu. He trained Fijian catechists to carry forward the circuit work he knew well in many parts of the group. Some conception of the brotherhood between early Tongan and Fijian missionaries in Fiji is conveyed by the names of a group of thirty of them who in 1869 signed a message to their departing chairman, William Moore. In 1865, when Bulu was at Waikava, 100 villages, with about 10,000 people, accepted Christianity in Fiji. Much of the hard work at local level was done by the kind of catechists he trained. The catechist (*vakatawa*) remains today an important figure in village church life; his name describes him as the sentinel of the *lotu*.

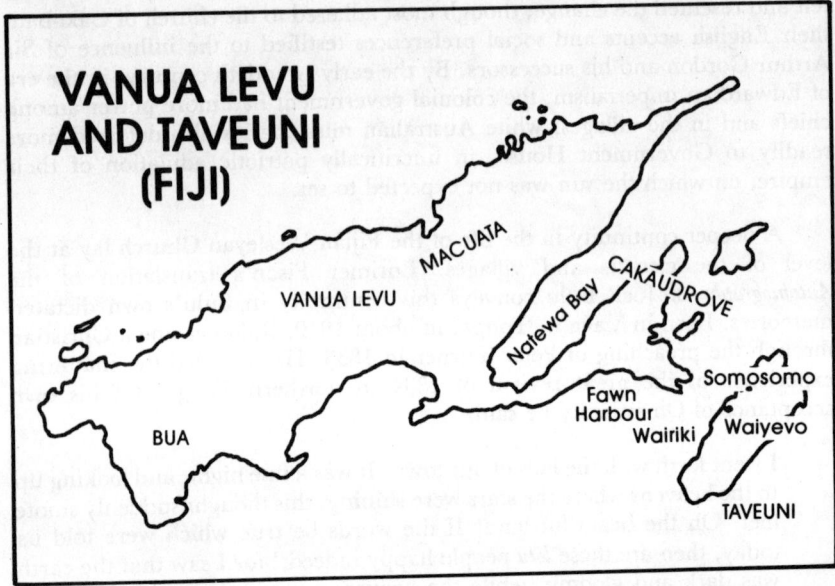

Bulu's second wife, Akesa, was a Fijian from Vanua Balavu in Lau, Ma'afu's headquarters, where Tongan influence was strong. By the time he remarried he had become part of the Fiji scene. When he described how two heathen chiefs made peace with him by the traditional presentation of a whale's tooth *(tabua)* he said: "They kissed my hands, sniffing at them, after our fashion in Fiji and Tonga." His arm bore the scars made by a shark during his early ministry at Rewa; the shark bit him on the thigh when he was swimming in the river after playing with a group of boys and a young chief, who were diverting themselves by pushing toy canoes. The shark transferred its jaws from thigh to arm. Bulu roused himself to anger and fought it. He pushed his hand down its throat, raised it out of the water, dragged it ashore and collapsed unconscious. Bulu recovered from the shark bite to live on into mellow later years on Bau as chaplain to Cakobau. There Miss Constance Gordon Cumming. a guest of Gordon, "a very tall, plain woman, a regular globe-trotter," rhapsodized about him in 1875:

His features are beautiful, his colour clear olive, and he has grey hair

Joeli Bulu in old age.

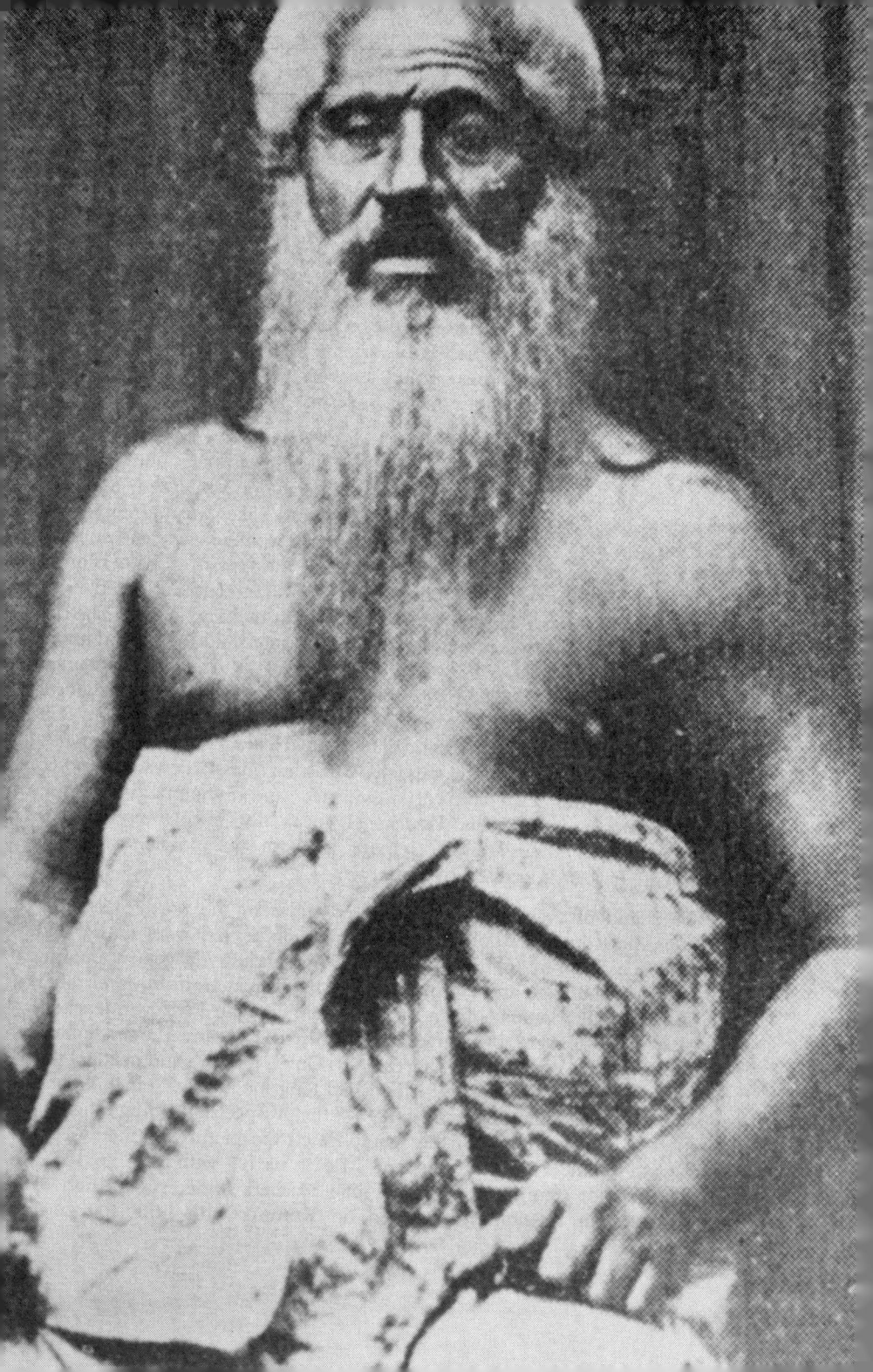

and a long silky beard. He is just my idea of what Abraham must have been, and would be worth a fortune to an artist as a patriarchal study.

Miss Gordon Cumming was present during Bulu's last days and at his funeral in May 1877. "He has been the old king's special teacher," she wrote, "— and many a difficult day he has had with him and all his handsome, strong-willed sons and daughters. They are all very much attached to him; and some of them are generally with him now, fanning or just watching beside him." Lady Gordon, the governor's wife, sent him "a parcel of jujubes and acid drops." He was buried beside his friend John Hunt on Viwa. Many other Fijian and Tongan ministers and teachers who were his friends have grave-sites effaced by hurricanes or lost in scrub.

When Bulu died some of Fiji's most able evangelists were going to New Britain. At home in Fiji the ardor of a second generation was cooling off. The mission met problems in the mountainous interior of Viti Levu, a region suspicious of the influence of Bau. In 1867 Thomas Baker was murdered and eaten trying, probably without adequate advance reconnaissance and cultural tact, to take Christianity into the area. In 1874, the year of Fiji's cession to Britain, Joeli Bulu and thirty other Islander missionaries clashed with Langham over their exclusion from the decision-making annual District Meeting of the church. In fact they carried great responsibilities and did much of the pioneering work. The western side of Viti Levu remained unevangelized as late as 1890. In Fiji, as in many parts of the Pacific, local religious reactions set in. During the 1880s, among the disaffected mountain people of Ra and Wainimala, a colourful cult called *Tuka,* combining elements of the old pagan religion with vaguely Christian messianic expectations, appeared under the leadership of a wizened and dynamic little man, Dugumoi, known as *Na Vosa Vakadua* (I speak but once). Its seditious possibilities and heresies raised tremors in both the mission and the government. It was suppressed by force.

The island of Rotuma, three hundred miles to the north, gave the Wesleyans and Roman Catholics further trepidation. Its first missionaries had been two teachers left by John Williams in 1839 on his last voyage to Vanuatu. Rotuma has a language and culture of its own, distinct from Fiji and other parts of the Pacific. Samoans from the LMS and Tongan Wesleyan teachers made slow progress there, even after Rotuma in 1841 became the missionary responsibility of the Wesleyans by agreement. Chiefs to south and north of the mountainous and heavily wooded island had long fought each other. When Roman Catholic missionaries arrived in 1847 the prospects of adding religious differences to old animosity further complicated the picture. Father Pierre Verne, with members of the pioneer Marist party, withdrew in 1853. Catholics did not return until 1868. Fijian teachers under supervision of visiting Wesleyan missionaries worked on Rotuma with little statistical success. However, between 1859 and 1864 a Rotuman, Serupapeli (Zerubbabel), who had become a Christian, using a translation of Matthew's Gospel in Rotuman, took up the task of teaching other Rotumans to read, imparted the Christian faith and organized a local church along Methodist lines. He opposed the priests of the island's old religion and became the effective pioneer of a lasting devotion to Methodist Christianity in the chiefly districts of the west and north of the island. In 1864 William Fletcher of the Fiji Wesleyan Mission arrived to reside, with four Fijian teachers. The return of the Catholic mission with Rotuman Catholics trained at Wallis and Futuna served to polarize old feuds between the districts, leading in 1871 and 1878 to savage fighting between Catholics and Protestants. The wars were frequently supported from behind by white missionaries of both parties, whose mutual venom contributed to the conflict. After the last sharp battle in 1878 Wesleyans and Roman Catholics on Rotuma lived in an uneasy peace. The island became administratively related to Fiji in 1881 while keeping its identity; the churches, today reconciled, became permanently related to Fiji's Catholic and Wesleyan communities.

In Fiji itself religious diversification increased during the 1880s and 1890s. In the old capital of the colony, Levuka, William Floyd, the Tractarian Anglican Irish chaplain to the white residents, sought wider association with other Anglicans in the Pacific, notably with the bishops of Melanesia, who handled his approaches with caution — Levuka was a centre for ships of the Melanesian labour trade. By agreement with the Wesleyans, Floyd and his successors abstained from any attempt to make Fijian converts within Fiji, though some high chiefs in time, unhappy with Methodist moralism and lack of ceremonial, became Anglican. Immigrant plantation workers from the Solomon Islands, and later some converts among Indian indentured labourers, expanded the nucleus of colonists within the church. In 1908, when the Diocese of Polynesia, with its bishop in Suva, emerged (page 264), the Anglicans of Fiji joined forces with Bishop Willis' small church in Tonga, and with scattered groups in Samoa and Kiribati. But the most important change in the religious life of Fiji came in 1879, when indentured labourers were introduced from India to work on plantations. Hinduism and Islam came to Fiji with the new wave of population, which has transformed the country in the twentieth century into a multicultural community in which almost exactly half the population is of Indian extraction.

Wesleyan activity among the migrants began in 1892; an Indian catechist from the United Provinces, curiously named John Williams, undertook slow and difficult work around Nausori on Viti Levu. In 1897 an Australian woman, Hannah Dudley, a single-minded conservative evangelical who had prepared herself in India, began to devote herself to Indian families in and around Suva, tirelessly helping the poor; she became a vegetarian to enforce the credibility of her concern. The enterprise she mothered, often combatively, until 1912, was not taken seriously at first by the Wesleyan missionary establishment in Fiji. The number of Fiji-Indians who became Christians was small from the beginning of the work among them. With important exceptions such as John Wear Burton, Richard Piper and W.R. Steadman, Australian Methodist missionaries to the migrant people from India complied with the dominant attitudes of their colleagues who served among Fijians. Under the chairmanship of Arthur James Small between 1900 and 1924 the mission deferred as a rule to the British administration and the Australian-based Colonial Sugar Refining Company rather than to the cultural, spiritual and political aspirations of their new neighbours from the Indian sub-continent.

FIJI'S ROMAN CATHOLIC CHURCH developed slowly. The poverty-stricken and ill-supplied Marist fathers of the early mission could not count on any large contingent of Pacific Islander missionaries to aid them. With the help of their lay brothers, also celibates, they refused to let years of local opposition and Protestant prejudice dislodge them. Their first leader, Jean-Baptiste Bréhéret, born in the Vendée, was in Fiji for forty-four years — an inextinguishable missionary with a passion for sailing, but a poor organizer. Bishop Bataillon brought him to Lakeba in 1844 with François Roulleaux-Dubignon; the bishop was then experiencing a flush of renewed hopes for concerted Marist advance in Central Oceania. The vessel that brought the priests was piloted from Tonga by Charles Simonet, a French Catholic friend of the mission. Two Lauan converts, one of whom had been baptized in Tonga *in extremis,* preceded them. Simonet's vessel also brought two Wallisian catechists, Pako and Apolonia. When they arrived at Lakeba, Tui Nayau, the high chief, who had the Tongan chief Finau with him at the time, declined to lodge or protect them. They went to Namuka, where they were little better received. They tried again at Lakeba, where they learned that one of the two Catholic converts who had preceded them in Fiji, the catechist Mosese, had defected to the Wesleyans. Their troubles increased; Finau's Tongans pillaged their root crops and stoned their house. Roulleaux suffered from bad dysentery; Bréhéret injured his leg; he limped for the remainder of his life. Lyth and Calvert, unimpressed by the slender material resources of the Marists, called them "resourceless vagabonds," but their distaste for papists was transcended by their common humanity; they came to the rescue with medicines. This, said Bréhéret, was "excessively kind." His perils and those of his companions continued throughout 1846 and were compounded in 1847 when a contingent of Ma'afu's Tongan troops arrived at Lakeba. They brought with them, in the view of a Catholic historian, "conversion by club and rifle butt" until "finally the Lau Group of islands found it had been converted to the Wesleyan sect."

EACH CHURCH DISTINCT II

Bréhéret's ill fortune as head of mission extended over a period of eleven years at a time when the Oceanian Company (pages 99-101) failed and Colin's grand scheme for expansion was drastically curtailed. From 1851 onward, when Bataillon brought him three new missionaries and three auxiliary brothers, Bréhéret, who was gentle, faintly eccentric, and generally liked by all, threaded the reefs westward in his small craft. When Bataillon went, on his advice, to try to gain favour at Bau (page 112) he was rejected. Stations were established at Wairiki on Taveuni and at Rewa; both had to be evacuated. A hope of holding on at Levuka remained. When Bataillon returned in 1855 he assembled his missionaries there to assess their discouraging reports. The battle of Kaba was won by Cakobau in that year with Tongan help. The imminent conversion of Cakobau to Wesleyan Christianity threatened the Catholics with the application of "Wesleyan varnish" to a multitude of nominal converts who would follow the example of their chiefs. The discouragements for the Catholics seemed mountainous. Bréhéret and two other priests, undeterred, settled down at Levuka, with one brother, to try again. They built a small schooner, *Vola Siga* (Morning Star), and found two whaleboats for coastal work in villages. "The land and sea for work, the heavens for rest," Bréhéret said, as he sailed with "one hand on the tiller and the other on his rosary." The missionaries cultivated Rewa again, and the Verata coasts of the main island. They visited the islands of Lomaiviti nearest to Levuka, Taveuni, the western tip of Vanua Levu, the Yasawas, Kadavu, and Lau once more. After two further years' work they reported 202 conversions.

In 1861 Bataillon made the last of his five visits. By then 4,000 were under Catholic instruction; 500 had received baptism. In 1863 the mission at Wairiki on Taveuni reopened with help from the then Tui Cakau — the powerful and wayward chief Golea — who had fought successfully against the Tongan Methodist soldiers, invaders of his kingdom of Cakaudrove. Bréhéret was named Prefect Apostolic for Fiji; it was a consolation prize for a pioneer who clearly did not have the administrative powers to be promoted to bishop, as his colleagues wished. With bald domed head, wispy beard, old soutane and faint smile, he appears in his portrait as a seasoned and lovable old-timer, remembered affectionately at Levuka after his death in 1898 by pious Methodists and by irreligious scalliwags — a saintly man, matured by sun, brine and wind. The whole town came out for his funeral.

The closing years of Bréhéret's term as prefect foreshadowed consolidation. In 1868 Brother Stanislas, the mission's builder, raised the first solid church building at Rewa. Another followed at Levuka in 1878. In 1881 teaching institutions were begun at Lomere and Suva. Sister Marie de Jésus, the leader of the Missionary Sisters of Mary who came to Fiji in 1882 as the first nuns, opened schools for girls and boys at Loreto on Ovalau in 1885 and

TO LIVE AMONG THE STARS

1886. The way opened up for the arrival of the first bishop, Julien Vidal, a direct and practical ruler and planner from the Marist Mission in Samoa, who was consecrated in 1888 after Bréhéret resigned his charge as Prefect Apostolic. Vidal brought with him to Suva the Marist Brothers of the Schools and Sisters of St. Joseph of Cluny. In the 1890s he planned and built his Cathedral of the Sacred Heart, using Pyrmont sandstone imported from Sydney. A Catholic mission to migrants from India began in 1895; two missionaries were sent to India to learn Hindustani. Vidal also introduced to Fiji Father Pierre Joseph Emmanuel Rougier, a suave controversialist, speculator and businessman, who distinguished himself as a missionary at Rewa and Namosi, did battle in the public press with distraught anti-Catholic Wesleyans over the burning of a stock of old Bibles at Naililili in the Rewa delta, and finally left Fiji and the Marists under suspicion of scandal to make a fortune in business at Papeete in Tahiti. At Suva Vidal flew the French flag; he was required by the governor to take it down. He extended and steadied the Catholic cause before he died in 1922. French missionaries were succeeded by Irish in many parishes and institutions. Local Fijian communities of auxiliary sisters and brothers spread through the group in the present century. A Catholic Church, no less rooted in the villages than the Wesleyans, and led today by a Fijian archbishop, has become the second largest Christian institution in the country.

KIRIBATI

IN KIRIBATI, Christianity began to be rent by rivalry in 1888 when Roman Catholic Missionaries of the Sacred Heart arrived, on orders from their superiors on Thursday Island (page 241). Their early Protestant opponents were led by American missionaries, who supervised the Hawaiians of the Evangelical Association (pages 148-155). Alfred Walkup, a former San Francisco boxer with fiery red hair and a capacity for protracted voyaging, stood out among them. His affections were with the Kiribati students he trained as teachers and stationed in northern Kiribati; he saw that the time had come for the Hawaiians to hand over to local leaders. Captain Walkup, as other whites called him, first sailed the schooner *Morning Star*, then later the steam-assisted *Hiram Bingham*. He did not linger on single islands. Catholic activity among his Kiribati teachers irritated his energetic Protestant soul. He defended himself with more than his fists; he hoped Kiribati would become an American sphere of influence, especially after he learned the Catholic missionaries had been visited, soon after their arrival, by a French gunboat, the *Fabert*. In 1909 Walkup acquired a new *Hiram Bingham*. In that year she foundered in a heavy squall on a journey from Banaba (Ocean Island). A Banaban named Teta graphically narrated privations of Walkup and his company of nine survivors in the badly overloaded ship's dinghy on an epic drift of three hundred miles, to Ebon in the Marshall Islands. On arrival Walkup, exhausted, died. The ABCFM's work in the north of the group was taken over by the LMS (pages 153-155) during the First World War.

The Roman Catholic pioneers, Missionaries of the Sacred Heart (MSC), were Father Edouard Bontemps, from Niort in Poitou, and Father Joseph Leray, from the vicinity of Nantes, with Brother Conrad Weber. They landed on Nonouti in 1888 and said their first mass on 10 May. They came by way of Samoa in response to appeals from small groups of Kiribati plantation workers who had become Catholics while in Tahiti and returned home to Nonouti, Beru and Abemama. Frank Even, a French Catholic trader on Nikunau, promised support; he provided land for a small chapel, leaving the site to the mission when he died in 1892. The small group that invited the mission, beleaguered by indignant Protestant neighbours, offered Bontemps, as head of the mission, restricted standing ground. He began work on Nonouti immediately, itinerating on foot in an effort to turn nominal Protestants from heresy to the Church; Leray stayed on Nikunau. They encountered stubborn Samoan pastors of the LMS, who were already serving in the central islands and had been indoctrinated in Samoa as to the perils of popery. The Samoans combated the Catholics by telling Protestants not to trade with Frank Even, whose business suffered.

In the first six years the founders of the Catholic Church in Kiribati, hampered by small numbers, ill health and lack of their own boat, struggled with small success. In 1893, when the Gilberts came within Bishop Couppé's newly established vicariate in New Britain (page 241), Bontemps went to Europe to recruit new missionaries, including eight nuns, the first of many whose work became a prodigy of patience under isolated conditions. When Bontemps returned, accompanied by the newcomers, he faced two unexpected shocks: he found he was suffering from serious kidney and liver ailments, then in 1896 word came that Leray had been appointed over his head as first bishop (Vicar Apostolic), which "did nothing to improve his health," but was, said the chronicler of his disappointment, "for the good of his soul." The record says that in spite of his devotion and the good work he did during his absence of nearly three years in Europe, Bontemps had a hot temper, was "domineering and rather egocentric" and "lacked practical sense." Leray, who reported 5,300 Catholics by 1894, was prone to agree with Bontemps' policy of widespread premature baptism. "We need not praise that system," remarked Ernest Sabatier, whose policy as one of their successors was to compensate for it by catechizing thoroughly. Bontemps, a pioneer with a tinge of the pathetic about him, died in November 1897, leaving Leray to do battle with W. Telfer Campbell, the British Resident Commissioner, and "the Protestants, the devil and his brood." Campbell, who was allegedly an Orangeman, in fact acted severely against both Catholics and Protestants, more on account of their tendency to assume control over the secular affairs of the people, who were, in civil terms, his wards.

Sabatier gave a memorable portrait of the bishop — a tender pastor to his flock and a fierce scourge for wolves beyond the fold. Leray suffered from hernia and asthma. He could not balance properly on a bicycle, did not pay attention to anything beyond his priestly duties, and lacerated his body with a small whip and chain to obtain graces for the mission. The bishop's English was never good; he spoke "a Gilbertese of his own invention." His oddities, accentuated by the isolated atoll life, earned him affectionate, and often amused submission from his hardy community of Catholic Islanders. "This poor missionary bishop," Sabatier wrote, "could not be refused help." Many of the fathers and brothers who worked with him were fashioned by the environment into equal idiosyncrasy. "His face," Sabatier recalled, "made one think of St. Benedict; a long thin face tended by a grey beard; he had a complexion burned by the equatorial sun, and skeletal yellow hands; a slow voice and a sad air about him." Leray, who retired in 1927, died in 1929. During his almost forty years in the islands a Catholic Church emerged, showing pride in its ceremonies, attached to the Rosary, but with few signs of producing a numerous local clergy. Today its adherents in Kiribati, the independent state proclaimed in 1979, slightly outnumber the Protestants.

Stephen J. Whitmee of the LMS in Samoa supervised the pastors in the southern islands from 1870 onward. William E. Goward, a forceful and often tactless resident missionary with thirteen years' previous experience in Samoa, took over in 1900 and stayed until 1919. In 1917 the LMS finally took over all the work of the American Board and the Hawaiian church in the central and northern islands. The LMS centralized the training of pastors at Rongorongo on Beru. In the twentieth century developing Kiribati Protestant church leadership, in co-operation with Samoan missionaries, of whom the best known was Pastor Iupeli, prepared the way under general LMS supervision for today's independent Kiribati Protestant Church.

At the turn of the century two high islands on the equator to the west, Banaba (Ocean Island) and Nauru, were disturbed out of their previous detached and tranquil way of life by the discovery of rich deposits of calcium phosphate. Banaba had before that time been an agreeable, if inaccessible, headquarters for Walkup of the ABCFM. Phosphate mining scraped and pitted the surface of both islands and changed the way of life of the people. Workers were brought in as miners from other parts of Kiribati and Tuvalu. Their church grew before 1900 under the care of Samoan, Kiribati and

Tuvalu pastors, or under the leadership of their own Banaban people. Tabuia, a Kiribati missionary, evangelized Nauru — which was administered by Germany after 1888 — between 1888 and 1899 without direct foreign missionary oversight on the island. William Harris, a beachcomber who had settled on Nauru in 1842 and married various local women, consistently requested Christian missionaries. He sponsored and helped Philip A. Delaporte, an American from Honolulu sent in 1899 by the Central Union Church in that city and by the ABCFM. Delaporte acquired good Nauruan, a unique distinct language. When Father Alois Kayser from Alsace arrived as a Catholic Sacred Heart Missionary in 1902 he and Delaporte, both born with German as mother tongue, became involved in long and bitter controversy as rival experts on Nauruan life and customs and as representatives of incompatible churches. Nauru's reversion to British control in 1914 preceded the take-over of missionary responsibility by the LMS in 1917. Since that time a majority of Nauruans has been attached to Protestantism. The National Protestant Church of Nauru and the Roman Catholic Church live side-by-side.

VANUATU

PRESBYTERIAN POLICY and outlook in Vanuatu (then known as the New Hebrides) during the later years of the nineteenth century reflected the strong personality of John G.Paton (pages 176-7), who spent limited time there, but heavily influenced the churches in Scotland and Australia in favour of the New Hebrides mission. Paton's pious eloquence and clamorous denunciations of the labour trade, Catholicism and the French helped to shape opinion in Britain and the colonies. The purple prose of his memoirs ran into many editions. Theologically, he radiated confidence in divine approval of his opinions. His public crusades implied that the British people had a God-conferred destiny — to make the world safer for the faith of the evangelical middle classes. He dramatized the transfer of responsibility for the mission from Scottish and Canadian to Australian colonial churches as "Australia's special call." The handover took place officially in 1866, when Paton's own ministerial accreditation was also transferred. In his public discussions of politics in the islands he did not stop to be subtle about many aspects of the power struggle for land between British and French speculators. He simplified the matter by alluding fierily to "the tyranny and Popery of the French." A true zealot, he and his Protestant contemporaries rarely credited any part of their opposition with good faith.

The Protestant and Anglican churches in Vanuatu, with little knowledge of French language and culture — and less inclination to acquire either — almost invariably aligned themselves with British naval and commercial

aspirations. French Catholics did the same with their government and countrymen after Marists re-entered Vanuatu in 1887. The published views of William Gunn, an ordained minister and medical doctor sent by the Free Church of Scotland, who arrived on Futuna in 1883 and worked there until 1917 before retiring to Sydney, may be taken as representing the climate of opinion in the Presbyterian Mission. He and most of his colleagues aggressively advocated British annexation. When their wish was thwarted by the ratification of the curious Anglo-French condominium in 1906 they became and remained strong critics of that surreal arrangement, which was an uneasy alliance of polite dislike. Presbyterians, Anglicans and representatives of the Churches of Christ met to condemn the condominium roundly in 1913. The Australian-based Churches of Christ began their work in 1903 on Pentecost (Raga) through the spontaneous witness of Toby Man Con, a returned labourer from North Queensland who had been converted while abroad. Their mission spread to nearby western Aoba through the preaching of Peter Pentecost, another returned labourer. White missionaries from Australia followed.

As an ironic variant in such a rigidly nationalistic scene, John Higginson, Anglo-Irishman, naturalized French citizen and an Anglican, promoted Roman Catholic missions in Vanuatu. This trim and cocky entrepreneur made his fortune by floating plantations and cattle-runs there — and the nickel industry in New Caledonia. The French bankers of the house of Rothschild stood behind him. Higginson spoke an assortment of French, English and Pidgin. His speculative support for French colonization through the formation of the French Society for the New Hebrides led logically to his advocacy of a Roman Catholic mission to offset his *bêtes noires,* the pro-British colonial Presbyterians. He urged his friend Bishop Ferdinand Vitte, the Roman Catholic Vicar Apostolic in New Caledonia, to follow the flag with the faith. In 1887 Father Charles Le Forestier, with three other priests and one brother, commenced work at Mele on Efate. The strength of the future church, however, soon lay to the north, in the area where French colonists were most numerous, on Malekula and Santo. Thus, as the mission extended, religious lines were drawn between two groups in their own islands: French-speaking Catholics and pro-British Presbyterians — Melanesian as well as European. Ingrained presuppositions and prejudices of the whites on both sides of the colonial divide transmitted themselves with the gospel into the growing churches. They were not notably transcended as Vanuatu moved toward independence, which it achieved in 1980.

Presbyterian consolidation in the central and northern islands nevertheless played an important part in giving people of previously separated

Monument to an activist tradition: Paton Memorial Church, Vila, Vanuatu.

islands, speaking different languages, a sense of common identity. Bislama, the widespread Pidgin of the group, increasingly prevailed as the conversational language of the mission. Australians, New Zealanders and Scots, within the tight-knit family of the mission, created a camaraderie as they plied hazardously up and down the island chain on the *Dayspring* and on smaller boats. Oscar Michelsen, a Norwegian who had worked in the gold mines in New Zealand, then served as a colporteur for the Bible Society in that country, began his ordained career as a missionary on Nguna in 1878. He learned the local language, making it a stepping-stone to his career of fifty-three years on neighbouring Tongoa, where the language was related to that of Nguna. He persuaded the people to build serviceable tracks between alienated villages and was a father to the church. He died in retirement in New Zealand at the age of ninety-two. Peter Milne, Michelsen's preceptor on Nguna when he arrived, was a Scot sent by Knox Presbyterian Church, Dunedin, New Zealand. He spent fifty-four years (1870-1924) as apostle of the island — and of nearby Emae and Makura. His grave is on Nguna, where he died, aged ninety-one, in 1924.

The Melanesian Anglicanism of the Banks Group in the north (pages 182-189) worked southward into the islands of Aoba, Maewo and Pentecost. A gentlemen's agreement between the Presbyterians and the Melanesian Mission in 1881 assigned these three islands to the Anglicans. Today the Anglican Church, with its own bishop, counts fourteen per cent of the population of Vanuatu. Its continuing links are with the Province of Melanesia, the wider church produced by the Melanesian Mission.

NEW CALEDONIA

ON THE MAINLAND OF NEW CALEDONIA little attempt was made by the LMS, preoccupied in the Loyalties, to follow up the early preaching and teaching of Polynesian teachers (pages 189-192). The field was left to the Marists (page 193) until New Caledonia in 1864 became a penal colony, to be swollen after 1871 by the arrival of convicts who had participated in the abortive Paris Commune following the Franco-Prussian War. François Lengereau, the French Protestant chaplain to the Noumea penitentiary, who began work in 1886, established a relationship with the LMS churches in New Caledonia and its dependencies. He watched over the situation on the island of Mare in the Loyalties when the church of the LMS took to the bush rather than surrender its direction to Pierre Cru, a missionary approved by the French government but not by the Paris Mission (page 205). When Cru left, Lengereau mediated with the chiefs on Mare and made contact with the church there. His son Jules-Ernest went to the Loyalties as a missionary teacher between 1891 and 1893, but proved a failure. The older Lengereau then helped Philadelphe Delord, who was sent, by agreement with the LMS, to Mare, as the first accredited missionary of the Paris Evangelical Society. Lengereau, in facilitating this change in the Loyalties, observed that Protestants from the Loyalty Islands, using old contacts with the scattered tribes of the eastern mainland, had infiltrated, contrary to French regulations, into the reserves set aside for these tribes, which spoke distinct languages. The missionaries from the Loyalties acted as evangelists, but did not form a constituted church — baptisms would have been against the law.

While visiting French colonists Lengereau, as a French citizen, baptized 150 of the converts of these teachers in 1897. They had been reached from Lifou by Mathaia, a missionary who used old contacts between his own people and those of Houailou on the central New Caledonian coast to train local catechists. The nucleus formed by Lengereau's baptisms then came under the care of Maurice Leenhardt, a Paris missionary, and an ethnographer of prodigious intelligence and industry. Leenhardt settled at Do-Neva near Houailou, among the people, in 1902. He became an authority on the Kanak customs and languages of New Caledonia's peoples, which differed greatly from the Polynesian-influenced cultures of the Loyalties. Leenhardt's background gave him a sense of locality; the Leenhardt family derived from Alsace; Maurice was born at Montauban. He grew up in the independent atmosphere of Protestantism in the French southwest, the Languedoc. Such qualities made him sensitive to the gentle but proud personalities of New Caledonian and Loyalty Island pastors. They shared his life on horseback as he made himself acquainted with the chiefs of the centre and north of the big island. Leenhardt preserved a report filed by three of these local colleagues — Jemes of Mare, an old man, and two younger men, Makonn of Lifou and Eleicha Nevayes of Neopimia on the mainland. Their journal, written in defective but moving French, described a visit to Aname, the high chief of the district of Poyes, who had earlier become Leenhardt's friend and had accepted Protestant missionary influence on his lands, though he had himself up till then been pagan rather than Catholic.

Leenhardt's relationship with Aname showed his admiration of the distinction and dignity of the myths and customs of Kanak people; to his sorrow he perceived they were being gradually destroyed by the pressure of incoming French colonial influences. His remarkable book *Do Kamo* expounded their beliefs about origins, ancestors, nature and the beginnings of the land. In the case of Aname, who was interned on the island of Wallis by the French colonial authorities on account of his alleged rebellion, Leenhardt expressed his wounded feelings over the behaviour of his fellow-countrymen. Aname was once arrested because he affronted a group of high colonial officials by remaining seated in their presence; they did not understand that being taller than they, and recognizing their authority, he had assumed, by sitting down, a lower position than theirs, thus conveying respect.

Notwithstanding the treatment he received, Aname enlisted in the First World War and died for France. Leenhardt, sharing the company of men like these, was a calm but committed champion of the rights of the Kanak people during their abortive revolts against French alienation of their lands for mining. He resisted French forced labour policy as a violation of his own country's traditional regard for human rights and struggle against slavery. His study of New Caledonian languages was not abstract, but stressed the functional purpose of words in conveying the identity of the people and the person. He translated the New Testament into Houailou, promoted the Blue Cross total abstinence movement among the alcohol-ravaged tribes, introduced systematic hygiene, and is credited more than any other person with saving the Melanesians from depopulation. He left New Caledonia in 1926 to teach in Paris at the Sorbonne, where he became the founder of a distinguished school of ethnology. Its pupils regarded themselves as his disciples.

In the present century a numerically strong Evangelical Church of New Caledonia and the Loyalty Islands has grown out of the work of the London and Paris missions. Waves of migration from the Loyalties to the mainland — workers in the mines, the nickel industry in Noumea, the cattle industry — have augmented its ranks in traditionally Catholic centres of influence. Its membership is largely Melanesian. In 1979, after years of silence about politics, its assembly came out in favour of distinctive Melanesian rights and New Caledonian national independence. The Roman Catholic Church, with its archbishop in Noumea, is more cosmopolitan, bringing together Melanesians, French settlers and migrants from other French Pacific territories and Indo-China. Its composition makes its attitude to national autonomy or independence less clear-cut; both churches are members of the Pacific Conference of Churches, remain in touch with each other, and are opposed to compulsory secularization of the curricula of their government-subsidised schools.

SOLOMON ISLANDS

SOLOMON ISLANDS ANGLICAN CHRISTIANITY in the last decade of the nineteenth century spread out from its central station at Siota, on Gela, where a white staff began to reside all the year round in 1895. Siota, isolated, though within convenient distance of Tulagi, the headquarters of the British Resident Commissioner Charles Morris Woodford, was at times a death trap on account of its setting and climate. Henry Welchman, an English medical man afterwards ordained, served for most of his time on Santa Isabel. When he was appointed to train local clergy at Siota he took his young wife there to live in 1897, only to see her die within six months. Many of his pupils at Siota suffered from dysentery. After 1900 he returned to work on Isabel, assuaging his loneliness by unremitting evangelistic and medical work. He travelled by boat and walked on Isabel in partnership with Soga, the Big Man of the southern Isabel district of Bugotu. Soga belonged to a dominant headhunting family founded by the trading and raiding of his father Bera, who had partly unified the island by terrorising its villages. Soga also afforded protection for those he subdued on Isabel against fearsome headhunting expeditions made by the Roviana people of New Georgia to the west.

The earlier evangelization of Isabel had been largely undertaken by Mano Wadrokal, a forceful teacher recruited by the Melanesian Mission on Mare in the Loyalties. He clashed with Bera, Soga's father; there was not enough room in the area for two strong-minded personalities engaged in their own attempts at conquest. Bera died unregenerate; but Soga extended his father's policy of subjugation after his death. Soga had heard of the adoption of Christianity by Cakobau in Fiji. He was impressed by the power of the new religion to unify by pacification rather than intimidation. Soga accepted baptism at the hands of Charles Bice in 1889. When Welchman came to Bugotu the two men, powerful personalities of different kinds, complemented one another. Welchman's years as a widower were spent living with the people, constantly travelling among them until his death in 1908. He lived in their houses, cured their ailments by his authoritarian medical magic, supervised Prayer Book worship (his basic theological position was more evangelical than Anglo-Catholic) and used a brusque manner to conceal a tender heart. He and Soga, both bearers of special *mana*, understood each other.

As a result Anglicanism put down roots on Isabel probably more firmly than elsewhere in the Solomons. The policy of unification and peace was expressed by the integration of many villages round new Christian shrines on the island. New Christian rituals took on the power of the old to ward off evil spirits. The ghosts of the dead seemed robbed of their power to haunt by the adoption of a new complex of benign spirits — Christ, his apostles, the saints — celebrated through the round of the Church's year. Crosses replaced charms round people's necks; catechists, working in partnership with government headmen, took the place of the older predatory Big Men of the headhunting era. Island-wide Mothers' Unions, Servers' Guilds and Men's Brotherhoods took the place of the older local secret societies. Charles Elliot Fox, a New Zealander whose career in the Melanesian Mission as teacher, priest and father-figure spanned almost three-quarters of a century, looked back on Welchman's work as an example of the close identification with the people of the Solomons Fox himself later achieved.

IN 1898 THE PROLONGED ANGLICAN missionary monopoly in the Solomons was broken by the arrival of Marist fathers, brothers and catechists from Fiji, Samoa, Wallis and Futuna. Their re-entry to a field they had abandoned in disarray in 1847 (page 181) was motivated partly by the incapacity of the Missionaries of the Sacred Heart, to whom Melanesia was assigned, to extend their work into the area. Bishop Julien Vidal of Fiji and Cardinal Moran in Sydney fretted over Catholic absence from a part of the Pacific where Quiros' ships had made their landfall and Epalle had shed his blood (pages 179-181). Vidal's approach from Fiji was supported from Australia. The ship bearing Vidal and the first party of missionaries set out from Sydney. Commissioner Woodford was not opposed to a Catholic mission, but he did not want it to intrude as a disunifying force on Anglican-occupied Isabel, where Epalle's remains lay buried. The Marists therefore first settled precariously on the small island of Rua Sura off northern Guadalcanal. Vidal visited the mission several times before 1903, taking with him altogether thirty Fijians, most of whose names and deeds are not prominently recorded. The death rate among them, coming as they did from a non-malarial group of islands, was high. Supervision on the spot passed to Jean-Ephrem Bertreux, who was at first named as Prefect Apostolic of the South Solomons and in 1912 became the first Vicar Apostolic and bishop. He prudently directed the steady development on Guadalcanal and Malaita of what was to become the most handsomely staffed and run mission in the Solomons.

Bertreux's co-pioneer Pierre Rouillac was an angular character, the antithesis of his colleague. Rouillac had not pleased Vidal in Fiji; he thought he had been sent to the Solomons by Vidal as good riddance. Rouillac acted as an advance guard for the entry of the mission along the Guadalcanal and Malaita coasts. He was a roving boatman descended from Breton fisherfolk, in his element at sea. One of his like-minded companions, Ferdinand Guilloux, was drowned while consolidating work begun at Tangarare in May 1902. "Gifted with robust health, full of life and drive, lovable and sprightly," Guilloux succeeded in winning the Tangarare people by the manner of his death; they became Catholics to make sure of requiting his departed ghost. Visale, another station on Guadalcanal, founded in 1904, symbolized the determination of the Marists to build for eternity. Its stone church, the first in the Solomons, spoke of solidity. Missionary Sisters of Mary staffed convents in each station; the training of catechists, a work Bertreux had supervised in Fiji, aimed to create institutional work of greater durability than the comparatively impecunious Anglicans were able to afford at the same period. Parallel missionary effort began in a separate Vicariate of the Northern Solomons, which had come under German rule by international agreement. With shrewdly judged support from Samoa, where German administrators were on good terms with the Roman Catholic mission, German Marists occupied the Shortland Islands in 1899 as a springing-off point for development on the east coast of the large island of Bougainville. They gradually extended their work, in competition with Methodists who also began a mission in the Western Solomons early in the twentieth century.

THE ROMAN CATHOLICS DID NOT ACCEPT the idea of comity — delineated spheres of influence for specific denominations. Neither did the Queensland Kanaka Mission, an Australian-based interdenominational faith mission led by Florence Young, an irrepressible evangelical maiden lady of a family of English Plymouth Brethren. Miss Young had served in China in Hudson Taylor's China Inland Mission; she accepted the CIM's theological and practical standards. Her family ran a sugar plantation at Fairymead near Bundaberg in Queensland. When some of the converts made by the Queensland Kanaka Mission among men from Malaita returned home to the Solomons she determined to extend the mission's work there. The best known of the QKM's Solomon Islander Malaita pioneers was Peter Ambuofa, the son of an inland Big Man, who first encouraged the extension to the Solomons in 1894. Miss Young and her helpers adopted Hudson Taylor's principle that the Holy Spirit should be implored to generate a locally led church as early as possible. In 1904 Queensland terminated all contracts for Islanders in the sugar fields. The mission changed its name to South Sea Evangelical Mission (SSEM) and worked through many of the QKM's returned converts who followed the example of Ambuofa in starting churches in their own villages.

The SSEM's white missionaries, who came from a variety of conservative evangelical backgrounds, but especially from among the Open Brethren, cultivated the wild coasts of Malaita. The church they nurtured, with upright doctrinal and moral solicitude, took its theology from beliefs upheld at the Keswick Convention and its Australian counterpart, the Katoomba Convention: verbal inspiration of Scripture, a substitutionary doctrine of Atonement, faith in intercessory prayer rather than in financial appeals as source of support, the priority of preaching over social service, expectation of the imminent personal return of Christ. In keeping with its aim of creating a genuine church of the people the SSEM used Pidgin, thus facilitating rapid growth across language frontiers. The missionaries' Puritan distaste for crosses, candles and religious medals led it into frequent local clashes with Roman Catholics and Anglicans, but its wide diffusion and its stress on moral trustworthiness contributed elements of unity and leadership within the emerging sense of identity of the Solomons under British rule. Miss Young was strong-minded and strict. Her admired early protégé Peter Ambuofa pained her by his later lapses — adultery and defiance of the authority of the SSEM, at Malu'u on Malaita. Other SSEM converts helped to inspire the anti-white millenarian movement known as Maasina [Marching] Rule, an assertion of local identity with political overtones. The SSEM's teaching about Christ's thousand year final reign of blessing on earth received an unexpectedly political, materialist and revolutionary twist in the Maasina Rule movement. The British protectorate government frowned — and suppressed it.

METHODISTS ENTERED the Western Solomons, Buka and Bougainville, as a result of the visit of George Brown, the general secretary of the Australasian Wesleyan mission board to the Roviana headhunters of New Georgia in 1899. Brown had for a long time considered the local chiefs open to receive a mission. He gained the unenthusiastic consent of Bishop Cecil Wilson (of the under-financed and over-extended Melanesian Mission) to a comity agreement endorsing Methodist work in the area. In 1902 Brown personally accompanied John F. Goldie as leader of the new mission to Munda in the Roviana Lagoon. The party consisted of four Australian missionaries accompanied by fourteen Pacific Islanders. The mission was thoroughly equipped with the housing and tools needed. John Wesley had taught practical Christianity. Under Goldie it took the form of what were then being referred to as industrial missions; he was an activist who lacked both contemplative calm and cultural sensitivity. Born in Tasmania, he conducted a school for evangelists in Sydney at the Central Methodist Mission, then worked in circuits in Queensland before volunteering for the Solomons. His gospel of hard work took definite shape in technical and farming schools. The mission invested in plantations and did well. Goldie, in partnership with local chiefs in his busy enterprises, accumulated local prestige and became a powerful man as he supervised the mission's expanding properties. Methodist missionaries from Fiji, Tonga and Samoa, Australians and New Zealanders, assisted in founding and building up the Methodist Church on Choiseul, Vella Lavella, Buka and Bougainville, which today forms part of the United Church in Papua New Guinea and Solomon Islands.

Goldie's highly definite and unsubtle personality made itself felt in the Solomons as a whole. He became a vocal member of the British Colony's Advisory Council. His spick-and-span manner and unresponsiveness to the finer points of local cultures led to the imposition of imported styles of worship and leadership in the church. In 1959 one of Goldie's pupils, Silas Eto, reasserted what he claimed to be genuine Methodism against the mission. Eto combined prophetic, charismatic, and pre-christian cultural influences in a schismatic Christian Fellowship Church in his home area. The tension thus generated in the birthplace of the Methodist mission in the Western Solomons continued to breed discussion and controversy into the 1970s.

Struggles between contending missions — Roman Catholic, Methodist, Seventh-day Adventists — in Melanesia paved the way in the first half of the twentieth century for proliferating competition for souls between various small faith churches. After the Second World War governmental regulations against unrestricted entry by new groups led such competing elements to draw closer to each other — and cautiously to explore agreements based on the Bible and the Christian creeds with the larger and more widely established churches in the region. The time of origins, even in the New Guinea Highlands, the last of the Pacific mission fields, drew to a close. Local cargo cults containing Christian elements continued to appear, more frequently in Melanesia than elsewhere. Though they were almost invariably judged by the missions to be heterodox they asserted a right of the evangelized to detach themselves from foreign cultural dominance and to have a church of their own.

Silas Eto's movement in the Solomons, one among many of these religious reactions, claimed to be loyal to Goldie's ghost. Most of the cults asserted that mission influence had distorted what God intended for the people involved in them. They began with prophetic visions and fresh local structures. Eto's own starting point was a vision in which he believed Goldie spoke to him. He possessed charismatic power. His followers addressed him as Holy Mama. To them it simply meant that divine endowment rested upon him as prophet and pastor; the missionaries believed that the use of the expression equated him with God and made him in effect a substitute Messiah. He modelled his kind of mastery over his followers on Goldie's — and launched out into forms of worship and communal economic enterprise embodying the customs of his people in protest against imported ways.

Local leaders within larger churches in many parts of the Pacific have achieved similar independence of action. Constitutionally, they stand free of foreign control; they are united with each other in their acceptance of the Bible and the substance of the Apostles' and Nicene creeds. Each church is distinct. As they meet each other the extended Christian community of Oceania continues to acquire a specific regional character of its own.

13

Toward Regional Identity

The Twentieth Century

MORE PACIFIC ISLANDERS than white missionaries spread Christianity across the Pacific. Their daily contacts proved deep and lasting. They slowly created a feeling of close kinship between the young churches of the region. Within two generations they were celebrated as pioneers of the faith, praised along with chiefs who had the wit to welcome them. In many islands their marriages formed bonds of flesh and blood. While such sentiments were forming, wider realization of the underlying unity implicit in Christian beginnings lay dormant. The nascent churches were already there; but effective and regular relationships between them were not as strong as their dealings with the foreign mission boards and societies to which they were still attached. Within the structure of the mission in each island group a church had been born, waiting for freedom to develop in its own way, to reach out toward other churches in the Pacific. Island societies and churches knew themselves better than missionaries knew them. The well known white missionary remark "I know these people" usually betrayed anxious self-reassurance, inability really to comprehend. Many island peoples, having become Christian, anticipated the departure of the mission with patience, much after the fashion of resident sea creatures in a tropical lagoon integrating the influence of transients into their ecology. In theological terms, the first baptisms sowed seeds of maturity for each church, and for an ultimate regional identity that united them, within the island world they shared, as a distinctive "communion of saints."

TOWARD REGIONAL IDENTITY

In the twentieth century regional solidarity sharpened its outlines under the influence of the international missionary movement, dating from the first world missionary conference at Edinburgh in 1910 and taking institutional shape in 1921 with the formation of the International Missionary Council (IMC). Study and awareness of Christianity in Oceania as a whole were promoted by World Dominion Press volumes, written in Australia and published in London. The *International Review of Missions* summarised developments in its annual surveys. When Germany's colonies in the region were dismantled and put in trust under other powers the German mission boards and societies involved negotiated handover and aid of their work to missions in Britain, Australia and New Zealand, mainly within the general context of the IMC.

When the second international missionary conference met at Jerusalem in 1928 autonomy for younger churches dominated the proceedings. In the Pacific, scattered Christian communities drew closer together. Descendants of pioneer missionaries from Fiji, Tonga and Samoa followed their parents or grandparents in the service of Melanesian and Micronesian churches in a second and third generation. War with Japan sent a shock of self-assertion through this emerging wider family. Battles were fought along coasts where local Christians and missionaries who came from other parts of the Pacific became partners in adversity. American and Australian troops observed the importance of church life in the islands; some Americans, including American blacks, encouraged Pacific peoples to be less subservient to foreign white men. After the war American missionaries, both Protestant and Catholic, came in larger numbers to work in Micronesia and some other parts of the Pacific. Fast travel by air between island groups increased the possibility of travel and consultation for local church leaders as mission control made way for independent churches.

Developments in New Guinea, the last part of the Pacific to be reached by missions, set the pace for other islands. After the Second World War the highlands region of New Guinea opened up to modernization and Christian missions. Roman Catholics, German and American Lutherans, Australian-based Methodists and Baptists, and many small faith missions cultivated the dynamic highland tribes, previously sealed off from outside contact. Fijians, Tongans and fellow-Melanesians among missionaries to the highlands continued a long tradition of migrant missionary presence, running from east to west. The first major organic union of denominations in the Pacific was concluded in Papua New Guinea and Solomon Islands. In 1962 the Papua Ekalesia, formed out of the work of the LMS, joined with the Methodists of Papua, New Guinea and Solomon Islands, and with the United Church in Port Moresby, to form the United Church. The two congregations of the Port Moresby church, catering largely for expatriate Methodists, Presbyterians and Congregationalists, had been part of the United Church of North Australia before the union.

While churches evolved toward greater independence of action, their ordained Pacific Island ministers and clergy progressed only slowly toward equal status with foreign missionaries. Long usage dictated that missionaries received, and generally expected to retain, greater deference and respect than local leaders. The transition to equality, not yet complete, can be gauged by the retention of older titles of address. Protestant missionaries from abroad frequently spoke to local ministers and clergy using their baptismal names; they were normally approached, or answered, by use of "Mr" before the surname, or by "Sir"; their wives received "Mrs." By the late 1970s this situation had changed. In the Roman Catholic Church, difference in status was widely covered over by use of the title "Father" between priests, though "Sister" and "Brother" helped to bridge the gap. The baptismal name, symbolizing equality of Christians in the sight of God, was rarely used by local Protestants to address white missionaries, though some greatly loved exceptions, such as James Chalmers, were addressed by affectionate local versions of their second names, in Chalmers' case by Tamate (page 270).

Few Roman Catholic Pacific Islanders achieved the status of priesthood. The jump out of local cultural experiences into scholastic and ascetic customs in the seminaries led to widespread defections from student ranks. Clerical celibacy raised a culturally strange demand; for many candidates the social solitude that went with it was harder to accept than renunciation of active sexuality. Since ordinations for local people were rare, Catholic missions necessarily depended on foreign staff. The nomenclature and jurisdictional setting of the episcopate were puzzling and exotic. Bishops were still technically Vicars Apostolic *in partibus infidelium* (in regions of non-christians). Their official titles derived from Mediterranean or North African cities where bishops of Roman allegiance had been stationed before the great schism and the Islamic invasions. This Latin fiction mystified most of the faithful. More lowly catechists and nuns, on the other hand, were often Islanders; their work in parishes and institutions maintained close links with island life. A serious problem arose on less accessible islands where Catholics lived without a resident parish priest. For long periods they were without the Eucharist; the reserved sacrament normally perishes quickly in tropical climates. In spite of such difficulties, expatriate Catholic priests and sisters had one important advantage: being generally committed for life to their mission they did not count on recurrent periods of leave and final retirement "at home," as did most Protestants. For many Catholic missionaries the Pacific became home for life.

TOWARD REGIONAL IDENTITY

In the administration of financial aid mission boards moved in the present century from denominational toward ecumenical policies. Although most donor agencies tended to treat their own denominations as a first priority, they tried to confer together and to help co-operative and regional projects presented by the churches acting together. When the World Council of Churches directed its member churches in affluent countries to the needs of the third world, direct non-mission inter-church aid on a larger scale slowly became available for many projects in the Pacific. From the 1950s onward, mission boards and agencies worked toward co-ordinating their giving with this new direct source of income. By the 1960s the missions responded to meet needs the newly autonomous churches in the Pacific expressed: a regional Pacific council of churches with adequate staff; a regional centre for united theological training at higher level. Before these changes in patterns of aid took place denominational families of churches in the Pacific remained ill-informed about each other. In the new context this has partly changed.

When the World Council of Churches was established at Amsterdam in 1948 the ecumenical movement influenced relationships between leaders of its Protestant and Anglican member churches in the Pacific who met each other as fellow members of the small South Pacific delegations to international meetings. Some studied in North American seminaries. Two Methodists, Setareki Tuilovoni of Fiji and Sione 'Amanaki Havea of Tonga, emerged as spokesmen for little known churches in Oceania. Both followed in the steps of Pastor Iupeli, a dedicated and physically imposing Samoan (page 290), who represented the Samoan churches of the LMS tradition at the third world missionary conference at Tambaram, Madras, in 1938. Iupeli, who had given long service as a missionary in Kiribati (Gilbert Islands), symbolized the spontaneous expansion of the church in the Pacific. Louis Vangeke of Papua (page 244), who eventually succeeded Alain de Boismenu as bishop in Papua New Guinea, showed that some local leaders and spokesmen were also coming forward within the Roman Catholic Church, though more slowly. In Polynesia Pio Taofinu'u of Apia, Samoa, now a cardinal, preceded him in elevation to the episcopate.

In 1960 the International Missionary Council was integrated into the structure of the World Council of Churches. As churches in the Pacific became fully autonomous, independent of foreign mission control, they gained the right to send representatives to meetings of the World Council. Under the revised constitution of the WCC, member churches in Europe and North America were required to ensure that people who represented foreign missionary concern were included in delegations to meetings of the Council's governing bodies. Asian, African, Latin American and Caribbean church representatives also participated more vocally. They prepared the way for others, from the Pacific, to insist that their churches' concerns be understood and shared.

Less predictable, but swift, changes altered the face of Catholic Christianity in the Pacific during the 1960s. In October 1962 Pope John XXIII convened the Second Vatican Council. The council's documents led to the re-structuring of the Roman Catholic vicariates of Oceania. Missions, the religious life, the liturgy, the use of scripture, ecumenism, the role of bishops in the church, the place of the laity and the official understanding of religious liberty were altered with astonishing speed. Protestants were obliged to shelve stereotyped hostilities — often virulent in the Pacific. Many Catholics declared they were ready for dialogue and expressed repentance for old attitudes. Protestant incredulity then gave way to positive response. The College of Propaganda in Rome was internationalized as the Congregation for the Evangelization of the Nations. The new and simplified Roman Mass was translated into Pacific vernaculars and celebrated with locally devised ceremony and music. More local bishops were consecrated. The bishops formed the Episcopal Conference of the Pacific (CEPAC), encouraged the development of parish councils, co-operated with the Bible Society of the South Pacific in Bible translation, and were accepted in January 1976 as full members of the Pacific Conference of Churches (PCC).

The PCC itself held its first assembly on Lifou in the Loyalty Islands in 1966 as a result of the request of the first conference of Pacific churches and missions at Malua, Western Samoa, in 1961. Following this meeting a Pacific Islands' Christian Education Curriculum was devised. In the 1970s the PCC recruited more local staff concerned with human and economic development, family welfare, the status of women, opposition to nuclear testing and advocacy of independence from colonial rule. From permanent headquarters in Suva the Conference began to work closely with the World Council of Churches. A second institution, the Pacific Theological College, was built in Suva in 1966 to provide advanced training for the ministry. Older local theological schools in the South Pacific send selected students for further training at the PTC. The Roman Catholic Church's Pacific Regional Seminary followed nearby. Students and faculty of the two schools shared in regular acts of worship and in selected courses. Both institutions belonged to the South Pacific Association of Theological Schools, which worked with the Melanesian Association of Theological Schools to set standards and keep in touch with theological education in other parts of the world.

The 1970s, the Pacific's decade of new awareness and desire for national identity, brought ministers and clergy forward in many places as national leaders. In Papua New Guinea, Roman Catholic priests and laity influenced by the teaching and example of Patrick Murphy, an Australian Missionary of

Tahitians Joel and Céline Hoioré: husband and wife, graduates, Pacific Theological College.

the Divine Word who directed the Holy Spirit Seminary at Lae — and afterwards at Bomana near Port Moresby — were prominent and often controversial public figures. John Momis and Leo Hannett, inspired by the documents of Vatican II and by Murphy's teaching, took a prominent part in politics as their country became independent in 1975. Murphy later acted as secretary to the Bishops of Melanesia, director of the Melanesian Institute and a staff member of the Pacific Conference of Churches Programme on Church and Society. He died tragically in a road accident at Port Moresby in 1978. The impetus he and his students gave to Christian political and social action in Melanesia was continued in the participation of other church leaders in politics. In Vanuatu Walter Lini, an Anglican priest, became prime minister when his country reached independence in 1980. Lini's colleague Gérard Lemayng, a Roman Catholic priest who belonged to the opposition French-leaning coalition, worked with him to devise the country's final constitutional disengagement from the condominium. Several Presbyterian ministers, graduates of the Pacific Theological College, were elected to parliament in Lini's first government. In New Caledonia Jean-Marie Tjibaou, a prominent social scientist of Catholic training and background, joined freely with Protestants in advocating Melanesian rights and political independence. Church leaders have been more directly involved in political action in Melanesia than in Polynesia or Micronesia, but in the longer established independent nations of Polynesia they have at times provided an ethical and theological critique of governments tempted by short-term material goals.

Foreign missionary categories of thought frequently placed an accent on the theme of individual salvation, reflecting the preoccupations of their own nuclear family life. In every part of the Pacific individual life, by contrast, drew its meaning from the greater reality of extended families, with multiple relationships and duties. Family trees in Oceania spread wider; they offered more than casual shade; cousins were classed as "brothers" and "sisters," descent through female relatives in many places could knit generations together tightly by reference to many known ancestors. Patrilocal and matrilocal patterns after marriage widened and strengthened the web of belonging together which sustained island societies in storm, drought or prolonged absence of any outside aid. These community values of the pre-christian period, never surrendered, have been reaffirmed in the second half of the twentieth century. Affinities with Old Testament tribal Jewish society have been invoked by church leaders, as they were (in oral contexts) by newly literate Bible readers in the nineteenth century. Island nationals have sought to articulate an Oceanian theology, for their own people and for the Christian

The church and politics in the Pacific: Prime Minister of Vanuatu, Anglican Father Walter Lini, with Presbyterian pastor and cabinet minister Sethy John Rengenvanu.

population of the Pacific as a whole. Inventive minorities have begun to experiment with the use of local ceremony, dress, music, church construction and the commemoration of Islander pioneers in the liturgy. Imported baroque or Anglo-Saxon styles are criticized by a generation intent on recovering its ancient cultural roots.

All over Oceania the Church, integral to village life, has been recognized as a strong, though sleepy, potential source of social change. Its members, while they remain on the land, maintain old ways of worship and social organization. They often seem only dimly aware of the meaning of immense changes pressing on their relatives who go in great numbers to work in cities and towns — transnational economic enterprise, emigration to Australia, New Zealand and North America, tourism, foreign aid and outside manipulation of local economies in the guise of development. The churches, the World YWCA and the YMCA have selected some villages where cash cropping, crafts and trades and the logic of self-help can be demonstrated in local and traditional terms rather than by reference to the specialized and baffling vocabularies and techniques of governments and international agencies. Pilot experiments have increasingly been kept in touch with one another. Local forms of leadership, simpler village technologies, and modest initial capital, with a lead given from within the church at village level, offer prospects for wider awakening of the semi-dormant Christian community.

Progress in breaking down language barriers between English-speaking and French-speaking Pacific Islanders within the Church has been slow. Southern Polynesian Christians share a common pool of linguistic expressions and customs; this helps to some extent in relationships between French Polynesians, Cook Islanders and New Zealand Maoris. Other Polynesians, Micronesians and Melanesians are less fortunate. They also find it hard to understand French categories of thought that have partly shaped the personalities of New Caledonians, many from Vanuatu, Tahitians and Wallisians. On the English-speaking side of the divide people have been brought up with often unacknowledged British cultural presuppositions. France's continued colonial presence and atomic testing policy further hinder them from responding rationally to Pacific Island Christians who are indebted to the cultural heritage of France. Much of the effort to cross the gulf in the life of the churches has come from the French-speaking side; French-speaking priests and ministers trained at the Pacific Theological College and the Pacific Regional Seminary have learned to speak and write English. In Vanuatu, where the English-speaking Presbyterian Church and the largely French-speaking Roman Catholic Church are able to converse in Bislama, the local *lingua franca*, both church life and political life would be enriched by understanding if more people on each side of the colonially created chasm could communicate across it in each other's second languages. Unfortunately for regional awareness, the Pacific Conference of Churches has so far worked and thought mainly in English. In Melanesia, the churches and people of three Pidgin-speaking nations — Papua New Guinea, Solomon Islands, Vanuatu — are increasingly bonded by common heritage; together they constitute about three quarters of the population of the Pacific islands.

Christianity's progress across Oceania has helped to articulate the region's growing awareness of its sources of cultural and geographical unity. Although other world religions are active in Fiji and a few other island countries, Christianity has almost everywhere contributed to "the Pacific way." Churches in town and country are well attended. Islanders who come to town find the church is a place where they feel at home with others like themselves. In capital cities worship and church life are a cosmopolitan jostling-ground for varied outer-island micro-cultures. Yet these are blended within the *lotu,* a synthesis of Christian good news and local tradition. Secular education at advanced level has sometimes separated secular and sacred in the lives of members of minority elites; most people, by contrast, retain strong underlying convictions about God. They may be occasional and casual in worship and behaviour, but they think of themselves as forgiven sinners, members of the church of the people. For them the union of natural and supernatural, as their ancestors knew it under pre-christian religions, persists within the church. They seek out divine power to reassure them and to relate them to the worlds of ancestors and children's children — especially through baptism, confirmation, marriage and funeral rites and customs. The Bible, preaching and sacraments are part of a heritage they do not wish to lose, centred in the vivid image of the Christ of the Gospels. This heritage was first accepted, then diffused, by Island forerunners they honour, who bore the message from east to west over the vast sea-distances of Oceania.

Acknowledgments

TO LIVE AMONG THE STARS is as much the product of a community of explorers as the work of a single author. In writing it I have been constantly supported and corrected by a host of friends and scholars — and by the encouragement of Pacific Islander colleagues and students too numerous to list. The personal names that follow the general acknowledgments of aid received give no detailed account of manifold services rendered. Unintentional omissions will cause me inevitable regret. With my thanks to all who have helped I give the assurance that remaining defects — which are inevitable in a book of wide scope — are strictly my own fault.

Libraries and librarians, patient and anonymous guides to lost authors, have been mentioned near the beginning of the list. The bare enumeration of individual names that follows, without honorifics or titles, is intended as a testimony to a wealth of friendships:

The South Pacific Association of Theological Schools, for commissioning the book; the Programme on Theological Education of the World Council of Churches, for a writing grant; the Australian National University, Canberra, for a visiting fellowship; staff members of the Mitchell Library, Sydney; the Houghton Library, Harvard; the Hawaiian Mission Children's Society Library, Honolulu; the Pacific Theological College Library, Suva; Faculty and Students of the PTC; the National Archives of Fiji, Suva; the Marist Province of Oceania, Suva; the Roman Catholic Archdiocesan Office, Suva; St. John's College, Library, Auckland; the Alexander Turnbull Library, Wellington; the National Library, Canberra; the Menzies and Chifley Libraries, ANU, Canberra; the Department of Pacific History, Research School of Pacific Studies, ANU, Canberra; the Auckland Library and Museum; the Fiji Museum.

Ahmed Ali, Robert Anderson, Paparai Arapari, Louis Beauchemin, Judy Bennett, Jim Bergquist, Lola Bourke, John Broadbent, Doug Brown, Jabez Bryce, Malcolm Campbell, Fergus Clunie, Shoki Coe, Coral Coleman, Marjorie Crocombe, Ron Crocombe, Geoff Cummins, Pastor Dariu and Dariu Vahine, Rex Davis, Gavan Daws, Sadrud Dean, John Doom, Charles W. Forman, Abdul Gaffar, Mark Garrett, Roberta Garrett, Stephen Garrett, Cyril Germon, Patrick Gilbert, Ken Gillion, Lela Goodell, Kim Gravelle, Cecil Gribble, Niel Gunson, Sione 'Amanaki Havea, David Hilliard, John Hosie, Jaffar Hussein, Shem Jimmy, Ward Kaiser, Tomasi Kanailagi, Tony King, Jan Kok, John Mavor, George Knight, Margaret Knox, Hmana Lalie, Bob Langdon, Jione and Rigamoto Langi, Hugh and Eugénie Laracy, Elizabeth Larsen, Robin Leamy, Walter Lini, Barrie Macdonald, P.D. Macdonald, Tim Macnaught, Francis Colm Maguire, Bob McCahill, Vince Mc-

ACKNOWLEDGMENTS

Carthy, Martha McIntyre, Daniel Mastapha, Nancy Morris, Jotama Muahea'he'a, Doug Munro, the late Patrick Murphy, Baiteke Nabetari, Jacques Nicole, Margaret Patel, John Pinson, Jovilisi Qasi, Alan Quigley, Sitiveni Ratuvili, Watalaite Ratuvili, Dorothy Rengenvanu, Sethy Rengenvanu, Aharon Sapsezian, the late Ratu Emosi Saurara, the late Ratu Meleti Saurara, chiefs and people of Daku village, Albert Schneider, Prem Shankar, Elsabe Smith, Wendy Smith, Ian Somerville, June Starke, Elia and 'Ane Ta'ase, Ioritana Tanielu, Lopeti Taufa, Mele Taufa, Arona and Elise Temu, John Thornhill, Andrew Thornley, Bernard Thorogood, Fred Timakata, Viliame Tohi, the late Simiki Tonga, Fred Trautmann, Finau Tu'uholoaki, Sevati Tuwere, Esau Tuza, Henri Vernier, Bob von Oeyen, Lukas Vischer, Robyn Walker, Hans-Ruedi Weber, Neal Whimp, the late C.W. Whonsbon-Aston, A. Harold Wood, Matt Wilson, Gary Winter.

JOHN GARRETT

Glossary

ANTI (Kiribati)	Haunting local spirits, demanding placation.
ARI'I, ALI'I, ARIKI	High chiefs.
ARIOI (Tahiti)	Companies of strolling players, devotees of the Raiatean god Oro.
ATUA (Polynesia)	A god.
BETE (Fiji)	Priest of a pre-christian God.
BURE ATUA (Tahiti)	People who pray to God.
BURE KALOU (Fiji)	House of the god, pre-christian temple.
BUROTU (Fiji)	The place of departed spirits.
ENEHMU (Lifou)	Welcomed and protected guest (of chief).
FA'A SAMOA	Samoan custom, the Samoan way.
FAIFE'AU (Samoa)	Pastor.
FALE (Samoa, Tonga)	House.
FONO (Samoa)	Council, deliberative meeting.
HA'A (Tonga)	Lineage.
HALE (Hawaii)	House.
HAU (Tonga)	Ruling chief of Tongatapu.
HEIAU (Hawaii)	Pre-christian temple space, open to sky.
HIMENE (Tahiti)	Ancient folk tune, adapted for Christian hymns.
'INASI (Tonga)	Festival of first fruits of yam in pre-christian Tonga.
KAHILI (Hawaii)	Feathered stave banners carried before high chiefs.
KAHUNA (Hawaii)	Pre-christian priest.
KEREKERE (Fiji)	Begging from a member of one's own group, with obligation to comply.
KUHINA NUI (Hawaii)	Royal dowager with executive power.
LALI (Fiji)	Ceremonial drum made from hollowed log.
LOTU	The Christian faith; also the Christian Church; hence, by extension, particular churches, e.g., *lotu Tahiti*, *lotu Tonga*. As a verb: to accept the Christian faith.
LOTU WESELE (Fiji)	The Wesleyan Methodist Church.
MAHU (Tahiti)	Effeminate male companion.
MANA	Spiritual power.

GLOSSARY

MANEABA (Kiribati)	Traditional community meeting house.
MARAE, MALAE	Pre-christian temple space, sometimes elevated, open to the sky; also, the village green.
MATAI (Samoa)	Titled family head, chief.
MISINALE (Tonga)	Annual communal voluntary festival with offering for mission of the church.
NATMASSES (Aneityum)	Local haunting spirits.
PALAPALA (Hawaii)	Reading, literacy.
PAPALAGI (Tonga)	White person from abroad.
PEROVETA (Papua)	Prophet; hence prophet song, locally devised Christian chant often based on Polynesian equivalent.
PICPUS (France)	Picpus Fathers and brothers were members of the Society of the Sacred Hearts of Jesus and Mary, with their mother house in the rue de Picpus, Paris.
PULE (Hawaii)	Prayer.
SUKWE (Mota)	Graded pre-christian society of rank, with initiations involving invocation of spirits.
TABU, TAPU, KAPU	Taboo, forbidden, with supernatural sanctions and aura of the holy.
TABUA (Fiji)	Whale's tooth, highly prized and presented as token of honour.
TALATALA (Fiji)	Ordained minister of the church; literally, messenger.
TAPWARORO (East Papua)	Acceptance of Christianity; literally, bending of the knee.
TA'UNGA (Cook Islands)	Pre-christian priest.
TUAROI (Tahiti)	Group dialogue using Bible texts in Protestant parish house.
TU'I, TUI (Tonga, Fiji)	Sovereign high chief, royal person.
TUKA (Fiji)	Name of a cult; literally, immortality, resurrection, agelessness.
TULAFALE (Samoa)	Orator.
VAKATAWA (Fiji)	Catechist; literally, sentinel.
VAKAVUVULI (Fiji)	Teacher; used of Fijian missionaries to Melanesia.
VARANI (Fiji)	France, French; name given to chief who captured French ship.

GLOSSARY

VASU (Fiji) — Relationship of boy with mother's brother, conveying rights of local residence in uncle's locality and possession, on request, of uncle's goods (with reciprocal duties attached).

VAVALAGI (Fiji) — White person from abroad.

VUNIVALU (Fiji) — Supreme commander, especially on chiefly island of Bau; literally, root of war.

Abbreviations

ABCFM	American Board of Commissioners for Foreign Missions
ADB	*Australian Dictionary of Biography*
AM	*Annales Maristes*, 1877-1921
AMO	*Annales des missions d'Océanie*, Société de Marie, 1837-1855
ANU	Australian National University, Canberra
APF	*Annales de la Propagation de la Foi*, Lyon
APM	Archivio Padri Maristi, Rome
ASAO	Association of Social Anthropologists in Oceania
ASC	*Annales de Notre Dame du Sacré-Coeur*
ASSCC	*Annales des Sacrés-Coeurs*
ATL	Alexander Turnbull Library, Wellington
CMS	Church Missionary Society
CDCWM	*Concise Dictionary of the Christian World Mission*
DNZB	*Dictionary of New Zealand Biography*
HJH	*Hawaiian Journal of History*
HMCSL	Hawaiian Mission Children's Society Library, Honolulu
JPH	*Journal of Pacific History*
JPS	*Journal of Polynesian Society*
JRH	*Journal of Religious History*
JSO	*Journal de la Société des Océanistes*
LMS	London Missionary Society
ML	Mitchell Library, Sydney
MMSAF/NAF	Methodist Missionary Society of Australasia, Fiji
MOM	Methodist Overseas Missions Archives, ML, Sydney
MSC	Missionnaires du Sacré-Coeur
NAF	National Archives of Fiji, Suva
NZJH	New Zealand Journal of History
ODCC	*Oxford Dictionary of the Christian Church*
PCC	Pacific Conference of Churches
PIM	*Pacific Islands Monthly*
PTC	Pacific Theological College, Suva
RHM	*Revue d'Histoire des Missions*
SIM	Sandwich Islands Mission
SM	Société de Marie
SOAS	School of Oriental and African Studies, London

ABBREVIATIONS

SPG	Society for the Propagation of the Gospel
SSCC	Congregation of the Sacred Hearts of Jesus and Mary
SSEM	South Sea Evangelical Mission
SSJ	South Seas Journals, LMS
SSL	South Seas Letters, LMS
TS	Typescript
UMCA	Universities Mission to Central Africa
WMMS	Wesleyan Methodist Missionary Society

Sources

SOURCES in this selective list are arranged alphabetically by author, then title, or by title alone where there is no stated author. Abbreviations are given in the preceding list.

In the Notes (page 340) only authors and/or abbreviated titles are given, for quick reference from the short citations to their sources.

Indication of major sources used in writing each chapter follow the chapter headings in the Notes.

ABCFM/ SIM, Sandwich Islands Mission Journal. Ms. Houghton Library, Harvard.
Abel, Charles W., *Savage Life in New Guinea*. London, 1902.
ADB. Australian Dictionary of Biography (eds. Pike, Douglas, Bede Nairn and A.G. Serle), Vols. 1-8 (proceeding). Melbourne, 1966-81.
Ahlstrom, Sydney E., *A Religious History of the American People*. New Haven and London, 1972.
Anderson, Charles Roberts, *Melville in the South Seas*. New York, 1939.
Anderson, Rufus, *History of the Sandwich Islands Mission*. Boston, 1870.
Anderson, Rufus, *Letters to Sandwich Islands Mission*. HMCSL.
Anon., *Pontife et Victime, Monseigneur Collomb de la Société de Marie* .... Lyon, 1934.
Atlas of the South Pacific. Prime Minister's Department. Wellington, 1978.
Auna, Journal (tr. from Tahitian by William Ellis), 11 May-2 July 1822. Facsimile, HMCSL.
Baker, L. and B. Shirley, *Memoirs of the Reverend Dr. Shirley Waldemar Baker, D.M., LL.D., Missionary and Prime Minister*. London, 1951.
Baker Papers, Wesleyan Mission Papers, Tonga, re charges against Rev. Shirley Baker 1876-1878. ATL.
Balleine, G.R., *A History of the Evangelical Party in the Church of England*, new edn. London, 1951.
Bassett, Marnie, *Realms and Islands, The world voyage of Rose de Freycinet in the Corvette Uranie, 1817-1820*. London, 1962.
Beaglehole, J.C., *The Exploration of the Pacific*, 3rd edn. London, 1966.
Becke, Louis, *Wild Life in Southern Seas*. London, 1897.
Bianquis, Jean, *Les Origines de la Société des Missions Evangéliques de Paris, 1822-1830*, 3 vols. Paris, 1930-1935.
Bingham, Alfred M., 'Sybil's Bones, a Chronicle of the Three Hiram Binghams,' *HJH*, 9, 1975, 3-36.

SOURCES

Bingham Family Papers. HMCSL.
Bingham, Hiram, *A Residence of Twenty-one Years in the Sandwich Islands*. Hartford & New York, 1847.
Bingham, Hiram, II, Bingham Letters. HMCSL.
Bingham, Hiram, II, *The Making of a Version of the Bible for Gilbert Islanders*. New York, 1893. HMCSL.
Bingham, Hiram, Jr., *Story of the Morning Star, The Children's Missionary Vessel*. Boston, 1866.
Binney, Judith, *The Legacy of Guilt, A Life of Thomas Kendall*. Auckland, 1968.
Binney, Judith, 'Christianity and the Maoris to 1840: A Comment,' *NZJH*, Vol. 3, No. 2, October 1969, 143-165.
Binney, Judith, 'Nukutawhiti: Thomas Kendall's drawing,' *Turnbull Library Record*, Vol. 13, No. 1, May 1980.
Bird, Isabella L., *Six Months in the Sandwich Islands* (1st edn., 1875), 7th edn. Rutland, Vermont & Tokyo, 1974.
Birtwhistle, Allen, *In His Armour, The Life of John Hunt of Fiji*. London, 1954.
Biskup, Peter (ed.), *The New Guinea Memoirs of Jean Baptiste Octave Mouton*. Canberra, 1974.
Blanc, Joseph, *Histoire religieuse de l'archipel Fidjien*, 2 vols. Toulon, 1926.
Blanc, René, Jacques Blocher & Etienne Kruger, *Histoire des Missions Protestantes Françaises*. Flavion (Belgique), 1970.
Bliss, Theodora Crosby, *Micronesia, fifty years in the island world, a history of the American Board*. Boston, 1906.
Bollen, J.D., 'English Missionary Societies and the Australian Aborigine,' *JRH*, 9, No. 3, June 1977, 263-291.
Bonwick Transcripts. ML.
Boutilier, James A., Daniel T. Hughes & Sharon Tiffany (eds.), *Mission, Church, and Sect in Oceania*. Ann Arbor, 1978.
Brenchley, Julius L., *Jottings during the Cruise of H.M.S. Curacoa among the South Sea Islands in 1865*. London, 1873.
Brewster, A.B., *The Hill Tribes of Fiji*. London, 1922.
Broadbent, John V., Attempts to form an indigenous clergy in the Catholic Vicariates Apostolic of Central Oceania (Wallis, Futuna, Tonga) and the Navigators' Islands (Samoa and Tokelau) in the nineteenth century. PhD, Louvain, 1976.
Broadbent, John V., Address to Suva Theological Club, 12 October 1976 (ms. notes in possession J. Garrett).
Brookes, Jean Ingram, *International Rivalry in the Pacific Islands, 1800-1875*. New York, 1941.
Brown, George, Letter Books. ML.
Brown, George & P.P. Fletcher, *Report of Commissioners to Tonga appointed by the Committee of Privileges of the New South Wales and Queensland Conference* [Wesleyan Church]. Melbourne, 1888.

SOURCES

Brown, George, *George Brown, D.D., pioneer missionary and explorer, an autobiography.* London, 1908.
Brown, George, *Melanesians and Polynesians, their life histories described and compared.* London, 1910.
Brown, Stanley, *Men from Under the Sky, The Arrival of Westerners in Fiji.* Rutland, Vermont, 1973.
Bromilow, William E., *Twenty Years among Primitive Papuans.* London, 1929.
Buck, Peter H., *Vikings of the Pacific* (5th impression). Chicago & London, 1972.
Bulu, Joel, *The Autobiography of a Native Minister in the South Seas, tr. by a Missionary* [Lorimer Fison]. London, 1871.
Burchett, Wilfred G., *Pacific Treasure Island, New Caledonia* .... Melbourne, 1941.
Burrows, Edwin G., *Ethnology of Futuna.* Honolulu, 1936.
Burton, J.W., *Modern Missions in the South Pacific.* Sydney, 1949.
Burton, J.W., *Our Indian Work in Fiji.* Suva, 1909.
Burton, J.W. and Wallace Deane, *A Hundred Years in Fiji.* London, 1936.
Butcher, Benjamin T., *We Lived with Headhunters.* London, 1963.
Buzacott, Aaron, *Mission Life in the Islands of the Pacific* .... London, 1866.
Cadoux, le R.P., *L'Apôtre des Papous: Mgr. Henri Verjus.* Lyon, 1931.
Calvert, James, *Fiji and the Fijians, Mission History* (ed. George Stringer Rowe). London, 1858.
Campbell, Malcolm Henry, A century of Presbyterian mission education in the New Hebrides. Presbyterian Mission educational enterprises and their relevance to the needs of a changing Melanesian society 1848-1948. MEd, Melbourne, 1974.
Carano, Paul & Pedro C. Sanchez, *A Complete History of Guam.* Rutland, Vermont & Tokyo, 1964.
Cargill, David, *A Refutation of Chevalier Dillon's Slanderous Attacks on The Wesleyan Missionaries in The Friendly Islands* .... London, 1842.
Cargill, David, *Memoirs of Mrs. Margaret Cargill.* London, 1841.
Carter, George G., *A Family Affair, A Brief Survey of New Zealand Methodism's Involvement in Mission Overseas 1822-1972, Proceedings of Wesley Hist. Soc. of N.Z.,* 28, 3 & 4. Auckland, 1973.
Carter, George G., *Misikaram, The Reverend John Arthur Crump, F.Z.S., J.P., Missionary to New Britain 1894-1904. Proceedings of Wesley Hist. Soc. of N.Z.,* 29, 1-4. Auckland, 1975.
Catalyst, Social Pastoral Magazine for Melanesia, Published by the Melanesian Institute for Pastoral & Socio-Economic Service, Port Moresby.
Centenaire des Missions Maristes en Océanie. Lyon & Paris, 1936.
Chadwick, Owen, *The Victorian Church,* 2 vols., Part I. London, 1966.
Chalmers, James, *Work and Adventure in New Guinea.* London, 1902.
Chalmers, James and W. Wyatt Gill, *Work and Adventure in New Guinea.* London, 1885.

SOURCES

Chanel, Pierre, *Ecrits du Père Pierre Chanel, missionnaire mariste à Futuna 1803-1841* (ed. Claude Rozier). Paris, 1960.

Chatterton, Percy, *Day That I Have Loved*. Sydney, 1974.

Chesher, Richard H., 'Holy Mama, Solomons Prophet ...,' *PIM,* Vol. 49, No. 7, July 1978.

Clark, C.M.H., *A History of Australia*, 5 vols. Melbourne, 1963-1981.

Clark, Paul, *'Hauhau,' The Pai Marire Search for Maori Identity*. Auckland, 1975.

Coan, Titus, *Life in Hawaii*. New York, 1882.

Cochrane, Glynn, *Big Men and Cargo Cults*. Oxford, 1970.

Codrington, R.H., *The Melanesians, Studies in their Anthropology and Folk-lore*. Oxford, 1891.

Colwell, James (ed.), *A Century in the Pacific*. Sydney, 1914.

Coppenrath, Gérald, *Les Chinois de Tahiti de l'aversion à l'assimilation 1865-1966*. Paris, 1967.

Corney, Bolton Glanvill (ed.), *The Quest and Occupation of Tahiti by Emissaries of Spain during the years 1772-1776 ...,* 3 vols. London, 1913-19.

Coste, J., *Lectures on Society of Mary History*. Rome, 1965.

Coste, J. & G. Lessard, *Origines Maristes (1786-1836),* 4 vols. Rome, 1960-67.

Courant, V., *Le Martyr de la Nouvelle-Calédonie, Blaise Marmoiton, Frère Coadjuteur de la Société de Marie (1812-1847)*. Lyon & Paris, 1931.

Cragg, G.R., *The Church and the Age of Reason (1648-1789)*. Harmondsworth, 1960.

Crawford, David and Leona, *Missionary Adventures in the South Pacific*. Rutland, Vermont & Tokyo, 1967.

Crocombe, Marjorie Tuainekore, 'Ruatoka: A Polynesian in New Guinea History,' *PIM,* Nov. & Dec. 1972.

Crocombe, Marjorie Tuainekore, Maretu's Narrative of Cook Islands History. MA, Univ. of Papua New Guinea, 1974.

Crocombe, Marjorie Tuainekore, *If I Live, The Life of Ta'unga*. Suva, n.d.

Crocombe, R.G. (ed.), *Land Tenure in the Pacific*. Melbourne, 1971.

Crocombe, Ron, 'Missionaries: sacred and secular.' Paper for symposium on mission activities in Oceania, Association for Social Anthropology in Oceania, March 1975.

Crocombe, R.G. and Marjorie (eds.), *The Works of Ta'unga. Records of a Polynesian Traveller in the South Seas, 1833-1896*. Canberra, 1968.

Crocombe, R.G., *The New South Pacific*. Wellington, 1973 (rev. edn., 1978).

Crook, W.P., Ms. Account of the Marquesas Islands. ML.

Cross, Whitney R., *The Burned-over District, The Social and Intellectual History of Enthusiastic Religion in Western New York, 1800-1850*. New York, 1965.

Cumming, C.F. Gordon, *At Home in Fiji* (4th edn.). London, 1882.

Cumming, C.F. Gordon, *A Lady's Cruise in a French Man-of-War,* 2 vols. Edinburgh & London, 1882.

SOURCES

Cummins, H.G. 'Holy War: Peter Dillon and the 1837 Massacres in Tonga,' *JPH*, 12, 1977, 25-39.

Cummins, H.G., School and Society in Tonga 1826-1854, A study of Wesleyan mission schools, with special emphasis upon curriculum content and influence on political and social development,' MA, ANU, Canberra, 1977.

Cummins, H.G. (ed.), *Sources of Tongan History*. Nuku'alofa, 1972.

Cummins, H.G., 'Missionary Politicians,' *JPH*, 10, 1975, 105-112.

Cyclopaedia of Fiji. Sydney, 1907.

Cyclopaedia of Samoa, Tonga, Tahiti, and the Cook Islands. Sydney, 1907.

Danks, Benjamin, *In Wild New Britain, the story of Benjamin Danks, pioneer missionary, from his diary* (ed. Wallace Dean). Sydney, 1933.

David, Mrs Edgeworth, *Funafuti* .... London, 1899.

Davidson, J.W., *Samoa mo Samoa, The Emergence of the Independent State of Western Samoa*. Melbourne, 1967.

Davidson, J.W. & Deryck Scarr (eds.), *Pacific Islands Portraits*. Canberra, 1970.

Davidson, J.W., *Peter Dillon of Vanikoro* (ed. O.H.K. Spate). Melbourne, 1975.

Davies, John, *The History of the Tahitian Mission*, 1799-1830 (ed. C.W. Newbury). Cambridge, 1961.

Daws, Gavan, *A Dream of Islands, Voyages of Self-discovery in the South Seas*. New York, 1980.

Daws, Gavan, 'Honolulu in the 19th Century, Notes on the Emergence of Urban Society in Hawaii,' *JPH*, 2, 1967, 77-96.

Daws, Alan Gavan, Polynesian religious revivals: a study with background. MA, Univ. of Hawaii, 1960.

Daws, Gavan, *Holy Man, Father Damien of Molokai*. New York, 1973.

Daws, Gavan, *Shoal of Time, A History of the Hawaiian Islands*. Honolulu, 1968.

Daws, G., 'The Great Samoan Awakening of 1839,' *JPS*, 70, No. 3, Sept. 1961, 328ff.

Delacroix, S., *et al.*, *Histoire Universelle des Missions Catholiques*, Vol. III, *Les Missions Contemporaines (1800-1957)*. Paris, 1957.

Dening, Greg (ed.), *The Marquesan Journal of Edward Robarts, 1797-1824*. Canberra, 1974.

Derrick, R.A., *A History of Fiji*. Suva, 1950.

De Salinis, A., *Marins et Missionnaires, Conquête de la Nouvelle-Calédonie* (2me edn.). Paris, 1927.

Dillon, Peter, *Letter to Richard More O'Farrell Esq* .... [London?], [1841].

Diya (Methodist Church in Fiji, Indian Division), souvenir issue to mark the eightieth anniversary of the coming of Miss Hannah Dudley .... Suva, August 1977.

SOURCES

Dodge, Ernest S., *New England and the South Seas*. Cambridge, Mass., 1965.
Don, Alexander, *Peter Milne (1834-1924), Missionary to Nguna* .... Dunedin, 1927.
Doucéré, Victor, *La Mission Catholique Aux Nouvelles-Hébrides* .... Lyon-Paris, 1934.
Dovey, J.W., *The Gospel in the South Pacific*. London, 1950.
Dunand, J., *Aux Iles Samoa, La Forêt qui s'illumine*. Lyon & Paris, 1934.
Dunstone, A.S. (ed.), *Report of the Inaugural Meeting of the Melanesian Association of Theological Schools*, April, 1969.
Dupeyrat, André, *Papouasie, Histoire de la Mission (1885-1935)*. Paris, 1935.
Dupeyrat, André, *Papuan Conquest*. Melbourne, 1948.
Dwight, Edwin, *Memoirs of Henry Obookiah* ... (reprint). Honolulu, 1968.
Dyson, Martin, *My Story of Samoan Methodism; or, A Brief History of the Wesleyan Methodist Mission in Samoa*. Melbourne, 1875.
Dyson, Martin, [Autobiography]. The Life of a Meltham Methodist ..., 1894. Ms. ML.
Eason, W.J.E., *A Short History of Rotuma*. Suva, 1951.
Eglise Evangélique en Polynésie Française, 166 ans d'histoire (1797-1963). Notre Lien. Papeete, 1963.
Elder, J.R. (ed.), *The Letters and Journals of Samuel Marsden 1765-1838*. Dunedin, 1932.
Elder, J.R. (ed.), *Marsden's Lieutenants*. Dunedin, 1934.
Ellis, Albert F., *Ocean Island and Nauru, Their Story*. Sydney, 1936.
Ellis, Albert F., *Adventuring in Coral Seas* (2nd edn.). Sydney, 1937.
Ellis, Albert F., *Mid Pacific Outposts*. Auckland, 1946.
Ellis, John Eimeo, *Life of William Ellis* .... London, 1873.
Ellis, William, *Narrative of a Tour through Hawaii* .... London, 1826.
Ellis, William, *Polynesian Researches*, 4 vols. (2nd edn.). London, 1831.
Ellis, William, *The American Mission in the Sandwich Islands; a Vindication and an Appeal*. Honolulu, 1866.
Ellis, William, *The History of the London Missionary Society*, Vol. I. London, 1844.
Erskine, John Elphinstone, *Journal of a Cruise among the Islands of the Western Pacific ... in Her Majesty's Ship Havannah*. London, 1853.
Evatt, H.V., *Rum Rebellion. A Study of the Overthrow of Governor Bligh* .... Sydney, 1938.
Farmer, Sarah S., *Tonga and the Friendly Islands*. London, 1855 (reprint, Canberra, 1976).
Fatiaki, Anselmo, *et al.* (eds.), *Rotuma, Split Island*. Suva, 1977.
Fiji Methodist Centenary Souvenir, 1835-1935. Suva, 1935.
Findlay, G.G. & W.W. Holdsworth, *The History of the Wesleyan Methodist Missionary Society*, 5 vols. (Vol. 3). London, 1921.
Fischer, John L., Saul H. Riesenberg and Marjorie G. Whiting (trs. and eds.), *The Book of Luelen — Luelen Bernart*. Canberra, 1977.

SOURCES

Fischer, John L., Saul H. Riesenberg and Marjorie G. Whiting (trs. and eds.), *Annotations to the Book of Luelen*. Canberra, 1977.

Fletcher, C. Brunsdon, *The Black Knight of the Pacific*. Sydney, 1944.

Forman, Charles W., *The Island Churches of the South Pacific: Emergence in the Twentieth Century*. New York, 1982 (forthcoming).

Forman, C.W., 'Theological Education in the Pacific Islands ...,' *JSO*, 25, 1969, 151-167.

Forman, Charles W., 'Tonga's tortured venture in church unity,' *JPH*, 13, 1978, 3-21.

Fortune, R.F., *Sorcerers of Dobu, the social anthropology of the Dobu Islanders of the Western Pacific*. London, 1932.

Fox, C.E., *Kakamora*. London, 1962.

Fox, C.E., *Lord of the Southern Isles*. London, 1958.

Fox, C.E., *Threshold of the Pacific*. London, 1924.

France, Peter, *The Charter of the Land, Custom and Colonization in Fiji*. Melbourne, 1969.

Freeman, J.D., 'The Joe Gimlet or Siovili Cult: An episode in the Religious History of Early Samoa,' *Anthropology in the South Seas* (eds. Freeman, J.D. and W.R. Geddes). New Plymouth, 1959, 185-200.

Frerichs, Albert and Sylvia, *Anutu Conquers in New Guinea*. Minneapolis, 1969.

Fullerton, L.D., From Christendom to Pluralism in the South Seas, Church-State Relations in the Twentieth Century. PhD, Drew Univ., Madison, N.J., 1969.

Gadd, Bernard, *The Rev. James Buller, 1812-1884. Proceedings of Wesley Hist. Soc. N.Z.*, 23, Nos. 1 & 2. Auckland, 1968.

Gallagher, Pat, *The Marist Brothers in New Zealand, Fiji and Samoa, 1876-1976*. Christchurch, 1976.

Garran, Robert R., *Prosper the Commonwealth*. Sydney, 1958.

Garrett, John, 'Australia in the Pacific: A Christian Interrogation,' *St. Mark's Review* (Canberra), No. 89, March 1977.

Garrett, John, *A Way in the Sea: Aspects of Pacific Christian History with reference to Australia*. Melbourne, 1982 (forthcoming).

Garrett, John and L.W. Farr, *Camden College, A Centenary History*. Sydney, 1964.

Garrett, John, 'A letter from Oceania,' *Voices of Unity, Essays in honour of Willem Adolf Visser 't Hooft* .... Geneva, 1981.

Garrett, John, 'Justice — a job for God or Caesar?,' *PIM*, Vol. 45, No. 12, 1974, 33-5.

Garrett, John, 'The Conflict between the London Missionary Society and the Wesleyan Methodists in 19th Century Samoa,' *JPH*, 9, 1974, 65-80.

Garrett, John, 'The Meeting of Religions in Fiji,' *Journal of Pacific Studies* (Suva), Vol. 5, 1979, 10-33.

SOURCES

Garrett, John, 'Wooing the Church in the New Hebrides ...,' *PIM*, Vol. 46, No. 7, 1975, 1-2.
Gast, Ross H., *Don Francisco de Paula Marin*, with *The Letters and Journal of Francisco de Paula Marin* (ed. Agnes C. Conrad). Honolulu, 1973.
Giles, W.E., *A Cruize in a Queensland labour vessel to the South Seas* (ed. Deryck Scarr). Canberra, 1968.
Gill, William, *Gems from the Coral Islands. Western Polynesia* .... London, 1855.
Gill, William Wyatt, *Life in the Southern Isles; or, Scenes and Incidents in the South Pacific and New Guinea*. London, 1876.
Gill, William Wyatt, *Historical Sketches of Savage Life in Polynesia, with illustrative clan songs*. Wellington, 1880.
Gill, William Wyatt, *From Darkness to Light in Polynesia*. London, 1894.
Gillion, K.L., *Fiji's Indian Migrants, A History to the end of indenture in 1920*. Melbourne, 1962.
Gillion, K.L., *The Fiji Indians, Challenge to European Dominance 1920-1946*. Canberra, 1977.
Gilson, Richard, *The Cook Islands 1820-1950* (ed. Ron Crocombe). Wellington and Suva, 1980.
Gilson, R.P., *Samoa 1830 to 1900, The Politics of a Multi-cultural Community*. Melbourne, 1970.
Goldman, Irving, *Ancient Polynesian Society*. Chicago & London, 1970.
Goodall, Norman, *A History of the London Missionary Society 1895-1945*. London, 1954.
Gordon, Arthur, *Fiji: records of private and of public life, 1875-1880*, 5 vols. Edinburgh, 1897-1912.
Goulter, Mary Catherine, *Sons of France, A forgotten influence on New Zealand history*. Wellington, 1958.
Grattan, F.J.H., *An Introduction to Samoan Custom*. Apia, 1948.
Greenslade, W.H., *John Whitely 1806-1869, Proceedings of Wesley Hist. Soc. of N.Z.*, 24, Nos. 3 & 4. Auckland, 1968.
Guiart, Jean, *Un Siècle et demi de Contacts culturels à Tanna, Nouvelles-Hébrides*. Paris, 1956.
Guiart, Jean, 'The Millenarian Aspect of Conversion to Christianity in the South Pacific,' Sylvia Thrupp (ed.), *Millennial Dreams in Action*. New York, 1970.
Guinard, Fr., S.M., The History of Namosi (ts. in French, Archives of Roman Catholic Archdiocese, Suva); rough tr. by Margaret Knox, June 1976.
Gunn, William, *The Gospel in Futuna*. London, 1914.
Gunson, Niel, 'An Account of the Mamaia or Visionary Heresy of Tahiti, 1826-1841, *JPS*, 71, No. 2, June 1962.
Gunson, Niel (ed.), *Australian Reminiscences & Papers of L.E. Threlkeld, Missionary to the Aborigines, 1824-1859*, 2 vols. Canberra, 1974.

SOURCES

Gunson, Niel (ed.), *The changing Pacific: Essays in honour of H.E. Maude.* Melbourne, 1978.

Gunson, Niel, 'Co-operation Without Paradox: A Reply to Dr. Strauss,' *Historical Studies, Australia and New Zealand,* XI, 1965, 513-34.

Gunson, Niel, Evangelical Missionaries in the South Seas, 1797-1860. PhD, ANU, Canberra, 1960.

Gunson, Niel, 'John Williams and His Ship: The Bourgeois Aspirations of a Missionary Family,' D.P. Crook (ed.), *Questioning the Past, A Selection of Papers in History and Government.* St. Lucia, Queensland, 1972.

Gunson, Niel, *Messengers of Grace, Evangelical Missionaries in the South Seas, 1797-1860.* Melbourne, 1978.

Gunson, Niel, 'Missionary Interest in British Expansion in the South Pacific in the Nineteenth Century,' *JRH,* III, 1965, 296-313.

Gunson, Niel, 'On the Incidence of Alcoholism and Intemperance in early Pacific Missionaries,' *JPH,* 1, 1966, 43-62.

Gunson, Niel, 'Pomare II of Tahiti and Polynesian Imperialism,' *JPH,* IV, 1969, 65-82.

Gunson, Niel, 'The Theology of Imperialism and the Missionary History of the Pacific,' *JRH,* V, 1969, 255-65.

Gunson, Niel, 'Victorian Christianity in the South Seas: a Survey,' *JRH,* VIII, 1974, 183-97.

Habel, Norman C. (ed.), *Powers Plumes and Piglets. Phenomena of Melanesian Religion.* Melbourne, 1979.

Hadfield, Emma, *Among the Natives of the Loyalty Group.* London, 1920.

Hadfield, Octavius, *[Pamphlets], One of England's Little Wars, A letter to the Right Hon. The Duke of Newcastle, Secretary of State for the Colonies.* London and Edinburgh, 1860; *The Second Year of One of England's Little Wars.* London and Edinburgh, 1861; *A Sequel to "One of England's Little Wars": being an account of the real origin of the war in New Zealand, its present stage, and the future prospects of the colony.* London and Edinburgh, 1861.

Hames, E.W., *Walter Lawry and the Wesleyan Mission in the South Seas, Proceedings of Wesley Hist. Soc. of N.Z.,* 23, No. 4. Auckland, 1967.

Handy, E.S. Craighill, *Polynesian Religion.* Honolulu, 1927.

Handy, E.S. Craighill, *History and Culture in the Society Islands.* Honolulu, 1930.

Havard-Williams, P. (ed.), *Marsden and the New Zealand Mission, Sixteen Letters.* Dunedin, 1961.

Haweis, H.R., *Travel and Talk* (Vol. II). London, 1896.

Henderson, G.C. (ed.), *Fijian Documents, Political and Constitutional.* Sydney, 1938.

Henderson, G.C. (ed.), *The Journal of Thomas Williams, Missionary in Fiji, 1840-1853,* 2 vols. Sydney, 1931.

Henderson, J. McLeod, *Ratana. The Man, The Church, The Political Movement* (2nd edn.). Auckland, 1972.

SOURCES

Henry, Teuira, *Ancient Tahiti: Based on Material Recorded by J.M. Orsmond*. Honolulu, 1928.
Hilliard, D.L., Protestant Missions in the Solomon Islands, 1849-1942. PhD, ANU, Canberra, 1966.
Hilliard, David, 'Bishop G.A. Selwyn and the Melanesian Mission,' *NZJH*, 4, No. 2, October 1970, 120-137.
Hilliard, David, *God's Gentlemen, A History of the Melanesian Mission, 1849-1942*. St. Lucia, Queensland, 1978.
Hocart, A.M., *Lau Islands, Fiji*. Honolulu, 1929.
Hocart, A.M., *The Northern States of Fiji*. London, 1952.
Hogbin, H.I., *Experiments in Civilization*. London, 1939.
Hogbin, H. Ian, 'Mana,' *Oceania*, Vol. VI, No. 3, 241.
Holmes, J.H., *By Canoe to Cannibal Land*. London, 1923.
Holmes, J.H., *In Primitive New Guinea*. London, 1924.
Holmes, J.H., *Way Back in Papua*. London, 1926.
Hopkins, A.I., *From Heathen Boy to Christian Priest*. London, 1949.
Hopkins, Manley, *Hawaii: the past, present and future of its island-kingdom*. London, 1862.
Hosie, John, The French Mission, an Australian base for the Marists in the Pacific, to 1874. MA, Macquarie Univ., Sydney, 1971.
Hosie, Stanley W., *Anonymous Apostle, The Life of Jean Claude Colin, Marist*. New York, 1967.
Howard, Alan, An annotated bibliography of Rotuman materials (ts.). Univ. of Auckland (n.d.). (Copy in NAF, Suva.)
Howe, K.R., *The Loyalty Islands, A History of Culture Contacts 1840-1900*. Honolulu, 1977.
Howe, K.R., 'The Maori Response to Christianity in the Thames-Waikato Area, 1833-1840,' *NZJH*, 7, No. 1, April 1973, 28-46.
Howse, Ernest Marshall, *Saints in Politics, the 'Clapham Sect' and the growth of freedom*. London, 1953.
Hunt, John, *Entire Sanctification: Its Nature, The Way of its attainment, and Motives for its Pursuit. In Letters to a Friend*. London, 1853.
Hunt, John, Journal 1839-1841 (transcribed by E.H.). ML.
Hunt, John, *Memoir of the Rev. William Cross* ... (2nd edn.). London, 1858.
Inglis, John, *In the New Hebrides, Reminiscences of Missionary Life and Work, especially on the Island of Aneityum, from 1850 till 1877*. London, 1887.
Inglis, John, *Bible Illustrations from the New Hebrides, with notices of the progress of the mission*. London, 1890.
Inglis, K.S. (ed.), *The History of Melanesia*. Canberra, 1969.
Jackson, K.B., 'Head-hunting in the Christianization of Bugotu 1861-1900,' *JPH*, 10, 1975, 65-78.
Jacomb, Edward, *France and England in the New Hebrides, The Anglo-French Condominium*. Melbourne, 1914.
James, A.T.S., *Twenty-five Years of the L.M.S. 1895-1920*. London, 1923.

SOURCES

Jarves, James Jackson, *History of the Hawaiian or Sandwich Islands*. London, 1843.
Jimmy, Shem, The Influence of Christianity among the people of Ponape. BD, PTC, Suva, 1972.
Jore, Léonce, *Un Belge au Service de la France dans L'Océan Pacifique* .... Paris, 1942.
Joyce, R.B., *Sir William MacGregor*. Melbourne, 1971.
Judd, Bernice, *Voyages to Hawaii before 1860*... (enlarged and ed. Helen Yonge Lind). Honolulu, 1974.
Kekela Letters. HMCSL.
Kennedy, T.F., *A Descriptive Atlas of the Pacific Islands* (3rd edn.). Wellington, 1974.
Kent, Harold Winfield, *Dr. Hyde and Mr. Stevenson*. Rutland, Vermont & Tokyo, 1973.
Keys, Lillian, *The Life and Times of Bishop Pompallier*. Christchurch, 1957.
King, Cecil J., *Copland King and his Papuan Friends*. Sydney, 1934.
King, Joseph, *Ten Decades, The Australian Centenary Story of the London Missionary Society*. London, 1895.
King, Joseph, *Christianity in Polynesia, a Study and a Defence*. Sydney, 1899.
King, Joseph, *W.G. Lawes of Savage Island and New Guinea*. London, 1909.
Knox, Margaret, Draft Bibliography: Time Line of the history of the Catholic church in Fiji. Catholic Archives, Suva, Fiji (ts.).
Kofe, Laumua, The Tuvalu Church: a socio-historical survey of its development towards an indigenous church. BD, PTC, Suva, 1976.
Korn, A.L., *The Victorian Visitors, an account of the Hawaiian Kingdom, 1861-1866* .... Honolulu, 1958.
Koskinen, Aarne A., *Missionary Influence as a Political Factor in the Pacific Islands*. Helsinki, 1953.
Kuykendall, Ralph S., *The Hawaiian Kingdom*, 3 vols. Honolulu, 1938-1967.
Langdon, Robert, *Tahiti: Island of Love* (4th edn.). Sydney, 1972.
Langdon, Robert, *The Lost Caravel*. Sydney, 1975.
Langi, Jione, The History of the Church in its Rotuman setting: an introductory outline. BD, PTC, Suva, 1971.
Langmore, Diane, *Tamate — A King, James Chalmers in New Guinea, 1877-1901*. Melbourne, 1974.
Laracy, Hugh, *Marists and Melanesians, A History of Catholic Missions in the Solomon Islands*. Canberra, 1976.
Laracy, Hugh M., Catholic Missions in the Solomon Islands, 1845-1966. PhD, ANU, Canberra, 1969.
Laracy, Hugh, 'Roman Catholic 'Martyrs' in the South Pacific, 1841-55,' *JRH*, 9, 1976, 189-202.
Latourette, K.S., *A History of the Expansion of Christianity*, 7 vols.; *The Great Century 1800-1914* (Vol. 4); *The Great Century in the Americas, Australasia and Africa* (Vol. 5). London, 1949.

SOURCES

Latukefu, Sione, *Church and State in Tonga, The Wesleyan Methodist Missionaries and Political Development, 1822-1875.* Canberra, 1974.

Laurenson, George I., *Te Hahi Weteriana, Three Half Centuries of The Methodist Maori Missions, 1822-1972, Proceedings of Wesley Hist. Soc. of N.Z.*, 27, Nos. 1 & 2. Auckland, 1972.

Laval, Honoré, *Mangareva, l'histoire ancienne d'un peuple polynésien.* Braine-le-Comte (Belgique), 1938.

Laval, Honoré, *Mémoires pour servir à l'histoire de Mangareva* (ed. C.W. Newbury and Patrick O'Reilly). Paris, 1968.

Lawry, Walter, *Friendly and Feejee Islands: a Missionary Visit to Various Stations in the South Seas ....* London, 1850.

Leenhardt, Raymond H., *Au Vent de la Grande Terre, Histoire des Iles Loyalty de 1840 à 1895.* Paris, 1957.

Leenhardt, Maurice, *Do Kamo, la personne et le mythe dans le monde Mélanésien.* Paris, 1947.

Lescure, Ph. Rey, *Abrégé d'Histoire de Tahiti et des archipels de la Polynésie Française* (2e edn.). Papeete, 1970.

Lesson, P.-A., *Voyage aux Iles Mangareva (Océanie).* Rochefort, 1844.

Levison, Michael, R. Gerard Ward and John W. Webb, *The Settlement of Polynesia. A Computer Simulation.* Canberra, 1973.

Levy, Robert, *Tahitians: mind and experience in the Society Islands.* Chicago, 1973.

Lewis, David, *We, The Navigators, The Ancient Art of Landfinding in the Pacific.* Canberra, 1975.

Liu, John, Mission Imperatives for Churches of Christ in the New Hebrides. BD, PTC, Suva, 1976.

Livingston, Theodore William, The Morning Stars: ships of the 'Gospel Navy' with a supplemental listing of missionary vessels around the world. MA, Univ. of Hawaii, 1971.

LMS/SSL. South Sea Letters, London Missionary Society. Mss. and microfilm. SOAS (microfilm, ML and NL).

LMS/SSJ. South Sea Journals, London Missionary Society. Mss. and microfilm. SOAS (microfilm, ML and NL).

LMS/SI. LMS letters from Sandwich Islands 1822-1834 (in HMCSL as Angus Transcripts, typed for Hawaiian Historical Society by Donald Angus).

Loomis, Albertine, *To All People, A History of the Hawaii Conference of the United Church of Christ.* Honolulu, 1970.

Lovett, Richard, *The History of the London Missionary Society, 1795-1895*, 2 vols. London, 1899.

Lovett, Richard, *James Chalmers, His Autobiography and Letters.* London, 1902.

Loy, Allan W., An Outline of the History and Present Situation of the Methodist Church among Indian People in Fiji. BD, Union Theological Seminary, New York, n.d.

SOURCES

Lundie, George Archibald, *Missionary Life in Samoa, as exhibited in the Journals of the late George Archibald Lundie, during the Revival in Tutuila in 1840-41*, edited by his Mother. Edinburgh, 1846.

Luxton, C.T.J., *Isles of Solomon*. Auckland, 1955.

Luxton, C.T.J., *The Rev. James Wallis of the Wesleyan Missionary Society, Proceedings of Wesley Hist. Soc. of N.Z.*, 21, Nos. 1 & 2. Auckland, 1965.

Lyth, Richard Burdsall, Journals, 1845-1850. ML.

Mackaness, George, *Life of Vice-Admiral Bligh*. Sydney, 1931.

Macnaught, Timothy J., Mainstream to Millpond? The Fijian Political Experience 1897-1940. PhD, ANU, Canberra, 1975.

McAuley, James, *Collected Poems 1936-1970*. Sydney, 1971.

McAuley, James, 'My New Guinea,' *Quadrant*, Vol. 5, No. 3, Winter 1961, 15-27.

McFarlane, Samuel, *Among the Cannibals of New Guinea: being the story of the New Guinea mission of the London Missionary Society*. London, 1888.

McFarlane, Samuel, *The Story of the Lifu Mission*. London, 1873.

McManners, John, *Church and State in France, 1870-1914*. New York, 1972.

Malinowski, Bronislaw, *Argonauts of the Western Pacific*. London, 1922.

Malo, David, *Hawaiian Antiquities* (2nd edn.), tr. B. Emerson. Honolulu, 1951.

Mander Jones, Phyllis (ed.), *Manuscripts in the British Isles relating to Australia, New Zealand, and the Pacific*. Canberra, 1972.

Mangeret, le R.P., *Mgr. Bataillon et les Missions de l'Océanie Centrale*, 2 vols. Lyon, 1884.

Marau, Clement, *The Story of a Melanesian Deacon*. London, 1894.

Marceau, M., *Des Missions Catholiques dans l'Océanie*. Lyon, 1845.

Marsden Papers. ML.

Marsters, Ned, Transcript of tape recording made at ATL between John Burland, Mr. Ned Marsters, head of Palmerston Island, and his daughter, Miss Pika Marsters, 2 February 1959. ATL.

Martin, Margaret Greer (ed.), *The Lymans of Hilo* (revised edn.). Hilo, 1979.

Maude, H.E., *Of Islands and Men, Studies in Pacific History*. Melbourne, 1968.

Maude, H.E., 'The Raiatean Chief Auna and the Conversion of Hawaii,' *JPH*, 8, 1973, 188-191.

Maude, H.E., *Slavers in Paradise, The Peruvian labour trade in Polynesia, 1862-1864*. Suva, 1981.

Maudslay, Alfred P., *Life in the Pacific Fifty Years Ago*. Canberra, Stanford and London, 1930.

Mauer, Daniel, *Aimer Tahiti*. Paris, 1972.

[Mayet, Claude], *Auguste Marceau, Capitaine de frégate, Commandant de l'Arche d'Alliance*, (Nouvelle édn.) 2 vols. Paris, 1862.

[Mayet, Claude], *Le Premier Vicaire Apostolique de la Nouvelle-Calédonie, ou*

SOURCES

Monseigneur Douarre, Evêque d'Amata et la Nouvelle-Calédonie, 2 vols. Lyon, 1879.

Miller, R.S., *Misi Gete, John Geddie, Pioneer Missionary to the New Hebrides*. Launceston, 1975. (Based on Geddie mss. in La Trobe Library, Melbourne).

Miller, J. Graham, *Live, a history of church planting in the New Hebrides to 1880*. Sydney, [1978].

Missionary Album, Portraits and Biographical Sketches of the American Protestant Missionaries to the Hawaiian Islands, Enlarged from the Edition of 1937. Honolulu, 1969.

MMSA/NAF. Methodist Missionary Society of Australasia, Fiji District records. NAF, Suva.

MOM. Methodist Overseas Missions papers (Australasian Conference). ML.

Monfat, A., *Le Missionnaire des Samoa, Mgr. L. Elloy* .... Lyon & Paris, 1928.

Monfat, A., *Les Origines de la Foi Catholique dans la Nouvelle-Zélande, Les Maoris*. Lyon, 1896.

Monfat, A., *Les Premiers Missionnaires de Samoa (Archipel des Navigateurs)*. Paris, 1923.

Monfat, A., *Les Tonga, ou Archipel des Amis et le R.P. Joseph Chevron, de la Société de Marie* .... Lyon, 1896.

Montgomery, H.H., *The Light of Melanesia. A Record, or, Fifty Years Mission Work in the South Seas*. London, 1904.

Montgomery, James (ed.), *Journal of Voyages and Travels by the Rev. Daniel Tyerman and George Bennet, Esq., deputed from the London Missionary Society to visit their various stations* ..., 2 vols. London, 1831.

Moors, H.J., *With Stevenson in Samoa*. London, n.d.

Morison, John, *The Fathers and Founders of the London Missionary Society* .... London, 1844.

Morrell, W.P., *Britain in the Pacific Islands*. Oxford, 1960.

Morrell, W.P., *The Anglican Church in New Zealand, A History*. Dunedin, 1973.

Morris, Nancy J., 'Hawaiian Missionaries in the Marquesas,' *HJH*, 13, 1979, 46-58.

Morrison, James, *The Journal of James Morrison, Boatswain's Mate of the Bounty* .... London, 1935.

Munro, Doug, 'Kirisome and Tema, Samoan Pastors in the Ellice Islands.' Scarr (ed.), *More Pacific Islands Portraits*. Canberra, 1979.

Munro, Doug, Ms. chart of Missionary voyages to the Ellice Islands 1865-1906 (photo-copy; original with author). 1977.

Munro, Doug, Ts. drafts for thesis on Tuvalu (formerly Ellice Islands). Lent by author, 1977.

Murray, A.W., *Forty Years' Mission Work in Polynesia and New Guinea, from 1835 to 1875*. London, 1876.

SOURCES

Murray, A.W., *Martyrs of Polynesia, Memorials of Missionaries, Native Evangelists and Native Converts, who have died by the hand of violence, from 1799 to 1871*. London, 1885.

Murray, A.W., *Missions in Western Polynesia, Being Historical Sketches of these Missions, from their commencement in 1839 to the present time*. London, 1863.

Murtagh, James G., *Australia, The Catholic Chapter*. Melbourne, 1969.

Nan Madol, a tour through the Venice of Madolenhihmw (ed. Carole Jencks). Ponape, 1970.

Neill, Stephen, *Christian Missions*. Harmondsworth, 1964.

Neill, Stephen, Gerald H. Anderson and John Goodwin (eds.), *Concise Dictionary of the Christian World Mission* [CDCWM]. London, 1970.

Newbury, Colin, 'Resistance and collaboration in French Polynesia: The Tahitian War: 1844-7,' *JPS*, 82, No. 1, March 1973, 5-27.

Niau, J.H., *The Phantom Paradise, the story of the expedition of the Marquis de Rays*. Sydney, 1936.

Nicholson, Robert B., *The Pitcairners*. Sydney, 1965.

Nisbet, Henry, Papers (mss.). ML.

Niue Island, Mss. Collection. ATL (MS papers 1273).

[ODCC], *The Oxford Dictionary of the Christian Church* (2nd edn., ed. Cross, F.L. and E.A. Livingstone, reprinted 1977). Oxford, 1974.

O'Farrell, Patrick, *The Catholic Church in Australia, A Short History: 1788-1976*. Melbourne, 1968.

Oliver, Douglas L., *The Pacific Islands*. New York, 1961.

Oliver, Douglas L, *Ancient Tahitian Society*, 3 vols. Honolulu, 1974.

Orange, James, *Life of the late George Vason of Nottingham, One of the Troop of Missionaries first sent to the South Sea Islands by the London Missionary Society in the Ship Duff*.... London, 1840. (Reprint, Nuku'alofa, 1975).

O'Reilly, Patrick and Edouard Reitman, *Bibliographie de Tahiti et de la Polynésie Française*. Paris, 1967.

O'Reilly, Patrick, *Calédoniens, Répertoire bio-bibliographique de la Nouvelle-Calédonie*. Paris, 1953.

O'Reilly, Patrick, *Essai de bibliographie des missions Maristes en Océanie Occidentale*. Paris, 1932.

O'Reilly, Patrick, *Imprints of the Fiji Catholic Mission including the Loreto Press, 1864-1954*. London and Suva, 1958.

O'Reilly, Patrick, 'La Société de l'Océanie (1844-1854),' *Revue d'Histoire des Missions*, 7, juin 1930, 227-262.

O'Reilly, Patrick, *Pomare, Reine de Tahiti*. Paris, 1972.

O'Reilly, Patrick and Raoul Teissier, *Tahitiens, Répertoire biographique de la Polynésie Française* (2me edn.). Paris, 1975.

O'Reilly, Patrick, 'Tentative d'évangélisation de Tahiti par les franciscains espagnols,' *Revue d'Histoire des Missions*, septembre 1933, 387-409.

Orr, J. Edwin, *The Second Evangelical Awakening in Britain*. London and Edinburgh, 1949.

SOURCES

Owens, J.M.R., *Prophets in the Wilderness, The Wesleyan Mission to New Zealand, 1819-27*. Auckland, 1974.

[PCC], *The Fourth World Meets, PCC Assembly, Davuilevu, Fiji, 1971*. Suva, 1972.

Pacific Islands Year Book & Who's Who, Tenth Edition (ed. Judy Tudor). Sydney, 1968.

Pacific Islands Year Book, Thirteenth Edition (ed. Stuart Inder). Sydney & New York, 1978.

Parsonson, G.S., 'The Literate Revolution in Polynesia,' *JPH*, 2, 1967, 39-57.

Parsonson, G.S., 'La Mission Presbytérienne des Nouvelles-Hébrides: Son Histoire et son Rôle Politique et Social,' *JSO*, 12, 1956, 107-137.

Paton, James (ed.), *John G. Paton, Missionary to the New Hebrides, An Autobiography*, 2 vols. London, 1889.

Patteson, John Coleridge, Letters. Ms. ATL.

Patteson, John Coleridge, Letters. Ms. St John's College, Auckland.

Phillips, Clifton J., *Protestant America and the Pagan World: The First Half Century of the American Board of Commissioners for Foreign Missions, 1810-1860*. PhD, Harvard, 1954. (Reprinted as No. 32, *Harvard East Asian Monographs*, 1968).

Pinson, W.J., Diocese of Polynesia, 1868-1910. BD, PTC, Suva, 1970.

Pionnier, Jean, *Une Page de l'Histoire des temps Héroiques de la Mission de Calédonie et le Sanctuaire de l'Immaculée-Conception*. Lyon & Paris, 1911.

Pisier, Georges (tr. et réd.), *Le Témoignage de Ta'unga, ou La Nouvelle-Calédonie vue par un "teacher" polynésien avant l'implantation européenne* ... (tr. from Crocombe, R.G. and Marjorie, *The Works of Ta'unga*). Nouméa, 1980.

Poignant, Roslyn, *Oceanic Mythology*. London, 1967.

Pompallier, Jean Baptiste François, *Early History of the Catholic Church in Oceania* (tr. Arthur Herman). Auckland, 1888.

Poncet, Alexandre, *Histoire de l'île Wallis*, tome 2, *le protectorat français*. Paris, 1972.

Powell, Thomas, *Savage Island, a brief account of the Island of Niué, and of the work of the Gospel among its people*. London, 1868.

Powell, Wilfred, *Wanderings in a Wild Country, or, three years amongst the cannibals of New Britain*. London, 1884.

Prout, Ebenezer, *Memoirs of the Life of the Rev. John Williams, Missionary to Polynesia*. London, 1843.

Ramsden, Eric, *Marsden and the Missions, Prelude to Waitangi*. Sydney, 1936.

Raucaz, L.M., *Vingt-cinq Années d'Apostolat aux Iles Salomon (1898-1923)*. Paris, 1925.

Reid, A.C., 'The Fruit of the Rewa, Oral Traditions and the Growth of the Pre-Christian Lakeba State,' *JPH*, 12, 1977, 2-24.

Reid, A.C., 'The View From Vatuwaqa, The role of Lakeba's leading lineage in the introduction and establishment of Christianity,' *JPH*, 14, 1979, 154-167.

SOURCES

Rere, Taira, *Genealogy of the Papehia Family*. Suva, 1977.
Rere, Taira, *History of the Papehia Family*. Suva, 1977.
Restarick, Henry Bond, *Hawaii 1778-1920 from the Viewpoint of a Bishop*. Honolulu, 1924.
Roach, Kevin J., 'Jean-Claude Colin and the foundation of the New Zealand Catholic Mission,' *NZJH*, April 1969, 74-83.
Robertson, H.A., *Erromanga, the Martyr Isle* (ed. John Fraser). London, 1902.
Robson, R.W., *Queen Emma, the Samoan-American girl who founded an empire in 19th Century New Guinea*. Sydney, 1965.
Ross, Angus, *New Zealand Aspirations in the Pacific in the Nineteenth Century*. Oxford, 1964.
Ross, R.M., *A Guide to Pompallier House*. Wellington, 1970.
Roth, G.K., *Fijian Way of Life* (2nd edn.). Melbourne, 1973.
Rowe, G. Stringer, *A Pioneer, Memoir of the Reverend John Thomas*. London, 1885. (New illustrated edn., Canberra, 1976).
Rowe, G. Stringer, *James Calvert of Fiji*. London, 1893.
Rowe, N.A., *Samoa under the Sailing Gods*. London & New York, 1930.
Rozier, Claude, 'Lano, Petit Séminaire,' *Missions des Iles* (Paris), 1962, No. 114, 52.
Rutherford, Noel (ed.), *Friendly Islands, A History of Tonga*. Melbourne, 1977.
Rutherford, Noel, *Shirley Baker and the King of Tonga*. Melbourne, 1971.
Sabatier, Ernest, *Astride the Equator, an account of the Gilbert Islands* (tr. Ursula Nixon, from *Sous l'Equateur du Pacifique*). Melbourne, 1977.
Sabatier, Ernest, *Sous l'Equateur du Pacifique, Les Iles Gilbert et la Mission Catholique*. Paris, 1939.
Saville, W.J.V., *In Unknown New Guinea*. London, 1926.
Scarr, Deryck, *Fragments of Empire, A history of the Western Pacific High Commission, 1877-1914*. Canberra, 1967.
Scarr, Deryck, *I, the very bayonet*, Vol. 1 of *The Majesty of Colour, A life of Sir John Bates Thurston*. Canberra, 1973.
Scarr, Deryck (ed.), *More Pacific Islands Portraits*. Canberra, 1979.
Schmidlin, Joseph, *Catholic Mission History* (tr. and ed. Matthias Braun). Techny, Illinois, 1933.
Schoofs, Robert, *Pioneers of the Faith, History of the Catholic Mission in Hawaii (1827-1940)*. Honolulu, 1978.
Schütz, Albert J. (ed.), *The Diaries and Correspondence of David Cargill*. Canberra, 1977.
Seemann, Berthold, *Viti: an account of a Government mission to the Vitian or Fijian Islands in the years 1860-61*. Cambridge, 1862.
Shanahan, Mary, *Out of Time, Out of Place, Henry Gregory and the Benedictine Order in Colonial Australia*. Canberra, 1970.
Shevill, Ian, *Pacific Conquest, The history of 150 years of missionary progress in the South Pacific*. Sydney, 1949.

SOURCES

Shineberg, Dorothy, *They Came for Sandalwood, A Study of the Sandalwood Trade in the South-West Pacific, 1835-1856*. Melbourne, 1967.
[SIMJ]. Sandwich Islands Mission Journals. HMCSL.
Sinclair, Keith, *A History of New Zealand* (2nd edn.). Harmondsworth, 1969.
Sinclair, Keith, *The Origins of the Maori Wars*. Auckland, 1961.
Smith, Bradford, *Yankees in Paradise, The New England Impact on Hawaii*. Philadelphia & New York, 1956.
Smythe, W.J. & Mrs., *Ten Months in the Fiji Islands*. London, 1864.
Spalding, Arthur Whitefield, *Origin and History of Seventh-day Adventists*, 4 vols. (Vols. 2 and 3). Washington, 1962.
Spooner, T.G.M., *Brother John, The Life of the Rev. John Hobbs, Proceedings of Wesley Hist. Soc. N.Z.*, 13, Nos. 2-4. Auckland, 1955.
South Sea Missions. ML (A 381).
Stacpoole, J.M., *A Guide to the Waimate Mission House*. Wellington, 1971.
Stair, John B., *Old Samoa, or Flotsam and Jetsam from the Pacific Ocean*. London, 1897.
Standish, M.W., *The Waimate Mission Station*. Wellington, 1962.
Starke, June, 'The Waitara Purchase,' *Turnbull Library Record*, Vol. 6 (n.s.), No. 1, May 1973.
Steel, Robert, *The New Hebrides and Christian Missions*. London, 1880.
Steven, Margaret, *Merchant Campbell, 1796-1846, A Study of Colonial Trade*. Melbourne, 1965.
Stevenson, Robert Louis, *In the South Seas*. London, 1900. (Facsimile edn., Honolulu, 1971).
Stevenson, Robert Louis, *Vailima Letters* (18th edn.). London, 1920.
Stewart, C.S., *Journal of a Residence in the Sandwich Islands during the years 1823, 1824, and 1825* (reprint of 3rd edn., 1830). Honolulu, 1970.
Stock, Eugene, *The History of the Church Missionary Society, its environment, its men and its work*, 3 vols. London, 1899.
Stock, Eugene, *The Story of the New Zealand Mission*. Nelson (N.Z.), 1913.
Ta'ase, Elia, 'Beyond Samoan Christianity, a study of the Siovili Cult and the problems facing the church in Samoa today,' BD, PTC, Suva, 1971.
Tagupa, William E., 'Soliloquies from the surviving; missionary notes from the Marquesas Islands, 1853-1868,' *JSO*, 60, XXXIV, September, 1978.
Talu, Alaima (*et al.*), (eds.), *Kiribati, Aspects of history*. Suva and Tarawa, 1979.
Taylor, C.R.H., *A Pacific Bibliography* (2nd edn.). Oxford, 1965.
Thompson, Laura, *The Native Culture of the Marianas Islands*. Honolulu, 1945.
Thompson, R. Wardlaw, *My Trip in the John Williams*. London, 1900.
Thomson, Basil, *Savage Island, an account of a sojourn in Niué and Tonga*. London, 1902.
Thomson, Basil, *The Diversions of a Prime Minister*. Edinburgh & London, 1894.

SOURCES

Thomson, Basil, *The Fijians. A Study of the Decay of Custom*. London, 1908 (reprinted, London, 1968).

Thornley, A.W., The Methodist Mission and the Indians in Fiji, 1900 to 1920. MA, Univ. of Auckland, 1973.

Thornley, A.W., Fijian Methodism, 1874-1945: the emergence of a national church. PhD, ANU, Canberra, 1979.

Thornley, A.W., '"Heretics" and "Papists": Wesleyan-Roman Catholic Rivalry in Fiji, 1844-1903,' *JRH*, 10, No. 3, June 1979.

Thorogood, Bernard, *Not Quite Paradise*. London, 1960.

Threlfall, Neville, *One Hundred Years in the Islands, the Methodist/United Church in the New Guinea Islands Region, 1875-1975*. Rabaul, 1975.

Threlkeld, L.E., *Australian Reminiscences and Papers of L.E. Threlkeld* (ed. Niel Gunson), 2 vols. Canberra, 1974.

Threlkeld, L.E., Reminiscences of Lancelot Edward Threlkeld, extracted from *The Voice in the Wilderness*, February-November 1852 and *The Christian Herald, and Record of Missionary and Religious Intelligence ...,* February 1853-April 1855 (ts. in possession of Niel Gunson, ANU, Canberra).

Thrupp, Sylvia L. (ed.), *Millennial Dreams in Action, Studies in Revolutionary Religious Movements*. New York, 1970.

Tippett, Alan R., *Oral Tradition and Ethnohistory, The Transmission of Information and Social Values in Early Christian Fiji 1835-1905*. Canberra, 1980.

Tippett, A.R., *People Movements in Southern Polynesia*. Chicago, 1971.

Tippett, A.R., *Solomon Islands Christianity*. New York, 1967.

Tippett, Alan R. and Tomasi Kanailagi (eds.), The Autobiography of Joeli Bulu, Tongan Missionary to Fiji. Professor/Associate Research Project, MA, Fuller Theological Seminary, Pasadena, n.d.

Tippett, A.R., *The Christian (Fiji 1835-67)*. Auckland, 1954.

Tippett, Alan R., *The Deep Sea Canoe, the Story of Third World Missionaries in the South Pacific*. South Pasadena, 1977.

Tjibaou, Jean-Marie, *Kanaké, the Melanesian Way*. Papeete, 1978.

Tohi, Viliami, A Study in the Nature of the Church as seen in the Anglican Church in Tonga. BD, PTC, Suva, 1972.

Tomkins, Dorothea and Brian Hughes, *The Road from Gona*. Sydney, 1969.

Tomlin, J.W.S., *Awakening, A History of the New Guinea Mission*. London, 1951.

Tucker, H.W., *Memoir of the Life and Episcopate of George Augustus Selwyn, D.D.*, 2 vols. London, 1879.

Tudor, Judy (ed.), *Papua New Guinea Handbook* (7th edn.). Sydney, 1974.

Tupouniua, Sione, Ron Crocombe and Claire Slatter (eds.), *The Pacific Way, Social Issues in National Development*. Suva, 1975.

Turner, George, *Nineteen Years in Polynesia: Missionary Life, Travels, and Researches in the islands of the Pacific*. London, 1861.

SOURCES

Turner, George, *Samoa a Hundred Years Ago and Long Before, together with Notes on the Cults and Customs of Twenty-Three other islands in the Pacific.* London, 1884.

Turner, J.G., *The Pioneer Missionary: Life of the Rev. Nathaniel Turner* .... Melbourne, 1872.

Turner, Peter, Private Journals. ML.

Verguet, L., *Histoire de la Première Mission Catholique au Vicariat de Mélanésie.* Paris, 1861.

Vernier, Charles, *Tahitiens d'autrefois, Tahitiens d'aujourd'hui.* Paris, 1934.

Viviani, Nancy, *Nauru, Phosphate and Political Progress.* Canberra, 1970.

[Wallis, M.D.], *Life in Fiji, or, Five Years among the Cannibals, by a Lady.* Boston, 1851. (Facsimile reprint, Ridgewood, N.J., 1967.)

Ward, Marion W. (ed.), *The Politics of Melanesia.* Canberra, 1970.

[Waterhouse, J.B.], *Secession and Persecution in Tonga.* Sydney, 1886.

Waterhouse, Joseph, *The King and People of Fiji.* London, 1864.

Watsford, John, *Glorious Gospel Triumphs as seen in My Life and Work in Fiji and Australasia.* London, 1900.

Watt, Agnes C.P., *Twenty-five Years' Mission Life on Tanna, New Hebrides* .... Paisley, 1896.

West, Thomas, *Ten Years in South-Central Polynesia: Being Reminiscences of a Personal Mission to the Friendly Islands and their Dependencies.* London, 1865.

Wetherell, David, Christian Missions in Eastern New Guinea: A Study of European, South Sea Island, and Papuan Influences, 1877-1942. PhD, ANU, Canberra, 1974.

Wetherell, David, 'Pioneers and patriarchs: Samoans in a nonconformist mission district in Papua, 1890-1917,' *JPH*, 15, Part 3, July 1980.

Wetherell, David, *Reluctant Mission: The Anglican Church in Papua New Guinea, 1891-1942.* St. Lucia, Queensland, 1977.

White, Geoffrey M., 'Symbols of Solidarity in the Christianization of Santa Isabel, Solomon Islands,' written for the symposium on Transformations of Christianity at the meetings of the Southwestern Anthropological Association. San Diego, April 1977. (Copy lent by Judith A. Bennett.)

White, Geoffrey M., 'War, Peace and Piety in Santa Isabel, Solomon Islands,' ts. for ASAO volume on Pacification in Melanesia, 1977. (Copy lent by Judith A. Bennett.)

White, Mrs. G.F., *Memoir of Mrs. Jane Tucker, wife of the Rev. Charles Tucker, Sometime Missionary to Haabai and Tonga* ... (ed. H.W. Williams). London, 1877.

Whitehouse, John Owen, *A Register of Missionaries, Deputations, Etc. from 1796 to 1896 (London Missionary Society) compiled for the use of the directors and missionaries of the Society, 1896.*

Whitmee, Samuel James (1838-1925), Recollections of a Long Life .... (Ts. transcribed Irene M. Fletcher, London Missionary Society), August 1964.

SOURCES

Whonsbon-Aston, C.W., *Pacific Irishman.* Sydney, 1970.
Wilkes, Charles, *The Narrative of the United States Exploring Expedition during the years 1838, 1839, 1840, 1841, and 1842,* 5 vols. Philadelphia, 1845.
Williams, John, *A Narrative of Missionary Enterprises in the South Sea Islands* .... London, 1837.
Williams, John A., *Politics of the New Zealand Maori, Protest and Co-operation, 1891-1909.* Auckland, 1969.
Williams, Ronald G., *The United Church in Papua, New Guinea, and the Solomon Islands.* Rabaul, 1972.
Williams, Thomas and James Calvert, *Fiji and the Fijians,* 2 vols. London, 1858.
Williams, Thomas, Journal 1840-49. Ms. ML.
[Wilson, James], *A Missionary Voyage to the Southern Pacific Ocean performed in the years 1796, 1797, 1798, in the ship Duff* .... London, 1799.
Wiltgen, Ralph M., *The Founding of the Roman Catholic Church in Oceania 1825 to 1850* Canberra, 1979.
Wood, A.H., *History and Geography of Tonga.* Auckland, 1943. (Reproduced, Wodonga, Victoria, 1972).
Wood, A. Harold, *Overseas Missions of the Australian Methodist Church,* 4 vols. (Vols. 1-3). Melbourne, 1975-80.
Wood, Arthur Skevington, *Thomas Haweis, 1734-1820.* London, 1957.
Woods, Gay (ed.), *South Pacific Dossier.* Canberra, 1978.
Worsley, Peter, *The Trumpet Shall Sound. A Study of Cargo Cults in Melanesia.* London, 1970.
Wright, Harrison M., *New Zealand, 1769-1840, Early Years of Western Contact.* Cambridge, Mass., 1959.
Wright, Louis B. and Mary Isabel Fry, *Puritans in the South Seas.* New York, 1936.
Yarwood, A.T., *Samuel Marsden, The Great Survivor.* Melbourne, 1977.
Yate, William, *An Account of New Zealand and of the Church Missionary Society's Mission in the Northern Island.* London, 1835. (Reproduced Auckland, 1970.)
Yonge, Charlotte Mary, *Life of John Coleridge Patteson, missionary bishop of the Melanesian Islands,* 2 vols. London, 1874.
Young, Florence S.H., *Pearls from the Pacific.* London & Edinburgh, [1925].
Young, Robert, *The Southern World, Journal of a Deputation from the Wesleyan Conference to New-Zealand and Polynesia* (4th edn., revd.). London, 1858.
Yzendoorn, Reginald, *History of the Catholic Mission in the Hawaiian Islands.* Honolulu, 1927.

Notes

IN THESE NOTES, citations for each chapter are preceded by a general chapter note on major sources.

Each note gives a short indication of author and title cited, as given more fully in the alphabetically arranged list of Sources (page 317).

Citations of manuscripts are confined to those actually used in writing the book. Full and useful listings of historical manuscript sources on Pacific history and the growth of Christianity in Oceania are at the Pacific Manuscripts Bureau, Research School of Pacific Studies, Australian National University.

Translations from the French in the text and the references are by the author unless otherwise indicated.

Chapter 1
A Curious New God
(Pages 1-31)

THE BEGINNINGS in the Marianas are summarized in Carano & Sanchez. For Tahiti, Oliver, *Ancient Tahitian Society*, and Handy's two listed works, with Henry's *Ancient Tahiti* (to be read in the light of Oliver's book on the same subject), give useful background. Lovett's *History of the LMS*, with constant reference to Gunson's *Messengers of Grace*, still provides good narrative framework based on sources. Davies, Ellis' *Polynesian Researches*, Wilson's *Voyage of the Duff*, James Montgomery's account of the LMS Deputation of Tyerman and Bennet, with Threlkeld's Reminiscences (extracted from religious periodicals in Australia), are by participants. O'Reilly and Teissier, *Tahitiens*, has biographical detail.

The main manuscript sources are LMS/SSJ and LMS/SSL, also available in microfilm.

Page
1   Papal bull, 1493: Neill, Anderson and Goodwin, *CDWMC*, 'Patronato Real,' 474.
     Impact of Spaniards: Langdon, *Lost Caravel*; cf. review by Peter Bellwood, *JPH*, 11, Nos. 3-4, 1976, 253-7; Yzendoorn, 12, 13 (and n.).

NOTES

2   First organized Catholic mission: Carano/Sanchez, 61-87.
    Guam's social pyramid: Thompson, L., *Native Culture of Marianas*.
3   About 5000 survived: Carano/Sanchez, 86.
    Spanish ships supplanted: Beaglehole, 108-315.
    Spaniards came twice to Tahiti: Corney.
4   Wallis, Cook, Bligh: Beaglehole; Mackaness.
    Calvinistic Evangelicals: *ODCC*, 244; Balleine.
    Haweis and the *Duff*: Wood, A.S., *Haweis*, 177-8.
    Castaways: Maude, *Of Islands and Men*, 134-177.
    Sio Vili: Ta'ase; Freeman.
    The Polynesian societies: Background in Oliver, *Pacific Islands*.
5   Local "prophets": Yzendoorn, Preface; Crocombe, M., Maretu's Narrative, 67-8. There are many other examples.
6   John Young: Daws, *Shoal of Time*, 34, 46.
    Hagerstein: Koskinen, 20.
    Miraculous signs on paper: Parsonson, 'Literate Revolution ...'
7   The condition of Tahiti: Wilson, 319-409.
    Pomare, Tu: O'Reilly/Teissier, *Tahitiens*, 'Pomare Ier'; Newbury in intro. to Davies, xxxvii-xl.
    Oro and the Arioi: Oliver, *Ancient Tahitian Society*, 759-765, 890-913; Handy, *History and Culture*, 61, 65, 72; Ellis, *Polynesian Researches*, 1, 229-247.
8   The Pomares' titles and power: Langdon, *Lost Caravel*, illust. and caption following 160.
    Evangelical Revival: Cragg, 141-173.
9   Calvinistic Methodists: *ODCC*, 224-5.
    Godly mechanicks: Gunson, *Messengers*, 31-46.
    Missionary Society: Lovett, *History of LMS*, 5ff.
    Calvinist Anglicans: Balleine; Howse.
10 The "funeral of bigotry": Lovett, *History of LMS*, I, 35-6.
    Fundamental Principle: Lovett, *History of LMS*, I, 50.
    "Disinterested benevolence": Phillips, 1-3.
    Not exactly millennial fever: Phillips, 8-13.
11 Haweis: Wood, A.S., *Haweis*.
12 The 1400 subscribers: Wilson, 421ff.
    Journal of James Morrison: text in Morrison.
    The list of missionaries: Wilson, 5-6.
13 Haweis versus Bogue: Gunson, *Messengers*, 64-78.
14 A scene of great oddity: Wilson, 56-59.
    "During sermon and prayer": Wilson, 57.
15 Cover's sermon: Wilson, 57.
    Conception of ceding land: Crocombe, R.G., *Land Tenure* (variously); but, on original Matavai cession, cf. Wilson, xcix.
    Harris and Crook in the Marquesas: Wilson, 141-2; Crook.

NOTES

"The suburbs of hell": Phillips, 115.
16 Vason's memoirs: Orange.
"So depraved are these poor heathens": Wilson, 201.
"You give me much paraow": Wilson, 224-5.
17 Defection of Lewis and Broomhall: LMS/SSL, Tahiti, 4 August 1798, 1 February 1799; Jefferson to Love, n.d. (1799?), Jefferson to Secretary, 13 January 1800; (on Broomhall), Jefferson to Directors, 31 December 1800.
18 Pomare I, "decidedly a *religious* character": Davies, 65.
Pomare II to LMS Directors: Lovett, *History of LMS*, 189.
Exiles in New South Wales: Letters to Rev. S. Marsden 1802-1836 re South Sea Mission, Marsden Papers (A1995), ML.
19 Marsden and the LMS: A.T. Yarwood, 'Samuel Marsden', *ADB*, 2; Yarwood; Gunson, *Messengers*, 115-117.
Robert Campbell: Stephen.
Pork and coconut oil: Jefferson to Directors, 29 August 1803. LMS/SSL; Maude, *Of Islands and Men*, 178-232.
Accusations of distilling rum: Henry to Orme, 30 December 1828, LMS/SSL; Gunson, 'On the incidence of alcoholism...'; Davies, 225-231.
Rum, a prized item of barter in NSW: Evatt.
"Many would be aspiring": Jefferson to Directors, 12 December 1804, LMS/SSL.
"By almost every vessel": Jefferson to Directors, 3 September 1803, LMS/SSL.
Nott as teacher of Tahitian: Youl to Platt, 1 October 1802, LMS/SSL.
20 "The writing is the King's": Eyre to Directors, 29 July 1805, LMS/SSL.
"No sincere desire of instruction": Davies, 89.
"Dangerous rebellion": Davies to Campbell, 12 November 1808, LMS/SSL.
21 Nott's custom marriage: Haweis, 284, 286; Gunson, *Messengers*, 202 (and refs.).
Nott's Sydney marriage: Nott to Haweis (from Sydney), 28 July 1812, LMS/SSL.
22 Tuahine and Oito: Davies, 157, 164.
Paofai a Manua: O'Reilly/Teissier, *Tahitiens*, 'Paofai'.
Paofai saved Shelley: Davies, 165-6.
Hostility from Fenuapeho: Davies, 309.
"These Islanders are Religious people": Davies to Directors, 7 January, 1814, LMS/SSL.
23 Battle of 12 November 1815: Davies, 191-2; Ellis, *Polynesian Researches*, 1, 146-153.
"The profession of Christianity having become national": Davies, 197.

NOTES

24 "Much prudence and caution": Davies, 214.
 A new and eager group of missionaries: Gunson, *Messengers,* 132-6.
25 "We refuse episcopal government": Wood, A.S., *Haweis,* 238.
 Pomare II and the press: Davies, 208-9.
26 Raiatea, central point of influence: Handy, *History and Culture,* 109.
27 The auxiliary societies: Gunson, *Messengers,* 308-312.
 Missionaries as law-givers: Gunson, *Messengers,* 284-287.
 Signs of Pomare's end: Crook, Journal, 6 February 1821, LMS/SSJ.
28 Tyerman and Bennet with Pomare: Montgomery, 1, 98-103.
 Ellis, indefatigable collector: Ellis, *Polynesian Researches.*
 Crowning of Pomare III: Montgomery, 2, 90-95.
 Queen Pomare IV: *Pomare, Reine de Tahiti.*
29 Raiatea under Threlkeld: Threlkeld, Reminiscences.
 Sabbath controversy: Henry to Threlkeld, 4 March 1823, LMS/SSJ; Gunson, *Messengers,* 125.
 Williams' quest for a ship: Gunson, 'John Williams and His Ship.'
 Growing and exporting tobacco: Williams, John, *Narrative,* 168.
 Williams invited to Hawaii: Bingham and others to Leeward Station, Society Islands, 20 February 1823, South Sea Missions, ML, A381, Item 157.
30 The Deputation's appeal for unity: Montgomery, 2, 112.
 Williams and Bourne Voyage to Hervey Islands: LMS/SSJ.
 "The vessel belonging to the United Chiefs": Williams and Bourne Journal (title).
31 Threlkeld among Australian Aborigines: Gunson, *Australian Reminiscences.*
 "'I said I shall die in my nest'": Threlkeld, Reminiscences, 150.
 "The caprice of irresponsible directors": Threlkeld, Reminiscences, 82.
 "For my part I cannot content myself": 30 September 1823, LMS/SSL.

Chapter 2
Christians in Hawaii
(Pages 32-59)

GENERAL HISTORY of the Hawaiian islands, with attention to the growth of the churches, is in Kuykendall and in Daws, *Shoal of Time.* Origins and theological background for the ABCFM are treated by Phillips. Hiram Bingham's recently re-issued *Residence,* based on his own manuscripts, is detailed and valuable, though tendentious. The *Missionary Album* is a mine of fact and background. Smith's *Yankees in Paradise* is useful and diverting.

NOTES

Catholic origins described by Yzendoorn are further explained, especially for the sending end, by Wiltgen. The sufferings of converts, with Hawaiian names and some detail, have been traced by Schoofs.

Morrell, *Britain in the Pacific Islands,* clarifies the Franco-British confrontations over Hawaii.

Manuscripts, chiefly ABCFM journals and correspondence, are in the Houghton Library at Harvard and in the Hawaiian Mission Children's Society Library, Honolulu, which is rich in materials. LMS/SSJ and SSL for the Leeward Islands and for the Sandwich Islands cast light on the important role of Society Islander missionaries from 1822 onward. Catholic sources are in *ASSCC* and *APF.*

Page

32 Davis and Young: Daws, *Shoal of Time,* 34ff.
    Pre-christian Hawaii generally: Kuykendall, Vol. 1; Jarves, 216-9.
33 Arrival; "men and women eating"; "if these are facts": ABCFM/SIM, 30 March 1820.
    Birth of the ABCFM: Phillips, 1ff.
    Maritime Boston and Salem: Dodge.
    Whitefield in America: *ODCC,* 'Whitefield'; Cragg, 179-181.
    Christ's millennial reign: Phillips, 9, 96.
35 Opukahaia: Dwight.
    Cornwall Mission School: Phillips, 91.
    Instructions from the Board: Kuykendall, 1, 101-2.
    Kalanimoku baptized: Yzendoorn, 19-20; Bassett, 158-9 (and illust. between 132 and 133).
36 Kalanimoku's baptism judged valid: Yzendoorn, 20.
    Spanish influences in Hawaii: Yzendoorn, Ch. 1, passim; Langdon, *Lost Caravel,* 272-280; Ellis, W., *Polynesian Researches,* 4, 437-441.
    Kaumualii's backsliding: Phillips, 100.
    Kaahumanu's self-consolidation: Daws, *Shoal of Time,* 66-7.
37 Rives: Daws, *Shoal of Time,* 71; Gast, 116.
    Marin: Gast.
    Bingham: *Missionary Album,* 41; Bingham, Hiram, *Residence,* generally.
    Thurston: *Missionary Album,* 190; Martin.
    Holmans "did not adjust": *Missionary Album,* 117.
    Names and details of pioneer ABCFM company: *Missionary Album.*
38 "The age of darkness ... passed": Bingham, Hiram, *Residence,* 577-8.
    Bingham denied return to Hawaii: Bingham, Alfred M., 'Sybil's Bones,' 10-11.
    "Without them the American flag": *Missionary Album,* 4.
    Castle and Cook: Daws, *Shoal of Time,* 175, 176-7.
    Mrs Dole's attainments: *Missionary Album,* 133.

NOTES

Members of second and later companies: *Missionary Album*, list, 7-12.
39 Fathers and mothers in Israel: see the portraits and memorials on the walls of Honolulu's Kawaiahao church.
Correspondence with LMS in the Society Islands: ABCFM/SIM, 12 May 1820, Houghton Library.
Auna: O'Reilly/Teissier, *Tahitiens*, 'Auna'; Davies, 177, 285, 286, 303; *JPH*, 8, 1973, 188-91 (H.E. Maude); Bingham, Hiram, *Residence*, 161-8.
40 Joy (and tight fit) in mission house: ABCFM/SIM, 16 April, 29 April 1822.
Kuakini's welcome on Hawaii: LMS/SSL, Sandwich Islands (Ellis to Burder, 9 July 1822; Ellis, *Polynesian Researches*, 4, 34-9.
Auna's wife's brother: Ellis, *Polynesian Researches*, 4, 39; Ellis to Burder, 9 July 1822, ABCFM/SSL; ABCFM/SIM, Journal, 9 May 1822.
Kaahumanu "produced for them a lodging": ABCFM/SIM, Journal, 9 May 1822. (Other quotes from same source).
42 Voyage of *Jenny*: Judd.
"Some of them wished to learn our prayers": Morrison, 83-4.
"Generally speaking they have cast away their idols": Ellis to Burder, 9 July 1822, LMS/SSL, Sandwich Islands.
"One of the most polished females": Stewart, 274.
Auna's journal: In LMS/SSJ, Sandwich Islands, 1822-3, 11 May-2 July, tr. Ellis.
"The voyage seemed to be marked out": Ellis to Burder, 9 July 1822, LMS/SSL, Sandwich Islands.
Kent's amorous attention: ABCFM/SIM, Journal, 8 May 1822; Bingham, Hiram, *Residence*, 161.
Matatore's wife died at sea: Montgomery, 1, 490.
43 Tours of Auna and Tahitians: Auna Journal, LMS/SSJ, 1822, Box 4, tr. Ellis; ABCFM/SIM, Journal, 31 July 1822.
"The King has declared his regard": Bennet to Hankey, 1 August 1822, PS dated 10 August, LMS/SSL.
Ellis' hopes for Liholiho: Ellis to Burder, 9 July 1822, LMS/SSL.
Auna's departure, 1824: Stewart, 274.
44 Betsey Stockton: *Missionary Album*, 186.
Over half population literate: Kuykendall, 109.
"*I believe* that all": Eli Chamberlain, Journal, 11 October 1825, HMCSL.
Richards opposed Buckle at Lahaina: Bingham, Hiram, *Residence*, 274.
Dolphin, riot at Honolulu: Bingham, *Residence*, 283-9.
45 Liholiho in London: Daws, *Shoal of Time*, 71-75.
46 Rives, in London and Paris: Yzendoorn, 29-31; Wiltgen, 1-7, 17-20; Jarves, 231-2.
Baptisms on the *Blonde*: Jarves, 234.

NOTES

Kauikeaouli's "Christian education": Jarves, 237.

47 Slow licensing of preachers: Kuykendall, 1, 339.
"Most teachers have lain with many": Lorrin Andrews, 1835, quoted by Smith, 191.
"The clothes the girls put on": Smith, 192.
Rufus Anderson: Neill, Anderson and Goodwin, *CDWMC,* 'Anderson, Rufus,' 21; Anderson Letters, HMCSL; Kuykendall, 1, 114, 335ff.
"*Our* standard by which to judge": Kuykendall, 1, 114.

48 America's "burned over district": Cross.
Sacred Hearts fathers and founders: *New Catholic Encyclopaedia,* 12, 827-8; Wiltgen, 5-6.

49 Voyage and arrival of Catholic mission: Wiltgen, 20-22; Yzendoorn, 30-34.
Boki's baptism on *Uranie*: Bassett, 158-9.

50 Jones and Coffin: Daws, *Shoal of Time,* 77-8.

51 ABCFM anti-catholic books: e.g., J.F. Pogue, *Thoughts on Popery* and *The True Church,* listed in *Missionary Album,* 158.

52 Boki's fatal voyage: Jarves, 264-6; Daws, *Shoal of Time,* 86-7 (and reference, 429).
Violent anti-catholic measures: Yzendoorn, 56-7; Schoofs, 25.
Forced labour on Waikiki wall: Schoofs, 25-35.

53 Bachelot's willingness to comply, lack of funds: Yzendoorn, 66, 64.
Appointment of Rouchouze: Wiltgen, 68-88.
Murphy: O'Reilly/Teissier, *Tahitiens,* 405; Yzendoorn, 87-8, 93-4.
Russell's agreement: Jarves, 389-90.

54 Bingham's "boorish" jostling: Bingham, Hiram, *Residence,* 508-9.
Maigret's death: Yzendoorn, 120.
Kekauluohi's persecution: Yzendoorn, 128.
Ultimatum from *Artémise*: Yzendoorn, 134-5.

55 Liliha's funeral: Yzendoorn, 143.
Coans and Lymans: *Missionary Album,* 70, 142; Bird, 63ff, 114ff; Martin.
Lyons: *Missionary Album,* 144; Bird, 149.
Finney: Cross, 151-169.

56 Sarah Lyman: Martin.
The outbreak of revival: Daws, *Shoal of Time,* 99-102; Daws, 'Polynesian religious revivals'; Smith, 202-212.

57 David Malo: Smith, 190, 233, 235-6, 252, 268, 272-3, 306-7; Malo; Kuykendall, 1, 259.
"The most effectual rebuke": Anderson, General Letter to SIM, 10 April 1846, quoted in Kuykendall, 337, n.7.
Twenty-two missionaries naturalized: Kuykendall, 340.
Hawaiian Evangelical Association: Kuykendall, 341.

NOTES

Anderson's stand against all foreign interference: Anderson to Clark, Confidential, 16 May 1862, HMCSL.

58 Anderson's other reasons for localizing: Anderson letters, generally, HMCSL.

"A *vernacular church*": Anderson to Hawaiian Missionary Society, 5 December 1856, HMCSL.

Edging out of Dole: *Missionary Album*, 84-5.

Anderson's requirement of economy: Anderson to Hawaiian Evangelical Association, 12 March 1864, HMCSL.

"Came to do good and did well": Dodge, 116.

59 Inflation and war between states: Anderson to Hawaiian Evangelical Association, 14 April 1864; to Hawaiian Board, 12 July 1864; HMCSL.

Anderson's topical book: Anderson, Rufus, *History of Sandwich Islands Mission*.

Mormons moving in: Anderson, *History*, 369; Daws, *Shoal of Time*, 221-5; Daws, *Dream of Islands*, 138ff.

Chapter 3
Points of Progress
(Pages 60-87)

THE IMPORTANCE OF SYDNEY as a new base is brought out in Gunson's *Messengers of Grace*. Marsden's role appears clearly in Yarwood's biography. The works of Ramsden and Elder deal with the CMS in New Zealand, as do Judith Binney's book on Kendall and Morrell's history of the Anglicans. Owens' study of the Wesleyan mission to New Zealand is clear and revealing. Findlay and Holdsworth generally treat Wesleyan early days in New Zealand and Tonga, with the same matter more critically covered by A.H. Wood and by chapters in Rutherford's composite volume. Stanley Hosie and Wiltgen describe Catholic initiatives; for New Zealand, Lillian Keys' book on Pompallier is laudatory, but useful.

Cummins' MA thesis and collection of sources on Tonga call for wider circulation. Latukefu's *Church and State in Tonga* clarifies many issues in Tongan terms. Monfat's book on Chevron covers Marist beginnings.

LMS arrival in the Cooks is in John Williams' *Missionary Enterprises*.

Manuscripts are LMS/SSL and SSJ, the collection of Marsden's papers in the Mitchell Library, Sydney, and (microfilm copied) CMS correspondence.

NOTES

APM sets the scene for closer study of Marist correspondence. Details not found in printed works appear for the Cooks in LMS/SSJ for 1823, 1830, 1832 and 1839.

Page
- 60 New Zealand background: Sinclair, *History of New Zealand,* 33-6.
  Hawaiki, mythic homeland: Buck; Langdon, *Lost Caravel,* 243-253.
- 61 Maori dignity and forebodings: Yarwood, 169; Ramsden, *Marsden and the Missions,* 160.
  The Church Missionary Society: Neill, Anderson and Goodwin, *CDCWM,* 111; Stock, *History of CMS.*
  Marsden on Australian Aborigines: Marsden to Pratt, 20 November 1811, reprinted in Havard-Williams, 41.
  Marsden on civilizing mission: Yarwood, 81-94, 115-6.
- 62 "My new leader and friend": Elder, *Marsden's Lieutenants,* 25.
  Peter Dillon: Davidson, *Dillon,* generally.
  Thomas Kendall: Binney, *Legacy of Guilt.*
- 64 Infidelity of Kendall's wife: Binney, *Legacy of Guilt,* 53-4.
  Kendall's quest for Maoris' inner soul: Binney, *Legacy of Guilt,* 125-157; Binney, 'Nukutawhiti'.
- 65 Kendall's last days: J.W. Davidson, 'Thomas Kendall,' *ADB,* 2.
  The Williams brothers: Morrell, *Anglican Church in N.Z.,* 8, passim.
  "Do not sign the paper": Keys, 125.
- 66 Character of Leigh: Owens, 26-29, 31.
  "Unequal to the conflict": Findlay and Holdsworth, 180.
  Attackers remnants of Ngatiuru: Owens, 105-115.
- 67 Hobbs, "second founder": Spooner.
  White dismissed from mission: Findlay and Holdsworth, 207, 210; Ramsden, *Marsden and the Missions,* 4.
  Wallis: Luxton, *Wallis.*
  Buller: Gadd.
  Comity disputes with CMS: Morrell, *Anglican Church in N.Z.,* 16-17, 35.
  Pompallier: Keys.
  Society of Mary: Coste/Lessard.
  Jean Claude Colin: Hosie, S.
- 68 Pompallier's voyage out: Wiltgen, 122-223, 246-266.
  Polding and the Marists: Shanahan, 76-80; Hosie, J., 30-62.
  Pompallier's chants and ceremonies: Wright, H.M., 153.
  Pompallier at Waitangi: Keys, 126-134.
  "The result of this long trip": Keys, 139.
- 69 His "well loved Maoris": Keys, 134.
  Murder of Chanel, handover to Bataillon: Keys, 184-90.
  Maori adoption of Christianity: Wright, H.M., Chapters VIII, IX; Owens, 116-147.

NOTES

70 The Papurihia and Pai Marire cults: Clark, Paul, *'Hauhau'*.
Hassall-Marsden-Lawry connections: See *ADB*, 1, under these names.
Walter Lawry: Hames.
Lawry in Tonga: Wood, A.H., *Overseas Missions*, 1, 19-25.

71 Tahitians in Tonga: Gunson in Rutherford (ed.), *Friendly Islands*, 109-11; Wood, A.H., *Overseas Missions*, 1, 26-32; Davies, 316-17.
John Thomas: Rowe, G.S., *A Pioneer*.
"What a raw, weak, uncultivated wretch": Findlay and Holdsworth, 3, 282.

73 Pita Vi with Taufa'ahau at Lifuka: Narrative of Pita Vi in West, 364.
Pulela'a: personal communication, S.A. Havea; White, G.F., *Jane Tucker*, 75.

74 Three supreme Tongan titles: Latukefu, 1-4.
"When I turn, they all turn": Findlay and Holdsworth, 3, 289.
Taufa'ahau baptized as George: Findlay and Holdsworth, 3, 300.
Revival on Vava'u: Schütz, 47-50; Wood, A.H., *Overseas Missions*, 1, 56-7.

75 Wesleyanism and Tongan culture: Cummins, School and Society, generally.
Bulu saw Taufa'ahau writhe: Bulu, 17.
Taufa'ahau as local preacher: He was instructed by a talented wife of a missionary — see White, *Jane Tucker*, 75-7.

76 The Ha'a Havea opposition: Latukefu, 151-3.
School books, sermons, journals: Cummins, 'Holy War'.
Pamphlet charges and counter-charges: Cummins, 'Holy War'.
Taufa'ahau put non-combatants to the sword: Cummins, School and Society, 178; Monfat, *Les Tonga*, 40-1.
WMMS embarrassed: Cummins, School and Society, 179; Cummins, 'Holy War'.

77 "King George is conqueror": Cummins, 'Holy War', 38.
"A choice young man and a godly": Thomas to Secretaries, 2 September 1831; Cummins, School and Society, 131.
Moeaki's invitation to Marists: Laracy in Rutherford (ed.), *Friendly Islands*, 139.
Roman Catholic settlement at Pea: Monfat, *Les Tonga*, 183-7.

78 Law code of 1839: Latukefu, 118ff.
Subdivision of Pompallier's jurisdiction: Wiltgen, 239ff.
Wallis as "Jerusalem": Poncet, 125.
Colin's Sydney supply centre: Hosie, J.

79 Taufa'ahau's Samoan designs: Garrett, 'The Conflict.'
"A fine young woman": John Williams, Journal, 5 November 1832, LMS/SSJ.

80 Ma'afu's power threatened Cakobau's: Scarr, *Pacific Islands Portraits*, 95-126, (Deryck Scarr).

NOTES

Violence and licence of Ma'afu's troops: West, 403-4; Wilkes, 3, 172; Seemann, 253.
Robert Young's tour: Young, Robert, *Southern World*.
81 "*Inasi* replaced by examinations: Cummins, School and Society, 210.
Misinale festival behaviour: personal observation, Vava'u, 1972.
Davies' list of outstations: Davies, 269-324.
82 Hiro: Langdon, *Lost Caravel*, 159-163.
Voyage of 1823: Bourne and Williams, Journal, July, August, LMS/SSJ.
"Old chief Tamatoa": Bourne and Williams (above), 4 July.
"A gang of fellows": Bourne and Williams (above), July.
"When that shipload of women arrived": Crocombe, M., Maretu's Narrative, 67-8.
"He manifested a true missionary spirit": Bourne and Williams (above), 20 July.
Papeiha's marriage and lands: Rere.
83 Tiberio's gun: Crocombe, M., Maretu's Narrative, intro., 24.
"Entered the harbour of Raiatea": Bourne and Williams, Journal, 7 August 1823, LMS/SSJ.
Faaori, "our native sailor": Williams, John, *Missionary Enterprises*, 104.
Aligning landmarks with stars: Williams, John, *Missionary Enterprises*, 96-97.
"Entirely of a moral character": Williams, John, *Missionary Enterprises*, 141.
Pitman as translator: Buzacott, 187; Lovett, *History of LMS*, 1, 358.
"This is the man we want": King, Joseph, *Ten Decades*, 84-5.
84 The Takamoa seminary: Buzacott, 131-2.
Decline at Raiatea: Gunson, 'John Williams and His Ship', 85-6.
Names of Islander teachers: Williams and Barff, Journal, 1830, 25 June, LMS/SSJ, (page 25 in typed transcript, ML).
"So great are the advantages": Williams and Barff, Journal, 1830, LMS/SSJ, (page 17 in typed transcript, ML).
85 "Giving the Samoans in general": Williams and Barff, 1830 (above), (page 27).
Makea "excited much attention": Williams, Journal of Voyage from Rarotonga to Navigators..., 1832, 20 October, LMS/SSJ.
Sabbath observed at Leone: Williams, Journal, 1832, 18 October, LMS/SSJ.
Sio Vili, "clever, artful, designing": Williams, Journal, 19 October.
"Appropriate from below": the phrase is R.G. Crocombe's.
Teava: Gill, W.W., *Life in the Southern Isles*, 126-7; Buzacott, 137-8; Murray, *Forty Years*, 19.
86 Williams in England: Gunson, 'John Williams and His Ship,' 90-93.

NOTES

Cultivating nobility and royalty: Williams, John, *Missionary Enterprises*, Dedication.

The detailed observations: See also Williams, *Missionary Enterprises*, Chapters 28-32.

"A man had two wives": Williams' Samoa Journal, 1832, 23 October, LMS/SSJ.

"Before it had been in my mouth": Williams, Samoa Journal, 1832, 24 October, LMS/SSJ.

87 Williams' last Journal: LMS/SSJ, 1839.

Chapter 4
Ave Maria or Hallelujah?
(Pages 88-115)

THE SACRED HEARTS (Picpus) Fathers Mission to the Gambiers is described and analyzed in detail in Laval's *Mémoires*, edited by O'Reilly and Newbury. Origins of the SSCC's coming to the Pacific have been explored by Wiltgen. Individual portraits and biographical details of participants, with further bibliography, appear in O'Reilly/Teissier, *Tahitiens*.

Marist origins, with the conflict between Pompallier and Colin, have been traced by Coste/Lessard, by Stanley Hosie and by John Hosie (whose thesis on the transfer of the Marist base to Sydney is important). Chanel's collected papers, edited by Rozier, are the prime source for Futuna. Mangeret's book on Bataillon and the Vicariate of Central Oceania needs supplementing by Wiltgen. Poncet's history of Wallis is revealing, but partisan.

Tahitian and Wesleyan arrival in Fiji have been dealt with in A.H. Wood's second volume on *Overseas Missions of the Australian Methodist Church*. Thomas Williams' *Fiji and the Fijians* is a notable work by a participant; others by Calvert and Joseph Waterhouse are equally useful. Schütz's editing of Cargill's Diaries and Correspondence explains many aspects of Wesleyan entry to Fiji, but has omitted theological material necessary for a full explanation of Cargill's character and fluctuating relationships.

Watsford and Mrs M.D. Wallis have vivid early detail from Viwa and Bau.

The background of European contact with the Fijians can be found in Derrick and Clunie, the latter giving much detail drawn from missionary sources.

SSCC archival materials and background are listed by Wiltgen and by the Pacific Manuscripts Bureau, ANU (PMB DOC. 330). Marist archival materials are in Rome and are in Wiltgen's list (page 549). The Marist

NOTES

Annales, printed records of progress *(AM),* have to be read alongside documents. The Marists' Provincial headquarters in Suva has material relative to Villa Maria in Sydney and to beginnings in Oceania.

Journals of the early Wesleyans in Fiji in the Mitchell Library, especially those of Hunt, Lyth and Thomas Williams, can be supplemented from manuscript resources in NAF, Suva, and from the records and correspondence of the WMMS. Gunson's note on sources, in his *Messengers of Grace,* 395-6, gives locations and evaluations.

Page

88   SSCC: Wiltgen, 4ff; Laval, *Mémoires,* xiii-xx.
     "Reductions": Neill, *Christian Missions,* 202-4.
     Coudrin: "Valparaiso, Gambier": Laval, *Mémoires,* xv.
89   Nobbs: Nicholson, 87-89, 93-95, 120, 161; H.E. Maude, 'George Hunn Nobbs,' *ADB,* 2.
     Caret: O'Reilly/Teissier, *Tahitiens,* 91.
     Murphy: O'Reilly/Teissier, *Tahitiens,* 405.
     "What could be more appropriate?": Laval, *Mémoires,* 25.
     Mary's burial: Laval, *Mémoires,* 25.
     "Erotic compositions": Laval, *Mémoires,* 23.
90   Island teachers from Rapa: Davies, 279-281.
91   Accusation of eating babies: Laval, *Mémoires,* 33-4, 34 n.11.
     "A retrospective glance": Laval, *Mémoires,* 60.
     Encounters with Nobbs: Laval, *Mémoires,* 71-81.
92   "National superiority": Laval, *Mémoires,* 84.
     "Under Constantine and others": Laval, *Mémoires,* 92.
     The bishop "came out of our lodgings": Laval, *Mémoires,* 108.
93   "Simple if you will": Laval, *Mémoires,* 138.
     Polynesian plainsong: Laval, *Mémoires,* 139.
     Laval's "stereotyped smile" and manners: Lesson, 27, 28-30.
     Twin towers of Akamuru church: Laval, *Mémoires,* Plate VIII and caption (following 641); Laval, *Mangareva,* 202.
     "Large-hearted athlete": Laval, *Mémoires,* xxiv.
     "Duel" of "barracks behaviour" and "conventual customs": Laval, *Mémoires,* xlviii.
     "There are times": Laval, *Mémoires,* xc-xci.
     Laval as ethnographer: Buck, 170, 207-8; Laval, *Mangareva,* generally.
95   Pignon, "Laval's nightmare": Laval, *Mémoires,* 206 n.13.
     Pignon affair and "state of siege": Laval, *Mémoires,* xcvii-cviii, 313-629, passim.
     De La Motte-Rouge report, "the sooner the better", etc.: Laval, *Mémoires,* cvii.
     "How bored I am": Laval, *Mémoires,* 629.
     Laval's last days: Laval, *Mémoires,* xxiv-xxvii; O'Reilly/Teissier,

NOTES

Tahitiens, 315.
96 Laval with Caret to Tahiti: Laval, *Mémoires,* 155-158.
"Preaching to the Mormons": Laval, *Mémoires,* 277.
"Now that the Mormons are thrashing": Laval, *Mémoires,* 280.
Fouqué in Tuamotus: O'Reilly/Teissier, *Tahitiens,* 188.
Pompallier visit, "a beautiful dream": Laval, *Mémoires,* 166.
"His Lordship and those with him": Laval, *Mémoires,* 167.
Chanel's short account: Chanel, 185-190.
97 Pompallier never professed as Marist: Hosie, John, 17 n.33; Coste/Lessard, 1, 930.
Colin nettled sorely: Hosie, Stanley, 163-179; Wiltgen, 246-266.
War between districts, Futuna: Burrows, 37-42; Laracy, 'Roman Catholic Martyrs,' 190-192.
98 "I ask nothing for my body": Chanel, 220.
"We could well wish": Chanel, 225.
99 The Oceanian Company: O'Reilly, 'La Société...,'; Marceau; [Mayet], *Marceau;* Hosie, Stanley, 181-220; Wiltgen, 449-50, 486-7.
New Vicariate, Central Oceania: Wiltgen, 224-245.
The Sydney Marist Procure: Hosie, John, generally, and esp. 73ff; Hosie, S., 181, 217; John Hosie, 'Jean Louis Rocher,' *ADB,* 6.
Marceau's booklet: Marceau.
"Quasi-monastic discipline": O'Reilly, 'La Société...,' 243.
"A very wretched manager": O'Reilly, 'La Société...,' 245.
101 Colin's withdrawal: Hosie, Stanley, 221.
Details of later history of Wallis/Futuna: Poncet, 24, 132, 207, and generally.
"Catholic and French": Poncet, 228.
102 Tongan influence in Fiji: Reid, 'The Fruit of the Rewa.'
"Expressed a strong desire": Davies, 289.
Tahitian missionaries: Rutherford, *Friendly Islands,* 110-111 (Niel Gunson); Wood, A.H., *Overseas Missions,* 2, 22-3; Schütz, 121-2; Reid, 'The View from Vatuwaqa,' 154-162.
Josua Mateinaniu: Reid, 'The View from Vatuwaqa,' 161; Wood, A.H., *Overseas Missions,* 2, 63-4; Schütz, 121-2.
103 Cargill: Schütz, generally; Wood, A.H., *Overseas Missions,* 2, 33-4.
Hazlewood: Wood, A.H., *Overseas Missions,* 2, 78-9.
Bau and Rewa: Derrick, 54-61.
Early whites in Fiji: Clunie, 77-80, 83-85, 87-96.
Beachcombers' morals, "of the poultry yard": Derrick, 45.
Congregation "of 300 or 400 Tonguese": Schütz, 83.
105 Six Tongan teachers: Wood, A.H., *Overseas Missions,* 2, 38.
Hunt, Calvert, Jaggar: Wood, A.H., *Overseas Missions,* 2, 41-46.
Jaggar's lapse: Gunson, *Messengers,* 158 (and reference, 378).

NOTES

Calvert's career: Calvert; Rowe, G.S., *James Calvert*.
Hunt's life: Birtwhistle.

106 Hunt: "The fact is...": Hunt, Journal, 2 September 1839.
Hunt: "I have more help...": Hunt, Journal, 7 June 1839.
Tui Cakau and Tui Kilakila: Derrick, 22, 83.
Lyth: Wood, A.H., *Overseas Missions*, 2, 46.
Hunt: "The god and the priest...": Hunt, Journal, 27 January 1840.

107 Hunt on chief "who was given to the God": Hunt, Journal, 27 January 1840.
Hunt: "We requested permission": Hunt, Journal, 27 July 1840.
"The songs on these occasions are very lewd": Hunt, Journal, 1841, ML, (ts., 207).
Margaret Cargill: Schütz, 182-200; Cargill, *Memoirs*.
"Our two good brethren": Hunt, Journal, March 1840, ML, (ts., 141).
Hunt's memoir of Cross: Hunt, *Memoir*.
Hunt: "I must object to Mr Cargill": Hunt, Journal, 10 June 1842.

108 Cargill's tribute to his wife: Cargill, *Memoirs*.
Cargill's death: Wood, A.H., *Overseas Missions*, 1, 85-6 and 2, 72; Schütz, 225-246; Gunson, 'On the Incidence of Alcoholism...'
Hunt on Tongans: "Christian men...": Hunt, Journal, 2 September 1839.
Hunt, Lyth, among Tongans at Somosomo: Somosomo report of mission, June 1841 (MMSA, CAK/B/1), NAF.
Tongan chief's "progress in Popery": Hunt, Journal, 1841, ML, (ts., 250).
"Many of them attend": Hunt, Journal, 1841, ML, (ts., 251).

109 "Until the king leads": Hunt, Journal, March 1841, ML, (ts., 251).
Requirement of "godly sorrow": Tippett, *The Christian*, generally.
Varani of Viwa: Derrick, 59; Wood A.H., *Overseas Missions*, 2, 65-67; Hunt, Bau and Viwa Circuit Reports 1840-1858,MMSA/VIWA/A/1, NAF), June 1845 (Varani's conversion); Wallis, 24; Lyth, Journal, 4 March 1846, 13 July 1846.
Varani "publicly bowed the knee": Hunt, Viwa Report (A/1, NAF) describing events of Good Friday 1845; Wallis, 65, 70-72.

110 Hunt: "His whole spirit...": Hunt, in MMSA/VIWA/A/1, NAF, June 1845.
Revival on Viwa: Hunt, Journal, 19 October 1845; Birtwhistle, 131-133; Wood, A.H., *Overseas Missions*, 2, 82-3.
"During the first week": Birtwhistle, 133.
Impending war, "a great deal of anxiety": Birtwhistle, 131.
Watsford: "blood and fire": Watsford, 52.
War with Rewa: Derrick, 86-7.

111 Cakobau's witticisms — "Ah, well!", etc.: Waterhouse, Joseph, 102-3;

NOTES

Wallis, 62.
Ordination of pioneers approved: Lyth, Journal, 20 September 1848, ML; Wood, A.H., *Overseas Missions*, 2, 89.
Fijian chanting: Wood, A.H., *Overseas Missions*, 2, 84; Tippett, *Oral Tradition*, 11-12, 27, 29, 34-5.
Noa of Viwa: Watsford, 59-60.
Hunt on sanctification: Hunt, *Letters*. Dr Niel Gunson owns a copy of this rare book.
Watsford's recollections of Hunt: Watsford, 60-63.
Hunt's death: Wallis, 321-4, 411-2; Wood, A.H., *Overseas Missions*, 2, 89-90; Hunt's last letter, annotated by Lyth, is included with Lyth, Journal, 85-87, ML.

112 Varani's death: Derrick, 109; Waterhouse, Joseph, 207-15.
Bau killing stone: Personal observation, 1969, Bau.
Mission wives confronted Tanoa: Erskine, 182-184.
Watsford confronted Cakobau: Watsford, 104-108.

113 Cakobau and Bataillon: Waterhouse, Joseph, 195-6.
Home site on Bauan summit: Waterhouse, Joseph, 225.
Young, deputationist: Young, Robert.
King George: "The rebel fortress": Waterhouse, Joseph, 229.

114 "I wish, Cakobau, you would *lotu*": Waterhouse, Joseph, 244.
Waterhouse's "unusually long interview": Waterhouse, Joseph, 257.
The fall of Kaba: Derrick, 113-115.

Chapter 5
Securing Polynesia
(Pages 116-138)

EARLY COOK ISLANDS CHRISTIANITY is not covered in any single book. The beginnings are bracingly described in John Williams' *Missionary Enterprises*, in Buzacott and in Joseph King's *Ten Decades*. Marjorie Crocombe's editing of Maretu's Narrative and R.G. and Marjorie Crocombe's *Works of Ta'unga* cast much light. Lovett's *History of the LMS* is a stand-by text. Gilson's *Cook Islands*, Chapters 2 and 3, gives useful background and social history.

LMS approach to Samoa has been set out in some detail by John Williams' *Enterprises* — and Lovett's *History* is again reliable as far as it goes. Murray and George Turner were early participants. Gilson's *Samoa* skilfully elucidates interactions between culture and church. Martin Dyson's *My Story of Samoan Methodism* gives documents and detail, faithfully balanced out by a wistful

NOTES

participant in crises. The first volume of A.H. Wood's *Methodist Overseas Missions* supplements Findlay and Holdsworth. George Brown's *Autobiography* has to be filled out by use of his Letter Books and Journals — and of Australasian Methodist Overseas Missions materials (in the Mitchell Library).

In the section on Niue, King's *Lawes,* Lovett's *History of the LMS,* Buzacott, Williams' *Enterprises* and the anonymous Niue Island manuscript in ATL, Wellington, have been general guides.

Gunson's *Messengers of Grace* provides reference on Protestants to 1860.

Catholicism in Samoa has been dealt with in Monfat's *Les Premiers Missionnaires* and his book on Elloy, together with Dunand. For deeper study they need comparison with sources and with the more general and analytical works by Broadbent and the Hosie brothers.

LMS/SSL and SSJ, and Marist sources, are detailed in lists provided by the Pacific Manuscripts Bureau, ANU, Canberra.

Page

116 Samoa and Rarotonga reacted to Williams' death: Murray, *Missions,* 182-3; Buzacott, 132-3; Gill, William, *Gems,* 118-9.
Bogue's divinity notes: Gunson, *Messengers,* 67.
117 "Instruction in general knowledge": Buzacott, 135.
118 Wives' "suitable course": Buzacott, 135.
Takamoa's roll, 1857: Buzacott, 136.
Teava: Buzacott, 137-8.
119 Hitchcock's sisters: Gunson, *Messengers,* 46.
Maretu, "They all embraced": Crocombe, Marjorie, Maretu's Narrative, 128.
Maretu on Manihiki: Crocombe, Marjorie, Maretu's Narrative, 127-8.
120 Erikana-Tauraki-Teina Materua-Ruatoka: Crocombe, Marjorie, 'Ruatoka,' and Maretu's Narrative, 189 n.
Maretu's "word of advice": Crocombe, Marjorie, Maretu's Narrative, 137.
121 *Papalagi:* Gilson, *Samoa,* 65.
Ned Marsters' interview: Marsters.
Sio Vili: See note to page 87, above.
122 Record of Tahitians: Gunson, *Messengers,* 357-364, under names.
Hymns used for dances: Williams, Journal, October 1832, LMS/SSJ.
Manono's Tongan connections: Garrett, 'The Conflict,' 65; Dyson, *My Story,* 28-31.
"Wesleyan aggression": G. Turner to Tidman, 24 September 1857, Samoa Letters, LMS/SSL.
123 Manono leaders, "What do we know of Tahiti?": Dyson, *My Story,* 31.

NOTES

Turner and Wilson removed: South Sea Missions, ML (Item 307).
Latuselu: Garrett, 'The Conflict,' 72.
Samoan society, run with finesse: Gilson, *Samoa*, 1-64; Grattan; Davidson, *Samoa*, 15-30.
124 Revolt of pastors, Tutuila: Gilson, *Samoa*, 128-132.
125 Heath: "I do not know": Heath to Secretaries, 30 April 1841, LMS/SSL.
126 Stevenson on Bible: "Not only": Moors, 69.
Barnden drowned: Murray, *Forty Years*, 100-102.
"A few rays of light" on Tutuila: Murray, *Forty Years*, 33.
Teava: Murray, *Forty Years*, 64-5, 110-111.
"His knowledge of the Samoan": Murray, *Forty Years*, 111.
127 Tutuila revival, 1839: Murray, Journals, 1839, 1840, LMS/SSJ; Murrray, *Forty Years*, 123; Lundie; Daws, Polynesian Religious Revivals, 105-111.
Revival "reached its height": Murray, *Forty Years*, 125.
"Ten or twelve sank down exhausted": Murray, *Forty Years*, 141.
"But a short time had passed": Murray, *Forty Years*, 141.
128 Resumption of Wesleyan Samoan mission: Wood, A.H., *Overseas Missions*, 1, 290-296; Garrett, 'The Conflict,' 74-80.
Martin Dyson: Dyson, *My Story* (and his Autobiography); Garrett, 'The Conflict,' 75.
Brown's arrival in Samoa: Garrett, 'The Conflict,' 79-80; Wood, A.H., *Overseas Missions*, 1, 297-313; Brown, *Autobiography*.
129 Catholics "exposed defenceless": Monfat, *Les Premiers Missionnaires*, vi.
130 Peloux: "I am the only brother": Monfat, *Les Premiers Missionnaires*, 184.
Violette on *Etoile* — "no shooting star": Monfat, *Les Premiers Missionnaires*, 190.
"Before we had been ashore": Monfat, *Les Premiers Missionnaires*, 189.
131 "My provisions were giving out": Monfat, *Les Premiers Missionnaires*, 264.
Elloy appointed as priest in Samoa: Monfat, *Les Premiers Missionnaires*, 325.
Corpus Christi, June 1862: Monfat, *Elloy*, 94.
Lufilufi disputation, July 1861: Monfat, *Elloy*, 96.
"A few complimentary remarks": George Brown, Journal, 11 July 1861, ML.
132 "The Pro-vicar drew the sword": Monfat, *Elloy*, 96.
"Popery soon afterwards drooped": Dyson, *My Story*, 90.
Clydesdale seminary: Hosie, John, 246ff., 268; Broadbent, Attempts (and Address); Monfat, *Elloy*, 125, 137-8.
Elloy named as bishop: Monfat, *Elloy*, 133-4.
134 Elloy's landing, 1870: Monfat, *Elloy*, 243; Brown to Weber, 1 Novem-

NOTES

ber 1870, Brown, Letter Book, ML.
"It would be pretentious to recall Constantine": Monfat, *Elloy*, 309.
Steinberger: "because more than anywhere else": Monfat, *Elloy*, 296.
135 Elloy's last days: Monfat, *Elloy*, 348.
Niue, generally: Lovett, *History of LMS;* Niue Island, ATL.
Williams and Barff, Niue, 1830: Williams, *Missionary Enterprises*, 298-9.
Crook's visit, 1831: Buzacott, 160.
136 The canoes "gave no encouragement": Buzacott, 158.
"A most bitter wail,"etc.: Buzacott, 159-60; Crocombe, R.G. and Marjorie, *Ta'unga*, 14-15.
Peniamina "intelligent" but "wanting," etc.: Niue Island, ATL, 12.
Fakafitiniu: Niue Island, ATL, 1.
"The conduct of Peniamina": Niue Island, ATL, 3; further details on teachers from same source.
137 Lawes, "prime minister, doctor": Morrell, *Britain in Pacific Islands*, 296-7.
Ships from Peru: Niue Island, ATL, 5; Maude, *Slavers*, 55-62.
All Lawes' students volunteered: Niue Island, ATL, 9.
138 Lano seminary and its problems: Broadbent, Attempts (and Address); Rozier.

Chapter 6
Micronesia: Missions Meet
(Pages 139-160)

HAWAIIAN AND AMERICAN MISSION in the Micronesian islands has been affectionately chronicled by Albertine Loomis. Other books include Crawford and Bliss. Shem Jimmy's thesis on Ponape is by a local writer. The *Missionary Album* and its 1937 edition list names and give some details about missionaries, as does Gunson's *Messengers of Grace*. Fuller information must be mined in the Micronesian Mission materials and personal papers in the extensive HMCSL collections in Honolulu. The Bingham family papers, read with Alfred Bingham's article in *HJH*, are especially important.

Maude and Sabatier interpret events in Kiribati. The files of the mission periodical, *The Friend,* Honolulu, provide consecutive reports.

Laumua Kofe's thesis, by a Tuvalu student, may be read alongside LMS/SSL and SSJ.

The LMS histories by Lovett and Goodall summarise developments in both Kiribati and Tuvalu.

NOTES

Page

139 Andrews and Paris as advocates: *Missionary Album*, 22, 152; Loomis, 53-57; Crawford, 1-29.
Gulick: *Missionary Album*, 106.
Sturges, Snow: Gunson, *Messengers*, 356.

140 Mission Children's Society: Loomis, 57.
Lahainaluna Seminary: Kuykendall, 1, 338-9.
Twenty-two missionaries became citizens: Kuykendall, 1, 340.
"The word auxiliary should be dropped": Anderson to Clark, 9 June 1853, HMCSL.

141 Opunui and Kaaikaula: *Missionary Album*, 1937 edn., 194.
Encounters with white predecessors: Mac and Leslie B. Marshall, 'Holy and Unholy Spirits, The Effects of Missionization on Alcohol Use in Eastern Micronesia,' *JPH*, 11, 1976, 135-166.

143 Structure of Ponape society: Fischer, *et al.*, *Book of Luelen* and *Annotations;* Jimmy, 13-17, 26-36.
Nose-flute music: Crawford, 102.
"There is a happy land": Loomis, 78.
Gulick forced to trade with tobacco: Loomis, 64-66.
Gulick's vaccine: Loomis, 73-75; Crawford, 66.

144 "WORKERS WANTED," etc.: Crawford, 223.
Bushnell, theologian: Ahlstrom, 610-11.
Sturges: "We gain nothing": Crawford, 74-5.

145 The *Morning Star*: Bingham, Hiram, II, *The Story;* Livingston.
Career of Gulick: *Missionary Album*, 106-7.

146 Reverses at home for ABCFM: See note to page 59.
Orramel Gulick: *Missionary Album*, 108-9.

147 Hezekiah Aea: Loomis, 98-100.
Other Hawaiians in Marshalls: List in *Missionary Album*, 1937 edn., 195-6.

148 Successive political occupations: Jimmy; Loomis, 85-93; Crawford, 236-7, 243, 258ff., 269.
Origins in Mortlocks and Truk: Loomis, 81-85.
Sturges — "Hawaii, the child": Loomis, 82.

149 Richard Randell: Maude, *Of Islands and Men*, 233-283.
Hiram Bingham, Junior: Bingham Letters, HMCSL; Bingham, Alfred M.
Bingham's weak eyes and throat: Bingham to Clark, 5 August 1858, HMCSL.

150 Randell-Bingham friendship: Maude, *Of Islands and Men*, 261-263.
Gilbertese society and government: See H.E. Maude's *The Evolution of the Gilbertese Boti: an ethnohistorical interpretation*. Polynesian Society Memoir 35, Wellington, 1963; Davidson and Scarr, 203, 204 (H.E. Maude).

NOTES

Wars on Abaiang: Loomis, 111-2.
151 Kiribati religion and the *anti*: Sabatier, *Astride the Equator,* 53-79.
Kanoa — *"a humble ... missionary"*: Bingham to Clark, 5 August 1858, HMCSL.
"The memory of my dear friend": *The Friend,* March 1897.
Mahoe shot: *The Friend,* March 1870.
152 Stevenson and Maka: "I have never known": Stevenson, *In the South Seas,* 227-8.
"I have great compassion": Bingham to Clark, 17 August 1860, HMCSL.
"Only about *half* a missionary": Bingham to Clark, 17 April 1861, HMCSL.
Happy Home "a complete wreck": *The Friend,* March 1870.
"We shall not soon forget": *The Friend,* 2 March 1868.
Hymn book "done at Samoa": *The Friend,* 2 March 1868.
"One of the sixty-four original copies of John": *The Friend,* 2 March 1868.
153 Two Nui women "able to read fluently": *The Friend,* 2 March 1868.
"The contrast": *The Friend,* 2 March 1868.
LMS/ABCFM agreement: Bingham to Pogue, 6 March 1871, HMCSL; *The Friend,* 1 April 1871.
Handover of Kiribati to LMS: Loomis, 140-1.
Abemama: Davidson and Scarr, 201-224 (H.E. Maude); Maude, *Of Islands and Men,* 258-260.
"A very short but decisive reply": *The Friend,* 2 March 1868.
Binoka, "a short thick-set corpulent man": Bingham to Pogue, 21 March 1874, HMCSL.
"One of the most famous": Bingham to Pogue, 21 March 1874, HMCSL.
154 "We will not send you away": Bingham to Pogue, 21 March 1874, HMCSL.
Permission "to land one or more": Bingham to Pogue, 21 March 1874, HMCSL.
"Bless the Lord!": Bingham to Pogue, 21 March 1874, HMCSL.
Moses Kanoaro: Davidson and Scarr, 213, 216-7 (H.E. Maude); Stevenson, *In the South Seas,* 286.
Binoka's syncretic religion: Davidson and Scarr, 217 (H.E. Maude); Sabatier, *Astride the Equator,* 275-277.
Arrival of Catholics on Abemama, 1891: Sabatier, *Astride the Equator,* 275.
Clarissa Bingham's itinerant pregnancy: Bingham, Alfred M., 26-29; Loomis, 127-8.
Completion of Gilbertese Bible: Bingham, Hiram, II, *The Making of a Version; The Friend,* May 1893; Bingham, Alfred M., 29-32.

NOTES

Kaure, "native pundit": *The Friend,* May 1893; see also *The Friend,* May 1891.

Clarissa Bingham, "born linguist": *The Friend,* May 1893.

155 Picture "a pleasant perpetuation": *The Friend,* May 1893.

"A brooch...a small purse": *The Friend,* May 1893.

Moses Kaure's misbehaviour: Loomis, 130-1.

Young son, Morning Star: Bingham, Alfred M., illustration facing 10.

Kaure's penitent letter: Loomis, 131.

156 Elekana's drift and mission: Kofe, 34-5; Murray, *Forty Years,* 375-424, covers early visits.

The *John Williams* line of ships: Livingston; Lovett, *History of LMS,* 471-473; Goodall, 409-411.

157 Voyages to Tuvalu: Munro, Ms. chart.

Kirisome and Waters, Nui: Kofe, 40 (with work of other teachers outlined, 39ff); Munro, Ts. draft and personal communication; Scarr, *More Pacific Islands Portraits,* 75-93 (Doug Munro).

"French windows": Munro, Ts. draft and personal communication.

Changes in copra business: Munro, Ts. draft.

158 Ioane of Nanumanga: Based on accounts of Turner and Powell, LMS/SSJ, 1875, and on Munro's Ts. draft.

159 Ioane's work "received unanimous praise": Munro, Ts. draft.

Tuvalu's assertion of independence: Kofe, 70-73.

Tuvalu's part in "evangelization of the world": Kofe, 59ff.

At least seventy-nine Tuvaluan missionaries: List in Islander Missionaries Memorial Chapel, Pacific Theological College, Suva.

Samoan district status dropped: Kofe, 70-74.

160 Dr Robert Ross: G.L. Lockley, 'Robert Ross (1792-1862),' *ADB,* 1.

Other Congregational Independents: e.g., Christine Walsh, 'Henry Hopkins,' *ADB,* 1.

Independence of the Tuvalu Church: Autonomy under local leadership was completed in 1969.

Chapter 7

Melanesian Footholds I

(Pages 161-178)

BACKGROUND FOR THE CHURCHES IN MELANESIA has been given in Tippett's *Solomon Islands Christianity,* with cultural and ethnological influences assessed.

The death of John Williams and early Pacific Islander work in Vanuatu are introduced by contemporaries in the works of Murray and George Turner.

NOTES

R.S. Miller's *Misi Gete* is a convenient editing of John Geddie's journal, woven together with other materials. The original of the journal is at the La Trobe Library, Victoria. The documents of the Presbyterian Mission are in Sydney and in Canada. Scarr's *Fragments of Empire* and Dorothy Shineberg's book on the sandalwooders both offer correctives to over-enthusiastic mission histories. The books of Inglis and Steel complement a study of Geddie and take the story further. Paton's autobiography, edited by his brother, needs cautious comparison with less pro-mission sources.

LMS/SSJ and SSL, with the large collection of Nisbet Papers in the Mitchell Library, are useful for more detailed study.

Page

161 The name, Melanesia: *Oxford English Dictionary*, 12 vol. edn., 'Melanesia.'
Melanesian cultural background: Tippett, *Solomon Islands Christianity*, 3-19; Crocombe, R.G., *The New South Pacific*; Codrington; Hogbin; Oliver, *Pacific Islands*, 36-63.

162 Sandalwooders' prior experience: Shineberg, generally.

164 Sandalwood expeditions to Erromanga: Shineberg, 16-22; see notes to 51-2; Murray, *Missions*, 191, 195-6, 204-208.

165 Murders of Williams, Harris: Prout, 577-583; Shineberg, 205-207; Murray, *Martyrs*, 89ff.
Turner did not stress specific revenge: Murray, *Missions*, 207-8 (account of George Turner); Turner, *Nineteen Years*, 383-385, 486-7.

166 Ovialo grieved at killing "man of God": Murray, *Missions*, 208.
Geddie on Kauiaui's recollection: Miller, R.S., 162-3.
Posthumous eulogy of Williams: Prout.
"This is a memorable day": Williams, Journal, 18 November 1839, LMS/SSJ.

167 "At a meeting": Murray, *Missions*, 182-3.
Arrival of Samoan teachers: Murray, *Missions*, 138-140.
Lasalo, Taniela and others to Erromanga: Murray, *Missions*, 182-3, 186-7.
Nivave "standing on the deck": Murray, *Missions*, 190-191.
Nivave "continued steadfast": Murray, *Missions*, 192.

168 John Geddie: Miller, R.S., generally; Miller, J.G., 69-104.
Secession and relief churches: *ODCC*, 'Scotland.'

169 LMS-Presbyterian co-operation: Geddie to Nisbet, 22 July 1867, Nisbet Papers, ML.
Dr Robert Ross' "eminently correct business habits": Miller, R.S., 232, 250; G.L. Lockley, 'Robert Ross (1792-1862),' *ADB*, 2.
Powell's withdrawal: Miller, R.S., 31, 52, 57.
Archibald's withdrawal: Miller, R.S., 57, 62, 71, 94, 100; Shineberg,

NOTES

      105 (and references, 263).
Paddon: Shineberg, 98-108.
Paddon showed "the greatest kindness": Miller, R.S., 40; cf. Shineberg, 104-106.
"A malignant state of feeling": Miller, R.S., 104.
"A torrent of abuse": Miller, R.S., 86.
170 Archibald's child refused baptism: Miller, R.S., 94-5.
Geddie, "blue Nose": Shineberg, 105.
Burning of mission house and sequel: Miller, R.S., 105-109.
Geddie: "I thought the pistol": Miller, R.S., 107.
"They were both at home in the language of Billingsgate": Miller, R.S., 107.
"They will have no more tobacco": Miller, R.S., 108.
"Our servants are Samoans": Miller, R.S., 39.
Simeona — interpreter, guide: Miller, R.S., 34, 50.
172 "His life was that of a Christian": Miller, R.S., 261.
"As there were French priests": Miller, R.S., 32; Doucéré, 55.
Catholic Sabbath "sporting": Miller, R.S., 54.
Geddie "kindly received": Miller, R.S., 49.
"Much struck with the bishop's dress": Miller, R.S., 57.
173 "Uniformly manifested a friendly disposition": Miller, R.S., 71-2.
"To win the unbelievers through Mary": Doucéré, 55.
John Inglis: Inglis, J., *In the New Hebrides* and *Bible Illustrations*.
Noahat: Miller, R.S., 138; Murray, *Missions*, 86, 124-127.
Waihit: Miller, R.S., 64-5 and passim.
Womra: Miller, R.S., 63-66, 81, 84; Miller, J.G., 46.
Recruiting of New Hebrideans: Inglis, J., *Bible Illustrations*, 219-233; Miller, R.S., 199-200; Miller, J.G., 93-100.
174 "I hope to see the day": Miller, R.S., 120.
"The first church ... in Western Polynesia": Miller, R.S., 123; Murray, *Missions*, 95.
"Trustworthy men" ordained deacons: Miller, R.S., 212.
Appointment of elders, 1860: Miller, R.S., 255.
"The tables are now turning": Miller, R.S., 113.
Remarriage of cast-off wives: Miller, R.S., 184.
"Possessed a kind of intuitive sagacity": Inglis, *In New Hebrides*, 253.
175 "Unsought, undesired, and underserved": Miller,R.S., 286.
A "sailing missionary": Steel, 61ff.
Measles epidemic: Gunson, *Changing Pacific*, 273-284 (Norma McArthur).
"Much languor of body": Miller, R.S., 174.
176 Rangi of Erromanga: Miller, R.S., 89, 264-5; Shineberg, 134-5, 266 (n. 24); Robertson, 42-44.
Deaths and difficulties of Gordons: Miller, R.S., 306-7, 326-7; Shine-

NOTES

berg, 210-211.
God's "terrible judgment": Shineberg, 210.
John G. Paton: G.S. Parsonson, 'John Gibson Paton,' *ADB*, 5; Paton.
177 *Curacoa's* bombardment and sequel: Miller, R.S., 283-285, 294-295, 300-301, 330; Paton, 299ff.; Steel, 171-179; Guiart, *Un Siècle*, 121-123; Geddie to Nisbet, 3 July 1866, Nisbet Papers, ML.
"Theology of imperialism": Gunson, 'The theology'.
"The step proposed is ... premature": Miller, R.S., 256-7, 268.
The "slave trade" and the mission: Scarr, *Fragments*, 139-146; Davidson and Scarr, 226-229, 251 (Deryck Scarr).

Chapter 8
(Melanesian Footholds II)
(Pages 179-205)

MELANESIAN BACKGROUND FOR THE SOLOMONS is handily summarized in Tippett's *Solomon Islands Christianity* and the first chapter of Laracy's *Marists and Melanesians*. Morrell's *Britain in the Pacific Islands* provides political contexts.

Wiltgen's ecclesiastical detail fills out the early Catholic frustrations described in the island setting by Laracy's *Marists and Melanesians*. Verguet, a suffering missionary, has given a measured account.

Hilliard's standard *God's Gentlemen* can be supplemented by reference to fuller information on adjacent Protestants in his doctoral thesis. Charlotte Yonge's biography of Patteson, with its period flavour, continues to be an important resource. Relationships between Anglicans of varying schools of thought in New Zealand, with sections on Melanesia, are given in Morrell's *Anglican Church in New Zealand*.

The Crocombes' *Works of Ta'unga*, revealingly annotated by other researchers, contains unique Islander material on the LMS in New Caledonia and the Loyalties. Dorothy Shineberg's book is a companion piece. Balanced assessment of Loyalty Island origins requires use of Howe's book and of Raymond Leenhardt's alongside McFarlane's detailed participant apologia.

Mayet's book on Douarre, read with Howe, de Salinis, Wiltgen and Morrell's *Britain in the Pacific Islands,* helps sort out complicated ups and downs of Marist commencement in New Caledonia.

Hilliard's book and thesis set out sources for study of the Anglican Melanesian Mission. Howe's book lists both LMS and Catholic primary sources.

NOTES

Page
179 "The tragedy ... where Solomon was wanting": Beaglehole, 75.
Epalle and his mission: Laracy, *Marists and Melanesians*, 11-31; Wiltgen, 330-346.
180 Murder of Epalle: Wiltgen, 336-341; Laracy, *Marists and Melanesians*, 17-18.
181 Xavier Montrouzier: Davidson and Scarr, 127-145 (Hugh Laracy).
Collomb: Laracy, *Marists and Melanesians*, passim; Wiltgen, passim.
Marists on Murua, Umboi: Laracy, *Marists and Melanesians*, 22ff; Wiltgen, 474-487.
Milan Fathers and their Society: Laracy, *Marists and Melanesians*, 28-31; Wiltgen, 545-548.
182 Selwyn: Tucker; Morrell, *Anglican Church in New Zealand*, 24-47.
Selwyn's comity agreement for Melanesia: Morrell, *Anglican Church in New Zealand*, 143-4; Gunson, *Messengers*, 22; Hilliard, *God's Gentlemen*, 7.
Patteson: Yonge; Hilliard, *God's Gentlemen*, passim; Davidson and Scarr, 177-200 (David Hilliard).
183 The Maori Wars: Sinclair, *The Origins*.
Gore Browne, Kingi: Sinclair, *The Origins*, 110-225; Starke, 12-25.
Octavius Hadfield: *DNZB*, 'Hadfield.'
Trio of tracts: Hadfield, *[Pamphlets]*.
"Unwise" language: Starke, 18-19.
184 Patteson's letters to England: Patteson Letters, ATL; Starke, generally.
"Between the mass of the English": Patteson to his father, 10 April 1860, ATL.
"The intolerable pride of race": Patteson to his sister, Joanna, 27 March 1860, ATL.
"Offer terms of peace": Patteson to his father, 5 February 1861, ATL.
"We start with the fullest belief": Patteson to "My dear Archdeacon," Easter 1866, St. John's College Library, Auckland.
Norfolk Island school: Hilliard, *God's Gentlemen*, 35-43.
R.H. Codrington: Hilliard, *God's Gentlemen*, passim; Codrington, *The Melanesians*.
George Sarawia: Hilliard, *God's Gentlemen*, passim.
186 John Palmer; Hilliard, *God's Gentlemen*, 300 and passim.
Sarawia and the *sukwe*: Hilliard, *God's Gentlemen*, 198-202.
Clement Marau: Marau (tr. Codrington).
Marau's behaviour on Ulawa: Hilliard, *God's Gentlemen*, 172-3.
187 Charles Brooke: Hilliard, *God's Gentlemen*, 189-90.
Joseph Atkin: Hilliard, *God's Gentlemen*, passim, esp. 65-67.
Death of Patteson and companions: Hilliard, *God's Gentlemen*, 65-75; Yonge, Vol. 2, 566-579.
188 Obscure motives for Patteson's murder: Davidson and Scarr, 198-9

NOTES

(David Hilliard); Hilliard, *God's Gentlemen,* 65-71.
Anglican attitudes to labour trade: Hilliard, *God's Gentlemen,* 101-107.
"White folks ... look ... bleached": Yonge, Vol. 2, 544.
Prejudice against Pidgin: Hilliard, *God's Gentlemen,* 104-5.

190 Edward Foxall's tip: Shineberg, 29.
A Tongan empire: Shineberg, 32.
Ta'unga at Tuauru: Crocombe, R.G. and Marjorie, 27-42.
Samoans were "bad tempered": Crocombe, R.G. and Marjorie, 40.

191 The *Star* massacre: Crocombe, R.G. and Marjorie, 43-54; Shineberg, 43 (and references).
Ta'unga to Touru, "Greetings" etc.: Crocombe, R.G. and Marjorie, 66.

192 Douarre and New Caledonia mission: Mayet, *Le Premier Vicaire,* esp. 1, 23-26; Wiltgen, 432-445, 463-473.
Blaise Marmoiton: Courant.

193 Flight of Marists: De Salinis, 43-54; Wiltgen, 464-473.
Bwaxat of Hienghène: Scarr, *More Pacific Islands Portraits,* 35-57 (Bronwen Douglas).
Death of Douarre: Montrouzier in *APF,* Vol. 26, 119-123.
Rougeyron at Bourail: Pionnier.
Patteson met Montrouzier: Davidson and Scarr, 140-1 (Hugh Laracy).

194 LMS suspicion of "Puseyites": Murray to Nisbet, 25 February 1853, Nisbet Papers, ML; Hilliard, *God's Gentlemen,* 46.
Solia of Tiga: Personal communication, Chépénéhé, 1975; Gunson, *Messengers,* 361.
Ta'unga on Mare and Lifou: Crocombe, R.G. and Marjorie, 77-85.
Yiewene Naisiline: Scarr, *More Pacific Islands Portraits,* 1-7 (Kerry Howe); Howe, *Loyalty Islands,* 22-25.
Ta'unga to Yiewene, "Don't you listen": Crocombe, R.G. and Marjorie, 81.

195 Paoo (Fao): Leenhardt, R.H., 27-36; McFarlane, *Story of Lifu Mission,* 25-46, 82-3.
"A bad example of a man": Crocombe, R.G. and Marjorie, 82.
Ta'unga and Navie: Crocombe, R.G. and Marjorie, 58n., 114-5.
Ta'unga's later career: Crocombe, R.G. and Marjorie, 117-148.

197 Palazy on Paoo, "a serious and elderly man," etc.: Leenhardt, R.H., 35-6.
Samuel McFarlane: McFarlane, *Story of Lifu Mission;* Leenhardt, R.H., passim.

199 Wainya's and Bula's "police": Howe, *Loyalty Islands,* 57-8.
Guillain, "passionate follower of Fourier": Leenhardt, R.H., 49ff.; (on Fourier see Alfred Cobban, *A History of Modern France,* Harmondsworth, 1965, Vol. 2, 120).
McFarlane's "successful paper war": McFarlane, *Story of Lifu Mission,*

NOTES

196-279, 347.
200 John Fairfax: Garrett and Farr, 2; J.O. Fairfax, 'John Fairfax,' *ADB*, 4.
John West: Garrett and Farr, 8, 71; John Reynolds, 'John West,' *ADB*, 2; Leenhardt, R.H., 68.
Guillain's 300 troops at Chépénéhé: Leenhardt, 50-57; McFarlane, *Story of Lifu Mission*, 150-189; Howe, *Loyalty Islands*, 57-59.
Appeal to Napoleon III: McFarlane, *Story of Lifu Mission*, 205.
201 Nathalo church: personal observation, 1975.
Alleged sacrilege at Nathalo: Leenhardt, R.H., 72-80.
202 Confrontations on Ouvea: Howe, *Loyalty Islands*, 46-56, 65-70; McFarlane, *Story of Lifu Mission*, 258-282; Leenhardt, R.H., 67-8, 86-92.
203 Wars on Mare: Howe, *Loyalty Islands*, 71-81; McFarlane, *Story of Lifu Mission*, 283ff.
204 Xavier Caillet: Leenhardt, R.H., 87-92; O'Reilly/Teissier, *Tahitiens*, 'Caillet.'
Caillet's notebook: Leenhardt, R.H., 197.
Beaulieu, long stayer: Howe, *Loyalty Islands*, 121.
205 Gospel incorporated with local mythology: Tjibaou, 10.
Jean-Pierre Cru: Howe, *Loyalty Islands*, 76-78.
John Jones: Howe, *Loyalty Islands*, 71-78.

Chapter 9
The Lure of New Guinea
(Pages 206-229)

LONDON MISSIONARY SOCIETY pioneering in New Guinea has been summarized in Lovett's *History of the LMS*. McFarlane, Murray and W.W. Gill treat early days in the mission.

Diane Langmore's study of Chalmers in New Guinea, with Lovett's biography of Chalmers and King's of Lawes, describe the two best known builders of the Papuan LMS church. Our knowledge of Ruatoka is enriched by the articles of Marjorie Crocombe, a fellow-Cook Islander.

Goodall and R.G. Williams bring the story into the twentieth century. LMS/SSJ, SSL and Papua Letters are vital primary sources.

George Brown's autobiography and Danks' *In Wild New Britain* go with Threlfall and R.G. Williams in the study of Wesleyan entry to the islands. Primary materials are in the Methodist Overseas Mission of the Australasian

NOTES

Church in the Mitchell Library.

Page

206 McFarlane in New Guinea: McFarlane, *Among the Cannibals* and *Story of Lifu Mission*, 355-386; Lovett, *History of LMS*, 431-440.
Murray and Gill in New Guinea: Lovett, *History of LMS*, 432, 440-446; Murray, *Forty Years*, 435ff; Gill, W.W., *Life in Southern Isles*, 247-269.

207 "Common sense, without which," etc.: McFarlane, *Among the Cannibals*, 39.
Darnley as McFarlane's Iona: Lovett, *History of LMS*, 437.
"Central station," McFarlane's strategy: McFarlane, *Among the Cannibals*, 81-2; Lovett, *History of LMS*, 447-449.
Gucheng and Loyalty Islanders: McFarlane, *Among the Cannibals*, 36; Lovett, *History of LMS*, 432-435, 437.
The *Ellangowan*: McFarlane, *Among the Cannibals*, 58; Lovett, *History of LMS*, 446.
"An able, plodding, cautious ... man": McFarlane, *Among the Cannibals*, 59.
"You know that Mac stands at the portals": Langmore, 53.

208 Chalmers: Lovett, *Chalmers;* Langmore, generally.
Chalmers' eloquence: Lovett, *Chalmers*, 257. Forsyth's speeches on missions are in his *Missions in Church and State*.
Landings of Islanders, cultural contact: Crocombe, Marjorie, 'Ruatoka'; Lovett, *History of LMS*, 441-446, 449-451.
Ruatoka: Crocombe, Marjorie, 'Ruatoka'; Lovett, *History of LMS*, 442; Lovett, *Chalmers*, 78, 132ff.

210 Aruadera and Teina Materua: Lovett, *Chalmers*, 132-138; Goodall, 435; Crocombe, Marjorie, Maretu's Narrative, 189n.
Role of Samoans in Papua: Personal observation and enquiry, January 1976; Wetherell, 'Pioneers.'

211 McFarlane's character and opinions: McFarlane, *Story of Lifu Mission*, 71-2, 89-90, 335-341.
J.H. Angas: Sally O'Neill, 'John Howard Angas,' *ADB*, 3.

212 "A great mistake has hitherto been made": Lovett, *Chalmers*, 257.
"Our trust is in Him": Lovett, *Chalmers*, 187.
Influence of Gilbert Meikle: Langmore, 2-3.
Four stages in Chalmers' career: Langmore, generally.

213 Queensland and British protectorates: Morrell, *Britain in Pacific Islands*, 249-262; Lovett, *Chalmers*, 202-224; Lovett, *History of LMS*, 461-466.
The Kalo massacre: Lovett, *History of LMS*, 460-1; Langmore, 29-31.
"Flag hoisting ... a white man's amusement": Lovett, *Chalmers*, 263.
Sir William MacGregor: Joyce, generally.

215 "Rather than go home": Lovett, *Chalmers*, 222.

NOTES

Toaripi murders, Chalmers' reaction: Langmore, 64.
216 Chalmers with Stevenson and Brown: Lovett, *Chalmers,* 359-60.
"Pioneer missionaries, splendid men": Lovett, *Chalmers,* 359.
Chalmers and Robert Bruce: Langmore, 60, 86-7, 88-91.
217 Chalmers' last months: Langmore, 99-104.
Chalmers' reasons for going to Goaribari: Langmore, 122-3.
218 Murder of Chalmers: Langmore, 105-138.
C.S. Robinson and his suicide: Langmore, 131-134; Morrell, *Britain in Pacific Islands,* 423-4.
Later LMS missionaries: Goodall, 425-438.
"Delectable" Delena: Chatterton, 42 (and 37-76).
Walker and Abel at Kwato: Wetherell, Christian Missions, 345ff.
Holmes, Saville, Butcher: see books under their names in Sources.
220 LMS church in Papua: Williams, R.G., 15-93.
"Don't forget that whenever our people wake up": Brown to Rabone, 22 August 1868, Brown, Letter Book 1865-1871, ML.
Henry Reed: Hudson Fysh, 'Henry Reed,' *ADB,* 2.
221 Brown's Samoan "old boys": Brown, *Autobiography,* 83.
Brown at Navuloa: Brown, Letter Book 1871-1876, 502-539, ML; Brown, *Autobiography,* 71ff.
"The ferocity of the natives": Brown, *Autobiography,* 75.
Bulu "gave them a very stirring address": Brown, *Autobiography,* 82; Brown to Chapman, 14 June 1875, Letter Book for 1875, ML.
222 "Sir, we have fully considered": Brown, *Autobiography,* 80.
Teachers' written declaration: Brown, *Autobiography,* 82.
Brown as frontiersman: Fletcher, generally.
223 Brown moved by Ravono's and Volavola's sermons: Brown, *Autobiography,* 85-87, 179-80.
"The natives often considered them as belonging to them": Brown, *Autobiography,* 229.
"Inveterate traders and pedlars": Brown, *Autobiography,* 113.
Pioneer groups of Islander teachers: Brown, *Autobiography,* 176.
Eduard Hernsheim: Scarr, *More Pacific Islands Portraits,* 115-130 (Stewart Firth), esp. 117-8.
Volcanic eruptions at Blanche Bay: Brown, *Autobiography,* 237ff.
Work "in some respects more beneficial": Brown, *Autobiography,* 246.
Murder of teachers on Gazelle Peninsula: Brown, *Autobiography,* 254-256; Threlfall, 42-47; Morrell, *Britain in Pacific Islands,* 246-248.
225 "Relish" for Talili to eat with Brown: Brown, *Autobiography,* 254-5.
Retaliation for murders: Brown, *Autobiography,* 256-266.
Talili's "natural force of character": Brown, *Autobiography,* 284.
"We only heard of the appointment": Brown, *Autobiography,* 275.
226 "Tarlily" etc.: Powell, W., 117-158.
"If Wesleyan Christianity obtains a foothold": Powell, W., 157.

NOTES

"There is not a native in the group": Brown, *Autobiography*, 269.
Danks witnessed first baptisms: Brown, *Autobiography*, 289.
Danks, "expert engineer": Brown, *Autobiography*, 290; Danks, 17-18, 87; J. Ann Howe, 'John Danks,' *ADB*, 4.
"A land ... full of glorious missionary possibilities": Danks, 24.
"The first quartette": Danks, 227; Threlfall, 50-59.
227 Eyre: Geoffrey Dutton, 'Edward John Eyre,' *ADB*, 1; see also James Morris, *Heaven's Command*, London, 1973, 301-317.
Brown's arraignment at Levuka: Brown, *Autobiography*, 299-320; Gordon, Vol. 3, 247-8, 255, 343-345, 430-434; Vol. 4, 104, 119-124 (with Gorrie-Gordon correspondence).
228 Gordon as "head" over court: Gordon, Vol. 4, Gorrie to Gordon, 10 November 1879.
"Here we are distressing ourselves": Brown, *Autobiography*, 312.
"I have yet borne a great deal of unmerited obloquy": Brown, *Autobiography*, 320.
Gorrie's lingering venom: Brown, *Autobiography*, 332.
"Best pundit," Peni Lelei: Brown, *Autobiography*, 378, 406.
Danks and labour trade: Danks, 242-246.
Marquis de Rays and New France: Niau; Robson, 225-230; Biskup; Brown, *Autobiography*, 353-370; Dupeyrat, *Papouasie*, 37-46.
A suburb for the nobility: Brown, *Autobiography*, 362.
229 De Lannuzel: Danks, 245; Dupeyrat, *Papouasie*, 39-41.
German missionaries, Fellmann: Williams, R.G., 130; Threlfall, 72-3, 86-88, 102.

Chapter 10
Partitioning Papua
(Pages 230-252)

GEORGE BROWN'S AUTOBIOGRAPHY and Bromilow's book of reminiscences provide groundwork for study of the Wesleyans in the Papuan islands. Aspects of the controversial partitioning of the field are dealt with by Brown, Wetherell and Dupeyrat. King's biography of Lawes touches on the agreement. R.G. Williams charts Wesleyan developments. Fuller interpretation of the cultural background and the place of Islander missionaries is in David Wetherell's thesis and other writings.

Joyce discusses the relationships between MacGregor and the churches. Morrell's *Britain in the Pacific Islands* has other political settings of some events.

The Catholic mission's inception and progress has been analyzed in detail in

NOTES

Dupeyrat's *Papouasie*. Cadoux presents additional material on Verjus and his startling austerities.

Wetherell's *Reluctant Mission* is a full and balanced assessment of Anglicanism in Papua. Tomkins and Hughes in *The Road from Gona* give additional human detail.

Wesleyan source materials are in MOM in the Mitchell Library; the Sacred Heart Mission's archives, formerly in France, are now at Rome, though sources in Sydney would be of interest for studying relationships with the Australian bishops and the Marists. Anglican sources are in Wetherell's book.

Page

230 "Full confidence" and "large and important" circuit for Brown: *Autobiography*, 409, 410.
    MacGregor and the missions: Joyce, 167-180.
231 MacGregor's Greek Testament, etc.: Bromilow, 267-274; Wetherell, Christian Missions, 40-42, 50.
    "Scratching old sores": Brown to Rabone, 22 February 1865, Brown, Letter Book, ML.
    Comity agreement, 17 June 1890: Brown, *Autobiography*, 465-467; Wetherell, Christian Missions, 32-34. Text of resolutions is in Brown, *Autobiography*, 468.
    "Now, Brown ... take care": Brown, *Autobiography*, 485.
    The Kula ring: Fortune; Malinowski.
233 Bromilow, good eating: Bromilow, 73.
    "The finest house in New Guinea": Brown, *Autobiography*, 492.
    Bromilow: Roderic Lacey, 'William Edward Bromilow,' *ADB*, 7; Bromilow, 19ff (earlier career); Wood, A.H., *Overseas Missions*, 2, 155.
    The *vasu* relationship: Roth, 75-77.
    "We three were Dobuans": Bromilow, 127.
    Fijian and Tongan local marriages: Wetherell, Christian Missions, 213.
    Saragigi: Bromilow, 130.
    Membership in Kula: Bromilow, 128-9.
    Peacemaker, Bwaidoka: Michael W. Young, 'Doctor Bromilow and the Bwaidoka Wars,' *JPH*, 12, 130-153.
234 "It was easiest and most natural": Bromilow, 103.
    "Is this house of yours...?: Bromilow, 106.
    Vakavuvuli, agents of change: Wetherell, Christian Missions, 100-143, 434-436.
    Simeoni Momoivalu: Bromilow, 251; Wood, A.H., *Overseas Missions*, 2, 385; Wetherell, Christian Missions, 131-2.
235 Joni Kuli: Bromilow, 159-163; Wood, A.H., *Overseas Missions*, 1, 240.
    "Then with a fine sweep": Bromilow, 163.

NOTES

Kuli "was the embodiment of leadership," etc.: Bromilow, 159-60.
Withdrawal from Kula ring: Bromilow, 264-5.
"The idea that these brown natives...": Bromilow, 244-5.
"Nicholas the Greek": Bromilow, 191-193.
236 Field and successor missionaries: Williams, R.G., 182-187.
Sailosi, Lasaro Banobano: Bromilow, 226-230.
M.K. Gilmour: Williams, R.G., 195-200; Malinowski's intro. to Fortune's *Sorcerers of Dobu*.
Lemeki Muiowei: Bromilow, 247.
Bromilow's return: Bromilow, 231-243. Martha McIntyre has confirmed aspects of the description of the mission, through her work on Tubetube (personal communication, May 1980).
237 Formation and background of MSC: Dupeyrat, *Papouasie*, 31-36; McManners, 55-73.
Early vagaries of founders of mission: Dupeyrat, *Papouasie*, 37-54. See also notes to pages 228-9.
238 Methodists not unfriendly, but galled: Threlfall, 59-60; Williams, R.G., 112-3.
Moran and the Austral Land: O'Farrell, 133-5.
Verjus: Cadoux; James Griffin, 'Henri Stanislas Verjus,' *ADB*, 6.
"Avid for martyrdom": Dupeyrat, *Papouasie*, 84.
239 "Deep in my heart": Dupeyrat, *Papouasie*, 83.
"Thursday Island cage": Dupeyrat, *Papouasie*, 83.
Mosby, "an old man": Dupeyrat, *Papouasie*, 85.
"The last episode": Dupeyrat, *Papouasie*, 86.
240 "Three shirts ...": Dupeyrat, *Papouasie*, 89.
"Image of the Infernal Prince," etc.: Dupeyrat, *Papouasie*, 89.
Scratchley: R.B. Joyce, 'Sir Peter Henry Scratchley,' *ADB*, 6.
LMS landed two teachers on Yule: Inglis, K.S., 284-5 (Percy Chatterton); Langmore, 52.
Douglas: R.B. Joyce, 'John Douglas,' *ADB*, 4.
241 Brother Rick, coffin maker: Dupeyrat, *Papouasie*, 140-1.
"A good religious": Dupeyrat, *Papouasie*, 188.
Verjus' self-mortifications: Cadoux, 277-303.
"Victimized to obtain the conversion": Dupeyrat, *Papouasie*, 208.
242 "Holy follies": Dupeyrat, *Papouasie*, 209.
Consecration signed in blood: Cadoux, 277.
Burns Philp: G.J. Abbott and H.J. Gibbney, 'Sir James Burns,' *ADB*, 7 (esp. conclusion, 491).
Verjus anaemic: Cadoux, 283.
Genocchi: Dupeyrat, *Papouasie*, 235-7, 246n.
Jullien, "comically lost": Dupeyrat, *Papouasie*, 239.
"Dévotions particulières": McManners, 22-3; see also Friedrich Heyer, *The Catholic Church from 1648 to 1870*, London, 1969, 177-183.

NOTES

243 Lavigerie: Neill, Anderson and Goodwin, *CDCWM*, 'Lavigerie.'
Foucauld: *ODCC*, 'De Foucauld.'
Alain de Boismenu: James Griffin, 'Alain Marie Guynot de Boismenu,' *ADB*, 7 (and references).
De Boismenu named bishop: Dupeyrat, *Papouasie*, 318-9.
"Spheres of influence": Dupeyrat, *Papouasie*, 254-272.
"Liberty to work": Dupeyrat, *Papouasie*, 286.

244 "Headquarters of heresy": Dupeyrat, *Papouasie*, 398.
"The spontaneity we might like to see": Dupeyrat, *Papouasie*, 391.
"Eyes and ears of the priests": Dupeyrat, *Papouasie*, 439.
De Boismenu and his "mountain road": McAuley, J., 'My New Guinea' and *Collected Poems*, 80-81.
Couppé: Hugh Laracy, 'Louis Couppé,' *ADB*, 7.

245 UMCA, Oxford Movement: Both (*s.v.*) in *ODCC*.
Ethos and flavour of mission: Wetherell, *Reluctant Mission*, generally.

246 Dipa and acquisition of Dogura: Wetherell, *Reluctant Mission*, 19-22.

247 Forty-five Melanesian missionaries: Wetherell, *Reluctant Mission*, 96-121 (and Appendix, 340-1).
Suppressed impatience of Melanesians: Wetherell, *Reluctant Mission*, 109, 306-7.
James Nogar: Wetherell, *Reluctant Mission*, 106-109.

248 Copland King: King, Cecil; Wetherell, *Reluctant Mission*, passim.
Stone-Wigg, Anglo-Catholic: Wetherell, *Reluctant Mission*, 54.
Saumarez Smith and Stone-Wigg's nomination: Wetherell, *Reluctant Mission*, 48-9.
Far from the pollution of towns: Personal communication, the late Camilla Wedgwood, 1944.
Rautamara, other candidates for priesthood: Wetherell, *Reluctant Mission*, 303-310.
LMS handover in Torres Strait: Goodall, 420.

251 Individualists flourished: Names and work in Wetherell, *Reluctant Mission*, passim; also Tomkins and Hughes.
Australian Proposals for Intercommunion: See Ruth Rouse and S.C. Neill (eds.), *A History of the Ecumenical Movement 1517-1948*, London, 1954, 482-484.
Sir John Guise: Tudor, 582.

Chapter 11

Each Church Distinct I

(Pages 253-278)

FOR THE SOCIETY ISLANDS the Pritchard affair has been explained by

NOTES

Langdon's *Tahiti* and in Morrell's *Britain in the Pacific Islands*. Jore and many entries in O'Reilly/Teissier are helpful. The LMS transfer to the Paris Mission is in Blanc/Blocher/Kruger. LMS missionaries, especially Orsmond, are discussed in Gunson's *Messengers of Grace*. Vernier and Mauer are useful, the latter also on Roman Catholicism in Tahiti. For Catholics, O'Reilly/Teissier has a store of information. Primary sources are LMS/SSJ and SSL, the headquarters of the Evangelical Church, Papeete, and SSCC archives (also set out by the Pacific Manuscripts Bureau, Canberra).

Kuykendall and Daws' general histories include material on the churches of Hawaii. Restarick's carefully weighed treatment of Anglicanism corrects the viewpoints of Manley Hopkins and Isabella Bird, and the bias of Rufus Anderson and William Ellis' books.

Hawaiian Catholicism has been chronicled by Yzendoorn and Schoofs — the second complementing the first to some extent. Daws' *Holy Man* and Kent's book on Hyde cast differing lights on Father Damien's agony. Honolulu libraries are rich in primary material.

Dening's writings, including his recent (unlisted in Sources) *Islands and Beaches,* Melbourne, 1980, deal with the Marquesas. Nancy Morris and Tagupa are valuable for Hawaiian missionaries. The LMS and ABCFM beginnings and encounters are in Loomis and in Lovett's *History of the LMS.* O'Reilly/Teissier and general Catholic mission histories introduce the Catholic mission and its personalities. LMS/SSJ and SSL, ABCFM and SSCC sources are as for previous chapters. HMCSL has the letters of missionaries from the Hawaiian Church.

Lovett's *Chalmers,* Gilson, Goodall, and the books of Wyatt and William Gill, supplement study of LMS/SSJ and SSL for the Cook Islands.

A.H. Wood's *Overseas Missions,* Volume 1, with books produced by Rutherford and Latukefu, introduce developments in Tonga. Cummins' Master's thesis has recently been carried further by his (unlisted) PhD on Moulton (Missionary chieftain, ANU, Canberra, 1980). Anglicanism's beginnings in Tonga are in Restarick and Tohi. MOM sources in the Mitchell Library and Marist archives, including those at the Marist Provincial House in Suva, are for further study.

Samoa's LMS church growth, seen from various angles, has been surveyed — Methodism apart — by Lovett's *History of the LMS,* Goodall and Gilson. LMS/SSJ and SSL, with documents in Samoan from the office of the Congregational Christian Church, Apia, are available.

Page

253 The Pritchard affair: Account generally based on Langdon, *Tahiti,*

NOTES

      135-185; Lovett, *History of LMS*, 306-325; Morrell, *Britain in Pacific Islands*, 71-88.

254 The Mamaia: Gunson, 'Account.'
Queen Pomare: O'Reilly, *Pomare, Reine*.
Caret and Laval with Pomare: Laval, *Mémoires*, 156-7.
Ultimatum from *Vénus*: Langdon, *Tahiti*, 140-142.

255 Utami, Tati, Hitoti, Paofai: O'Reilly/Teissier.
"What is dear to Tahitian hearts": O'Reilly/Teissier, 430.

256 Revolt on Tahiti: Newbury; Lovett, *History of LMS*, 321-325.
"My government is taken away": Newbury, 8.
Orsmond: See especially the 'Old Orsmond MS,' ML.
Howe: O'Reilly/Teissier; Gunson, *Messengers*, passim; SSL, Tahiti, 1852, statement by Howe on the mission; Lovett, *History of LMS*, 327-335; Vernier, 166-172.

257 Arrival of French missionaries and handover: Lovett, *History of LMS*, 335-339; Vernier, 173ff.
Arbousset, Atger: Blanc/Blocher/Kruger, 16ff; O'Reilly/Teissier, under names.
Viénot: O'Reilly/Teissier.

258 Members of Vernier family: O'Reilly/Teissier, under names.
"His disquiet over the danger": O'Reilly/Teissier, 590.
Mediation in revolt on Raiatea: O'Reilly/Teissier, 'Teraupoo,' and 'Vernier, Frédéric.'

260 The *Me, himene, tuaroi*: Vernier, 186-193, 202-211; Mauer, 98-99, 104, 107; also personal observation, Uturoa (Raiatea), March 1977.
Tahitian Catholicism: Mauer, 116-138 and personal observation.
"Perfectly integrated into the décor": O'Reilly/Teissier, 'Gimbert, Prosper.'
Jaussen, Montiton: O'Reilly/Teissier, under names.

262 Work with Chinese: Coppenrath.

263 "Southward, on his way of benediction": Hopkins, Preface, xii.
"A hidden want": Hopkins, 373.
"A religious clique": Hopkins, 376.
Manoeuvres of Anderson and Ellis: Kuykendall, 2, 92-94; Ellis, W., *The American Mission*; Rufus Anderson to Clark, 16 May 1862 (Confidential); Anderson to Hawaiian Board, 11 November 1865, HMCSL.

264 Priscilla Sellon: *ODCC*, 'Sellon.'
"A pining and sickly exotic": Quoted in Restarick, 144.
"I am told that it is above the desires": Bird, 27.
Damien: Daws, *Holy Man*.
"Father Damien's *humaniora*"..."a great baptist": Yzendoorn, 203, 204.

NOTES

266 Stevenson, Damien and Hyde: Daws, *Holy Man*, 11-16, 224-232; Kent, 258-280, 344-376. See also George Mackaness, *Robert Louis Stevenson, His Associations with Australia*, Sydney, 1935, 12-20.
Mother Marianne Kopp: Daws, *Holy Man*, 128-9; *Dream of Islands*, 161.
Damien's Nunc Dimittis: Yzendoorn, 211.
The Marquesan background: Greg Dening's *Islands and Beaches: Discourse on a silent land: Marquesas 1774-1880*, Melbourne, 1980, is an additional source, now available; Dening, *Marquesan Journal of Robarts*.
Names of LMS and ABCFM missionaries: Gunson, *Messengers*, passim; *Missionary Album*; Davies, 285-288.

267 Names of Roman Catholic missionaries: O'Reilly/Teissier, under names.

268 Hawaiian missionaries to Marquesas: Tagupa; Morris; Loomis, 142-178.
Bicknell: Gunson, *Messengers*, 356; Loomis, 41, 43, 48, 147, 156, 165-169.
Kekela, Kauwealoha: Letters in Hawaiian are in HMCSL and being translated by Nancy Morris; most previously tr. Henry P. Judd. The story of the mission's inception is in Kauwealoha to Emerson, 18 February 1891 (tr. Nancy Morris).
Kekela's rescue of Whalon: Loomis, 161-163 (with illustr.); Maude, *Slavers*, 179; Stevenson, *In the South Seas*, 87-90.

269 Tahitian tales of Kekela: Personal communication, Pastor Dariu, Borabora, 10 March 1977.
Tute: Lovett, *History of LMS*, 345-6; O'Reilly/Teissier, 'Tute' and 'Tehuiarii'; Daws, *Shoal of Time*, 89, 126 (Sumner).

270 Moral and spiritual decline in Cooks: Goodall, 397-404.
Evangelization of Australs: Davies, 273-283.
"The Rarotongan standards next to the Bible": Lovett, *Chalmers*, 81.
"A perfect host": Lovett, *Chalmers*, 67; John Earnshaw, 'William Henry Hayes,' *ADB*, 4.
"If you were near me": Lovett, *Chalmers*, 70.
"Tamate": Lovett, *Chalmers*, 70; etymology of word, personal communication, Ron Crocombe.

271 "The medium of military evolutions": Lovett, *Chalmers*, 98.
Maretu "a prince of men": Lovett, *Chalmers*, 77.
Piri: Lovett, *Chalmers*, 128-132.
"I think it is time": Lovett, *Chalmers*, 109-110.
"I have been on every mountain-top": Lovett, *Chalmers*, 102.
"Of course subscriptions...declined": Lovett, *Chalmers*, 117.

272 The role of the church in the Cooks: Thorogood, generally; Goodall, 397-404.

273 Shirley Baker: Rutherford, *Baker and King of Tonga*, generally.

NOTES

Moulton: See Cummins, G., *Missionary chieftain: James Egan Moulton and Tongan society, 1865-1909*, PhD, ANU, 1980; Wood, A.H., *Overseas Missions*, 1, esp. 126-131, 133-134, 164-206, 174-177.

274 Baker, constitutional adviser: Latukefu, 203-220.

275 Attempted assassination of Baker: Wood, *Overseas Missions*, 1, 188-190.
"The King is Mr Baker": Brown to Symonds, 12 September 1889, Brown Letter Books, ML.
"These poor people have suffered enough": Brown to Thurston (Private and Confidential), 25 September 1889, Brown Letter Books, ML.
Thurston had Baker removed: Scarr, *Fragments*, 107.
Reunion of Tongan churches: Wood, A.H., *Overseas Missions*, 1, 216-225; Forman, 'Tonga's tortured venture.'

276 Baker and Anglican beginnings: Rutherford, *Shirley Baker and King of Tonga*, 173-4; Pinson, 18-39; Tohi, 32-79.
Willis: Restarick, 172-209; Morrell, *Anglican Church in New Zealand*, 209-212.

277 Stevenson's estimate of missionaries: Stevenson, *In the South Seas*, 84-86.
"The excellent William Clarke": Stevenson, *Vailima Letters*, 146.
"Christianizing but not Anglicizing": Goodall, 357.
Samoan cricket: Lovett, *History of LMS*, 399; also personal observation, Upolu, December 1969.

Chapter 12
Each Church Distinct II
(Pages 253-278)

DEVELOPMENT OF FIJI METHODISM, as traced by A.H. Wood's second volume, is explored also in Thornley's theses. Derrick and the recollections of Gordon, with documents he includes, add non-ecclesiastical spice to the record. Joeli Bulu's autobiography is a gripping account; there are many references to Bulu's role in works by visiting and resident whites. Joseph Blanc's first-hand account of Fiji's Roman Catholic Church demands translation. Gallagher fills out a picture that calls for closer study in Marist archives and the Archdiocesan collection in Suva. Wiltgen gives some guidance on location of sources in Europe. For Methodism, MOM (ML) and MMSAF (NAF) are rewarding. Anglican records are in NAF.

Loomis and Sabatier, with the serviceable bibliography of the translation of

NOTES

the latter and Goodall's section, outline a story still to be filled in by work with documents in Tarawa, Apia, and HMCSL, Honolulu. LMS/SSJ and SSL are again revealing. Kiribati Protestant and Catholic history need local researchers in the vernacular. The PTC, Suva, houses the G.H. Eastman collection.

Much information about Vanuatu Presbyterianism is in Steel. Parsonson's writings (not all listed) take account of local forces at work. Hilliard's *God's Gentlemen* includes material on Vanuatu Anglicanism. Doucéré's book on Roman Catholic arrival can be supplemented by reference to individual portraits in O'Reilly's biographical dictionaries, *Hébridais* and *Calédoniens*. Scarr's *Fragments of Empire* has much political and social interpretation.

Blanc/Blocher/Kruger narrate developments for mainland New Caledonian Protestantism. Works by Jean Guiart (some not listed) illuminate both cultural and historical settings. The pivotally important roles of Loyalty Island missions and of Maurice Leenhardt are clarified in *JSO*, March-June 1978. O'Reilly's *Calédoniens* provides indications for writing both Protestant and Catholic history of New Caledonia, with help from Paris Mission sources in France, church offices in Noumea, and the Marist Provincial House in Suva.

For the Solomon Islands churches Tippett's book and those of Raucaz, Laracy (*Marists and Melanesians*), Fox and Hilliard have been consulted. Brown's *Autobiography*, Luxton's *Isles of Solomon*, R.G. Williams and Tuza assist study of Methodism in the Western Solomons. Florence Young's founder's account of the SSEM needs assessment in the light of parts of Hilliard's thesis, which also describes the Methodist/Adventist encounter and the personality of Goldie. SSEM sources, listed in Hilliard's thesis, and records of MOM (ML) and the United Church in Port Moresby and Honiara will repay study. The Pacific Churches' Research Centre in Vila can also assist.

Page

279 Consolidation and moralism: Wood, A.H., *Overseas Missions*, 2, 141ff; Thornley, Fijian Methodism, generally.
"Of securing the promotion of civilization": Deed of Cession, quoted in Derrick, 251.

280 "The cardinal": Gordon, Vol. 1, 506.
Fison's governmentally received version of land rights: France.

281 Bulu's *Autobiography*: see also Tippett and Kanailagi.
"I went forth with the lads of our town": Bulu, 10.
"I used to think Ono was a little heaven": Bulu, 49.
Bulu at Waikava: Bulu, 60; Tippett and Kanailagi, 75 (n.15), 85 (n.25).
Signatories of farewell to Moore: Bulu, 79.
Statistics, 1865: Tippett and Kanailagi, 89-90.

282 "They kissed my hands": Bulu, 41.
Fight with shark: Bulu, 27-31.

NOTES

"A very tall, plain woman": Maudslay, 84.
"His features are beautiful": Cumming, C.F.G., *At Home*, 112.
284 "He has been the old king's special teacher," etc.: Cumming, C.F.G., *At Home*, 312, 316-7.
Clash of Bulu and teachers with Langham: Thornley, *Fijian Methodism*, 58-61.
Tuka cult: Brewster, Chapter XXIII; Worsley, 27-39.
Rotuma: Langi, generally; Wood, A.H., *Overseas Missions*, 3, 113-142; Blanc, Joseph, Vol. 2, 253-280.
William Floyd: Whonsbon-Aston, generally; Pinson; Gordon, passim.
Anglican abstention from proselytism: Formal agreement with Methodists is in Memorandum of Conversation of Bishop J.R. Selwyn and Floyd with Langham and Webb, 19 June 1880, MMSAF (M-/12), NAF.
Wesleyan and Indo-Fijian population: Thornley, The Methodist Mission and the Indians in Fiji; Wood, A.H., *Overseas Missions*, 3, 1-109; Garrett, 'The Meeting.'

286 Catholic arrival: Blanc, Joseph, Vol. 1, 136ff.
"Resourceless vagabonds": Blanc, Joseph, Vol. 1, 146.
"Excessively kind": Blanc, Joseph, Vol. 1, 146.
"Conversion by club and rifle butt": Blanc, Joseph, Vol. 1, 150.
287 "Wesleyan varnish": Blanc, Joseph, Vol. 1, 180.
"The land and the sea for work": *Centenaire*; Blanc, Joseph, Vol. 1, 202.
Bréhérét's portrait: Blanc, Joseph, facing 20.
Catholic consolidation: Blanc, Joseph, Vol. 2 generally.
288 Rougier: Blanc, Joseph, Vol. 2, 165-177; O'Reilly/Teissier, 'Rougier.' Rougier's correct full name was kindly supplied by P.D. Macdonald from a copy of his birth certificate.
Bible-burning at Naililili: Thornley, "'Heretics.'"
Alfred Walkup: Loomis, 132-134; Sabatier, *Astride*, 224-226.
289 Teta's narrative of drift: Ellis, Albert F., *Adventuring*, 180-195.
"Did nothing to improve his health": Sabatier, *Astride*, 216.
"Domineering and egocentric", etc.: Sabatier, *Astride*, 217-8.
"We need not praise that system": Sabatier, *Astride*, 219.
290 Telfer Campbell: Scarr, *Fragments*, 278-281, 317.
"The Protestants, the devil and his brood": Sabatier, *Astride*, 317.
"A Gilbertese of his own invention": Sabatier, *Astride*, 174.
"This poor missionary bishop": Sabatier, *Astride*, 324.
"His face": Sabatier, *Astride*, 323-4 (tr. corrected).
Whitmee, etc.: Goodall, 385-392.
Banaba and Nauru: Goodall, 393-397; Viviani, 25-28; also personal observation and enquiry.
291 "Australia's special call": Paton, Vol. 2, 98.
"The tyranny and Popery of the French": Paton, Vol. 2, 101.

NOTES

293 Gunn: Gunn, *The Gospel in Futuna*.
Protestant condemnation of Condominium: Gunn, 299-308.
Churches of Christ: Liu.
Higginson: O'Reilly, *Calédoniens*, 'Higginson'; Doucéré, 57ff.; Scarr, *Fragments*, 182-184.

294 Milne: Don. Other names are in Steel.
Gentlemen's agreement, 1881: Hilliard, *God's Gentlemen*, 98-101.
Lengereau: Blanc/Blocher/Kruger, 212-214.
Leenhardt: O'Reilly, *Calédoniens*, 'Leenhardt, Maurice'; *JSO*, 58-59, Tome XXXIV, mars-juin 1978, *Centenaire de Maurice Leenhardt*.
Aname and Leenhardt: Documents in *JSO*, 58-59, 1978.

296 Followers of Leenhardt: O'Reilly, *Calédoniens*, 'Guiart.'
Woodford: Scarr, *More Pacific Islands Portraits*, 193-209 (Ian Heath).
Welchman: Hilliard, *God's Gentlemen*, 87ff., 173-176; Jackson; White, G.M., 'Symbols' and 'War, Peace and Piety'; Fox, *Lord of Southern Isles*, 196-199.

297 Fox: see titles listed under his name in Sources.
Inception of Catholic re-entry to Solomons: Laracy, *Marists and Melanesians*, 37ff.; Raucaz; Blanc, Joseph, Vol. 2, 153-160.

298 "Gifted with robust health": Raucaz, 113-4; Laracy, *Marists and Melanesians*, 42.

299 Florence Young and the SSEM: Young, Florence S.H.; Hilliard, *Protestant Missions*, 349-409.
Maasina Rule: Hilliard, *Protestant Missions*, 397ff. Hugh Laracy's book on the movement is to be published in Suva in 1982.

300 Methodist-Anglican comity in New Georgia: Hilliard, *God's Gentlemen*, 136-138.
Goldie: Luxton, *Isles of Solomon*, passim; Hilliard, *Protestant Missions*, 236-247.
Eto and the Christian Fellowship Church: Tippett, *Solomon Islands Christianity*, esp. 212-266, passim; Tuza; Williams, R.G., 270-272; Chesher; Boutilier/Hughes/Tiffany, 232-250 (Frances Harwood).

Chapter 13
Toward Regional Identity
(Pages 302-311)

THIS CONCLUDING EPILOGUE deals only with unitive trends implicit in the pattern of Christian expansion. Some of the same ground is covered informally in Garrett, 'A letter from Oceania.' Citations given are background

NOTES

rather than chapter and verse. Forman's forthcoming *The Island Churches* will provide detail.

Page

303 The international missionary movement: See W.R. Hogg, *Ecumenical Foundations*. New York, 1952.
World Dominion Press volumes: J.W. Burton, *Missionary Survey of the Pacific Islands*. London, 1930; Dovey.
United Church in Papua New Guinea and Solomon Islands: Williams, R.G.

304 Roman Catholic problems and advantages: Based on many personal communications from Catholic priests and laity.

305 Amsterdam 1948 and the World Council of Churches: Neill, Anderson and Goodwin, *ODCC*, 'Assemblies, Ecumenical,' (with references).
Iupeli: Goodall, 379, 380, 389.
Integration, New Delhi, 1960: W.A. Visser 't Hooft (ed.), *The New Delhi Report....*London, 1961.

306 Reforms of Second Vatican Council: Walter M. Abbott, *The Documents of Vatican II...With Commentaries and Notes by Catholic, Protestant and Orthodox Authorities*. London-Dublin, 1966.

308 Vanuatu Christian leadership: Brian Macdonald-Milne and Pamela Thomas (eds.), *Yumi Stanap, Leaders and Leadership in a new Nation*. Suva, 1981. Portraits and biographies.

310 Experiment in Pacific Island worship: *PCC*, 107-108. The Roman Catholic Cathedral, Papeete, and the Roman Catholic Parish Church, Raiwaqa, Suva, show architectural adaptation. There are other examples, especially in Melanesia.
The churches and social change: See publications of the Pacific Conference of Churches, the Melanesian Institute and the Institute of Pacific Studies, University of the South Pacific, Suva.

311 Christian sources of cultural and geographical unity: Tupouniua, Crocombe and Slatter, 165-182.

Index

A

Abaiang, 145; Binghams on, 150-1; wars with Tarawa, 150, 151; 154, 155
Abbot, Wilfred, 247
Abel, Charles W., 218
Abemama, 153; Bingham at, 153-4
Aborigines, Australian, Threlkeld and, 31; Marsden and, 61
Acculturation of Christianity, 69; in Tonga, 73-75; 80-1; in Gambiers (SSCC), 93; in Fiji, 110-114; by Cook Islander missionaries, 117; in work of Maretu, 119-20; in Samoa, 122, 123-4, 277-8; in Tutuila revivals, 127; in Polynesia (LMS), 138; on Ponape, 143, 144-5; in Marshalls, 147-8; in Kiribati, 151, 152, 160; in Tuvalu, 158-9, 160, 171-2; Anglican in Melanesian Mission, 182, 183, 184-5, 186, 189; Polynesian in Melanesia, 190; in Loyalty Islands, 194, 204-5; in LMS Papuan field, 220; New Britain, 223; Papuan Islands, 233-5, 236; in MSC Papuan field, 243, 244; in Anglican New Guinea Mission, 246, 247, 249, 252; in Pacific generally, 253; in Tahitian Protestantism, 256-260; in Tahitian Catholicism, 260-2; in Australs, 270; in Cooks, 272; in Anglican work on Isabel, 297; in Western Solomons, 301
Adamu, (Cook Islander pioneer in Papua New Guinea), 208, 271
Aea, Hezekiah and Debora (Kaaikaula), (Hawaiian missionaries to Marshalls), Lahainaluna training, 146; Hezekiah assists Coan; pioneer in Marshalls, 146-7. *See also* Kaaikaula
Afareaitu, 25, 28
Agana, 2
Age, The, 226
Air travel, 303
Aitutaki, 30, 82, 120; Royle on, 120
Akamuru, 88, 91, 92, 96
Akarongo (missionary to Palmerston), 121
Akatangi (Rarotongan missionary), on Erromanga, 167
Akoneriko (Hawaiian Catholic), 52
Alcohol, 16; Pomare II and, 21; George Kaumualii and, 36; Liholiho and, 43; Cargill and, 108; control of, 125, 296; and ABCFM on Ponape, 141-3; on Abaiang,

150-1; Chalmers and, 208, 216, 217; George Brown and, 222; MacGregor and, 231; orange liquor on Rarotonga (and Chalmers), 270-1; and Fiji Methodism, 281; Leenhardt and Blue Cross, 296
Aleamotu'a (Tongatapu chief), as Tu'i Kanokupolu, 74, 75, 77; baptized Josiah, 74; 76, 77; death, 77; father of Ma'afu, 80; 102
Alexander, William Patterson, 266-7
Ali'i (arioi, ariki, 'eiki), 4-5; Tahitian, 7, 16, 18, 19; Hawaiian, 40; Samoan, 123
Ambon, MSC pioneers at, 237
Ambuofa, Peter, and SSEM, 299; lapses, 299
American Board of Commissioners for Foreign Missions (ABCFM), 10, 28; arrival of mission in Hawaii, 33, 37-39; background of pioneer company, 33-35, 38; and LMS, 33, 35; founding of 33-35; instructions to SIM, 35, influence on Hawaii, 38; wives of missionaries, 38; second and later companies, 38-39; 50; and Catholics, 51; Rufus Anderson of, 57; naturalization of missionaries, 57; creation of Hawaiian Evangelical Association, 57; role in Marquesas and Micronesia, 58, 139, 140-1; financial reverses, 59, 146; detaches Hawaiian Board of Missions, 146; agreement with LMS in Kiribati, 153, 156
American frontier, 55, 58
American influence in Pacific, Hawaii, 50, 55, 58; Kiribati, 288; in World War II, 303
Amherst College, 24
Amsterdam Assembly, 305
Anaa, 81; Montiton on, 260
Aname (chief of Poyes), and Leenhardt, 295; interned on Wallis, 295; dies in World War I, 296
Anderson, Rufus, 47; and Hawaiian church autonomy, 57-59; resists foreign interference, 57; visits Hawaii, 58, 59; book on Hawaii, 59; urges Hawaiian missions to Pacific, 140; campaigns against Reformed Catholic Church, 263
Andover Seminary, 38
Andrews, Claudius B., 139
Andrews, Lorrin, 47
Anederea (Cook Islander missionary), 208
Aneityum (Vanuatu), 167, 169-178; Geddie arrives on, 169; sandalwooders on,

383

INDEX

169-171; Samoans on, 167-172
Anelgauhat, 169-177; mission house burned, 170; church built, 174; church and school burned, 175
Angas, John Howard, and McFarlane, 211
Anglicans, Anglicanism, Calvinistic, 9; Marsden, 19; missions, 19; 46; in Hawaii, 57, 59, 263-4; in New Zealand, 61-67, 68, 183-85; Oxford Movement, 182, 245; in Papua New Guinea, 231, 245-52; Anglo-Catholics, 245, 263, 264; Anglican Communion, 245, 276; Diocese of Polynesia, 264, 276, 285; beginnings of Tongan church, 276; in Fiji, 285; in Vanuatu, 294. *See also* Melanesian Mission
Anglican New Guinea Mission, 245-252; leadership and ethos, 245-6, 248; Melanesian missionaries in, 246; ecumenical relations, 251-2
Aniwa, 167
Anti (Kiribati), 151
Apia, celebration of Germany's 1870 victory, 134; Catholic schools, 134; Binghams at, 154
Apolonia (Wallisian catechist), 286
Arbousset, Thomas, pioneers for Paris Mission in Tahiti, 257
Archibald, Isaac, 169; adultery and withdrawal, 169; with sandalwooders and Geddie, 169
Are language and people, and Tomlinson, 251
Arioi, 7, 14, 15, 16, 22, 39, 89. *See also* Oro
Armand, Abraham, 48
Arminians, Arminianism, 8, 9, 212
Armitage, Elijah (cotton weaver), 30
Armstrong, Richard, 58, 267
Arona, Prince Regent, 95
Aruandera (first baptized Papuan), 210
Arue (Raiatean missionary), 122
Ata (Tongan chief), 71, 72, 73
Atger, Emile, 257
Atiu, 82, 83
Atkin, Joseph, 187; death, 187
Atoll culture, 146, 159
Attale, Brother, 77
Atua, 15, 69
Auna (missionary to Hawaii from Huahine), work in Hawaii, 40-43; welcomed by Hawaiian chiefs, 40, 42; succeeded by Tute, 269
Australasian, The, 228
Australasian Methodist Missionary Society.

See Wesleyan Methodists
Austral Islands, 24, 29, 31, 71, 258; early evangelization, 270
Australian Board of Missions (ABM), 245, 248
Auxiliary societies (Raiatea), 26, 27, 29

B

Bachelot, Alexis, 48-54; confirmed as Prefect Apostolic, 53; adversities in Honolulu and death, 54
Baigona religion (northern Papua), 249
Baiteke, Tem (of Abemama), and Hiram Bingham II, 153-4
Baker, Thomas, murdered, 284
Baker, William, 199
Baker, Shirley Waldemar, 80; arrival in Tonga and personality, 272-3; helps frame Tongan constitutions, 273, 274; elected chairman, 273; and Godeffroys, 273; and Moulton, 273, 274; personal claims and opportunism, 273-4; designs flag, 274; replaced as chairman, 274; and Tongan king, 273-5; Premier in Tonga, 274-5; attempt to assassinate, 275; removed from Tonga, 275; return, founds new church, death, 276
Balade, 172, 181; Marists at, 192; mission house burned, 192
Baledrokadroka, Aminio (Fijian missionary), speech at Navuloa, 221; 225
Banaba (Ocean Island), 289; phosphate discovered, 290; evangelization of, 290-1
Banks Islands, 185-6
Banks, Sir Joseph, 12
Banobano, Lasaro (Papuan Islands pastor), 236
Baptism, discipline of, Hawaii, 57; Papua New Guinea (LMS), 211; Kiribati (Catholic), 289
Baptists, in New Guinea highlands, 303
Barave, Timoci (Fijian missionary), murdered on Gazelle Peninsula, 224
Barff, Charles, 24, 27; voyage with Williams, 84; and WMMS in Tonga, 84; in Samoa, 126; touches Niue, 135
Barnden, George, drowned, 126
Barriol, Eugène, censured on Ouvea, 203
Bataillon, Pierre, 68, 69; becomes bishop, 78, 98; priest on Wallis, 97; character and strategy, 101; visits Cakobau, 112-3, 287; sends Marists to Samoa, 129; visits Samoa, 131; visits Rome, 131; acquires

384

INDEX

Clydesdale Seminary, 132, 138; 192; sends Marists to Fiji, 286-7; visits Fiji, 287
Bau, 79-80; 103-115; importance for missions, 103; Cross visits, 105;109; war with Rewa, 110; killing stone on, 112; Bataillon visits, 112-3; Taufa'ahau visits, 113; church accepted on, 114
Baudichon, Joseph-Paul, 267
Bay of Islands (N.Z.), 60, 62, 65, 66, 68, 72, 81
Bazit (chief of Ohwen), 201, 202, 203
Beachcombers, in Tonga, 15, 68, 73; in Samoa, 85; at Bau, 103; on Ponape, 141-3; on Nauru, 291
Beaulieu, François, 203, 204
Belcher, Edward, 53
Bennet, George, 27, 28, 30, 31, 39, 42
Bera (Big Man of Bogutu), 297; clash with Wadrokal, 297
Bernard, Jean, 197; on Ouvea, 202-3; censured and withdrawn, 203
Bertreux, Jean-Ephrem, Prefect Apostolic, Vicar Apostolic, 298
Bete (Fiji), 110
Bible, in Samoa, 124, 128; and Pratt, 125-6; Stevenson in Samoa and, 126; Kiribati, 154-5; Vanuatu, 174-5; Papua New Guinea, 215, 220; Dobuan, 236; in Anglican New Guinea Mission, 249, 251; revision of Tahitian, 257; and Tahitian language, 260; Tongan, 273; in Pacific, 311. *See also* Bible translation and use
Bible Society, British and Foreign, 126, 294
Bible Society of the South Pacific, 306
Bible translation and use, Tahiti, 27, 257; Cooks, 83, 84; Fiji, 106; Samoa, 124-5; Niue, 137; Kiribati, 150, 152, 154-5; Tuvalu (Samoan Bible), 157, 158; Vanuatu, 175, 177; Lifou, 197, 201; Loyalties, 205; Papua New Guinea, 215; New Britain, 226, 228, 229; Papuan Islands, 236; into Are language, 251; drama in Cooks, 272; Tonga, 273; Rotuma, 285; burning of Bibles in Fiji, 288; Houailou, New Caledonia, 296; 308
Bice, Charles, 297
Bicknell, Henry, 12, 17, 21, 24; baptizes Pomare II, 27
Bicknell, James, of Oahu, 268; in Marquesas, 268; in Honolulu, 268
Big Men (in Melanesia), 162, 185, 186, 247, 297, 299
Binandere people, 247; Copland King and, 248

Bingham, Hiram, I, 37; character and career, 37-8; writes to LMS, Tahiti, 39; 43, 44-5, 50; and Catholics, 51; 53; jostled by sailors, 54; denied second term, 38
Bingham, Hiram, II, 145; physique, 149, 152, 154; settles on Abaiang, 150; translation work, 150, 152, 152-3, 154, 154-5; and Richard Randell, 150; in wars on Abaiang, 150; persistence, 152; encounters LMS in Tuvalu, 152-3; and Abemama, 153; completes Bible translation, 154-5; work in Honolulu, 154, 155; death, 155
Bingham, Minerva Clarissa, 150; translator, 152, 154-5; teacher, 153; pregnancy, 154; birth of Hiram III, 154; at completion of translation, 154-5
Binoka, Tem (of Abemama), 153; and Kanoaro, 154
Bird, Isabella, 264
Bislama (Vanuatu Pidgin), 294, 310
Blanche Bay, volcanic eruptions in, 223; 225
Bligh, William, 4, 7, 11, 13, 16
Blohm, Hans, 224
Boog, Thomas (beachcomber), 68; accompanies Pompallier to Wallis, 97
Bogue, David (of Gosport), 9; differences with Haweis, 13; 24, 25, 117
Bogutu, Soga and Welchman at, 297
Boianai, Gill at, 251
Boismenu, Alain Marie Guynot de, origins and early career, 243; arrival at Yule Island, 243; bishop, 243; restructuring of MSC Papua mission, 243; and Navarre, 243; archbishop, 243; appearance and character, 243; rejects comity, 243-4; missionary principles, 244; 305
Boki (high chief), 46; and Catholic mission to Hawaii, 49-55; baptism of, 49; lands at Waianae, 51, 54; sandalwood expedition and death, 52, 164; his party, 52-55
Bondu, Melchior, 51, 53
Bontemps, Edouard, 241; pioneer for MSC in Kiribati, 289; early difficulties, 289; encounter with Samoans of LMS, 289; recruits in Europe, 289; ill health, 289; disappointments and character, 289; death, 289
Borabora, 21, 26, 27, 28
Borabora (missionary), 71
Bordeaux, 49
Boston, ABCFM Headquarters, 34, 35, 45, 57, 58, 59, 139, 160
Boti (Huahine missionary), 84, 122
Bougainville, Marists and Methodists on,

385

INDEX

298, 300
Bourail (New Caledonia), 193
Bourjade, Léon, 244
Bourne, Robert, 24, 26, 29; visits Cooks, 82-3
Bowell, Daniel, 15
Bréhéret, Jean Baptiste, 113; career in Fiji, 286-7; at Lakeba, 286; early reverses, 286-7; and Wesleyans at Lakeba, 286; moves westward, 287; slow progress, 287; made Prefect Apostolic, 287; appearance and personality, 287
Breton, Marin (hermit of Neiafu), 132
British Government influence and Christianity, Hawaii, 57; New Zealand, 65-6, 183-4; in Melanesia, 177, 182; in Loyalties, 204; in Papua New Guinea, 213-215, 230-3, 240; Kalo massacre, Papua, 213; reprisal at Toaripi, 215; in Crown Colony of Fiji, 221-2, 280-1, 286; in Papuan Islands, 230-3; in Anglican New Guinea Mission, 246; in Tahiti, 255, 273, 291; in Vanuatu, 293; in Solomon Islands, 300
Bromilow, Lilly, 233; and women on Dobu, 233, 236; adopted into Kula ring, 233
Bromilow, William, on Dobu, 233-6; adopted into Edugaula tribe and Kula ring, 233, 235; pacifying role, 233; called *Saragigi*, 233; with Tongans and Fijians, 233-4; protected by Gagunamore, 233, 235, 236; translates Bible into Dobuan, 236; absence and return, 236
Brooke, Charles, 187
Broomhall, Benjamin, 12, excommunicated in Tahiti, 17; leaves Tahiti, 17
Brothers, Catholic, early, 101; Marist of the Schools, 101; of Ploërmel, 260; in Fiji, 286-7; Marist in Fiji, 288
Brown, George, 94; in Samoa, 128-9, as strategist, 128; with Elloy at Lufilufi debate, 131-2; 134; and Samoan high titles, 134; with Stevenson and Chalmers, 216; personality, 216, 222; inspires New Britain mission, 220; recruits in Fiji for New Britain, 220-22; physique, 222; and Islander missionaries, 223; leads armed expedition in New Britain, 225-6; meets Talili, 225; and consequences of raid, 225-8; evacuated for ill health, 227; in Levuka court case, 227-8; return to New Britain, 228-9; at Port Breton, 228; appointed Australasian Mission board's general secretary, 230; travels to America and Britain, 230; and MacGregor, 231-3; in Papuan Islands, 231-3; party to comity in Papua, 231; 239; and Shirley Baker, 275; and J.B. Thurston, 227, 275; and Western Solomons mission, 300
Bruce, Robert, personal vagaries, 216; resigns, 216; Chalmers and, 216
Buchanan, Ebenezer, 168
Buchanan, Francis de Sales, 251
Buckle, William, 44
Buddle, James, 67
Bula (blind chief of Losi), 195, 196
Bula the younger (chief of Mu, Losi), 197, 199
Buller, James, 67
Bulu, Akesa, 282
Bulu, Joeli, 75; sent to Fiji, 105; 111, 114; and students at Navuloa, 221; work in Fiji, 281-4; *Autobiography*, 281; longs to "live among the stars", 281; on Viwa with Hunt, 281; at Ono, 281; in Vanua Levu, 281; and Ma'afu's troops, 281; trains catechists at Waikava, 281; puts down roots in Fiji, 281-2; fights shark, 282; last years on Bau as teacher of Cakobau, 282-4; death, 284; clashes with Langham over participatory church government, 284
Bunting, Jabez, 222
Burder, George, 25, 39
Bure atua (Tahiti). *See* Praying people
Bure kalou (Fiji), 107
Burns Philp Company, 242, 252
Burotu (Fiji), 112
Burton, John Wear, 286
Bush Brotherhood, 249
Bushnell, Horace, 144
Butaritari, 151, 152
Butcher, Benjamin T., 218
Butler, John, 64, 65
Buzacott, Aaron, 82; manual skills, 83-4, 85; 116-8, 120; in Samoa, 126; at Niue, 136; 270
Bwaidoka, Bromilow visits, 233; Ambrose Fletcher at, 236
Bwaxat (chief of Hienghène), 193

C

Caillet, Xavier, 204
Cakaudrove (Fiji), 102, 106, 287
Cakobau, Seru (*vunivalu* and king), 79, 80, 103; Cross meets, 105; warlord on Bau, 109, 111, 113; and Varani, 109, 110; wit,

386

INDEX

110-11, 112-13; and Hunt, 110-11; character, 112; at widow strangling, 112; installed as *vunivalu,* 113; accepts Christian faith, 114, 279; baptized, 114; claims to supremacy in Fiji, 115; as king, 279; 297
California, Hawaii's Catholic missionary pioneers in, 49, 52
Calinon, Pierre, 78
Calvert, James, 105; at Levuka, 113; and Cakobau, 113; 280
Calvinistic Evangelicals, 4, 19, 71
Calvinistic Methodists, 9, 19, 24, 25
Calvinists and Calvinism, British, 9, 212; Anglican, 9; American, 10, 34, 37, 144, 152; Moderate, 10; Dissenters, 71, 160; Independents, 121; and revivalism, 128, 168
Campbell, Robert, 19
Campbell, W. Telfer, 290
Cannibalism, New Zealand, 60; Fiji, 107, 110, 112, 113, 115; Erromanga, 166; Ta'unga's observations in New Caledonia, 194, 195; in murder of Chalmers, 218; in murders in New Britain, 225; 233; and women on Dobu, 233
Caret, François d'Assise, 88-96; in Mangareva, 89, 90; poor boatman, 91; school, 92; mission on Tahiti, 96, 253-4
Carey, Jesse, 221
Carey, William, 8, 13
Cargill, David, in Tonga, 74, 76; sent to Fiji, 79, 102; training and character, 103, 106; and Fijian alphabet, 103; at Lakeba, 105; 104, 106; loss of wife, 107; leave in England, 107; tribute to first wife, 108; death, Vava'u, 108; alcohol- and drug-dependence, 108
Cargill, Margaret, death, 107; tribute to, 108
Castle and Cooke, 38
Castle, Samuel Northrop, 38, 58
Catholic missions, *see* Roman Catholic missions
Celibacy, 138, 244, 304
Central Oceania, Vicariate of, 78, 99, *see also* Bataillon, Marist missions, Vicariates
Chabot, Joseph, 242, 243
Chalmers, James, 137; in New Guinea, 206-18; on McFarlane, 207; partners Lawes, 208; character, 208, 215, 216; Ruatoka and, 208-10; critical of Motu as *lingua franca,* 211; identifies with Papuans, 212; on clothing, 212; opinions and piety, 212; and Kalo massacre, 213; and alcohol, 215, 217; in Britain on deputation, 215; at Toaripi, 215; marriages, 212-13, 215; visits Rarotonga, 215; and Stevenson, 208, 215-6; in Strait and Western District, 216-8; at Saguane, 217; murdered, 218; repercussions of death, 218; and colleagues, 216, 218; earlier work on Rarotonga, 270-71; and Bully Hayes, 270; called Tamate, 270; and Royle, 270-71; and Rarotongan youth, 270-71; uses coconut milk for communion, 271; views and practice on church self-government, 271; fund-raising practice, 271; 304
Chalmers, Jane, 212-13; death, 213
Chalmers, Sarah Elizabeth (Lizzie), 215; visits Rarotonga, 215; ill-health and English respite, 216; return to Saguane, 216; final illness and death, 217
Chamberlain, Daniel, 37, 40, 44
Chamberlain, Eli, 44
Chamorri (Marianas), 2
Chanel, Pierre, 68, 69, 79; on Mangareva, 96; on Futuna, 97-9; hardships, 97-8; conversions, baptisms, 98; murder, 98; relics to Rome, restored to Futuna, 98; canonized, 98-9; background in France, 99; character, 99; 101
Chapman, Benjamin, 227
Charlotte (wife of Taufa'ahau), 75, 79
Charlton, Richard, 50, 53
Chépénéhé, Wainya of, 196; importance of, 196, 199; military measures at, 199-200; LMS seminary at, 201, 205; students in New Guinea, 206
Chester, Henry, 239
Chevalerie, Henriette de la, 48
Chevalier, Jules, 237, 238, 242, 243
Chevron, Joseph, 77, 78; character and origins, 78; work in Tonga, 79; on Wallis, 97
Chiefs, welcoming role of, 5; material expectations of, 6; wars of, and Christianity, 6; and Tahitian church, 20; in Tahiti, 21; Hawaiian, 35, 36, 40, 42, 43; and Catholics in Hawaii, 52; and Treaty of Waitangi, 65-6; role in Tonga, 72, 73, 74, 77, 273; on Raiatea, 82; in Cooks, 82-3; on Mangareva, 91; at Lakeba, 102; in Samoa, 84, 85, 130; on Bau, 103, 105; John Hunt and, 105, 109; on Mangaia, 120; in Samoa (and LMS) 120, 122, 124; and Marists in Samoa, 130, 131, 134; on Ponape, 141-43; on Tarawa and Abaiang, 150; in Tuvalu,

387

INDEX

156, 158; on Aneityum, 170, 173; as labour recruiters, 177; and Marists in Solomons, 181; and Anglicans in New Zealand, 183-85, Tuauru and Isle of Pines, 190; Bwaxat of Hienghène, 193; Loyalty Islands, 194, 195, 196, 199, 201-05; Ta'unga's dealings with, 191, 194, 195; Talili (New Britain), 224-5; Yule Island, 242; at Dogura, 246; and Mamaia cult (Tahiti), 254; and French (Tahiti), 256; and Hawaiian Protestantism, 262-3; Nukuhiva, 267; Hivaoa, 268; Fijian, 279, 281; Fijian and Gordon, 280; Fijian and Anglicanism, 285; Fiji, 286, 287; and Leenhardt (New Caledonia), 295-96; on Isabel (Solomons), 297; in Western Solomons, 300

Christian Fellowship Church (Western Solomons), 300, 301, *see also* Eto

Church self-government and autonomy, Hawaii, 57-59; Tuvalu, 159, 160; Geddie's views on, 174, 177; slowness in Vanuatu, 177; retarded in Melanesian Mission, 187; in Papuan Islands, 236; Chalmers on, 271; free Church of Tonga, 274-5; Waterhouse and (Fiji), 279-80; Bulu, Tongans and Langham clash over, 284; SSEM and, 299; generally, 301, 302, 303

Churches of Christ (Australia), in Vanuatu, 293

Church of England, 4, 263

Church of Tonga, 276

Church Missionary Society, 19; and Marsden, 61; 64; New Zealand mission, 61-66, 182; and Wesleyans (New Zealand), 66-7; and Patteson, 183

Civil War, American, 59, 146

Civilizing mission, Haweis on, 11; Marsden on, 11, 61

Clark, Ephraim, 140, 152; baptizes Prince Albert Edward, 263

Clarke, William, 277

Clothing, 47, 174; and measles on Aneityum, 175; Chalmers on, 212; Bromilow on, 235

Clydesdale Seminary, 132, 138

Coan, Titus, character and career, 55; in Hawaiian revival, 56

Coconut oil trade, 19, 27

Codrington, R.H., 185; 186, 188

Colin, Jean Claude, 67, 68; tension with Pompallier, 78, 97; requirements of missionaries, 97; forms Oceanian Company, 99; collapse of plans, 101; withdrawal and death, 101, 131; 179, 287

College of Propaganda, 49, 52, 53, 78, 99; internationalized, 306

Collomb, Jean-Georges, 181; consecrated in New Zealand, 181; dies, 181

Colonial Sugar Refining Company, 286

Comity of missions, WMMS-LMS, 84; Melanesian fields, 182; in Loyalties, 193, 197; in Papua, 231, 240, 243, 245; LMS-ABCFM in Marquesas, 266; Rotuma, 284; in Vanuatu, 294; in Solomon Islands, 299, 300

Condominium, Anglo-French (New Hebrides), and missions, 293; 308

Cook Islands, 29, 30, 31, 60; missionaries from, 85, 116-18, 120; link with Tahiti and New Zealand, 120, 270; development of church in, 269-72, *see also* Pacific Islander missionaries

Communion, Holy, McFarlane's practice, 211; Chalmers' practice, 271

Congregationalists, Congregationalism, and LMS, 11, 12, 24, 121, 220; and ABCFM, 33, 46; New England, 46, 58; dominance in Tuvalu, 156; Australian and LMS, 160; Scottish and LMS, 168; Wesleyan influence among, 212

Congregation for the Evangelization of the Nations, 306

Constantine (Samoan Catholic catechist), 129; wife, Amelia, 130

Convicts, escaped, 194

Cook, James, 3, 7, 9, 13, 16, 32, 36, 45, 60, 135

Cooke, Amos Starr, 38, 58

Copeland, Joseph, 175

Cornwall (Connecticut) Foreign Mission School, 35, 38

Corpus Christi festival, 48, 131

Cotton trade (Raiatea), 27, 29

Coudrin, Pierre, 48-9, 52, 88

Countess of Huntingdon, Selina, 4, 9

Couppé, Louis, 238, and MSC organization in Sydney, 238; opens Mekeo for MSC, 240; named bishop for New Britain, 241; estimate of Verjus, 241; 244, 289

Cover, James Fleet, 12, 15, 16

Cramaille, Théophile, 238

Crey, Cyprien, 181

Cricket, 277-8

Crook, William Pascoe, 12; in Marquesas, 15, 266; at Pomare II's baptism, 27; and

388

INDEX

Niue, 135
Croker, William, 77
Cross, William, in Tonga, 72, 73; and John Williams, 79, 84; sent to Fiji, 79, 102; goes to Bau and Rewa, 105; character, 105, 106; differences with Cargill, 107; death, 107
Cru, Jean-Pierre, 205, 295
Cruz, Hipolito de la, 2
Cults and religious reactions, 4, 70, 301; Sio Vili, 4, 85, 121; Papahuria, 69-70; *Pai Marire* (*Hauhau*), 70; Baigona and Taro cults, 249; Mamaia, 253; *Tuka* (Fiji), 284; Maasina Rule, 299; Christian Fellowship Church (Etoism), 300, 301
Cultural alienation, on Mangareva, 96; on Ponape, 143; on Abaiang, 155; in Tuvalu, 159; Anglicization, 183, 184, 188; in Papuan Islands, 235; 244; in Tahiti, 262; Western Solomons, 300
Cumming, Constance Gordon, on Bulu, 282-84
Cunningham (Mate of Camden), 164-5

D

Damien de Veuster, work (and death on Molokai), 264-66; and R.L. Stevenson, 266; successors on Molokai, 266
Dancing, in Samoa (night dance), 122, 125, 127; Niue, 137; on Abaiang, 155; in Papuan Islands, 235; in Cook Islands, 272
Danks, Benjamin, 226; handyman, 266; at Kabakada, 226; 228
Danks, Emma, 226, 229
Darling, David, 24, 26, 27, 266, 270
Darnley Island, 206, as McFarlane's Iona, 207
Dartmouth College, 34
Daru, 217; seminary for Kiwai teachers, 218
Dauncey, Harry M., 218
Davies, John, 17; complains of neglect by London, 18; and Tahitian language, 19-20; frank reports to London, 20, 22; 21, 22; on importance of religious decisions, 22; 24; translator, 24; cultivates outstations, 24; 26; on Huahine, 26; 31, 39; sends missionaries to Tonga, 71; 81; sends missionaries to Fiji, 102; 255, 269, 270
Davis, Isaac, 32
Deacons (in LMS system), 24, 29, 39, 82, 124, 220, 256, 260
Delaporte, Philip A., on Nauru, 291
Delena (Papua), 218

Delord, Philadelphe, 295
Depopulation, *see* Population decline
Deputation, LMS, 27, meets Pomare II, 28; reports on Leewards, 28; present at Pomare III's coronation, 28; 29, 30; in Hawaii, 39, 42, 43
Desnoës, Gustave, 242
Dévotions particulières, 242
Dillon, Peter, takes *Active* to New Zealand, 62; and Tongan wars, 76-7; takes Cross to Bau, 105
Dipa, Abrieka, and Dogura land, 246
Directors (LMS), *see* LMS Directors
Disinterested benevolence (theological concept), 10, 34
Doane, Edward T., missionary record, 145, 146; visit to Mortlocks, 148
Dobu, Wesleyans on, 232-36
Dogura, acquisition of land at, 246; Maclaren's remains at, 247; schools, 249; clergy trained at, 249-51; Tomlinsons' role at, 251
Dole, Charlotte, 38
Dole, Daniel, 38, 58
Dole, Sanford Ballard, 58
Do-Neva, Leenhardt at, 295
Dordillon, René Ildefonse, 268
Douarre, Guillaume, 172; at Balade, 192; character, 192; as bishop, 192; absence from New Caledonia, 193; death, 193
Douglas, John, and MSC, 240
Drummond, George, 168
Dubreul, *see* Freydier-Dubreul
Dudley, Hannah, 285-6
Dugumoi (*Na Vosa Vakadua*), and *Tuka* cult, 284
Duke of York Island, 222
Dumont d'Urville, J.S.C., 109
Du Petit-Thouars, Abel, 53, 254
Durin, Joseph, 237; at Manila, 237; at Macassar, 237-8, death, 238
Dyson, Martin, and WMMS Samoa mission, 128-9; disputation with Elloy at Lufilufi, 131-2.

E

Eastern Oceania, Vicariate of, 53
Ebon, 145, 146, 289
Ecumenical movement, 303-11
Edinburgh Conference (1910), 303
Edinburgh Missionary Society, 17
Edwards, Jonathan, 10, 33-4
Efate, 167
Elder, James, 17

INDEX

Elders, role in Vanuatu Presbyterianism, 174, 177
Eleicha Nevayes (New Caledonia missionary), 295
Elekana (Cook Islander missionary), 120, 155-6; removed, 157; father of Teina Materua, 210
Elephantiasis, *see* Filariasis
Elia (missionary to Niue), 136
Ella, Samuel, on Ouvea, 201-2; joins appeal to Napoleon III, 202
Ellice Islands, *see* Tuvalu
Ellis, William, 24; sets up press, 25; 26, 27; on Huahine, 28, 39; ethnographer, 28, 94, 29, 31; *Polynesian Researches,* 31; LMS Foreign Secretary, 31; and Hawaii, 38, 39-43, 45, 81; Hawaiian hymns, 44; campaign against Reformed Catholic Church in Hawaii, 263; commends Tute to Hawaiian royalty, 269
Elloy, Louis, 131; style in Samoa, 131; disputation with Wesleyans, 131-2; at Clydesdale, named bishop, 132; solicits in Australia for Samoa, 132-3; return to Apia (1870), 134; and Mata'afa Iosefo, 134; and Steinberger, 134; and high Samoan titles, 134; travels to Wallis, Fiji and Rotuma, 135; to USA, 135; received by Pius IX, 135; death, 135
Epalle, Jean Baptiste, 179; earlier life, 180; death, 180; successor, 181; 298
Epidemics, measles, 164, 171, 175-6, 176, 221; influenza, 164; malaria, 164, 167, 181, 191, 194
Episcopal Conference of the Pacific (CEPAC), 306
Erikana, *see* Elekana
Erromanga, 52, 116; murder of John Williams on, 164-67; sandalwooders at, 164, 176; measles epidemic, 176; Rangi of, 176; Gordons on, 176; murders on, 176
Erskine, John, 173, 213
Eto, Silas, and Christian Fellowship Church, 300, 301; visions and role as prophet, 301
Evangelical Academies, 13
Evangelical Church of French Polynesia, 260
Evangelical Church of New Caledonia, 296
Evangelical Revival, 4, 8
Even, Frank, trader on Nikunau, 289; welcomes MSC, 289; business suffers, 289
Exeter Hall, 27, 188, 200, 227, 228, 260
Eyre, Edward John (Governor), and Gorrie 227

Eyre, John (LMS missionary), 12, 17, 20, 21

F

Faaori (Raiatean sailor), 83
Faaruea (Tahitian missionary), 102
Fa'a Samoa, 121, 124; in Papua, 210
Favre, Laurent, with Paoo at We, 197
Faife'au (Samoa), 124
Fakafitiniu (Niue missionary), 136
Fale (Samoa), 278
Faleono, Victor (Vitolio), 132
Falealili (Samoa), Teava at, 126
Fanea (Niue), 135
Fao, *see* Paoo
Faone, Sailosi (Tongan missionary), 105
Fatu (Tongan chief), 70
Fauea (Samoan chief), 84-5
Favre, Julien, succeeds Colin, 131
Fawn Harbour, *see* Waikava
Febvrier-Despointes, Admiral, 193
Feipi, Battle of, 23, Auna at, 39
Fellmann, Heinrich, 229
Fellows, S.B., 234, 236
Fenuapeho (Tahaa chief), 22
Field, J.T., 233, on Tubetube, 236
Fietoa, 77
Fiji, 24, 31, 69, 79; Tongan migrations to, 79, 102; Tongan missionaries in, 80, 81; Catholic Church in, 101, 286-88; WMMS enters, 102-115; connections with Tonga, 102; *lotu* in, 111; Tongan warriors in, 79, 80, 103, 108, 112, 114, 281; Methodism in, 114; labour trade, 177; Crown Colony, 221; cession to Britain, 279, 284; Anglicanism in, 285; Indian population and Christianity, 285-6
Filariasis, Pomare II, 27; John Williams, 29; George Brown, 224
Finau Ulukalala, 71, 73, 74, 286, (also 275)
Finney, Charles Grandison, 55, 56
Firearms, 16, 19, 65, 103, 109, 150, 153, 170, 181, 189, 192, 212; used by Brown in New Britain, 225-6; 232, 233, *see also* Muskets
Fison, Lorimer, 221; mediates between Waterhouse and Langham, 280; as anthropologist, 280; and land rights in Fiji, 280; theological and sociological thought, 280
Fletcher, Ambrose, 236
Fletcher, William, 227; on Rotuma, 285
Floyd, William, at Levuka, 285; abstention from proselytism, 285; seeks wider Anglican links, 285
Fono (Samoa), 123, 277

INDEX

Foucauld, Charles de, 243
Fouqué, Clair, 96
Fox, Charles Elliot, 297
Foxall, Edward (sandalwood informant), 190
Franciscans, in Tahiti, 3; in California, 52
Franco-British confrontations, Tahiti, 29; Vanuatu, 291-93
Franco-Prussian War, 95; effects in Apia, 134
Fransoni, Cardinal Giacomo, 99
Free Church of Tonga, under royal patronage, 274-5; reunited with Wesleyans, 275; continuing remnant, 275
Free Wesleyan Church of Tonga, 275
Frémont, Jean-Pierre, 180, 181
French Government, support for Catholic missions, 50, 54, 192, 193; ultimatum at Tahiti, 54, 254-5; ultimatum at Honolulu, 54-5; support of Pompallier in New Zealand, 68; support for Marists in Tonga, 77; confrontation with Laval, Mangareva, 95; annexes New Caledonia, 193; influence in Loyalties, 197; military interventions on Lifou, 199-200; naval and military measures in Tahiti, 254-56; and Tahitian Catholicism, 262; annexation of Marquesas (and attitude to opium trade), 268; policy in Pacific, 273; support for MSC in Kiribati, 288; 293; influence in Vanuatu, 291-93; Leenhardt and (New Caledonia), 295-6
French Polynesia, Roman Catholic Church in 96, 260-62; Evangelical Church in, 256-60
Freycinet, Louis de, 36, 49
Freydier-Dubreul, Antoine, 99, Pro-Vicar in Samoa, 131
Fromm, Mesmin, 238
Funafuti, 156
Fundamental Principle of LMS, 10
Futuna, 6, 68, 69, 96-101; culture related to Samoa, 97; Chanel on, 96-99; 193
Futuna (Vanuatu), 167; Waihit sent to, 174; Gunn on, 294

G

Gaireka (chief of Dogura), 246
Gaitcha, 199
Gambier Islands, 88-96, see also Mangareva
Gasbara, Salvatore (Kala), 239, at first mass in Papua, 240; work and character, 241
Gaulton, Samuel, 15
Gazelle Peninsula, 223; George Brown's raid across, 225-6; MSC pioneers on, 238
Geddie, Charlotte, 168-9; and Paddon, 169-71; and Marists, 172, 173
Geddie, John, 137, 166, 168-178; home influences, 168; with LMS Scots in Samoa, 168; and LMS, 169; and Paddon, 169-71; declines to baptize Archibald's child, 170; and Selwyn, 170; mission house burned, 170; and Marists, 172-3; and chiefs, 170, 173; trains local missionaries, 173, 175; forms first church, 174; chooses deacons and elders; 174; as missionary, 174; translator, 174-5; doctorate, 175; and measles epidemic, 175; church and school burned, 175-6; and Gordons, 176; and bombardment of Tanna, 176; opposes Paton, 177; last years, 177-8; death and estimate, 178
Gela (Florida), Melanesian Mission station, 187
Genocchi, Jean, 242
George, (Te Araa), (Maori chief), flogged, 62; 66; son flogged, 66
George III, King, 71, 74
George Tupou I, see Taufa'ahau
German Government and its influence, in New Britain, 228, 229; annexation of New Britain, 229; interests in Tonga, 273; Shirley Baker leans toward, 275; in Samoa, 277; in Solomons, 298; 303
Giles, John (cotton planter), 30
Gill, George, 120
Gill, Stephen Romney, 251
Gill, William, 120
Gill, William Wyatt, 94, 120; in Papua New Guinea, 207, 208; investigations on Mangaia, 271
Gilmour, M.K., 236; work at Salamo, 236
Glew, E.J., 236
Goaribari, death of Chalmers at, 217
Godeffroy and Son, Samoa, 134; Tuvalu, 156, 157; and Shirley Baker, 273
Goldie, John F., 300-01; and industrial missions, 300; personality, 300; previous career, 300
Gold rush (Papua New Guinea, 1878), 210, 213
Goodenough Island, 232
Gordon, Arthur, Governor of Fiji, 225; High Commissioner, 225, 227; and George Brown, 227-8; and Langham, 280
Gordon, George N. (and Ellen), 166, 175; preaching on Erromanga, 176; character, 176
Gordon, James, 176, present at Tanna bom-

391

INDEX

bardment, 177
Gore Browne, Thomas, Governor, 183
Gorrie, John, in Fiji, 227; Brown charged with manslaughter before, 227-8
Gosport, theological course, 116-7, *see also* Bogue
Goujon, Prosper, on Aneityum, 172-3
Goward, William E., 290
Goyon, Dr, assists Emma Danks, 229
Grange, Jérôme, 78
Gray (Tutuila beachcomber), 85
Great Commission, The, 8, 9, 34
Great Revival (Hawaii), *see* Revivals
Guadalcanal, Marists on, 298
Guam, 2-3
Gucheng (Loyalty Island missionary), 207
Guillain, Charles, and McFarlane, 199-201; politics, 199; military measures on Lifou, 199-200; opinions, 201; and Marists, 201; sends troops to Ouvea, 201, 202; replacement as governor, 201; censured in French reports, 201, 202; and Mare wars, 204
Guilloux, Ferdinand, drowned, 298
Guise, John, 252
Guitta, Jérôme, 203
Gulick, Luther Halsey (and Louisa), background, training, 139; on Ponape, 141-43; at Metalanim, 143; uses vaccine, 143; on Ebon, and later career, 145; 148
Gulick, Orramel (and Ann Eliza), 146
Gulick, Peter Johnson, 139
Gunboats, *see* French Government, British Government, German Government, Naval intervention, Firearms
Gunn, William, 293

H

Ha'a Havea chiefs, 76, 77
Ha'apai, 72, 73, 74, 75, 276
Haavi (Tahaa missionary), 82
Hadfield, James, 203
Hadfield, Octavius, 183; and Waitara Purchase, 183-4
Hagerstein, Peter, 6, 7, 15, 32
Haina, George (Hawaiian missionary), 152
Hakakarioi (Mangareva), 89
Hale Palani (Honolulu), 50
Hall, William, 61, 62, 63
Hanalei (Princeville), 263
Hankey, William, 43
Hannett, Leo, 308
Hanuabada village (Port Moresby), 208
Hape (Tahitian missionary), 71; on Rapa, 71

Hardie, Charles, 119, 126
Harper, Samuel, 15
Harris, James, 164-5
Harris, John, 12, 15, 17
Harris, William (of Nauru), 291
Hassall, Otoo, 12
Hassall, Rowland, 12, 16, 70
Hassall, Thomas, 19, 70
Hatai (Tahitian missionary), 102
Hau (Tonga), 76
Hauhau, *see* Cults
Havea, Semisi, 105
Havea, Sione 'Amanaki, 305
Hawaii, Ellis and LMS Deputation visit, 28; 32-59; Roman Catholic Mission, 46, 48-55; revival, 55-6; Republic, Territory, 58; annexation and statehood, 58; Anderson book on, 59; Mormons in, 59; 262-66
Hawaii (big island), 33, 36, 40, 43; revival on, 55
Hawaiian Evangelical Association (HEA), 57
Hawaiian language, Ellis and, 28; 36; Lyons and, 56
Hawaiian missionaries, *see* Pacific Islander missionaries and individual names
Hawaiian Mission Children's Society (HMCS), 58, 140
Hawaiian royalty, leans toward Britain, 57, *see also* Kamehameha, Kaahumanu, Kamehameha I, II, III, IV, V, Kamamalu, Kalakaua, Liholiho
Hawaiki (Maori homeland), 60
Haweis, Thomas, 4, 11; differences with Bogue, 13, 25; mentor of Nott, 21; 24, 25, 61
Hayes, William Henry (Bully), 208; and Chalmers, 270
Hayward, James, 17, 21, 24
Hazlewood, David, 103
Heath, Thomas, 125, 126, 167
Heiau (Hawaii), 33
Henderson & McFarlane, 157
Hendrick, Brother (Rick), 241
Heneri (Cook Islander missionary), 208, 271
Henry, Samuel P., 164
Henry, William, 12, 16, 21, 27; anoints Pomare III, 28
Hermon (pastoral school, Papeete), 258
Hernsheim and Co., 222, 224, 227, 238
Hervey Islands, *see* Cook Islands
Hienghène, 193
Higginson, John, promotes Marist mission in Vanuatu, 293; commercial enterprise, 293

392

INDEX

Hihifo (Tongatapu), 71, 72, 73
Hilo, 44, 56
Himene (Tahiti), 260
Hiro, 81, 82
Hiro (Rarotongan missionary), 217
Hitchcock, George, 119
Hitoti (Tahitian chief), writes to Queen Victoria, 255; fights and dies with France, 256
Hobbs, John, 66, 67
Hokianga (New Zealand), 66, 68
Holman, Thomas, 37, 44
Holmes, John Henry, 217, 218
Hongi Hika (Maori chief), and Kendall, 62, 63, 64; visit to England, 64; death, 65; 67
Honolii, John (ABCFM first company), 43
Honolulu, 36, 40, 44, 53, 54
Hopkins, Manley, Hawaiian consul in London, 263; book on Hawaii, 263; on Hawaiian Protestantism, 263; on Hawaiian Catholicism, 263
Hopkins, Samuel, 34
Hopu, Thomas (ABCFM first company), 35, 43
Houailou, 295
Houma (Tonga), 77
Howe, William, 256-7; revises Tahitian Bible, 257; opposes government control of church, 257; advocates French missionaries, 259; inducts Arbousset, 257
Huahine, 20, 21, 22, 23, 26, 28, 39, 43, 84, 122
Hula (Hawaiian), 33; revival as surrogate for, 56
Hullett, Nellie, on Naniu Island, 251
Hunt, Hannah, 106, 107
Hunt, John, 105; personality and career, 105-6, 111; and chiefs, 106; translations, 106; at Somosomo, 106; understanding of Fijians, 106, 111; and cannibalism, 106; and pre-christian priests, 107; mediates between Cross and Cargill, 107; role in Varani's conversion, 109-11; and Watsford, 110; and Cakobau, 110-11; death, 111; *Letters on Entire Sanctification*, 111; 280, 284
Huntingdon, Selina, Countess of, 9
Hutchinson, John, 71
Hyacinthe, Brother, murdered, 181
Hyde, Charles McEwen, and Stevenson's Open Letter, 266

I

Iakopo (Samoan missionary), 194

Imperialism and missions, 176-7; Geddie and, 176-7; theology of, 177, 291
'Inasi (Tonga), 81
Independents, Congregational, 24, 121
Infantile sexuality, problem to LMS on Tahiti, 28
Inglis, Jessie, 174
Inglis, John, 173; travel in Melanesia, 173; stationed at Aname, 173; forms church, 174; translator-editor, 174-5; doctorate, 175; at shelling of Tanna, 177
Intercommunion, Australian Proposals for, 251-2
International Missionary Council (IMC), 303, 305
International Review of Missions, 303
Ioane (of Nanumanga), 158
Ioane (on Nukulaelae), 156
Isabel (Solomons), 179-80; murder of Epalle on, 180; Anglicanism on, 296-7
Islander missionaries, *see* Pacific Islander missionaries and individual names
Isle of Pines, 189, 190, 191, 193, 195, 203
Issoudun, cult of, 237-8
Itia, 16
Iupeli, Pastor (Samoan missionary), 290, 305

J

Jacobinism (accusation), 24
Jacquet, Claude, murdered, 181
Jaggar, Thomas, 105, 109
Jaussen, Etienne, 94, 95; as bishop at Papeete, 260
Jefferson, John, 12, 17, 18; death, 20; role as leader, 20
Jemes (of Mare, missionary), 295
Jerusalem Conference (1928), 303
Jesuit mission to Marianas, 2-3
Jesuit reductions (Paraguay), 88
Jesuits (Protestant misnomer), 51, 173
Jiear, A.H., and Chalmers, 217-18
Joachim (Samoan Catholic catechist), 129
Joe (Erromangan at Malua), 167
John Williams, see Ships, missionary
Jones, John Coffin (consul), 50
Jones, John (LMS missionary on Mare), 197, 202; and wars on Mare, 204-5
Jones, John (trader on Wallis), 129
Judd, Gerrit P., 57, 58
Jullien, André, 242, 243

K

Kaahumanu (*kuhina nui*), 36, takes husbands

INDEX

from Kauai, 36; 40, 42, 43, 44, 45; role as regent, 46; and Catholic missions, 50-53; Liliha rebels against, 52; persecutes Catholics, 52; death, 53; 262

Kaaia, Solomon P. and Kanoho (Hawaiian missionaries), 147

Kaaikaula, Berita and Debora (later Aea), (Hawaiian missionaries), 141, 147

Kaba, 114, battle of, 80, 287; revolt against Bau, 113; Cakobau repelled from, 114

Kabakada, 224, 225, Danks stationed at, 226

Kaelemakule, J.W. (Hawaiian missionary), 147

Kahaa, S. Kamakahiki (Hawaiian missionary), 141

Kahelemauna, Samuel (Hawaiian missionary), 147

Kahili (Hawaii), 33

Kahuna (Hawaii), 32

Kailua, 40, 44

Kala, *see* Gasbara

Kalaaauluna, John E. Phelps (ABCFM third company), 38

Kalaioulu, Richard (ABCFM second company), 38

Kalakaua, King, 262

Kalanimoku (Hawaiian chief), 35-6, baptism, 36, 42, 49; 40, 44, 50

Kalawao (leprosy settlement), 264-66

Kalo, massacre at, 213

Kalola (Hawaiian Catholic chief), 52

Kaluka (Luke), tends Kusaie church, 146

Kamamalu (Hawaii), 45, 49

Kamehameha I, 6, 32, 33, 36, 46, 49

Kamehameha II (Liholiho), *see* Liholiho

Kamehameha III (Kauikeaouli), 46, 53, 57, 263

Kamehameha IV (Alexander Liholiho), 57, 263

Kamehameha V (Lot), 263

Kamooula, William (ABCFM second company), 38

Kanoa, J.W. and Kaholo (Hawaiian missionaries), 149, 150; Bingham and, 151

Kanoaro, Moses (Hawaiian missionary), on Abemama, 154

Kanokupolu, *see* Tu'i titles, Tongan

Kapali, David and Tamara (Hawaiian missionaries), 147

Kapu system (Hawaii), 33, 36, 42

Kapu, W.P. (Hawaiian missionary), 152

Kauai, 35, 36

Kauiaui (Erromanga assassin), 166

Kaumualii, George (Hawaiian chief), and ABCFM, 35, 36; revolt and death, 36; 40

Kaumualii of Kauai (husband of Kaahumanu), 40

Kaunaka, Luika (Hawaiian Catholic), 52

Kaure, Moses, assists Bingham as translator, 154-5; lapse and penitence, 155

Kauwealoha, Samuel (Hawaiian missionary), in Marquesas, 268-9

Kawaiahao Church (Honolulu), 152, 263

Kayser, Alois, on Nauru, 291

Kekauluohi, 54

Kekela, James Hunewell (Hawaiian missionary), 47, at Kahuku (Oahu), 140; on first voyage to Micronesia, 141; in Marquesas, 268; rescue of Whalon, 268-9; rewarded by Lincoln, 269; descendants in Marquesas, 269

Kekuanoa (Hawaiian chief), 46

Kekuewa, Samuel W. and Miriama (Hawaiian missionaries), 147

Kendall, Thomas, background and character, 62; and Hongi, 62, 64; and Maori mythology, 64-5; visit to England, 64; receives Holy Orders, 64; lapse, censure and dismissal, 65; death, 65

Kent, Captain (*Mermaid*), 42-3

Kerekere (Fiji), 103, 106

Keswick Convention (and Katoomba Convention), 299

Kielaa, George Tyler (ABCFM third company), 38

Kinau (Hawaiian female chief), 52, 54

King, Copland, 245, and Maclaren, 245; lands at Dogura, 246; career in Papua New Guinea, 248; declines nomination as bishop, 248; on Mamba, 248; translator, 248; botanist, 248

King, John, 61, 62, 63, 65

Kingi, Wiremu (Waitara chief), 183

Kiribati, ABCFM/Hawaiian mission, 148-155; warriors of, 150; culture and prechristian religion, 151; ABCFM relinquishes work in, 153, 289; LMS in, 152-3, 290-91; MSC in, 288-90

Kiribati Protestant Church, 290

Kirisome (Samoan missionary), 152, 156; and Waters, 157

Kiriwina, Nicholas the Greek on, 235; Fellows on, 236

Knapp, Horton, 38

Knox Presbyterian Church, Dunedin, 294

394

INDEX

Kohimarama, *see* St. Andrew's College; *see also* Mota
Kopp, Marianne, work on Molokai, 266
Koro (Fiji), Tongan Wesleyan exiles on, 274
Kororareka, 68
Kuakini (Hawaiian chief), 40, 43
Kula ring, 232, 235, 236
Kuli, Joni (Tongan missionary and boatman), in Australia, 235; in Papuan Islands, 235; personality and record, 235
Kupelii (ABCFM second company), 38
Kusaie, 141, church on — and Marshalls, 146
Kwato Evangelical Association and Mission, 218, 251

L

Labour trade, 176, 177; Patteson and, 184, 187-8; and death of Patteson, 188; in New Britain, 228; at Levuka, 285
Lady Huntingdon's Connexion, 9
Lahaina, 44, 47
Lahainaluna, 47, mission seminary, 57, 140
Lakeba, 71, 77, 79, 102-05
Lalolangi (Samoan missionary), on Tanna, 167
Land (cessions, sales, alienations of), 1, Tahiti, 15; Cooks, 82-3; New Zealand (Waitara Purchase), 184; alienation in PNG, 213; cession by New Guinea Governor to missions, 231; on Yule Island to MSC, 240; donations to MSC (Papua), 243-4; at Dogura, 246; on Tahiti, 256; Lorimer Fison on, 280; 291; in New Caledonia, 296
Langham, Frederick, 228, as chairman of Fiji district, 280; colonial background, 280; and Gordon, 280; personality and opinions, 280; clashes with British administration, 280-1; moralism, 281
Langi (of Tongatapu), 102
Langi, Wesele (Vesile), (Tongan missionary to Fiji), 105, 111
Lannuzel, René-Marie de, and Wesleyans, 229; and MSC, 237; returns to Europe, 238
Lano Seminary, 138
La Place, Cyril P.T., 54
Lasalo (Samoan missionary), killed in *Star* massacre, 191
Latour de Clamouze, Alphonse de, 93, architect-educator, 93
Latu, Selemaia (Tongan missionary), 105

Latuselu, Penisimani (Benjamin), 79, in Samoa, 123; character, 123
Lau Group (Fiji), 79, 80, 102-05
Laumahina (Niue chief), 136
Laval, Louis (le Père Honoré), 88-96; 88, 89, 90; recalls first Christmas on Gambiers, 91; poor seaman, 91, 94; in charge on Mangareva, 93; manners and character, 93-4; influence of Chartres and Beauce on, 93; creates miniature Christendom, 93; clashes with pearlers and administrators, 94-5; writer, translator, ethnographer, 94; builder, 94; and Maria Eutokia, 95; and military occupation, 95; French report on, 95; retirement to Papeete and death, 94, 95; mission on Tahiti, 96, 253-4; mission in Tuamotus, 96
Lavelua, 97
Lavigerie, Charles de, 243
Lavinia, Chiefess, 276
Law codes, Tahiti (Nott), 24, 27; Raiatea, 27; Huahine, 27; Tonga, 78
Lawes, Frank E., 137
Lawes, William George, 136; translator of Niue New Testament, 137; 206; arrival in Papua New Guinea, 207, 208; strategy, 211; career in Papua, 212-18; furlough, 213; and Motu Bible, 215; and controversy over Bruce, 216; and George Brown, 231; 239
Lawry, Walter, 70, and Leigh, 70; 102
Layard, Edgar, 221-2
Lee, Samuel, 64
Leenhardt, Maurice, enthnographer, 295, 296; background in France, 295; writes *Do Kamo*, 295; and Aname of Poyes, 296; defends Kanak rights, 296; promotes Blue Cross and hygiene, 296; teacher at Sorbonne, 296
Leeward Islands, 8, 20, 23, 24, 25, 29, 30; LMS mission from, 81; 254; revolt in, 258; conserve traditions, 258
Le Forestier, Charles, begins Marist mission to Vanuatu, 293
Leigh, Samuel, with CMS in New Zealand, 66; informs on Kendall, 66; character, 66; withdrawal, 66; and Lawry, 70
Lelei, Peni (of Duke of York Is.), 228
Leleo, G. (Hawaiian missionary), 152
Lemayng, Gérard, 308
Lengereau, François, 294-5
Lengereau, Jules-Ernest, 294
Leone (Tutuila), 85, Teava at, 126; Vidal at,

INDEX

132
Leray, Joseph, pioneers in Kiribati for MSC, 289; on Nikunau, 289; appointed Vicar Apostolic, 289; personal characteristics, 290
Lesson, Pierre Adolphe, 93
Leulumoega, 125, talking chiefs, 128
Levuka, 109, Calvert at, 113; Taufa'ahau at, 114; Bingham transits, 154; 221; Brown before court at, 227-8; Floyd at, 285; labour trade and, 285; Marists settle at, 287
Lewis, Thomas, 12, defects, murdered, 17
Liausu, Chrysostome, 53
Liausu, Cyprien, 92, medical work, 93; head of Gambier mission, 93; departure, 93
Lifou, Melanesian Mission school on, 183, 186; Ta'unga on, 195; Paoo on, 195-97; Polynesian migrations to, 195; McFarlane and LMS on, 198-201
Lifuka, 73
Liholiho (Kamehameha II), 33, 35, 36, 42, 43, visit to England, 45-6, 49
Liliha, 46, and Catholic mission, 52, 54; death, 55
Lincoln, Abraham, rewards Kekela, 269
Lind, Cornelius, 7, 15, 32
Lini, Walter, 308
Literacy (and writing), 6, 17-18, 25, 43, 44, 56, 69, 80, 83, 84, 91, Fijian alphabet, 103; 109, 114; 136; Ponape, 143; Kiribati, 149; Tuvalu, 152-3, 158; New Britain, 226; Wedauan people, 248; Rotuma, 285
LMS (London Missionary Society), 4, 8, change of name from Missionary Society, 9; foundation, 9-11; social composition, 11-13; subscribers to *Duff* volume, 12; pioneer party for Tahiti, 12, 17; break in contact with Tahiti, 17; success in Tahiti, 23; and ABCFM, 33; 34; and WMMS in Samoa, 79, 84, 122-3, 128-9; westward expansion, 81-87; on Mangareva, 89-91; in Samoa, 121-28, 277-8; in Niue, 135-38; in Tuvalu, 152-3, 155-60; in Kiribati, 152-3, 290-91; agreement with ABCFM in Kiribati, 153, 156, 290; Ellice as Samoan District, 159; involvement in Vanuatu, 164-78; helps Presbyterians in Vanuatu, 168; reaction to death of Patteson, 188; Polynesian missionaries in New Caledonia, 189-92; Polynesians in Loyalties, 193-205; and Melanesian Mission, 193; in Loyalty Islands (mission and wars), 197-203; in Papua New Guinea, 206-220; flag of, 220; and MSC on Yule Island, 240; 248; and Franco-British conflicts over Tahiti, 255-6; hands over to Paris Mission in Tahiti, 257; May meetings of (and Tahiti), 260
LMS Directors, inquire into Tahitian reverses, 18-19, informed that Pomare opts for Christianity, 21; complain of progress, 22; and younger Tahiti missionaries, 24; question trade by mission, 27, 29; and John Williams, 30
Locke, John, 10, 34
Logan, Robert W. and Mary, 148
Lolohea, 73
Lomaiviti Group (Fiji), 80, 102, 114
Lono (Hawaii), 33
London Missionary Society, *see* LMS
Loomis, Elisha, 37, 40, 44
Lotu, Joeli Bulu decides to, 281; as church in in Papuan Islands, 233; in Fiji, 281, 282; in the Pacific, 311
Lovoni (Fiji), 112, 113
Loyalty Islands, 161, 189; Marists and LMS in, 193-205; Polynesian influences in, 194; LMS-Marist and Franco-British encounters, 197-205
Lufilufi, talking chiefs of, 129; Catholic-Methodist disputation at, 131-2
Lundie, George Archibald, 127
Luvu, Peni (Fijian missionary), murdered, 225
Luzy, Joseph, 68
Lyman, David, 55
Lyman, Sarah, 56
Lyon (France), 67, 99
Lyons, Lorenzo, 55-6, character, 56; hymns, 56
Lyth, Mary Anne, 107
Lyth, Richard Burdsall, at Somosomo, 106; 280; and Marists at Lakeba, 286

M

Ma'afu, Henele (Enele), power in Fiji, 80; Tu'i Lau, 80, 115; with Cakobau at Kaba, 114; 281, 282; and troops in Fiji, 79, 80, 103, 108, 112, 114, 286
Maasina Rule, 299-300
Macdonald, Alexander, 126, 136
McFarlane, Elizabeth, charged with sacrilege, 201
McFarlane, Samuel, 197, supports Wainya and Bula, 199; opposes Guillain, 199-201;

INDEX

wages "paper war", 199-201, 202, 207; in New Guinea, 206-212; missionary strategy, 206-08; use of Loyalty Islanders, 207; writes *Story of the Lifu Mission*, 207; on Lawes, 207; character, 197; 208; in Torres Strait, 211; returns to England, 211, 216; awarded doctorate, 211; theology and opinions, 211-12; and Verjus, 239

MacGregor, William, 215, and missions, 215; and Wesleyans in New Guinea, 230-33; and MSC, 242, 243; and Anglicans, 245

McKean, Thomas, killed in Tahiti, 256

Maclaren, Albert, 231, 245; and Copland King, 245; at Dogura, 246; death, 247; remains interred at Dogura, 247

Mahoe, J.H. (Hawaiian missionary), shot, 151, 152

Mahu (Tahiti), 16, 27

Maigret, Louis, 54, 92, 254

Maka, Robert (Hawaiian missionary), Stevenson describes, 152

Makea (Rarotongan high chief), 82, welcomes Papeiha, 82; condones land acquisition, 83; helps LMS, 83; visits Samoa, 85; 86

Makonn (Lifouan missionary), 295

Malaita, 298, 299

Malaria, 168, 169, 172, 175-6, 181, 182, New Caledonia immune from, 189; in Papua, 208, 213, 215, 241, 246, 247; in New Britain, 223, 224, 228; 298, *see also* Epidemics

Malietoa Laupepa, and Protestants in Samoa, 134

Malietoa Vai'inupo, 84, 85, welcomes LMS, 85; 121

Malinowski, Bronislaw, 218

Malo, David, 57

Malua Institution, preceded by Takamoa, 119; 120; and Samoan ministry, 124; 125; LMS Missionaries trained at, 126; 128, 136, 137, 138, 156; Tuvalu pastors at, 159; Erromangans trained at, 167; Marriott and Newell at, 277; first Pacific Conference of Churches and Missions held at, 306

Mamaia cult, 254, and chiefs, 254

Mana, 6, 7, 23, and cannibalism, 60; 73, 97, 109, 121, 158; in Melanesia, 162; 170, 297

Mana (Erromangan trained at Malua), preaches at Dillon's Bay, 167; on Erromanga, 167

Man Con, Toby, 293

Maneaba (Kiribati), 150

Mangaia, Maretu on, 119, 120; Gill brothers on, 120

Mangareva, 53, 68, SSCC on, 88-96; first baptisms of children, 89; on Aukena, 89; LMS Rapa teachers on, 90; chants in vernacular on, 91, 93; cutting of chiefs' hair, 91; Nobbs on, 91; winning of high chiefs, 92, 93; visit of Bishop Rouchouze, 92; smashing of idols, 92; building projects, 93; convent, 93; influence of Chartres and the Beauce on Laval's church, 93; annexation and protectorate, 94-5; French soldiers on, 95; effects of work ethic on, 95-6; depopulation, 96

Mangungu (N.Z.), 67

Manila, MSC pioneers at, 237

Manipulation of missionaries, 16, 18, New Zealand, 65; Tonga, 72; Samoa, 84-5; Fiji, 105; Ponape, 143; Solomons, 181; New Caledonia, 192; Loyalties, 194, 197, 205; Anglican New Guinea Mission, 246; on Hivaoa, 268; on Rotuma, 284-5

Manono, 79, 85, connections with Tonga, 79, 122, 123, 125, 128

Manua, 85

Manumanu (Papua), landing of Cook Islanders, 208

Maori people, New Zealand, 60-61; Cook Islands, 60; and New Zealand missions, 62-70; and Catholicism, 68-9; and Patteson, 183-85

Maori Wars, 183-85, *see also* Patteson, Hadfield

Maputeoa, 89, 90, attends mass in Gambiers, 91-2; attends school, 92; as Catholic king, 94

Mara (chief of Rewa), 113, 114

Marae (malae), 7, 26, 33, 73, 82, 92, 158

Marau, Clement, 186-7; work on Ulawa, 186; late ordination, 186; lapses, 186

Marau, Martin, 186

Marceau, Auguste, 99, visit to Rome, 99; book, 99; poor management, 99-101; 131

Marconi, Nicola, 239

Mare, 189, 194, Ta'unga on, 194; Yiewene Naisiline of, 194, 195; John Jones on, 197; LMS-Marist involvement in wars on, 204-5; Lengereau and, 294

Maretu, 82 (Cook Islander missionary), work in Cooks, 119-20; on Mangaia, 119, 120; on Manihiki and Rakahanga, 119-20; Chalmers' tribute to, 271

Maria Eutokia (regent), 95; appeals to French

397

INDEX

Empress, 95
Marianas Islands, 1-4
Marie de Jésus (MSM), leads sisters in Fiji at Loreto, 287-8
Marist Brothers of the Schools, 101, 134, *see also* Brothers
Marin, Francisco de Paula, 37, 50
Marist missions, New Zealand, 67-70; Tonga, 77-79; Wallis and Futuna, 96-101; Samoa, 129-134; privations in Pacific, 78-9, 97-8, 130, 131, 179, 192-3, 199, 286; Vanuatu (Aneityum), 172-3; Solomon Islands, 179-82, 297-99; rule of life, 180, 181, 192; New Caledonia and the Loyalties, 192-94, 197-205; on Rotuma, 284-285; in Fiji, 286-88
Mark, Harry (Melanesian missionary), 246
Marmoiton, Blaise, murdered, 192
Marquesas Islands, 15, 18, 24, 31, 39, 42, 47, 58-9, 81; Laval protests military conquest of, 94; 122, 145, 258; SSCC in, 260; cultural problems for missions, 266; LMS/ABCFM division of, 266; Tahitians, Catholics, Hawaiians in, 268-9
Marriage with Tahitians (and LMS), 11, 17, 21
Marriott, John, 277
Marsden, Samuel, 16-17, 19; appointed LMS Sydney agent, 19; voyages to New Zealand, 19, 61-65; co-operates with Campbell, 19; acquires *Active*, 19, 61, 62; 21, 26, 29; and New Zealand missions, 61-66; and Maoris, 61, 62; Anglican-Calvinist-Methodist, 61; views on civilizing mission, 61-2; visit to England, 61; and trade, 62, 70; and Ruatara, 62; arrival in New Zealand, 63; second and third visits to New Zealand, 64; dismisses Kendall, 65; and Wesleyan mission to New Zealand, 66-7; and Tonga, 70
Marshall Islands, 139, 145, 146-48; pastors trained on Kusaie, 148
Marsters, Ned (and family), 120
Martyrs and martydom, 192, *see also* Chanel, Montrouzier, Williams (John), Patteson, Verjus
Marziou, Michel-Victor, 99, 101
Massim people (Papua), 232, 233, 235, 246, 248
Mata'afa Fagamanu (Samoan high chief), protects Marists, 130
Mata'afa Iosefo (Samoan high chief), and Elloy, 131; 132; builds Falefa church, 138;

compared with Constantine, 134
Matai (Samoa), 121, 128, 124; and Samoan pastoral status, 124, 125; 277
Matapang (of Guam), 2
Matatia (Samoa missionary), 156
Matatore (Huahine missionary), 39, 40
Matavai, 12, 15, 22
Mateinaniu, Josua (Fijian missionary), importance, 102, sent to western Fiji, 103; 111
Matetau (chief of Manono), 79, 85, 122, 129
Mathaia (missionary from Lifou), 295
Matheson, John W. and Mary, 175
Matua (chief), 91, favours SSCC on Mangareva, 91; authorizes iconoclasm, 92
Matupit, 223
Matuunui (chief of Hivaoa), 268
Mauke, 82
Maupiti, 26, 254
May Meetings, 27, 200, 260
Me (Tahiti), 260
Measles, *see* Epidemics
Medicine, missionary, Lyth in Fiji, 106; Gulick's hospital on Ponape, 143; Pierson on Kusaie and Ebon, 145; in Papuan Islands, 236; Paul Vernier in Marquesas, 258; Damien on Molokai, 264-66; Welchman on Isabel, 296-7
Medina, Luis de, 2
Meikle, Gilbert, 212
Mekeo, district and people, and MSC, 240-1, 244
Melanesia, name, 161; character of region, 161-64; religion in, 162-64; Anglican Province of, 294
Melanesian Association of Theological Schools, 306
Melanesian Institute, 308
Melanesian Mission (Anglican), 182-89, 296-7; ethos, 184-5, 188; finances, 185, -188, 300
Mendaña, Alvaro de, 1, 179
Mere Lava, 186
Metalanim, 143
Methodists, Methodism, *see* Wesleyan Methodist Missions, etc.
Methodists (Roman Catholic misnomer), 48, 51, 130, 173
Michelsen, Oscar, on Nguna and Tongoa, 294
Micronesia, Hawaiian missions to, 47, 57, 139-155; Hawaiian Board of Missions and, 146
Middlebury College, 34, 38
Milan Fathers, 182

INDEX

Millennialism, 10-11; Napoleonic Wars, French and American Revolutions and, 34
Mills, William, 126, 168
Milne, Peter, of Nguna, Emae and Makura, 294
Misieli (Samoan missionary), death in New Britain, 224
Misinale festivals (Tonga), 81
Missionary Album (ABCFM), 39
Missionary Enterprises (John Williams), 86
Missionary Herald (ABCFM), 34
Missionary Society, The, *see* LMS
Missionary Sisters of the Third Order of Mary, 101, 134
Mitiaro, 82
Moe (Jack), (Tahitian seaman), 40, 42
Moea (Moia?), (Huahine missionary), 84, 122
Moeaki (Tongan chief), 77
Moerenhout, Jacques Antoine, 253, American Consul at Papeete, 254; and SSCC missionaries, 254
Momis, John, 308
Momoivalu, Simeoni (Fijian missionary), from Yasawas, 234; at Panaeiti, 234
Montiton, Albert, 260
Montrouzier, Xavier, speared on San Cristobal, 181; recovery, 181; at Douarre's deathbed, 193; and annexation of New Caledonia, 193; on Lifou, 193; meets Patteson, 193
Moorea, 8, 15, 20, 21, 22, 23, 25, 26, 27, 28, 39, 40
Moore, Elizabeth, 277
Moran, Patrick Francis, 238, and Austral Land of Holy Ghost, 238; and Solomons Mission of Marists, 298
Morgan, Captain J.C., 166
Morineau, Philippe de, 49
Mormons (Latter Day Saints), Hawaii, 59; Tuamotus, 96
Morrison, James (of ship *Bounty*), 12
Morse, Jedidiah, 34
Mortlock Islands, 148; first missionaries from Ponape, 148; students sent to Ponape, 148
Mosby, Edward (Yankee Ned), 239
Mose (Samoan missionary), on Tanna, 167
Moses (missionary to Etal and Truk), 148
Mota, language, 185, 186, 188; Kohimarama village on, 186
Mota Lava, 185
Motte-Rouge, Commandant de la, and Mangareva, 95
Motu (Papuan *lingua franca*), 208, adopted by Lawes, 211; New Testament in, 215
Moulton, James Egan, and Baker, 273, 274; teacher, hymn-writer, translator, 273; chairman of Tonga district, 274; maintains Wesleyan Church against king, 274; withdrawal from Tonga, 275; return as Wesleyan chairman, 275
Mu'a 70, 77, 275
Mu, younger Bula of, 197; Baker's station, 199
Moveave, 215
Muiowei, Lemeki (of Dobu), 236
Mulinu'u, 130
Munamunu (Samoan missionary), 170
Murphy, Columban, 53, 54, 89, 90, 91
Murphy, Patrick, 306
Murray, Archibald Wright, 126, and Tutuila revivals, 126-28; career and writings, 126, 200, 206; and Teava, 126; in Tuvalu, 156, 157; with Geddie in Samoa, 168; in New Caledonia, 192; in New Guinea, 206-7
Murray, Hubert, 243
Murray Island, 206, McFarlane's industrial school on, 211
Murua (Woodlark), 181, 232, E.J. Glew on, 236; 237
Muskets, 60, 63, 85, 103, *see also* Firearms
Musumusu (assassin, Futuna), 98

N

Naboro, Livai (Fijian missionary), murdered, 224
Nahnken (Ponape), 143
Naisiline, Yiewene, 194, 195; Nidoish, 203-4; Yiewene (II), 205
Namosimalua (chief of Viwa), 109, 110, 112
Namwarkis (Ponape), 143
Nantua (France), 78
Nanumanga, Ioane on, 158-9
Napoleon III, petitioned over Loyalties crises, 200
Napoleonic Wars, and communication with Tahiti, 17, 19; and Millennialism, 34
Nathalo (Nasalo), 197, church, at, 201
National Protestant Church of Nauru, 291
Natmasses (Aneityum), 167
Naturalization (of ABCFM missionaries in Hawaii), 57
Naucukidi, Sailasa (Fijian missionary), murdered on Gazelle Peninsula, 224
Naulivou (of Bau), 103
Naulivou, Siuliasi (missionary to Fiji), 105
Nauru, phosphate on, 290, evangelized by

INDEX

Tabuia, 291; ABCFM and Catholic rivalry on, 291; transferred to LMS, 291
Naval interventions, French, 50, 54-5, 68, 77, 95, 112-3, 254-5, 288; British, 176-7, 213, 226, 227, 254-5; German, 131, 226, 275 (proposed by Baker)
Navarre, André-Louis, 237, at Manila, 237; at Macassar and Batavia, 237-8; in Sydney, 238; in New Britain, 238; on Thursday Island, 238, 240; made Vicar Apostolic, Archbishop, 241; visits Europe to reinforce mission, 241, 242; character and role, 241, 243
Navie, and Ta'unga, 195
Navuloa, training institution, 221-2
Nawaa, S.P.K. and Mary (Hawaiian missionaries), 147
Neiafu, 74, hermit of, 132
New Britain, 81; Wesleyans in, 220-29; MSC in, 238, 244
New Caledonia, LMS Polynesians in, 189-92; Marists in, 192-3; annexed by France, 193, 204; Paris Mission and Evangelical Church in, 294-96; penal colony, 294; Evangelical Church of, 296; internal migration in, 296; Roman Catholic Church in, 296
Newell, James E., 277
New England, 32, Puritanism, 33, 34; 37; Congregationalism, 46; 55, 56, 57, 148
New France, *see* Rays
New Georgia, 300
New Guinea Mission (Anglican), *see* Anglican New Guinea Mission
New Hebrides, *see* Vanuatu
New Ireland, 223, colony of New France on, 228; and MSC, 237
Newton, Henry, trains priests at Dogura, 249; previous career, 249; character, 249; as bishop (Carpentaria), 249; as bishop (New Guinea), 251
New Zealand, 19, missions to, 60-70, 183-85; as base for Melanesian Mission, 183
Ngatangiia, 83
Ngatiuru tribe (New Zealand), 66
Nihiang (alleged incendiary, Aneityum), 175-6
Nisbet, Henry, 168
Niuafo'ou, 79, 122
Niuatoputapu, 79, 122, Taufa of, on Mare, 194
Niue, 84, 117, 135-38; population characteristics, 135; first LMS contacts, 135;

Samoans and Rarotongans on, 136; W.G. Lawes and F.E. Lawes on, 136-7; Peruvian slavers at, 137; and Samoan labour, 137; missionaries to Papua, 137; missionaries to Vanuatu, 137
Niuliki (Futuna chief), 97
Nivavave (Erromangan at Malua), 167
Nivelleau, Charles, 78
Nizier, Marie, 68
Noa (of Viwa), 111
Noa (Samoan missionary), 190
Nobbs, George Hunn, 89, 90, 91
Noblet, Marie-Thérèse, 242, 244
Nogar, James (Melanesian missionary), origins and Australian experiences, 247; in Papua New Guinea, 247
Nohoat, and Geddie, 170, 173
Norfolk Island, 89, base for Melanesian Mission, 185, 187, 188
Nott, Henry, 12, 17, 18; and Tahitian language, 19-20; friendship with Pomare II, 20; alone on Tahiti, 21; writes to Haweis, 21; marries in Sydney, 21; travels to Leewards, 23; drafts law code, 24; translator, 24, 27; cultivates outstations, 24; as chaplain to Pomare II, 24; crowns Pomare III, 28; 31; revision of his Bible translation, 257; 270
Noumea, 190, 201
Nui, visit of Binghams, 152-3; Gilbertese spoken, 152-3, 156; Kirisome on, 156
Nukapu, death of Patteson on, 187-8
Nuku'alofa, 71, 72, 73
Nukufetau, 156
Nukuhiva, 15
Nukulaelae, 155, 156

O

Oa (Oua, Owha), 148
Obookiah, *see* Opukahaia
O'Brien, Jack, 156
Oceanian Company, 78, formation by Colin, 99; organization and financing, 99; supporters, 99; collapse, 101, 131, 193, 286
Ocean Island, *see* Banaba
'Ofa (Tongan female chief), 26
Offerings for missions and church, incorporate old festival ways, 27, 81; in LMS churches in Samoa, 124; coconut oil in Marshalls, 148; in Cooks, 271; in Tonga, 273, 274
Oito (Tahitian convert), 22
One (San Cristobal), 181, feud with Toro peo-

INDEX

ple, 181
Oneata, 102
Opatinia and Obediah (missionaries to Mortlocks), 148
Opoa, 7, 26
Opukahaia (Obookiah), 35
Opunui, Daniel and Doreka (Hawaiian missionaries), 141
Orators, Samoan, 123, 128, 130, 132
Ordination of Islanders, Hawaii, 47, 57, 140; Tonga, 73; Fiji, 111; Samoa, 124; Tuvalu, 159; Vanuatu (Geddie), 174; by Melanesian Mission, 186; in Papuan Islands (Bromilow), 236; in MSC Papua mission, 244; in Anglican New Guinea Mission, 247, 249, 251; retarded in Tahiti's Catholic Church, 262; slow in Catholic Church in Kiribati, 290; in nineteenth century Roman Catholic Church, 304
Oro (Raiatean god), 7, 8, 18, 21, 26, 33, *see also* Arioi
Oro people and language (Papua New Guinea), 240
Orsmond, John Muggridge, 24, character, 25, 26, 256; on Borabora, 28; on Moorea and Tahiti, 31; critic of older missionaries, 31; critic of LMS Directors, 31, 256; sends missionaries to Tonga, 71; 81; takes service under French, 256; knowledge of Tahiti, 257
Ovalau (Fiji), 109, 113
Ouvea (Loyalty Islands), 190, 195; French troops on, 201; Marists on, 201; migrations from Wallis (Uvea), 201, 204
Ovialo (assassin), 166

P

Pacification (and Christianity), 69, Cooks, 119; Samoa, 124; on Aneityum, 170; Melanesian Mission, 189; in Loyalties, 204; in Papua New Guinea, 213; in New Britain, 223; Wesleyans in Papua, 233; Anglicans in Papua New Guinea, 248; Anglicans in Solomons, 297
Pacific Islander missionaries, Raiatean, 26; Hawaiian, 47; Maori, 69; Tahitians in Tonga, 71, 80; Tongans in Samoa, 79; Tongans in Fiji, 80, 105; Tongans in Melanesia, 80; from Tahiti, 81; from the Cooks, 84; use of, 84; from Rapa on Mangareva, 90; LMS to Samoa (*lotu Tahiti*), 85; Cook Islanders, 85, 116-18, 120, 136, 194, 211; Tahitians in Fiji, 102; Tongans in Fiji, 105, 111, 281-84; training at Takamoa, 116-18; as cultural mediators, 117-18, 171-2, 208-10, 223, 247; Samoans, 120, 136, 157, 211; Tahitians, Cook Islanders in Samoa, 122, 127; Samoan Catholic, 129; to Niue, 135, 138; Samoans, Niueans, Rarotongans on Niue, 136; from Niue to Tokelaus, 137; from Niue to Vanuatu, 137; Hawaiians to Micronesia, 140-154, 160; Hawaiians in Marshalls, 146, 160; Micronesians to Mortlocks and Truk, 148, 160; Hawaiians to Kiribati, 151-52, 155-60; Samoans to Tuvalu and Kiribati, 152-3, 155-60; from Tuvalu, 159; Samoans to Vanuatu, 167-172; Rarotongans to Vanuatu, 167, 168; in relation to white missionaries, 172; Melanesians in Melanesian Mission, 182-3; Polynesians in New Caledonia, 189-92; Polynesians in Loyalties, 193-205; Loyalty Islanders to new Guinea, 201, 206-10; Rarotongans in Papua New Guinea, 207-220; Niueans in Papua New Guinea, 210; Samoans in Papua New Guinea, 210-11; Wesleyan Fijians and Polynesians in New Britain, 221-27; Polynesians and Fijians in Papuan Islands, 233-36; Torres Strait Catholic catechists in Papua, 244; Melanesians in Anglican New Guinea Mission, 246-7; Tahitians in Marquesas, 266, 269; Hawaiians in Marquesas, 268-9; LMS on Rotuma, 284; Rotumans and Fijians on Rotuma, 285; Wallisian-trained Rotumans on Rotuma, 285; Wallisians to Fiji, 286; Kiribati within Kiribati, 288; Samoans in Kiribati, 290; Kiribati to Nauru, 291; Loyalties to New Caledonian mainland, 295; Fijian, Samoan, Wallisian Catholics to Solomons, 298; Fijians, Tongans and Samoans in Western Solomons, 300; 302, 303; to New Guinea Highlands, 303; 311
Pacific Conference of Churches (PCC), 296, 306, 311
Pacific Islands Christian Education Curriculum (PICEC), 306
Pacific Regional Seminary, 306, 310
Pacific Theological College, 306, 310
Paddon, James (sandalwooder), on Aneityum with Geddies, 169-71
Padel, Louis, 131
Paele, Kimeone, 52

INDEX

Page, Rodger, 275
Paget, Jean, murdered, 181
Pago Pago, revivals, 126-28
Pai Marire, see Cults
Pako (Wallisian catechist), 286
Palapala (Hawaii), *see* Literacy
Palauli, Macdonald at, 136
Palazy, François, at We (with Paoo), 197; on Ouvea, 202
Palmer, John, 186
Palmerston Island, 121
Paloo, Samuel J. Mills (ABCFM third company), 38
Pantutun, Robert, 186
Paofai (Tahitian chief), 22, writes to Queen Victoria, 255
Paoo (Fao), (Aitutakian missionary), 120, on Lifou, 195-97; with Ta'unga, 195; and blind Bula, 195; and chiefly rivalries, 196; moves to We, 196; prepares for white successors, 197; visited by Patteson, 197; entertains Marists at We
Papahurihia, see Cults
Papalangi, 86, 121
Papaoa, 28
Papara, 70, 102
Papeete, 3, 27, 29, 68, Caret and Laval at, 253-54; French naval ultimatum at, 254
Papeiha (pioneer missionary in Cooks), 30, 82; on Aitutaki, 82; on Rarotonga, 82
Papetoai, 22, 39
Papua Ekalesia, 303
Papua New Guinea, 81, 124, 206-29; Polynesian cultural influences, 207; tribal feuding, 211, 215; Queensland, Britain, annex, 213
Pare, 22
Parker, Benjamin, 267
Paris Evangelical Missionary Society (Paris Mission), 204, 205, sends missionaries to Tahiti, 257; traditions of and Tahiti, 257; sends missionaries to New Caledonia, 295-96
Paris, John, 139
Parkes, Henry, 274
Paseta (Samoan missionary), death in New Britain, 224
Paton, John G., 175, sent from Scotland, 175; related to Australia, 175; on Tanna, Aniwa, 176; character and talents, 176, 291; at shelling of Tanna, 176; confronted by Geddie, 177; and labour trade, 176-7; anti-Catholicism, 177; as fund-raiser, 177, 291

Patteson, John Coleridge, 182-88, 182, 183, linguist and ethnologist, 183; background and qualities, 183; and Waitara Purchase, 183; and labour trade, 184, 187; convictions and mission policy, 184, 188; choice of Norfolk Island, 185; financial resources, 185; failing health and forebodings, 187; death on Nukapu, 187; accounts of murder, 187-8; reactions to death, 188; on Lifou, 185-6, 193, 197; meets Montrouzier, 193; 263
Patteson, Sir John, 184
Patuone (Maori chief), 67
Paula (missionary to Niue), 136
Paulo (missionary to Niue), 136
Pea, 77
Peloux, Jacques, 129-30
Peni (Samoan missionary), on Vaitupu, 157; withdrawal, 157
Peniamina (of Niue), 135-6
Pentecost, Peter (Churches of Christ missionary), 293
People's churches, Hawaii, 56-7, 262-3; Tonga, 74-5, 80-81; Fiji, 114; Tahiti, 258-60; Cook Islands, 272
Percival, John, 44-5
Peroveta (Papua New Guinea), 210
Persecutions, of Hawaiian Catholics, 53, 54; of Tongan Wesleyans, 275
Peruvian slave trade, Niue, 137; Tuvalu, 156; Marquesas, 268-9
Peu (Samoan missionary), 152
Pidgin, in Solomons, 189; in Anglican New Guinea Mission, 248-9; in Vanuatu (Bislama), 294; used by SSEM, 299
Pi (Cook Islander missionary), 213
Pieplu, Alfred, 78
Pierson, George and Nancy, medical work on Kusaie, Ebon, 145
Pilgrim's Progress (Bunyan), and anti-Catholic reports, 91
Piper, Richard, 286
Piri (Rarotongan missionary), 208, earlier record on Rarotonga, 271
Pitcairn, 89, 91
Pitman, Charles, 82, 83, as translator, 83; character, 83; 119, 120, 270
Platt, George, 24, 26, 27
Plymouth Brethren, and SSEM, 229
Polding, John Bede, 68
Politics, churches and, 308
Polygamy, John Williams and, 86, John Geddie and, 174; Simioni Momoivalu and, 234
Polynesia, Anglican Diocese of, 264, 276,

INDEX

285
Polynesian outliers (in Melanesia), 161
Pomare (Samoan missionary), death in Vanuatu, 167
Pomare I (Tu), 6, 7, 12, 15, 16, 17, 18, death, 19, 269
Pomare II, 6, character of, 8, 15, 21; 16, 17; under instruction, 18; writes to LMS Directors, 18, 20; relationship with Nott, 20; uses mission to advance aims, 20, 21; retires to Moorea and Raiatea, 20, 22; as second Constantine, 20; letter in Tahitian to Haweis, 21; opts for Christianity, 21; baptism delayed, 21, 23; military conquest, 23-4; idols sent to London, 24; establishment of church, 24, 25; and printing press, 25; builds *Haweis*, 26; moral and physical decline, 27, 29; baptism, 27; alcoholic addiction, 27, 28; dallies with *mahu*, 27; death, 27; 29; frowns on cotton project, 30; 39, 254, 269
Pomare III, education, 28, coronation, 28; death, 28
Pomare IV (Queen), 28, Pritchard and, 29; 31, 54, 94; Caret, Laval and, 253-4; and Britain, 255-6; writes to Queen Victoria, 255, 256; exile from Tahiti, 255; calls on chiefs to resist France, 255; capitulates to France, 256
Pomare line, 8, 12, 16, 26
Pompallier, Jean Baptiste, 67, not professed Marist, 67, 97; route to New Zealand, 68; Protestant opposition, 68; proselytism in New Zealand, 68; 77; tension with Colin, 78; and subdivision of jurisdiction, 78; visit to Gambiers (SSCC), 96; 97, 99
Ponape, 53, 54, 68, 141, missionaries in clash with whites on, 141-43; church's missionaries sent to Mortlocks, 148
Poncet, Alexandre, 101
Popes, Alexander VI, 1; Pius VII, 49; Leo XII, 49; Gregory XVI, 99; Leo XIII, and MSC, 237, 242; Pius IX, 99, 193, 240; John XXIII, 306
Popohe, Stephen (Tahitian in third ABCFM company), 38
Population decline, Hawaii, 47, 56; Mangareva, 95-6; arrested by vaccinations (Ponape), 143; on Aneityum, 175; in Marquesas, 268, 269; in New Caledonia, 296
Pork trade, 19, on Raiatea, 27
Port Breton colony, 228, Brown at, 228

Port Moresby, 208, 210, 211, 212; Chalmers at, 213; Catholic parish of, 214; 303
Pouebo, 193, death of Douarre at, 193
Pouvanaa a Oopa, 258
Powell, Thomas, on Aneityum, 169
Powell, Wilfred, supports Brown, 226
Poynton, Thomas, 68
Pratt, George, 125, linguist and translator, 125-6, 137; 129, 130; on Niue, 136
Praying people (Tahiti), 22, 23, 269
Presbyterian missions, Vanuatu (New Hebrides), 168-178, 291-94; assisted by LMS, 168; in Vanuatu (and church backgrounds), 168; Scottish influences, 168; government and discipline, 168; and labour trade, 178
Presbyterian party (LMS), 13, 24
Presbyterians, Presbyterianism, Scottish, 12, 177; American, 33; Cargill forsakes, 74; in Nova Scotia (Canada), 168, 177; Free Church of Scotland, 173; Secession Church, 168, 173; New Hebrides (Vanuatu) ethos, 173, 291-94; Reformed Presbyterian Church (Scotland), 175
Priesthood, Islander aspirants to Catholic, 132, 134, 138
Princeville (Kauai), 263
Printing and presses, 6, Moorea, 25; Tonga, 74; Fiji, 105; Samoa, 125, 128, 152; Cooks, 271
Pritchard, George, 29, 253, and Catholic missionaries, 254; pleads cause of Queen Pomare in Britain, 255; 270
Procure, Marist (Australia), 99, *see also* Villa Maria
Propagation of the Faith, Association for the (France), 99
Prophets, local, 5, in Hawaii, 35; on Rarotonga, 82; in Samoa, 127; on Lifou, 195; in Tahiti, 254; in Western Solomons, 300-01
Prostitution and missions, *see* Sex
Protestant Episcopal Church in the USA, takes over Hawaii's Reformed Catholic Church, 264
Pule (Hawaii), 43, 56, *see also* Literacy
Pulela'a (Tonga), 73
Punahou (Hawaii), 47, 58, Bingham's house at, 154-5
Propaganda, *see* College of Propaganda
Puritanism, New England, 33, 34; doctrines, 46
Pusey, Edward, 246

INDEX

Puseyites (Protestant reproach), 193-4, 263
Puu (Hawaiian sailor in Marquesas), 268

Q

Qaraniqio (of Rewa), 109
Queensland Kanaka Mission (QKM), 299
Quélen, Abbé de, 35
Quipuha (chief of Agana), 2
Quiros, Pedro Fernandez de, 1, 179, 238, 298

R

Racism and missions, 184, 188, 235
Raiatea, 7, 18, 20, 21, 22, 23, 26, church on, 26; mission from, 26, 29-31, 81-87, 122; auxiliary societies of, 26-7; Congregational churches of, 29; Auna from, 39; chapel built on, 82; return of Williams and Bourne to, 83; navigational skills on, 81, 83; decline of church on, 84; 122; Pomare IV in exile on, 255; 256; revolt on, 258
Raivavae, 81
Rake (Aitutakian missionary), 84
Randell, Richard, 148, and Hiram Bingham II, 150, 155; and Baiteke of Abemama, 153
Rangi (Rarotongan missionary), 190, dies in *Star* massacre, 191
Rangi, Toriki (of Erromanga), 176
Rangihoua, 63, 70
Rapa, 71, 81, LMS teachers from on Mangareva, 90
Rarotonga, LMS reaches, 82; Takamoa Institution on, 116-18; coral lime building style, 118; LMS strategy on, 125; Chalmers on, 213, 215
Rau (Cook Islander missionary), 208, 271
Rautamara, Peter, first local Anglican priest in New Guinea, 249
Ravono, Elimatama (Fijian missionary), 223
Rays, Charles de Breil, Marquis de, 228, and MSC, 237
Reed, Henry, 220
Reformed Catholic Church of Hawaii, 263-4
Relief Church (Scotland), and LMS, 168
Religious decision, importance of, 18, 22, 159, 194
Religious liberty, Papua, 243; Tahiti, 254, 255, *see also* Comity
Revivals, Hawaii, 47-8, 55-6; Tonga, 74-5, 78; Viwa (Fiji), 110; Tutuila (Samoa), 126-28; influence of Scots on, 127, 168
Rewa (river and province), 103, 106, war with Bau, 110; 287
Richards, William, 44, 57, 58

Richerie, Gaultier de la, 95, 204
Rickard, R. Heath, 226
Ritual, ritualism, Catholic, 51, 68, 172, and Melanesian Mission, 185; in Loyalties, 205; Anglo-Catholic in Papua New Guinea, 248; appeal in Tahiti, 262; high church Anglicanism in Hawaii, 264; and SSEM in Solomons, 299
Rives, Jean, 36-7, 45-6, sponsors Catholic mission, 49; dissociation from mission, 49
Roberton, John, 68
Roberts, Ephraim P. and Myra, 145
Robinson, C.S., 218
Rocher, Jean Louis, 99
Rodgerson, John, 266
Rodriguez, Maximo, 3
Roman Catholic missions, Hawaii, 48-55, 264-66; arrival in Hawaii, 50; reverses, 52-55; deportations, 52; protection by France, 54; persecutions in Hawaii, 53, 54; Hawaiian catechisms, 55; New Zealand, 67-70; Mangareva, 88-96; Tonga, 77-79; Wallis and Futuna, 96-101; Samoa, 129-34, 278; Kiribati, 154, 155; 288-90; Tuvalu, 156; Vanuatu (Aneityum), 172-3, 293; Solomon Islands, 179-82, 297-99; Murua and Umboi, 181-2; New Caledonia and Loyalties, 192-94, 296; and comity in Papua, 231; in Papua New Guinea, 237-44; in Tahiti, 96, 253-4, 260-62; in Marquesas, 267-8; on Rotuma, 284; in Fiji, 286-88. *See also* Sacred Hearts (SSCC) missions, Marist missions
Roman Curia and missions, 49, 95, 99, *see also* College of Propaganda, Popes
Rongomatane (chief of Atiu), 82
Rongorongo, training of pastors at, 290
Ron Kiti, Sturges at, 144-5
Rooney, Isaac, 226
Ross, Robert, LMS colonial agent, 160; agent for Presbyterians, 169
Rotuma, Rotumans, 52, 97, 164, 244; Wesleyans and Marists on, 284-5; comity with LMS on, 284; wars between mission districts, 284-5; Serupapeli evangelizes, 285; united administratively to Fiji, 285
Rouchouze, Etienne, 53, 54, 68, 92, arrival at Gambiers, 92; departure, 93; 267
Roudaire, Gilbert, 129
Rougeyron, Pierre, on Aneityum with Geddies, 172-73; at Bourail, 193
Rougier, Pierre Joseph Emmanuel, career in Fiji, 288; and burning of Bibles, 288;

INDEX

leaves Marists and settles at Papeete, 288
Rouillac, Pierre, and Vidal, 298; boatman, 298
Roulleaux-Dubignon, François, 97, 113, at Lakeba, 286
Rourou convent (Mangareva), 93
Roviana area and people, 297, 300
Royal School (Hawaii), 47
Royle, Henry, of Aitutaki, 120; and Chalmers, 270
Rua Sura, 298
Ruatara (Maori chief), and Marsden, 62, 63; death, 63
Ruatoka (Cook Islander missionary), 120, lands on Papua coast, 208; role and career in Papua New Guinea, 208-10, 218, 271; in gold rush, 210
Ruggles, Samuel, 37, 43
Rum trade (Tahiti-Sydney), 19
Russell, Lord Edward, 53

S

Sabatier, Ernest, 289, on Leray, 290
Sabbath, 14, controversy over in Tahiti, 29, 85; element of taboo, 42, 69, 81, 172, 190; in Tonga, 81; in Cooks, 82, 272; in Samoa, 85, 125; in Tuvalu, 158; on Aneityum, 172; McFarlane and, 212
Sacred Heart Missionaries (MSC), in Kiribati, 154, 155, 288-91; in Papua New Guinea, 237-44; inception and background, 237; and Sydney, 238; in New Britain, 238, 244; Sydney Procure of, 238; and LMS on Yule Island, 240; in Torres Strait, 241; in Kiribati, 289-91; 298
Sacred Hearts (SSCC), Congregation of, 48; French Revolution, Napoleonic Wars and, 48; in Hawaii, 48-55, 264-266; assigned Eastern Oceania, 53; 67, 68; in Gambier Islands (Mangareva), 88-96; origins and ideals, 88; in Tahiti, 96, 253-54, 260-62; in Tuamotus and Marquesas, 260-62; in Marquesas, 267-68
Sacrilege, charges of at Nathalo, 201
Sailosi (Papuan Islands pastor), 236
St. Andrew's College (Auckland), 183, 184
St. Barnabas' College (Norfolk Island), 185
Saipan, 2
Sakaio (Samoan missionary), 170
Salamo, Wesleyan training centre, 236
Salata (wife of Taufa'ahau), 79
Salomea (Samoan missionary), death on Tanna, 167
Salote Tupou III, Queen, and Methodist reunion, 275
Samoa, Wesleyans in, 79, 84, 122-3, 128-9, 278; LMS in, 84-86, 117, 121, 123-28, 277-8; culture related to Futuna, 97; Marists in, 101, 129-35, 278; social structure and LMS, 121, 123, 277; prechristian religion, 121; pastors in, 124; LMS missionaries in, 124, 277; church building in, 125, 277; diffusion of LMS in, 125; Marists in, 129-35; *sunami* in (1868), 134; cricket in, 277-8
Samuela (missionary to Niue), 136
San Cristobal, 180, 187
Sandalwood trade, Hawaii, 32, 52; Vanuatu, 169-71; New Caledonia, 189-90, 192
Sandwich Islands (and Sandwich Islands Mission), *see* Hawaii, American Board
Santa Cruz Islands, 187
Sanvitores, Diego Luis de, 2-3
Sapapali'i, 85
Sarawia, George, 185-6, on Norfolk Island, 186; first Melanesian priest, 186; and *sukwe*, 186
Satupa'itea, 122, 123, 128
Saudeleur dynasty (Ponape), *see* Nahnken, Namwarkis
Savage, Charlie, 103
Savai'i, 85, 122, 125, 129, 130
Saville, William James, 218
Schools, LMS in Tahiti, 28; Hawaii, 46-7; Hilo, 56; Punahou, 58; Tonga, 78, 81; Mangareva (SSCC), 92; Wallis and Futuna, 101; Fiji, 108, 287; Rarotonga, 118; Leulumoega (Samoa), 125; Lufilufi (Samoa), 129; Marist in Samoa, 134; on Kusaie, 148; on Ponape, 148; in Tuvalu, 158; on Aneityum (Geddie), 175; of Melanesian Mission, 183, 184, 185; LMS on Lifou, 199, 200; in Papuan villages, 211; industrial on Murray Island, 211; Sacred Heart Sisters, Melanesia, 238; Anglican at Dogura, 249; Protestant in Tahiti, 257; Catholic in Tahiti, 260, 262; Papauta (LMS, Samoa), 277
Schultze, Valesca, 277
Scott, William, 17, 21
Scratchley, Peter, 240
Sea otter trade (Hawaii), 32
Secession Church (Scotland), and LMS, 168, 173
Self-government (of churches), *see* Church self government
Self-support (of churches), Marshall Islands,

INDEX

148, Tuvalu, 157; Rarotonga, 271; Tonga, 273
Selina, Countess of Huntingdon, 4, 9
Sellon, Priscilla Lydia, 264
Selwyn, George Augustus, and Aneityum, 170, and Melanesian Mission, 182; missionary convictions, 182; and Nonconformist missions, 170, 182; and Waitara Purchase, 183-4; 185
Seminaries and training institutions, see Chépénéhé, Clydesdale, Daru, Dogura, Hermon, Lahainaluna, Lano, Lufilufi, Malua, Navuloa, Rongorongo, Salamo, St. Andrew's, St. Barnabas', Siota, Takamoa, Vatorata, Waikava
Serupapeli (Zerubbabel), work on Rotuma, 285
Seventh-day Adventists, 300
Sex (and missions), 28, 44, 47, Thomas Kendall, 64-5; 69; and dancing (Samoa), 81; and prostitution, 44, 44-5, 142-3; 105; on Abemama, 154; 169; 187; in Loyalties, 194, 195; venereal disease, 44, 143, 212; 216, 235; on Rarotonga, 270; in Tonga, 274; in Fiji under Langham's rules, 281
Shalong, L.H. Gulick at, 143
Sharp, Gerald, Bishop of New Guinea, 249; and local cults, 249; work in New Guinea, 249; resigns to become Archbishop of Brisbane, 251
Shelley, Elizabeth, 70
Shelley, William, 12, 15, 16, 22, 70
Ships (missionary), LMS strategy with, 118, 126, *Duff*, 4, 7, 16, 17; voyage, subscribers to volume on *Duff*, 12; arrival in Tahiti of *Duff* 13-14; *Duff* captured, 17; *Endeavour*, 30, 81; *Haweis*, 26, 29; *Thaddeus*, 35, 36; *Notre Dame de Paix*, 54; *Messenger of Peace*, 83; *Arche d'Alliance*, 99, 131; *John Williams*, 126, 136, 156, 166, 167, 173, 190, 206; *Etoile de la Mer*, 129-30; *Morning Star*, 145, 146, 148, 150, 152, 153, 288; *Star of Peace*, 149; *John Williams II, III*, etc., 156-7, 195; *Dayspring*, 156, 177, 294; *John Knox*, 175; *Southern Cross*, 183, 185, 187; *Ellangowan*, 207, 240; *Henry Reed*, 220, 223, 226; *John Wesley*, 227, 228; *Lord of the Isles*, 232, 233; *Mayri*, 212; *Niue*, 218; *Dove*, 235; *Pius* (formerly *Gordon*), 239-40; *Albert Maclaren*, 248; *Vola Siga*, 287; *Hiram Bingham*, 288
Ships (general), *Actaeon*, 53; *Active*, 19, 26, 61, 62; *Aguila*, 3; *Aigle*, 45; *Aimable Joséphine*, 109; *Alice* (launch), 227; *Anonyme*, 181; *Ariadne*, 226; *Artémise*, 54; *Blonde*, 46; *Blue Bell*, 176; *Bounty*, 12, 40, 42, 89; *Brampton*, 65; *Bucéphale*, 192; *Beagle*, 226; *Boyd*, 62, 63, 66; *Caroline*, 141, 145, 148; *Clémentine*, 53; *Comète*, 49; *Curacoa*, 177; *Daedalus*, 7; *Danae*, 227; *Daniel*, 44; *Dolphin*, 44; *Dove*, 235; *Eleanora*, 32; *Eliza*, 103; *Emma Bell*, 188; *Fabert*, 288; *Fair American*, 32; *Favourite*, 77; *Gordon*, 239-40; *Havannah*, 173; *Héros*, 49; *Hibernia*, 20; *Jenny*, 42; *Marian Watson*, 180, 181; *Matilda*, 7; *Mermaid*, 39, 43; *Merrie England*, 231, 233, 247; *Montreal*, 139; *Prince Regent*, 39; *Pylade*, 93; *Royal Admiral*, 16, 17, 18; *Sandfly*, 226; *Star*, 191; *Star of the East*, 226; *Susanne*, 157; *Uranie*, 35; *Vénus*, 54, 254; *Vincennes*, 52; *Waverley*, 52; *Wolverene*, 213
Short, Patrick, 48-54
Shortland Islands, Marists in, 298
Siasia a Vika (Church of Victoria, Tonga), 276
Simeona (Samoan missionary), role on Aneityum, 170-71; Geddie's tribute, 171
Simonet, Charles, 68, brings Marists to Lakeba, 286
Siota, Melanesian Mission station and seminary, 296
Sio Vili cult, 4, 85, 121
Sisters, Missionary, of Third Order of Mary, 103, 134; Wesleyan Methodist, 236; Daughters of our Lady of Sacred Heart, 238, 243, 289; Papuan Catholic, 243; Australian Anglican in Papua New Guinea, 246; of St. Joseph of Cluny, 260; 288; Society of the Most Holy Trinity, 264; Franciscan of St. Joseph of Syracuse, 266; Catholic in Cooks, 272; Missionary of Mary, Fiji, 287-8; Solomons, 298; local in Fiji, 288; 304
Smith, William Saumarez, 245, 248, and Stone-Wigg appointment, 248
Snow, Benjamin and Lydia, 139, 141, 146, and Marshalls church, 146; and Mortlocks, 148
Society for the Propagation of the Gospel in Foreign Parts (SPG), 245
Society Islands, 10-11, 22, 26, 32, 39, see also Tahiti
Society of Mary (S.M.), 67, French background, 67, 78; requirements of missionaries, 97; Sydney Procure, 99; early reverses in Pacific, 99; reliance on Australia, 101, see also Colin, Marist missions, Vicariates

INDEX

Soga (Isabel Big Man), and Welchman, 297
Solia (Samoan missionary), on Tiga, 194
Solomon Islands, visits of Mendaña and Quiros, 179; Marist missions to, 179-82, 297-99; Anglican Melanesian Mission in, 182-189, 296-7
Somosomo, 105, 106-09
South Pacific Association of Theological Schools, 306
South Sea Academy, 28
South Sea Evangelical Mission (SSEM), 299-300, personnel, 299; theology, 299; encounter with Marists and Anglicans, 299; ethics, 299
Spaniards in Pacific, 1-3, 34, 144, 146
Spanish expeditions to Tahiti, 3
Spheres of influence policy (Papua New Guinea), *see* Comity
Stack, James, 66
Staley, Thomas Nettleship, 263, arrival in Honolulu as Bishop, 264; introduces nuns, 264; resigns, 264
Stallworthy, George, 266
Stanislas, Brother, builds Rewa church, 287
Star massacre, 191
Steadman, William Reginald, 286
Steinberger, Albert B., 134, pro-Catholic, 134-5
Stevenson, Robert Louis, on Samoan Bible, 126; on Robert Maka, 152, and Chalmers, 208, 215-6; on Brown and Chalmers, 216; on Damien (*Open Letter*), 266; and LMS in Samoa, 277
Stewart, Charles, 44
Stockton, Betsey, 44
Stockwell, Richard, 64
Stone-Wigg, Montagu, 247, as bishop in New Guinea, 248; previous career, 248
Sturges, Albert A. and Susan, 139, 141-46, hymns translated by on Ponape, 143, innoculates Nahnken, 143; work ethic, 144; theology, 144-5; first baptisms, 146; visits Mortlocks, 148
Suau, Chalmers at, 212-3
Sugar trade (Tahiti), 19; in Hawaii, 58
Sukwe (Mota grade society), 186
Sumner, Mrs William, daughter of Tute, 269
Sydney, pioneer Tahiti missionaries' flight to, 16; 18, 19, 21, 29; Williams' visit to, 29-30; 60, 61, 62, 72, 73; base for Marists, 78; 81; base for New Hebrides (Vanuatu), 169; base for MSC, 238
Sydney Morning Herald, 200

T

Ta'aroa (Tahitian god), 7
Taataori (Taatu Ori), (Raiatean missionary), 84, 122
Taboo, *tapu, tabu,* 7, 106, 111, 124
Tabua (Fiji), 107, 112, 282
Tabuia (Kiribati missionary), evangelist of Nauru, 291
Tafeta (Tahitian missionary), 71
Tahaa, 22, 26, 29, 82
Taharaa (Tahitian missionary), 102
Tahiti, 3, 6, 7-8, 9, 10, 13-31, revolt against Pomare II on, 20, Mamaia cult on, 254; Franco-British conflicts over, 254-56; French protectorate, 255; rebellion of chiefs, 255-56; French annexation, 258; Protestant Church in, 256-60; Catholic Church in, 260-1; Chinese in, 262. *See also* Society Islands
Tahiti, Henry (Tahitian in ABCFM third company), 38
Tahitian church of LMS (*lotu Tahiti*), protector of culture, 22, 256, 257, 258-60; as an establishment, 24, 25, 28; expands to Tonga, 71, 72, 73; expands to Cooks, 81; expands to Samoa, 85, 86, 121, 123, 127; and Mamaia cult, 253
Tahitian language, 17, 18, 21, Ellis' command of, 28; French Protestants acquire, 257; preserved by Bible, 260
Tahitian missionaries, *see* Pacific Islander missionaries
Tahitian mission of LMS, 4-31
Tahuata, 15
Tahunga (Maori), 65
Taiarapu, 39
Taiere (Taihaere), missionary from Borabora, 84, 122
Takai (chief from Lakeba), 102
Takamoa (theological and mission institution), 84, 116-18, curriculum, 116-7; record of early students, 118; 138; Chalmers at, 271; 272
Talatala (Fiji), 111
Talili (Gazelle Peninsula chief), directs murders, 224-5; attracts armed reprisal, 225; meets Brown, 225; 226
Tamatoa I, 26, 27, 29, 30, 82, 83, travels with Williams, 82-3
Tambaram (Madras) Conference, 305
Tane (Tahitian god), 7
Tangarare, 298
Taniela (missionary to Erromanga), 167

INDEX

Taniela (Samoan missionary), 190
Taniela (of Tutuila, Samoan missionary), killed in *Star* massacre, 191
Tanna, 167, Nohoat of Aneityum and, 173; 175; Paton on, 176; British bombardment of, 176-7; 247
Tanoa (chief of Bau), 103, 105, 112; death, 112
Taofinu'u, Pio, Cardinal, 305
Taravai (Gambier Islands), 91
Tapu, 64, 69, 81, 157, 172
Tapwaroro (Massim term), 233
Tarawa, wars with Abaiang, 150
Taro religion, 249
Taroaniara, Stephen (San Cristobal missionary), 187, death, 187
Tati (Tahitian chief), 28, writes to Queen Victoria, 255; opposes revolt, 256
Taua (Tahaa missionary), 82
Taufa'ahau (King George Tupou I), 6, 72, and John Thomas, 72-78, 79-80; questions old gods, 73; and Pita Vi, 73; baptism, 74; and Tu'i Kanokupolu title, 74; takes name George, 74; in Tongan revival, 75; at war on Tongatapu, 76; becomes Tu'i Kanokupolu, 77-8; and Samoa, 79, 122; expansionist aims, 79; visit to Lakeba, 79; sends warriors to Fiji, 80; treaty with France, 80; visits Sydney, 80, 113; with John Williams, 86; sends missionaries to Fiji, 105; visits Cakobau, 113; urges Cakobau to become Christian, 113-14; and Shirley Baker, 272-75; and foreign powers, 273; and Free Church of Tonga, 274; persecution of Wesleyans, 275; recall of Wesleyan exiles, 275; death, 275
Ta'unga (Rarotongan missionary), pupil of Pitman, 83; 120; in New Caledonia, 190-1; style of preaching, 190; descent from priests, 190-91; confronts Touru, 191; on Mare and Lifiou, 194; second stay on New Caledonian mainland, 195; and Navie, 195; return and later career, 195; hymns written for Lifou, 196
Tataio (Samoan missionary), 194
Tauraki (Cook Islander missionary), murdered, 210, 215; and Ruatoka, 210; and Chalmers, 215
Taurino, Joseph, 244
Taute (Borabora missionary), 71
Tautira, 3, 253
Taveuni, 80, 102, 103
Taylor, Hudson, and Florence Young, 299

Te Araa, *see* George
Teao (and Hue), Mamaia prophets, 254
Te Atua Wera (Maori prophet), 70
Teava (Cook Islander missionary), on Manono, 85, 122, 126; character, 85; 118, 119; on Tutuila with Murray, 126-7; grasp of Samoan, 126
Tehuiarii, Tute, *see* Tute
Teina Materua (Cook Islander in Papua), 120, 210
Tenui, William (ABCFM first company), 35
Teraupoo (rebel chief of Raiatea), and Frédéric Vernier, 258
Tessier, Samuel, 17
Testard, Jules, 197
Thero (Aneityum incendiary), 170
Thomas, John, background and character, 71; distaste for Calvinism, 71; Tory convictions, 71; at Hihifo, 71-2; at Ha'apai, 73; and Taufa'ahau, 73-78, 79-80; baptizes Taufa'ahau, 74; and wars in Tonga, 75-6; 79; visits England, 80; leaves Tonga, 80; effects re-entry to Samoa, 128, 272, 272-3
Thompson, Ralph Wardlaw, 213-15, 216
Thomson, Robert, 266
Threlkeld, Lancelot E., 24, character, 25-6; on Raiatea, 26, 28, 29, 31; controversy over trade, 29; quest for ship, 29, 30, 31; and Australian Aborigines, 31; 81, 84
Thurston, Asa, 37, 40, 44
Thurston, John Bates, 221-2, and Brown, 227, 275; critical of Shirley Baker, 275; removes Baker from Tonga, 275
Thurston, Lucy, 37
Tiberio (Raiatean missionary), 83
Tiga, 194
Tioka (Hivaoa deacon), 258
Timoci (Fijian missionary), death in New Britain, 224
Tindall, Charles, 71
Tinian, 2
Titles of address for missionaries, 304
Tjibaou, Jean-Marie, 304
Toaripi, murders at, 210, 215; Chalmers at, 215-6; Catholic parish opened at, 244
Tobacco, export from Raiatea, 29; trade currency for ABCFM, Ponape, 143; and Geddie on Aneityum, 170; Chalmers and, 208, 212; in Papua New Guinea land sales, 240, 246
Tokelau Islands, Catholics on, 132; Niue missionaries (LMS) on, 137; Catholic catechist from in Tuvalu, 156

INDEX

Tomkins, Oliver, 217, death with Chalmers, 218

Tomlinson, Elizabeth (Sina), 251

Tonga, 6, 15, 18, 19, 31, and Marsden, 61; 66, 69; Wesleyan origins in, 70-81; navigators of, 73; revivals in, 74-5, 78; Methodism in, 74-5, 80-81, 84; missionaries from (*lotu Tonga*), 79, 80, 81, 84, 122-3, 128-9, 221-27, 233-36; warriors from in Fiji, 79, 80, 103, 108, 112, 114, 286; culture related to Wallis, 97, 102; Marists and, 79, 101; marriage and dynastic ties with Fiji, 102; voyagers to New Caledonia, 190, 194; Anglicanism in, 264; Baker and Moulton in, 272-75

Tongatapu, 15, 70, 71, 72, 73, 74, 75, 76, 77

Tories, Wesleyan, 71, 113, 273, High Church, 188

Toro people (San Cristobal), feud with One, 181

Torres Strait Islands, LMS in, 206-08, 211, 216-7, 249; MSC in, 241; LMS churches assigned to Anglicans, 249; Newton at, 249

Totiara, 68

Touru (Isle of Pines chief), 190-91

Trade and traders, questioned by LMS, 27, 157; on Raiatea, 29; sea otter (Hawaii), 32; sandalwood, 32, 164-66; 169-71, 176, 189-90, 192; Hawaiian ABCFM missionaries and, 58; Marsden and, 62; in arms (New Zealand), 65, 153; and missionaries in Tonga, 72; Marists and, 78; and Sio Vili cult, 85: Laval (and pearl traders), 94; Oceanian Company and, 99-101; Tonga-Wallis, 102; Tonga-Fiji, 79, 102; on Ponape (and ABCFM), 143; in coconut oil (Kiribati), 148, 150, 153; copra (Kiribati), 154; copra (Tuvalu), 156, 157; Australian trade and missions, 157, 160; Melanesian aptitude, 162, 223; and missions in Melanesia, 162; Paddon's sandalwood and Geddie, 169-71; Rangi's sandalwood (Erromanga), 176; labour trade, 176, 177, 184, 188, 228, 285; in Solomons, 184; Patteson and, 184; Melanesian Mission and, 189; Papuan trade and LMS, 208; in land and gold, Papua, 213; in New Britain, 222, 224, 228, 238; in Papuan Islands, 235; and Burns Philp, 242; in opium (Marquesas), 268; Peruvian slave trade, 137, 156, 268-9; and Cession of Fiji to Britain, 297; in Kiribati, 289; and church in Western Solomons, 300-01

Trade goods and material possessions, 16, 18, 19, 32, 62, 65, 72, Sio Vili cult and, 85; John Williams and, 86; and Fijian chiefs, 109; and new Caledonians, 192; Chalmers and, 212; used to acquire Dogura, 246; among Islander missionaries in Anglican New Guinea mission, 246; on Hivaoa, 268

Training institutions, *see* Seminaries, Schools

Truk, pioneered by Moses (of Etal), 148

Tuamotus, 22, 24, 96, 204, Catholics in, 260

Tuaroi (Tahiti), 260

Tuauru, 190

Tubuai, 81

Tucker, Charles, 75

Tui Cakau (of Cakaudrove, Fiji), 102, 103, 106; Golea, 287

Tui Dreketi (of Rewa, Fiji), 105

Tui Kilakila (of Cakaudrove), 106, 108

Tuinaula (chief of Satupa'itea, Savai'i), 122

Tui Nayau (Lakeba, Fiji), 102, 286

Tuilovoni, Setareki, 305

Tu'i titles, Tongan, 74, 75, 76, 77-8

Tungaroa (Maori girl of high rank), 65

Tupou (Nuku'alofa), *see* Aleamotu'a

Tupou I, George, *see* Taufa'ahau

Tupou II, George, King, 276

Tu (Pomare I and II), *see* Pomare

Tuahine (Tahitian convert), 22

Tuava (Samoan missionary), 84

Tuka cult (Fiji), 284

Tulagi, 296

Tungane (wife of Ruatoka), role and death in Papua, 208-10; and Aruandera, 210

Tungaru (Gilbert Islands), 148

Turner, George, 119, 126, writings, 126; at Malua, 126; on death of Williams, 164-66; 168, 192

Turner, Nathaniel, 66, 72, 73; and Leigh, 73; and John Williams, 79, 84

Turner, Peter, 74, 75; in Samoa, 79, 122, 123, 128; preaching converts Bulu

Tute (Tahitian missionary and royal chaplain), missionary, 269; Hawaiian royal chaplain, 269; adopted by Pomare I, 269; successor to Auna, 269; estate on Oahu, 269

Tutuila, 85, revolt of LMS pastors on, 124 Murray on, 126-28; revival on, 126-28; Teava on, 126; Elloy visits, 132

Tuvalu, Elekana's mission to, 120, 155-6; Samoans in, 124; Bingham II visits, 152; Polynesian culture of, 152; affinity of language with Samoan, 152, 155, 156;

INDEX

Samoan missionaries and LMS in, 124, 155-60; British protectorate over, 157; within Gilbert and Ellice Colony, 159
Tyerman, Daniel, 27, 28, 30, 31, 39, 42

U

Ukeneso (chief of Wet), 195, 197, receives Marists, 197, 199; 201
Ulladulla (NSW), Kendall drowned at, 65
Ulawa, 186
Ultramontanism, 88, 243
Umboi, 181-82, 237
Umia (Raiatean missionary), 84, 122
Underwood, Edward (sandalwooder), 169, 170
Unitarianism, Unitarians, 33, 50, 58
United Church in Papua New Guinea and Solomon Islands, 300, 303
United Church of North Australia, 304
Universities Mission to Central Africa (UMCA), Maclaren and, 245; New Guinea Mission and, 245
Upaparu, *see* Paofai
Upolu, 79, 122, 125, 129
Utami (Tahitian chief), 28, writes to Queen Victoria, 255; joins revolt in Tahiti, 256; surrenders to French, 256
Utui (Vava'u), 74
Uvea, *see* Wallis

V

Va'a (Rarotongan missionary), on Erromanga, 167
Vahapata (Raiatean missionary), 30, 82
Vaiofanga (Samoan missionary), 167
Vaitupu, 152, 156
Vakavuvuli (Fijian), 234
Vakatawa (Fijian Methodist catechist), 281
Valeriano (Hawaiian Catholic), 52
Valparaiso, 53, 65, 67, 88
Vancouver, George, 32, 36, 45
Vangeke, Louis, Archbishop, 244, 305
Van Rooij, Stanislas (Tani), 241
Vanua Balavu, 282
Vanua Lava, 185
Vanua Levu, 80, 102, 103, 112
Vanua/Matanitu/Lotu (Fiji), 114
Vanuatu (New Hebrides), 52, 86, Presbyterian Mission in, 161-78, 291-94; Marists enter, 293; Churches of Christ in, 293; Anglicanism in, 294
Varani (chief of Viwa, Fiji), 109-113, conversion, 109-10; and Hunt, 109; and Cakobau, 109, 110, 111, 112; at death of Hunt, 111; death, 112, 113; example, 112, 114; 282
Vason, George, 12, Tongan experiences and later life, 15-16
Vasu relationship (Fiji), and Dobu, 233
Vatican Council I, Infallibility Decree, 95, and Elloy, 132-33
Vatican Council II, 205, 306
Vatorata, Lawes' training school at, 211
Vava'u, 68, 71, 73, 74-5, 132
Vea, Paula (Tongan missionary), 111
Verjus, Henri Stanislas, 238, desire for martyrdom, 238-9, 240; on Thursday Island, 239; pioneer on Yule Island, 239-40; visits Mekeo, 240-41; self-mortifications, 241-42; forms New Guinea Victims of Sacred Heart, 242; goes to Europe, 242; death, 242
Verne, Pierre, on Rotuma, 284
Vernier, Charles, in Tahiti and France, 258
Vernier, Henri, in Tahiti, 258; at Pastoral School of Hermon, 258
Vernier, Jean Frédéric, in Tahiti, 258, mediates in Raiatea revolt, 258
Vernier, Paul, in Marquesas, 258, 269; at death of Gauguin, 258
Veuster, Damien de, *see* Damien
Vi, Pita (Tongan minister), baptized at Nuku'alofa, 73; and Taufa'ahau, 73; ordained, 73
Vicariates and Vicars Apostolic (Oceania), Central Oceania, 78, 99; Eastern Oceania, 52-3; Melanesia, 179, 237, 241; Micronesia, 181, 237, 241; North and South Solomons, 298; 304; re-structuring of, 306
Victoria, Queen, and Pomare IV, 255, 256; godmother to Hawaiian prince, 263
Vidal, Julien, in Samoa, 132; in Fiji, 288; brings teaching brothers and sisters, 288; builds Cathedral, 288; opens mission for Fiji Indians, 288; flies French flag, 288; and mission to Solomons, 298
Viénot, Charles, and Tahitian Protestantism, 257
Villa Maria (Marists' Sydney base), 99, refuge for MSC, 238
Violette, Théodore, 129, 130
Visale, Marists at, 298
Viti Levu, 103, 105, 114
Vitte, Ferdinand, 293
Viwa, printing press on, 105; 106; Hunt at, 109-11; Varani of, 109-13; revival on, 110

INDEX

Volavola, Livai (Fijian missionary), 223
Von Werner, Captain, 226
Vunivalu (Fiji), 112, 113

W

Wadrokal, Mano (Loyalty Islander missionary), on Isabel, 297
Waihit, and Geddie, 170, 173; mission to Futuna, 174
Waikava (Fawn Harbour), training school for catechists, 281
Waikiki wall, 52
Waimea (Is. of Hawaii), 56
Waimea (Kauai), 43
Wainiqolo, agent of Ma'afu in Fiji, 281
Wainya (of Chépénéhé), 196, 197, and McFarlane, 199
Wairiki, 287
Waitangi, Treaty of, 65, 68, 183
Waitara Purchase, Patteson and Hadfield criticize, 183-85
Walker, Frederick W., 216, 218
Walkup, Alfred, career in Kiribati, 288-9; drift at sea and death, 289; Banana headquarters, 290
Wallis, James, 67
Wallis (Uvea), 68, 69, 78; 96-101; as headquarters of Vicariate, 101, 129; culture related to Tonga, 97, 102; Tongans from in Fiji, 108; Marists sent to Samoa, 129; Catholic help to Mata'afa, 130; and Ouvea (Loyalties), 190, 201
Walsh, Arsenius, 53, 54
Wanigela, Abbot and Nogar at, 247
War of 1812 (Britain-America), 35
Wars, manipulation of missions for, in Tahiti, 16; in New Zealand, 65; in Tonga, 75-77; in Fiji, 80, 108-9; in Samoa, 121-2; on Abaiang, 150; in Solomons, 181; in New Caledonia, 189; on Lifou, 196-201; on Ouvea, 201-03; on Mare, 203-05; on Rotuma, 284
Waterhouse, Joseph, 113, interviews Cakobau, 114; 221; controversy with Langham, 279-80; drowns, 280; writes *King and People of Fiji*, 280
Waters, Robert (Bob), and Kirisome, 157
Waters, William, 17
Watkin, Jabez Bunting, and chairmanship of Tongan Wesleyan District and Church, 274; chairman of Free Church, 275; death, 275
Watkin, James, 74, 75
Watsford, John B., with Hunt on Viwa, 110-

11; and Cakobau (at widow strangling), 112; 226; visits New Britain, 226
We (Paoo's station), 196, visit of Marists, 197
Weber, Conrad, pioneer brother in Kiribati, 289
Weber, Theodore, 226
Wedau people and language, 246, 248
Weiss, John, 72
Welchman, Henry, 296, at Siota, 296; on Isabel, 296-7
Wesley, Charles, 71, 111
Wesley, John, 4, 9, 71, 111, 114
Wesleyan Methodist Missionary Society (WMMS), *see* Wesleyan Methodists
Wesleyan Methodists, 8, Oceania missions, 17, 19; New Zealand, 66-7; visited by Marsden, 66; New Zealand mission house burned, 66; and CMS in New Zealand, 66-7; 68; Tonga mission, 70-78, 79-81, 84, 272-76; WMMS and Tongan wars, 76-7; WMMS and Samoa, 79; WMMS handover of field to Australasia, 80, 113, 272, 279; WMMS-LMS Samoa agreement, 84, 122; Australasian Methodists enter Oceania, 80; Fiji mission, 103-115, 279-86; requirement of personal repentance and faith, 109; in Samoa, 122-3, 128-9; in New Britain, 220-29, 238; declaration of confidence in Brown, 227; 248; Australasian Conferences and Shirley Baker, 272-75; persecution of Wesleyans in Tonga, 275; deputation sent to Tonga, 275; colonial influences in Fiji, 280; deference to Fiji Crown Colony Government, 281; on Rotuma, 284-5; among Fiji's Indian migrants, 285-6; in Western Solomons, 299, 300-01
Wesleydale, 66, 67
West, John, 200
Western Pacific, High Commissioner for the, 225, 225-6, 227-8, 274, 275
Western Solomons, 81, Methodism in, 300
Whangaroa, 62, 63, 66
Whenegay (of Fayawe, Ouvea), 195, 202
White, William, 66, 67
Whitefield, George, 4, 9
Whitmee, Stephen J., 153, 157, 290
Whitney, Samuel, 37, 43
Widow strangling, 112, 169
Wilberforce, Samuel, 263
Williams College, 34
Williams, Henry, 65

INDEX

Williams, John (LMS), 24, 26, on Raiatea, 26, 28, 29; quest for ships, 29, 30, 31, 86; controversy over trade, 29; and ill health, 29, 86; invitation to Hawaii, 29; to Cook Islands, 30-31, 83-3; character, 30, 81-2, 84, 86, 166-7; relationship with LMS Directors, 30, 31; and older missionaries, 30; wide vision, 31; and John Thomas, 71; in Tonga, 79, 84; 81, 82; travels with Tamatoa, 82-3; builds vessel at Rarotonga, 83; neglects Raiatea, 84; on use of Islander missionaries, 84; voyage with Barff, 84; pioneer in Samoa, 84-86; visit to England, 86; writes *Narrative*, 86; tact and humour, 86; last voyage, 86; death, 87, 116, 161, 164-67; 119, 120, 122, 123; repercussions of death, 126, 167; touches Niue, 135; presentiments of end, 166; 167; and Rotuma, 284
Williams, John (Indian catechist in Fiji), 285
Williams, Thomas, 107
Williams, William, 65
Willis, Alfred, as Bishop of Honolulu, 264; in Tonga, 276; and Diocese of Polynesia, 264, 276, 285
Wilson, Charles, 17, 21, 27
Wilson, Captain James, 14, 29
Wilson, Cecil, 300
Wilson, Matthew, 123
Windward Mission (Tahiti), 28, 30
Womra (of Ipece, Aneityum), and Geddie, 173, goes to Samoa, 173
Woodd, Basil, 64
Woodford, Charles Morris, 296, and Marists, 298
Woodlark, *see* Murua
Woon, William, 74
Women, status of, 174, on Dobu, 233; and Lilly Bromilow, 236; 306
Work ethic, Laval and, 95-6; Sturges and, 144; McFarlane and, 211; Brown, 224; in Cooks, 272; Goldie and, 300
World Council of Churches, 305, 306
World Dominion Press (and movement), 303
World War II and churches, 303
Worship, localization of, 306, 310
Writing, *see* Literacy, Printing
Wyllie, Robert Crichton, 57, and Reformed Catholic Church of Hawaii, 263

XYZ

Yale, 34, 35, 37, 149
Yankee Ned, *see* Mosby
Yate, 193, 195
Yonge, Charlotte, 183, 188
Youl, John, 17
Young, Florence, 299-300, and Queensland Kanaka Mission, 299; in China Inland Mission, 299; and SSEM, 299
Young, John, 6, 32
Young, Robert, 80, on Bau with Taufa'ahau, 113
Yule Island, MSC pioneers reach, 239-40; LMS claims, 240; 241
Zekaraia (Rarotongan missionary), on Lifou, 195
Zeula (of Gaitcha, Lifou), 199
Zorobabela (Borobora missionary), 71

Photo-computer typeset in 10 point on 11, Baskerville II, printed and bound by Oceania Printers Ltd., Suva, Fiji, South Pacific